SENATOR
MANSFIELD

The Extraordinary Life *of a*
Great American Statesman *and* Diplomat

SENATOR
MANSFIELD

DON OBERDORFER

SMITHSONIAN BOOKS ✴ Washington and London

Copy editor: Joanne S. Ainsworth
Production editors: Duke Johns and Robert A. Poarch
Designer: Janice Wheeler
Compositor: Brian Barth

Library of Congress Cataloging-in-Publication Data
Oberdorfer, Don.
   Senator Mansfield : the extraordinary life of a great statesman and diplo-
mat / Don Oberdorfer.
          p.   cm.
   Includes bibliographical referernces and index.
   ISBN 1-58834-166-6 (alk. paper)
      1. Mansfield, Mike, 1903–. 2. Legislators—United States—Biography.
3. United States. Congress. Senate—Biography. 4. Statesman—United
States—Biography. 5. Diplotmats—United States—Biography. 6. United
States—Politics and government—1945–1989. 7. United States—Foreign
relations—20th century. I. Title.
   E840.8.M2O24 2003
   328.73'092—dc21
   [B]   2003045553

British Library Cataloguing-in-Publication Data available

Manufactured in the United States of America
10 09 08 07 06 05 04 03   5 4 3 2 1

∞ The paper used in this publication meets the minimum requirements of
the American National Standard for Information Sciences—Permanence of
Paper for Printed Library Materials ANSI Z39.48-1984.

For permission to reproduce illustrations appearing in this book, please corre-
spond directly with the owners of the works, as listed in the individual cap-
tions. Smithsonian Books does not retain reproduction rights for these illustrations individually, or maintain a file of addresses for photo sources.

Frontispiece: Mike Mansfield as Majority Leader of a very different Senate: he
broke all records for longevity in office and for the respect and affection of his
colleagues. Photo by James K.W. Atherton, *The Washington Post.*

CONTENTS

PREFACE

For most of his ninety-eight years, Mike Mansfield did not want this book to be written. Asked by journalists how he would like to be remembered, he responded, "When I'm gone, I want to be forgotten," and he may actually have meant it. Although he was among the most visible and most admired figures of twentieth-century American politics and diplomacy, he was a man of genuine humility who rejected all pretension and claims to greatness—which, in the view of all who knew him, made him all the greater. Serving with great distinction as Majority Leader of the U.S. Senate during the administrations of Presidents John F. Kennedy, Lyndon B. Johnson, Richard M. Nixon, and Gerald R. Ford and as a renowned U.S. ambassador under Presidents Jimmy Carter and Ronald Reagan, he consistently rejected all suggestions that he write his memoirs or cooperate with an oral history project or biography of his remarkable life.

I asked him in early 1998 to grant me a series of interviews covering his life and work. Standing tall as always despite his advanced years, fingering his beloved briar pipe filled with the common man's Prince Albert tobacco, he fixed me with his keen and level gaze and rejected my request out of hand, saying he had neither time to devote to such a project nor interest in it. But then, surprisingly, he served me a cup of the instant coffee that he always prepared for visitors, sat me down at a plate of cookies, and recounted a fascinating conversation with President Johnson four days before Johnson's weighty 1968 decisions that became the turning point of the U.S. war in Vietnam. Later I discovered that Johnson had secretly taped the conversation. Mansfield, delighted at this news, helped me obtain access to the recording, which even now has not been released by the Lyndon B. Johnson Library. The recording demonstrated that Mansfield's recollection, thirty years later, was astonishingly accurate.

When I told his close friend, former Senate aide Charles Ferris, that Mansfield had rejected my request for a series of interviews, Ferris advised me, "Don't ask him, just *do* it." I then began what turned out to be a series of thirty-one more meetings with Mansfield over the last three and one-half years of his life. I never again asked, nor did he ever volunteer, permission to proceed with this activity. He certainly knew what I was doing and helped me gain access to documents I could not have obtained on my own, but he never inquired about my work on this project nor asked to see a word I had written. On the one occasion when I inadvertently mentioned the dreaded word *biography*, he quickly responded, "It's unauthorized!"

A history major at the University of Montana and later a professor of Asian history, he possessed a historian's sense of the importance of events he witnessed, especially in the field of foreign affairs. He wrote personal notes for his files immediately after many of his meetings with presidents and other important officials. He wrote memos, some scrawled on legal pads, of his own ideas and conclusions as they evolved, documenting the changes in his view of the developments of the day. Without setting out to do so, Mike Mansfield left a remarkable record of his extraordinary life and work, especially of his half-century involvement in United States relations with Asia, a vital part of the world he studied more energetically and understood more deeply than any other political figure of his time.

Mansfield had served in the lowest ranks of all three then-existing U.S. military services, the Navy, Army, and Marines, during and shortly after World War I. Having seen military life and action firsthand from those vantage points, he was unusually skeptical of the use of force in international affairs and always in the forefront of those urging political solutions to international ills. Among those with direct and frequent access to the Vietnam War presidents from Kennedy to Ford, he was among the most consistent, persistent, and articulate critics of the ill-fated commitment of American troops in Indochina. He understood better than almost anyone else the central role of China, a country that had fascinated him from his brief service there as a Marine in 1922. He played a significant although largely unknown part in Nixon's opening to Beijing. But as revealed in tape recordings secretly made by Nixon and recently released by the National Archives, their collaboration on China was not free of the fierce passions and double-dealings that eventually brought Nixon down.

Many histories of international events tend to neglect the important role of Congress. This is due partly to the journalistic and historical focus on the White House and the predominance of presidential power in foreign affairs and partly to the greater availability of the records of the executive branch of government. The story of Mike Mansfield, who amassed and bequeathed probably the most extensive record of substance of any congressional leader in contemporary times, helps to redress that imbalance.

Mansfield's work continued during his nearly twelve years as ambassador to Japan under Presidents Carter and Reagan after his retirement from Congress. As ambassador, most of his communications with Washington were in the form of State Department cables, many of which were declassified at my request under the Freedom of Information Act. At the same time, he continued to communicate directly, at times completely outside of normal government channels, with the two presidents he served. The records of those interventions have also been made available.

In my quest for a complete picture of this extraordinary man, I was aided by the firsthand accounts of many persons who interacted with Mansfield, from former presidents and prime ministers, senatorial colleagues and staff members, to constituents in Montana. I also received invaluable assistance from his daughter, Anne, who made available family papers; from the custodians of the voluminous Mansfield Archives at the University of Montana; from the Senate Historical Office; and from the National Archives. These and many other contributions are recognized in the acknowledgment section of this book.

Mike Mansfield had a sophisticated understanding of politics and international relations, but he also understood and mastered the power of simplicity. He was among the simplest of men in his life style, and he advanced simple, honest, and straightforward positions in unadorned speech that left no doubt of what he thought or where he stood. As a result of his widely recognized integrity, he gained a moral authority on Capitol Hill of a sort that has virtually disappeared from public life today. It is inconceivable that a party leader in the contemporary Senate could obtain a unanimous vote of that body to investigate the election misdeeds of a sitting president of the other party—but Mansfield did that to begin the Watergate investigation in 1973. It is hardly likely that a U.S. ambassador, appointed from the political ranks, could obtain and retain the confidence of successive presidents of opposing philosophies and political parties—but Mansfield did that as ambassador to Japan under both Jimmy Carter and Ronald Reagan. His life is a great American story, the saga of a remarkable person who came up from the lowest ranks of the military services and out of the deep and dangerous copper mines of Butte, Montana, to the leadership of Congress and the first rank of American diplomats abroad. This record of what he stood for and what he said and did in his long career will help to frustrate his oft-expressed wish. He will not be forgotten.

GOOD-BYE TO
PRIVATE MIKE

I It was a U.S. Marine funeral from start to finish. Handsome young leathernecks in dress uniforms guided Washington's powerful, including thirty-four members of the U.S. Senate and eight former members, into the Memorial Chapel at Fort Myer across the Potomac River from the capital. In measured step a Marine sergeant, accompanied by an Army sergeant, both richly decorated with medals and ribbons, wheeled the casket on a carriage down the center aisle and, when the prayers and the eulogies were said, back up the aisle.

Outside, through the forest of headstones at the adjoining Arlington National Cemetery, 115 more Marines stood at attention to the slowed, sweet strains of the familiar "Marines' Hymn"—"From the halls of Montezuma to the shores of Tripoli"—as the casket was lifted from the hearse. This task was performed in perfect cadence by an unusual mixed team of pallbearers from every military service, in recognition of his service during and immediately after World War I in the Navy, Army, and Marines—every branch of the U.S. military then existing. They bore the casket to the grave site, under a sheltering oak on the forward slope of a gentle hill a few feet from the grave of Rear Admiral Richard Byrd, the first to fly over the North Pole, and of General Daniel "Chappie" James, the first black American to reach the four-star rank, and other celebrated heroes of American history. From a grassy spot nearby, seven Marines raised their rifles on command and fired three rounds each into the early autumn air, the traditional twenty-one-gun salute, followed by a bugler's haunting rendition of taps. Four stars glistening on his shoulders, General James Jones, the commandant of the Marine Corps, supervised the ceremonial folding of the flag that had decorated the casket and presented it with words of comfort to the next of kin. Thus did his family, friends, and the nation say farewell to Mike Mansfield, age ninety-eight, the Majority Leader of the U.S. Senate for longer than anyone else in American history and one of the last of the great figures of a generation of Senate giants.

Mansfield owed much to the Marines, and they to him. The Corps sent him first to China in 1922 as a Marine private, part of a U.S. expeditionary force to protect the foreign enclave of Tientsin from the ravages of Chinese warlords. Brief as it was, his taste of the Middle Kingdom captured his interest and imagination forever more. Fascination with East Asia was a central theme of his life as a professor of Far Eastern history, a leading Asia expert of the U.S. House of Representatives and Senate and, later, ambassador to Japan. Counseling presidents from Franklin D. Roosevelt in 1944 to Ronald Reagan in 1988, he was deeply involved for nearly half a century in American decision making in regard to China, Indochina, and Japan, bringing empathy, understanding, and insight at many crucial moments. At the same time, he represented the best of America in the minds of many Asian leaders.

Despite all his attention and advice, the great failure of his life was his inability to head off and later to contain U.S. military intervention in Indochina, whose folly he saw so clearly from the early 1960s. He had some success in warning his friend President John F. Kennedy against expanding the U.S. engagement there, but he was ineffective in his efforts to dissuade President Lyndon B. Johnson, who had been his close associate in the Senate, from plunging America deeply into the war that ultimately destroyed his presidency. As Johnson made crucial decisions in 1964 and 1965, Mansfield was an articulate but lonely island of opposition in three important White House meetings, the only person in the room who spoke out against the President's plans to bomb North Vietnam and to send American ground troops into war. After initially supporting President Richard M. Nixon in the hope he would terminate the fighting, Mansfield lost confidence in the President's intentions and helped enact legislation that forced the withdrawal of U.S. troops and brought the war to its final, inglorious end. As the battles raged, Mansfield kept a card in his breast pocket with the latest figures of American dead and wounded, which he called "a tragic waste" and for which he felt an agonizing measure of responsibility.

There were triumphs, too, including his little-known role in the reopening of U.S. relations with China under Nixon and his satisfaction in leading the first official delegation to the People's Republic after the restoration of U.S. ties. And not least, his special relations with Japan, where he served as U.S. ambassador under Presidents Jimmy Carter and Ronald Reagan, who rarely agreed on anything else, and where he became the most revered foreign envoy of all time among the Japanese people. "A Giant Walks among Us," one of the Tokyo newspapers declared early in his nearly twelve-year tenure.

In addition to Asian affairs, Mansfield made history in many other ways. As the Senate's leading Democrat, he played a key role in passing some of the most important legislation of his times, including civil rights acts of historic renown. He fought for more than a decade to bring the operations of the Central Intelligence Agency under serious legislative scrutiny, an effort that finally succeeded only after scandals erupted in the middle 1970s. He sought repeatedly to bring large numbers of American troops out of Europe, an effort bitterly contested by Presidents Johnson, Nixon, and Gerald Ford. He conceived and brought about the creation of the Watergate investigating committee, whose work led to the resignation of Nixon.

As a senior member of the Senate, he personified character and integrity in a fashion that had been almost forgotten in the current era of big media and big money. Representing the thinly populated and impecunious state of Montana, he financed his campaigns for office on a few thousand dollars each and gave a portion of the funds he did not need to other Democratic candidates who could use help. When he became a close friend of one very rich metals magnate, he instructed his campaign officials not to accept any of his money. He refused to see lobbyists for any private interests other than those in Montana, whom he felt obliged to hear although not necessarily to heed. "In an age of alarums, of strident voices and personal image-building, old-fashioned words like honest, fair, humble, quiet, guileless, nice, unassuming and patriotic cling to him like stubborn vines," wrote Saul Pett, the senior feature writer of the Associated Press in 1970. Pett called him "the last of the low profiles, a man so singularly uncolorful and so indifferent to personal charisma that he is, in these days, singularly colorful."

The participation of the Marine Corps commandant and the abundant presence of Marines at his funeral was, in a sense, partial payment of an old debt. Mansfield in the House of Representatives and Paul Douglas in the Senate, both of whom had seen service as Marines, sponsored the 1952 law that guaranteed the permanent existence of the Corps at a strength of no less than three divisions and three air wings. It put a halt to moves, following the unification of U.S. military forces, to reduce drastically the size of the Marine Corps and subordinate it fully to the Navy Department. The Douglas-Mansfield act was the lifeline for a strong and independent Marine Corps after an unsympathetic President Harry S Truman called it "the Navy's police force" and complained that it had "a propaganda machine that is almost equal to Stalin's."

Characteristically, Mansfield allowed none of his political or diplomatic achievements to be celebrated on the granite headstone he had chosen, the smallest and simplest available, for his grave at Arlington National Cemetery. Engraved on the stone were the words:

Michael
Joseph
Mansfield
Pvt
U.S. Marine Corps
Mar 16 1903
Oct 5 2001

On the back of the same stone was the inscription for the woman who had guided his ascent from the deep copper mines of Butte, Montana, into academe and the political life, and who had preceded him into the soil of Arlington a year before:

> Maureen
> His Wife
> Mar 23 1905
> Sep 20 2000

Although he held the highest party office in the Senate, Mansfield was the least partisan of men. Democrats and Republicans, liberals and conservatives, sat together in the front rows of the Fort Myer chapel. The white-maned Robert Byrd of West Virginia, dean of the Senate Democrats and Mansfield's immediate successor as Majority Leader, sat next to Tom Daschle of South Dakota, the Majority Leader at that time. The previous day, Byrd had declared in the Senate that "Mike Mansfield personified both America and the American dream." Daschle, for whom Mansfield was a model in the operations of leadership, had told the Senate that Mansfield "understood that in this body of loquaciousness, there is an eloquence to simplicity, that in this place of debate there is always an opportunity for decency, that in this location, as we consider those who are more prominently seen throughout the country in positions of leadership, there is that quiet strength that came from a Mike Mansfield."

Sitting two rows back was Ted Kennedy of Massachusetts, brother of the assassinated President who had been Mansfield's friend and who had insisted that he accept the leadership of the Senate Democrats in 1961, only to quarrel briefly with him later over the deepening war in Vietnam. Next was Dan Inouye of Hawaii, the Japanese-American political leader and wounded veteran of World War II, who had accompanied Mansfield on a globe-girdling trip to Paris, Moscow, Southeast Asia, and Japan and who Mansfield recruited, against his will, for an important role on the Senate Watergate Committee. Jesse Helms of North Carolina, the Republican conservative and frequent Senate obstructionist, who nevertheless had had cordial relations with Mansfield, shuffled into the chapel leaning heavily on a metal cane and on the arm of an attendant. Mansfield, while still in the Senate, had written to him in appreciation for his courtesy and consideration, adding, "It is true that we belong to different parties and many times we vote in opposition to each other, but after all, that is what this Republic is all about."

There were younger senators, too, who had never served with Mansfield, including Democrat Hillary Rodham Clinton of New York, the former first lady. Both she and Republican Kay Bailey Hutchison of Texas, seated at her left, had frequently contrived to sit next to the former leader when he attended the biweekly prayer breakfasts in the Senate, his only regular excursion to Capitol Hill in the last years of his life. Only one seat was reserved at the intimate and off-the-record breakfasts—Mansfield's seat. As a mark of respect, no one else would sit there unless it was clear he wasn't going to attend.

Across a narrow aisle at the funeral service was Republican Ted Stevens of Alaska, now among the most senior members of the Senate. Mansfield had rescued Stevens from political embarrassment in 1970 after the Alaskan had been a lawmaker a little more than a year. To fulfill a promise in his home state, the novice senator had prepared an amendment to an ocean fishery bill being debated on the Senate floor and secured a commitment from the manager of the bill, the prestigious Edmund Muskie of Maine, that he would have a chance to submit and debate it. To his shock, he reached the floor as the final roll call on the bill was in progress—without his amendment. He blew up at Muskie on the floor and called him "a son of a bitch." Mansfield upbraided Stevens for his anger and his language, but after learning what had happened, he took the almost unprecedented step of interrupting the roll call in progress and obtaining unanimous consent to consider Stevens's amendment. It was accepted without debate on the strength of the Majority Leader's support. When the bill had passed, Mansfield walked over to Stevens on the Republican side of the Senate and said, "We are all equal on this floor, and a senator must keep his word." Stevens never forgot what Mansfield had done that day. "He treated everyone alike, without regard to politics or seniority."

Hurrying down a side aisle as the funeral service began was Democrat Joseph Biden of Delaware, chairman of the Foreign Relations Committee, on which Mansfield had served during his entire Senate career. Biden, whose wife and daughter had been killed in an automobile accident six weeks after his election in 1972, would never have sat in the Senate without Mansfield's intercession. Shortly after the tragedy, the thirty-year-old Biden informed Mansfield in a telephone call that he couldn't "be the father I want to be" to his two young sons, both of whom had been severely injured in the crash, and also be a U.S. senator, and therefore he had decided to resign and permit the Democratic governor of Delaware to name a successor. The Majority Leader called Biden repeatedly at the hospital to persuade him to serve, arguing that he owed it to his late wife, who had worked hard for his election and that he would only have to commit himself to six months' service while Mansfield organized the Senate. (In fact, his vote was not needed to keep the Senate Democratic.) Biden reluctantly agreed but declined to come to Washington to be sworn in on the opening day of Congress in early January—so Mansfield sent Frank Valeo, then secretary of the Senate, to Wilmington to administer the oath of office to Biden in the hospital room of four-year-old Beau, who was in a body cast, and three-year-old Hunter, who had suffered a severe skull fracture. When Biden finally took his seat, Mansfield appointed the neophyte freshman to the important Democratic Steering Committee, which rules on committee assignments for Democratic senators, and then arranged to place him as the only freshman on the then-coveted Foreign Relations Committee (as Mansfield had been when he had come to the Senate twenty years earlier). "He knew that work was the only thing that would save me," Biden recalled. "He was constantly taking my pulse, keeping me engaged and involved." During Biden's entire first year, the Majority Leader arranged for the two of them to speak privately, usually in his office, for at least a few minutes every week. "I thought it was everyone [who conferred with the leader this way] but after a while I learned I was the only freshman he was talking to like this." Other senators showed their sympathy to him in their own ways. Hubert Humphrey of Minnesota lavished special favors on Biden and shed tears of his own while consoling the young senator; Ernest Hollings of South Carolina arranged social evenings to engage Biden in Washington society. Mansfield was Biden's unseen sponsor and a caring but businesslike tutor in the life and lore of the Senate. He never mentioned the tragedy or acknowledged that because of it, Biden was being treated differently from every other senator. He played an unheralded and most unusual role and was the most important person in Biden's Senate career.

The funeral in the Fort Myer chapel was attended by eighteen Senate Democrats, fifteen Republicans, and Vermont Independent James Jeffords, whose recent exit from the Republican Party had placed the Senate once more under Democratic control, to Mansfield's private delight. The senators present made up more than one-third of the current members of America's most exclusive legislative body, although only a fraction of them had begun their service before Mansfield had retired from politics twenty-four years earlier. The day before the funeral, all 100 senators had affixed their names as sponsors of a resolution memorializing the former leader as "a man of integrity, decency, and honor, who was loved and admired by the Nation."

Present, too, were former senators, including two former presidential nominees of their respective parties, Republican Robert Dole and Democrat George McGovern, both fast friends of the departed leader. Dole, who served in the Senate with Mansfield for eight years and was among his successors as Majority Leader when the GOP was in control, recalled the astonishment of one of his staff aides when she encountered Mansfield at the Capitol at 6:15 one morning. At that early hour, she was on a recreational jog, but Mansfield was arriving for work. McGovern, who was the Democratic Party's candidate for president in 1972, recalled what happened when he traveled surreptitiously to Mansfield's house late at night in an attempt to persuade him to accept the vice presidential nomination in place of Thomas Eagleton (who had been forced out after the revelation that he had had electric shock treatment for mental illness years earlier). "Mike came to the door in his pajamas, kind of sleepy," McGovern recalled. "When I told him what I had in mind, he said, 'Well, George, I don't want that job. I don't want to be vice president, I don't want to be president, I want to be a senator from Montana. That's all I've ever been, and all I ever want to be.'" McGovern tried but was unable to convince him otherwise. Unlike other potential vice presidential nominees who were subsequently approached, Mansfield never revealed the incident to the press.

Seated behind five rows of senators was the former foreign minister of Japan, Ikeda Yukihiko, who had been sent from Tokyo to the funeral as the special representative of his government and people. Across the aisle was the South Korean ambassador, Yang Sang Chul, who brought a written letter of condolence from President Kim Dae Jung, winner of the Nobel Peace Prize and a figure highly praised by Mansfield in his last years.

Mansfield had never employed a press secretary but journalists had always been an important focus of his public life. A careful and voracious reader of newspapers, he had declined most classified government briefings since his early Senate days, insisting that he could learn as much about sensitive matters from the press without being bound to secrecy. He was the most accessible of major political figures, although he was renowned for his short answers, often "yep," "nope," or "don't know." Reporters who appeared with him on *Meet the Press* and other Sunday morning television programs came armed with several times as many questions as they did for other guests because of the brisk way Mansfield disposed of them. Among the journalists in the chapel were former CBS anchor Roger Mudd; the former Washington bureau chief of the Associated Press, Walter Mears, and of the *Wall Street Journal*, Al Hunt; and the syndicated columnist and Public Broadcasting regular Mark Shields, who had described Mansfield on the air as the last survivor of the legislative giants of the mid-twentieth century. In the back of the chapel, making notes for a report on the funeral in the next day's paper, was the *Washington Post* veteran political correspondent, David Broder, who had written two years earlier, "I had lunch last week with the man I think may be the greatest living American . . . Mike Mansfield, the former Senate Majority Leader and Ambassador to Japan. One thing I know for sure. There are few American lives that match the one Mansfield has lived."

In tribute to him, the national flag at Fort Myer and at every federal building and military installation throughout the nation and the world was at half-staff, as it had been from the day of his death to the end of his funeral, by order of President George W. Bush. Those attending the service had been asked to assemble at the chapel at least a half-hour early, advice that proved to be essential. Military posts were under extraordinary security due to the terrorist attack on the World Trade Center and the Pentagon four weeks earlier and the U.S. bombing of Afghanistan, which had begun three days before the funeral. Troops in fatigues thoroughly searched—inside, outside, and underneath—each automobile entering Fort Myer, an exercise that caused long lines of mourners' cars to form outside the one gate left open for the public.

Preceded by the red-jacketed members of "the President's own" U.S. Marine Corps band were the blue-jacketed Marines, resplendent in white trousers, white military caps, and white gloves and bearing polished rifles with fixed and gleaming bayonets. They arrived at the Fort Myer chapel to the roll of drums and the tread of marching feet just ahead of the hearse. Almost everyone inside was seated by the time they heard the muffled command from just outside, "Bearers halt!" As the Marine Band outside played the hymn "Faith of Our Fathers" and the mourners inside stood, the casket was slowly wheeled down the center aisle, the Army sergeant at its head, the Marine sergeant at its feet.

"The gathering today is a testament to a great man, but all of you who knew Mike understand that he would have been embarrassed by such a fuss," began Stephanie Shea O'Connor, Mansfield's grandniece, who presented a eulogy on behalf of the family. She recalled that in 1976, just before his retirement from the Senate, he had arrived at the chamber to find his colleagues assembled to deliver remarks in praise of their departing friend and leader. "When he realized the purpose of the session, Mike stood up and walked out, leaving his admirers to celebrate without him. He meant no disrespect, of course, but it was Mike's well-known, profound humility that forced him from the Senate chamber that day. And it is with that humility that he considered himself throughout his long life, not as Mr. Ambassador, not as Senator, not as Majority Leader, but as Private First Class Mike Mansfield."

Stephanie O'Connor went on to describe a childhood "with a Dickensian characteristic" after his mother died in New York City and he and two younger sisters were sent to live with relatives far away in Montana. He ran away from the only home he knew to join the Navy at age fourteen, falsifying his age to participate as a seaman in World War I. Later he joined the Army and finally the Marines, which he honored with unstinting loyalty because it sent him to China, making it possible to fulfill his boyhood ambition to see faraway places. She recounted how after his military service he lived the prototypical Irish immigrant story as a copper miner in Butte, Montana, for nine years. There he learned that copper miners cautioned one another to "tap 'er light" when setting a dynamite charge that could either expose a rich vein of ore—or, if the blast was premature or its force more powerful than planned, bring a rockslide and sudden death. O'Connor recalled that throughout the rest of his life he said "tap 'er light" to signal his caring and affection when saying good-bye to friends .

Stephanie O'Connor's grandmother, Anne Hayes, had introduced Mike Mansfield to her sister, Maureen, in 1928. He was twenty-five, a penniless miner with a seventh-grade education living in a rooming house, and she was twenty-three, the college-educated daughter of a well-known business-man and local political figure living in a house near the top of the Butte hill. The resulting love affair, so improbable by today's standards, was described by Maureen's grandniece as "a burst of romance when he met his beloved

Maureen, with whose help he walked out of those mines and into school. He became a teacher, a professor, and then their ambitions took him on to politics. To the House of Representatives. To the Senate. To the Leadership. To our nation's representative to Japan under two presidents. And at the age of 86, into the private sector. Could there be a better example of fulfilling the American dream?"

There was stillness in the chapel among the senators, diplomats, journalists, friends, as Mansfield's grandniece concluded: "If I could speak to Mike directly right now, on behalf of the family, I would say this: Mike, with all apologies and love, we cannot view you with the same degree of humility that you viewed yourself. You are our giant. Our hero. A colossus in the continuum of our nation's history. But you are also our Uncle Mike, whom we will mourn and miss.

"And to you, friends and admirers of him, I say this: that even after accomplishing so much, after going so far, Mike was mindful that what passes for important is often unimportant, that fame holds no significance, that money need not be a motivator, and that simplicity can be a means of success. . . . Tap 'er light, Private Mike."

Then came the second of the two eulogies, this one by Charles Ferris, who had been chief counsel to Mansfield's Democratic Policy Committee in the Senate from 1963 to 1977, and his close friend and private attorney in recent years. Ferris remembered a Majority Leader who "never twisted an arm but touched the conscience of his colleagues." By his openness, character, and reason, "he transformed a Senate of power brokers"—a body historically dominated by the seniority system and the famous Senate club of favored insiders—"into a Senate of equals. His was a leadership rooted in clarity of motive, honesty of purpose and respect of his fellow Senators."

Ferris recalled that Mansfield's emphasis on equality extended beyond the Senate to America itself. "He was at the helm of the Senate at the height of fundamental achievement—the Nuclear Test Ban Treaty, the Civil Rights Act of 1964, the Voting Rights Act of 1965, the passage of Medicare, federal aid to education, the 18-year-old vote—all deeply controversial at the time, many requiring the then-dreaded two-thirds cloture vote" to close debate and choke off filibusters. In each instance, he made sure a different senator received most of the accolades. "Mike Mansfield always gave the credit to others; his satisfaction came from within; his approbation from Maureen." Without his leadership, however, the historic accomplishments would have been impossible or diminished.

There was method as well as generosity in his willingness to cede the acclaim to others. Ferris remembered the day when the chief of staff to "a Midwestern Democrat" (Paul Douglas of Illinois, another much-admired senator) complained that bipartisan strategy meetings with Justice Department officials on the Voting Rights Act of 1965 were held regularly in the office of Senate Minority Leader Everett Dirksen, an Illinois Republican who was highly partisan on his home turf. After each meeting the loquacious GOP leader was given center stage by Mansfield at a press conference outside the Republican leader's office. Douglas's aide pleaded that at least half the meetings should be held in Mansfield's office so that Democrats could share the limelight, but Mansfield was not moved. "Charlie, last year the Republican Party drifted far from the mainstream during the presidential election," Mansfield responded to his aide. "If the public can see the Republican Leader each day reporting on the progress of what hopefully will be the most significant civil rights legislation ever, it will be very beneficial for the country to grasp that this bill was being drafted by both parties, even in an overwhelmingly Democratic Congress." In discussing the issue on another occasion, Mansfield observed that Republican votes were essential to passage of civil rights bills in the face of Southern Democratic opposition. To win the day, the Democratic leader was willing to cede the credit to his Republican counterpart because "Dirksen is the one who had to get the votes."

Ferris then recounted an incident from Mansfield's service as ambassador to Japan in which he uncharacteristically sought the limelight for his own purposes. After the nuclear submarine USS *George Washington* accidentally sank a Japanese freighter and ran off without attending to the dead and injured in 1981, Mansfield exerted heavy pressure on the U.S. Navy for a full report. When it was received, he delivered it in person to Foreign Minister Sunao Sonoda. Surprisingly, he asked Sonoda to permit the press and cameras to remain after the opening few seconds of their dialogue. Mansfield then executed a very deep bow from the waist, close to forty-five degrees, in presenting the report. "As he knew," Ferris continued, "this symbol in the Japanese culture has great significance. The sincerity and depth of the apology was visually conveyed. That five seconds was played and replayed on Japan's TV stations many times over—obviously seen by everyone in Japan with a television. The political issue ceased to exist."

After Mansfield's return from Tokyo in 1989, Ferris became the closest of friends, almost like a son, seeing him daily when he accepted a job as an adviser on Asia to the international financial firm of Goldman, Sachs. Mansfield maintained a remarkable mental acuity throughout those years as he reached his upper nineties. "At the hospital three days before he died, he was resting comfortably, his eyes closed. He had been informed the day before that he was on his final lap. I went to his bedside and took his hand and quietly asked how he was doing. He opened his eyes, strained to focus, and said, 'Oh, Charlie, how are you?' A moment later, 'What day is it?' Monday, I said." Mansfield asked about the performance of former Boston College quarterback Doug Flutie, now a professional football player, whom Ferris and Mansfield often discussed. "It was as if this were a normal day, another visit, nothing unusual. In looking back, this final chat I believe was much more. He was not a man of idle gestures or wasted words. He knew the wheels were about to touch down. But like remaining in the background at joint press conferences, or bowing below the waist to the Foreign Minister or with a stern look repairing a parliamentary abuse, I believe he was conveying a message. That he was mentally comfortable and spiritually content; that he had no fear about what lay beyond the horizon. In effect, he remained a mentor to the very end—still more interested in giving comfort than seeking it—teaching again by example the final lesson of dying with serene dignity."

At Maureen's funeral in the same chapel at Fort Myer twelve months and fourteen days earlier, her husband had delivered the eulogy himself in the strong, spare, high-politics voice that had been so familiar for so many years in the halls of Congress. After praising her unstintingly and giving her nearly all the credit for his success in life, he choked up at a heartfelt ending to his most important relationship: "I will not say good-bye to Maureen, my love, but only 'so long' because I hope the Good Lord will make it possible that we will meet at another place in another time and we will then be together again forever." After her funeral, his secretary, Barbara Hickey, often entered his office to see him staring as if in reverie at her photograph on his desk. After her death, he rejected all proposals for medical intervention to stave off the slowly progressing congestive heart failure that finally brought his long life to a close.

"Mike has gone to Maureen. Together again with the love of his life," said Ferris in ending his eulogy, shortly before the flag-draped casket was rolled away in the care of the Marines to the graveside ceremonies just down the hill at Arlington National Cemetery.

"In the world where politics is so often so self-regarding and so many so self-absorbed, Boss, you set a different, higher standard. You tapped 'er light but left the deepest imprint."

THE EARLY YEARS

2

As the twentieth century dawned, the rapidly developing United States was taking in millions of immigrants to fill its ranks. Its population and economic development were spreading from the East Coast steadily westward across the continent. The story of Mike Mansfield exemplifies both trends. His parents, Patrick Mansfield and Josephine O'Brien, arrived from Ireland on the eve of the new century. After Josephine died in New York, Patrick arranged to send young Mike and his two sisters to live in faraway Montana, where an uncle had earlier followed the railroads west to seek his fortune. As America burst out of its continental bounds in the Spanish-American War, it established the beginnings of an empire farther westward in the Pacific with the seizure of the Philippines and the annexation of Hawaii. Teenager Mansfield, who ran away from home to see the world, finally achieved his goal as a U.S. Marine in the Philippines and, briefly, in China. These encounters left a deep impression and engendered his lifelong fascination with Asia.

The earliest thing Mike Mansfield remembered was being in a park in New York City with a woman when a bird flew over. That is all he could recall of his mother, whose death propelled him to a life in rustic Montana, far across the continent and a world away from the sidewalks of New York. Until almost the end of his long life, he did not know why she died nor was he sure how old he was at the time. He had often said—and most of his obituaries erroneously repeated—that he was three years old. At my final meeting with him ten days before he died, he was fascinated to learn from a copy of his mother's death certificate, which I had obtained from the Municipal Archives of the City of New York, that she had died of nephritis, a kidney disease common at the time, on November 24, 1910, at age twenty-seven. He was seven years old.

Mike Mansfield's youthful experiences and his rise from obscurity to prominence comprise a classic American adventure of the early twentieth century. He was born in New York City in 1903, the year of the first short airplane flight by the Wright brothers. He lived beyond the end of the century, well into the era of mankind's exploration of outer space, of the rise of instantaneous mass communications and of powerful weapons of mass destruction.

There was nothing about his birth or his difficult childhood that suggested potential prominence or renown of any sort. His father was a construction worker, later a hotel porter, and eventually a maintenance man for a municipal water department. He barely knew his mother. Although not a neglected or abandoned child, he lacked parents or close relatives he could rely on during most of his youth. He spent a year in a home for wayward and orphaned children, in essence a reform school, and eventually struck out on his own by running away from home shortly after his fourteenth birthday to ride the rails in empty boxcars like a hobo. He joined the Navy before his fifteenth birthday by falsifying his age and matured in his country's uniforms, serving in all three military services of the United States before he was out of his teens.

In retrospect, his boyhood experiences are a key, however hidden, to his remarkable attributes in later life, some of which are close to being unique in a political leader. Having come from the ranks of ordinary working folk, he never sought to escape them but sought them out and was entirely com-

A note on Chinese names: The English language spellings of Chinese names of persons and places have changed over the years. I have retained the pre-1949 spellings in common usage when referring to persons and places at that time. For discussion of persons and places after 1949, I have generally followed the *pinyin* system now in use, except for the names of certain well-known people, such as Chou En-lai and Mao Tse-tung. In those few cases I have used the old spellings, which appear frequently in Mansfield's speeches and correspondence.

fortable with them throughout his career. He was a self-reliant, straightforward man, completely lacking in pretension, unsophisticated in his values
and sentiments, although not in his intellect or knowledge. He bought his
clothes off the rack from the least expensive store available; his preferred
luncheon, even as a powerful Senate leader, was a hamburger by himself in
his office. On visits to Montana from Washington, he often dropped in
alone and unannounced to workingmen's bars, accepting conversation from
whoever happened by. His favorite haunt in the university town of Missoula
was the Oxford Bar and Grill, where gambling took place in the basement,
reachable through the meat locker. Typically he would show up for breakfast and sit quietly at the lunch counter there until someone took the initiative to engage him in conversation, not always about politics. On one
occasion in early 1952, the year of his first race for the Senate, he was temporarily tossed out of Sonny O'Day's bar in the small town of Laurel because
the proprietor, Sonny himself, did not recognize the seedy figure wearing a
rumpled jacket and rumpled hat and mistook him for a bum seeking refuge
from the weather.

As stated at his funeral, Mansfield was so uncomfortable with public praise
that he fled from the Senate floor when his admiring colleagues began a series
of speeches designed to express their appreciation for his leadership. He was
unusually sensitive to the feelings of others, whether colleagues or workaday
persons far beneath his station in life, but he kept his own feelings to himself.
"There has always been something held back and unreachable in his character," said his former student and Senate aide Stan Kimmitt, one of the handful of persons closest to Mansfield. Remarkably for a successful politician,
Mansfield told me in one of our interviews that he had been "sort of a loner
all my life." Probably only one person—his wife, Maureen—was ever given
access to his innermost thoughts. It was she alone who recognized his character and intellect early in life, who launched him into academia and later into
politics, and whose approbation he sought far beyond that of all others.

A TROUBLED BOYHOOD

Both his parents, Patrick Mansfield and Josephine O'Brien, had come
through Ellis Island from Ireland, although they did not know one another
when they landed in America. Patrick was a tall, lanky, taciturn young man

who had slipped away from his parents' farm and boarded a cattle boat for New York in 1897. He had almost no money, no contacts, and no prospects. His reasons for leaving remain uncertain; surprisingly, his son never asked him, nor did he ask when or why Josephine died. As the firstborn of six children, Patrick would have eventually inherited the farm. In view of his primogeniture, one of his grandchildren was offered a share of the property during a rare visit to the Irish relatives nearly a century later. The offer was declined. Even less is known about Josephine, except that she was seven years younger than her husband and came from Limerick.

Michael Joseph Mansfield, their first child, was born on March 16, 1903. Two sisters, Kate and Helen, quickly followed. Then Patrick fell from a thirty-five-foot brick wall while employed as a construction worker. Severely injured, he was slowly nursed to health by nuns in a Catholic hospital. The crowning blow came with the death of Josephine. Suddenly left with three small children and no way to care for them, he wrote for help to his nearest relative in the United States, his uncle Richard in faraway Montana, with an appeal to take the children under his care. A few weeks later Richard's wife, Margaret, came East and packed up the children and their few belongings. In three days and nights on the train, she brought young Mike and his sisters from New York City, a heavily populated, increasingly cosmopolitan metropolis, to the small western town of Great Falls, Montana, where she and her husband had established a neighborhood grocery store several years earlier.

Great Falls in 1910, the year that Mike and his sisters arrived, was Montana's second largest city but had fewer than 14,000 inhabitants and was only a few decades removed from frontier America. The great falls of the Missouri River, which gave the city its name and its reason for existence, had been among the most important landmarks of the celebrated American explorers, Meriwether Lewis and William Clark, who had discovered the falls in June 1805 on their journey of exploration. Lewis called it "the grandest sight I ever beheld" because it confirmed that he was on course for what he thought would be the Northwest Passage to the Pacific coast. With Montana's admission to the Union as a state in 1889, only a little more than two decades before Mike's arrival, Great Falls had become a processing point for rich lodes of copper from the mines of Butte, 150 miles to the southwest. The 506-foot-high smokestack of the Boston and Montana Smelter, said to be the highest in the world, was visible for miles around. Encouraged and enabled by the Enlarged

Homestead Act passed by Congress in 1909 to provide free land to settlers, the population and the agricultural production in the area were increasing rapidly, and Great Falls was becoming a substantial trading center.

When the Mansfield children arrived in the care of Aunt Margaret, horses and buggies were more in evidence than automobiles, of which there were fewer than three hundred in town. Mike remembered in one of our conversations many decades later, "Wooden sidewalks—dirt roads—cowpunchers coming into town on Saturday, raising hell. Ranchers—gophers galore, three miles from home. All gone now."

"Uncle Richard" was a man of the frontier. After arriving in New York from Ireland at age sixteen, he had followed the gradual progress of the Great Northern Railroad west across the country, arriving in Great Falls in 1885, the year after the city's founding. Following his marriage in 1890, he opened a saloon in Barker, a mining town on the outskirts of the city, obtaining the license in his wife's name. He purchased barrels of whiskey and port wine for $497 from a wholesaler in San Francisco, but instead of paying for them and other goods, he bought land and began speculating in silver mining. Hauled into court by his creditors, he lost nearly everything as a result of court action and the silver crash of 1893. By 1897 he was reduced to working as a laborer in Great Falls. But a few years later he and Margaret managed to establish a small grocery story in a working-class neighborhood on the less-than-fashionable south side.

The Mansfield grocery was the front room of a one-story frame building whose door opened to the sidewalk. Inside were barrels of sugar and flour; an icebox, replenished in regular visits by an ice wagon, containing fresh fruit and meat; and boxes of candy, tea, and spices. It was the forerunner of what today would be called a convenience store, a haven for purchases between trips to larger, better-stocked establishments downtown. When Mike and his sisters arrived, there was no indoor plumbing or electricity. Lighting came from kerosene lamps, and heat during the long, harsh winters was supplied by a pot-bellied stove near the back wall, which also served as the partition to the family kitchen, dining room, and living room. The children slept in the attic and Richard and Margaret occupied a separate but tiny frame house in back. Richard's brother, James, lived next door.

Young Mike helped deliver groceries, first accompanying Richard or James on a horse-drawn wagon and later, when times were tougher and he was bigger, relying on his own strength to push a two-wheeled cart. Occasionally, he made deliveries to the rustic home of Charles M. Russell, the increasingly famous artist of western frontier scenes, whose picturesque Old West way of life was exciting to the young boy. In the summers he sold empty beer bottles for reuse to the Mint Saloon, where he saw Russell's portraits and drawings lining the walls. Despite the time devoted to work, Mike made friends among his elementary school peers and often played with them amid the sagebrush, gullies, and creek beds at the edge of town.

In 1912, two years after the Mansfield children moved to Montana, Uncle Richard died. Aunt Margaret had her hands full with the store as well as the children. Nearly fifty years old and never having had children of her own, she found dealing with an energetic and sometimes headstrong young boy particularly difficult. Although Mike had virtually no recollection of his mother, he probably idealized her. In contrast, he found his great aunt to be unacceptably stern and demanding.

Impressed by the crude physical power of the drifters who often came to town, young Mike began imitating them on a junior scale. "At the drop of a hat or the flick of a stick, up came my fists," he recalled. The feisty transplant from New York won a frightened respect in the schoolyard until he encountered Bill Scott, who was older and heavier, and who refused to be cowed when Mike growled as fiercely as he could and raised his fists. "In the next instant, I sat on the ground holding my broken nose. Tears of pain streamed down my face. Bill came over, picked me up and set me on my feet and walked away." The broken nose healed but the comeuppance cured him of aggressive arrogance, which he never again displayed.

Mike's behavior may have contributed to his grandaunt's decision in the fall of 1913, a year after her husband died, to take him out of public school and place him in the stricter St. Mary's parochial school, where he was taught by nuns. Feeling mistreated, he ran away from home the following summer. He got as far as Ulm, a farming community nine miles from Great Falls, where he was caught by sheriff's deputies. He was held in the city jail overnight, possibly in an attempt to scare him, before being sent home. He repeatedly begged the mother of a schoolmate, Walter Davidson, to adopt him, but she refused. In the fall of 1914 Aunt Margaret had Mike committed to the state home for wayward and orphaned children at Twin Bridges, nearly two hundred miles to the south, where he spent nine months and the sixth grade. The commitment papers reported the child to be destitute, which he certainly was not, given his aunt's store, but gave no other explanation for her act.

Returning to Aunt Margaret's home and store in mid-1915, young Mansfield was placed in the seventh grade of a Great Falls public school. He was an average performer in school, but outside of classes he began to be an industrious reader as an escape from his unhappy life. He was especially fascinated with the historical novels of Sir Walter Scott and other popular authors of the day, whose books stimulated his dreams of great adventures and faraway places. He became entranced with places he longed to see— Tibet, Kilimanjaro, Mount Everest, the Amazon. "I had quite an imagination and I always saw something green beyond the horizon," he recalled later in life. In more tangible diversions from the reality of his boyhood, he began cutting classes and disappearing to the home of his friends the Davidsons or the house or hayloft of an ex-policeman who lived a few doors away. He usually came back after a day or two, sometimes as truant officers were searching for him.

When the United States entered World War I in 1917, the young teenager made his break to independence in a spirit of high adventure. The newspapers in Great Falls were filled with patriotic fervor and reports of Americans proudly joining the armed forces. Mike had just celebrated his fourteenth birthday, but within weeks he left home for good. In June, after telling his sisters that he was leaving to see the world, he walked to Shelby, about ninety miles north. With less than a dollar in his pocket, he could buy only a few small cans of pork and beans. From Shelby he rode the rails on the main line of the Northern Pacific west to the Cascade mountains near the Pacific Coast, living in or atop freight cars under the guidance of hobos, who were common at the time. In Leavenworth, Washington, he was able to land a job at a lumber camp as a whistle blower, signaling lumberjacks with a whistle when a tree was about to fall.

While off the job, he met members of the Oregon National Guard who had been placed in the vicinity to guard bridges and tunnels against potential wartime enemies. They came to appreciate the blue-eyed kid from Montana who attached himself to their squad. Ordered to travel to an East Coast military depot, en route to military service in Europe, they smuggled their young friend aboard their troop train across the country to a camp on

Long Island, New York. One morning Mike left them and made his way alone into New York City. There he found his father.

INTO THE MILITARY SERVICES

In a stately New York neighborhood, a few steps off lower Fifth Avenue on East 11th Street, three blocks south of Union Square, stood the Hotel Van Rensselaer. Built shortly after the turn of the century, it was named after one of the old Dutch families which, like the Roosevelts, were the true aristocrats of New York. In the decade of the 1910s it advertised "quiet, homelike accommodations, making it an ideal stopping place for tourists, professional men and those desiring a location both choice and convenient." The tariff was $10 and up for a single room with private bath and $22 and up for a suite that included a parlor, bedroom, and private bath; full board of three meals daily from the hotel dining room was $9 extra.

Patrick Mansfield, who had never entirely recovered from his construction accident, was a porter at the Van Rensselaer hotel when Mike reappeared in his life around the turn of the year 1918. Then forty-one years old and living in a small apartment a few blocks away in Greenwich Village, Patrick had remarried the previous year. His new wife, Mary Tracy, another Irish immigrant, was a chambermaid at the hotel. Father and son, both men of few words, had a joyous reunion.

Mike stayed with his father and stepmother while trying to enlist in the armed forces. In despair after being turned down as too young, he asked his father to make a false declaration of his age in order for him to qualify, but Patrick refused. Undaunted, Mike went to the Roman Catholic church where he had been baptized, obtained a copy of his birth certificate, and changed the notation of his birth date, claiming to be born February 18, 1900, more than three years earlier than his actual birth date. In a period when the military services were searching for warm bodies to fill their ranks, a Navy recruiter accepted him as an apprentice seaman on February 23, 1918. According to Navy records, he was five feet four inches tall and weighed 122 pounds. In fact, Seaman Mansfield had not yet celebrated his fifteenth birthday.

By any standard, Mansfield's military service record is extraordinary. During a period of less than five years—all before he was twenty years old—he served in all three U.S. armed services then existing, first the

Navy, then the Army, and finally the Marine Corps. As far as is known, he was the only member of Congress ever to achieve that distinction. Because of his underage enlistment, he was among the youngest veterans of World War I and at his death in 2001 among only a handful of surviving veterans of that war. He can truly be said to have grown up in the U.S. military, which substituted for the comfortable family circle he rarely enjoyed. His experience contributed to a strong respect for authority and lawful command. His intimate knowledge of the armed forces from the bottom ranks, however, would not incline him to accept military judgments or to advocate military solutions to international problems; rather, he would be unusually suspicious of both.

After initial training at Newport, Rhode Island, he made three wartime voyages aboard the USS *Minneapolis,* a cruiser assigned to convoy duty, across the North Atlantic, which was infested with German submarines. A month after the war ended in November 1918, Mansfield made his first contact with high political authority. The lowly seaman wrote directly to Montana's powerful U.S. senator, Thomas J. Walsh, later famous for directing the investigation that uncovered the Teapot Dome scandal of the early 1920s, asking for his help in being released from military service. "I am not asking you to do this because I got a streak of yellow but now that the armistice is signed I would like to return to home and school," he wrote. Walsh sent the letter on to Secretary of the Navy Josephus Daniels, saying that it "appeals to me strongly" and recommended favorable action. Daniels, however, bucked the issue to the commanding officer of the *Minneapolis,* who did not dismiss the seaman until eight months later. His memory of this unhappy episode prompted Mansfield as a member of Congress to strongly support U.S. servicemen in China who asked to be mustered out quickly after the end of World War II.

Mansfield returned from the Navy to a Montana devastated by a catastrophic flu epidemic that cost the lives of more than 1,200 people in the state, followed by a disastrous drought that brought widespread crop failure, shattering the previous economic boom. Unwilling to go back to the eighth grade that he had fled two years earlier and finding no attractive jobs available, Mansfield joined the Army after less than three months of civilian life. In view of his undiminished thirst for foreign travel, he was excited when the Army recruiter suggested he would be sent to occupation duty in

Germany. Instead the Army assigned him to Fort McDowell, a hospital base
on Angel Island in the San Francisco Bay, where the commander, learning
he was from Montana, put him in charge of taking care of his horse.
Swallowing this disappointment, Private Mansfield served out his time in
the Army. The day his one-year enlistment was over, he took a ferry boat
across to San Francisco. The next day he joined the U.S. Marines for a two-
year hitch. He was seventeen years old.

The Marine Corps sent him to Subic Bay in the Philippines, a naval base
that was an important site and symbol of America's colonial presence in the
Pacific. There in the spring of 1922 he was among those selected from the
ranks for temporary duty in China, where an armed struggle between two
Chinese warlords was menacing American business interests and missionaries in the foreign-dominated coastal city of Tientsin. Mansfield was
delighted. His wanderlust had already taken him three times across the
North Atlantic as an underage Navy seaman and then to the San Francisco
Bay as an Army recruit. Now in the third of America's three military services, he was finally on the way to exotic and faraway places, the stuff of his
boyhood dreams, in this case the ancient and fabled Middle Kingdom, also
known as China.

A MARINE IN CHINA

On the sunny afternoon of May 5, 1922, Private Mansfield was among 150
Marines aboard the USS *Huron,* flagship of America's Asiatic Fleet, who
landed at Taku on the Chinese coast. As they traveled in a British tugboat
up the Pei-ho River to the landing, they saw bodies of Chinese soldiers in
padded cotton jackets floating in the water. In late afternoon, the nineteen-
year-old U.S. Marine from landlocked Montana watched the tug maneuver past dozens of square-rigged junks, fishermen's sampans, and ocean-
going freighters flying European, American, or Japanese flags to land at the
dock of the British Concession. Mansfield wore a wide-brimmed campaign
hat, a khaki uniform with canvas leggings and shouldered a well-oiled
Springfield '03 rifle. As he trotted down the gangplank, his eyes danced over
an exotic and most unfamiliar scene: swarming Chinese stevedores, a
bustling wharf, and a cityscape of warehouses and solidly built monumen-
tal buildings just beyond.

The U.S. military column briskly marched the short block to Victoria Road, a wide, tree-lined street named by the British in honor of their revered queen. On their right as the Marines turned into the thoroughfare was the majestic three-story structure of the Chartered Bank of India, Australia, and China, one of thirteen banks from Europe and Asia that handled the thriving business of the city. On their left the Marines passed the equally imposing headquarters of the ninety-year-old British trading company of Jardine Matheson, the leading foreign firm of the China trade, with its high Corinthian columns guarding a classic entrance that would have been in style on the streets of London. The Marines marched on, past the elaborate and rosy façade of Jardine's most important rival in China, Butterfield & Swire Co., Ltd., whose building stretched an entire city block. A little further were the elaborate balustrades and balconies of the Astor House hotel, established in 1863, where European royalty and visiting business leaders stayed. Further on, the Marines passed the British Club, housed in a massive Georgian mansion, and on to Strasse 5 (Street 5) on the edge of the area formerly occupied by Germany. There the leathernecks unloaded their packs and put down their rifles at the headquarters of the U.S. Fifteenth Infantry regiment, a block-long compound of brick and masonry barracks dominated by turrets and towers of officers' quarters and headquarters buildings.

The milieu into which Mansfield and his fellow Marines had been thrust seemed, at first glance, to partake as much of Europe as of Asia, as much of the nineteenth century as the twentieth. The European-dominated section of Tientsin was a world of its own, to a great degree insulated from the China all around it. Like Shanghai, it was among a handful of "treaty ports," whose political and commercial concessions had been wrested from the militarily weak Chinese after the Opium Wars in the mid-1800s. These ports operated under the principle of extra-territoriality, in which foreign governments applied their own laws, not those of China, to their people and activities therein. Tientsin's fifteen thousand foreign residents in the early 1920s dominated close to a million Chinese inhabitants of the city. Tientsin was the main port and business center of North China and the gateway to the inland capital of Peking, which was only eighty-three miles away. When Mansfield arrived, in addition to the dominant British, separate concessional areas were occupied by Belgians, French, Japanese, and Italians. The United States had earlier occupied a concession area, but in 1896 had given it back as impractical and unnecessary. However, U.S. businesses and missionaries continued to be present and prominent in Tientsin.

To protect American lives and property and do their share of guarding the railway and other points of access to the foreign diplomatic missions and enclaves in Peking, the troops of the Fifteenth Infantry regiment had been stationed in Tientsin since 1912, the year following the Chinese revolution that overthrew the last imperial dynasty, the Ch'ing, and initiated a period of chaos and warlord rule. The Marines were sent in as reinforcements after a civil war broke out near the city between two of the most prominent warlords, Marshal Wu Pei-fu, a Confucian conservative whose troops dominated a large area south of Peking, and Marshal Chang Tso-lin, a former bandit who wore a black satin skullcap adorned with a huge pearl, whose troops dominated the region of Manchuria north of the Great Wall.

The arriving Marines joined an international group of reinforcements for the city's diverse foreign business interests: a battalion of Japanese troops, detachments of Indian Sikhs brought by the British from Hong Kong, and detachments of Vietnamese soldiers supplied by the French. The senior officer was Japanese General Suzuki; for perhaps the only time in history, American troops were under the nominal command of a Japanese officer. Mansfield and his fellow Marines were assigned in pairs to patrol the outskirts of the city. They were also sent to guard the outposts of the United States: the compounds of the Standard Oil Company, the Texas Oil Company, the Dollar Lumber Company, and the Methodist Mission, as well as the Tientsin Power Plant.

Living at the barracks of the Fifteenth Infantry was considered "great duty" by the young Montanan. There was no kitchen police or other such chores, because Chinese "boys" hired by the permanent residents did this work for minimal pay, small pocket change for the Americans. Headed by a number-one boy dressed in a long blue gown and black skullcap, Chinese servants shined the shoes, made the beds, cleaned the barracks, cooked the meals, and even shaved officers and enlisted men. The infantrymen had their own Chinese tailors, who made their uniforms to order from cloth provided by the U.S. Army. During normal periods of tranquility, officers of the Fifteenth Infantry enjoyed tea and dinner dances and polo at the racing club. Tientsin also offered hundreds of bars, many staffed by White Russian girls whose families had fled from the Bolshevik Revolution. The venereal disease rate among enlisted men was reported to be three times that of the U.S. Army as a whole.

As it turned out, Mansfield and his fellow Marines had little need to fight. According to contemporary newspaper reports, Marshal Wu's troops fiercely attacked those of Marshal Chang the day before the Marines landed. After the shootout, the losers fled in panic. The British-owned *Peking and Tientsin Times* called it an "absolute debacle," whose principal danger to the city was that of marauding stragglers, "men of the type who constitute a menace to the towns and villages through which a retreating army passes in China." The Marines, though, heard a different version. Mansfield recalled that one morning he awoke to discover that both warlord armies had disappeared. The Marines were told that during the night some pieces of silver, Mexican dollars, had changed hands and both armies had gone home.

Four days after the Marines arrived, their patrol duty was called off. Mansfield and his fellow leathernecks were given liberty to explore the cobblestone streets of the city, where a few motorcars contended with ox carts, sedan chairs for the wealthy, and rickshaws pulled by muscular men stripped to the waist. In contrast to the broad streets and stately buildings of the foreign enclaves, the older and more heavily populated Chinese city was a warren of small lanes and narrow alleyways, redolent of incense covering a dozen other odors and alive with the sights and sounds of hawkers of every description.

After a little over a week in Tientsin, the Marines picked up their packs, reshouldered their rifles, and marched back to the dock. The *Huron* then sailed to Shanghai, where the Marines were given five days of liberty in China's largest and most economically developed city before sailing back to routine duty in the Philippines.

Mansfield's service in the Philippines and especially his brief sojourn in China made a deep impression. It was responsible, he later wrote, "for my developing an intense personal interest in China, in particular, and the Far East, in general. Because of that experience, I majored in Far Eastern history at the University [of Montana], did my thesis for my Masters on U.S.–Korea Relations, 1866–1910, and taught Far Eastern history from 1933 to 1943. My interest was based on population, geography, culture, affection and the fact that we were looking too much eastward and not enough westward where, I think, in many respects the future of this nation lies."

After less-than-satisfying experiences in the other two services, the Marines won his lasting admiration and loyalty for taking him to Asia and, after he was elected to the House of Representatives, promoting him to his highest military rank, that of private first class. As a member of the House, Mansfield co-sponsored the legislation that established a strong and permanent foundation for the modern Marine Corps. As a member of Congress, as an ambassador, and in retirement, he loyally continued to wear a Marine Corps lapel pin or tie clasp nearly every day of his life. Affixed to a red tie, his Marine tie clasp went with him to his grave at Arlington National Cemetery.

TO THE MINES AND
THE LOVE OF HIS LIFE

3

*A growing America was being wired for electricity and tele-
phone lines in the early decades of the century, and copper
was essential. The purest and most extensive veins of this precious metal were found in Butte, Montana, where thou-
sands of miners wrested ore from rock far beneath the surface of "the richest hill
on earth." In the 1920s young Mike Mansfield, recently out of military service,
toiled in the mines of Butte. As the Great Depression sapped economic life,
he abandoned the mines for a university education at the urging of a win-
some young woman who became the dominant figure in his life. As a professor
of Far Eastern studies at the University of Montana, his attention turned
again westward across the Pacific. There, Japan was flexing its muscles, invading China and eyeing the natural resources of Southeast Asia. If conflict developed in the Pacific, Professor Mansfield told his students, "the Japanese might
be the ones we would go to war with."*

In December 1922, only a month after his discharge from the Marines,
Mansfield took the train from Great Falls, where jobs were hard to find in

the postwar recession that afflicted most of the West, to the mining city of Butte, 150 miles to the south, where jobs were available for able-bodied men. From the station he gazed up the lengthy slope at an amazing panorama—dozens of skeletal frames, looking like lopsided oil derricks, on the skyline of a giant hill, which was also dotted with mine buildings and smokestacks belching smoke or steam. The derricks, known as gallows frames because of their resemblance to places of execution, held the elevator apparatus for lowering men in narrow shafts far into the bowels of the earth, where they blasted or chiseled copper ore from the volcanic rock. The mines were operating twenty-four hours a day, emitting the constant rumble of machinery, the roar of crackers of ore, and the sharp, shrill music of industrial whistles. The site of this vast works was known far and wide as "the richest hill on earth," at the time the most important industrial facility in the western United States. The giant hill dominated the city physically, economically, and socially and dominated Mansfield's life for the next decade.

"My ten years in Butte as a mucker, miner and sampler were ten years well spent and despite the heat, the copper water, and the copper dust, Butte still holds the number one place in my heart," Mansfield declared in a Labor Day speech in 1939, when he was contemplating his first run for public office. Once in office, Mansfield relied on Butte as a solid political base, furnishing large majorities for him at the ballot box in every race and in his one close race a powerful 68 percent endorsement that was the key to his victory.

He went to work at age nineteen as a mucker, whose job it was to shovel rock and ore into heavy metal cars deep underground for shipment to the outside. He made $4.25 per day, an excellent industrial wage for unskilled labor and more money than he had ever made in his life. After five years in the U.S. military services at about $30 per month, "I thought I was on the road to riches," he recalled, "but one shift in a stope [the narrow horizontal tunnel where rock and ore was gouged from the walls] on the 2800 level [the depth in feet below ground of the job at hand] washed away literally any illusions I may have had and brought me back to reality."

Wearing an open-flame carbide lamp on his hat to provide light, the young miner began his day lowered thousands of feet underground in a "chippy," a narrow elevator cage holding three to five other men crammed together with barely enough room to exhale. He typically spent eight and a half hours in the lower depths, including a half-hour to eat from the lunch bucket he brought down with him. At the end of the shift he emerged filthy from the grimy work, covered with sweat, and often exhausted from hard labor and bad air. Yet he and most others considered it a good living while it lasted.

Beneath the surface of the hill was a honeycomb of more than two thousand miles of tunnels alive with activity twenty-four hours a day. Above ground and down the slope, beyond the mining works, was another side of life: the rose-colored brick buildings and wooden structures of commercial and residential Butte, including banks, bars, brothels, and churches in profusion. Joseph Kinsey Howard, the state's most celebrated historian, described Butte as "huge, sprawling, chaotic—a very bully of a city, stridently male, blusteringly profane, boisterous and boastful." Yet it also was, as the Montana Writers' Project described it, "a city of paradox—virtuous yet wanton, vindictive and forgiving, hard headed or charitable, kind, cruel, religious, agnostic, sordid, exalted, gay and tragic."

When the mines were operating full blast, as they were during most of Mansfield's stay, the streets were thick with people day and night. Butte boasted, for it was never shy, a thriving red light district several blocks long and more than one hundred bars—more than twice as many as churches. There were forty-five miles of electric streetcars and eight thousand automobiles, about one for every eight residents. The city was served by four transcontinental railroads supplying its industrial needs and transporting the riches from its hill.

Butte had been established as a gold-mining camp in the 1860s and had enjoyed a brief boom of silver mining in the 1870s. In 1882 a prospector named Marcus Daly, exploring the depths of a played-out silver mine, "the Anaconda," discovered a rich vein of copper at the 300-foot level. Daly's purchase of the mine for $30,000 was supported by three California investors, the leader of whom was George Hearst, whose son, William Randolph Hearst, later turned his share of the Butte-based family fortune into a publishing empire. After decades of intense maneuvering, nearly all of the burgeoning mines on the hill were the property of Daly's Anaconda Copper Mining Company—known in Butte simply as "the Company"—which eventually also owned smelters, foundries, brass mills, coal fields, coke ovens, timberlands, sawmills, the Butte, the Anaconda and Pacific Railway, and most of the daily newspapers in the state. From the 1890s through World War I, passionate and often violent conflict for or against the Company, fought with bullets and bombs as well as angry words, erupted in Butte. At one point the headquarters of the Butte Miners' Union was blown up with twenty-five blasts of dynamite; a leader of the radical International Workers of the World, known popularly as the Wobblies, was lynched. The Company hired private Pinkerton operatives to enforce its dominance, among them the future novelist Dashiell Hammett, creator of Sam Spade and other fictional tough guys.

The biggest boom town in the West attracted legions of immigrants, especially the Irish who had experienced declining copper mines in the home country and the Cornish who had left depleted tin mines. Census figures from 1920 reported that 27,695 of the 60,313 residents of Butte and its environs were immigrants or the children of immigrants. By far the largest single group were the 7,556 Irish, but the records also identified significant numbers (more than 200 each) from Austria, Canada, Denmark, England, Finland, France, Germany, Greece, Hungary, Italy, Norway, Russia, Scotland, Serbia, Sweden, Switzerland, Turkey, and Wales. In addition, there were Chinese and Japanese, who were not counted, and small numbers from a variety of other countries. "No Smoking" signs in the mines were in English and sixteen other languages. This melting pot was the industrial and financial heart of Montana and the largest city in the five-state region of the northern Rockies and plains.

When Mike Mansfield arrived in Butte, its population had declined by a third from its high point of 90,000 in 1916, but nearly three dozen mines were in operation, employing about 5,000 miners daily. In his career as a miner, from December 1922 to December 1931, he would work in at least eighteen different mines, being laid off at times and at other times moving from one mine to another in search of better working conditions. On one occasion he was fired for reasons now obscure, but it did not seem to interfere with the next employment. "It was no trouble to get jobs in those days and when the going got a little too tough for us we would just pack our 'turkeys' [work clothes] and rustle another job," he recalled.

One mine where he worked, the Mountain Consolidated, or "Mountain Con," was 6,135 feet above sea level at its highest point with a shaft that eventually penetrated 5,291 feet underground, giving it and Butte fame as a mining town "a mile high and a mile deep." Below ground the heat was often intense, ever more so the deeper into the rock the work took place. Danger from underground fires that could cause asphyxiation, such as a disastrous fire in 1917 that killed 166 men, and from falling earth and rock, which killed many minors instantly, was part of daily life. The life of constant peril gave rise to the miners' greeting, originating in caution about the use of dynamite underground, that Mansfield carried into later life: "Tap 'er light."

Macabre humor inspired the creation of another expression. Loosened rocks plummeting down from above, the most common cause of death in Butte mines, were known as "Larry Duggans"—the name of Butte's most prominent undertaker. Between 1914 and 1920, 559 Butte miners died underground, an average of almost two per week; a heavy toll persisted into the 1920s and beyond. In December 1922, the month that Mansfield arrived, a thirty-six-year-old miner was killed instantly at the 2,400-foot level of the Colorado mine, where Mansfield first went to work. The incident was so commonplace that the *Butte Miner* recorded it in a one-paragraph story on page six. Victor Segna, an Italian immigrant who began working in the mines in 1922, said, "Once you got on that cage, you never knew if you'd come out of there. You never knew it. You got on there and you got down there, you may come up and you may not."

Even greater danger than sudden death was the long-term threat of silicosis, the often deadly scarring of lung tissue resulting from inhaling rock dust. In 1916 federal investigators examined 1,018 miners who appeared voluntarily for check-ups and found that 42 percent of them suffered from silicosis, popularly known as "miner's con," short for miner's consumption. The powerful Anaconda Copper Mining Company claimed to everyone's disbelief that the sky-high rate of respiratory illness and death in Butte was due to unsanitary living conditions. Although safety improvements were being made in the 1920s, including ventilating fans and wet drilling to keep down rock dust, foul air was still a daunting hazard, and many miners found the wet drills impractical. Mansfield saw many men coughing their lungs out; the plight of one man made an indelible impression.

Gus Erickson [he wrote years later] was one of the strongest men I've known. For most of 1926 we stayed in the same rooming house. . . . We ate together, loafed together, talked together. And together we sweated in the dust-filled air of the copper mines. Gus died of silicosis that year. The dust had gotten into his lungs. I watched his weight and muscle disappear. I saw him doubled over in bed, coughing and choking until his face was deathly white. At his funeral, I kept thinking: this could be me . . . this could be me.

During the travail of Gus Erickson, Mansfield decided to seek a better future. In mid-1926 he walked a dozen blocks across the hill from his boarding house to the Montana School of Mines, whose opportunities for education to become a mining engineer offered the most readily available means of advancement. Despite his lack of a high school education, he was accepted as a provisional student. That fall he attended school by day while working six nights a week in the mines; finding it was more work than he could sustain, he dropped out after a month but returned in the fall of 1927. This time he managed to complete the school year and was rewarded with promotion in 1928 to the job of sampler by the Company, which was receptive to advancing promising workers from within. Later in 1928 Mansfield was promoted again, to the post of assistant mining engineer.

MEETING MAUREEN: THE TURNING POINT

A vitally important turning point for Mansfield, who often said it was the most important event of his life, took place in 1928 outside the mines. Through her younger sister, Anne, whom Mansfield dated briefly, he met Maureen Hayes, the eldest daughter of Francis Fairclough "Frank" Hayes, a prominent businessman and political figure. Maureen was a confident, vivacious young woman with copper-colored hair, two years younger than he. Although he had not completed the eighth grade in school, she had an unusually extensive educational background for a woman of that era: high school and two years of college in private schools in Iowa and a year at the University of California at Los Angeles (UCLA) before obtaining her bachelor of arts degree at St. Mary's College, the female side of Notre Dame University. Returning to town as the English teacher at Butte High School, she lived with her family in a spacious frame house near the top of the hill and was a choice catch for any young man. No doubt to the surprise of her friends and at least some of her family, she and the solitary miner who lived in a rooming house fell in love. Somehow, she recognized a strength and potential in him that others, probably including himself, had not seen.

There was and remains considerable mystery about their powerful bond and unusual relationship. A photograph of the couple from this early period in their lives together provides a clue: a tall, slim, serious young man with downcast eyes and a sharp, almost triangular face, his hands self-consciously in his pockets, and a broadly smiling young woman with bobbed hair, keeping an affectionate grip on his arm and holding him close. "I had always been a loner who kept his thoughts to himself," Mike observed, "but Maureen brought out the talk in me. . . . Suddenly, I had a new friend, perhaps the only genuinely close friend in my life."

Before they met, his ambitions as well as his possibilities had been severely limited. It was her urging, in many cases her insistence, that propelled him from the mines to the university, and from there to the forefront of political life in Washington. Without her it is highly unlikely he would have undertaken any of those leaps, and even if he had tried, less than likely that he would have succeeded. "She literally remade me in her own mold, her own outlook, her own honest beliefs," he said at her funeral. In his opinion, she was solely responsible for his longevity. At the time of his birth, the life expectancy for American males was 47.9 years, and for a miner doubtless less, yet Mansfield lived to more than twice the expected age. By demanding that he leave copper mining for academia, "Maureen doubled my life span, at least," he told me.

She was chatty; he was quiet, often so silent as a member of Congress that he was the despair of hostesses, who could not decide what patient woman to seat next to him. According to Salpee Sahagian, a longtime Mansfield staff member, "He always consulted her. He always worshipped her. She had lots of nice things to say about him all the time. . . . He was her guardian and she was his consultant." Sophie Engelhard Craighead, a young family friend who worked as an intern in his Senate office and saw a great deal of the Mansfields at home in the late 1960s and early 1970s, observed, "They were co-dependent on each other. She was happy when he was happy. He beamed when she was near. They had a true love affair."

He could not remember his mother and had had an unhappy relationship with the grandaunt who had taken him in. He told me toward the end of his life that he realized that Maureen had been both a mother and a wife to him, that she "had taken the place of the mother I had never known." When she developed Alzheimer's disease several years before her death, he cared for her himself in their Washington apartment with minimal help. When eventually she had to be placed in a nursing home for twenty-four-hour care, he visited her every morning on the way to his office and every afternoon on the way home, even when she slipped so deeply into the disease that she no longer was certain who he was. When she died, his motivation to live on diminished. He forbade his doctors to do anything to prolong his life after that. He died in little more than a year later.

He gave her extraordinary and unparalleled tribute on every possible occasion, insisting, for example, that the library at the University of Montana be named the Maureen and Mike Mansfield Library and that a foundation established in his honor by Congress be named the Maureen and Mike Mansfield Foundation. He also refused to permit a commemorative statue to be placed in the Montana State Capitol unless it depicted both him and Maureen, not him alone as the sponsors proposed. Yet he forever maintained that he had failed to give her sufficient credit, that he reaped all the honors and acclaim when a large share should rightly have been hers.

That the teacher in a house at the top of the hill and the miner living in a cold water rooming house could fall in love and remain together for a lifetime is a testament to the American romantic ideal. It is also a tribute to the flexible social structure of Butte in the early part of the twentieth century. Although there were important distinctions between the many ethnic groups that contributed to the polyglot city, there was an easy tolerance and respectful recognition among most of them. Men of all backgrounds worked together in necessary harmony below ground and usually got along back on the surface. Perhaps for this reason, Butte was remarkably democratic. A social register of the supposedly elite was established in 1901 but abandoned after one year for lack of support. "There isn't a man, woman or child in the community who doesn't believe that he or she is as good as his neighbor. The miner or mucker doesn't look up to the banker or merchant, and the banker or merchant doesn't look down on the miner," wrote the authors of a Butte survey by the depression-era Writers' Project of the federally sponsored Work Projects Administration. Discrimination was limited mostly to Orientals and blacks, who were banned from most mines.

Nonetheless, Mike was not the choice of Maureen's father, who did not think the solitary miner from no discernable family was good enough for his talented and beautiful daughter. Hayes, a handsome and energetic man, had been born in 1874 in Michigan of Irish ancestry and came to Butte shortly after the turn of the century, when people were still putting down mining claims in much of the surrounding area. A speculator and plunger, he never struck it rich in mining properties but he successfully operated a coal and ice supply business, Western Fuel Company, until the coming of natural gas deprived it of its most important residential customers. Hayes was good at math and fascinated with politics. He had been auditor of the city early in his residence there; he was elected as a Democratic representative to the state legislature in 1914 and ran unsuccessfully for the Democratic nomination for mayor in 1923 and as a minor candidate for the Democratic nomination for governor in 1936. "He was always dabbling in politics. The house was always talking politics all the time," said his grandson and namesake, Frank Hayes.

Maureen's mother, Mary Frances Sullivan Hayes, had been born in Canada of Irish immigrant parents around 1881. Her parents died young, leaving two-year-old Mary Frances to be raised by an aunt and uncle in Duluth, Minnesota—a situation remarkably similar to that of the young Mike Mansfield. One of her granddaughters, Maureen Shea, described her as a strong influence in the Hayes household. "She would only use real linen, not cotton; real silver, not tin. She was not a snob, but she knew what was good." She made sure that each of her four children, two girls and two boys, of whom Maureen Hayes was the eldest, went to college, and private colleges at that. In early 1927, a year before Maureen met Mike, Mary Frances died of a stroke, leaving this twenty-two-year-old high school teacher the leading woman of the household. By then her father's financial reverses had set in, and her paycheck was an important source of income for the family.

By the time he met Maureen, Mike had been in Butte six years and had established himself with many friends. Handsome, serious, and studious— friends remember him spending many hours reading at the public library—he lived in a variety of rooming houses, each one a little better than the last. He took his meals for six dollars a week at Mary Fleming's Boarding House, owned as was often the case by a widow whose husband had been killed in the mines. Socially, he had become part of an informal group who went together to baseball games, to the popular Columbia Gardens amusement park or to one of the city's many dance halls. One of Mike's frequent dancing partners and dates was a secretary and bookkeeper whose father was the Butte sheriff. Another was a bank teller. Other members of the crowd were an electrician and a teacher. Unlike him, nearly all his friends had completed high school or higher education.

From their first meeting, Maureen was someone very different from these friends, with a much more powerful magnetic attraction. Before returning to Butte, she had learned in a letter from her sister, Anne, that she was dating "an older man" whose name was Michael Mansfield (he was twenty-five; Maureen was twenty-three; Anne was nineteen). Maureen considered it a beautiful name, and she was enchanted by the sight of the handsome miner heading up the Butte hill to the mines from his rooming house. Long afterward, on his eightieth birthday, Maureen wrote to Mike, in a letter that suggests her role in their courtship, "I thank God every day for my glance of you going up Washington Street, and my decision then that I was going to have you." Her sister, who went away to college that year, was shortly out of the picture. As Maureen and Mike began to date steadily, she would sit at the piano at home until he came into view and then would play "To a Wild Rose," the popular and brief piano solo by the American composer Edward MacDowell. They went dancing at the Winter Gardens, a local hall open on weekends that imported orchestras from Sioux City and elsewhere, and chose Vincent Youmans's "Tea for Two" as their favorite song. When Maureen died at age ninety-five, Mike arranged to have both tunes played at her funeral service.

When he met Maureen, Mike was in his first full academic year at the School of Mines, hoping for advancement in mining, while continuing to work six nights a week below ground. He spoke to Maureen about his early love of history, about the adventure books he had read and his life as a sailor, soldier, and Marine. Encouraged by Maureen to expand his horizons, he applied in October 1928 to Montana State University in Missoula, 120 miles northwest of Butte. He discovered to his dismay that because he had never attended high school, he would be considered only as a provisional or "special student" despite his military service and attendance at the School of Mines. The following summer he resigned from the Company, where he had been promoted to an assistant mining engineer, in order to attend the university. But after the summer semester, in which he received C's in each of his courses except for swimming, where he was awarded a B, he went back to work in the mines. With serious layoffs under way in Butte, he was deeply worried that he would soon be out of work. When Anaconda offered three-year contracts in the Chilean mines it had bought from the Guggenheim interests early in the decade, Mike applied for a job in Chile.

Until this moment of decision, his future seemed destined to be bound up in copper as tightly as the twisted pairs of wires that carried the voices of the telephone customers of the day. Then Maureen intervened. When he told her what he had done, she was thoughtful for more than a minute. In a soft, serious voice she asked, "Mike, are you sure you really want a career in mining?" She suggested that in view of his love for history and reading, he should take the money he had been saving and apply himself full time to obtaining a university degree. "But what about us?" Mike countered. "We couldn't afford to get married for years." Maureen responded, "The most important thing is for you to find yourself; we'll talk about marriage later." He tried to object, but she kept on insisting and finally won the debate. He dropped the application to go to Chile. At the same time, however, he considered a full-time college career starting at his age, without even a high school education, to pose almost insurmountable hurdles and, in fact, to be "absurd." Maureen argued on and began tutoring him in correspondence courses to prepare himself for the university.

Professor Walter Scott of the School of Mines, who administered several exams for his correspondence courses, wrote the Montana State University Admissions Committee in August 1931, "Mr. Mansfield in some respects is not a very gifted student but he impresses me as being very much in earnest about getting more education. He found our work in engineering very difficult but he may have more capability in other lines. He works at his studies and will do his best to make good." The committee admitted him on the condition that he complete a high school equivalency course before receiving his college degree. In late 1931 he again quit his job as an assistant mining engineer, which by then was paying him the very good salary of $220 per month and began a new life as a full-time university student.

INTO THE ACADEMIC LIFE

Founded in 1895, Montana State University (later renamed University of Montana, and referred to that way in the rest of this book) comprised nineteen buildings on one hundred acres of well-tended campus at the foot of Mount Sentinel, whose steep, grassy slopes towered above the university,

much as the "richest hill on earth" towered above Butte. There the similarity ended between the gritty industrial city Mansfield had left and the liberal arts academic setting in the pleasant small city of Missoula that was to
be the center of his life for the next twelve years. "A sense of quiet and peace-
fulness" pervaded the oval at the heart of the campus, he wrote in an essay
toward the end of his first year as an undergraduate. "The green grass, the
leafy trees and the stateliness of the buildings are all conducive to this feeling. . . . They form a picture that impresses itself upon the mind of the
undergraduate and visitor alike. It is one that will loom large and clear in
our memory for years to come."

The twenty-eight-year-old freshman, who was older and more experienced in the world than his classmates, rented a room in a house near the
campus and spent many of his waking hours at a table in the university
library. Taking a full load of college courses on top of correspondence courses
and high school equivalency tests to make up for his lack of academic preparation, he had little time for anything but study. Through diligence, a trait
he displayed throughout his life, he earned an A (in history of Rome), two
B's, and a C in his first quarter and kept up creditable if not outstanding
grades throughout the rest of his undergraduate career. He was a serious student and an avid reader, a habit he had formed much earlier and would continue throughout his life. His professor in European history commented that
Mansfield as a student "did a *vast* amount" of reading.

Maureen was still teaching in Butte during his first year at Missoula, and
the two communicated only through the mail. By the fall of 1932, the separation had become too painful for them both. Maureen quit her job and drove
to Missoula, where they were married at St. Anthony's Church on September
13. Both had been saving as much money as possible in preparation for their
campus life, but they had to struggle to get by in the depths of the depression.
A $700 bonus paid to veterans of World War I helped greatly but was not
enough. At one point Maureen decided to cash in her life insurance, worth a
little over $1,000, to shore up their sinking finances. As her husband began
to protest, she shook her head angrily: "Be sensible, Mike—keeping you in
school is our insurance for the future." One night Mike saw three pounds of
hamburger on sale for twenty-five cents and bought it for a treat, only to have
Maureen break down in tears when he brought it home because they had no
icebox in their small apartment in which to store it. Shortly before his gradu-

ation in the spring of 1933, after six quarters of full-time university work and remedial high school study, Mike applied for high school teaching positions in two towns in western Montana where he believed he had good prospects. His applications were rejected, apparently because of his religion. The Ku Klux Klan was active in Montana at the time; not against blacks, of which there were few, but against Roman Catholics.

Brokenhearted, he faced the prospect of receiving his B.A. degree in history at age thirty with no job and few prospects at a time when about one-fourth of the state's population was on relief and faculty salaries, already low, were being cut. At this moment, his career took another fateful turn. Paul C. Phillips, chair of the history department, who had been following the work of the ex-miner with interest, offered him a job as graduate instructor of two freshmen history courses for a total of $22.50 per month to pay the rent while Mansfield pursued a master's degree on a scholarship leading to an academic career. Although rarely given to expressive emotions, Mansfield decades later could still recall the joy and excitement he felt. "Here was the goal for which Maureen and I had been striving. At last, I was truly a part of the world of books and ideas." Maureen was working in the kitchen when he returned from the meeting with Phillips. "Tonight, Mrs. Mansfield," he said with mock severity as he untied her apron, "we are going out for a steak dinner." In the spring of 1934 Maureen, who had been taking graduate courses in English, won her master's degree in English after successfully completing a thesis on biographies of Emily Brontë. In June Mike was awarded his master's degree in history.

His thesis, on U.S. diplomatic relations with Korea from 1866 to 1910, was an early display of his continuing interest in Asia. After meticulously tracing the interaction of American diplomats, military officers, and missionaries with Korea as the country began to open to the outside and came under the increasing control of Japan, Mansfield ended by observing that the U.S. government, despite an earlier "Treaty of Amity and Commerce" with Korea, refused to intervene or even protest when Japan annexed its less powerful neighbor. "After all," he wrote, "we had no imperialistic designs in Korea; we had no class clamoring for a commercial or political foothold; we had no real and vital interests in the country; therefore, the treaty of 1882 notwithstanding, we had no business there. Thus, we departed and left Korea to her fate." Mansfield's concern for U.S. national interest, overriding other considerations, would dominate many of his later views on U.S. foreign policy in Asia.

With his M.A. in hand, Mansfield dispatched copies of his academic transcript to five other universities and such leading institutions as the Carnegie Endowment for International Peace, but no teaching prospects were forthcoming. Once again, Phillips stepped in to arrange a part-time job as assistant to the registrar at $100 per month plus $25 monthly for teaching history classes. After nearly three years with this makeshift arrangement, the university agreed to sponsor summer semesters toward a Ph.D. in history, which Montana did not offer, at the University of California at Los Angeles, on the understanding that he would specialize in Far Eastern and Latin American history, which were of increasing interest but not taught at Montana. Mansfield attended UCLA in the summers of 1937 and 1938, earning nearly straight A's in those subjects while auditing additional courses.

When Mansfield returned from his first summer at UCLA, he began teaching full time. His most important and most popular offering was history of the Far East, concentrating on the modernization of China, Japan, and the Philippines. It was the first time that such a course had been offered at Montana and one of the few courses in that subject to be offered in the United States at the time.

With his experiences in China and the Philippines as a Marine and his continuing fascination with Asia now reinforced by a solid academic background, Mansfield was a popular and highly successful teacher. His mastery of his material; his extraordinary memory for facts, figures, and names; and his ability to organize his ideas and information into powerful presentations—capabilities that were later on display in his political and diplomatic careers—won excellent reviews from both faculty and students. Noting that he made the seemingly obscure subject of Far Eastern history come alive, one former student recalled that "I've never before, or since, been so taken with subjects that I wasn't aware of time, but with Mike, the period always ended before you expected it." Another recalled that "I took a minor in history because of him. Everything he threw out, you understood it. . . . Everybody wanted to be in his classes." Beginning in 1937, Mansfield taught Far Eastern history nearly every quarter for the next five years—as long as he was at the university—while also occasionally teaching Hispanic-American history, European history, background of the French Revolution, and other history courses, all of which later contributed to his expertise and interest in international affairs.

As war clouds gathered at the end of the decade, Mansfield was preparing to make another major shift in his career, from academe to the life of a public man.

INTO THE
POLITICAL WORLD

4 *Within months after their invasion of China in 1937, Japanese
forces attacked and sank the* Panay, *an American ship anchored near Nanking, and Japanese troops besieged and rav-
aged that city in what has been known since as the Rape of
Nanking. U.S. public opinion began to turn sharply against
Japan, even as it turned against Germany as Adolf Hitler's troops rampaged
through Europe. In Asia, Japan seized more Chinese cities and, after the German
occupation of France, moved troops into French Indochina. This prompted
President Franklin D. Roosevelt to impose a U.S. embargo on sales of scrap iron
and steel to Japan and later to freeze Japanese assets. Japan, having signed an
"axis" partnership with Germany and Italy, attacked the U.S. naval base at
Pearl Harbor, Hawaii, on December 7, 1941. This was the start of the American
participation in World War II, which brought a massive buildup of
American military power and fundamental changes in the American role in
the world. It also brought about great changes in the life of Mike Mansfield.*

It was not Mike Mansfield's idea to go into politics. As he told me on several occasions, from his boyhood days he was always "sort of a loner." The
ambition and the impetus came from Maureen, "who pushed me, prod-

ded me and encouraged me." In response, the popular assistant professor and assistant university registrar began to discuss the possibility of a
political future with a few trusted friends as early as 1936. Sitting in his
office in Main Hall, the Romanesque administration building of the
University of Montana, he asked the advice of Peter Meloy, a politically
experienced law student four years younger than he, about whether it
made more sense to run for Congress or for state superintendent of
schools. Meloy, who ran unsuccessfully that year for a seat on the
Montana Railroad and Public Service Commission, recommended that
he run for Congress. About the same time, Mansfield discussed the pros
and cons of a race for Congress with Philip Roberts, a recent law school
graduate and a neighbor. Mike initially decided he was not yet ready for
such a contest, but at the same time "I felt that if I did go into politics I
should try for something really responsible and because of that made the
decision to go for Congress."

In retrospect election to Congress was almost an impossible dream for a
virtually unknown instructor with no money and no experience in politics.
The would-be congressman was tall and handsome in a gawky, angular way,
reminiscent of photographs of the young Lincoln. His most appealing asset
was a lack of pretension. He was a shirtsleeve figure who dressed in the garb
of the common people from whom he had come, never quick to speak and
notably willing to listen. His ability to remember names after a single meeting, no matter where or how the next meeting took place, was a politically
valuable talent that never left him.

While studying at UCLA in the summer of 1937, Mansfield made his first
visit to Washington, D.C., the city where he was to spend much of the rest
of his life. He bought a round-trip cross-country bus ticket for $90 and
embarked on a reconnaissance mission, calling on Montana's two U.S. senators, James E. Murray and Burton K. Wheeler, and Representative Jerry
O'Connell, who represented Montana's western district, including Missoula
and Butte. O'Connell, six years younger than Mansfield and at twenty-eight
one of the youngest members of Congress, was making a name for himself
as a flamboyant liberal with his militant support of the Loyalist fighters in
the Spanish Civil War and other causes. Mansfield later acknowledged that
he was already considering a run for O'Connell's House seat when he made
the trek to Washington.

At this time, Mansfield was participating in a different sort of politics. Angered by the arbitrary actions of the newly installed president of the university, twenty-seven of the eighty-four members of the faculty in April 1937 revived a dormant chapter of the American Federation of Teachers, which was affiliated with the American Federation of Labor. Mansfield, who was just making the transition from part-time to full-time teaching, was among the most active members of the teachers' union and became its first treasurer. He also served as the union's liaison with other labor groups, whose leaders found the straight-talking former miner different from what they expected from the campus—a professor they could talk to, and support.

Mansfield's work as a miner in Butte from 1922 to 1931 predisposed him to an interest in the cause of labor. He had not, however, been a labor union member at the time because internecine warfare had destroyed the Butte Miners' Union in 1914 and it was not reestablished until 1934. When Mansfield worked in Butte, the Anaconda Copper Mining Company was essentially an open-shop enterprise, but there were few clashes between the miners and the Company. He got along well both with his fellow workers and with management, which awarded him several promotions.

In November 1938 Representative O'Connell suffered a surprise defeat in his bid for reelection. It had been widely expected that in 1940 he would challenge Wheeler, who had been transformed from a New Deal supporter to President Roosevelt's number one enemy by leading the successful Senate fight against FDR's 1937 court-packing plan. Wheeler and his friends in the Democratic stronghold of Butte reacted to O'Connell's potential challenge by crossing party lines en masse to elect O'Connell's Republican opponent, a political novice named Dr. Jake Thorkelson.

In December 1938, a month after O'Connell's defeat, Mansfield resigned as an officer of the teachers' union and began traveling and speaking extensively throughout the western congressional district. The president of the teachers' union, Professor Edmund Freeman, wrote an enthusiastic letter about Mansfield as a potential Democratic congressional candidate to Montana's junior senator, Jim Murray, an avid New Dealer with much influence in Butte:

Everybody who knows him likes him. Many of us love him. His [sic] is honest and immediately impresses people as honest. He is patient and persistent. I have not seen him slight or avoid any hard or unpopular job—and a number of them come up in our community and our organization. As a member and officer of our union he has been invaluable—for his zeal, his tact and his faithfulness. He makes friends and has many connections. He is keenly interested in politics and is a very thoughtful person. I simply do not know how well he would do in the public-speaking phase of the job. He does fine classroom work and would do excellent work on the radio—and he might do well on the public platform. In making profitable contacts I think no one would surpass him.

Murray, although impressed that Mansfield had a "very excellent likelihood of making headway in public life," responded that he would remain neutral in the coming Democratic primary. Months later, after hearing from a political ally that Mansfield preferred him over Wheeler, Murray wrote back that "I think he has got the intelligence, the ability and the integrity that would make a good Congressman" and authorized his ally to pass that word to Mansfield.

Remembering what had happened to O'Connell when he crossed the senior senator and his allies, Mansfield wrote Wheeler in March 1940 that he hoped for his "friendly interest" in his campaign although he realized he could make no endorsement in the primary race. Mansfield went on to emphasize that "my entry into the race was my own idea; that I will be under obligation to no person or organization; and that if elected I will be my own man." Wheeler responded simply that he was taking "no part in the primary campaign whatsoever."

Mansfield seemed well positioned for the congressional race. He believed that, as a previous inhabitant of the Democratic stronghold of Butte, he had "much support" there, and he pointed this out to Wheeler. To help him translate acquaintanceship into votes, he secured the assistance of James "Jimmy" Sullivan, with whom he had formed a friendship while living at the boardinghouse of Sullivan's mother-in-law, Mary Fleming. Sullivan was a house painter and paper hanger—and a man with many friends in Butte. He agreed to help Mansfield and eventually became a full-time aide and his closest Montana political adviser.

As Mansfield also wrote Wheeler, his university connection was "a decided help." Robert Pantzer, who was student body president at the time and much later the university's president, was among a group of students who distributed leaflets and undertook other chores for the professor-candidate. "I was not in his classes, but we all knew Mike and said, 'Let's try to help him.'"

As it turned out, this support was not enough. Instead of being the sole alternative to O'Connell, who ran again, Mansfield was faced with two additional candidates, who split the votes. O'Connell, a native of Butte, came out on top, and Mansfield finished third in a field of four for the Democratic nomination. The Republican nomination went to Jeanette Rankin, the first woman elected to the U.S. Congress and a legendary pacifist who had voted against World War I during her one previous term in Congress in 1917–1919. With the United States again on the brink of a world war and the Democrats deeply divided, Rankin went on to win the general election by a comfortable margin.

At Maureen's insistence, Mansfield continued campaigning the day after his election defeat. On one celebrated occasion he visited the tiny town of Wolf Creek. Asked what possible business he had there, Mansfield replied that he had received one vote in Wolf Creek in the previous Democratic primary, while O'Connell got forty-nine. "I want to see the one person who voted for me, and thank him." He did not find the one supporter, but the story got around political circles in the state.

At this point a dramatic external event—the Japanese attack on Pearl Harbor on December 7, 1941—intervened in a way that would change Mansfield's life. A year earlier he had campaigned on a "peace and preparedness" theme. "I was in a certain sense an isolationist at the time. I did not believe we should become involved in wars outside our shores. But once Pearl Harbor happened, my opinion and the opinion of many others changed." Suddenly his experiences as a professor of Far Eastern history and as a veteran of military service in World War I became major political assets. He utilized them, along with his history and contacts as a miner in Butte, still the most important Democratic stronghold in the state. Mansfield traveled widely throughout the district speaking about the battle against Japan to any group that would invite him. While he traveled, Maureen compiled lists of his former students and prepared "Dear Fellow Student" letters to them emphasizing his qualifications and asking for support. "I feel that we are now engaged in a life and death struggle—a struggle for existence," Mansfield declared in a standard letter in his own name. "As one of the youngest veterans of the last War, I have an understanding of the problems of today and sympathy for our young men in the Service."

The coming of the war brought an end to the political career of the pacifist incumbent, Jeanette Rankin, who stuck by her principles and became the only member of Congress to vote against declaring war on Japan despite the attack on Pearl Harbor. Her solitary act was hailed by some as a "brave folly," but it doomed her chances for reelection; she did not even enter the Republican primary in 1942. On the Democratic side, O'Connell once again tried to return to office, but his defeats in 1938 and 1940 and the continuing opposition of the Wheeler faction of the party destroyed his chances to make a comeback. Thus both major political obstacles to Mansfield, the Republicans under Rankin and the left-wing Democrats backing O'Connell, were eliminated, clearing the way for the miner-professor.

Mansfield easily won the 1942 Democratic nomination for Congress from the Western District. His Republican opponent was Howard K. Hazelbaker, a state senator with little appeal, although his uncle had been governor and his campaign was expected to be well-heeled. Mansfield had won a resounding primary victory in July, but protests to the university about his energetic activities as a politician forced him to go on leave without pay. He had no other source of income and virtually no money in the bank. He was left to face the fall campaign with no reliable source of campaign funds.

At this point an acquaintance from Butte, James Rowe Jr., emerged as an important figure in that campaign and the rest of Mansfield's political career. Although they shared roots in Butte, the two came from very different backgrounds. Rowe was the son of a prosperous real estate man and had attended Harvard University and Harvard Law School. He and Mansfield had met at a cigar-store hangout in Butte while he was on summer vacation from Harvard and Mansfield was still working in the mines. On graduation from law school, Rowe was law clerk to former Chief Justice Oliver Wendell Holmes. This launched him on a brief but prominent career in government, first as a White House assistant to FDR and then by 1942, assistant to Attorney General Francis Biddle. After leaving government following wartime service in the Navy and postwar service at the Nuremberg Trials of the Nazi war criminals, Rowe went on to become a well-connected corporate lawyer in Washington and an influential Democratic Party insider, a close friend and confidential adviser to Lyndon Johnson in his congressional career and in the White House. He served either officially or unofficially as

Mansfield's finance chairman in nearly all of his campaigns. Even though Rowe was six years younger, Mansfield once said he "in a sense, was my political godfather." Mansfield described him as "a man of great honesty . . . of great cynicism. A man whom you could talk to in confidence and know that it would be held in confidence. A man you could trust."

In 1940 Rowe had mused about coming home to Montana to run for Congress, but he lacked contacts in the state and was reluctant to give up his exciting life in New Deal Washington. Seeing a potential winner, he urged Mansfield to run in 1942. After his friend won the Democratic nomination, Rowe set about to help him in ways that made possible not only the financing of his successful campaign but his identification as a promising new political figure with the leaders of the Democratic Party, including House Speaker Sam Rayburn; Democratic National Chairman Ed Flynn, the political boss of the Bronx; and even President Roosevelt.

In a fund-raising letter to Flynn, Rowe said Mansfield "is a very poor man and the money crowd has shown no interest in him." In response to a personal appeal from Mansfield, Rowe had his wife, Elizabeth, wire him $750, which, he said, came from unidentified "private individuals" with "absolutely no strings upon it" other than Rowe's assurance that Mansfield would be a pro-Roosevelt liberal Democrat. The source of the money is not known, but Rowe had access to political funds from organized labor and, through his friend Representative Lyndon Johnson, from corporate sources in Texas and elsewhere. Rowe, through Rayburn, arranged for the Democratic Congressional Campaign Committee to send Mansfield $1,000 more, which was the maximum provided for any House candidate that year. The records of spending reports for that period in Montana have been discarded and no other records could be found, but the likelihood is that these two contributions provided the bulk of Mansfield's campaign funds. According to an Associated Press account immediately after the election, Mansfield's preliminary campaign finance statement reported contributions of $1,150, including $1,000 from the Democratic committee. At Rowe's suggestion, Mansfield also wrote an appeal for funds directly to Johnson, who had been the chief fund-raiser for House Democratic candidates in 1940, with Rowe serving as his liaison with the White House. By 1942, however, Johnson was no longer in that role. As far as can be determined, Johnson did not respond directly to Mansfield's letter, but it was the first contact between two men whose futures would be linked in ways that neither could then imagine.

Rayburn had previously complained to Rowe about the quality of representation from the western Montana district. In his appeal for funds to the powerful speaker, Rowe wrote that "Mansfield has a lot of common sense, and in fact has many of the qualities of Lyndon in his ability to get around. He has carefully kept away from getting into a factional fight with either the Murray or Wheeler factions in Montana. If he comes to Congress, and I am sure he will with some help, I know you will be proud of him, and know also that the good name of Montana will be vindicated in your mind." To FDR, Rowe sent along a copy of a letter from Mansfield reporting, among other things, that Roosevelt's nemesis, Wheeler, had failed to show up for the State Democratic Convention. With this tidbit a point of interest, Rowe described Mansfield in the first of two memos to the President as "an intelligent New Dealer with an international point of view [who] combines the excellent background of a hard-rock copper miner and history professor." These contacts and Rowe's enthusiastic endorsement would prove to be crucial in Mansfield's Washington career.

A week before the election, Mansfield delivered the only radio address that he could afford during the campaign. "I have tried to meet as many of you as I possibly could over the last three years," he said. "I have nothing to hide, as my cards have always been on the table and my position known. I entered this campaign clean, and I come out of it the same way. I want you to have the same faith and confidence in me that I have in you."

On election day, Mansfield won easily with nearly 60 percent of the vote, although nationally the Democratic Party lost forty-seven seats in the House and only narrowly retained its majority. Rowe wired his victorious friend: I AM DELIGHTED. I AM GLAD SOMEBODY I KNOW WON DESPITE THE REPUBLICAN SWEEP. I AM SURE THIS IS THE BEGINNING OF A LONG AND DISTINGUISHED CAREER FOR YOU. From Floyd J. Hughes of Manhattan, Montana, came a more intimate reaction: "From 'Mucker' to 'Congressman' pretty darn good, if you ask me. So—just keep the feet on the ground, or better still just be Mike Mansfield, your going around Manhattan, hat and coat off shirt collar unbuttoned, pipe in your mouth and calling everyone by their first name was a vote getter, believe me, as a lot of the folks said that fellow is a regular guy and I'm going to vote for him. . . . You can be

Congressman as long as you want IF you will always be just Mike Mansfield. . . ."

ON TO WASHINGTON

In late December 1942 Mike, Maureen, and their three-year-old daughter, Anne, who had been born as Mike began to campaign in the 1940 race, left Missoula. In their battered 1936 Ford with their belongings packed in the back they drove across the vast, forbidding northern part of the country to arrive half-frozen nearly a week later in Washington, D.C. The United States had been at war for a year, and the capital had been transformed from a sleepy southern city to a swollen metropolis as war-related agencies grew and government workers arrived month by month. Housing was so scarce that newcomers crowded around newspaper offices at press time to obtain the first copies of the papers to check out ads for rooms to rent. High-ranking officials, heads of war agencies, and many members of Congress were living in hotels. The Mansfields felt lucky to find a house in suburban Chevy Chase, Maryland, even though the rent was exorbitant by their standards and their new home was ten miles away from the House Office Building, a far cry from the convenience of academic life in Missoula.

Through the personal initiative of Speaker Rayburn, Mansfield was named to the prestigious Committee on Foreign Affairs, his first choice. Newspapers at home reported he was the first member of the House from Montana ever to serve on that committee. From the beginning, he served with enthusiasm and diligence. In committee meetings, he said little about issues and areas unfamiliar to him but spoke up confidently and unhesitatingly about Asia. Journalists on Capitol Hill quickly learned he was easily approached and both knowledgeable and quotable.

In early February, less than two weeks after joining the committee, he was quoted by the Associated Press and Washington newspapers, saying that the war in the Pacific was as important as that in the Atlantic, which had first priority under U.S. war plans, and calling for greatly stepped-up aid to China. In early March he played a surprisingly prominent role in the House debate on Lend-Lease supplies to China and was even more prominent in the news accounts. "The Chinese are being starved out and worn out because of our inability to get materials to them," Mansfield told the

House. He took issue with the thesis that it would be impossible to do more, saying, "this war is going to be won by doing the impossible."

By the end of April, the freshman congressman was considered a sufficient authority on the war in Asia that the National Broadcasting Company asked him to deliver a radio address. His first exposure to a nationwide audience, "What Are We Going to Do about the Pacific?" was broadcast over NBC's Blue Network on April 30, 1943. It was largely a repetition of things he had said in House hearings, emphasizing the vital importance of China. "Today Japan holds China in the grip of a blockade by land, sea and air. . . . China is barely hanging on, fighting to stave off disaster until help can reach her. . . . Let us give to China—and soon—the tools she needs. We can rest assured that *she* will do her utmost to finish the job." As for Japan, Mansfield totaled its impressive gains in area and population since Pearl Harbor and maintained that "Japan now has the resources to wage a war for many years to come." At one point Mansfield uncharacteristically bought into the racist sentiments of the day, referring to "these small, myopic, buck-toothed sons of Nippon" as "the most dangerous enemy we have ever faced." At the end of the speech he called for instituting "a realistic press policy" on the serious situation in Asia rather than continuation of a policy of "what the people don't know won't hurt them." Not surprisingly, the address won praise from the press as well as the public. It led to two more national radio addresses in succeeding months.

In speeches over three local radio stations after returning home that summer of 1943, Mansfield spoke in detail of his work for his district and the state, but then he discussed the war and set forth the great importance that he placed on China, which would become a central theme for the rest of his life. At this stage, he was remarkably optimistic.

> The defeat of Japan—and it will be difficult—is only one small part of the "war" for the future of the Pacific. The great stabilizing, balance force in the Pacific world after the war, must be a China able to participate on equal terms with Russia, Britain and the United States—in fact, not on paper.
>
> Quite apart from China's strategic position, tradition, and size, there's a compelling reason for this. China is the only Asiatic power which has of its own gumption shared our experience of revolution—which has the slightest understanding of what it means to struggle and die for the rights of man.

Japan is fully aware of China's importance—aware that China is a greater potential danger to Japan, over the centuries, than all of us put together. For Japan and China represent diametrically opposite ideas. We need have no fear of a strong China; rather, we should fear a weak China because then we might not be able to stay out of Asia. China's strength would be an asset, not a menace, so long as it is used to promote the rights, and not the servitude, of man. This, China is trying to do.

China appeared much less democratic and its future much less promising from the vantage point of the executive branch of the U.S. government, which was experiencing deepening frustration with its leader, Generalissimo Chiang Kai-shek. He was holding back his best troops to checkmate the growing communist guerrilla forces in northwest China rather than fight the Japanese, and the troops he did commit to battle often refused to fight under their ineffective and corrupt commanders. Mansfield, however, continued to campaign for additional U.S. aid to Chiang's government as a spearhead of the fight against Japan.

WORKING FOR MONTANA

Although foreign policy had been and continued to be his greatest interest as a lawmaker in Washington, his most pressing concern was practical assistance to his constituency, which he considered his first and most essential job.

Montana is one of the largest states in area and among the most politically divided among all those in the United States. It covers 580 miles from east to west at its northern border which it shares with Canada, roughly the distance between New York City and Columbus, Ohio. It is 275 miles from north to south. Until the admission of Alaska in 1958, it was the third largest state after Texas and California. By itself, Montana is considerably larger than Greece or Italy.

Physically it is sharply divided. Its western third, which Mansfield represented as a member of the House of Representatives, is a rugged land of heavily forested peaks and valleys dominated by the Rocky Mountains. The eastern two-thirds is part of the prairie of the Great Plains, broken by a network of valleys and low mountains, stretching across the middle of the continent.

Montana was and is thinly populated. In 1940 the entire state had only 559,000 inhabitants, an average of 3.8 persons per square mile. Beginning even before it became a state in 1889, the two major political parties and political tendencies had been evenly matched as conservative corporate interests, ranchers, and merchants contended with miners and other industrial workers and small farmers, some progressive and some radical.

For many decades Montana's economic giant, the Anaconda Copper Mining Company, and its brotherly behemoth, the Montana Power Company, had been among the most important and most controversial factors in the state's politics, with many issues decided by the intervention of the Anaconda Company or by coalitions for or against it. Anaconda owned not only the Butte copper mines but also the smelters, refineries, and reduction works that processed the ore; it possessed hundreds of thousands of acres of timberland, and as late as 1959 it held the predominant financial interest in daily newspapers in Billings, Butte, Helena, Livingston, and Missoula.

Because of the decline of metal mining in the state and the Company's diversification outside, Anaconda's political role was receding when Mansfield entered public office in 1943. Instead of battling ruthlessly and openly against those who declined to do its bidding, the Company's newspapers and political operatives simply ignored political figures who were beyond its control, such as Mansfield. The Company held detailed records on Mansfield's early career as a miner and did not consider him an enemy. "They never went after me, I never went after them. They never asked me to do anything. I never made any move in their direction," he told me, although he did consistently back U.S. duties on copper and aid to western mines in the interest of his constituency. Except for the *Great Falls Tribune,* which was independently owned but outside of his congressional district, Mansfield was given the silent treatment by the state's prominent daily papers during his early years in Congress.

Throughout his career in public life, Mansfield managed to float above the shot-and-shell of Montana partisanship and become a widely respected, even beloved politician with a constituency stretching across normal political lines—even while other state and congressional offices rotated between Republicans and Democrats, conservatives and progressives, with regularity and in fierce contention. After his first election to Congress in 1942, this unpretentious yet authoritative figure, universally known as Mike, won every contest by comfortable, usually lopsided majorities, with a single exception. That was his 1952 race, when he narrowly won election to the U.S. Senate for the first time in the face of the Eisenhower landslide and despite a smear campaign masterminded and personally brought to the state by the anti-communist demagogue, Senator Joseph R. McCarthy.

When, in 2000, the *Missoulian,* the daily newspaper of the university town, selected the 100 most influential Montanans of the twentieth century, it singled out Mansfield together with his wife, Maureen, as first on the list. In the late 1990s, at the initiative of the state's Republican governor, Marc Racicot, the Montana legislature provided the authority and most of the funds (the rest from public subscription) for a statue of the Mansfield couple in the state capitol building—the only such statue there except for one of the famed pacifist politician Jeanette Rankin. The statue was dedicated with ceremony shortly after Mansfield's death. One of the great mysteries of his political career is how and why he was able to attain this extraordinary stature, which began in his first term in Congress, in an otherwise partisan and bitterly divided state. This achievement has been examined with wonder by Montana historians and political scientists, and with admiration sometimes mixed with envy and occasional irritation by other politicians in the state.

Part of the answer was his industriousness in pursuit of the individual and collective interests of his constituents and his success in keeping an unexcelled and untroubled relationship with very many of them. Representing a thinly populated state a long way from the U.S. capital, Mansfield's congressional office was legendary for its attentiveness to constituents. Mansfield's practice throughout his many years in Congress was to read every letter sent to him from Montana and make sure it received a suitable answer, signed in his own hand. He refused to permit use of the auto-pen, a mechanical device popular among congressional offices for automatically affixing what looks to be an individual signature, and he often appended handwritten personal notes to routine letters his aides had prepared. According to Peggy DeMichele, who was an assistant to Mansfield during nearly his entire congressional career, "he believed the reason people sent him to Washington was to attend to the little things." No request was too insignificant, as when a young boy in Billings asked for some snow from Washington to complete a project comparing different kinds of snow. "So, we packed up some snow and sent it to him," DeMichele recalled.

Members of his office staff assiduously combed Montana's daily and even weekly newspapers for obituaries and stories of notable achievement by constituents. Each received a letter of condolence or congratulation from Mansfield. For many years he sent out Christmas cards featuring sketches of capital scenes drawn by Maureen, until the list became too unwieldy. However, aides continued to collect and respond to the Christmas cards he received and saved them all, now contained in seventy-nine archival boxes in his congressional papers.

In the *Missoulian's* profile for its top 100 list, Steve Doherty, Democratic leader of the state senate, declared, "Whenever a Montanan was in the service and something needed to be done, a message, a leave, Montanans knew that Mike would make it happen. He is and always has been for many of us that magical person who knew the ways of Washington, but embodied the core values we aspire to. He navigated through the sometimes twisted hallways of power in order to make better our lives. . . . In his public life, Mike connected with us like few others have." Peggy DeMichele recalled his visits to Montana cities and small towns when Congress was out of session, often meeting people at local bars or cafés and writing down their requests for government assistance on the spot, sometimes on nothing but the back of a book of matches, and sending it to his office for action. The secret of his success, DeMichele believed, was that this unpretentious, unassuming person "made everybody feel that they were more important than he was."

Another factor in his popularity throughout his career was a phenomenal memory. John Buzzetti, who had been a student in one of his classes in 1941, was in a hotel in Great Falls in his Army uniform en route to the Philippines when Representative Mansfield spied him across the lobby and called out to him by name—three and a half years after the last time they had met. Norma Keil, a Democratic precinct committeewoman in northwestern Montana who had met Mansfield only once before, was amazed to see him coming across the street with his hands outstretched, greeting her and her husband by name, on the way to a county Democratic meeting in the mid-1950s. Greg Morgan, who like scores of other Montanans worked temporarily for Mansfield as a junior aide, recalls Mansfield in the halls of the Capitol greeting by name two women from Montana he had not seen in fifteen years. On another occasion, when Morgan introduced Mansfield to fifteen young people from Montana visiting the Capitol, the lawmaker asked each his or her name and home town and then inquired by name about their parents, close relatives, and even neighbors. An official of the U.S. Embassy in Tokyo was astonished to see then-ambassador Mansfield greet a large group of Montanans who were traveling in Asia and call each by name, mentioning the last time they had met and asking questions about their family and friends. Later the official asked the ambassador how he possibly remembered all those names. "When you're a politician, you remember people's names," was the reply—but few other politicians ever remembered them as extensively or as readily.

Seeking to maintain a relationship with all sides, Mansfield kept his distance from most of the divisive clashes that mobilized the energies and unleashed the passions of other Montana politicians. Michael Malone, one of the state's most celebrated historians of twentieth-century politics, described Mansfield's consistent posture in Montana as that of "a hardworking guardian of his constituents' interests and a non-partisan master of the big issues." In a report written with Montana State University colleague, Pierce C. Mullen, Malone observed that this permitted Mansfield "to be non-combative and watch quietly while others fought the dragons." This stand often infuriated those in the trenches of the fierce political struggles in the state. In 1944, as Mansfield was running for reelection after his first term in the House, an exasperated Senator James Murray, a leading liberal with whom Mansfield agreed more often than not, complained bitterly to Roosevelt that the congressman was remaining aloof from the state Democratic Party: "He has declined to state any program on which he is running. In his public statement he only says, 'I pledge my best for the welfare of Montana and the Nation.'" Murray and his allies were particularly miffed at Mansfield's failure to take a stand on the proposed Missouri Valley Authority (MVA), which had been sponsored by Murray and which was the most contentious issue in Montana politics from 1944 through most of the decade, even though it never became a reality. Lowndes Maury, a Butte attorney and adviser to Murray, wrote to the senator in 1946 that "Mansfield deliberately, on all occasions, dodges [the MVA issue]; he sits on the fence, and he will not come down on either side." Mansfield had considered his position well and concluded that this proposal was too divisive.

"I never get a Mansfield-type campaign," Lee Metcalf, his Democratic colleague in the U.S. Senate, and an outspoken battler for public power and other controversial causes, complained in 1971. "I don't have any campaigns when I can do nothing but talk about being in three branches of the service, and about how Maureen was my childhood sweetheart and how she put me through college. Every time I go into a campaign it's rough, it's mean, it's vicious. Mansfield and I vote pretty close together, but I am a dangerous radical and Mansfield is a fine, conservative fellow."

In a letter to Arthur Lamey, a Montana political associate, Mansfield defined the most desirable candidates as "individuals who are neither tied to the extreme right or the extreme left but who will try to look at all the angles in a situation and on the basis of their best judgment, arrive at the best possible solution of the question at hand." Whether conscious or not, that was an apt description of his own political philosophy and of his judicious approach to most issues. To a written inquiry from Professor Eric Goldman of Princeton University, Mansfield described himself as "a conservative-liberal." He added, "I believe in slow evolutionary changes and in some instances, would vote as a conservative in the hope that in so doing, the desired changes, once achieved, would be more acceptable, and as a result would be of a more durable nature." Most of his constituency in Montana, and the national constituency in Washington, applauded his lack of ideology and his cautious political view.

When I asked Mansfield in 1999 what had been his greatest satisfaction as a member of Congress, he immediately responded that, although it might surprise me, it was "saving Flathead Lake." In the early 1940s, he energetically battled against a proposal from the Army Corps of Engineers and the Bonneville Power Administration to raise the level of the dam at Flathead Lake, the largest freshwater lake west of the Mississippi River. The project would have flooded several small Montana towns, parts of the cities of Kalispell and Polson and some 50,000 acres of rich farmland in order to provide additional power, much of which would be transmitted to the West Coast. Public opposition was immediate and fierce. Mansfield led the fight against the plan in Congress, on the grounds that Montana's natural resources were being stripped away unfairly for the benefit of other areas.

In July 1943 Mansfield addressed an impassioned letter in very personal terms to President Roosevelt to "do everything in your power to stop this iniquitous activity and to assure the people of western Montana that nothing will be done to alter the status quo." To give it greater emphasis, he added that "this is the most important letter I have ever written in my life." Although he claimed that "it is not a matter of politics with me but it is a matter of look-ing after the welfare and security of the people of western Montana," his suc-cessful campaign proved to be one of the most politically important things Mansfield ever did at home, remembered by Montanans many decades later. Although Mansfield did not know it at the time, due to extraordinary wartime secrecy, the additional power that the project would have provided was almost certainly destined for the giant plutonium production works at Hanford, Washington, which produced the fissionable material for the atomic bomb. However, even if he had known this, he told me, it would have made no dif-ference in his attitude.

A related campaign that elevated Mansfield's popularity was his sponsor-ship of a dam on the south fork of the Flathead River, a few miles east of the lake, which could provide power without flooding any area of importance. Building the Hungry Horse Dam, as it came to be known, would provide added assurance that Flathead Lake would not be expanded to provide addi-tional power. The project had the approval of the federal power authorities and much local backing, including that of the Kalispell newspaper editor, Harry J. Kelly, but was opposed by the Montana Power Company, which saw it as public power competition. This was a rare case in which Mansfield fired back in personal terms against political opponents. At various stages of the fight for Hungry Horse, he condemned the private power company's "spite-work tactics," "dog-in-the-manger attitude," and "predatory and per-nicious interests." With support from the Roosevelt administration, the bill authorizing construction of the dam passed both House and Senate in the spring of 1944. On June 5, 1944, Mansfield was among thirty-six members of Congress invited to an informal meeting with FDR at the White House. He was eager for news of the signing of the Hungry Horse bill. Outside the Oval Office Maurice Latta, the White House executive clerk, told him it had not yet been signed but that it was on the list for early action. The meeting with the President was in a lighthearted vein, with the lawmakers doing most of the talking. FDR did not look healthy, and his hands shook continuously. After about twenty minutes the meeting ended, and the congressmen filed out, with Mansfield last in line.

I noticed Judge Latta come in and lay something on the President's desk [Mansfield wrote for his files later the same day]. The President said "What, another Bill?" and I looked over my shoulder, saw a letter on the outside which I did not recognize and therefore thought that the bill was certainly not the Hungry Horse one. However, I had hardly walked ten feet before the President yelled "Mansfield!" Like a good soldier I trooped back and said "Yes, sir." He said "Would you like to see your Bill signed?" "I would be delighted, Mr. President," I said, and watched him put down the date and affix his signature. I said "Mr. President, I can't tell you how happy I am about your signing this Bill, I want you to know that it will make the father of this project 'Hungry Horse Harry Kelly' of Kalispell, a happy man when he gets the news." He leaned back in his chair, roared and said "Hungry Horse Harry Kelly. I have heard many good names in my day but this is the best one yet."

The one curious note in the meeting was an off-hand remark by FDR to the lawmakers, who did not grasp its significance. He said that in connection with his forthcoming radio address that night he wished he could get something over to the American people without alarming them but he didn't know how to do it. In his "fireside chat" a few hours later, the President spoke with satisfaction about the taking of Rome by the allies and praised the American troops who participated, but then ended on a prayerful note, "May God bless them and watch over them and over all of our gallant, fighting men." The following day—June 6, 1944—Roosevelt again broadcast to the nation. He revealed that as he was speaking the previous evening, he had known that 4,000 ships and landing craft of U.S. and allied forces were crossing the English Channel to Normandy in the greatest amphibious assault in history, to drive the German forces from western Europe. This time he asked Americans to join in a more extensive prayer for the success of this "mighty endeavor," known as D-Day, which proved to be the decisive turning point of World War II.

MISSION TO CHINA

By 1944 the tide of World War II had turned decisively against the Axis powers in Europe and against Japan in the great naval battles of the Pacific. Still, Japanese forces continued to occupy the cities and supply lines of eastern China and to mount new offensives to extend their reach. To the frustration of Washington, Generalissimo Chiang Kai-shek, the Chinese Nationalist leader, still held back the bulk of his forces from battle against Japan in order to check the growing strength of the Chinese communists under Mao Tse-tung, whom he feared more than the Japanese. In October 1944 a protracted struggle over strategy and tactics between Chiang and the U.S. commander in the region, General Joseph W. "Vinegar Joe" Stilwell, ended with President Roosevelt's reluctant decision to recall Stilwell. At this point the U.S. President sent Mansfield to China as a personal envoy.

The single most important event of Mike Mansfield's career in the House, elevating him from obscurity to national prominence, was his mission to wartime China in 1944 as the personal envoy of President Roosevelt. It was the product of an intense interest that had been kindled in his visits to

Tientsin and Shanghai as a U.S. Marine, deepened in his academic studies and teaching of Far Eastern history at the University of Montana, and intensified as a member of the House of Representatives and its busy Committee on Foreign Affairs. From his arrival in the House in 1943 until his retirement from the Senate in 1977, he followed Chinese affairs closely and consistently when few other members of Congress and indeed few American policymakers displayed more than episodic interest. Mansfield always accorded a central place in his thinking to the Middle Kingdom, the central power in Asia.

In March 1943, three months after being sworn in, Mansfield addressed a personal letter to the Chinese ambassador, Wei Tao-ming, requesting detailed information on the status of the war against Japan "which might be of value in spreading the gospel of greater action in the Far East among my colleagues and the people at large." Greatly exaggerating his two-week visit as a Marine in 1922, he wrote that "I have spent several years in China" as well as teaching Far Eastern history "with special emphasis on China" at the university. There is no record of Wei's response.

Frustrated by the lack of progress toward revisiting China, he teamed up with John M. Vorys, a conservative Republican from Columbus, Ohio, also a member of the Foreign Affairs Committee, in seeking to arrange an official trip. Vorys, who was in his third term in the House, had been a teacher in China in 1919–1920, shortly before Mansfield's brief visit as a Marine in 1922. Undersecretary of State (later Secretary of State) Edward Stettinius advised the veteran Republican and the freshman Democrat to obtain an invitation from the Chinese government, which could be the basis for U.S. arrangements. When they took their plan to Ambassador Wei, however, he gave them scant encouragement, promising only to "bring the matter to the attention of my Government."

Mansfield heard no more during the summer recess, which then was a standard feature of the congressional schedule, but on October 1 he received a call from the White House summoning him to a meeting with Roosevelt the following day. In a memorandum written immediately after the event, Mansfield said that after greeting the President, "I brought the matter of the China trip to his attention and he agreed that I should go to China on official business for him, leaving Great Falls two or three days after the election, and report back to him personally on my findings." The memorandum said that he and

Roosevelt then discussed the political situation in Montana and the nation, including FDR's race for his fourth term in office that fall. "He didn't look too well, in fact he looked very worried but I suppose that would be expected when one considers the responsibilities he must be carrying on his shoulders in addition to conducting a political campaign," Mansfield wrote.

As suggested in his claim of spending "several years" in China, at this early stage of his career Mansfield was not above exaggerating or even fabricating aspects of his foreign experiences. He had told his constituents in the 1942 election campaign that he had served overseas in "China, the Philippines, Japan and Siberia." Although he had served in the first two locales, he had only been in Japan overnight when the naval vessel bringing him home from the Orient in 1922 stopped for fuel at Nagasaki, and he had never been in Siberia at all. When I asked him about his Siberian service—which he once claimed had extended for six weeks—he responded, "That was a lie." I was so stunned by this confession from a man known for his truthfulness and candor that I did not ask the obvious follow-up, to determine why he had lied.

Regarding the genesis of his China mission, Mansfield told a colorful—and concocted—version to Washington columnists Drew Pearson and Richard L. Neuberger and later to others, in which the initiative came from Roosevelt because of the congressman's expertise in Asia. In this version, FDR called him in and said, "Mike, I have asked you to come here to request that you undertake a special confidential mission for me to China. I have had economic and military reports but what I want is an overall picture of the situation and I think you are the man to get it for me." Yet his own contemporaneous account of the meeting makes clear that it was he rather than the President who took the initiative. When I discussed the conflicting versions with him in 1999, Mansfield said it was "fair enough" that he had initiated the idea and obtained Roosevelt's assent.

Mansfield's motivation in seeking the trip was clear. He was fascinated by China and the war in Asia, which he regarded as more vital to the United States than the European battles that had greater priority and greater attention. As a member of Congress, he believed he was in a position to help to rectify this error, at the same time rising from obscurity to a prominent place in wartime Washington. To return to China, this time as a personal representative of the President, was everything he could have hoped for.

Roosevelt's motivation was less obvious and, on the surface, more difficult to fathom. He barely knew Mansfield, having met him once at a White House reception for new members of Congress and once more on the occasion when he signed the Hungry Horse Dam bill. In view of extensive official reporting he did not need more information about the difficult situation in China—in a sense he already knew more than he wanted to know. The U.S. military chief in the region, General Stilwell, had scant regard for Chiang, whom he privately referred to as "Peanut." In the spring of 1944 a Japanese offensive in China generated deep concern, even alarm, in Washington about the future of the Middle Kingdom. FDR had been increasingly frustrated by Chiang's refusal to accept Stilwell's demands that he launch serious attacks against the Japanese. Since September 23 Roosevelt had been immersed in a political-military crisis brought about by Chiang's insistence that Stilwell be removed. The very day before FDR saw Mansfield, his close aide Harry Hopkins had told a Chinese official in Washington that the President would agree, very reluctantly, to Stilwell's ouster. This decision put Roosevelt deeply at odds with his own military adviser, the Army chief of staff General George C. Marshall, and led the senior U.S. military ranks in Washington to downgrade the possibility that China could play a major role in defeating the Japanese in East Asia.

Clearly, FDR had something else in mind in sending a freshman congressman into this maelstrom halfway around the world as his personal emissary. The existing evidence suggests that Roosevelt was motivated by political and personal factors—a wish to enhance Mansfield's stature in hopes that in the elections of 1946 two years later the congressman would slay FDR's personal dragon, Montana's senior U.S. senator, Burton K. Wheeler.

Wheeler, a dedicated progressive, had been one of the first promoters of Roosevelt's candidacy for president and a strong backer of FDR in his first term but split with him in 1937 over the President's controversial plan to "pack" the U.S. Supreme Court with additional justices favorable to embattled New Deal legislation. Later, Wheeler became a leading opponent of U.S. involvement in World War II. In Senate debate in 1940 he charged that the President's Lend-Lease plan to aid the British was the international equivalent of its politically controversial policy of plowing under agricultural surpluses, stating that the consequences of Lend-Lease "will plow under every fourth American boy." An angry Roosevelt responded that he regarded Wheeler's statement as "the most untruthful, as the most dastardly, unpatriotic thing . . . the rottenest thing that has been said in public life in my generation." He sought to deny his former friend federal patronage and privately mused that it wouldn't be bad "if somebody kidnaps Wheeler and shanghais him on board an outgoing steamer for the Congo."

FDR's former aide Jim Rowe had alerted Roosevelt to Mansfield's political potential in two memoranda in 1942 that also mentioned Wheeler, although the memos did not explicitly describe Mansfield as a potential Wheeler-killer. There is no known record of such a conversation, but it is likely that Rowe spoke to Roosevelt about his hopes for Mansfield as a candidate against Wheeler. On several occasions Rowe urged Mansfield to run against Wheeler when the senator's term was up in 1946. By the time of the Roosevelt-Mansfield meeting on the China mission in 1944, Rowe had left Washington for service in the U.S. Navy in the Pacific, so it appears unlikely that he directly instigated that session, however much its initial inspiration may have come from him.

A Montana editor, quoting a Teamsters Union official, reported later that Mansfield had been selected to run against Wheeler in a meeting in which Roosevelt participated in late 1944, and that part of the strategy was to build up Mansfield with a trip to China. The editor, Dan Whetstone of *Cut Bank Pioneer Press*, was a Republican critic of Mansfield, but the story has the ring of truth. Records in the Roosevelt Library show that in the weeks leading up to his meeting with Mansfield, Roosevelt met three times with the president of the Teamsters Union, Dan Tobin, who was his close political friend, but all three meetings were designated by the President as off the record. No details survive.

Mansfield told me he did not know Tobin and did not recall hearing of a presidential meeting designating him as the potential opponent to Wheeler, nor did Roosevelt discuss that possibility with him. Mansfield did seriously investigate running against Wheeler in 1946 but decided he was "too much of a novice" after only two terms in the House and that the race would be too expensive. As it turned out, Wheeler was defeated in the Democratic primary that year by Leif Ericson, a liberal. Wheeler then threw his support to the Republican Zales Ecton, who won election to the six-year U.S. Senate term. Ecton was Mansfield's opponent when his term was up.

THE LAUNCHING OF AN EMISSARY

After obtaining President Roosevelt's sponsorship of his trip in October 1944, Mansfield was treated to a private chat two days later with one of China's most powerful officials, H. H. Kung, Chiang Kai-shek's brother-in-law, who was recurrently Chiang's finance minister and always a financier looking out for himself. After a talk in his apartment in the Shoreham Hotel, Kung took the congressman off to a lobster and squab luncheon at Twin Oaks, China's wooded Washington estate.

Mansfield sat at the head of the table with Kung who, according to Mansfield's notes, "was affability itself." At the foot of the table, below the salt, was the Chinese ambassador Wei Tao-ming, the functionary to whom Mansfield had unsuccessfully addressed his earlier travel requests. Also around the table were Washington insiders on China issues, including Leo Crowley, head of the Foreign Economic Administration, the agency responsible for providing foreign aid; Lauchlin Currie,* a White House economist who often served as a presidential contact point with China; and John Carter Vincent, chief of the China desk at the State Department.

On October 6 Mansfield had a longer and more serious luncheon conversation with Vincent, who had previously been counselor of the U.S. Embassy at Chiang's headquarters in Chungking. Vincent told him (in Mansfield's words) that "the nub of the whole problem over there was Chinese-Russian relationships which were centered on the Chinese Communistic and Chungking governments getting together." Mansfield offered his initial assessment that there was "no close working relationship" between the Soviet Union and the Chinese Communists, who "seemed to be interested primarily in problems indigenous to China itself . . . centered on the land and land-lord system." Vincent agreed, and said the Soviets would work with any group who could unite China against the Japanese.

The same day, two officials of the U.S. aid program visited Mansfield and recommended, among other things, that he take $500 to $1,000 in $50 and $100 bills and exchange them in China on the black market to avoid the unrealistic Chinese government-imposed exchange rate. Before he departed, Lieutenant Sidney Wald from the Army's Air Transport Command came to his office and sheepishly collected fifty cents from the congressman, explain-

---

*Currie was later revealed to have been a secret informant of Soviet intelligence, whereas Vincent, one of the most prominent China hands in the State Department, was later falsely accused of being a security risk and forced to resign in the anticommunist hysteria that followed the Communist victory in China.

ing that all passengers were charged twenty-five cents each for two catered meals served in flight. He also told Mansfield he was listed as a VIP on travel documents and would have a plush seat. Characteristically, Mansfield said he would take his chances on ordinary seats and did not consider himself to be a Very Important Person.

As a boy he had dreamed of seeing the world, but until this point he had seen only bits of it. Now at age forty-one a circuitous journey in a Douglas C-54, a four-engine Army transport plane, provided kaleidoscopic glimpses of a broad swath of the world at a time when such rapid and extensive travel was rare. Because Southeast Asia and coastal East China were occupied by the Japanese, the route to the area of Chinese Nationalist forces was across the Atlantic to Africa, the Middle East, and India, China's back door, rather than across the Pacific. After stops in Bermuda, the Azores, Casablanca, Cairo, Abadan, and Karachi, he landed at New Delhi early on November 19, five days after his trip had begun. He was put up at a suite in the Imperial Hotel, which the former enlisted man noted, to his strong disapproval, was off limits to enlisted men but not to officers. "What a shame!" he wrote in the diary that he meticulously kept in a clear, neat, steady hand in a plastic-covered datebook for 1943 from a Helena, Montana, insurance agent. When his remarkably detailed notes were typed by his secretary at the end of the trip they came to sixty-nine single-spaced pages. It is evident that Mansfield believed at that point that his mission to China for FDR was the most important episode of his life.

His exploration of the situation in China began with a meeting in New Delhi with Major General Frank Merrill, who had become famous as leader of the American commando regiment in Burma popularly known as "Merrill's Marauders," the first and only U.S. ground combat unit in the area. Promoted as a result of battlefield leadership from major to major general, the tall, heavyset veteran soldier used big maps in the war room of the India-Burma Command to illustrate the central military issue of the day: the problem of supply to the Chinese Nationalist forces.

After the Japanese pushed Chiang Kai-shek's forces into southwest China in 1938 and captured the major ports in the east, the Nationalist lifeline became a nine-foot-wide dirt road, scarcely more than an oversize trail, hacked out of the jungle into Burma almost by hand. This route, linking up with British-built roads bringing supplies from the port of Rangoon, was known as the Burma Road. It was shut down in early 1942, when the Japanese seized Rangoon and parts of southern Burma. At that point, Roosevelt, Chiang, and the U.S. high command authorized herculean efforts to provide supplies through ports in India, including enlarged airfields and more airplanes to fly supplies into China over the Himalayas, the highest mountain range in the world, and the building of a new road from Ledo, in northeast India, through northern Burma to hook up with the path of the old Burma Road into southeastern China. The Ledo Road, as it was called, faced fearsome obstacles: harsh mountainous terrain and seemingly impenetrable jungles occupied by Naga headhunters and subject to torrential rains and the dangers of snakes, tigers and leopards, leeches and disease-bearing insects of all sorts, as well as opposition from the Japanese Army.

Merrill offered to fly Mansfield to Ledo to begin a trip over the rugged road to Myitkyina, a Burmese town and key junction point that U.S. and Chinese forces had finally taken from the Japanese after a long frustrating and bloody struggle. Mansfield jumped at the chance, and Merrill arranged for him to be issued Army fatigues for the trip. "A former buck private like myself, we hit it off fine," Mansfield wrote of Merrill in his diary.

The Ledo Road was a very rough track. Mansfield's jeep often crawled along at five to ten miles per hour, eating the dust of other vehicles or of whole convoys. "Bump, bump, bumpety, and dust, dust, dust. . . . Saw a jackal and some wild chickens. Dense jungles and lots of bamboo," Mansfield wrote. It was "the roughest ride I have ever undertaken," he reported at the end of the trip.

He visited eight U.S. military hospitals along the road, most of them with dirt floors, thatched roofs, and sides made of bamboo and rough cloth. At every stop there, he sought out soldiers from Montana for pictures and special words that he put in letters he sent home to his delighted constituents. This rangy figure smoking his pipe, his uniform topped with a soft Army fatigue cap, became a familiar figure to both GIs and generals along his route. His appreciation for their efforts was recorded on a slip of paper placed inside his diary: "From the Bible—'I will liken him unto a wise man, which built his house upon a rock; And the rain descended, & the floods came, & the winds blew, & beat upon that house; & it fell not; for it was founded upon a rock.' And that rock was American ingenuity, skill & courage & is now known as the Ledo-Burma Road."

Mansfield was beginning to understand the reality of Nationalist China, a far cry from the society in a revolutionary struggle for the rights of man that he had idealistically described the year before. "Under present system being conscripted into Chinese army is like receiving a death sentence—no training, no food, no equipment," he wrote in his diary. "Soldiers are starved and poorly equipped because of graft up above. Commanders hang on to stuff, then flood black market and enrich themselves but also make it tough on their own people." Rich men's sons could buy their way out of conscription for about $100, he learned, and $1,000 could buy a position as a regimental commander.

On November 26 he flew to the wartime capital of Chungking. Later that day he wrote, "When I started on this trip I thought China's chief problem was supply but now I am beginning to think it is cooperation among the Chinese themselves and that this has always been the case." It was becoming increasingly clear that the future of the war against the Japanese in China—and more broadly, the future of that vast country itself—depended on the relative strengths of the Nationalist regime headquartered in Chungking and those of the Communist regime centered in the caves of Yen-an, and the relationship between these two centers of power. These political factors increasingly dominated his exploration.

Chungking is a very old city, going back five centuries before the time of Christ as a regional capital, and had been an important port even before steamboats made their way there from the coast early in the twentieth century. It sits atop hills at the confluence of two rivers, the Chialing coming down from the north and the mighty Yangtze, the country's longest and most important river, which flows from its headwaters near Tibet across China to the sea. The old walled city, replete with hundreds of narrow alleyways, was home to 200,000 people before Chiang Kai-shek made it his capital when fleeing from the Japanese. Within an astonishingly short time, the city had ballooned to nearly a million, including people from every part of China, many of whose dialects were impenetrable to others. Everything, from whiskey, women, and opium to political and military favors, was for sale. Mansfield was both fascinated and appalled by what he saw. He wrote poetically in his diary his Chungking impressions:

Three men to a rubber wheeled cart going down hill—one to steer and two to hold back.

The terraced fields, the poverty, the cheerfulness of children.

The Yangtze and its river boats.

The Chialing which the Embassy overlooks.

The murky weather compared to Kunming's sunshine.

The work the Chinese do and the loads they carry compared to the Indians.

British Embassy 300 feet above American Embassy.

Hand directions for motor cars in China.

COMMUNISM IN CHINA: THE CRUCIAL ISSUE

A central issue for Mansfield and American policymakers at the time was the nature of the Chinese Communist regime, which was much less clear at the time than it became later. Mansfield's pre-trip judgments that the Communists had "no close working relationship" with Moscow and were primarily oriented to China's agrarian problems were supported by most Americans he saw on his trip. General Claire Chennault, who had organized and commanded the unofficial Flying Tigers (later the official Fourteenth U.S. Air Force) and who would become an anticommunist icon in the 1950s, told Mansfield that "he rates the Communists highly and declares there is no connection with Russia." Merrill and others said much the same, although some also cautioned that the situation would probably change if the Communists came to power.

Of all the American and Chinese views that Mansfield recorded in his detailed diary, only those of Chennault's thirty-four-year-old aide, the future columnist Joseph Alsop, expressed a harshly negative assessment of the Chinese Communists. Alsop, who had been deeply involved in the intrigue against Stilwell on behalf of Chennault, had been commissioned a first lieutenant at the direct order of his cousin, President Franklin D. Roosevelt, and had been promoted to captain the day Mansfield first met him. In most unmilitary fashion he wore a lieutenant's single bar on one shoulder and a captain's double bars on the other. He told Mansfield that "Russia was very much interested in the communist movement, that Mai Tseng-tse [Mansfield's initial attempt to spell Mao Tse-tung] was an ardent and fanatical follower of Moscow, and that Russia still had designs on Manchuria." Mansfield immediately disliked the future Washington columnist, judging him to be "blasé, opinionated and not to be trusted."* In contrast, Mansfield came to appreciate and trust the observations of *Time* correspondent Theodore H. White, who had an illustrious career ahead of him as the chronicler of "the making of" American presidents. White told him that "the Communists look upon America as their great allies," that "their communism is not Marxism but is tied to purely local reform." Many of White's observations about the political situation in China were repeated without attribution by Mansfield in his post-trip reports. In turn, White was so trustful of Mansfield that he asked him to be his courier for an anguished and angry letter to his publisher, Henry Luce, protesting *Time's* watering down of his positive views of the Communists and the twisting of his criticisms of the Chiang Kai-shek regime into praise. The article in question had been rewritten by *Time's* new foreign editor, Whittaker Chambers, a former communist operative who would later become famous for accusing Alger Hiss. After reading the letter, Mansfield prudently decided not to become involved in White's private war with his publisher and declined to convey it to New York.

In his report to Roosevelt following the trip and a slightly expurgated public report to the House, Mansfield said the Communists are "quite democratic" in ruling the area under their control, and described them as "more reformers than revolutionaries" and "not Communists in the sense that Russians are as their interests seem to focus on primarily agrarian reforms." Ironically, during the early stages of his career Mansfield had been better acquainted with the history of the Chinese Communist movement than most of his on-the-ground informants. Notes he took in the mid-1930s, which formed part of the basis for his course in Far Eastern history at the University of Montana, portray the Communists as "nearer to Soviet Russia

---

*Mansfield wasn't Alsop's favorite person either. Nearly thirty years later, in a column devoted to controversy about U.S. bombing in Cambodia, Alsop described the Senate Majority Leader as "what Russian peasants used to call 'a holy idiot'"—one who sincerely believes in idiotic ideas.

tho little aid was received." His notes also contain a prominent warning about information on the status and leanings of the Communists: "Beware of Russian reports. Beware of Chinese reports. Beware of Correspondents' reports." In 1944, wanting to see for himself, he asked to go to Yen-an to meet the Communists but was unable to do so. Although he listed "my inability to get into Yen-an due to weather conditions" as first among his disappointments at the end of his trip, there is no indication he made a determined effort to get there.

The true policies of the Chinese Communists, and especially the party's relationships with the Soviet Union, became a highly politicized issue in the United States following the Communist victory in China in 1949. Mansfield's comments on the Communists as agrarian reformers would come back to haunt him. It is very clear now that the Chinese Communist leaders were not democratic in any Western sense of the word and were not merely agrarian reformers. Contemporary historians, however, have reached no consensus on the nature of the Chinese Communist relationship with the Soviet Union during World War II. It is clear that Moscow provided little tangible assistance to the Communists but did provide aid to Chiang Kai-shek and his Nationalist forces in an effort to contain the Japanese threat to the U.S.S.R. Soviet leader Joseph Stalin told Ambassador W. Averell Harriman in the summer of 1944 that Chiang was the best leader available in China and that the Chinese Communists were only "margarine" Communists, not real ones. Nevertheless, Moscow maintained a Soviet liaison officer and a secret radio link with the Communist leaders; the nature and extent of this relationship was carefully hidden from the American diplomats visiting Yen-an.

Indeed, a recent study based on previously unavailable Chinese Communist Party documents led its author to conclude that, at variance with the views of most on-the-spot American diplomatic observers at the time, "Mao and his comrades were internationalists loyal to the Moscow-led world revolution," that Mao was in close touch with Stalin during this period, and that he consistently cleared his party's decisions with the Soviet Union. However, other scholars who have examined recent evidence believe Yen-an's ties to Moscow were complex and tenuous before 1945. In this context, the views expressed by Mansfield during and after his mission were not as reliably erroneous as they seemed at the height of the cold war.

The months of November and December 1944, when Mansfield was in

China, saw the onset of the first intensive negotiations between the United States, the Chinese Communists, and Chiang and his inner circle. The negotiations were initiated and conducted by Patrick J. Hurley, a colorful Republican political figure who had been secretary of war under President Herbert Hoover but who was on good terms with FDR. Hurley kept Roosevelt personally informed and to some extent the State Department, especially after FDR designated him as U.S. ambassador to China in mid-November. He told Mansfield little, however. In their first meeting in Chiang's capital at Chungking on November 27, "we talked for three hours—Pat for two hours and 47 minutes and I for 13 minutes, which was just the way I wanted it," Mansfield wrote in his diary. "He feels quite optimistic about the Chinese situation, but I wonder. He tells me that the Gimo [Chiang] and the Communists are going to get together. Just how I do not know." On reflection, Mansfield was "amazed at the optimistic attitude" of Hurley and doubted that he understood the critical situation facing China. Later the same day, Hurley was meeting Chou En-lai, the chief Communist negotiator even then, who was visiting Chungking, but he did not explain to Mansfield the issues under discussion. For his part, Mansfield made no effort to see Chou, despite his previously expressed wish to travel to Yen-an.

Evaluating the controversial Hurley, Mansfield on first meeting called him "a smooth and talkative customer" and later wrote in his diary that "Pat talks too much, is too playful, and likes the grand manner though with me he is very, very friendly." Regardless of these misgivings, Mansfield praised Hurley in his report to Roosevelt, saying that "No better choice could be made for this very important position" of ambassador to China.

A year later, when a dispirited and bitter Hurley resigned as ambassador, he charged that his efforts had been sabotaged by State Department careerists siding with the Chinese Communists, an explosive statement that helped give rise to the conspiracy theory that came to dominate American politics in the 1950s. As he prepared to resign, Hurley told Mansfield he had recommended to President Truman and Secretary of State James F. Byrnes that Mansfield be his successor in China. When Hurley asked if he would take the job, the congressman was noncommittal, saying, "it was a tough job and I had a family and my own future to look after." There is no record of such a recommendation from Hurley, and the ambassadorship to China was never offered; if it had been, it is doubtful that Mansfield would have accepted at that stage of his career. In any case it would have been the kiss of death for Mansfield, because Truman and Byrnes were infuriated by Hurley's resignation and his charges.

In his mission to China, Mansfield's most important meetings were two conferences with Chiang Kai-shek and his participation as a guest of Chiang on a social occasion. The generalissimo, as Chiang was called, initially received Mansfield at dusk on November 30 at his hilltop villa overlooking Chungking, in an airy room decorated with rare Ming vases and Chinese tapestry and scrolls. A picture of Sun Yat-sen, the leader of the 1911 revolution, which deposed the last Chinese imperial dynasty, and the man who gave Chiang his start as a leader, hung over the fireplace.

"Chiang has a closecropped head of gray hair, gray mustache, eyes alive . . . immobile face, an occasional hearty laugh," observed Mansfield. The Chinese leader wore a plain olive drab uniform of good cloth with no decorations. As Mansfield spoke and his words were translated to Chinese, Chiang interjected sounds of encouragement—"hah," "oh" or "uh"—but spoke mostly in generalities. Mansfield said the United States had recently sent to China its best men in their respective fields—Hurley the diplomat; General Albert C. Wedemeyer, who had replaced Stilwell as U.S. commander and as Chiang's chief U.S. military adviser; and Donald M. Nelson, former head of the U.S. War Production Board, who was in China at the head of an economic advisory mission. Chiang interjected that if they had come a year ago the situation would be different now. Mansfield did not argue but said, "We must forget the past and look to the future." He said the United States "had a great admiration for China and wanted to see her strong so that she could prove herself a bulwark for peace."

In those early winter days, the military situation in China was extremely tense. The broad Japanese ground offensive, which had started in the spring, was making worrisome gains as Chinese Army resistance melted. Panic was setting in. The Chinese in Chungking had begun selling their clothing and valuables. The U.S. Embassy, in consultation with the military command, was making plans to evacuate its personnel, destroy its confidential files, and move further inland.

The day after seeing Chiang, Mansfield confided to his diary:

China has very little more space to trade for time, and time is the most important element now. Time to reorganize the Chinese army, to give

Wedemeyer a chance, to bring cooperation in China, and to build the road. The feeling between the GI's and the Chinese is bad and some GI's would rather kill a Chinese than a Jap. The divisions at Kweilin—American armed—didn't fight but took the equipment and went into the hills. The graft is terrible. . . . If Chiang is forced back China will become a Communist country— a *Chinese* Communist state—but inevitably relations with Russia will get stronger and with the U.S. weaker. I am not interested in ideologies here. I'm only interested in keeping China in the war; in shortening the struggle as much as possible, and in saving American lives. That is the most important consideration and to me the only one. All else is of secondary importance.

On December 1 Mansfield joined Hurley, Nelson, and others at Chiang's villa for tea. The generalissimo said the crisis would come to a head in the next fifteen to twenty days but expressed a belief that his forces would hold the line at Kweiyang, a city on the approaches to K'un-Ming and Chungking. In fact, they did so, backed up by the warplanes of Chennault's Fourteenth Air Force. A counterattack beginning December 10 turned the tide against what turned out to be the high-water mark of the Japanese advance into Chinese territory.

Mansfield saw Chiang again for an hour and ten minutes on December 11, the day before his departure, to convey his conclusions. He maintained that the United States had done everything within its means to assist China, because of its desire to see a successful conclusion to the war and to save American lives. He recounted U.S. efforts, from the provision of supplies over the hump and the Ledo Road to financial aid and military training and advice. Mansfield declared that America's attitude toward China had changed with the relief of Stilwell at Chiang's insistence. China must now assume its full share of responsibility, he said, and "now we expect results."

In fact, the U.S. priority was rapidly shifting away from China. As American military leaders saw it, Chiang's refusal to take Stilwell's direction and the dimming prospects for a working arrangement between the Nationalists and Communists sharply diminished the chances of major Chinese offensives against Japanese forces. In the meantime the spectacular success of U.S. arms in the fierce battles of the Pacific seized Washington's attention. By November 1, the Japanese fleet had been defeated and General Douglas MacArthur had landed more than 100,000 troops in the

Philippines. With the first atomic bomb still untested, Roosevelt and the Joint Chiefs of Staff also began placing greater emphasis on bringing Russia into the war in the Far East to deliver a knockout blow against Japan. The conviction was growing in Washington that it would be safe—and certainly more satisfying—to bypass the complex and unresolved situation in China and take the war to Japan on other fronts.

In his discussion with Chiang, Mansfield continued to emphasize the paramount need for cooperation among the Chinese people. Chiang immediately understood the reference to an accord with the Communists, of whom he continued to be very leery. "The Japanese are a disease of the skin; the Communists are a disease of the heart," Chiang had said earlier in explaining why he had given priority to blockading his domestic enemies over attacking the foreign enemies. His sentiments had not changed. Although he insisted he would continue to try for a settlement with the Communists, Mansfield felt "he was so dead set against them that chances of success are small." When Mansfield pointed out several possibilities for compromise with Yen-an, Chiang said he had considered them all. "Americans expect the government to make all the concessions. Why not try to get the Yen-an group to make some?" he asked. "This sounds like a good suggestion," Mansfield commented in his report to Roosevelt.

"The weaknesses of Chiang's government are apparent; its durability is in question; and its honesty is open to the gravest sort of doubt," Mansfield wrote in his diary. In his report to Roosevelt, he detailed the results of some of Chiang's failures: the use of as many as sixteen divisions to blockade the Communists rather than fight the Japanese; the deterioration of China's military strength through corruption and ineptitude; the uncontrolled inflation and profiteering in civilian life; the continued impoverishment of the peasantry through high rents and high rates of interest. Despite this realistic understanding, Mansfield in the end accepted and even endorsed Chiang's leadership, writing that Chiang "is the *one* leader in China. . . . He and he alone, can untangle the present situation, because on the basis of what he has done and in spite of some of the things he has done, he is China." A similar acceptance of authority, no matter how flawed, would later contribute to Mansfield's unwavering support for the Vietnamese leader Ngo Dinh Diem despite all signs of his stubbornness and incompetence.

In comments throughout his mission and in his final report, Mansfield highlighted his antipathy to colonial powers in Asia and his opposition to U.S. military intervention for any reason other than fighting the Japanese. He was especially critical of the British, whom he accused of failing to carry their share of the load and of caring only about their postwar colonial interests in Singapore and Hong Kong, and for this reason preferring a weak China. Unlike the European powers, Mansfield asserted in his talks and his report, the United States has "no ulterior motives" in China: "We are in China to help China and ourselves against a common enemy; we intend to get out of China just as soon as victory is won." (In fact, this did not prove to be the case, to Mansfield's unhappiness. See Chapter 6.)

With his China mission at an end, Mansfield flew to India on December 14 and proceeded to the Persian Gulf, the Middle East, Italy, and the Azores, close to the same route he had traveled a month earlier. At the end of the trip he recorded with satisfaction in his diary that, among members of Congress, he was "First over Ledo-Burma Road" and "First [to accomplish] official mission to China." His plane landed at Washington at 5 P.M. on December 22, 1944.

REPORTING TO ROOSEVELT

Immediately after Christmas Mansfield completed his report and began calling the White House for an appointment to deliver it to the President who had sent him to China. After getting no response for nearly two weeks, he resorted to contacting First Lady Eleanor Roosevelt for help. She spoke to FDR, who agreed to see him for fifteen minutes on January 9.

The President greeted Mansfield warmly, saying he was glad to see him and wanted to hear about the trip. Mansfield handed him the report—a twenty-three-page typescript accompanied by ten pages of annexes on the Ledo Road and on a parallel fuel pipeline under construction. Roosevelt asked what Mansfield thought about Chiang Kai-shek. Mansfield responded that Chiang had his virtues but also his faults. "Who else is there in China?" Roosevelt asked, succinctly highlighting the failure to identify other potential noncommunist leaders, which was a serious limiting factor on American policymaking. Mansfield said there was no one else but expressed optimism that Chiang would attempt necessary military reforms. He repeated, as he had told Chiang and had written in his report, that cooperation among the Chinese factions was the greatest imperative in China. Roosevelt agreed emphatically. Harboring the view that Mansfield and many others also had accepted, FDR said he had tried to explain to congressional leaders in a meeting earlier the same day that the Chinese Communists were not communists in the Russian sense but, in reality, agrarian reformers.

Out of the blue, Roosevelt then raised an issue that was recurrently on his mind and that would occupy much of Mansfield's activity and thoughts in years to come: the future of Indochina. After asking Mansfield what he had heard on his trip about Indochina, FDR reported that Chiang had assured him at the Cairo Conference in November 1943 that China had no designs on Indochina, saying that "these people were not Chinese." However, the President said he had had a much more difficult time with Winston Churchill at the same wartime meeting. The British prime minister favored returning Indochina to the French colonizers, which Roosevelt adamantly opposed. FDR told Churchill, he recounted to Mansfield, that "the French have gotten at least one dollar out of that country for every five cents put in; that they are poor administrators and that they will resume their policy once they are allowed to regain their former colony."

Since at least 1942 Roosevelt had strongly favored an international trustee-ship for postwar Indochina and opposed the return of the French. In the fall of 1944, he had received reports outlining British intentions to bring the French into the war in Asia as a means of assisting their reconquest of Indochina. FDR wanted no part of this, and refused to authorize U.S. participation in any such action. This was the background of his question to Mansfield and his explanation that followed.

The subject of Indochina had come up briefly in Mansfield's conversation with General Merrill in New Delhi on the way home from China. With the war against Japan rapidly moving toward its conclusion, Merrill voiced the belief that U.S. forces should stick to supplying war material to China and avoid becoming involved in the reassertion of British and French colonial power in India, Burma, and Southeast Asia. Merrill was particularly concerned about the possibility that the United States could become involved "in a way we do not want" if the U.S. Army Air Force were to drop propaganda leaflets into "French Indochina" or if the Office of Strategic Services

(OSS, the wartime predecessor of the CIA) were to send agents into Indochina. In his written report to Roosevelt, Mansfield adopted these concerns as his own, closely paraphrasing what Merrill had told him. In his talk with the President, Mansfield said only that "the American military were very fearful of becoming involved in that [Indochina] area in which we had no interest." As the cold war began to germinate shortly after Roosevelt's death, President Truman reversed FDR's policies toward Indochina and aligned the United States with the returning colonial French, thus beginning the ultimately tragic U.S. intervention there.

At the end of his conversation with Roosevelt, Mansfield urged the President to read his report, saying that, while he was neither a military expert nor a China expert, it was "an honest report with no axes to grind." Roosevelt promised to read it, but it is doubtful that he did. There are no notes or other markings on the White House copy of the report to suggest Roosevelt had done so. He was failing noticeably by the time Mansfield saw him in January 1945. Three months later he would be dead.

Mansfield's China mission was an important learning experience for him with extraordinary consequences for the rest of his career. In China in 1944, the former professor came face to face for the first time with military and political realities abroad and the personalities of those who were shaping it, all at a very high level and involving consequential issues of war and peace that would deeply affect the postwar era. He also had an opportunity to observe the dismal reality of the lives of the great majority of the Chinese people, an observation that played an important role in his assessment of the achievements of the Chinese communist system in the 1970s. His first experience in congressional travel abroad whetted his appetite for more and convinced him of the utility of on-the-spot exposure to the lands and situations that were the subjects of his interest. When he later became a senator, he traveled widely on official trips, often obtaining, as in 1944, presidential sponsorship of his journey.

From a career standpoint, the China mission put him on the map in Washington. Starting with an hour-long speech on the House floor on January 16, in which he provided a public version of his report, he buttressed and embellished his reputation as a leading congressional expert on the Far East. Newspapers and wire services wrote articles about his mission and report. Under the headline, "Chiang Is China," *Time* on January 22, 1945, carried a story that covered more than a full page and included a flattering picture of Mansfield, with the exaggerated information that he had served "a two-year tour in Peking and Tientsin 23 years ago." (Columnist Drew Pearson, on the eve of his mission, had reported that Mansfield was "one of the handful of Americans who speaks Chinese," which was also untrue. In fact, the congressman was not even adept at eating with chopsticks.) Mansfield never corrected these misstatements.

Capitalizing on the notoriety, Mansfield wrote an article on his mission for Montana newspapers and sent telegrams to radio stations in Montana, the Montana legislature, Montana State College at Bozeman, and high school principals in widely separated parts of the state requesting time to speak about his China mission. All responded positively. "Mike is hot stuff right now," said the station manager of one Montana radio station.

In Washington, Mansfield called on General George C. Marshall, the Army chief of staff and leader of the U.S. war effort, to present and discuss his report, and he supplied a copy to Secretary of State Edward Stettinius. He also compiled a handwritten list ten pages long of persons to be contacted about the trip or to be sent copies of the *Congressional Record* version of his report, from journalists and government officials to people he had met along the way. As in his travels throughout the rest of his career, Mansfield sent letters of commendation to the department heads or other superiors of officials who had assisted him.

After he attained high positions in Congress and the U.S. diplomatic service, Mansfield became allergic to self-promotion. At this early stage, however, he worked industriously and imaginatively to use the China mission to gain a reputation as an Asia expert. After returning from China, he made a speech in the House on developments in Asia once each month until the end of World War II on August 15, 1945. In his mission to China, he saw his chance to break out of the pack on a subject of his greatest interest. He succeeded beyond anyone's expectations.

THE TRUMAN YEARS

6

The surrender of Japan in August 1945 ended World War II and cleared the way for a new, turbulent, and lengthy era in United States foreign relations known as the cold war. In Asia, the struggle was joined first in China, where Communist forces finally vanquished Chiang Kai-shek's Nationalists in 1949 and proclaimed the People's Republic. The outbreak of the Korean War the following year and Chinese intervention to save North Korea from defeat saw mainstream U.S. and Chinese military forces in battle against each other for the first time. At home, a hunt for Soviet spies was spurred by the conviction of Alger Hiss, a pillar of the foreign policy establishment, for lying about his participation in espionage. Three weeks later Senator Joseph R. McCarthy unveiled sensational charges that "reds" in the State Department and elsewhere had brought about the triumph of communism in China. For Mansfield, the early postwar years saw his continued development as a congressional expert on foreign relations but also his greatest political travail as McCarthy led a campaign to prevent his election to the Senate in 1952.

Mike Mansfield had a knack for being at important places at historic times.

On the morning of August 10, 1945, when the United States rejoiced at the first news of the surrender of Japan, Mansfield was at the White House conferring with President Truman. Just hours earlier, word had been received in Washington, first from government code breakers and then from Tokyo's official news agency, that Japan was ready to surrender, subject only to maintaining the emperor as a "sovereign ruler." As Mansfield entered the executive mansion, excited crowds were gathering in Lafayette Park across the street to await an official announcement of the end of World War II. Military police, who had been withdrawn months earlier, returned to their posts to safeguard the White House from overzealous celebrants.

A little less than twenty-four hours earlier, past midnight Tokyo time, Emperor Hirohito had told the civilian and military leaders of his government, gathered in a stuffy bomb shelter underneath the Imperial Palace, that the time had come to "bear the unbearable" and sue for peace. A subsequent cabinet meeting confirmed Hirohito's decision, which was then announced in cables to its wartime enemies through neutral nations and in news agency broadcasts. As Mansfield bided his time in a White House waiting room, the President was discussing the U.S. response with his inner cabinet, including Secretary of State James Byrnes, Secretary of War Henry Stimson, and Secretary of the Navy James Forrestal. Later the same day Truman replied that the supreme commander of the Allied powers, who was to be General Douglas MacArthur, would possess ultimate authority in defeated Japan rather than the emperor. It took three more days to gain clear-cut Japanese acceptance of the surrender and three more weeks to arrange the formal ceremony of surrender, at which MacArthur presided aboard the USS *Missouri* in Tokyo bay.

In the Oval Office, Mansfield and Truman briefly discussed the Japanese offer to surrender. Mansfield recalled that he expressed the view that Japan should be allowed to keep the emperor, lest the country be engulfed in chaos. Nonetheless, the congressman pointed out that Japan's Kwangtung Army had obtained the permission neither of the emperor or of the civil government in Tokyo before invading Manchuria in 1931 or attacking China in 1937, and therefore the army might keep fighting, whatever the emperor said. Speaking to a new president who, he knew, was relatively unfamiliar with Asia, Mansfield also referred to "the general picture in Mongolia, Manchuria, Outer Mongolia and Sinkiang" on the extremities of China. On the way out, he told reporters that Truman was "keenly aware" of the problem of the Kwangtung Army and was determined to accomplish its outright capitulation. It is unlikely that many of the reporters had heard much—or anything at all—about Japan's expeditionary army.

Mansfield's purpose in seeing Truman on that momentous morning in August 1945 concerned China rather than Japan. His 1944 mission under the sponsorship of President Roosevelt had reacquainted him with the Middle Kingdom but, as the rest of his career demonstrated, nothing could quell his strong desire to see and learn more of China. The trip also transformed the obscure junior lawmaker from Montana into an expert on the Far East in the eyes of his colleagues and the press. Determined to return once again, if possible as a presidential emissary, he began making his request directly to Truman on May 23, 1945, only five months after returning from his earlier trip and six weeks after Truman became president on the death of Roosevelt.

As was the case with his earlier trip, Mansfield's aspirations in foreign affairs were assisted by circumstances in domestic politics. A special election had been scheduled for June 5 to replace a recently deceased member of Congress from Montana's Eastern District, which was a hotly contested area politically. It would be the first election of a member of Congress since Truman became president and was attracting national interest as a possible indicator of political sentiment in the coming 1946 congressional elections. The previous November, Mansfield had won reelection in the Western District with a startling two-thirds of the vote, instantly becoming a highly important Democratic figure in the state. It was logical, therefore, that Truman wished to discuss the forthcoming vote in the Eastern District with Mansfield, whom he had met during a barnstorming tour of Montana as FDR's vice president the previous winter.

They began by discussing Montana politics and the possibility of siting a new Veterans Administration hospital at Miles City in eastern Montana, a decision announced by Mansfield in the course of the special election campaign in that area. Mansfield noted that the state's senior senator, James Murray, had gone to Montana to campaign, but he predicted Murray would lose votes rather than win votes for the Democratic candidate in the special election by emphasizing his favorite program, the controversial Missouri Valley Authority for public development of the area. "I told [Truman] I wasn't even going to mention the MVA and he said that was a good thing because the issue is too hot and as this race is very vital we should do everything we can to win it," Mansfield recorded. Truman said he liked Jim Murray but that he realized Murray "did not have any political sense." (As it turned out, the Democratic candidate lost the special election.)

Mansfield then turned to the China trip, telling Truman that FDR had asked him "in strict confidence" to make a second trip to China as his emissary in the summer of 1945, although there was no indication of this in his earlier memoranda and it is doubtful that the dying Roosevelt made such a statement. According to Mansfield's notes, Truman readily agreed to send him back to the Middle Kingdom after Congress adjourned for the summer, although the new President cautiously rejected the congressman's proposal that Mansfield immediately inform newspaper reporters in the White House lobby of this decision. Mansfield outlined the political benefits of his returning to China, saying that "it is of vital importance that we have somebody on our side in the House to explain the situation and the policy in the Far East because conditions out there are going to be more embarrassing as time goes on." If he were able to speak with the enhanced authority of a new mission to China "it would help the President because I would be prepared to take the floor on any occasion," Mansfield added. Truman said he'd like to see Mansfield again to discuss the issue in about a month.

Continuing his pursuit of a new China mission, Mansfield persistently reminded Matthew Connelly, Truman's appointment secretary, of the President's commitment to see him after Congress adjourned. On May 26 he also sent a copy of his 1944 China report to the President's daughter, Margaret, on the grounds that she could appreciate it as a student majoring in history at George Washington University. On the House floor, Mansfield praised Truman for his performance at the Potsdam Conference with the British and Russians. The efforts seemed to be paying off. Connelly told him in a face-to-face encounter in July that "the White House like[s] me [Mansfield] very much."

In their meeting on August 10, the day of the Japanese surrender offer, Mansfield told Truman there were only three men in Congress "with any real knowledge of the Far East": Republican House member Dr. Walter Judd, a former medical missionary in China; Democratic Senator Elbert Thomas, a former teacher in Japan; and himself. According to his notes made at the time, Mansfield said, as he had earlier, that there was a need for "someone on our side to back up our policies out there." He told the President that "I wanted to go as his personal representative and report back to him, and then to Congress. My background fitted me for this job. I also pointed out even if the war was over, a greater need for understanding China was necessary."

The President agreed with those general points but said that because of the turn of events, he could not send Mansfield at that time. In office only four months, Truman was already involved in diplomatic maneuvering without the sometimes unwanted participation of members of Congress. The Soviet Union had declared war on Japan two days before the Japanese offer to surrender, and Truman was waiting to hear the latest reports of Chinese Nationalist negotiations with Stalin currently taking place in Moscow. The conflict between the Nationalists and the Communists, which Mansfield had observed in late 1944, was still growing. Referring to the controversial Patrick Hurley, who would resign three months later, touching off charges that procommunists in the State Department had "lost China," Truman said he had "a prima donna ambassador in China" whom he could not change at the moment. He did not think it wise to send a personal representative into that situation. Maybe later, he said in consolation.

Disappointed as he was by Truman's decision, Mansfield did not lessen his interest in U.S. policy, especially involving postwar China. However, he began to be notably more critical of the administration, saying in the House that he was unable to discover what the United States sought to do in Asia, except in the case of Japan. Recalling his unease in being retained in the Navy against his will at the end of World War I and fearing U.S. involvement in the great power politics of Asia, he delivered two House speeches in October asking for the removal of American forces as rapidly as possible from China, India, Burma, and Korea. He advocated that the Chinese, presumably Chiang Kai-shek's Nationalist forces, occupy Korea, the subject of his M.A. thesis at the University of Montana eleven years earlier, on grounds that "they would understand far better than we the situation there."

Mansfield was especially critical of the postwar landing in China of 53,000 U.S. Marines to help Chiang Kai-shek's Nationalist forces accept the surrender of the Japanese in North China before Communist troops could take over. The First Marine Division had landed at Taku, downriver from Tientsin, repeating the landing that Private Mansfield and his Marine detachment had made in 1922. The Sixth Marine Division landed at Tsingtao, further down the Chinese coast, and five U.S. cruisers were stationed offshore. In speeches on the House floor, Mansfield called this a "gunboat policy" and an "unwarranted interference" that might cause the Soviet Union to cancel its commitments to withdraw from China. He also took his objections to the China landings to the State Department, where he told his old acquaintance John Carter Vincent, who was now director of the Office of Far Eastern Affairs, that any prolonged use of the Marines in China would be "most unwise."

Having had no success in affecting U.S. policy, Mansfield wrote to Truman on November 7 enclosing his House speeches and asking for a meeting to explain his views. When the meeting was granted on November 27, he found a president who was already engaged in the cold war geopolitics that would dominate U.S. policy for many decades to come. Mansfield said he had learned that the State Department had known nothing of the military decision to send the Marines to China, that the deployment had caused "terrible discontent" among servicemen in the Far East and people at home, and that "if we kept the Marines in China, we would surely become involved." To Mansfield's plea to set a definite date for their withdrawal, Truman bluntly refused, saying, "I cannot do that. The situation over there is more serious than most people know. We have promised to back Chiang Kai-shek and we will." The President harshly criticized Russia for stripping machinery and equipment from Asian areas it had occupied and said Moscow was looking for an excuse to remain in Manchuria and is making it difficult for Chiang to assume control.

Mansfield responded that the United States should continue to back Chiang but that "we could become involved unwittingly" in a civil war. He then presented Truman in blunt fashion with what he called his personal conclusions: "Do away with secret diplomacy and tell the truth. . . . Get the Marines out of China at a *definite* time. . . . Let China use 40 American equipped [Nationalist Chinese] divisions to do the job of disarming the Japanese soldiers and assume control in North China and Manchuria. . . . Send China a strong American Military Mission which could be large enough to take over some of the jobs now being done by the Marines. . . . China should settle her own internal problems." On the last point, Truman pointed out that Chiang and his government "do not trust Russia or Britain. They trust only us and we got to carry the commitments through to the finish."

In the face of the divergence of views between the two men, there was no more talk of a Mansfield mission to China. They ended the meeting on a friendly note, however, discussing the practical politics of foreign policy. Mansfield mentioned a report in *Newsweek* that Truman had approved a Chilean appeal to reduce U.S. tariff rates on copper imports by 50 percent. The former copper miner from Butte told the President that if this were done, the impact on the U.S. mines would bring about the defeat of Democratic members of Congress from Arizona, Montana, Nevada, New Mexico, and Utah who had voted for a three-year extension of the reciprocal trade bill Truman had requested. The President said the news report was erroneous. "I am not going to put any of you boys on the spot, . . . " Truman responded. "I certainly do not intend to lose what Democratic votes we have in the West over a matter of this sort."

RIP VAN WINKLE GROWS IN STATURE

"Mike Mansfield, sometimes described as Montana's spare, slow-spoken congressman, is six feet tall, has blue eyes and is slight of build," wrote John Buzzetti, in his research paper "The Honorable Mike Mansfield" in early 1948. "Actually his manner of speaking is brisk if measured by Western-drawl standards. His articulate pronunciation—especially of Chinese names such as Chiang Kai-shek and Kuomintang—is accentuated by a bobbing Adam's apple. When talking before a group or to an individual he speaks directly and with an eye-contact that is as friendly as is his handshake." To Francis R. "Frank" Valeo, who later became Mansfield's closest aide, the studious congressman was a gangling figure from the hinterland who reminded him of Ichabod Crane, or perhaps Rip Van Winkle. His clothes looked as though they came from J.C. Penny, a low-budget store, Valeo recalled, and in fact that was where he often bought clothing items for many years.

Mansfield's keen attention to constituent affairs and his growing national prominence won him strong political support at home. In the 1946 election the Republican Party trounced the Democrats nationally amid the postwar transition, winning control of both houses of Congress for the first time since the Great Depression. Mansfield was opposed by a popular war hero, W. R. "Barney" Rankin, who campaigned on a promise of a 20 percent cut in income taxes and whose anticommunist political advertising maintained, "The $64 question is, Will you string along with Uncle Joe [Stalin]? Or will you vote American?" Despite these appeals, Mansfield survived with a comfortable 57.5 percent of the vote.

Buzzetti, a student of Mansfield's at the University of Montana before the war, conducted interviews about the congressman in the aftermath of the 1946 election. He found that Mansfield had benefited from being perceived as an opponent of the Montana Power Company and its corporate twin, the Anaconda Copper Mining Company as a result of his outspoken advocacy of rural electrification and the Hungry Horse Dam. A Missoula barber told Buzzetti that "I don't like the Democrats' policies but I vote for Mike because I know him and they need some educated men [like] him there." A bartender said he backed Mansfield because he was "a school teacher so I figure he's honest," while a customer said, "I hear that he's against Montana Power and that's enough for me." Many Montanans had direct contact with their congressman. Although Washington was far across the country, Mansfield estimated in response to a questionnaire from Buzzetti that about 4,500 Montanans had visited him at the capital in his first five years in Congress. He knew many of them by name.

Mansfield's popularity at home continued to rise. In his successive House campaigns in 1948 and 1950, he exceeded 60 percent of the total vote on each occasion despite partisan Republican attacks. His voting record in the House was solidly Democratic, with few deviations from party positions. With assistance from Mansfield, Truman carried Montana in his upset victory over Republican Thomas E. Dewey in the 1948 presidential election. Nationally, the Truman victory resulted in the return of Congress to Democratic control.

Two weeks after the 1948 election, Mansfield wrote to House Speaker Sam Rayburn and Majority Leader John McCormack, asking that he be considered for the post of majority whip, the third highest leadership position among Democrats in the House. The previous whip, Percy Priest, was from Tennessee, and no one from the West had been designated for the chairmanship of any legislative committee, despite the strong support given in the West to Truman. Mansfield wrote that he did not wish to displace Priest if he wished to continue, but his ambition for party office was clear. Mansfield's longtime friend and political sponsor, Jim Rowe, followed up with a letter to Rayburn. Rowe's law partner, former New Deal insider and lobbyist Thomas G. "Tommy the Cork" Corcoran both telephoned and wrote to Rayburn and also wrote to McCormack in Mansfield's behalf. Corcoran commented on his activity in a wry note to Rowe: "If you took half as good care of my business as I take care of yours, how much better off I'd be." Rayburn and McCormack responded with cordial letters to Mansfield and his sponsors, but when Congress reconvened, Priest decided to continue as Majority Whip. Mansfield, however, was named chief assistant whip, a sign of his good standing among Democratic Party regulars. Because of his reputation for rectitude, the Democratic leadership chose him in 1950 to be chairman of the House's Special Committee to Investigate Campaign Expenditures in that fall's campaigns. Mansfield chose Rowe as the committee's general counsel.

The growing respect in which he was held led to offers from outside Congress as well. In October 1949, Truman and Secretary of State Dean Acheson asked him to become assistant secretary of state for public affairs, in charge of the press and public side of American diplomacy. The offer was quickly reported by newspapers in Washington and Montana. Jimmy Sullivan, Mansfield's home state political aide, advised him not to accept the alluring job. The people he had seen were all against it, Sullivan wrote from Montana. "Many of them wonder if the powers that be in the State have not used their influence to have you liquidated in this way . . . the people of Montana are for you more than ever; but not the major officer holders." Montana's political establishment, dominated by the conservative mining interests of the Anaconda Company on the one hand, and the organized liberals of the AFL-CIO and the Farmers Union on the other hand, found Mansfield too independent for its taste. "You have been the pilot of your own canoe: you have piloted it a long way up the stream, sometimes against rapid currents," Sullivan wrote in his letter. "I have no doubt but that you can go a lot further with the same piloting." He pointed out that should Mansfield accept the State Department job but then wish to return to state politics, "you would have 2 strikes against you for the reason that you walked out on them." Mansfield turned down the job in a public statement that despite his continuing interest in national and international affairs, "I believe that it is my first duty to continue to work for the development of our State's resources and the betterment of our people." The following year he was offered the position of undersecretary of the interior and asked by the chair of the search committee to apply for the presidency of the University of Montana. He turned both down, citing reasons similar to those he had expressed in connection with the State Department post.

A PRIMA DONNA AND THE A-BOMB

If he could not undertake a second presidentially sponsored mission to China, Mansfield was determined to find other ways to broaden his detailed knowledge of world affairs through traveling abroad. Late in 1946, he arranged to attach himself to a four-member subcommittee of the House Naval Affairs Committee on a month-long tour of Japan, China, the Philippines, and the Micronesian islands in the mid-Pacific. A three-hour luncheon in Tokyo on December 1 with General Douglas MacArthur, who did nearly all the talking from his seat at the head of the table, left him impressed with his host's policies in the occupation of Japan and the "magnificent job" he was doing. Nonetheless, he confided to his travel diary that the general is a "primadonna" who "seems to enjoy his role as an American emperor." He noticed that MacArthur used silver dinnerware of his own with "D MacA" embossed on the plates. Little did Mansfield know that three decades later he would be living in the same spacious ambassadorial residence where he had been the general's guest and would then be revered among many Japanese as the greatest U.S. representative in Tokyo since MacArthur.

Mansfield's most searing experience in his return to Asia came as the special U.S. Air Force plane circled Hiroshima, where the first atomic bomb had been dropped sixteen months earlier. Mansfield wrote in his personal diary:

Devastation over a large area—4 square miles. Some large modern buildings, probably 8 or 10 standing and some wooden houses going up. No signs of gardens in bombed area. I do not feel good about the bomb and I think it was a mistake to use it on people. What did the ordinary person have to do with bringing on a war? Why should they have to always suffer for some individuals or small groups mistake? War is responsible for bringing about all the bad things we fear and few of the good things we want.

The atomic bomb had made a deep impression on Mansfield from the first time he heard of it, shortly after the initial explosion over Hiroshima on August 6, 1945. In a statement written in longhand and released to Montana news media in the aftermath of the Japanese surrender, he immediately recognized that the world had changed in fundamental ways. "The B-29, the robot bomb & finally the Atomic Bomb have all brought home to us the fact that isolation is dead—and dead forever. . . . We must cooperate with the other nations of the world because we know now that what has happened to Hiroshima & Nagasaki could conceivably happen to us." He idealistically observed that the fears and hopes engendered by the bomb reinforced the unity among nations, but at the same time he approved U.S. legislation to keep "the formula for the Atomic bomb" in the hands of the U.S., British, and Canadian governments.

On November 8, three months after the bomb was dropped, in a briefing by leading atomic scientists for members of Congress he learned that "the formula (for the atomic bomb) never was a secret and cannot be either kept or given away" and that the technical designs and production methods are only temporarily the exclusive property of the three governments because "all the principal industrial countries can achieve them." With his early hope for international unity fading, Mansfield said in a lengthy letter to Montanans that he was most afraid of "an atomic armaments race." He told his constituents that the atomic scientists who briefed him seemed to be "scared stiff" because "the Frankenstein they had made frightened them." Mansfield became an advocate of civilian control of atomic energy in the United States and international control abroad under the United Nations.

His experience in Hiroshima and his understanding of the power of atomic weapons confirmed Mansfield's view that it was essential for the United States to engage productively and extensively with other nations in the nuclear age, although he was also opposed in most circumstances to U.S. military intervention abroad. (An exception was the U.S. decision to fight in Korea, which he supported from the first in reaction to the North Korean invasion.) Later, President Lyndon Johnson, frustrated by Mansfield's opposition to the Vietnam War, and Henry Kissinger, fiercely opposed to Mansfield's proposal to bring large numbers of U.S. troops home from Europe, would lambaste him in private as an isolationist. Following the onset of World War II and especially after that of the nuclear age, this characterization was wrong.

In his journey with the Naval Affairs Committee, Mansfield was discouraged by what he found in his five days in China, which was very likely the principal objective of the trip from his standpoint. General George C. Marshall was nearing the end of his unsuccessful year-long mission to avert all-out civil war by bringing the Nationalists and Communists together. With both sides dug in against substantial concessions, Marshall was preparing to return home to become secretary of state, which he did in early January 1947. Mansfield's private view, confided to his diary, was pessimistic:

> No matter what we do we stand to lose. If we stay in we just sit tight and do nothing; if we get out, our mission is a failure. Madam Chiang now has no influence on Gimo [her husband, Chiang Kai-shek] and had adopted a defeated attitude. . . . Communists very anti-American and have posters in Yenan showing American marines shoving Chinese off streets, raping Chinese women etc.

The one bright spot in the picture for Mansfield was that the U.S. military presence in China had been rapidly reduced from a high point of 113,000 in late 1945, when he was complaining about it to Truman, to 12,000 only a year later, and the reductions were continuing. He saw little chance of the American military playing a useful role as long as the Nationalists and Communists were so far apart. Publicly, he told the House that the civil war would continue "as long as we, or any other great power, will underwrite a victory for one side or the other." Mansfield proposed that the United States initiate a four-power conference including the Soviet Union, Britain, and China to strengthen and unify China and guarantee it against foreign intervention. No such meeting was ever held.

As the Nationalists' position continued to deteriorate and U.S. proposals were ignored, Mansfield in October 1947 wrote Marshall, who was now secretary of state, that he was committed to making a speech in New York on the subject but that "I must admit at the present time I do not know exactly what the Chinese Policy of the United States is. . . ." He asked for a meeting with Marshall to discuss it, and State Department documents indicate this was granted in early November after subordinates reminded Marshall of the congressman's long interest in China and his "close relations" and "in general . . . friendly attitude" toward the State Department.

No record of the meeting with Marshall can be found, but it appears to have been effective. Mansfield's address to the annual meeting of the Academy of Political Science in New York on November 12 was an unswerving defense of U.S. policy, including Truman's decision to send U.S. troops to assist Chiang Kai-shek to disarm and evacuate the Japanese, which Mansfield had earlier criticized. "We extended this help in spite of strong counter-pressures at home and in the face of violent opposition from the Chinese Communists," Mansfield declared, —not mentioning that his had been among the counter-pressures. He praised Marshall for his painstaking efforts to negotiate an end to the Civil War raging in China, but he criticized the growing calls at home for U.S. intervention to halt the spread of communism now that the talks had broken off. Such a course would ultimately involve "a return of American forces to Chinese soil in large numbers," Mansfield warned. It would show "an abysmal or arrogant indifference to one of the most powerful forces in China today—nationalism." He ended by asking his listeners in effect to trust the government "to apply measures necessary to support China's sovereignty against any outside powers," but to do so while considering the full array of international problems it faced and of U.S. resources to deal with them "in the light of reality."

In September 1947 Mansfield took part in a five-week Senate-House trip through Western and Eastern Europe to assess the need for a U.S. information program in that part of the world. By this time Maureen had become resentful of his extensive travel while she was at home with Anne, now seven years old and suffering the usual childhood sicknesses. As the four-engine military transport plane flew across the North Atlantic at 3 A.M. on the first leg of the trip, Mansfield imparted to his journal an unusually introspective view of the life he was leading;

A man thinks of a lot of things in space—his family & their welfare, people of all kinds & how good life can be for some & how cruel for others. One can also think of politics & how, if successful, one is rewarded—in a sense—but how that reward affects one's personal life in relation to his family sometimes has a devastating effect. If I were not in politics I could be with my family always. In politics I am lucky to average 9 months a year at home. These trips I take are not easy because I have a normal man's fear of what may happen &, to me, there is very little pleasure in them. However, I must look to the future & the security of my family & I feel that if anything happens to me in politics I must be in a position to have as much background as possible to go back teaching tho I do not think I would like it. . . .

I have a lovely wife & daughter & I know that I am favored above all people in these respects. But life is hard & competition is keen. I have spent too many years in poverty & want & I do not intend in the years remaining to revert back to that. I must, & will, do what I can to assure for my family a decent security and a comfortable future. I must, & I will, do the best I know how to represent my people & do all in my power to be the kind of Congressman the people deserve.

The dawn is just coming up & the red colors seem to be rising from out of the ocean itself. All the group is asleep except the crew.

His concern for family life was intensified in Vienna, where he received an angry letter from Maureen, "so bitter and so unexpected," that haunted him and caused him to fear that she was looking with suspicion on everything he did. He was relieved to receive another letter from her eight days later in Athens with a completely different tone and message as well as a separate letter from Anne. Between the two letters, he decided to abandon plans to join a projected trip to the Far East. The cutback in overseas travel was temporary, however. From then until the senatorial election year of 1952, he traveled overseas with congressional delegations or on his own at least once each year and twice in two of the years.

In his first extensive taste of Europe, Paris in 1947 looked good to Mansfield, with "the most beautiful women in the world, the finest & most decorative streets & the best food I have ever tasted." The lawmakers went to the Folies Bergere on their first night in town, "a good enough show with a bevy of beautiful girls & a minimum of clothing," but Mansfield and his colleagues were tired and left at intermission. Elsewhere, though, Europeans were suffering from the effects of World War II. The Germans are "sullen" and without much hope, he observed, "the people are poorly clothed & there is not much food. . . . It broke my heart to see little children going barefoot in this cold weather." In Soviet-dominated areas, political conditions were much worse. Devastated Poland was "a police state in the strict sense of the word. If you talk to two persons at once the third may be an informer." Romania, he discovered, was "a country of fear, whispers & intimidation." The economic and political conditions Mansfield found in Europe near the onset of the cold war provided a benchmark that persuaded him that the prosperous and relatively stable

Europe of the 1960s and 1970s could do without such massive numbers of remaining American troops.

On this trip and those to come, Mansfield was developing his views about the nature and causes of communism, which increasingly was the great political issue of the day. In April 1948 he turned to Latin America, another region he had studied and later taught about at the University of Montana. As one of two official observers from the U.S. Congress, he attended the Ninth Conference of Inter-American States at Bogotá, Colombia, the historic meeting that created the Charter of the Organization of American States, a body that remains a significant factor in hemispheric politics more than half a century later. The headlines of 1948, however, were about the near-revolution that had broken out in Bogotá days before Mansfield's arrival as a result of the assassination of the Colombian liberal leader Jorge Gaitán. The murder was widely blamed on communists, although the true culprit is a matter of contention even in the twenty-first century. Many historians date the outbreak of a decade of civil war in Colombia, known as the *Violencia,* to the killing of Gaitán, and some suggest it was the spark for a guerrilla war that still continues.

Mansfield's fellow congressional observer, Donald L. Jackson, a conservative Republican from California, drew the lesson that "the Red tide last week touched the shores of the Western Hemisphere, and with the sword and torch the agents of international aggression have laid waste a capital city of one of the American Republics." Jackson was so concerned for his own safety that he carried a .45-caliber pistol, and gave Mansfield a .32-caliber pistol and fifty rounds of ammunition for self-defense. Mansfield thought that his colleague had "tremendously" overestimated the danger.

Writing in his diary, Mansfield agreed with Jackson that the perpetrators were communists, but he saw the causes and the eventual cures in more nuanced fashion:

> The situation here and elsewhere in Latin America is not too difficult to understand. It is the difference between the wealthy few interested only in themselves and the poverty-stricken masses trying to make a bare livelihood. . . . The people, by and large, are not communists. They are supposed to be living under a democracy but they're not; they know their presidents are, in the main, totalitarian minded and they are groping in the dark looking for something new to hang their hopes on. The Communists, very few but very

shrewd, exploit the weaknesses of all governments except their own, and they use the regularly constituted parties to achieve their own ends.

As the China issue heated up politically after the Communist triumph on the mainland in 1949 and Chiang's retreat to the island of Formosa, Mansfield opposed additional military aid to Nationalist China (a total of $2 billion having already been supplied since the end of World War II), saying in House debate that it "would be followed by military combat assistance in the not too distant future. . . . [I]t will only be a short time before you will be sending American boys to China, and if you get into a war over there you will get into something you cannot win, in my opinion, no matter what you do." By now thoroughly disillusioned with Chiang, he told a Washington Town Meeting in February 1950 that the failure in China was not due to American policy but "due to the incredible ineptitude of the Nationalist Army command . . . to the inability or unwillingness of the Chinese Government to take the necessary and repeatedly advised measures of social, economic, political and military reform . . . [and] due to the downright corruption in official circles."

After Truman interposed the U.S. fleet between Taiwan and the mainland following the outbreak of the Korean War in June 1950, Mansfield reversed himself and approved resumption of military aid to the Nationalists on the grounds that "there is some hope" it can prove effective. Still, "under present circumstances and at the present time, I do not believe we ought to back Chiang Kai-shek in an adventure on the mainland." He condemned "get in or get out" sentiment regarding China as "extremism" and called for a middle course of limited assistance.

THE UGLIEST CAMPAIGN

By the early 1950s, the American public had been jarred by a series of setbacks in the cold war, including the Communist triumph in China in 1949 and the detonation of the first Soviet atomic bomb the same year, and in 1950 the onset of the Korean War and the massive Chinese military intervention. At home, the 1950 perjury conviction of Alger Hiss, accused of spying for the Soviet Union, and the arrest of Julius and Ethel Rosenberg as spies a few months later, contributed to an atmosphere in which charges of widespread conspiracy were taken seriously by many Americans. More than half a century later, it is difficult to appreciate fully the fear produced by these events in the early years of the cold war. A black-and-white view of international relations, especially regarding faraway Asia, was dominant among U.S. policymakers and commentators. "We felt, as did everybody else in this country at the time, that the world had disappeared except for the Soviet Union and ourselves," recalled Frank Valeo. "And that anything that happened in the world, any threat in the world, came from Moscow and went through a hierarchy." This was the climate in which Senator Joseph R. McCarthy and others sought to use anticommunist sentiment against political opponents, diplomats, and scholars who saw a more complex picture.

McCarthy was the most prominent purveyor of the theory that treason at home was the cause of setbacks abroad. The movement that McCarthy symbolized was used politically by the conservative wing of the Republican Party, out of power in the White House since the 1932 election and determined this time to win at all costs. The Republicans had managed to recruit Dwight D. Eisenhower, a highly popular wartime leader, as their presidential candidate. Ike was a political moderate, but the party tolerated and even sponsored McCarthyite attacks on Democrats as the party of treason. The battle cry against the Democrats was, "Who Lost China?" As always, the Middle Kingdom was an intensely emotional issue in American politics.

Mansfield's 1944 mission to China and his outspoken interest in Asia policy had been instrumental in bringing him to prominence in Washington, but they had not always played well in Montana, where political opponents, calling him "China Mike," attacked his report as naïve or worse and charged that he was concentrating more on faraway foreign policy issues than on the home front. Mansfield had effectively countered this with his sponsorship of the Hungry Horse Dam and energetic contacts with and activities for his constituents, but it remained one of his few political vulnerabilities. In the contest for his House seat in 1950, amid the national uproar over China, his Republican opponent, Ralph McGinnis, the debate coach at the University of Montana, quoted Mansfield's 1944 characterization of the Chinese Communists as "agrarian reformers" and charged that Mansfield's "appeasement" had led to debacles abroad. Mansfield easily turned aside the challenge and won with 60.2 percent of the vote, but the issue did not go away.

Mansfield had been asked to run for the Senate in 1946 against Burton K. Wheeler but declined. Six years later Maureen, Jim Rowe, and others urged him to undertake the 1952 race for the U.S. Senate seat held by Republican Zales N. Ecton. Mansfield knew from the first it would be difficult but did not expect it to be as ugly as it proved to be. A wealthy farmer and rancher who had previously served as chairman of the State Republican Central Committee and spent fourteen years in the state legislature, Ecton was well known statewide, whereas Mansfield's contacts and supporters were concentrated in the western half of the state, which he had represented in Congress since 1943. Even though Ecton had a lackluster record in his six years in the Senate (*Redbook* magazine had listed him among the twenty-four "worst" members of Congress), he had the advantage of incumbency. He also had an unfortunate stutter, which sapped his strength as a public speaker.

While traveling in Montana to assess prospects for the race, Jimmy Sullivan was forewarned about Republican tactics in the eastern part of the state. Frank Whetstone, the son of a prominent Republican editor, told Sullivan, as recorded in his notebook, that the GOP plan was "to try to connect [Mansfield] with Red China and Communism. . . . They tried to pin Red on him in the western Dist[rict] it did not stick. Mike's neighbors knew him, they knew he was no communist. It is different here where he is not know[n] and the time is too short to have Mike meet the people of the eastern Dist like he met them in the western Dist. House to House contact. It would take him three years to do that in this dist. The Republicans have plenty money & you know the things they say or print don't have to be true."

Like many other Democrats, Mansfield had tried to protect himself from Republican charges of pro-communism by co-sponsoring legislation, along with many other liberal Democrats, to outlaw the Communist Party U.S.A. and by making it clear that he had no sympathy with the Russian or Chinese regimes. Mansfield was also provided by Truman with the most effective shield the administration had available—the opportunity to oppose Soviet representatives in prominent debate at the United Nations. As early as January 1947, Mansfield had asked Truman in a White House meeting and a subsequent letter "as a younger member of the [Democratic] Party" to be appointed an alternate delegate to the United Nations, a post usually given to members of

Congress. In a handwritten note on his letter of application, Mansfield wrote, "Keep punching, Mr. President. You've got the Republicans on the ropes & they're showing it." Truman did not appoint him then but did so for a special session of the UN General Assembly that convened in Paris late in 1951. In a debate on economic development of underdeveloped countries, Mansfield departed from the State Department's prepared text to speak as a former "copper miner, a farm hand, a smelterman and a lumberjack" about the aspirations of the downtrodden. In response, A. A. Aritunian, a senior member of the Soviet delegation, rebuked Mansfield for "talking like a lumberjack or a miner" rather than as a diplomat. With a grin on his face, Mansfield bowed slightly toward his adversary and said he deemed the charge a compliment since, in fact, he had done both those jobs in his career. The exchange was picked up by the international press.

The most well publicized debate pitted Mansfield against Soviet foreign minister Andrei Vishinsky, who had been chief prosecutor at Joseph Stalin's purge trials a decade earlier. Vishinsky was photographed wagging his finger at Mansfield, which prompted former first lady Eleanor Roosevelt to praise the congressman in her syndicated newspaper column for remaining "as calm and as cool as a cucumber" in the face of an "infuriated" Vishinsky. "I'd like to have this particular congressman with me if I were fighting for something really good, and I'd hate to have him against me," wrote Mrs. Roosevelt, who was also a member of the U.S. delegation.

In the Senate campaign that followed these well-publicized encounters, Mansfield took pride in having debated this "arrogant man who stands in New York today thundering against the free nations of the world" and for "the praise I received from the nation's newspapers and the world press for beating the Russian Vishinsky." Truman, campaigning for Mansfield in Montana, declared that after he sent Mansfield to the United Nations "he stood right up to the Russian Vishinsky and slugged it out with him and beat down a Russian attack on the foreign policy of the United States. . . . Mike has always known that communism was dangerous—and that we had to take measures to stop it." Such statements, however, proved to be an incomplete defense against his attackers.

Going into the election of 1952, the Senate was almost equally divided, 49 to 47 in favor of the Democrats in the 96-member Senate, and Montana was among fifteen battleground states. Both parties sent their top national political figures into the state to campaign, including President Truman and presidential and vice presidential nominees Adlai Stevenson and John Sparkman for the Democrats, and nominees Eisenhower and Richard Nixon plus sixteen incumbent senators for the Republicans. Both Senate candidates campaigned in nearly all of Montana's fifty-six counties, with Ecton relying on support among cattlemen and businessmen, and Mansfield on the support of organized labor, the Farmers Union, and a hard core of former students and friends from Butte.

With the war in Korea raging, the Ecton campaign made much of Mansfield's description of the Chinese Communists as "agrarian reformers," and charged in official advertising that Democratic policies upheld by Mansfield "compelled the surrender of all Asia to the communists—resulting in more than 115,000 American casualties and thousands of Americans tortured in Communist prison camps." A circular sent by mail to Montana households by Ecton allies charged that "Mansfield Aided *Communist* Line WHICH LED TO KOREAN WAR!" Newspaper advertisements attacking Mansfield "From a Father Whose Son Was Killed in Korea" were widely circulated. In a highly emotional thirteen-minute radio appeal, a Great Falls woman whose husband, an Army sergeant, was being held in a North Korean prison camp, blamed Mansfield's "blunders" about Chinese communists for his plight. It was broadcast more than two hundred times in the three weeks before election day.

The Mansfield campaign was also beset by anonymous telephone calls in which the callers would say, "Mike Mansfield is a communist" and then hang up. In other whispering campaigns, references were made to his Catholicism. At one stage, Mansfield staff members suggested that Jimmy Sullivan be kept out of the campaign in the Eastern District because his Irish brogue and typically Irish face might remind voters who did not know him of the candidate's religion. Mansfield refused to hear of it. "The Senate is not worth losing Jimmy as a friend," he said.

The big gun of the Republican smear campaign was McCarthy himself, who was at the height of his renown as a political dragon-slayer. After rolling to a lopsided victory in the Wisconsin primary, which virtually guaranteed his own reelection, McCarthy campaigned widely in other states and was credited (or blamed) for the defeat of four Democratic incumbents that fall, including his strongest opponent in the Senate, William Benton of

Connecticut, and the Senate Democratic leader, Ernest McFarland of Arizona. Addressing an overflow crowd in Missoula on October 14, McCarthy pulled out copies of the Communist Party's *Daily Worker* in which Mansfield was mentioned favorably, charging that he was not necessarily a communist but was "either stupid or a dupe." He described the political opposition as the "Commiecrat Party." To those who criticized his methods, McCarthy volunteered that "you don't hunt skunks with a top hat and a lace handkerchief" and "the more successful the skunk hunting is, the worse you smell."

To augment the GOP drive to discredit Mansfield, Harvey Matusow, a former Communist for hire, was brought into the state at McCarthy's request. Years later, Matusow wrote that "McCarthy had a violent hatred for Mansfield and told me that if he was elected 'you might as well have an admitted Communist in the Senate, it's the same difference.'"

Matusow had joined the Communist Party in 1947 but was soon disillusioned and became an undercover informant for the FBI. He surfaced as a witness in the federal trial of alleged communists in 1952 and became a paid witness for the Justice Department, the Subversive Activities Control Board, and others. Later he confessed that his testimony at various trials and hearings had been false. In Montana, he traveled to civic clubs, parochial schools, and American Legion halls in nine cities and made a radio broadcast "as an expert on the subject of communism in the U.S.A.," all paid for by the Ecton campaign. Matusow's tactic was to dip dramatically into his briefcase and bring out the photostat of an article attributed to Mansfield in the Communist Party's front publication *New Masses,* charging that it showed Mansfield's support for communism; actually the "article" was a reprint of a portion of Mansfield's report from his 1944 China trip as published in the *Congressional Record.* Matusow, like McCarthy, also used an old editorial from the *Daily Worker* favorably mentioning Mansfield to prove the candidate's "unrealistic attitude toward communism." As he later admitted, Matusow as a Communist had known nothing about Mansfield and was given the articles in question by members of McCarthy's staff.

The atmosphere became so heated that for the first (and only) time in Mansfield's life, he observed people he knew crossing the street to avoid meeting him, something that appalled him. Looking defeat in the face, Mansfield with encouragement from Jimmy Sullivan decided to fight back with a statewide radio address on Sunday night, November 2, thirty-six hours before balloting began. With unusual passion, Mansfield told the voters:

> If I win this election, I want to win it honestly and on the record. I can look every man and woman in Montana in the eye because I have done nothing I am ashamed of nor have I spoken evil of my fellow man. I have exercised restraint in this campaign until the 16 outside Republican senators sent into this state to defeat me had been heard; until the man who admitted he was a Communist had been brought into Montana by my opponent and his group and had attacked my patriotism, my character, my religious faith, my integrity; and, until my opponent, who, himself, and his friends had made all of his charges and made all the falsehoods known.
>
> What in heaven's name has happened to us as Americans? What have we done that a public servant should be so defiled and defaced? Is it not intolerable that a man seeking high office with its agonizing burdens would have to suffer the indignity of having to defend, not his political beliefs, but the very honor of his soul? How in these perilous times can we get decent men and women to run for public office if they are going to be subject to these vilifications?

With that, he blasted back at Ecton and his charges, describing his China report in some detail and recalling that General Frank Merrill was the author of the phrase "agrarian reformers" in describing the Chinese Communists in his 1944 China mission report. He cited praise from U.S. generals and prominent Republicans for his reporting and his stands on Asia. Then he attacked Ecton as a "do nothing" senator who had voted against a long list of Montana programs, principally public power projects, including the speeding up of the Hungry Horse Dam.

The broadcast probably saved the day. In the balloting, a powerful Republican tide brought Eisenhower and a Republican Congress into office nationally. Montanans overwhelmingly cast their votes for Eisenhower and elected a Republican governor. Nonetheless, Mansfield was elected to represent Montana in the Senate. His margin of victory was fewer than 6,000 votes out of 262,000 votes cast—by far the closest election he would ever have. Had he known how nasty it would be, he told me on several occasions, he would not have run. The day after the election, he was so worn out that he almost ran off the road several times driving the 120 miles from Missoula to Butte and had to stop at a hotel along the way to sleep.

In Washington several months later, McCarthy encountered the recently sworn-in Senator Mansfield on the underground trolley between the Senate Office Building and the Capitol. "How are things in Montana, Mike?" asked the garrulous Wisconsin senator in an attempt to break the ice. Mansfield, who rarely spoke harshly to anyone, snapped back with feeling, "Much better since you left." McCarthy wanted to make up, he thought, but for himself "the hurt was too deep." A year after the election Matusow, who subsequently wrote a book admitting that he had been paid to lie about Mansfield and others, sought an appointment with the Montana senator to apologize, telling Jimmy Sullivan that "his conscience was bothering him." Mansfield refused to see him. "Some things you can't apologize for," he said.

Remarkably, however, when McCarthy died in 1957, Mansfield participated in the proceedings of his funeral held in the Senate chamber at the request of McCarthy's widow. Standing before the flag-draped coffin placed at the front of the chamber where McCarthy had been censured for his conduct in 1954 and where he had few remaining friends, Mansfield expressed sorrow for the late senator's family. "We know, of course, that in his way he did the best he possibly could to keep the affairs of this country on an even keel," Mansfield asserted. His generous remarks concluded, Mansfield did not follow McCarthy to his final resting place in Wisconsin. He had done enough for his former tormentor.

INTRODUCTION TO
INDOCHINA

7 *Within weeks after the inauguration of Dwight D. Eisenhower as U.S. president in 1953, Soviet dictator Joseph Stalin died, leading to a decision by his successors to terminate the stalemated war in Korea. Once those guns were stilled, the former general provided vigorous leadership of cold war alliances but avoided committing U.S. troops to hot war situations. In Asia, Eisenhower chose not to use U.S. forces to stave off the defeat of the French in Vietnam by Vietminh insurgents, but he provided U.S. economic support and military advice to Ngo Dinh Diem, the first president of postcolonial South Vietnam. Mansfield, having been elected to the Senate as Eisenhower won the presidency, grew rapidly in stature within legislative ranks and quickly became its leading expert on Asia. After visits to Vietnam, he worked intimately with the Republican administration to bolster Diem. Without his help, Diem might have been abandoned or overthrown in the mid-1950s, potentially averting the prolonged tragedy that was to come.*

On the afternoon of September 22, 1953, General Henri-Eugene Navarre, supreme commander of France's forces in its embattled colonial empire in Indochina, welcomed Senator Mike Mansfield to his headquarters in Saigon.

The general, immaculately attired in a white tropical uniform, briefed Mansfield on his ambitious plans to take the offensive against the elusive Communist-led Vietminh insurgents, baiting them into joining a conventional battle in the remote countryside, where French firepower would destroy them. Two months later, French forces parachuted into their chosen base for combat, a desolate mountain valley at Dienbienphu. Mansfield, on the first journey to a land that would consume many of America's hopes and fears for decades to come, was greatly impressed. Navarre was "really brilliant," he concluded, and his strategy so sound that, with continued U.S. support, it might bring the long, inconclusive war to a successful end "within two years."

Mansfield went from Navarre's briefing about his venturesome military strategy to a sumptuous four-course dinner, including the best French wine and champagne, worthy of a fine Parisian restaurant, at the residence of the French governor general. In "the Paris of the East," as Saigon was then known, security was very much as Fowler, the erudite character in Graham Greene's fictional classic *The Quiet American,* explained to Pyle, the idealistic American newcomer: "The French control the main roads until seven in the evening; they control the watch towers after that, and the cities, part of them. That doesn't mean you are safe, or there wouldn't be iron grilles in front of the restaurants." From the palatial Majestic Hotel, Mansfield could look out under slowly revolving ceiling fans to the crowded docks of the Saigon River and, on the other bank, a lush landscape of banana and coconut trees dominated by the Vietminh. These two sides of the river, as the French journalist Lucien Bodard wrote, were irreconcilable: "On the one hand there was the huge expanse of Saigon, flooded with light; and over against it a great area of shadows, without so much as a gleam. You saw the riding lights of the ships, and beyond them nothing—everything was night. That dark stretch of stagnant water and marsh vegetation with villages scattered about in it was the battlefield for the 'dirty war.'" As in the American era later, the war seemed far away, and yet at the same time so very close.

By the time Mansfield returned to Vietnam a year later, Navarre's troops had been surrounded, besieged, and defeated at Dienbienphu and were going home in ignominy. Having conceded the northern half of the country to the Vietminh regime at the 1954 Geneva Conference, France was leaving the rest to the squabbling southerners and the mercies of arriving Americans. The abject failure of the French military plans that sounded so good contributed to pervasive skepticism—in retrospect, realism—in Mansfield's views of military designs in Indochina from that time on.

Following the French defeat, Mansfield played his most effective role in dealing with Indochina in his two decades of involvement. In public and in private he so strongly backed the newly anointed indigenous leader of South Vietnam that he would be called, not without reason, the godfather of Ngo Dinh Diem. In a diplomatic dance that became known only with the declassification of government documents decades later, the Eisenhower administration repeatedly used Mansfield's support for Diem to thwart external threats to the new South Vietnamese leader in his early years in power. Remarkably, on several occasions this first-term senator was the sole member of Congress consulted and cited in the policymaking about Vietnam within the executive branch of the U.S. government and between the United States and other governments.

Without Mansfield's support for Diem, the United States might have terminated its efforts to sustain an anticommunist regime in Saigon in the mid-1950s rather than in 1975, either because a successor to Diem would have been an abject failure unable to compete with North Vietnam, as Mansfield believed, or because Washington might have decided to cut its losses and withdraw rather than continue to back Diem, as suggested by Eisenhower's envoy, the retired general J. Lawton Collins. In either case the course of history would have been changed dramatically. The irony is that Mansfield eventually became one of the most articulate and determined opponents of a U.S. military intervention that, but for his strong support for Diem, might never have taken place.

A FAST-RISING FRESHMAN

Owing to his interest, his background, and his energy, Mike Mansfield had been an influential foreign policy spokesman in the House. Coming to the Senate, which had more authority and prestige in foreign affairs, he was anxious to continue that role. Soon after the 1952 election, probably at the instigation of his friend and political mentor, Jim Rowe, Mansfield wired his support to Lyndon Johnson, who was breaking out of the pack to run for minority leader now that the previous leader, Ernest McFarland, had been defeated at the polls. Mansfield's support was remarkable because LBJ's potential competitor for the leadership was Mansfield's venerable senior colleague from Montana, James E. Murray. According to Rowe, Mansfield's public backing for Johnson had wrecked the incipient liberal rebellion against the Texan being organized around Murray's candidacy by Senators Paul Douglas and J. William Fulbright. In return, Rowe lobbied Johnson, his old friend, to obtain a place for Mansfield on the Foreign Relations Committee, then one of the Senate's most coveted assignments. It was rarely given to freshman senators and in this case had been requested by several Democrats with seniority, who, according to normal procedure, had an undeniable claim on any vacancy.

Beyond his gratitude to Mansfield and Rowe, Johnson was anxious to strengthen the Democratic side of the committee, especially since Robert Taft, the new majority leader and the leader of the conservative Republicans in and out of the Senate, had opted to leave his dominant role on the Labor Committee for what threatened to be a crucial partisan position on Foreign Relations. Through an early display of his political legerdemain, Johnson managed to persuade senior Democrats to take other assignments that he opened up for them or for other reasons to give up their claims to Foreign Relations. That done, he arranged for the freshman Mansfield, a foreign policy expert who, he said, could "out-think" Taft, and the loquacious Hubert Humphrey, in his third year in the Senate, who could "out-talk" Taft, to join the coveted committee. This prompted a thank-you note from Rowe to LBJ: "Dear Lyndon: I don't know *how* you did it, but I know *who* did it. . . . And so does Mike."

Election to the Senate opened new doors to Mansfield personally as well as politically. During his ten years in the House of Representatives, the Mansfields had rented a succession of apartments and houses, never convinced that they would be permanent residents of the capital. After his election to the Senate with its six-year term, they began to believe they were in Washington to stay, at least for a long time, and for $4,500 bought a house on Dexter Terrace in the pleasant Wesley Heights section of the District of Columbia. Except for official Senate-related functions, they were not active in the Washington social scene and did little entertaining. Anne, now a teenager, was a day student at Marymount, a Catholic high school, in nearby suburban Virginia.

The house, a three-bedroom red brick structure on a corner in a quiet suburb, contained a piano, which Maureen and Anne played, and a "high fidelity" record player, a typical musical furnishing of that day. Anne's tastes ran to symphonic music, but her father reveled in the honky-tonk, barroom-style piano sounds of Knuckles O'Toole and Joe Finger Carr. In pleasant weather, he found relaxation on the screened porch of the house, listening to the music, smoking his pipe filled with his favorite Prince Albert pipe tobacco, and reading a murder mystery, "the bloodier, the better."

The Mansfields were careful about money, which was never theirs in abundant supply, and especially about any expenditure of public funds. When he traveled abroad, Mike kept a meticulous record of his purchases, no matter how small, and of spending on meals and lodging. When they traveled together on such delegations, Maureen kept the books. In 1964 a former State Department official made confidential accusations against several members of Congress, including Mansfield, charging that they had used government-owned foreign currency, known as "counterpart funds," for personal expenditures while traveling abroad. The FBI was assigned to investigate the charge that the Mansfields—fifteen years earlier—had used such funds to purchase a small statue for their personal use in Vienna in 1949. Amazingly, within a day or two of being notified of the charge Mansfield was able to produce Maureen's small trip notebook listing each expenditure, including $110 for the statue, along with notations of the cashing of traveler's checks in close proximity to the purchase. The investigation was closed, but the small Meissen china statue of an angelic figure with a crown of flowers and two cherubs wound around her remained a valued possession that the Mansfields took with them to Tokyo in his ambassadorial days.

Mansfield's personal qualities as much as his expertise in foreign policy led to his growing prestige within the Senate. Jack Anderson, the leading investigative aide (and later the successor) to Washington columnist Drew Pearson, called Mansfield "a rock of integrity, conscientious about his duties, courageous in his convictions" in a remarkable personal memo to Pearson at the end of 1956. "Incorruptible, Mike is poor by Senate standards. Not until two years ago was he able to scrape up enough money for a down payment on his own home. His sense of values lies in principle, not pocketbook. This rugged integrity has made Mike a power in the Senate. He is a Senator's Senator, liked and respected by his colleagues. They know

his word is Bible. They trust his motives, listen to his advice," Anderson
reported to Pearson, the premier gossip columnist of his day.

ENTER THE COLD WARRIOR

Because of his background and interest in Asia as a Marine, a university professor, and a member of the House, Mansfield was described as early as 1954
in the *Washington Post* as "probably the Senate's leading authority on the complex situation in the Far East." There was little competition. In Washington
of the 1950s, few knew anything much, or anything at all, about faraway lands
with which the United States had no historical relationship. During World
War II Franklin Roosevelt had strongly opposed the postwar return of the colonial French to Indochina (see Chapter 5). Although Harry Truman reversed
that policy and supported the returning French with military aid, he did not
commit U.S. power or prestige in Indochina. Eisenhower, in collaboration
with senior members of Congress, including Lyndon Johnson but not including Mansfield, decided not to intervene militarily in the spring of 1954 to save
the French at Dienbienphu. Only a handful of other members of Congress
visited Indochina in the early 1950s and none repeatedly, as Mansfield did in
1953, 1954, and 1955. Mansfield issued a public report to the Foreign Relations
Committee each time, full of straightforward, quotable conclusions, and made
speeches in the Senate to supplement his views.

For those familiar with Mansfield's dogged opposition to the Vietnam
War in the 1960s and 1970s, his thoughts and actions in the mid-1950s are
surprising. Before and during his early visits, he saw Indochina in cold war
terms. On February 19, 1953, only seven weeks after being sworn in as a senator, while most U.S. attention was still focused on the windup of the three-
year war in Korea, he wrote a memo for his files, the gist of which he conveyed to the *New York Times:*

Indo-China is at this time the most important area on the Continent of Asia. Its
loss would start a chain-reaction extending to the Persian Gulf and would give
to the Soviets and the satellites the rubber, the tin and the oil which are in such
short supply within the Soviet Union and which mean so much in the conduct
of a war. Indo-China itself would furnish only a small amount of the rubber but
its loss would open the area in Southeastern Asia which contains the riches which

the Soviets so badly need. In addition the loss of Indo-China would entail grave political consequences in the countries to the East, Malaya, Thailand, Burma, India, Pakistan, Iran and perhaps, beyond.

Because of the importance of Indo-China in the common struggle against Soviet encroachments, I believe that military shipments should be stepped up considerably to that area.

Mansfield had much company. As the only freshman senator given a place on the Foreign Relations Committee, he heard Secretary of State John Foster Dulles and French Defense Minister Pleven explain in secret sessions in early 1953 that the "loss" of Indochina would bring about the nearly automatic toppling of other noncommunist governments in Asia—what became known as the "domino theory." In August 1953 President Eisenhower's National Security Council, concerned about the possibility that France would sue for peace, concluded that "under present conditions any negotiated settlement would mean the eventual loss to Communism not only of Indochina but of the whole of Southeast Asia. The loss of Indochina would be critical to the security of the U.S." A briefing paper handed to Mansfield at the U.S. Embassy in Saigon the following month declared that the war in Indochina "essentially is a struggle to halt the Soviet Communist bloc's drive for world hegemony as manifested in Southeast Asia."

With his proclivity for traveling abroad, Mansfield was determined to see for himself. In mid-1953, he asked Frank Valeo, who had assisted him with Asia research in the House, to accompany him on visits to all three Indochinese countries, Vietnam, Laos, and Cambodia, then still French colonies. At that point, Valeo had never been to Indochina and knew little about it, but on this trip he formed a relationship with Mansfield that shaped his life and deeply affected that of Mansfield. Valeo, like Mansfield, was born in New York of immigrant Roman Catholic parents, but in 1916, thirteen years later than Mansfield. Valeo had studied Asian affairs in the graduate school at New York University and, like Mansfield, first visited China while in military service, but as a U.S. Army sergeant in World War II rather than as a Marine in 1922. In the early 1950s Valeo was the sole Asia specialist of the Library of Congress's research arm, the Legislative Reference Service. During the rest of Mansfield's congressional service, he was Mansfield's overseas traveling companion and closest foreign policy aide, eventually joining

Mansfield's staff full-time and becoming secretary to the Democratic majority and finally secretary of the Senate under Mansfield's leadership. Over two decades of working together, they forged a close collaborative relationship, especially on drafting speeches and memoranda to be sent to presidents and others. Mansfield would initiate the process by deciding that something needed to be said, based on news accounts or other sources, and would outline his ideas. Valeo would then draft a paper and bring it back to Mansfield for revision or issuance. At times, however, Valeo was the idea person.

Mansfield obtained authorization for his 1953 trip from the Foreign Relations Committee and assistance from the State Department, which arranged an itinerary and cabled U.S. diplomatic posts of Mansfield's wish to obtain "first-hand knowledge of the political, economic, military and psychological climate." Mansfield asked that 60 percent of his time be free from formal briefings and inspections, that entertainment be kept "to an absolute minimum," and, emphasizing his seriousness of purpose, that there be "no publicity" in connection with his visit. Nonetheless, Mansfield's schedule suggests that his ability to go beyond official views on his initial trip was very limited. He spent most of his time with French military and civilian officials, U.S. diplomatic officials, and high-ranking French-appointed Vietnamese. The closest he came to contact with the reality of the war was a flight in a military plane over the Red River Delta from Hanoi to the Roman Catholic bishopric of Bui Chu, accompanied by a French general and other ranking officials. Like many from Washington who came after him, he never experienced or even examined the war on the ground.

Mansfield had great confidence in and rapport with journalists, whom he found usually more candid and often more informative than government officials. Before his early trips to Indochina, he compiled lists of leading U.S. correspondents in Paris and the Orient and made a point of contacting them, asking their views and advice, and keeping in touch after the trips were over. On this first trip to Vietnam, however, he met only a few journalists, including the veteran Australian reporter Denis Warner, who was pessimistic about the outcome. Warner recalled that when he expressed doubt about the French strategy, Mansfield, whom he called "an ardent interventionist," repeated, "I'm sure you can't be right, I'm sure you can't be right"

Nonetheless, it was in many respects a pioneering visit. The crew of the six-seat U.S. Navy Beechcraft that took him from Cambodia to Laos in 1953 was so unfamiliar with the territory that the plane flew back and forth at low altitude above the Mekong River searching for the Laotian capital of Vientiane, which was little more than a village with a few paved streets. When the plane finally put down on the grass landing strip on the outskirts of the town, no immigration officials were on hand. Had there been, they would have seen that Mansfield carried visa number one to the Kingdom of Laos, the first such document ever issued in the United States by the Laotian legation, which was in the process of receiving symbolic authority from the French. The U.S. diplomatic establishment in Laos consisted of two diplomats living in a rented house; Mansfield later remarked that he and Valeo had temporarily doubled the American presence.

In Laos he met for the first time Prince Souvanna Phouma, then prime minister, the greatest modern leader and statesman of that thinly populated, mostly primitive country. A shrewd and ambitious aristocrat who was in and out of power for decades, Souvanna wore a white linen suit, the essential diplomatic costume of 1950s Indochina. He was attempting to maintain domestic peace by balancing the various Lao factions, not least the Communist-backed Pathet Lao, headed by his own half-brother, Prince Souphannouvong. Like Mansfield, the prime minister was a man of reticence. The two sat together, smoking their pipes. "One would make a remark, and then the other would make a remark, and gradually there emerged some kind of meeting of the minds between them," according to Valeo, who acted as interpreter between Souvanna's French and Mansfield's English.

The French, who were very much in charge, treated the Lao as little more than children. A French military commander told Mansfield and Valeo, in a lament that would be echoed by American advisers later, that "we have two battalions that we are training and we tell them that they must stay in camp, but on the weekends they want to go home and they go. . . . We will never make soldiers here."

In Cambodia, a country whose ultimately tragic fate would engage Mansfield for many years, the shrewd and energetic head of state, Prince Norodom Sihanouk, had gone into seclusion to protest France's reluctance to provide the promised full independence. In the presence of the U.S. ambassador to Indochina, Donald Heath, Mansfield delivered a stern lecture to Prime Minister Penn Nouth about the dangers of neutrality in the war against the Vietminh, declaring that independence from France would be "meaningless if it was won only to be lost to Communist attack." According to a report of the conversation by Heath, Mansfield left no doubt that he believed "Cambodia should join cause with all free nations in common struggle against international communism." Even more surprising in view of his later stance, Mansfield told French officials in Paris during a stopover on his way home that French forces in Vietnam would be justified in taking "whatever military steps" were necessary to protect their operations in Cambodia and remarked to an American official that a "get tough" policy would be justified.

But it was Vietnam, the most populous and most important country of the three Indochinese states, that most seized Mansfield's attention. He returned home with optimism bordering on enthusiasm for what he heard from General Navarre and others of the French-led struggle. With additional U.S. aid, planned increases in military manpower, including conscription of more Vietnamese anticommunist fighters, and French devolution of full sovereignty to the noncommunist governments, he wrote in his formal report in October 1953, "only an outright invasion by the Chinese Communists would be likely to rescue the Vietminh from defeat." He told the Senate on February 8, 1954, that "in my opinion, the French will not lose the war in Indochina." Mansfield endorsed Eisenhower's decision to send U.S. Air Force technicians to Indochina, calling it "a logical extension of a practice already underway," despite the objections of a respected colleague, Senator John Stennis of Mississippi, that the action could place the United States on "a road to direct intervention with armed manpower in the Indochinese war."

Mansfield received a trickle of critical mail about his position, including a handwritten letter from a political supporter, William B. Ellis, a cattle rancher in Cascade, Montana, who protested that "this is the beginning of another war and with your consent," and asked that Mansfield, as "a powerful man in Washington" use his talents more constructively. Mansfield responded that he had really not become so powerful, and then added, "When I taught at the University of Montana, I could find answers to any question easily—from the book. Since I have been back here I have had to face up to many problems and I must admit in all candor that the ready answers have been few and on most occasions, the answers have been hard to find."

Nonetheless, he continued his support of Eisenhower administration policy. When Undersecretary of State Walter Bedell Smith and Admiral Arthur

W. Radford, chairman of the Joint Chiefs of Staff, appeared in closed session before the Foreign Relations Committee, Mansfield expressed "every confidence" in Navarre and his aides. As to the U.S. policy of aiding the French, he said, "I am very glad that this government is spending $1,200 million this year in Indochina, and as far as I am concerned, I will vote for another billion or so next year." Shortly thereafter, when Secretary of State Dulles was under fire from Senator Hubert Humphrey and others in a closed Foreign Relations Committee hearing for inconsistent testimony and lack of a coherent plan regarding Indochina, Mansfield came to Dulles's defense. "I think our policy has been sound to date, and that the reason we do not know what to do in the future is that no one can find that answer at the present time," he told the Secretary.

His confidence was short-lived. On March 13, the Vietminh began their two-month siege of the exposed French position at Dienbienphu. About the same time, Mansfield learned more about the precarious political situation in France. On March 18 he wrote in a memo for his files, "The war in Indo-China cannot be continued indefinitely and at the present time, no armed victory is in sight for either side. As a result the war-weary French are ready to settle with the Communist Viet Minh on almost any terms." The only way he could see to stave off a communist victory was "the creation of a truly independent Vietnamese Government based on a much broader foundation than the present regime," one that could compete seriously with Ho Chi Minh. Such a truly independent regime could provide an alternative for Vietnamese nationalists "who are at the present time on the side of Ho Chi Minh and who are with him because they look at him not as the communist he is, but as the leader of the anti-colonial–anti-French forces," he wrote.

It was clear from the memo that he had begun to see the situation in Vietnam as fundamentally an internal problem with political roots that could not be solved by military means alone. This important perception was at the heart of his support for Ngo Dinh Diem as long as he felt that Diem had a strong political base, and it was at the heart of his subsequent opposition to massive U.S. military intervention. On the CBS program *Man of the Week* on April 25, 1954, he declared that if the war in Vietnam is to be won, "it is not going to be won by French troops and American aid, or American troops. It is going to be won or lost by the Viet Namese people themselves. They are the ones who have to get in and show the determination and fight for their own independence and their own liberty." Sooner or later, many others would make similar statements. Mansfield was among the first to grasp the basic problem of the Vietnam War and, unlike others, he consistently advanced it.

FINDING NGO DINH DIEM

In the 1950s, liberal Democrats, most of whom were genuinely anticommunist, were doggedly seeking a "third force," an alternative to both colonialism and communism in the developing world. Backing such groups and leaders seemed the way to compete with communism and also to provide political cover from the smear tactics pioneered by Senator Joseph McCarthy that "pro-communist" Democrats had brought about the "loss" of China. In the case of Vietnam, Mansfield quickly found a third-force leader on whom he was able to pin his hopes; surprisingly, it was a person he had met in Washington the year before. For most of the next decade, his views of Vietnam and his hopes for its future revolved around Ngo Dinh Diem, who remains one of the most controversial figures in contemporary Vietnamese history.

Ngo Dinh Diem was born in 1901 in Hue, the imperial capital in central Vietnam, the son of Ngo Dinh Kha, a respected mandarin who had been minister of rites and grand chamberlain to Emperor Thanh-Thai. When the emperor was deposed by the French in 1907 in favor of his ten-year-old son, the family became stridently nationalistic and anti-French, views that Diem embraced throughout his adult life. He also inherited an unusual combination of Confucianism from the Ngo Dinh family traditions and Catholicism from the family's conversion to Catholicism in the seventeenth century. Diem was deeply religious and took a vow of chastity while young. He never married, was uncomfortable in the presence of most women, and is believed never to have engaged in sexual relations. Despite the hedonism of upper-class Vietnam, he poured all his energies into work and study, much of it solitary, for which he became widely known. He rose rapidly in public service and served as minister of interior under the newly anointed emperor Bao Dai in 1933; he resigned when it became clear the French would not cede real powers to the imperial administration.

Well known within the country for his uncompromising nationalistic stands, he declined an offer from the occupying Japanese to become prime minister in 1945. When Vietnam was briefly governed by the Vietminh after the outbreak of the full-scale war against the returning French later that year, he refused an offer from Ho Chi Minh to become his minister of interior, and in 1949 he rejected an effort from Emperor Bao Dai to enlist him as prime minister of his postwar government. After learning that he had been sentenced to death by the Vietminh, and after the French refused to provide him protection, Diem went into self-imposed exile abroad in 1950, relying on his Roman Catholic connections to assist him.

Mansfield first heard of Diem in July 1951 from Representative Edna F. Kelly, a Democratic congresswoman from Brooklyn and a colleague on the House Foreign Affairs Committee. She passed along an appeal from Diem for U.S. aid to a third force in Vietnam, opposed to both communism and colonialism, centered in the Roman Catholic enclaves of Phat-Diem and Bui-Chu. Diem was living at the time at the Maryknoll Seminary in Lakewood, New Jersey, meditating and seeking to drum up U.S. support for his cause. On May 7, 1953, he was guest of honor at a luncheon for nine people given in his chambers by U.S. Supreme Court Justice William O. Douglas, who had traveled extensively in Southeast Asia and who had heard of Diem in Vietnam. Among the guests were two freshman senators, Mansfield and John F. Kennedy, both of whom would later loom large in Diem's future, one who defended and protected him ardently, and the other who eventually signed his death warrant by approving the military coup that brought about his overthrow and assassination.

Diem declared at the luncheon that "nothing less than an immediate promise of Dominion status [similar to Canada or Australia] will satisfy the Vietnamese population that they have something to fight for in Indochina." The trouble in Vietnam, he said, was that there was "no rallying point between the Communists and the French." Creating such a third way was his mission. Mansfield, impressed with Diem's sincerity and his anti-French convictions, was "left with the feeling that if anyone could hold South Vietnam, it was somebody like Ngo Dinh Diem."

A State Department memorandum on the luncheon conversation, written by Edmund Gullion, then a member of the Policy Planning Staff, referred to Diem as "Catholic Vietnamese Nationalist leader," and there is no doubt that his Roman Catholic connections were central to his support in the United States. Francis Cardinal Spellman, the most powerful American Catholic leader of his time, and Joseph P. Kennedy, a powerful Catholic lay leader and father of the future president, played important roles in organizing support for Diem. Mansfield was an observant but not notably devout Roman Catholic; he never traded on his religion in politics. When I asked him to what extent Diem's Catholicism affected his estimate of Diem's ability, Mansfield responded, "Not at all. . . . If he had a friendship with Cardinal Spellman, and he might have, it would have made no difference to me. His religion meant nothing. It was the man who impressed me."

On May 7, 1954, one year to the day after the Supreme Court luncheon, the French garrison at Dienbienphu surrendered, and the Indochina situation changed dramatically. The following day, the Indochina phase of the international peace conference of major powers convened at Geneva. The principal results were a cease-fire throughout Indochina and the "temporary" division of Vietnam at the seventeenth parallel, halfway up the peninsula, with internationally supervised elections to unify the communist North and the anticommunist South scheduled to be held within two years, by July 1956. While the Geneva conference was under way, Bao Dai appointed Ngo Dinh Diem prime minister of South Vietnam with extensive theoretical powers over what remained of his empire—which in reality extended only to parts of Saigon and a few other cities. The rest was effectively controlled by the Binh Xuyen, a well-organized criminal syndicate based in Saigon; the Hoa Hao and Cao Dai, two sects with private armies and their own base areas; or in much of the countryside, southern elements of the Vietminh.

RETURN TO VIETNAM 1954

Mansfield's return to Indochina came at a moment of transition in the divided country. He and Valeo arrived in Hanoi, the principal city in northern Vietnam, in September 1954, a month before the French evacuated it under the Geneva agreement. Vietminh troops had already encircled the city in preparation for the transfer; and only skeleton French forces remained to stand guard and operate sparsely manned government offices. The city "had already taken on the aspects of a ghost town," he reported later.

The French-appointed Vietnamese governor in Hanoi gave a dinner for the visiting U.S. senator in the French style, with the hosts wearing white suits and providing sophisticated cuisine of a high French standard. "We might as well at least have a good dinner, since we have to leave now," a rueful dinner guest told Valeo as they dined. Outside, the streets were eerily quiet at night but in daylight full of frantic Vietnamese selling their possessions at bargain prices before fleeing. Some who planned to stay were producing paper copies of Picasso's dove of peace to be displayed in welcome to Ho Chi Minh. Some of the panic was induced by a U.S. covert operations team, under counterinsurgency expert Colonel Edward G. Lansdale, which launched false rumors and produced fake Vietminh leaflets to alarm the population. Mansfield said that he knew nothing of this at the time.

At the time of Mansfield's visit 250,000 Vietnamese had been evacuated from the North. U.S. Navy ships operating from Haiphong to Saigon, along with French vessels and aircraft, ferried the refugees, whose number eventually reached 860,000 over the ten months when such emigration was permitted. In Saigon harbor Mansfield went aboard the USS *Montrail*, which was carrying several thousand refugees, mostly Catholics who were led by their parish priests. Mansfield was impressed that "they had chosen to come to the south with nothing but the rags on their backs rather than to live under the Communists." The influx of Catholics furnished Diem with a relatively small but intensely loyal Catholic and anticommunist constituency in the South.

In Saigon, Diem needed all the help he could get in the face of pervasive pessimism. The French, who barely tolerated the new and nationalistic prime minister, freely discussed his weaknesses and predicted he would quickly fail. En route to Indochina, Mansfield had been told by the U.S. ambassador to France, Douglas Dillon, of the widely held view in Paris that Diem "lacks what it takes and may soon be confronted with a coup d'etat." The French consensus, Dillon said, was that "some coalition of religious sects, underworld leaders and assorted military figures offers the only hope of holding the area." On the airliner from Europe to Asia, Scripps-Howard correspondent Jim Lucas, who had arrived in Vietnam in January, told Mansfield that Diem had neither "the drive or capacity" to rally the nationalists and predicted he could be ousted by a coup "at any time." J. Graham Parsons, chargé d'affaires of the U.S. Embassy in Bangkok and the first diplomat Mansfield saw in Asia, reported that the Thais "have written off Viet Nam entirely to the Communists. . . ." Sifting such portents, a CIA National Intelligence Estimate earlier in August concluded that "the chances are poor" for the French and Vietnamese to establish a strong regime in South Vietnam, even with firm U.S. support. "The situation is more likely to continue to deteriorate progressively over the next year," the intelligence estimate said. A CIA report from Saigon on the eve of Mansfield's arrival said, "Diem does not have control over finances, the military, customs, immigration, diplomatic representation, the judiciary and police matters or the security forces."

Mansfield called on the new prime minister at his private lodgings on September 2 and found him "a virtual prisoner in his residence," where he lived and worked because the official Norodom Palace was still occupied by the French. Although Diem spoke of problems with the Vietminh and French commercial interests, he emphasized that his greatest hazards were domestic—the national army, whose French-inclined chief of staff, Nguyen Van Hinh, was politically ambitious and a recognized threat to Diem, and the sects with their separate armies. Nevertheless, Diem told Mansfield that the Army chief appeared to be "coming around" and if so, he and the Army together could deal with the sects. Ambassador Heath was perplexed by Diem's optimism—he had found it necessary to warn Hinh personally twice in the previous four days against mounting a coup—but guessed that Diem played down the dangers "in order that the Senator should not have too dark a picture of situation here."

Mansfield found Saigon to be a city seething with intrigues and rumors. He reported to the Senate that "the political plotting goes on in army circles, government circles, foreign circles, in party headquarters, in police headquarters, and even in the demimonde of ill-disguised gangsters, pirates and extortionists." In this situation, Diem's program of attacking corruption and social inequity existed only on paper because of "a kind of conspiracy of non-cooperation and sabotage by those who oppose him." Diem's obvious faults, which Mansfield heard from nearly every side, included the fact that he was a native of Central Vietnam rather than the South, and his "political rigidity which makes it difficult for him to compromise." He made no mention of the fact, which became so prominent later, that Diem was a Roman Catholic in a largely Buddhist country. In the mid-1950s Diem's religion appeared to be an advantage due to his strong backing from the refugee population and the absence of conflict at that time with Vietnam's Buddhists.

Just about the only person Mansfield met who was sanguine about Diem's future was Diem himself. Self-centered, uncompromising, and determined to follow his own star, he infuriated the French and, increasingly, exasperated senior Americans who dealt with him. Heath told Mansfield that Diem was "utterly honest but tended to operate in a cloister." Wesley Fishel, the Michigan State University professor who had befriended Diem in the early 1950s and was his most intimate foreign adviser and promoter in 1954, told Valeo during Mansfield's visit that Diem accepted the premiership "with his eyes opened and closed at the same time," explaining that "Diem knew the difficult situation confronting him but somehow believed his own unimpeachable honesty and integrity, his moral rectitude would triumph." In this he was mistaken, Fishel said. However, "there are some dramatic things which Diem could do immediately if he wanted to unbend a bit." Unaccountably, he was refusing to do so.

Mansfield concluded from his 1954 Saigon experience that although Diem had serious defects, as with Chiang Kai-shek a decade earlier he could see no viable alternative. Impressed with Diem's determination and yearning to support a third force between communism and colonialism, Mansfield saw Diem as the only hope, as some Americans in Saigon suggested. "If Diem goes, there is not a replacement for him in sight," he was told by Ambassador Heath. Paul E. Everett, head of the U.S. aid mission, said, "Our only chance is with the present government. There is no one else available with national stature. . . . If he fails, only the old discredited hacks are available, and we should begin figuring our losses in preparation for getting out." Even Diem's friend Fishel said, "We do not have a good chance here, we have a chance." He added, in what became a key element in Mansfield's thinking, that "if the present government goes, then we can look forward to a succession of temporary governments which will be rehashes of past governments, ending finally in Vietminh control of the entire country."

THE SEATO TREATY AND
A THREAT TO BOMB CHINA

Midway through his second visit to Indochina in September 1954, Mansfield flew to Manila to meet Secretary of State John Foster Dulles, who had invited him to be one of two congressional participants in the international conference establishing the Southeast Asia Collective Defense Treaty and its treaty organization known as SEATO. This was the beginning of a close and most unusual working relationship between the Republican Secretary of State and the Democratic senator most keenly interested in Asian affairs.

Mansfield had first met Dulles during the Truman administration, when Dulles was negotiating the U.S. peace treaty with Japan as ambassador-at-large and Mansfield was chairman of the Subcommittee on the Far East of the House Foreign Affairs Committee. When Dulles resigned in 1952 to become an adviser to the Republican campaign for president, Mansfield wrote a personal "Dear Foster" letter of praise for his "ability, energy and knowledge" in performance of a "difficult task in the spirit of the highest American traditions." Dulles responded with a "Dear Mike" letter: "I always had the feeling that we worked together in a spirit of cordial cooperation" which "influenced in important ways" U.S. policies in Asia. When Dulles became secretary of state and Mansfield a member of the Senate Foreign Relations Committee in 1953, the senator, as noted earlier, came to the Secretary's defense when he was under fire on Indochina policy from Humphrey and others.

The two remained on cordial terms throughout Dulles's term of office. Mansfield, true to his nature, usually spoke warmly of Dulles personally even when he disagreed with his policies, and he deferred in the end to the primacy of the President and Secretary of State in foreign policy. When, however, right-wing Republicans at the end of the Geneva Conference in July 1954 sought to blame the failure of Indochina policy on the Democrats, Mansfield led a heated Senate Democratic counterattack on an administration policy of "bluster and retreat . . . under the guidance of bluffers, blusterers and buffoons." He was harsh and at times sarcastic in his criticism of Dulles for agreeing to participate in the conference that divided Vietnam. "Geneva was a mistake; and the result was a failure of American policy. It is a profoundly humiliating result," Mansfield declared. Dulles took Mansfield's remarks seriously enough to have an answer prepared by aides, responding that "Geneva may have been a mistake but if so it was not a United States mistake. The United States has not the power and if it had could not wisely exercise the power to force France to go on fighting after its will and power to fight had gone. We might ourselves have stepped in and taken over the fighting but that apparently is not what Senator Mansfield wanted us to do." Perhaps because he had other things in mind for Mansfield, Dulles never issued the answer his aides had prepared.

Shortly thereafter, Dulles began preparing for the launching of the Southeast Asia regional alliance, which had originated in his unsuccessful call for "united action" by the "free community" against the Vietminh during the siege of Dienbienphu in April. Faced with Eisenhower's caution and congressional opposition, the administration had declined to intervene with U.S. military forces to rescue the French, but the idea of a collective security arrangement for Southeast Asia lived on in State Department consultations with the British, French, and a few other allies. By mid-summer the initiative had been watered down to a relatively toothless accord with more of a political than military meaning. It was accepted by eight nations, including only Thailand and the Philippines from Southeast Asia, although a protocol to the treaty stipulated that South Vietnam, Laos, and Cambodia would be covered even though they were not signatories. Dulles and others hailed it as a potential bulwark against the spread of communism.*

Realizing that the treaty might be controversial in the Senate, Dulles decided on a most unusual means of improving its chances to obtain the constitutionally required two-thirds vote for ratification. He decided to invite a Democratic and a Republican senator to participate along with himself as signers of the document—the only time that members of Congress were signators to a U.S. treaty except for the San Francisco treaty of 1945 establishing the United Nations. On August 13 Dulles telephoned Republican senator Alexander Wiley, chairman of the Foreign Relations Committee, who recommended Mansfield as the Democratic participant. Dulles immediately telephoned the ranking Democrat on the Foreign Relations Committee, the prestigious Walter George, who told him that Mansfield "would be good, he is developing and will be a great fellow in the Senate." With the endorsement of the two senior senators, both of whom had been impressed by Mansfield's knowledge, industriousness, and unassuming nature, Dulles was comfortable with this choice. The following day, without mentioning the SEATO delegation, Mansfield departed from a speech on an unrelated subject to clear the air with Dulles, publicly apologizing as a "matter of conscience" for having

---

*Ironically, the only time the SEATO treaty gained any importance was when the Johnson administration two decades later proclaimed it to be a justification for U.S. intervention in Vietnam. Faced with Mansfield's dissent from his war policies, Johnson rarely failed to point out that among his justifications was "the SEATO Treaty signed by Senator Mansfield." Mansfield insisted that the treaty furnished "no justification whatever" for U.S. military involvement. During the Nixon administration, he went even further, declaring the treaty to be "not merely an inconsequential relic of the past, but a devastatingly costly enterprise and a positive hazard to the interests of this nation."

"slipped momentarily into partisanship" in his recent speech chastising the Secretary of State. Mansfield told the Senate, "It is time to stop making a whipping boy out of the incumbent of that office, whoever he may be and to recognize that his job is and will always be difficult at best."

The assignment to accompany Eisenhower's Secretary of State to an international conference added to Mansfield's prestige in narrowly divided Montana, much to the dismay of the state's Republican leadership, which feared that Mansfield's enhanced stature would be put to use behind Democratic candidates on the ballot in November. "Why did the Administration have to pick on us?" a Montana Republican asked a visiting *Washington Post* reporter. "If they had to send a Democrat to Manila, why didn't they send a Democrat from the South, where it wouldn't have made any difference—somebody like [J. William] Fulbright of Arkansas?"

Mansfield flew to Manila from Saigon on September 4 and went immediately to a reception at the residence of the American ambassador, retired admiral Raymond A. Spruance, who had been an illustrious World War II fleet commander in the Pacific. He had time only to greet Maureen, who had traveled from Washington with the official party, when he was told that Dulles wished to see him. The two men went off to a quiet corner of the room. Mansfield recalled the incident so vividly that when describing it to me nearly a half century later, he remembered not only the substance of the conversation but even the fact that Dulles had a glass of rye whiskey, his favorite, in his hand as they spoke.

The subject at hand was the first post–Korean War crisis with China. The previous day mainland Chinese artillery had commenced heavy shelling of two small islands, including the island of Quemoy, which were held and heavily manned by Chiang Kai-shek's Nationalists even though they hugged the Chinese coast as close as two miles away. President Truman at the outset of the Korean War had interposed the U.S. fleet between the Communist mainland and the island of Formosa (Taiwan) 100 miles off the coast, where Chiang and his forces had retreated in 1949 after being defeated in the Chinese civil war, but the status of the offshore islands was ambiguous. In its first weeks in office the Eisenhower administration provocatively announced it would "unleash Chiang" by permitting Nationalist attacks on the Chinese mainland while the U.S. fleet still guarded against Communist Chinese raids in the other direction. In November 1953 Eisenhower's

National Security Council secretly agreed to encourage and assist the Nationalists to launch raids from the offshore islands against mainland Chinese commerce and territory. The following month Chinese leader Mao Tse-tung, finally freed from military exertions in Korea, decided to increase the pressure against Nationalist-held coastal islands as part of a campaign to eventually liberate Taiwan. As Dulles was en route to Manila on September 3, 1954, Chinese artillery opened up on the islands with an unprecedentedly heavy barrage, killing two U.S. military advisers stationed there and touching off a high-level debate in Washington about what to do.

The Joint Chiefs of Staff, meeting at the Pentagon, agreed to authorize Chiang's air force to attack Chinese military targets from which the shelling originated, a recommendation that was approved by Eisenhower, who was at the time on vacation in Denver. This was followed by a second recommendation, supported by Admiral Arthur Radford, chairman of the Joint Chiefs, and backed by the Air Force and Navy chiefs, that Chiang be permitted to bomb mainland Chinese targets farther from the coast as he had requested and that, if China then retaliated against the offshore islands or Formosa itself, U.S. planes should attack China. The Army chief of staff, General Matthew Ridgway, however, dissented, believing the exchanges would lead to all-out war with China. Undersecretary of state W. Bedell Smith, a former Army general who had been left in charge at the State Department in Dulles's absence, also opposed the Joint Chiefs' plan.

All this Dulles briefly conveyed to Mansfield in the impromptu conversation. The Secretary of State supported the Joint Chiefs' plan, reporting to Washington his belief that the loss of Quemoy "would have grave psychological repercussions" that could "gravely jeopardize [the] entire off-shore position." He favored U.S. military action even if, as he suspected, it might lead to "constantly expanding US operations against [the] mainland." His one doubt was whether, even with U.S. aid, Quemoy was defensible, a military judgment he could not make from Manila. Dulles, like Eisenhower, was very conscious of the need to obtain support in Congress for military actions, recalling the bitter partisan disputes about the Korean War and other military issues that had bedeviled the Truman administration. Thus, even before Mansfield's arrival in Manila, Dulles recommended that congressional leaders be consulted on the issue as a matter of urgency. As a first step, he had already explained the situation to Senator H. Alexander Smith, the Republican representative at the launching of the Southeast Asian treaty and a senior congressional figure. Smith approved the plan to authorize a U.S. attack on the Chinese mainland, as Dulles promptly reported to Washington.

Mansfield, always sensitive to conflicts with China because of his experiences as a Marine and as FDR's emissary, reacted vigorously against the military plans. Without hesitation, he told Dulles he agreed with Ridgway and Smith rather than the Joint Chiefs of Staff majority and that in his opinion U.S. attacks on the Chinese mainland would be "madness." Before the administration took such a momentous action, Congress should be called back into session or, at the very least, Eisenhower should summon the Democratic and Republican leaders of the House and Senate to Denver for consultations. Mansfield asked that Dulles transmit his views to Eisenhower. The Secretary promptly reported his views, without the "madness" comment, to his deputy, W. Bedell Smith, who passed them on to Eisenhower.

On September 8 Dulles, Smith, and Mansfield joined the representatives of seven other nations in signing the Southeast Asia treaty. Mansfield, looking surprisingly casual with two locks of hair flopping down from his forehead, affixed his signature to the treaty. Using a special Sheaffer fountain pen supplied for the occasion, its gold-plated top suitably inscribed, he wrote his name in bold script. Dulles and Smith hovered over him as he did so.

The following day the Secretary and his party (without Mansfield, who returned to Saigon) left for home with a brief stopover in Taipei. In the meantime, Eisenhower had called a meeting of the National Security Council at the Officers Club at an Air Force base in Denver for September 12, when the Dulles party would reach the Colorado city.

Dulles came to the meeting with a memorandum of talking points he had drawn up en route, expressing much greater caution than he had displayed to Mansfield. "It is doubtful that the issue [of defending the offshore islands] can be exploited without Congressional approval," Dulles's memo said; even to present such an issue would result in "a sharply divided Congress and nation" in the current congressional election period. In the meeting Dulles went even further, telling Eisenhower that "If we act without Congress now we will not have anyone in the United States with us." In answer to a strong appeal for military action by Admiral Radford, Eisenhower said he was certain that this would precipitate a war with China. In a decisive comment he went on to say that this, in the absence of congressional authorization, "would be logical grounds for impeachment." The notes of the meeting do not mention Mansfield by name, but it is likely that his objections had made an impact.

As in the case of the proposal to intervene militarily at Dienbienphu earlier in the year, congressional considerations played a role in Eisenhower's decision to reject the Joint Chiefs of Staff majority advice, this time without a meeting with the Senate and House leadership. Mansfield had not been among the members of Congress consulted in the Dienbienphu crisis, probably because he was not a ranking member of the leadership or of any relevant committee, but his counsel was notably important in the first stages of the offshore islands crisis with China in September 1954. Eisenhower's decision not to authorize the bombing of China, together with a decision to take the matter to the UN Security Council and the easing of Chinese shelling ended the immediate crisis. However, the confrontation over the offshore islands continued into 1955, flared up again in 1958, and became an item of U.S. political contention in the presidential race between Kennedy and Richard Nixon in 1960.

Although he might not have initially welcomed Mansfield's views on the conflict with China, Dulles continued to place high value on their relationship. While en route home, he sent a cable to the vacation White House recommending that Eisenhower make a special gesture of greeting Maureen when the traveling party arrived in Denver to express thanks for her husband's "effective service" as a delegate to the Manila Conference and to emphasize the bipartisan character of the delegation. The President did so, to her surprise and delight. Two months later, after the congressional elections that were a triumph for the Democrats, Maureen sent a wooden tray with a carving of an elephant, the Republican Party symbol, to Dulles's wife, Janet Dulles, as a thank-you for her thoughtfulness and that of her husband during the Manila trip. Maureen had acquired the tray four years earlier and decided to save it for "her favorite Republican." Now "I've found you and Foster," she wrote, hoping the tray could find a place in the Secretary of State's office. John Foster Dulles responded warmly that "I am proud to be the Republican whom you honor by making me the recipient" of the elephant tray.

CONTENDING WITH THE FRENCH

The conversation between Dulles and Mansfield in the corner of the ambassador's residence in Manila on September 4 also dealt with Vietnam in a way that would have accelerating consequences for relations between Washington and Saigon and would begin to carve out an extraordinary role for Mansfield. As Dulles sipped his rye whiskey, Mansfield offered an assessment of the situation he had just left behind. Despite all his shortcomings and difficulties, he said, Diem might be "the last chance" for a prime minister who could be effective. When, two days later, Dulles heard the view of the French minister of state for Indochina, Guy La Chambre, that Diem was "totally ineffective" in building a broad base of support and should be replaced, the Secretary responded that he "did not believe any useful purpose would be served in getting rid of Diem since no better substitute had been advanced." He capped his argument by stating that "Senator Mansfield had recently been in Indochina" and quoting Mansfield's view that Diem was the "last chance."

This was the first of many occasions when Dulles and his subordinates in the State Department cited Mansfield's views on Diem to back up their own. From that day on, the Montana senator was the State Department's principal interlocutor on support for Diem in the mid-1950s, and the most important backer in Congress of the Saigon leader.

La Chambre was not persuaded by Dulles's remarks. Making it his business to see Mansfield while they both were in Manila, he quoted Jean Daridan, the French deputy commissioner general in Saigon as saying that Diem was "totally ineffectual" and "although a man of goodwill, he is not a man of will." Mansfield stood his ground, responding that "change in government every few weeks in Vietnam [would be] extremely unhealthy" and that in the absence of a good alternative, Diem should be supported and encouraged to broaden the basis of his government.

The French, who were antagonized by Diem's independent words and deeds and who were acutely aware of Diem's weaknesses, prepared to send diplomats to Washington to persuade the American administration to dump Diem. Knowing what was afoot, the State Department reached out to Mansfield to protect its position. "We realized we had to proceed carefully with the French," according to Kenneth Young, chief of the State Department's Southeast Asia office, so "we sent a cable to Senator Mansfield, who was abroad, asking him what he thought of Diem as premier. . . . We knew what the answer would be in advance, of course." Dulles's personal message urgently requesting Mansfield's judgment of Diem's ability reached the senator in Berlin after he had departed from Southeast Asia. Mansfield,

who probably guessed what was afoot, responded by giving Diem the benefit of all doubts and placing the onus on the French:

> The political crisis in south Vietnam arises from the insistence of Diem on form-
> ing a government that is free of corruption and dedicated to achieving a genuine
> national independence and internal amelioration. . . . [O]nly a govt of the kind
> Diem envisions—and it would be a govt worthy of our support—has much
> chance of survival, eventually free of outside support because only such a govt can
> hope to achieve a degree of popular support as against the Viet Minh. If Diem
> fails, the alternative is a govt composed of his present opponents, no combination
> of which is likely to base itself strongly in the populace. Such a govt would be
> infinitely dependent on support of the French and could survive only so long as
> the latter are able to obtain Viet Minh acquiescence in its survival.
>
> Most of those who oppose Diem have a long history of intimate working
> relations with the French in Indochina and have been amenable to the latter's
> guidance in the past. The fundamental question, therefore, may well be not
> can Diem form a worthy govt but do the French really want Diem and what
> he stands for to succeed? Even if Paris were so inclined, the French Govt
> would have to be willing to deal firmly with its large political and military
> bureaucracy in Indochina. Otherwise, Diem's prospects of achieving success
> could be constantly undercut by their activities and machinations in Saigon,
> regardless of official French policy.

The morning after Mansfield's cable arrived, Dulles cited it at a top-level
meeting of State Department, Defense Department, and foreign aid officials
to plan the talks with the French. Mansfield's appraisal "is in support of our
analysis," the Secretary of State said, adding that "the senator's views would
carry a lot of weight in the Foreign Relations Committee, especially with the
Democrats." Later that day, in a small private and preliminary meeting with
La Chambre, who headed the visiting French delegation, Undersecretary
of State Smith began his discussion of Diem by reading Mansfield's cable
aloud. Smith emphasized, as Dulles had, that Mansfield's views "would have
great influence in Congress, particularly with Democrats." Mansfield's cable,
according to Kenneth Young, "stunned the French."

In the meetings that followed, the French, in a difficult position due to
their need for U.S. financial aid to maintain their dwindling troop presence

in Indochina, reluctantly agreed to a secret commitment to support Diem and to urge all anticommunist elements in Vietnam to do the same. Declassified U.S. documents detailing the talks make no mention of any member of Congress other than Mansfield or indeed any other source of public or political opinion in the United States. State Department officials were using Mansfield's views, most of which they shared, as surrogate for all U.S. viewpoints outside the executive branch.

Two weeks after the conclusion of the U.S.-French conference, Mansfield published his 1954 report to the Foreign Relations Committee, with a final conclusion that drew much press attention and also became a central reference point for Dulles and the State Department. After asserting that the situation in Vietnam had reached the stage of "acute crisis," Mansfield forecast that if Diem were forced out of office, the replacement for his regime would probably be "a military dictatorship" unacceptable to the Vietnamese people and incapable of standing up to the Communists. Then came the jarring conclusion:

> In the event that the Diem government falls, therefore, I believe that the
> United States should consider an immediate suspension of all aid to Vietnam
> and the French Union forces there, except that of a humanitarian nature, pre-
> liminary to a complete reappraisal of our present policies in Free Vietnam.
> Unless there is a reasonable expectation of fulfilling our objectives the contin-
> ued expenditure of the resources of the citizens of the United States is unwar-
> ranted and inexcusable.

The U.S. Embassy in Saigon reported that "Diem and his supporters are jubilant. Anti-Diem groups are angry." So delighted was Diem that he printed and distributed 100,000 copies of Mansfield's report. Inside the U.S. government, the State Department's Far East Bureau reported to Dulles that Mansfield's report "should greatly strengthen the Diem Government and give its opponents pause to consider. Mansfield's criticism of American policy is not unbearable, it is put forward in an effort to help and is not partisan in nature."

Robert Cutler, President Eisenhower's assistant for national security affairs, after reading news accounts of Mansfield's report, suggested Vietnam as a topic at the next National Security Council meeting, saying that Eisenhower had been unaware of the seriousness of the situation. The issue was taken up at the National Security Council (NSC) meeting on October 22, with Eisenhower presiding. Concerned that "time is running out" for Diem and that the French had not been helping, Eisenhower sent word to Dulles, who was in Paris, to talk tough to the French prime minister, Pierre Mendes-France, about doing more to support Diem. Echoing Mansfield's position, Dulles was instructed to say that if Diem were ousted or prevented from developing a broad government, "the US will have to reconsider its aid to Vietnam and in particular whether it will continue even limited, short term assistance to prevent a critical emergency." In this respect, the cable of instructions went on to say that the "conclusions of Senator Mansfield are relevant. At this time we see no satisfactory alternative governmental solution [in Vietnam] insofar as effective US assistance or forthcoming Congressional support are concerned."

In a conversation the following day, Dulles reminded Mendes-France of Mansfield's report "and the importance it would have on congressional opinion and decisions regarding further aid to Indochina." Dulles told aides that Mendes-France was "aghast" when informed that if Diem fell, the United States would probably pull out of Vietnam entirely. The shaken prime minister said that, although he doubted that Diem could succeed, new instructions were being sent to French representatives in Saigon to get behind him, as had been agreed in Washington.

The October 22 NSC meeting that had been prompted by Mansfield's report was also notable for another reason. As a result of the NSC discussion, Ambassador Heath was instructed to deliver a letter from Eisenhower to Diem offering to provide U.S. aid directly to the Vietnamese government for the purpose of "developing and maintaining a strong, viable state, capable of resisting attempted subversion or aggression through military means." Although the United States had already been supplying assistance, principally through the French, this offer of direct and expanded aid, which was delivered by Heath to Diem on October 23 and made public by the White House two days later, has often been cited, especially in the Kennedy and Johnson administrations, as the beginning of the formal U.S. commitment to South Vietnam.

Ironically, a few hours before Heath was instructed to deliver the letter, the ambassador had addressed a swan song cable to Washington expressing doubt that Diem could ever succeed. Due to Diem's "lack of personality, his inability to win over people of opposite views, his stubbornness and intransigence, his general political ineptitude and his slowness in decision and action," he had lost ground among the articulate sections of the Vietnamese community, Heath reported. He recommended working as rapidly as possible to find a successor, because "everyone in Embassy is convinced that Diem cannot organize and administer strong government." Three weeks later, Heath was on his way home and Diem was still Washington's favorite.

CONTENDING WITH COLLINS

Mansfield's views in late 1954 and early 1955 played an even more remarkable role in the struggle over Vietnam policy inside the U.S. government than in the discussions with the French. This time his unshakable backing for Diem was deployed against General J. Lawton Collins, a celebrated figure with great prestige and authority. Remarkably, each time Collins delivered a negative assessment of Diem, the State Department solicited from Mansfield a contrary opinion, which was then used to sustain Diem in the high councils of the administration.

General J. Lawton "Lightning Joe" Collins had been one of Eisenhower's corps commanders in World War II, Eisenhower's chosen deputy when he was Army Chief of Staff, and a successor to Eisenhower as Army Chief of Staff during the Korean War. In November 1954, disturbed by the continuing controversy about Diem within the U.S. government, Eisenhower personally selected Collins as "Special United States Representative" in Vietnam with the rank of ambassador and armed him with broad authority to stabilize and strengthen the Diem government and U.S. policy. In Dulles's initial meeting with Collins, he called the newly minted adviser's attention to Mansfield's recent report, saying it "deserves serious consideration." That consideration had become all the more serious because the day before Collins's appointment, the Democrats had regained control of both the Senate and the House of Representatives in congressional elections. This meant that Mansfield henceforth would be a member of the majority party in Congress and thus a more important figure than before.

In early December, after a month in Saigon, Collins set forth his initial conclusions. "Diem still represents our chief problem," he reported to Washington, and his impression of Diem's weaknesses "has worsened rather than improved." Collins said the "time may be approaching rapidly" when thought should be given to "possible alternatives." He declared that "we shall be forced" to begin a search for a replacement if Diem had not demonstrated he was capable of governing by about January 1, which was three weeks off.

The morning after receiving Collins's cable, Dulles sent three State Department officials, including Kenneth Young and Walter Robertson, the assistant secretary for the Far East, to Mansfield's office with a copy of the top secret cable to solicit Mansfield's reaction. As had been the case three months earlier, Dulles and his aides had a good idea what the senator would say. As expected, Mansfield continued to back Diem strongly, saying that he "represented what small hope there may be in building something in Vietnam." Mansfield opposed relinquishing "even the small chance we have with Diem for some unknown and untried combination." On one of the few occasions when he referred to Diem's Catholicism, Mansfield told the U.S. diplomats that he was "certain the refugees and many of the Catholic bishops and church officials [in Vietnam] would oppose the replacement of Diem." He added that the idea that Diem would have to prove himself within the next few weeks "was playing with 'political dynamite' because it was giving Diem such an awfully short time in which to show results or be replaced." His statements were immediately reported to Dulles for use within the administration and cabled as well to Collins in Saigon.

Undeterred, Collins transmitted another long report a week later detailing his most recent frustrations with Diem, who continued to find ways to balk at appointing Phan Huy Quat, an effective candidate backed by the United States and France, to take over the key post of defense minister. For the first time, Collins raised the possibility that the U.S. effort in Vietnam might be doomed to fail and that the United States might better cut its losses and gradually withdraw if a solution to Diem's intransigence, either through reform or replacement, could not be found. Although that course "is least desirable, in all honesty and in view of what I have observed here to date it is possible this may be the only sound solution," Collins wrote on December 13. In that case, he wrote, "it may be wise to concentrate effort on saving Laos-Cambodia-Thailand-Burma-India line—if possible with latter's active support."

Like clockwork, a day after receiving the top secret cable, Assistant Secretary Robertson was back in Mansfield's office to solicit his views. For all Diem's faults, the senator said, it was necessary to persevere in view of his "honesty, incorruptibility, patriotism and self-evident anti-Communism." If Diem fails or the French impose a deal with the communist Vietminh, Mansfield added, then the "only choice for US is withdrawal effort [to] bolster Free Vietnam," with the realization that this could have "tremendous repercussions [in] Cambodia, Laos and Thailand." Mansfield endorsed the candidacy of Quat for defense minister and expressed willingness to permit U.S. officials in Saigon to pass his endorsement along to Diem, believing it might carry some weight with the Vietnamese leader.

Before Collins could discuss Mansfield's endorsement with Diem, the prime minister decisively rejected Quat as his defense minister, fearing that such a strong figure could compete for authority in his government. To Collins, this was "the final development that convinces me that Diem does not have the capacity to unify divided factions in Vietnam." In desperation, he proposed in still another top secret cable to bring Bao Dai, the playboy emperor living in the French Riviera, to Saigon to establish personal leadership, or failing that, to prepare for gradual U.S. withdrawal from Vietnam.

Predictably, within hours after receiving it, the State Department officials were once more back in Mansfield's office—for the second time in three days—with Collins's latest cable. This time Mansfield agreed to dictate a memorandum of his views rejecting any role for Bao Dai, partly out of concern he might cooperate with the Communists. Mansfield was dubious that "personality squabbles" in Saigon required the United States to consider seriously withdrawing from Vietnam.

By this point in December 1954, Mansfield had begun to display uneasiness about the role in which he had been placed. His memorandum, worded more tentatively than his previous expressions, began by cautiously saying his views were predicated "on basis of facts contained in dispatches shown me." He also went out of his way to say that, in view of the importance of the issues involved, "I cannot advise on the making of these judgments from an office in Washington." Nonetheless, Mansfield also said that if the United States does withdraw as suggested by Collins, "we may expect in my judgment that [the] Diem Government will fall and that the French will choose its successor with an eye to carrying out whatever policies they have in mind in connection with Viet Minh Communists under Ho Chi Minh."

After further consideration in Washington and three-way consultations in Paris by Dulles with the French prime minister, Pierre Mendes-France, and the British prime minister, Anthony Eden—during which the Secretary of State prominently mentioned that Mansfield had "strong feelings" and "believes in Diem"—it was decided to make no dramatic changes in Vietnam for the immediate future.

When the next—and most serious—crisis erupted in the spring of 1955, the State Department again looked to Mansfield to back Diem and validate the status quo. This time the trouble was not from the Vietnamese National Army, which had been brought under Diem's control the previous November, but from an alliance of the French, the Binh Xuyen vice lords who controlled the National Police, and the two armed sects, the Cao Dai and Hoa Hao, all of whom had temporarily united to oppose Diem. And this time Collins was more determined than ever—and more effective than before—in his conclusion that Diem must be replaced.

On March 31, fearing that a clash between Diem and the factions would split the Vietnamese army with intolerable results, Collins sent a lengthy cable to Washington insisting again that Diem be replaced either by Bao Dai, who would be brought from France for the purpose, or by one of two senior Vietnamese political figures, Tran Van Do or Phan Huy Quat. In Washington, Dulles telephoned Eisenhower to apprise him of this news, read him some of the cable, and suggest that "we ought to talk to Mansfield about it and see what line he will take." After first resisting such consultation, Eisenhower agreed that Dulles should see Mansfield while the administration sought to determine its course.

Mansfield was invited to the State Department the following day, where Dulles, Robertson, and Young described a situation in Saigon "getting progressively worse." When they outlined the options offered in the latest Collins cable, Mansfield responded that all the alternatives "were worse than keeping Diem in office; that we did not have much time; that if Diem quit or was overthrown, there would very likely be civil war; and that as a result Ho Chi Minh could walk in and take the country without any difficulty."

After this and further soundings in Washington, including two conversations with Eisenhower, Dulles counseled Collins to go slow in moving against Diem. Although sympathizing with his frustration, Dulles told Collins by cable that Congress was not likely to authorize more money for a South

Vietnam that was ruled by a successor to Diem who would seem to have a "French imprint." The administration's domestic legislative program was in the balance on Capitol Hill, and Dulles was seeking Democratic support on contentious Taiwan issues. It was not a good time for a fight with Congress.

Three days later, however, Collins was back with two strong cables, one reporting the decision of his French counterpart in Saigon, General Paul H. R. Ely, that "in order to save Vietnam for free world, Diem must be replaced," and quickly, because "continued delay can only compromise [the] future of Vietnam." The other cable announced Collins's own considered judgment that "despite several fine qualities . . . [Diem] lacks the personal qualities of leadership and the executive ability successfully to head a government that must compete with the unity of purpose and efficiency of the Viet Minh under Ho Chi Minh." He too said in effect that Diem had to go.

Following the now-familiar track, Kenneth Young was back in Mansfield's Senate office with Collins's cables the next day. To nobody's surprise, after reading them the senator declared, "The US should stick to its guns in continuing to support Diem. . . . Ngo Dinh Diem and Ho Chi Minh are the only two national leaders in Vietnam. To eliminate Diem will leave the field to Ho."

After talking to Eisenhower, Dulles cabled Collins that "we are disposed to back whatever your final decision is but before you actually finalize we want to be sure you have weighed all of the factors which concern us here." One factor was that "there will be very strong opposition in the Congress" if Diem is replaced: "Mansfield, who is looked upon with great respect by his colleagues with reference to this matter, is adamantly opposed to abandonment of Diem under present conditions." Collins responded with a lengthy restatement of his conclusions and added, "I have no way of judging Mansfield's position *under present conditions* [emphasis in original]. These conditions are rather different than those existing when he visited Vietnam in September, 1954 when he feared military dictatorship as only alternative to Diem. . . . As practical politicians, I would think that Mansfield and his colleagues on Senate committees would give considerable weight to the arguments I have advanced in my recent telegraphic letter to you, and other pertinent messages." Collins did not mention, and perhaps he did not know, that despite the State Department's reliance on Mansfield as an exalted expert, he had spent only six days in Vietnam in 1953 and six days in 1954.

Collins finally appeared to have won the day. On April 9 Dulles discussed the situation with Eisenhower, who expressed undiminished confidence in his former deputy, noting that he had sent Collins to Vietnam to use his judgment and that "we have to go along with it." The same day, however, Mansfield told the Associated Press that "Vietnam is perhaps only days away from events that could mean a civil war. . . . Chaos in this southern half of the Indochina Peninsula would open the gates for the Communist drive toward rich Southeast Asia." Without the U.S.-backed Diem, Mansfield added, "there is no one who can keep Vietnam free."

At this juncture Collins was summoned home from Saigon for a fateful week of deliberations about the future of Diem. Beginning with Collins's arrival on April 21, Mansfield was on the receiving end of pleas and pressures from a variety of directions: from the French Embassy, which sent its minister, Pierre Millet, to see him on April 21 to say Diem must be replaced; from Wesley Fishel on April 25 on behalf of Diem, who passed on optimistic views and said Diem would succeed if he had continued U.S. support; and from Collins, who met Mansfield personally on April 27 and told him Diem was so "completely uncompromising, ascetic and monastic" that he could not deal with reality.

In a memorandum for his files on the visit by the French minister, Mansfield observed that "I still feel [Diem] is the only man who stands a chance and it is a long chance of keeping South Vietnam free." However, it appeared to him that the administration was placing "the major responsibility on me" in connection with its Vietnam policy and he did not wish to be in that position. "As to what our future decision will be vis-à-vis the retention or overthrow of Diem I pointed out to Mr. Millet that the responsibility lay with the President and Secretary of State and that it was up to them to assume that responsibility. All I could do was to make my views known."

At 6:10 and 6:11 P.M. on April 27, 1955, top secret cables went out from the State Department to the U.S. embassies in Paris and Saigon setting in motion a process that was intended to lead to the ouster of Diem and his replacement by a new government to be established in Saigon by Collins and Ely, the French high commissioner. The cables specified that every effort was to be made to make the new regime appear to have originated with the Vietnamese rather than the Americans and French. Diem was to be told that "as a result of his inability to create a broadly based coalition government, and because of Vietnamese resistance to him," the United States and France "are no longer in positions to attempt to prevent his removal from office."

In a manner that is still mysterious, Diem quickly learned of the intention to oust him. He and his brother, Ngo Dinh Nhu, having consolidated their control of the army, had been preparing for several months to move against the Binh Xuyen. Within hours after the secret instructions went out, probably at Diem's instigation, the showdown battle with Binh Xuyen broke out. Cables on the military action from Edward Lansdale in Saigon prompted Dulles at 11:56 P.M. to cancel the earlier directives calling for Diem's ouster six hours after they had been issued. The most recent thorough account, in David L. Anderson's book, *Trapped by Success,* published by Columbia University Press in 1991, suggests that Lansdale may have tipped off Diem to the ouster orders and convinced Washington by his urgent cables that Diem's forces were winning the showdown battles. Some key documents on Lansdale's role remain classified. A thorough search of Lansdale's papers in the Hoover Institution Archives, including his handwritten notebooks and journals from early 1955, shed no light on his role in these crucial military events. In any case, the plan to depose Diem was put in abeyance after his cables and as the battle in Saigon continued. When Collins left Washington for Saigon by plane on April 29, it was still unclear if Diem would be overthrown or emerge triumphant.

Mansfield on April 29 issued a hard-hitting statement, which was accorded prominent attention in the *New York Times* and the *Washington Post,* backing Diem as the leader of "a decent and honest government" and characterizing the opposition to Diem as built on corruption and private armies, "the power of the Black Hand, the pirate, the mercenary, the racketeer, and the witch doctor." He also went out of his way to place the full responsibility for U.S. policy on Eisenhower and Dulles, saying it is "entirely possible" they may "find it necessary to alter the present direction of our policy in Vietnam" and if so, "it will certainly lie within their responsibility." His fellow Democratic senator, Hubert Humphrey, also issued a statement backing Diem, and others in the Senate and House were reported to be backing Diem as well.

By the time Collins landed in Saigon, the tide of battle in the streets and the policy struggle in Washington had both turned decisively in Diem's favor. Dulles cabled Collins on May 1 that owing to the rapidly changing events, Diem "rightly or wrongly" was becoming a popular hero in the United States and the symbol of Vietnamese nationalism struggling against French colonialism and corrupt backward elements. As a result, "Since your departure U.S. public and Congressional opinion, in view of Diem's apparent success in the current military and political battle, is now even less likely than before to support or countenance a removal of Diem forced from without. There is increasing Congressional support for Senator Mansfield's views with which you are familiar. . . . For us at this time to participate in a scheme to remove Diem would not only be domestically impractical but highly detrimental to our prestige in Asia." His recommendations rejected and his mission at an end, Collins left Saigon in frustration two weeks later. The effort to depose Diem was over—only to return with remarkable similarity eight years later, in late 1963. Only this time, there was no last minute reprieve to a secret telegram that sealed his fate.

On May 4 Diem wrote Mansfield an effusive thank-you letter, expressing appreciation for his firm stand and strongly worded opinion "at a time when we were facing a crisis unparallel[ed] in the history of this government." Diem continued, "If I am permitted to quote Confucius, the sage said, 'Only in winter do we know which trees are evergreen.' Figuratively speaking, you are the evergreen, as luxuriant as always. . . . We are very much moved and touched by your ever-understanding gesture." Mansfield responded that "you have stood steady as a rock in behalf of your country and freedom. . . . We are proud a man of your ability and patriotism has been able to withstand the aggressive attacks of the Communists, Communist-sympathizers and colonialists, who have tried to make things difficult for you in Free Vietnam." Then reverting to theological references that he rarely employed with other public figures, Mansfield wrote, "I hope this letter finds you in good health and that God in his wisdom will be kind to you in the difficult days ahead. May His hand always guide you. . . . My prayers are with you on the long road ahead."

Mansfield returned to Indochina in September 1955 for his third trip in successive years. In his report to the Foreign Relations Committee he termed the survival of the Diem government "the predominant factor in the current situation in south Vietnam." As a result of Diem's leadership, "the tide of totalitarian communism in Vietnam has slackened. . . . There is today a reasonable chance of the survival and development of a free Vietnam." In the Diem government, he concluded, "there now exists for the first time a genuine alternative to the authoritarian regime of Ho Chi Minh." In an article in *Harper's Magazine* following his trip, Mansfield was even more optimistic. He wrote that Diem, who had seemed almost powerless a year earlier, this time "exuded an air of self-confidence and authority, and with good reason, for he had taken what was a lost cause of freedom and breathed new life into it." He added that "Diem's star is likely to remain in the ascendancy and that of Ho Chi Minh to fade—because Diem is following a course which more closely meets the needs and aspirations of the Vietnamese people."

Mansfield's enthusiasm for Diem was matched by a small but significant group of American backers who were organized in the fall of 1955 as American Friends of Vietnam (AFV), which became known informally as the Vietnam Lobby. It was initiated by Joseph Buttinger, an Austrian-born socialist who helped organize an anti-Hitler underground in the 1930s and who married the wealthy American Muriel Gardner, the model for Lillian Hellman's fictional anti-Nazi character Julia. With help from Cardinal Spellman and Joseph P. Kennedy, Buttinger met Mansfield and other prominent political and media figures in 1955 to organize support for Diem. Unlike the parallel China Lobby backing Chiang Kai-shek, the prominent members of AFV tended to be more liberal than conservative in their political orientation, even including for a time Norman Thomas, the perennial Socialist Party candidate for president.

Mansfield did not initially join AFV, which was assisted by a New York public relations firm hired by Diem's government. When the organization planned its first high-profile public event in mid-1956, however, Mansfield was asked to deliver the keynote address on America's stake in Vietnam. He evidently declined to do so, and the address was delivered instead by his friend, Senator John F. Kennedy, who had traveled to Vietnam as a member of the House in 1951 and returned deeply skeptical of French policy. Like Mansfield, he was an advocate of a third force. In his AFV address, which was Kennedy's last known speech on the subject before becoming president, he declared Vietnam to be "the cornerstone of the Free World in Southeast Asia, the keystone to the arch, the finger in the dike." Kennedy ended his address with a close paraphrase of Diem's comment a year earlier to Mansfield, whom Kennedy referred to as "a great friend of Vietnam," saying that "It is only in winter that you can tell which trees are evergreen." Mansfield was listed on the AFV letterhead beginning in 1959 as a member of its 108-person National Committee but later did not recall having joined.

Meanwhile Diem, following his victory over the Binh Xuyen and the sects, was continuing to cement his authority in the south. He officially deposed Bao Dai as chief of state after an elaborately staged and rigged referendum in October 1955 and proclaimed the Republic of Vietnam, with himself as president. In 1956, with U.S. backing and the approval of Mansfield, Diem refused to hold the Vietnam-wide elections mandated by the Geneva Conference two years earlier, out of concern that North Vietnam was better mobilized for voting and that Ho Chi Minh was probably the most popular figure in the country. When Diem made a triumphal state visit to Washington in 1957, Mansfield gave him an enthusiastic and hyperbolic greeting in the Senate, declaring that he "is not only the savior of his own country, but in my opinion he is the savior of all of Southeast Asia . . . a man of the people; a man whom the Vietnamese admire and trust; and a man in whom the United States has unbounded confidence." Praise abounded for Diem in the American press, including editorials in the *New York Times,* the *Washington Post,* the *New York Herald Tribune,* and the *Christian Science Monitor,* editorials that Mansfield inserted in the *Congressional Record.*

At home, Diem began cracking down with increasing severity on opposition, communist and noncommunist, but compared with the past the South seemed relatively stable and secure. Until nearly the end of the decade, leaders in North Vietnam advised their southern comrades to forgo armed attacks, on grounds that the time was not ripe for revolution. It appeared to official Washington as though the advance of communism in Southeast Asia, which had seemed inexorable after Dienbienphu, had been halted at the seventeenth parallel in Vietnam. For better or worse, Diem remained in power nearly a decade before being ousted in a U.S.-orchestrated coup in 1963. He was a formative and ultimately tragic Vietnamese figure in the long, futile struggle to maintain a regime allied to the United States.

CONGRESS AND FOREIGN POLICY

Mansfield's deep involvement in U.S. policy toward Diem brought to a head his concern about the relationship of Congress to the executive branch in the field of foreign affairs, a subject of great importance to him. Until he swung hard against President Nixon's continued prosecution of the Vietnam War in the 1970s, he was an outspoken supporter of the constitutional primacy of the President in executing foreign policy. At the same time he was a leading exponent and practitioner of the congressional role in examining, assessing, and supporting or opposing U.S. policies and actions abroad. Although he was not shy about suggesting, publicly or privately, what he believed the executive branch should do in specific situations, he also maintained that the decisions were fundamentally the responsibility of the executive branch.

In the case of Diem in the mid-1950s, he had a deep and intimate involvement in the policymaking process that he had never experienced before and would never again experience to the same degree as a member of Congress. On reflection, he felt he had crossed an invisible but important line between executive branch action and congressional reaction almost without realizing it. As he looked back, he came to believe that Dulles "leaned a little bit too heavily on me" in their relationship on the issue of Diem—"to such an extent that I felt [the relationship] had to be broken off, because it was outside the ken of my responsibility and entirely within the purview of the executive branch under the Constitution." In a reflective 1966 oral history in which he discussed their ties, he said that he and Dulles "mutually broke off" their relationship regarding Diem.

If the decision to pull back regarding Vietnam policy indeed was mutual, Dulles did not give up seeking to forge special ties to Congress through Mansfield. As problems in the Middle East heated up early in 1956, Dulles suggested to Walter George, who had become chairman of the Foreign Relations Committee following the Democratic sweep in the previous congressional election, that Mansfield serve as an informal liaison between the administration and the committee. Mansfield came to mind, Dulles said, because he seemed least likely to inject "a partisan note" into the sensitive Middle East issue. Mansfield declined.

Later in the year, after Eisenhower intervened to stop the British and French from seizing the Suez Canal, Dulles suggested to the President that Mansfield and Republican H. Alexander Smith, the two senators who had accompanied him to the Manila meeting in 1954, join his U.S. delegation to an international conference in London of users of the canal. Eisenhower responded enthusiastically, but Mansfield rejected this bipartisan project in the approaches to the 1956 presidential election, saying he "had more urgent business elsewhere." He explained to Dulles that the urgent business was the Democratic National Convention in Chicago, where "I have to look after my state's interest" lest he be criticized at home for spending too much time on foreign affairs and not enough on Montana affairs. Dulles seems to have taken this decision in good grace. The following year, he met Mansfield three times in August and September to discuss a mini-crisis in Syria. On two of those occasions, no other member of Congress was present.

With the Democrats in the majority in Congress following his first two years in he White House, Eisenhower as well as Dulles was greatly concerned about the executive-legislative relationship in foreign affairs. While out of power the Republicans had often vehemently challenged both the authority and wisdom of Presidents Roosevelt and Truman in the field of foreign affairs; the first GOP president since the 1930s feared the same could now happen in reverse. When China resumed heavy bombing of the offshore islands in January 1955, Eisenhower asked Congress to pass a resolution backing his authority to use force, "as he deems necessary" to defend Formosa and the nearby Pescadores against attack. In January 1957 Eisenhower proposed a similar resolution regarding the use of force in the Middle East, which had become unusually volatile after the Suez crisis. In both resolutions Congress was asked to agree in advance that the President was "authorized" to use U.S. military power. Some in Congress and the press argued in both cases that Congress was being asked to pass "a predated declaration of war."

With a concern for separation of powers, Mansfield argued in both cases that such an authorization by Congress was unnecessary because the President already possessed all the authority he needed to undertake military action as commander-in-chief and that awarding this "authority" might suggest that he lacked such a capability until Congress acted. The Senate brushed aside this objection in regard to the Formosa Resolution, which then passed by a large majority in 1955 amid the continuing conflict in the Taiwan Strait. Mansfield was among those voting for it "because circumstances leave us no other choice."

His objection fared better in connection with the Middle East Resolution, which was amended on his motion on a party-line committee vote in 1957 to declare that the United States "is prepared" to use military forces against aggression from any country in the area "controlled by international communism," leaving the President's authority to do so untouched. *Time* magazine said Mansfield had scored "a major triumph" for the majority Democrats with his amendment, giving them something to show for their "nagging" about the measure. In the end Mansfield voted for the resolution, which passed handily. Later the two presidentially initiated resolutions established the precedent for the Tonkin Gulf resolution of 1964, which played a major and controversial role in the deepening involvement in Vietnam.

Mansfield's brand of foreign policy cooperation, especially from a Democrat whose views were taken seriously within his own party, was welcome in the Republican administration, all the more so because they were usually devoid of personal animus or a search for partisan advantage. In a Senate speech in February 1957 he sought to define his view of the separation of powers on issues beyond the water's edge: "Under the guidance of the President, the functions of foreign policy are shared functions, shared between the legislative and the executive branches of government. They can be effectively discharged only when there is leadership in the Presidency and when there is mutual will to cooperate between the executive branch and Congress." He added, "We shall proceed as the Senate ought always to proceed in vital matters of foreign policy. We shall proceed in independence but with full deference for the leadership of the President." Recognizing the appeal of his position, the *New York Times* pictured a serious, pipe-smoking Mansfield in March 1957 and described him as emerging as one of the "most powerful" members of the Senate Foreign Relations Committee. "He is critical of the Administration, yet disinclined to 'rock the boat' in world affairs," the *Times* explained.

Nonetheless, executive branch activities that took place outside the framework for effective congressional supervision bothered Mansfield, as was the case with the powerful, secret, and free-wheeling Central Intelligence Agency. In July 1953, after just six months in the Senate, he proposed establishment of a joint Senate-House committee to oversee the activities of the CIA. Mansfield's proposal came two weeks after an abortive and highly publicized effort by Senator Joseph McCarthy to subpoena and investigate William P. Bundy, then a CIA official and a friend of Mansfield. One of Mansfield's motivations was to protect the agency from such irresponsible investigations, even while subjecting it to serious and consistent congressional oversight.

Mansfield repeated the proposal the following year with a stronger statement that "an urgent need exists for regular and responsible congressional scrutiny of the Central Intelligence Agency. . . . Once secrecy becomes sacrosanct, it invites abuse." The powers that be in the Senate, particularly Richard Russell, who had been a principal overseer and sponsor of the CIA under the very informal arrangement with his Armed Services Committee then existing, resolutely opposed the Mansfield resolution, as did the CIA director Allen W. Dulles, the brother of the Secretary of State. In 1956 the resolution was co-sponsored by fifty-four senators, enough to bring it to the floor for a vote and seemingly enough to guarantee its passage. After Russell and other Senate elders expressed their strong opposition, however, it was defeated 59 to 27. Republican Leverett Saltonstall, one of the handful of lawmakers briefed periodically and informally by CIA directors, conceded in floor debate with Mansfield that he and other senators were reluctant to ask questions at the secret briefings because "we might obtain information which I personally would rather not have."

Despite the rejection, Mansfield persisted in calling attention to the problem of unchecked power at the CIA. After the Soviet Union downed a U-2 spy plane in 1960, the CIA operation that aborted the summit meeting that year between Eisenhower and Soviet leader Nikita Khrushchev, Mansfield renewed his appeal for a watchdog committee, declaring that "not a single member of the Cabinet nor the President exercised any direct control whatsoever over the ill-fated U-2 flight at the critical moment at which it was launched." He declared that the flight "owes its origin more to bureaucratic inertia, lack of coordination and control and insensitivity to its potential (diplomatic) cost than it does to any conscious decision of politically responsible leadership." Mansfield tried again in 1966, working with Fulbright to establish a new Senate committee to oversee the CIA, but once again the proposal was stymied by Russell's successful demand that intelligence oversight remain in the exclusive (and permissive) hands of his committee.

Despite Mansfield's efforts, it would not be until the mid-1970s, following revelations of CIA involvement in domestic spying and the Watergate cover-up, that the Senate and House would establish full-time committees to investigate and monitor intelligence operations. In introducing the legislation that created the Senate committee, its author, Abraham Ribicoff of Connecticut, recalled that Mansfield had been seeking congressional oversight of the CIA for twenty years. "If we had accepted his recommendation, the problems that have developed over the years would have been eliminated and the intelligence agency and this body would have been better off for it," Ribicoff said.

Throughout the 1950s, Mansfield was intensely active on the Foreign Relations Committee and absorbed in the issues it considered. He traveled abroad while Congress was out of session each summer and fall—which was its relatively relaxed schedule in those days—and reported in writing on each overseas trip. Based on a study of his records, a *Time* correspondent calculated in 1957 that Mansfield had made eighteen trips abroad for the House or Senate foreign policy committees in his fourteen years in Congress—five to East Asia, seven to Western Europe, two to North Africa, and four to Latin America— gaining him the distinction of being Congress's most traveled member.

In 1956 Mansfield made ten lengthy speeches on the Senate floor review- ing, one by one, U.S. policies in every part of the world and with virtually every important country. They were serious, substantive speeches that did not attract many listeners on the Senate floor but that were recognized and often analyzed by foreign policy experts. In 1957 he spoke at length in January on foreign pol- icy challenges around the globe and as Congress adjourned for the year in July spoke even more extensively in a forty-nine-page address, "The Next Stage in Foreign Policy." In the spring of 1958 he devoted a series of four lengthy Senate speeches to creating "a durable peace" in Europe, the Middle East, and the Far East. Although often critical of Eisenhower administration policy, his speeches were restrained in rhetoric and tone and often suggested alternatives. In their depth and breadth, they were scholarly speeches of a sort rarely heard in the Senate in that day and almost never since. In addition, Mansfield wrote articles on foreign affairs for a wide variety of prestigious publications, including the quarterly journal *Foreign Affairs* and *The Annals of the American Academy of Political and Social Science*. Social commentator Benjamin DeMott, in a lengthy article decrying the absence of intelligent commitment in Congress, cited Mansfield as an exception, calling him a scholarly senator "of impressive asce- tic quality." Valeo observed that "he thought like a historian" rather than as a lawyer, the professional training of most other senators.

INTO THE LEADERSHIP

In January 1957 Lyndon Johnson, who had become majority leader when the Democrats won control of the Senate two years earlier, selected Mansfield to fill the number two leadership post, that of majority whip, after the defeat of Earle Clements of Kentucky. Several versions exist of how and why he was chosen, but there is no doubt that Jim Rowe, Mansfield's friend and political booster, lobbied his other friend, Johnson, about the job. It was widely believed that LBJ's first choice had been George Smathers of Florida, but according to some accounts he was vetoed by Johnson's fellow Texan, House Speaker Sam Rayburn, because of Smathers's dirty campaigning against the well-respected Claude Pepper in the 1950 Florida Democratic primary.

Smathers, who in the frequent absence of Clements had actually been performing many of the whip functions after Johnson suffered a heart attack in 1955, said later that he had declined the post after it was offered by LBJ. In an oral history for the Senate Historical Office many years later, Smathers said that "Johnson really worked my tail off" as a makeshift aide to the point that his wife insisted that Johnson had destroyed his life. When he surprised Johnson by saying he did not want the whip post, "it was just as though you had unleashed an awful smell of something. His nostrils flared, his eyes looked sort of funny," and he started to bolt from the room in search of another candidate. Before he did so, Smathers told him that only "that angel, Mansfield," would be able to put up with his demanding and imperious ways.

Unlike his push for a position as Democratic whip in the House of Representatives, Mansfield had no ambition for this post, being content with his senatorial responsibilities and his growing prominence in foreign affairs. He accepted the job reluctantly after intense pressure from Johnson. "Lyndon insisted I had to take it because I was the least objectionable to most of the Democratic senators," recalled Mansfield. "It was not a flattering argument, but after several meetings I finally lost my resolve against becoming whip."

As Johnson's argument suggested, his decision for Mansfield seems to have been made in part on the basis of regional and political balance. Although Mansfield was a moderate liberal from the Northwest, he got along well with the conservative senators from the South and Southwest who then dominated the Senate and its leadership positions. He was particularly close to two Georgians of immense prestige within the Senate, Walter George (who was leaving the Senate in 1957) and Richard Russell. Mansfield believed it was Russell who proposed him for the job.

The West-South cooperation had been highlighted in an unusual political deal in 1956. Mansfield and three other western liberal Democrats had voted to bottle up a civil rights measure in the southern-dominated Judiciary Committee in return for southern Democratic votes the next day on a bill that authorized the controversial Hell's Canyon high dam in Idaho, a public power project adamantly opposed by the Eisenhower administration. Each side obtained something it ardently wanted. Mansfield, like most of his western colleagues, had little commitment to the cause of civil rights at this stage.

In fact, the post of majority whip under Johnson carried almost no power. Mansfield acquired a spacious office in the Capitol in addition to his Montana office in the Senate Office Building and was able to hire Valeo full time as his closest legislative aide, focusing on foreign affairs. In the Senate chamber, he moved from a rear seat to a front row desk next to that of Johnson. Otherwise, life was not much different, as Johnson was not only floor leader but also chair of the Democratic Conference and of the Policy and Steering Committees. He tended to operate the leadership from his back pocket and continued to rely heavily on Clements, his former whip, whom Johnson provided with an office in the Capitol even after his defeat. The task of keeping track of senators' probable votes on upcoming issues and lining up a majority was performed in most instances by Bobby Baker, the former Senate page and Johnson acolyte who was secretary of the Senate majority. When Mansfield attempted to move legislation forward during Johnson's absence, Baker was known to circulate through the chamber asking senators to delay voting until LBJ returned. "I was really a figurehead," Mansfield recalled.

Nonetheless, the title of Senate Majority Whip added to Mansfield's prestige, especially at home, as his selection to participate with Dulles at the signing of the Southeast Asia Treaty in 1954 had done and as his appointment by Eisenhower to be a member of the U.S. delegation to the United Nations General Assembly would do in 1958. But unlike lawmakers who became entranced with their positions and powers in Washington to the detriment of their political base, Mansfield continued to give high priority to Montana affairs and was always ready to meet any visitor or group that traveled to Washington from the faraway state, often greeting each person by name as an old friend.

Even while maintaining his preferred demeanor as a man of few words, he was sure-footed and confident in protecting the interests of his con-

Young Mike Mansfield and his sisters, Kate (left) and Helen, in New York City shortly before being taken to faraway Montana to live with relatives after their mother died in 1910. (Photo 2002-35, K. Ross Toole Archives, University of Montana)

His great-aunt Margaret and her husband's brother, James, pose with Mike's sisters, Helen and Kate, in front of the neighborhood grocery in Great Falls, Montana, where they lived and worked. After Mike ran away and was returned by sheriff's deputies, Margaret had him placed for a year in the state home for wayward children. (Courtesy Sheila Mansfield Miller, family collection)

Following service in the U.S. Navy and Army, Mansfield (left) found delight in the U.S. Marines, which sent him to the Philippines and briefly to China in 1922. This was the beginning of a lifelong fascination with and involvement in Asia. (Courtesy Sheila Mansfield Miller, family collection)

At a turning point in his life the young copper miner, who had not finished even the eighth grade, met college-educated Maureen Hayes, the English teacher at Butte High School. She grasped his arm and reordered his future to a life of leadership in academia, politics, and diplomacy. (Courtesy Bernice Hayes Lanspa, family collection)

Maureen, Anne (age four), and Mike on the U.S. Capitol grounds shortly after he came to Washington as a member of the House of Representatives from Montana in 1943. (Photo 2002-17, K. Ross Toole Archives, University of Montana)

The artistic Maureen sketched holiday greeting cards that were sent to friends and constituents each year during Mike's decade in the House. (Courtesy Anne Mansfield, family collection)

In his first important venture in foreign affairs, Mansfield persuaded Franklin D. Roosevelt to send him to war-torn China as a presidential fact-finding envoy in 1944. He met U.S. troops along the Ledo Road in Burma and, later, Nationalist Chinese leader Chiang Kai-shek at his mountaintop headquarters in Chungking. (Photo 85-208, K. Ross Toole Archives, University of Montana)

Republicans pulled out all stops in the dirty campaign of 1952, bringing demagogue Joseph R. McCarthy and a communist-for-hire to Montana in an unsuccessful attempt to portray Mansfield as a communist dupe. He narrowly won his Senate seat in a year when most Democrats lost. (1952 campaign scrapbook, K. Ross Toole Archives, University of Montana)

Freshman senators—and friends—Henry "Scoop" Jackson, John F. Kennedy, and Mike Mansfield met for softball on a Washington playground in the early 1950s. Mansfield quickly recognized Kennedy as "a charmed person" and a future president. (Photo 85-211, K. Ross Toole Archives, University of Montana)

Already established as a foreign policy expert in the Senate, Mansfield was selected to sign the Southeast Asian Treaty (SEATO) for the United States in 1954, while Secretary of State John Foster Dulles and an aide (right) and Republican Senator H. Alexander Smith (left) look on. Mansfield would later turn against the treaty. (Photo 1998-974, K. Ross Toole Archives, University of Montana)

Mansfield's unwavering support for Ngo Dinh Diem (here with an interpreter) was an important factor in fending off demands from French and American officials that the stubborn South Vietnamese president be removed from office. When Diem was finally overthrown and killed, Mansfield grieved. (Courtesy Anne Mansfield, family collection)

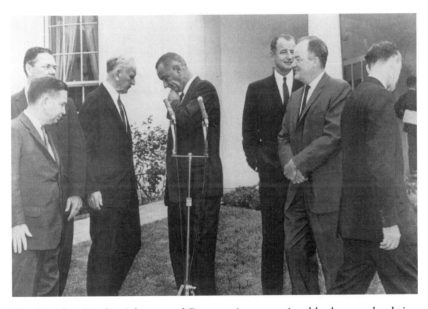

Vice President Lyndon Johnson and Democratic congressional leaders ponder their statements outside the Kennedy White House in 1962, while Mansfield exits the scene. On the left, Representatives Carl Albert, Hale Boggs, and Speaker John McCormack; on the right, Senators George Smathers, Hubert Humphrey, and Mansfield. Kennedy presented Mansfield with a copy of this photograph inscribed, "For Mike, who knows when to stay and when to go." (Photo 88-0067, K. Ross Toole Archives, University of Montana)

After his fourth trip to Indochina, Mansfield warned Kennedy against deepening involvement in the growing war. The President initially disputed his friend's assessment but later told Mansfield that he had changed his mind and, in a statement that has led to much historical speculation, confided that he planned to remove U.S. troops in his second term. (Photo by George Tames, *New York Times*)

stituents. Robert E. Wolf, a forester then working for the Senate Interior Committee, recalled what happened in 1958 when major forest industry interests quietly lined up House Republicans to kill a small business provision that had been sponsored in the Senate by Mansfield and other Western Democrats to aid lumbermen in the West. Learning about the situation, Wolf immediately informed Mansfield. "Without a second's hesitation, Mike picked up the phone and called Clements, the retired senator from Kentucky, who was then working for Johnson. Mike told Earle he was sending me in to see him on a matter important to the Western Democrats." When Wolf entered Clements's office he had only started to explain the provision when Clements cut him off, merely asking the number of the amendment in question as he picked up the phone and called his former Kentucky colleague, Representative Brent Spence, chairman of the House Interior Committee. "Brent, Mike and the boys have an amendment they'd like you to accept," said Clements, providing its designation number to the House chairman. After a very brief pause, Clements responded, "Thank you very much Brent, Mike and the boys will appreciate it." Turning to Wolf, the former senator said, "Tell Mike it's taken care of." To the surprise and disappointment of the forest industry lobbyists, the amendment was approved in the House committee in spite of their secret spadework and became law. "Mike had what I call a 'bear trap' mind. Given a situation he immediately knew what to do and who should do it," according to Wolf.

Mansfield went home to Montana every year while Congress was in recess, walking the main streets of the towns to greet people and stopping at local haunts for coffee and discussion with whoever came by. If Mike was otherwise engaged, Maureen would tour small Montana towns by herself. Not blessed with her husband's extraordinary recall for names, she would skim the local telephone book when arriving in town to spot the names of people she knew. In 1958, when he was up for reelection, Mansfield appeared so unbeatable that Montana Republicans had a hard time fielding a candidate to run against him. The best they could find was Lou W. Welch, a thirty-one-year-old smelter worker from Anaconda, near Mansfield's stronghold of Butte. Welch's only political experience was fourth place in a field of four contenders for his party's nomination for Congress.

During the campaign Richard Nixon, vice president at the time, stopped in Billings as part of a western tour in which he persistently raised the "soft on communism" theme against Democratic candidates. Nixon praised the Republican running against an incumbent Democrat in the eastern Montana district but did not say a word about the Senate race. Informed of Nixon's omission, Mansfield managed a wry smile and a typically terse observation, "He's learning."

Among the few issues raised by Welch was criticism of Mansfield's steadfast support of Diem, based on an attack in the right-wing magazine *American Mercury* by Hilare du Berrier, who had once worked for Diem's brother, Ngo Dinh Luyen, but had become disillusioned with Vietnam's powerful family. Du Berrier, who had earlier corresponded with Mansfield, sent letters to several Montana editors asking that Mansfield be defeated because of his "stubborn insistence on forcing Ngo Dinh Diem down the throats of a nation that does not and never did want him." Mansfield expressed surprised at the reaction to this attack, which was rare at the time. He wrote to a Montana editor that "I certainly have no apologies to make whatsoever for my part in keeping South Vietnam away from the communists."

The election result in 1958 was the most lopsided victory ever recorded in a Montana Senate race. Mansfield won more than three-fourths of the entire vote and carried each of the state's fifty-six counties, a far cry from his narrow margin in the face of the McCarthy-sponsored smear campaign and Eisenhower's national landslide in 1952. In the course of a single Senate term, he had become the most popular politician in the history of the state.

INTO THE LEADERSHIP
FOR KENNEDY

8

The day before John F. Kennedy was inaugurated as President in January 1961, President Dwight D. Eisenhower told him the unresolved conflict in Laos was "the cork in the bottle," where a communist victory would lead to irreversible gains throughout the Far East. With Mansfield's help and advice, Kennedy decided to negotiate rather than fight in Laos, but also to establish next-door Vietnam as the crucial battleground of the area. After a trip to Saigon in 1962, Mansfield informed Kennedy that U.S. policies were not succeeding and opposed greater U.S. intervention. Kennedy later told Mansfield that he planned to remove American forces from Vietnam, a statement that has given rise to intense debate among historians about Kennedy's intentions for his second term as President. In November 1963, South Vietnamese President Ngo Dinh Diem was ousted with Kennedy's approval and killed a few hours thereafter. Later the same month, Kennedy succumbed to an assassination in Dallas, Texas.

The election of his friend John F. Kennedy to the presidency marked the ascension of Mike Mansfield to the foremost post of the Democratic Party in the Senate and also the beginning of his strongly felt personal and political opposition to U.S. military intervention in Indochina. For Mansfield, leadership and dissent at the same time was an uneasy fit during the tenure of Kennedy and his successor, Lyndon B. Johnson, yet he persisted on both paths simultaneously. He maintained his powerful position in the Senate partly by insisting that the leadership had been thrust upon him through no decision or desire of his own, which was true, and that he would willingly give it up to other claimants. In sixteen years as Senate majority leader, the longest such stint in American history, no one ever challenged him for the post.

It all began with Kennedy, who sat next to him in the back row of the Senate in 1953, when the two of them came at the same time from the House of Representatives. Both were Roman Catholics of Irish descent but from vastly different, indeed contrasting, backgrounds. Kennedy had been brought up amid glamour and opulence as the son of one of the richest and most prominent men in America, and Mansfield, a virtual orphan, had had to make his own way. Kennedy exuded social ease, charm, and self-confidence; Mansfield, to the despair of Washington hostesses, was untroubled sitting at a table for hours without exchanging more than a few compulsory words with his dinner partners. Although both were progressive Democrats with a similar political outlook, they were from opposite ends of the country, Massachusetts and Montana, and Mansfield was fourteen years older.

Despite the differences, they were comfortable with one another and developed a great degree of mutual respect. When Kennedy became president, he insisted that Mansfield become Senate Democratic leader, the steward of his legislative program in the Senate. According to his brother Robert, John Kennedy "loved" Mansfield and considered him a loyal friend even when there were occasional disappointments in Mansfield's political performance. He gladly sponsored Mansfield's trips abroad and gave serious consideration to his advice on foreign policy. Mansfield, a loner who did not develop many close friendships, developed an unusually warm relationship of trust and confidence with Kennedy. In late 1963 Mansfield played a key role in saving the President from a White House sex scandal that could have devastated Kennedy's reputation shortly before an assassin ended his life.

Early in their Senate days the Montanan was surprised and amused when Kennedy, who had suffered an injury to his back and recurrent malaria from his World War II service in the Pacific (and had a variety of other ailments, which were carefully hidden), complained to Mansfield about the high costs he was encountering at George Washington University Hospital, including a charge of $5 or more for an aspirin pill. Something had to be done about medical costs for the majority of people, he said, presaging his fight to initiate Medicare. At the time, Kennedy was worth about $10,000,000 from trust funds provided by his father, while Mansfield was living on his Senate salary of $15,000 a year, which was more than he had ever made before. For several years Maureen worked part time in his Senate office for $5,000 per year.

The Kennedys and the Mansfields inhabited disparate social worlds. The Kennedys lived in an elegant house in the most prestigious part of Georgetown and were the toast of Washington society. The Mansfields lived in the pleasant three-bedroom house they bought when Mike was elected to the Senate. Even as Majority Leader, he was nearly always home by 10 P.M. because he often rose before 5 A.M. to get to his office around 6, when he opened the mail himself and sorted it into piles for answers or actions. Given his position as one of the most prominent and powerful men in Congress, his was a simple life.

In the mid-1950s, the two senators and other friends, in and out of politics, met occasionally on Sunday afternoons for softball or touch football games on a public playground. A photograph from 1954 depicts three emerging leaders of the time, all freshmen senators: at bat, Henry M. "Scoop" Jackson, swinging hard but high at the softball; the catcher, a young, tousle-haired John F. Kennedy, wearing khaki shorts, down on one knee behind the plate waiting for the ball; and Mansfield standing behind them as umpire, squinting into the sun, his right arm raised and extended to call a strike.

About this time, when they had been in the Senate only a year or two, Mansfield told John Newhouse, then a correspondent for *Collier's* magazine, that Kennedy was a charmed person and would be president some day. It was not until 1956, when he made a strong but unsuccessful bid for the vice presidential nomination at the Democratic National Convention, that Kennedy came to broad national attention. At the convention Lyndon Johnson asked Mansfield to enter the vice presidential race, but he declined and actively supported Kennedy. Shortly after the race, won by Senator Estes Kefauver, he wrote a "Dear Jack" note of congratulations on "the tremendous showing, the well-deserved national recognition which you received, and the anticipation that your star is just beginning to shine and that in the future the Democratic Party will be tied to it more securely." Although it would have been a great honor for Kennedy to have been nominated for vice president, Mansfield wrote, "I think in all honesty, that in the long run, it was a break that you were not." (The Stevenson-Kefauver ticket was handily defeated by the incumbent team of Eisenhower and Nixon.) Kennedy responded, in a handwritten note, "Your letter explains why you are the most respected member of the Senate."

When the 1960 Democratic National Convention took place, Mansfield was Johnson's number two person in the Senate leadership hierarchy. He was formally pledged to support Johnson in his race against Kennedy, but even before the balloting began he candidly described Johnson as a "long shot" and predicted that Kennedy was likely to win the Democratic nomination. Of Montana's fourteen convention votes Johnson received only two and Kennedy the rest. Kennedy went on to win the nomination and, with Johnson's help as his vice presidential running mate, to win the presidency.

BECOMING MAJORITY LEADER

On November 11, 1960, three days after his election victory, Kennedy telephoned Mansfield and insisted that he take the post of majority leader, saying he had "talked it over with Johnson and others and he wanted [Mansfield] to do it." Characteristically, Mansfield said he didn't want the job. Mansfield told his friend, the new President-elect, that he had put him "into a very delicate situation" but that "I would consider it and let him know later." Kennedy asked him to make no statement until he had reached a decision, and he reiterated that he wanted it to be in the affirmative.

A short time afterward, Johnson called from the LBJ Ranch in Texas to repeat Kennedy's proposal. He made it plain in the conversation that he intended to continue to mastermind Senate activity, if not run it, as in the past. As taken down by a secretary on another line in Mansfield's office, the conversation went like this:

> Johnson: Listen, now, I want you to take this Leadership. Everybody wants you to. Have you talked to Jack this morning? Did he tell you the same thing?
> Mansfield: I don't want to do it, Lyndon, but I will think it over.
> Johnson: Why?
> Mansfield: I watched you too long and saw what happened.

Johnson: People respect you and [Senator] George Smathers will help you and I am going to sit in on the Policy and Steering Committee and I will do everything for you at any time. If you don't, you will break up this party. [Senator Richard] Russell and everybody are for you. . . . You have a president who will help you and I will be there every week and I will do everything you want me to do.

Under high-pressure appeals from Johnson that went on for several minutes, Mansfield asked three times for time to think it over. Several days later, he agreed to take the post.

Why did both Kennedy and Johnson want Mansfield as Majority Leader? In the case of Kennedy, the most obvious answer is that JFK respected and completely trusted him. This is clear in many interactions and in the retrospective remarks from Kennedy's brother Robert and from Kennedy aides Arthur Schlesinger Jr. and Theodore C. Sorensen, in their books about the Kennedy presidency. After Kennedy's assassination his widow, Jacqueline, wanted Mansfield—and only Mansfield—to deliver a eulogy at the memorial service held in the rotunda of the Capitol.

Kenneth O'Donnell, perhaps Kennedy's closest confidant in the White House, presented another reason in his memoirs published nine years after the President's death: that Kennedy wanted Mansfield to lead the Senate because he did not want the domineering Lyndon Johnson to continue in the job. O'Donnell related that he angrily protested on learning that Kennedy had offered the vice presidential nomination to Lyndon Johnson, whom O'Donnell considered an "old hack machine politician," anathema to JFK's supporters. The widespread belief then, and especially later when Johnson's appeal helped win Texas and most of the old South in a razor-thin victory margin, was that Kennedy had picked LBJ in a calculated bid for those votes. However, O'Donnell wrote that Kennedy cited very different reasons when he took him into the most private place in the suite, the bathroom, closed the door, and told him something which he was instructed never to reveal (and which, in the light of recent revelations about Kennedy's health, seems particularly questionable):

I'm 43 years old, and I'm the healthiest candidate for President in the United States. You've traveled with me enough to know that. I'm not going to die in office. So the Vice-Presidency doesn't mean anything. I'm thinking of something else, the leadership in the Senate. If we win, it will be by a small margin, and I won't be able to live with Lyndon Johnson as the leader of a small majority in the Senate. Did it occur to you that if Lyndon Johnson becomes the Vice-President, I'll have Mike Mansfield as the leader in the Senate, somebody I can trust and depend on?

An oral history interview with Robert Kennedy, who was often at odds with Johnson, gave support to this view, quoting JFK as often saying he was lucky to have Johnson as vice president, because otherwise he would be majority leader "and that would be just impossible. Lyndon Johnson would screw him all the time." In contrast, "Mansfield was loyal to him. So he was very pleased."

For his part, the evidence suggests that Johnson expected Mansfield to be an easily led subordinate, with Johnson continuing to exercise the real power in the Senate, as he had done during the four years when Mansfield was his nominal deputy as Democratic whip. Johnson also expected Bobby Baker, who had been his protégé and right arm legislatively, to remain. At Johnson's direction, Baker telephoned Mansfield on November 14 to urge him to take the leader's job and offering his resignation and those of other leadership aides. Mansfield indicated that if he took the job, he wanted Baker to stay on.

Although Baker had been the point man of a very different style of leadership, Mansfield considered him essential to the operation of the Senate. Later, he formally asked Baker to remain and, after some hesitation, Baker agreed.

Meeting in December with several close Senate friends, including Richard Russell, Robert Kerr, George Smathers, and Hubert Humphrey, Johnson unveiled an unorthodox plan to have himself elected chairman, or presiding officer, of the Senate Democratic Conference, or caucus, and thus be in position even as vice president to exercise continuing influence if not control over the workings of the Senate. Reflecting this initiative, LBJ told Bobby Baker that the operation of the Senate is "gonna be just the way it was." Johnson presented his proposal to Mansfield, who would normally be expected to preside over the caucus as Majority Leader. The self-effacing Mansfield accepted the plan in the belief, as he told Kennedy in a conversation in advance of the meeting, that LBJ clearly understood the line that divided the Vice President, as a member of the executive branch, from the

Senate and that Johnson would preside at caucuses only in an advisory capacity. It would be merely a "pro forma" position, Mansfield believed. Kennedy, evidently primed by Johnson, told Mansfield he thought it was "a fine idea" and that he was glad it was being considered.

Johnson's scheme came a cropper in the initial meeting of the Senate Democrats on January 3, 1961, more than two weeks before Inauguration Day. LBJ, who had not yet resigned as senator from Texas, presided over the meeting of the sixty-five Senate Democrats while they elected Mansfield by acclamation as Majority Leader and two other Johnson favorites approved by Mansfield—Hubert Humphrey and George Smathers—as Majority Whip and secretary of the Democratic Conference, respectively. That done, Mansfield rose to present the idea that Johnson continue to chair the caucus as vice president—only to meet an eruption of opposition that soared to what one participant called "a crescendo of denunciation, sarcasm and indignation." His face flushed, Albert Gore Sr., a moderate from Tennessee, cited a long list of indignities that he attributed to Johnson and declared angrily, "We might as well ask Jack Kennedy to come back up to the Senate and take *his* turn presiding." To Johnson's surprise and embarrassment, several longtime members of his senatorial inner circle joined in the general criticism. Many of the objections were couched in Constitutional terms, on grounds that Johnson henceforth would be an official of the executive branch rather than a member of Congress, but the passions expressed were deeply personal. Johnson had ridden herd on the Senate Democrats like the overseer of Texas ranch hands for nearly a decade, persuading, insisting, mastering the political nuances of every senator's vote, intimidating the recalcitrant with what became known as the Johnson Treatment. They were eager to be relieved of his oppressive presence and appalled that he might somehow continue to afflict them. The very thought created a spontaneous revolt.

Mansfield quickly assured the aroused and skeptical Conference that he had no intention of sharing either responsibility or authority as Majority Leader with Johnson and that the proposal was merely intended to give the former leader a measure of recognition. In his self-effacing way, Mansfield claimed the proposal had been his own idea and expressed regret for any embarrassment caused Johnson. He said he had obtained approval of the plan in advance from Humphrey and Smathers but did not say—if indeed he knew—that Johnson had secretly lined them up in advance. After the bitter debate, a face-saving substitute motion was approved to permit Mansfield as Majority Leader to request Johnson—or any Democratic senator—to preside over the Conference; seventeen senators voted against even that proposal.

The event was a stunning manifestation of Johnson's loss of legislative power as he shifted to the feckless post of vice president. The idea he had expressed to Mansfield on November 11, that he would "sit in on the Policy and Steering Committee and . . . do everything for you" proved completely unacceptable to his former colleagues. "I now know the difference between a caucus and a cactus," Johnson was quoted as saying bitterly. "In a cactus all the pricks are on the outside." Deeply humiliated, Johnson rarely attended a Senate Democratic meeting after that. The effect of the meeting may have been the opposite of what Johnson intended: it established and confirmed Mansfield's authority as Senate majority leader, free of the overweening influence of Lyndon Johnson.

CHINA IS FOR THE SECOND TERM

On December 15, 1960, Mansfield came to lunch at the President-elect's elegant house on N street in Georgetown, walking past the police lines and the swarms of reporters and photographers who came every day to hear Kennedy announce his choices for high government office from the doorstep. Inside the house, the future president and future Senate Democratic leader compared notes in an intimate conversation over clam chowder, lamb chops, spaghetti, green peas, and red wine—a great contrast to Mansfield's usual Senate lunch of a hamburger and coffee. "I left with a full stomach," Mansfield wrote in a memo for his files on the occasion.

Mansfield's greatest interest continued to be foreign policy, especially U.S. policies in Asia. After discussing prospective appointments and several legislative issues, Mansfield turned the conversation to the Far East, which was at the top of the list in his pocket of "Possible Points of Discussion on Foreign Policy." A key item was a report on U.S. policy toward China, always a subject of great importance to Mansfield, who, unlike many others, continued to see China as the most crucial actor in the region and one not beyond the possible reach of the United States. Mansfield had prepared a report on China policy earlier in the month suggesting modest U.S. efforts to repair the breach, only to decide out of political caution not to make it public. Instead he had sent a single confidential copy to Senator J. William Fulbright, chairman of the Foreign Relations Committee. Now he handed a second copy to Kennedy, explaining that it was confidential and "for him alone."

Mansfield's interest in China had never flagged through the years. Nonetheless, he was wary of public advocacy of improved U.S. relations following his narrow victory in the 1952 senatorial campaign, in which Republican attacks on his alleged "soft-on-China" views were a central feature. After the 1952 campaign "the only question that I ever found Mansfield really afraid of was the China question," according to his close aide Frank Valeo. "Whenever questioned by the press, he would give the stock answers that everybody else was using at that time. He wouldn't separate himself from the mainstream on it—not for a long time." In Manila in 1954 he had privately objected to the plan to bomb China in the offshore islands dispute. Publicly, however, he took an unswerving stand against U.S. recognition of the People's Republic of China and against its admission to the United Nations. In 1955 he joined the Committee of One Million Against the Admission of Communist China to the United Nations, an anti-Beijing lobby group.

In June 1959, in the first sign of his positive engagement on China, he and Fulbright addressed a joint letter asking the Eisenhower administration to supply emergency food aid to alleviate starvation due to severe floods on the mainland. The State Department rejected the proposal on the grounds that China would probably refuse to accept the aid, citing the fact that it had rejected an aid offer from Taiwan through the International Committee of the Red Cross. The State Department also argued that providing humanitarian aid might create the false impression among "some of our friends" (Taiwan) that U.S. policy toward China was changing. In April 1960, in a separate initiative, Mansfield called in a Senate speech for "new approaches" toward the People's Republic, specifically a reciprocal exchange of journalists and for U.S. recognition of Mongolia as a window on both its neighbors, China and the Soviet Union.

Now, during the lunch in Georgetown, the President-elect expressed "great interest" in exploring the possibility of an exchange of journalists, even though he understood that those coming to the United States would certainly be communist agents. Kennedy also seemed "very interested" in the possible recognition of Mongolia, which caused Mansfield to go into detail about its potential as a listening post for both the Soviet Union and China. In March 1961 Kennedy's State Department would test the waters with Beijing by proposing to accept the assignment of Chinese journalists in the United States. The Chinese, however, would refuse even to discuss the matter until the United States severed its relations with Taiwan. The same year, the State Department would explore the possibility of establishing relations with Mongolia but would drop the idea because of Taiwan's opposition.

Unknown to Mansfield, Kennedy told Secretary of State Dean Rusk in May 1961 that he would make no major changes in China policy in his first term owing to the narrow margin by which he had been elected and the highly controversial nature of any move he might make. Later he told McGeorge Bundy, his national security adviser, that "China is for the second term." For the rest of the Kennedy administration, to Mansfield's regret, there would be no break in the hostility between the United States and China. The same was true in the Johnson administration as the United States became increasingly embroiled in Vietnam against the policy and interests of China.

A PALM BEACH INTERLUDE

On December 19, four days after their meeting in Georgetown, Mansfield interrupted a Florida vacation to travel to the President-elect's compound at Palm Beach for dinner at Kennedy's invitation. Kennedy and Lyndon Johnson, who was also present, had not returned from golf when he arrived, so Kennedy's secretary, Evelyn Lincoln, said she would show him to his room for the night. Mansfield demurred, saying he would return to Miami after dinner. A little later Kennedy arrived and asked him to stay the night for discussions the next morning involving House Speaker Sam Rayburn, who was also a guest.

"I explained to [Kennedy] that I was going back that nite and would come down by plane next morning, that I had not brought clothes or toilet articles along," Mansfield wrote immediately after the visit. "He said nonsense & told Evelyn to lay out some of his shirts, sox, underwear etc. & shaving materials for me. I felt embarrassed but acceded."

Before, during, and after dinner, Kennedy, Johnson, Rayburn, and Mansfield discussed high-level appointments, legislative strategy, and rules changes. They were joined at dinner by Lady Bird Johnson but not by

Jacqueline Kennedy, who was under doctor's orders to remain secluded, having delivered John Jr. less than a month earlier. Later they watched a movie. The following morning, after a press conference at the compound, Rayburn went fishing. "Jackie came in. Looked good but was weak," wrote Mansfield. He saw John Jr., now seven pounds, and assessed him to be "OK." Then Caroline, three years old, made her appearance. "You haven't got any hair," she said to the bald Speaker. "That's right and I'm glad of it," responded Rayburn. "You've got a lot of hair; let's see what you do with all of it."

In late morning, Robert Kennedy and his wife, Ethel, arrived for lunch. "Bobby talked about his chances for confirmation [as attorney general] without too much of a fight. I said I thought good & I'd talk to Dirksen & Sam Ervin & let him know."

"Kennedy—confident and assured
"Johnson—confident and eager
"Speaker—himself."

After lunch Mansfield was driven to the airport and put aboard a private plane for Miami. When the pilot asked who should get the bill for the flight, Mansfield replied, "Senator Kennedy."

THE STRUGGLE OVER LAOS

Mansfield played an important role in Kennedy's first foreign policy crisis, over the landlocked Indochinese country of Laos, an issue that consumed more of the new President's time than any other in his first two months in office. For the first time, Mansfield spoke up in a White House meeting to oppose U.S. military intervention in Indochina. On this occasion, the views of the Majority Leader, who was better qualified by experience and interest to deal with the subject than anyone else present, carried weight with the President.

For nearly everyone else around the table in the Cabinet Room, Laos was a bristling battlefield of opposing armies marching into cold war battles. Mansfield saw it very differently. Beginning with his September 1953 visit, when he carried visa number one and his U.S. Navy plane had a hard time locating the capital, Mansfield had visited Laos three times in successive years. Although his visits were brief, adding up to total of only four days, he had had a sense of the Laotian reality. It was, as he wrote after his 1955 trip, a land "sparsely populated, completely undeveloped in a western sense, and its way of life virtually unchanged over centuries of time."

He had repeatedly met some of the leading Lao personalities, especially Prince Souvanna Phouma, the hardy political leader and recurrent prime minister, who sought to maneuver between communist and anticommunist elements to create and maintain a neutralist position. Throughout the 1950s Mansfield continued to follow the convoluted events in Laos and occasionally speak out on the subject. He was particularly critical of the rapid growth in the U.S. presence and in U.S. aid, mostly military assistance to anticommunists, as the United States became deeply involved in the politics of the country. By the end of the decade U.S. aid totaled $300 million, or close to $1,500 for each Laotian, whose annual per capita income was less than $50 per year at the time.

In the U.S. presidential election year of 1960, the fragile and complex political and military situation in Laos was blown apart by a military coup headed by Kong Le, an obscure paratroop captain, touching off a bout of intensified struggle among existing right, centrist, and leftist factions, the right supported by the United States and the left by North Vietnam and its communist allies, the Soviet Union and China. In December, a Soviet airlift of arms and supplies to Kong Le's forces, which had made common cause with the leftist Pathet Lao, raised the specter of a communist victory. Under the cold war worldview then prevailing, the potential "loss" of Laos was seen as a serious blow. The Eisenhower administration, in its final weeks in office, considered overt U.S. military intervention but decided to leave the problem to its successors.

On January 2, 1961, almost three weeks before his inauguration, President-elect Kennedy raised the Laos situation with Mansfield by telephone from Florida, calling it "pretty lousy" (was a pun intended?) and asking his advice. Mansfield responded with a tightly written two-page memorandum observing that the problem in Laos "is partly of our own making," the result of a U.S. attempt "to steer that country away from what was essentially a course of neutralism, inclined toward the West, to a course which has made Laos a bone of possible military contention, in the Cold War." Mansfield recommended that the United States join international backing for the centrist leader, Souvanna Phouma, and aid him in seeking a neutralist solution. The alternative would be "a bloodbath" as contending Thai, North and South Vietnamese, and possibly Cambodian troops fought over the hapless country, with the United States supplying arms to one side and the Russians and Chinese to the other. "If the situation gets really bad we may be actually drawn into the fighting as well as the Chinese Communists," he wrote.

President Eisenhower, briefing Kennedy on January 19, his last full day in office, described Laos as the "cork in the bottle" for Southeast Asia and said that its "loss" would have devastating repercussions in the region. It remains a matter of historical debate just what Eisenhower advised Kennedy to do, if anything, because of different versions of the conversation in the notes or understanding of various participants at the meeting. However, it is clear that Kennedy and the other members of his small entourage got the impression that Eisenhower was ready to fight to maintain the status quo. The President-elect recorded in his contemporaneous notes that "I came away from the meeting feeling that the Eisenhower administration would support intervention—they felt it was preferable to a communist success in Laos."

During the transition period Mansfield received a personal and confidential letter from Souvanna Phouma, who had taken temporary refuge in Cambodia. "America has never understood me," lamented the Lao political leader. He decried the "outmoded" U.S. policy of "making use of anti-communism" as its principal weapon, a policy that he pronounced a dangerous failure in Laos and that he hoped Kennedy would abandon. "In view of the geographic situation and the temperament of its people, a policy of strict neutrality is the only one which can save my country from chaos," he wrote.

On January 21, Kennedy's first full day in office, Mansfield forwarded Souvanna's letter to the President, endorsing its conclusions. The only way to avoid an unlimited U.S. commitment or military involvement, Mansfield wrote, would be "an active attempt by this country to neutralize Laos in the pattern of Burma or Cambodia." Specifically, Mansfield recommended efforts to establish a neutralization commission consisting of Asian nations as arbitrators between the warring Laotian factions, and at the same time avoid greater U.S. involvement by reducing U.S. military aid and substituting French military trainers, who might be acceptable to Souvanna and the Laotian king, for Americans on the ground. Two days later Mansfield sent Kennedy a second memo with details of the proposal for a neutral commission. Such a commission "may permit us to extricate ourselves from an untenable over-commitment in a fashion which at least holds some promise of preserving an independent Laos without war," he wrote.

Kennedy's initial effort in early February was a partial step in the direction Mansfield suggested. Handed to the king of Laos for him to put forward as his own idea, the U.S.-drafted plan called for establishing a neutral commission composed of Cambodia, Burma, and Malaya to end the fighting and work out a negotiated solution. The hitch was that it continued U.S. support for the rightist faction, headed by a royal prince, as the legitimate government. Cambodia and Burma, which had not been consulted in advance, immediately rejected the plan as disguised support for the rightists. A U.S.-backed military offensive by the rightist forces, intended to maximize their bargaining position, was a complete failure. To increase the pressure on the communist side, the Defense Department on March 9 drew up a seventeen-point plan of U.S. military actions, just short of direct intervention with American troops. Kennedy withheld final approval for the actions but authorized the movement of U.S. forces in the Pacific closer to Indochina and the dispatch of a Marine helicopter unit to Thailand.

Later in March new White House meetings considered large-scale U.S. military intervention in Laos. Based on a background interview with "reliable informants" (in reality, Kennedy's pro-intervention adviser Walt W. Rostow), the *New York Times* reported on March 21 that Kennedy was resolved to "take whatever steps are necessary . . . and accept whatever risks are involved" to save Laos from communist domination. The following day Mansfield weighed in with a new memorandum "on the highly dangerous implications of an effort at [a] military solution," which he handed to Secretary of State Dean Rusk and also sent to Kennedy. In a prescient analysis, he argued that U.S. armed intervention in Laos could provoke counteraction from North Vietnam and China, resulting in "a costly and prolonged involvement on our part and a decimation of the Laotian people for which we may well be held primarily responsible in Asian opinion."

Virtually the only reason for official U.S. concern about faraway Laos was the fear that a communist victory there would lead to the toppling of one after another of the nearby Asian governments like a row of dominoes cascading down upon each other. In the early 1950s Mansfield had accepted and espoused the domino theory, as it was called, but by the end of the decade he had acquired greater experience and insight. In his memorandum to Kennedy on March 22 he wrote that "the domino theory, of the communist advance in Southeast Asia, so popular a few years ago has not proven accurate and may be less valid than a concept of checkmate by indigenous governments (i.e. Cambodia, Burma, Thailand) with some popular base, and drawn together by common purpose." Eisenhower, however, had invoked the domino theory in his briefing for Kennedy, and JFK, who had endorsed it publicly, wasn't sure it was wrong. As the first Democratic president since the "loss" of China, Kennedy was deeply concerned about potential political costs at home, even if most Americans had never heard of Laos before it leaped into the headlines.

On March 23, the day after Mansfield's memorandum, Kennedy opened an unusual prime time, televised news conference with a strong statement and three giant maps of Pathet Lao gains. "My fellow Americans, Laos is far away from America, but the world is small," he declared. He threatened a U.S. response under the aegis of the Southeast Asian alliance, SEATO, which Mansfield had signed in 1954, if communist forces continued to advance, but defined the U.S. objective in Laos as "a truly neutral government and not a Cold War pawn."

A new bout of high-level U.S. decision making was touched off by a Pathet Lao seizure in late April of Muong Sai, an obscure opium-trading village on the approaches to the Lao royal capital of Luang Prabang. On April 26 U.S. ambassador Winthrop Brown, who previously had counseled patience and negotiations, responded in panic with a recommendation that American B-26 bombers be brought into action, "probably followed up by U.S. or SEATO troops." Brown conceded that U.S. intervention would "blow wide open" international negotiations to resolve the situation peacefully. Nonetheless, he saw "no alternative" if the Pathet Lao pressed onward.

On receiving the cable, Kennedy immediately convened his top diplomatic and military advisers. In a lengthy session, Kennedy placed initial emphasis on diplomatic responses, sending messages to British and French leaders with whom he had been in regular contact on Laos and initiating diplomatic approaches to the Soviet Union. Brown's proposal for bombing the Pathet Lao was denied, but Kennedy did not rule out U.S. military intervention, saying it was the only card left to be played in an effort to exert pressure for a cease-fire. The following morning, April 27, he summoned a full-scale National Security Council meeting, in which his uniformed military advisers urged that U.S. ground troops be dispatched to Laos. A skeptical Kennedy questioned the practicality and consequences of the plan.

At this juncture Kennedy, even while the meeting was under way, decided to summon congressional leaders of both parties to discuss the possibility of U.S. intervention. Earlier in the month, Kennedy had consulted only Fulbright, and that on the spur of the moment, before the disastrous U.S.-sponsored invasion of Cuba at the Bay of Pigs. (Fulbright alone had dissented when Kennedy brought him into a planning meeting at the State Department with his national security team.) The only president since the Civil War who had served in both the House and Senate (although a relatively junior member in both), Kennedy understood the crucial importance of Congress in the U.S. constitutional system of separated powers, especially in the commitment and use of military forces. On this occasion, he had already received Mansfield's repeated warnings of the dangers of intervention in Laos and may well have expected that other senior lawmakers would also counsel caution.

The President began by reading aloud Brown's cable, starting with its melodramatic announcement, "Moung Sai has fallen," and continuing with Brown's recommendation of U.S. B-26 bombing in Laos, which, he said, had not been approved. Kennedy went on to describe the diplomatic contacts with the British, French, and Soviets he had initiated but which did not seem likely at that point to succeed. Secretary of Defense Robert McNamara described U.S. capabilities for immediate intervention, but he noted that the Joint Chiefs of Staff believed that U.S. forces "would not be able to win by conventional weapons alone" if the North Vietnamese or Chinese joined the battle. Kennedy added that earlier in the year, the Joint Chiefs had told him that "the communists could put into Laos five men to our one." Acting Secretary of State Chester Bowles reported that "some time ago the Chinese Communists had flatly stated that they would enter Laos if we did so." The President did not say what he was inclined to do but turned to the assembled lawmakers for their advice.

There was a long silence. Finally Mansfield spoke up, saying that if no one else chose to comment, he would do so. He had been thinking about Laos for a long time, he said. "The worst possible mistake we could make would be to intervene there. The Chinese Communists would come in and we would face a situation far worse than Korea." He analyzed at length the political and military situation in Laos, with which he was more familiar than any other member of Congress and most of the administration officials around the table. Fulbright and then Humphrey said they agreed with Mansfield.

Admiral Arleigh Burke, the chief of Naval Operations, spoke for the advocates of intervention. He began by agreeing with Mansfield that if the United States goes into Laos, "we have to be prepared for a war with China. . . . However, if we do not go into Laos we stand to lose all of Southeast Asia." He added, "If we go into Laos and find that we cannot hold our position we will eventually have to fight the Laotian war elsewhere, such as in North Viet-Nam, Hainan, and China." He then spoke of the possibility of using nuclear weapons in a spreading war. The choice, as he saw it, was "between what would likely be a long, tough, hard war or losing Southeast Asia without war." Under questioning, Burke amplified his view of the falling dominoes in Southeast Asia. Diplomat U. Alexis Johnson, who had been U.S. ambassador in Thailand, spoke of the dangers to Thailand and South Vietnam if Laos were overrun.

Burke's conversation about nuclear weapons and war with China, which Mansfield feared above all else, prompted the Majority Leader to speak up again, even more forcefully. When he had first visited Laos in 1953 only two American officials had been assigned there, but in the meantime "hundreds of millions of dollars had been spent and we had nothing in return." Mansfield agreed that if the United States intervened, "we may eventually have to face the possibility of using nuclear weapons." Reading portions of a *Washington Post* editorial that had been inserted into the *Congressional Record* by the Republican senator Everett Dirksen, the Senate Minority Leader, Mansfield declared flatly that no U.S. victory was possible in Laos.

Dirksen then spoke up in opposition to intervention, saying, "We would be fighting a war 11,000 miles from home and when we got through we would have nothing to show for it." Conservative Republicans Styles Bridges, Bourke Hickenlooper, and Leverett Saltonstall made clear they did not favor intervention. The crowning blows came from the highly respected Richard Russell, chairman of the Senate Armed Services Committee, who called war in Laos "an incredible fantasy from the beginning" and declared, "We should fight the first time and place where we have a commitment and an ally willing to fight for itself." Russell said, "[W]e should get our people out of Laos and write the country off." The powerful Speaker of the House of Representatives, Sam Rayburn, added that "the size of the war that we would face if we went into Laos was alarming" and questioned whether Laos was worth it.

At the end of the meeting, it was clear that the congressional leaders opposed military intervention, most of them strongly. This may well have been what Kennedy had hoped for, since a consensus of senior Democrats and Republicans in Congress might protect him from charges from the right that he had failed to act to save Laos. Before they departed, the President asked the lawmakers to keep their discussion confidential, saying that his "only card" in this difficult situation was "the threat of U.S. intervention and the uncertainty of the other side in this regard." He had made no decision, he pointed out, but the U.S. position would be seriously weakened if it were thought he had decided not to intervene.

Still deeply concerned, despite the unanimous view of the congressional leadership, Mansfield met privately for an hour with Kennedy in the early evening of May 1. There he handed the President his longest memorandum yet on the Laotian crisis—a six-page, single-spaced appeal for increased emphasis on diplomatic efforts to achieve a workable cease-fire and against U.S. military intervention. In the memo he made a plea not to oppose neutralist leader Souvanna Phouma, who was widely discounted or denounced in Washington circles but whom Mansfield described from personal experience as "a nationalist . . . an extremely astute man, skilled in eastern court politics and not without considerable knowledge of the West."

There had been much discussion in the official meetings on Laos about Vietnam as a better place to draw a line against the spread of communism in Southeast Asia. Ironically in view of later developments, Mansfield joined this chorus, writing that the United States should "concentrate our principal efforts in a place like Viet Nam where there is some hope for the future." He proposed that some of the military aid devoted to Laos be diverted to Ngo Dinh Diem's South Vietnam "in order to stiffen resistance to meet an anticipated increase in sabotage and terror." However, he also continued to place central importance on the political side of the Vietnamese problem, writing that military aid to Vietnam should be adjusted "at a level which is high enough to act against Viet Minh sabotage but not so high that it atrophies the will of the Viet Namese government to do what it must do to strengthen its ties among the Vietnamese people." Mansfield conceded it would take "great astuteness" to make such an adjustment and called for assignment of an "exceptional" diplomatic mission and aid team to Vietnam.

In those days of decision about Laos, the United States had been pressing urgently for a cease-fire between the U.S.-backed rightist forces and the leftist Pathet Lao. Ninety minutes before meeting Mansfield on May 1, Kennedy had received the first word from the CIA that a Pathet Lao delegation had made contact in the field with rightist troops, saying they wished to discuss a cease-fire. Two days later military commanders on both sides issued a cease-fire order. According to Arthur Dommen, a respected historian of the struggles in Laos, this marked "a definite transition of Western policy from a military to a political orientation." The Geneva Conference on Laos involving the three Laotian factions and major international participants on all sides, including the United States, China, and Soviet Union, convened on May 16. It took fourteen months of negotiations, pressures, and military muscle flexing after that, but the eventual result was an international agreement on a coalition government of the right, left, and center, headed by the neutralist Souvanna Phouma.

As the conflict in Indochina escalated, the desolate eastern part of Laos became home to the North Vietnamese supply line known as the Ho Chi Minh trail, close to the border of South Vietnam. U.S. bombing and other intervention concentrated heavily in that area for most of the war. Souvanna remained the nominal leader of a fragile government for most of the period before the communist victory in Vietnam in 1975. Shortly thereafter, the Pathet Lao seized power and proclaimed the Lao People's Democratic Republic.

Mansfield's views in April 1961 played a significant role in Kennedy's decision not to intervene militarily. Mansfield's several memoranda are the only materials regarding Laos from a member of Congress or any American outside of the administration that were found after Kennedy's death in the President's Office Files, the select group of documents kept for handy reference in the Oval Office. Many other factors also influenced the decision: the difficult military situation in Laos, the reluctance of Asian nations to contribute troops to U.S. operations under the theoretical umbrella of the Southeast Asian Treaty, the opposition of the other congressional leaders consulted by Kennedy, the views of U.S. allies in Britain and France, and the growing willingness of the Soviet Union to negotiate an accord. One of the most important factors stemmed from unrelated events on the opposite side of the world from Laos and ninety miles from American shores. The failure of the CIA-sponsored Bay of Pigs invasion of Cuba in mid-April had shaken Kennedy's confidence in his military advisers and in military solutions. After that, he was more skeptical and more willing to question assumptions and predictions. "Thank God the Bay of Pigs happened when it did," the President told his close aide, Ted Sorensen, in September 1961. "Otherwise we'd be in Laos by now—and that would be a hundred times worse."

A VERY DIFFERENT LEADER

The position of majority leader of the Senate is not mentioned in the U.S. Constitution or, until the aftermath of World War II, in any of the formal regulations established for the upper house of the U.S. Congress. It did not exist until the second decade of the twentieth century, when President Woodrow Wilson, who had been an academic observer and critic of "congressional government," supported a Democratic ally, John Worth Kern of Indiana, in the post of majority party floor leader, establishing the institution. Since then, according to historians of the Senate, the evolution to prominence of the post and of the parallel leadership position for the minority party, has been "the most significant institutional development of the Senate's history." Stripped to its essence, the power of the Majority Leader is based on senatorial courtesy and custom and especially on the right to be recognized first by the presiding officer ahead of all others seeking to speak on the Senate floor. This power of first recognition is more potent than it sounds, for it permits the Majority Leader to outflank any other senator in offering motions or amendments, and also to have the most important voice, rarely overruled, in shaping the nature and timing of Senate business.

No two majority leaders have been alike in their performance of the job, and no two were more dissimilar than Mansfield and the man he succeeded. Lyndon Johnson established an all-encompassing, all-consuming, and very personal leadership, which, after the Democratic Party returned to control of Congress following the 1954 congressional election, Johnson built to rival and often rebut the power of the Republican presidency of Dwight Eisenhower. Hardly anything or any vote was beneath the notice of this dominating and at times domineering leader. John G. Stewart, a political scientist who once served on the Senate staff, observed that Johnson "set for himself no less an objective than *running* the Senate, in fact as well as theory, by wielding decisive influence in generating majority support for the issues he permitted to come before the Senate for decision."

Johnson, during his final years as Majority Leader, had used his power to occupy a large suite of rooms close to the Senate chamber and redecorate them at taxpayers' expense so lavishly that the press and Capitol aides referred to the luxurious spread as the Taj Mahal. Here Johnson had met legislators and lobbyists requesting favors and entertained allies and, frequently, journalists following legislative victories on the nearby Senate floor. Summoned from the Press Gallery to such a celebration after a Johnson victory in my early days as a Washington reporter, I was awed by the easy access to senators and their top aides and the impressive flow of spirits from an open bar. After becoming vice president, Johnson initially refused Mansfield's request to vacate the Taj Mahal.

Rather than make an issue of it, Mansfield established his Majority Leader's office in a much smaller and less splendid suite that Kennedy as presidential candidate had used as an office during the post-convention session of Congress in the summer of 1960. Mansfield disapproved of the heavy drinking that had often lubricated the Johnson Senate and initially instructed Oscar Morris, an elderly African-American who was his major domo in the Capitol suite, to serve only coffee and soft drinks. Uninterested in fancy food or elaborate presentation, Mansfield surprised a White House lobbyist who stopped in to see the Majority Leader at lunch time: alone in a chair by the window, Mansfield was eating a hamburger over his trash can so that the meat juices would not spill onto the floor. When Maureen was out of town, staff members volunteered to prepare supper. "No, that's all right. I'll open up a can of beans," he told his Capitol office assistant, Salpee Sahagian.

In the role of majority leader as in his presidency later, Johnson was a dramatic, flamboyant, and towering figure, imposing and larger than life. Mansfield presented a stark contrast. Physically, he was "almost completely colorless," wrote journalist Frederick Collins, in an otherwise admiring profile of the Majority Leader in mid-1961 under the title, "How to Be a Leader without Leading," for the *New York Times Sunday Magazine.* "He is slightly built. The hue of his suits would depress an undertaker. His hair is dark and only adequate as coverage. His face is almost as pale as his shirt front, where a dark tie lies like a shadow. His smile is only a slight defrosting. He never cracks jokes or slaps backs."

Philosophically, Mansfield considered himself the leader of a Senate of individuals who were essentially his equals, with equal rights and responsibilities, rather than chess pieces to be moved around on a legislative board of his mastery. He privately abhorred Johnson's powerful pressures on senators to bend or conform, even to switch positions on legislation while the roll was being called to provide crucial votes. "I could not stand the way he dealt with people. . . . He was always getting something for your vote," Mansfield said later in life. He said and believed that the most effective persuasion in the long run, and the only sort he was willing to wield, was the appeal to logic and the public interest. "I don't collect any IOUs," he said. "I don't do any special favors. I try to treat all senators alike, and I think that's the best way to operate in the long run, because that way you maintain their respect and confidence. And that's what the ball game is all about."

Bobby Baker, the former Senate page from South Carolina whom LBJ had lifted to the position of secretary to the majority as his premier vote counter, manipulator, and confidant, observed that "working for Mike Mansfield, compared to working for Lyndon Johnson, was like lolling on the beach as opposed to picking cotton." After he left the Senate in disgrace in 1963 because of financial manipulations that eventually sent him to prison, Baker complained that when he wanted Mansfield to make decisions and deals, he found the leader sitting alone in his office, puffing his pipe and reading. Harry McPherson, a senior aide to both leaders in the Democratic Policy Committee, called the transition to Mansfield from Johnson "like going home to mother after a weekend with a chorus girl."

When he assumed the leadership, Mansfield announced that there would be few night or Saturday sessions and promised annual summer vacations rather than the long hours and uncertain schedules of the Johnson era. The response, according to McPherson, "was what one might expect from boys in a prep school when an old tyrannical headmaster, who believed in the redeeming power of work, was replaced by a permissive young don. . . . It was like a holiday for a time, and it inspired cooperation out of gratitude. Later there was grumbling that his reins were too loose, but there was no move to replace him; he was too much respected, no one else was so broadly accepted, and to discard him would have been a despairing judgment on the Senate itself—for he had permitted it to be what it was, a hundred disparate adults who ought to have been able to deal efficiently and responsibly with public affairs." Those who preferred the Johnson method, and even some who were repelled by Johnson's ways, questioned whether Mansfield was tough enough to be an effective majority leader. Asked by columnist Stewart Alsop whether his critics were right in this respect, Mansfield removed the pipe from his mouth and replied with characteristic terseness, "Yes."

From the first, Mansfield began to dismantle Johnson's highly centralized apparatus for exerting personal power in the Democratic majority. Faced with dissatisfaction about the allocation of places on leadership committees among northerners, westerners, and southerners, liberals and conservatives, Mansfield at the January 4 Democratic Conference made a commitment, formalized by a motion he himself proposed, that he would fill vacancies on the Policy and Steering Committees in a way "as representative as possible of the geographic and philosophic composition" of Senate Democrats as a whole. This he proceeded to do, but the fundamental change was in the operation rather than the membership of those bodies. Under Johnson, the committees met to ratify decisions that the leader had already made, often in the interest of enhancing his clout. Mansfield, however, listened to what others said in the Policy Committee about the merits and scheduling of legislation, usually accepted the consensus recommendations and delegated to others the responsibility for working out remaining snags and disagreements. In an even more radical change, Mansfield relinquished personal control over assignments to the Senate's legislative committees, leaving it to staff to match senators' requests with available vacancies, and resolving conflicts by consensus or secret ballot in the Steering Committee.

For all this, Mansfield was always clear about his own agenda. "He would sit back and smoke his pipe, and sphinx-like watch what happened," said Joseph R. L. Sterne, a *Baltimore Sun* correspondent who covered the Senate throughout the 1960s. "He always knew what he was doing. I think he had a very subtle mind. . . . He always enjoyed being under-estimated."

Unlike Johnson, Mansfield was "a conventional leader . . . a normal leader," according to George Smathers, who worked closely with both men. Smathers recalled that Mansfield "would call a meeting and say, 'Fellows, we've got this problem and here's what it looks like. Here's this side of it, and here's this side of it. So far as I can understand the Republicans are going to be here, and the President is going to be here, now what do we want to do?" This was completely different, he added, from his predecessor's method. "Johnson didn't believe in that kind of business. He had the Johnson program for all of this. . . . Mansfield was a consensus man. Johnson was the consensus."

By tradition, the Senate Majority Leader sits in the aisle seat in the front row of the majority side, and the Minority Leader sits across the aisle in parallel position. Johnson rarely left his privileged post except to button-hole recalcitrant senators while major business was at hand, and he virtually never let anyone else use it. Mansfield, however, turned over floor debate and management of most bills to the legislative committee chairman or other sponsor, who temporarily occupied the Majority Leader's chair. At such times Mansfield sat in the back of the chamber or left the floor entirely. His indifference to publicity and refusal to accept credit were sources of his strength within the institution; other senators appreciated the fact that he would leave the headlines to them.

Mansfield's relationships across the aisle were of crucial importance. Although a liberal Democrat in his voting record, he was never considered a strong partisan and was well respected by Republican senators. Beginning with his first year in the Senate, he ate breakfast nearly every working day with George Aiken, the Vermont Republican, who became probably his closest friend in the Senate. Both Mansfield and Aiken were early risers and had a habit of eating in the Senate cafeteria about 8 A.M. after working earlier in their offices. One day Aiken and his future wife, Lola, who was on Aiken's staff, came over to the table where Mansfield was eating alone and asked if they could join him. From then on, it was a regular breakfast date, in which Lola often joined. Aiken, like Mansfield, was an unassuming and widely respected figure and a skeptic, later an opponent, of the war in Vietnam. Neither was a strong partisan. Mansfield maintained they most often discussed the news of the day rather than politics, but there is little doubt he benefited from the sharing of viewpoints and intelligence with his Republican friend. Mansfield conceded after leaving the Senate that Aiken sometimes helped him politically "when I got into some sort of a difficulty."

Mansfield realized, as Johnson had before him, that Republican votes were essential to the passage of controversial legislation opposed by the conservative southerners, who made up about a third of the Democratic majority of the late 1950s and early 1960s. The Kennedy White House calculated that despite the nominal Democratic majority, pro-administration Democrats made up less than 50 percent of the Senate votes. Like Johnson, Mansfield was especially attentive to the conservative but pragmatic Minority Leader, Everett Dirksen of Illinois, whom the press corps dubbed "the wizard of ooze" because of his theatrical manner. Although Dirksen courted public attention assiduously and "did a good deal of acting on the floor of the Senate," Mansfield observed, he did a "good deal less acting in the back rooms when we met to discuss the potentials."

Mansfield went out of his way to praise Dirksen publicly before the 1962 election, when the GOP leader was opposed for reelection by the Democratic representative Sidney Yates. In discussions with the Kennedy White House, Illinois Democrat Paul Douglas objected that Mansfield's tribute had done "immeasurable damage" to Yates's campaign. The President, who also courted Dirksen, helped guarantee the GOP leader's reelection by sending an Air Force plane to bring him to the White House for high-level briefings on the Cuban Missile Crisis shortly before the election. Dirksen let it be known to the press that Kennedy had told him, "you've got [the election] in the bag." On the very eve of the election, Mansfield announced that Kennedy would provide a presidential airplane for the two Senate leaders to make a trip together to crisis areas of the world. This was "the final blow" to Yates's unsuccessful campaign, according to Douglas. As it turned out, Dirksen did not take the globe-girdling trip with Mansfield to Europe, the Middle East, and Asia immediately after the election, although three other members of the Senate did.

RELATIONS WITH KENNEDY

As Democratic leader of the Senate working with a Democratic president, Mansfield was in intimate and nearly constant communication with John Kennedy and his staff. Records at the John F. Kennedy Library list forty-two meetings of the two men following Kennedy's inauguration in 1961, fifty-three meetings in 1962, and fifty meetings in 1963, the last a breakfast in the living quarters of the White House on November 20, the day before the President departed on his ill-fated trip to Texas. The great majority of these were weekly presidential meetings with his congressional leadership while Congress was in session, but others were in-depth discussions of foreign affairs, such as the April 1961 meeting on Laos, or intimate talks of the two men alone or with only a few others. Mansfield also accompanied Kennedy in a state visit to Mexico in June 1962; met with him at Palm Beach, Florida, in December 1962; and accompanied him on a visit to Montana, including a stop at the Mansfield family home in Great Falls, in September 1963.

Coming after the relative inactivity of the Eisenhower years, during the last six of which Eisenhower was faced with a Democratic Congress, the Kennedy administration saw a torrent of legislative initiatives, more than a thousand legislative requests in three years, that seem modest only in comparison to the outpouring of activity under the Johnson presidency, which followed. The House of Representatives, where the old conservative coalition of Republicans and southern Democrats still held sway, was Kennedy's greatest legislative problem, but there were troubles in the Senate as well, particularly the defeat of the Medicare bill, for which the President had campaigned energetically. Walter Jenkins, for years the closest aide to Lyndon Johnson, said LBJ was disappointed in Mansfield's performance as Majority Leader, considering him "an introspective, sometimes perhaps impractical, theoretical fellow who may have been guided by the things the way he'd like to see them rather than things the way they are." Gerald Siegel, another Johnson aide, said Mansfield "didn't lead, really. He was kind of a coordinator. . . . It was seldom that he could take an issue and go out and build a campaign and win it. In fact, Mike's philosophy, I think, was, 'It's my role as Leader to make it possible for every senator to do what he wants to do.'"

Kennedy himself was at times frustrated by Mansfield's low-key, low-pressure approach, according to his domestic affairs aide, Ted Sorensen, and by what he felt were Mansfield's "excessive pessimism, caution and delays." Yet overall, Sorensen concluded, the President was "deeply appreciative of Mansfield's loyalty and labors, held him in close personal affection, and felt that no Senate leader in those years could have done better in the long run." The legislative accomplishments of the administration make a lengthy record, including the nuclear test ban treaty, trade expansion, tax reduction, an increase in the minimum wage, establishment of the Peace Corps, the Alliance for Progress to aid Latin America, and creation of the national educational television and communications satellite organizations, among others. In an extensive study of voting in the Senate, political scientist John G. Stewart concluded that "despite the dispersal of many tasks of party leadership and the generally permissive if not at times passive attitude displayed by the majority leader in managing the legislative program" the performance of Senate Democrats under Mansfield in 1961–1964 compared favorably and often surpassed their performance under Johnson in 1957–1960. Of course, having a president of one's own party made a huge difference.

Kennedy knew Mansfield well enough to appreciate how different he was from other political leaders. In striking pictorial illustration of this is a candid photograph of Vice President Johnson and congressional leaders as they completed a briefing for the press after a White House breakfast in September 1962. Johnson is holding his left hand to his chin pensively as he faces House Speaker John McCormack. Hubert Humphrey looks exuberantly toward his colleagues, while George Smathers looks pleasantly in the direction of the camera. Mansfield, however, has turned away from the others and is walking swiftly out of the picture, with only the back of his head to identify him. Kennedy had the photograph blown up to giant size and presented it to Mansfield with the affectionate inscription, "To Mike, who knows when to stay and when to go." Mansfield hung it in a place of honor in his office.

Mansfield was politically secure after his initial election to the Senate, yet he never failed to pay attention first to Montana affairs. As Majority Leader he continued to begin work very early every weekday morning in his Senate Office Building office, which was devoted to Montana affairs, usually by opening the mail himself and giving priority to anything from Montana. He almost never saw lobbyists for private interviews, except for those who were from Montana or represented Montana interests. In the envious position of representing a state that was far away, yet with a mere fraction of the population of the coastal states of the West or East, Mansfield was required to spend much less time and effort on constituent services than most of his Senate colleagues.

When Montanans did come to Washington and wish to "meet Mike," they would be guided by a junior staff member from the Senate Office Building to the ornate Senate Reception Room, where a page would be sent into the chamber to notify the Majority Leader that visitors had come to call. James Grady, at the time a junior aide to Mansfield's Senate colleague from Montana, Lee Metcalf, and later a well-known novelist (*Six Days of the Condor*) was frequently called upon to guide such groups. "After a few minutes, Mike would stroll out in one of those almost undertaker like suits, a striding confident, quiet motion. . . . Often Mike knew their names, so he did his own introductions. He led them over to the left hand corner seat, where he'd sit in the window box, and in the next 10 minutes say maybe two

things: 'Did you fly?' and something like 'Have you been taken care of?' The
constituents, usually led by one or two, would positively babble at him, usually general stuff, because they'd lobbied or special interested themselves out
to staffers before. Then—out could come a Senate page, a cookie-cut young
boy who the Montanans would adopt in a heartbeat, and usually in a voice
they didn't recognize as fairly staged and rehearsed, he'd say, 'Senator
Mansfield, they need you on the floor.' Mike would hold up his hand: 'I'll
be there in a minute. I'm busy with my friends now.' The page would walk
away. The constituents would tremble in awe at the respect/honor Mike
was showing them. They'd urge him to go, apologize for keeping him."
Mansfield would stand, say his farewells, and turn them over to Oscar
Morris, his major domo, with instructions to take them to the Family Galley
overlooking the Senate floor where they could observe their Mike as the center of authority. The story of their adventure would be recounted over and
over to everyone in earshot in Montana.

Because Montana was (and is) less affluent than the national average
and is the site of large U.S. forests, parks, and Indian reservations, the federal government played a large role there. The most important job of a senator or representative in the eyes of the Montana electorate "is to bring
home the bacon," according to Don Spritzer, a historian of the state's politics. "Mansfield was very good at that." A newsletter from his office in
October 1960, shortly before he became majority leader, reported that
Montana received $280 million in federal expenditures, with agricultural
expenditures and military spending at two large Air Force bases leading
the lists, compared with $144 million in federal taxes paid by residents.
The two-to-one ratio diminished only slightly during the Kennedy and
Johnson presidencies, although the amounts of U.S. spending and of U.S.
taxes each more than doubled due to inflation and increased economic
activity.

Both the Kennedy White House and the Johnson White House kept meticulous and detailed records of "favors granted" members of Congress. In
Mansfield's case they were almost all normal government contracts or projects,
invitations to White House bill-signing ceremonies or other meetings with the
President, and such minutiae as special sightseeing tours of the White House
for visiting constituents. The "favors" for Mansfield in 1961–1963 covered
eleven pages single-spaced and for 1963–1965 another nine pages. A March 1963

memo to Larry O'Brien, Kennedy's legislative liaison chief, from Chuck Daly, one of his aides, said, "This is one Senator who asks too little."

CUBA AND BERLIN

Even while dealing with the operations of the Senate and the demands of his constituents, Mansfield's greatest interest continued to be foreign affairs. After becoming majority leader, the demands on his time did not permit him to be as active as before on the Foreign Relations Committee. He rarely attended committee meetings, tending instead to operate alone in his interaction with the White House. Carl Marcy, the respected staff director of the Foreign Relations Committee, managed to recruit Mansfield to chair the Africa Subcommittee, a vacant post that for many years had evoked no interest from other Democratic members, despite the growing importance of independence movements on the continent. The Majority Leader accepted on the condition that the subcommittee would never meet. It did not do so during Mansfield's chairmanship.

Mansfield was active on the two foreign policy issues outside of Asia that dominated the agenda of the Kennedy administration: Cuba and Berlin. He had long been interested in Latin America, from the days at the University of Montana, where he had taught Latin American as well as Far Eastern history. As previously noted, he was a U.S. delegate to the 1948 Bogotá Conference, which established the Organization of American States. He was a delegate almost every year to the annual meeting of the Mexico–United States Interparliamentary Group, beginning with its inaugural meeting in 1961, and he acted as chairman of the U.S. delegation from 1969 until his retirement from the Senate in 1977.

He was taken aback by the disastrous Bay of Pigs invasion by U.S.-supported Cuban exiles in mid-April 1961. Immediately after the debacle, the initial foreign policy setback in the Kennedy administration, he was among a handful of congressional leaders called to two meetings with Kennedy to discuss the consequences. His was a voice of calm, in contrast to the intense frustration of the President and the bitterness bordering on hysteria among those who had played a part in the spectacularly unsuccessful venture. Amid growing talk of an outright invasion by U.S. troops to oust Castro, Mansfield drew up a four-page, single-spaced memorandum entitled "The Cuban

Aftermath" and took it to the President in person in the early evening of May 1, the same occasion when he handed him his written advice about Laos.

"The problem for us," he wrote, "is to face up to the fact that we have made a mistake. If we react in frustrated anger we are likely to intensify the mistake . . . if we yield to the temptation to give vent to our anger at our own failure, we will, ironically, strengthen Castro's position with his own people, jeopardize our relations with much of Latin America and do further damage to our position throughout the world." This is not to say, he continued, that the use of force by the United States should be ruled out in all circumstances. He believed that it could be justified if Cuba sought to take over the U.S. base at Guantanamo Bay by force, if Cuba invaded another country, or—showing remarkable prescience about what was to come and how it would be resolved—if force were required "to prevent the establishment of Soviet missile or any other kind of base *for Russian forces* in Cuba, *provided* we are seriously re-evaluating our own base policies on the rim of the Soviet Union" (emphasis in original). Seventeen months later Kennedy would learn that the Soviet Union had surreptitiously deployed missiles in Cuba. The United States threatened massive use of force and settled the argument with a secret but essential commitment to reduce U.S. missiles in Turkey on the rim of the Soviet Union.

When the missiles were discovered and Kennedy decided to demand their removal in October 1962, Mansfield was on vacation with Maureen in Florida. A military helicopter was sent to take him to McDill Air Force Base at Tampa, where an Air Force plane was waiting to fly him and George Smathers to Washington for a crisis conference with Kennedy. The two senators had no idea what the subject was and speculated it might be the hostilities between China and India. In the White House Cabinet Room immediately after their arrival, CIA experts briefed them on the placement of Soviet missiles in Cuba, and Kennedy told them about the blockade of Soviet shipping and other measures he planned to take. Mansfield said little in the meeting, except to disagree with the idea of an immediate U.S. invasion of Cuba that was advanced by Fulbright and Russell. Kennedy left the meeting to announce the crisis and his plans in a televised address, which Mansfield watched at the White House from Larry O'Brien's office. He thought that the speech was "excellent" and that it brought home to the American people the grimness of the situation. Later that evening he issued a statement that in this situation "the President's hand has been forced" by the Soviet buildup in Cuba. He reported that Kennedy's decision to confront the Soviet Union had the full support of the congressional leadership. In keeping with his deference to presidential authority in foreign affairs, Mansfield said the leaders recognized that "[Kennedy] and he alone had to make the decision in the light of all the facts available."

After another meeting of congressional leaders with Kennedy two days later, during which it was announced that some Soviet ships appeared to be turning way from Cuba, the lawmakers dispersed. When Mansfield traveled to Montana the next day, he noticed that military planes from Malmstrum Air Force Base in Great Falls, a Strategic Air Command base, had been dispersed to civilian airports in case of attack. The word several days later that the Soviets were removing the missiles came as a great relief.

A principal concern during the missile crisis had been the possibility of Soviet counteraction in that premier cold war flashpoint, Berlin. The East-West confrontation in Germany had long been a major concern of Mansfield's, who before becoming majority leader had made frequent speeches on the subject advocating negotiated solutions. In the spring of 1961, a renewed crisis was brewing over the strategic and symbolic city, divided between communist East Berlin and capitalist West Berlin. The topic was certain to be central to the late May summit meeting between Kennedy and the garrulous Soviet leader, Nikita Khrushchev, in Vienna.

Shortly before the summit meeting, Mansfield was informed by Kennedy's aide Ted Sorensen that diplomatic cables from Moscow predicted Khrushchev would take "a very hard and tough line." This prompted Mansfield to dispatch a lengthy memo of personal advice to his friend in the White House about the meeting, which, he believed, would set the tone for U.S.-Soviet relations for years ahead. His hope, he wrote Kennedy, was for a meeting of "an older man and younger man, each with great power and responsibility, ready to explore together soberly and without bombast new ways of achieving a more durable peace." But "if the meeting degenerates into a slug-fest of words, with each trying to prove he is stronger and more adamant than the other, then it would have been better had the meeting not taken place." In view of the reports of Khrushchev's hard line, he recommended that Kennedy inform the Soviet leader that the meeting should be postponed unless he was ready for "serious, sober, frank but quite preliminary discussions of the problems of peace," and that the President be prepared to walk out if the meeting degenerated into a propaganda exercise.

At the same time Mansfield let Kennedy know he was not happy with the new administration's initial foreign policy performance, which included the internal struggles over Laos and the dramatic failure at Bay of Pigs. "I am frank to say that our record in foreign relations since January, in my opinion, leaves much to be desired," he wrote. Although he approved Kennedy's "outstanding " statements on foreign affairs, "the performance of the bureaucracy is still little improved over the Eisenhower days. In some respects it has been worse. . . . Our remedies have been those of our predecessors, only more of the same."

The results of the Kennedy-Khrushchev summit were more serious than Mansfield imagined. Although they agreed to pull back from the confrontation over Laos—the one positive outcome of the meeting—in other respects it was close to a disaster. As Mansfield feared, Khrushchev sought to threaten and intimidate Kennedy, especially on the subject of Berlin, and "the younger man" left with the impression that "the older man" had succeeded in pushing him around.

Mansfield, who was briefed personally by Kennedy after the President's return to Washington, felt the summit had revealed to both sides "the hard kernel" of the Berlin problem. He decided to return to a proposal he had made more than two years before, during an earlier phase of the Berlin struggle: that a "third way" be found between the United States and the Soviet Union by neutralizing all of Berlin, both East and West, making it a free city with unrestricted access to both sides, guaranteed by all the great powers. In February 1959, Mansfield's proposal had attracted only modest interest, but now things were different. In the meantime he had become Democratic leader of the Senate and was known to be a friend and intimate adviser of the President, so the idea touched off an immediate and intense debate. Both East Germany and West Germany saw the plan as a threat to their sovereignty and ambitions and quickly rejected the proposal. West Germany sent its ambassador to the State Department asking that the idea be publicly disowned, which Secretary of State Dean Rusk did by stating that Mansfield had been speaking as one "individual senator" and that U.S. policy was unchanged. In the meantime Mansfield received an outpouring of mail,

which ran four-to-one against his ideas, and much editorial comment, ranging from praise from the *Washington Star* for his "fresh approach" to condemnation by the *New York Herald Tribune* for his "foolish impracticality"
that contributed to "a serious diplomatic blunder."

Mansfield maintained then and ever after that his proposal was his own
idea, not discussed in advance with Kennedy or any of his advisers. Being
essentially a repeat of what he had said—but under very different circumstances—two years earlier, that was understandable. After the controversy erupted, he defended his ideas in Senate debate, saying that he
would continue to advance his personal views despite his high position,
which on this occasion was "a cross I have to bear." He added, "Before any
senator is a majority leader, he is the senator of the state from which he
comes, and he is a senator of the United States. Before a senator has
responsibilities to any administration, he has responsibilities to the people
of the United States in the light of his conscience." However, he turned
down an invitation to be interviewed on Berlin on national television and
rejected an invitation to meet the Soviet ambassador, Mikhail Menshikov,
whom he had seen on several previous occasions, in order not to add fuel
to the fire. From that point on, the Majority Leader shied away from making controversial public proposals on most foreign policy issues while
Democrats held the presidency, although he continued to send confidential memoranda to the leaders on his views.

VIETNAM: THE FAULTY COMPOUND

The struggle in Vietnam, which was to dominate U.S. policy and eventually U.S. public opinion for a decade from the mid-1960s, was far from a top
priority in Washington in the early months of the Kennedy administration.
Only experts paid much attention to the growing insurgency in South
Vietnam following the decision by the Vietnamese Communist Party to
renew armed struggle in 1959 and the establishment of the National
Liberation Front as the struggle's political arm in December 1960, a month
before Kennedy came to office. Although the new President made some early
decisions to increase U.S. aid to the Saigon government, Laos rather than
Vietnam was initially the focus of U.S. attention in Southeast Asia. The disastrous Bay of Pigs invasion of Cuba in mid-April, followed by Kennedy's

decision to negotiate for a neutral coalition government rather than fight in Laos, created a crisis of confidence on the part of anticommunist regimes around the world, especially the embattled and increasingly unpopular South Vietnamese government of Ngo Dinh Diem.

In the summer and fall of 1961, many of Kennedy's senior aides pressured him to authorize much greater U.S. military involvement in Vietnam. At each point he delayed, disapproved, or watered down such moves.* A deterioration of morale in Saigon prompted a serious sense of crisis in September. Diem blamed U.S. policy in Laos, but more objective U.S. and Vietnamese officials blamed the regime's internal weaknesses. The sense of crisis was exacerbated by a sharp increase in Vietcong attacks. On September 18 a large force of guerrillas briefly occupied a provincial capital for the first time, publicly beheaded the province chief, and burned and ransacked provincial headquarters buildings. The *New York Times,* which placed an Associated Press account on its front page, commented in an editorial that the attack suggested the beginning of a new phase in the war, and that "Washington will face crucial decisions in the coming months not only over Berlin but in Southeast Asia as well."

In these circumstances, Mansfield addressed his first confidential memorandum to Kennedy on Vietnam on September 20. Characteristically, Mansfield began with his central idea about the struggle in South Vietnam, emphasizing its domestic political and economic roots: "The Vietnamese problem since 1955 has been a compound in which one part has been military and several non-military. Yet the remedy which has been applied to this problem has been a compound in which several parts have been military and only one part non-military." Mansfield would consistently

---

*Immediately after being pummeled by Khrushchev in their Vienna summit meeting in June, Kennedy told James Reston of the *New York Times* that it was necessary to prove to the Soviet leader that his leadership and U.S. power were credible, "and Vietnam looks like the place." This has given rise to the widespread belief that Kennedy was propelled into a deep commitment to Vietnam in 1961 by the desire to prove his manhood to Khrushchev. However, Robert Johnson, who was dealing with Vietnam and other Southeast Asian matters on Kennedy's National Security Council staff, told me there was no sign at the time that the President's concern about Khrushchev's attitude had extended to Vietnam or had caused him to alter his views on Vietnam, although it is well documented that he stiffened his policies toward Berlin, which was the principal bone of contention in the Vienna summit meeting. This view is reinforced by the extensive documentation on decision making in this period, especially the Pentagon Papers, which do not suggest a notable shift in Kennedy's attitudes or decisions on Vietnam following the Vienna meeting with Khrushchev.

emphasize this fundamental point throughout the policymaking about Vietnam. The presidents and their advisers would frequently give lip-service to this proposition but in fact give precedence to military solutions, considering the military difficulties to be more urgent and the nonmilitary problems, both political and economic, to be too intractable to be given top priority.

The recommendation to emphasize nonmilitary issues and means to deal with them was counter to the advice Kennedy was receiving from most of his senior aides. Beginning in October 1961, Kennedy came under strong pressure from U.S. officials to send American troops to reverse a deteriorating situation in Vietnam, where Diem for the first time agreed to accept U.S. combat forces under the guise of a "combat-training mission." In response, Kennedy dispatched his personal military adviser, General Maxwell Taylor, a former Army Chief of Staff, to Saigon to examine the situation and make recommendations. From the Philippines en route home on November 1, Taylor cabled his highly confidential recommendation to Kennedy that he deploy "an initial contingent" of 6,000 to 8,000 U.S. ground troops, with more to come if needed, to bolster Diem. Taylor's mission was well publicized, but his conclusions were not.

The day after the White House received Taylor's report, Mansfield weighed in with a strong and confidential memo to Kennedy "on this most important, delicate and dangerous situation." Sending U.S. troops "should be approached with the greatest caution" and "could become a quicksand for us" in view of potential Chinese intervention, Mansfield argued. He repeated the approach he had presented six weeks earlier and added more:

> While Viet Nam is very important, we cannot hope to substitute armed power for the kind of political and economic social changes that offer the best resistance to communism. If the necessary reforms have not been forthcoming over the past seven years to stop communist subversion and rebellion, then I do not see how American combat troops can do it today. I would wholeheartedly favor, if necessary and feasible, a substantial increase of American military and economic aid to Viet Nam, but leave the responsibility of carrying the physical burden of meeting communist infiltration, subversion and attack on the shoulders of the South Vietnamese, whose country it is and whose future is their chief responsibility. . . .

An involvement on our part can lead to four possible adverse effects:
(1) A fan-fare and then a retreat.
(2) An indecisive and costly conflict along the Korean lines.
(3) A major war with China while Russia stands aside.
(4) A total world conflict.

Against these four adverse possible consequences, there is the barest possibility of one salutary outcome. U.S. combat forces (not SEATO allied forces) might provide the bare margin of effectiveness which would permit a solution of the guerilla problem in South Viet Nam or prevent further encroachments southward—assuming of course that the Chinese Communists, let alone the Russians, do not become involved. Even then, we will have achieved a "victory" whose fruits, if we would conserve them, will cost us billions of dollars in military and aid expenditures over the years into the future.

Kennedy was pulled and hauled in opposite directions by his advisers as he approached the response to Taylor's recommendations. In the closest circle around him were his Secretary of State, Dean Rusk; his Secretary of Defense, Robert McNamara; his National Security Adviser, McGeorge Bundy; and Bundy's deputy who had taken special responsibility for Asia at the White House, Walt Rostow. All of these, in addition to the Joint Chiefs of Staff and the overwhelming majority of those elements of the national security bureaucracy consulted in this situation, advocated an explicit U.S. commitment with whatever it took to prevent the fall of South Vietnam to communism, including the deployment of U.S. troops. Arguing for caution rather than commitment were advisers in a second ring of access and power: Undersecretary of State George Ball, who had closely followed the futile struggles of the French in Indochina from a vantage point in Paris; Ambassador to India John Kenneth Galbraith, a skeptic about military action, who was in close contact with the Indian prime minister, Jawahjarlal Nehru; Senator Richard Russell, who had objected to U.S. military involvement in Vietnam from its start, when the Eisenhower administration had sent in military advisers; and Mansfield.

With the exception of Ball, the senior figures expressing opposition or caution to Kennedy about the use of American troops were "outside the loop" of day-to-day government reporting on conditions in Vietnam—reporting that eventually was proven to be faulty but that seemed at the time to be compelling. William Bundy, an important secondary figure in the first circle from his vantage point as Deputy Assistant Secretary of Defense, told me many years later that Mansfield had not been listened to seriously because "he didn't seem to have any expert knowledge of the immediate tactical situation" being discussed. Despite his perspective and wisdom, Bundy said, Mansfield had "no fingertip feel." This applied as well to most other advocates of caution.

Given the lineup of advisers and the political pressures for a muscular policy, especially in light of unpopular compromises in Laos, Kennedy made what seemed at the time to be a remarkably cautious set of decisions. In the climactic meeting with his advisers on November 11, nearly all of whom, except for his brother Robert, were on record as favoring stronger action, the President refused to accept the joint Rusk-McNamara recommendation for a formal U.S. commitment, including potentially unlimited numbers of ground troops, to prevent the fall of South Vietnam. Raising an issue that had been posed by Mansfield and others, Kennedy asked if the dispatch of U.S. troops would "mean a war with China." He also noted congressional problems in sending troops, because "Senator Russell and others are opposed." The only record ever found of this meeting, the sketchy notes by General Lyman Lemnitzer, chairman of the Joint Chiefs of Staff, did not specifically mention Mansfield.

Kennedy did agree to what seemed at the time to be secondary recommendations, modest compromises with his military-minded advisers: to provide immediately a variety of military support activities, such as U.S. helicopters with their crews, air reconnaissance personnel and equipment, and additional U.S. military aid and advisers, and to authorize Pentagon planning for full-scale deployment of ground troops if needed later. These steps were seen later as important moves down the slope to full-scale U.S. military intervention, although it is doubtful that Kennedy realized it at the time. An extensive study by the authors of the Pentagon Papers concluded that while debate raged over the deployment of ground troops, approval of the other measures was "apparently taken for granted." The first two companies of U.S. Army helicopter forces, numbering about 400 men, arrived in Saigon on December 11, 1961, one month to the day after Kennedy's decision. Nine days later the *New York Times* reported that uniformed U.S. troops and specialists were operating in battle areas with South Vietnamese

188

SENATOR MANSFIELD

forces and authorized to fire back if fired upon. By December 31, U.S. military personnel stationed in Vietnam had grown from 900 a year earlier to 3,205, and more were arriving day by day.

An important condition of the decisions Kennedy made in November had been obtaining Diem's agreement to implement basic political, economic, and military reforms, including broadening the political base of his regime and permitting greater U.S. involvement in Vietnamese decision making. After Diem refused to accept these changes, Washington proceeded with its military augmentation anyway rather than face a showdown with the Vietnamese leader. In January 1962, in a major expansion of the U.S. role, the Pentagon decided to place American military advisers with every battalion of the Vietnamese army, and at every province headquarters. Nonetheless, the arrival of more American military personnel did not halt the deterioration in South Vietnam.

Neither Congress nor the news media were paying much attention to Vietnam in early 1962, but Mansfield was watching the deepening U.S. involvement with growing apprehension. In June he seized public and official attention by speaking out against the trend in a commencement address at Michigan State University. The site for the speech was significant. A team of Michigan State experts led by Professor Wesley Fishel had been Diem's most important foreign advisers in the 1950s, operating under a contract with the Vietnamese government, and Fishel was one of Diem's most influential foreign friends. The relationship broke down as Diem became increasingly impervious to domestic and international opinion. When Fishel made a visit to Saigon in January 1962 after an absence of two and one-half years, he observed "a most profound and distressing deterioration there, politically, socially, and psychologically." Its contractual relationship and intimate ties at an end, Michigan State was pulling out of Vietnam as Mansfield spoke.

After briefly praising Diem as "a man for whom I have the highest respect and the deepest admiration," he went on to raise powerful objections to the course and results of U.S. policy. "After years of enormous expenditures of aid in south Viet Nam, that country is more, rather than less, dependent on aid from the United States," he declared, and its independent survival "less rather than more secure than it was five or six years ago." To avoid what Mansfield feared was "a collision course" to military conflict in Southeast Asia "of indefinite depth and duration, dependent largely on our forces for its prosecution," he proposed that the United States lighten its commitments in the region through vigorous diplomacy, using the neutralization accord with Laos as a model.

The speech caused concern in Washington and intense dismay in Saigon, especially because Diem's most important defender and protector of the mid-1950s could not be shrugged off as an irresponsible critic. Diem and his increasingly influential younger brother, Ngo Dinh Nhu, were particularly unsettled by Mansfield's contrast of embattled Vietnam with the relative peace and stability of the neutralist regimes in Cambodia and Burma, which were receiving little or no U.S. assistance. According to John Mecklin, chief public affairs officer of the U.S. Embassy, Diem and Nhu erroneously assumed that the speech had been cleared with Kennedy and represented a turnabout in high-level U.S. opinion. Jumping to the conclusion that the source of their problem was faulty reporting by the U.S. press, with which they were already at odds in Saigon, they intensified harassment of correspondents, which of course made matters worse.

Shortly after the speech, the Vietnamese ambassador in Washington, Tran Van Chuong, asked to see Mansfield's aide, Frank Valeo, to convey his views to the senator without doing so directly. Both Chuong, who served as Vietnamese ambassador to the United Nations, and his wife had an unusual inside view of their government because they were the parents of Madame Nhu, Ngo Dinh Nhu's flamboyant and controversial wife. Madame Chuong had written a letter of protest to Mansfield following the speech, arguing that "the instability in Viet Nam is definitely not home grown, it is master minded by the Communist world." Her husband, however, told Valeo that "the Diem government is in very deep trouble and has little prospects for survival" due to "family control, Diem's obliviousness to the realities around him [and] his mandarin tendencies which discourage any but relatives and 'secretaries' from working for him." Recalling how Mansfield in 1955 had demanded a cutoff of all U.S. aid if Diem were ousted, he appeared to be trying to discern Mansfield's attitude toward a likely coup. Valeo was noncommittal, saying the senator would probably follow the lead of the President.

Four months, later, on the eve of a trip by Mansfield to Vietnam, both Ambassador Chuong and his wife expressed even graver concern in a follow-up meeting with Valeo. Chuong said that despite the rapid increase in U.S.

military aid and activity, "there was not one chance in a hundred of eliminating the Viet Cong." The reason was the current structure in Saigon, which was dominated by their own son-in-law and daughter, Nhu and his wife, who were "absolutely drunk with power" to the detriment of Diem. When Valeo asked Madame Chuong if she had discussed her concerns with her daughter, she answered that she "didn't dare." If she raised such issues with her daughter, "she's crazy and probably will kill us," Valeo was told. He was amazed and dismayed, "because I really don't think of a daughter being that kind of threat to her parents." Ironically, both parents were murdered in 1986, apparently by their mentally disturbed son, Tran Van Khiem, who was found incompetent to stand trial.

BACK TO SAIGON

On November 29, 1962, at the most important point in a six-week trip through Germany, Greece, Egypt, Turkey, Iran, India, Hong Kong, and the Philippines, Mansfield arrived in Saigon for his first visit to Vietnam since 1955. He was greeted by greater U.S. official optimism than he had ever heard before, about a situation which seemed to him to have deteriorated alarmingly. Accompanied by Valeo and three Democratic senators, Claiborne Pell of Rhode Island, J. Caleb Boggs of Delaware, and Benjamin Smith of Massachusetts, he heard the U.S. ambassador Frederick (Fritz) Nolting declare in the course of an exhaustive four-hour briefing at the embassy that "we can see the light at the end of the tunnel"—the same optimistic phrase General Henri-Eugene Navarre had used in 1953. Nolting and the U.S. military commander, General Paul Harkins, predicted that the creation of armed "strategic hamlets," a plan that the United States and Vietnam had adopted from British tactics in Malaya, would be the turning point toward control of the Vietcong insurgency and should take place within the coming year.

Mansfield was not impressed, and even less so after his next appointment, a mind-numbing two and one-half hour meeting with Diem at the Presidential Palace. Instead of seriously discussing the problems facing the country, Diem launched into his standard monologue of his own history and that of Vietnam, his regime, and its activities. There seemed to be no recognition that Mansfield had carefully followed the Indochina situation for years or that Mansfield was the person whom he had first met in 1953, who had saved him from being ousted by the French and Americans in 1954 and

1955, with whom he had corresponded several times since, and who had publicly praised him in almost every speech he had made about Vietnam. After this one-sided harangue and a brief talk at a black tie dinner that Diem hosted for the delegation, Mansfield wrote in a memorandum for his files that "President Diem is a depressed man and I think he has a feeling of lack of accomplishment." Later he recalled that "Diem seemed to have turned into a recluse. . . . He wasn't the Diem I knew, so the only conclusion I could come to, and it was at best a guess, an estimate, was that he had fallen under the influence of his brother and his wife, and they were taking over control."

The following day Mansfield met Diem's powerful brother, Ngo Dinh Nhu and, separately, his flamboyant wife. Nhu claimed that two-thirds of the South Vietnamese population would be living in strategic hamlets within a month, a far-fetched claim. Separately, both Nhus sharply criticized the tiny American press corps in Saigon as the source of their troubles in Washington. "The Nhus are very aggressive but are, I believe, whistling in the dark to keep up their hopes," Mansfield wrote in his memorandum.

On the second and last full day of his visit, Mansfield met alone at a lengthy lunch with four of the journalists who had been the subjects of the Nhus' complaints, David Halberstam of the *New York Times,* Neil Sheehan of United Press International, and Peter Arnett and Malcolm Browne of the Associated Press. Mansfield considered journalists an important source of information, often more credible than government briefings. As was often the case in his travels, he initiated the private meeting in Saigon to hear their views. The reporters gave him an earful of their problems with the Diem regime and the U.S. mission, which sought to discourage or rebut any negative reporting. Halberstam, who did much of the talking, said the Vietnamese army was losing, not gaining, ground and that Diem was disrupting the war effort rather than leading it. Halberstam recalled, "We were quite pessimistic, but in terms of what was to come later, we were reasonably mild. . . . What was clear was that Mike Mansfield was really listening. He wanted to know."

At Tan Son Nhut airport the following morning, Mansfield rejected a suggested departure statement the embassy had drafted for him expressing "real encouragement" about what his delegation had found and congratulating the government and people of Vietnam "on your notable progress toward victory." Instead he delivered a statement praising Diem as a man of integrity and honesty but making no comment about the status of the war. Privately he wrote, "I came away with a feeling of depression and with the belief that our chances may be a little better than 50-50, being that the decision and initiative rest not with the United States but with Vietnam itself." Halberstam reported Mansfield's refusal to accept the embassy departure statement in the *Times*, which accompanied the story with a photograph of Mansfield under the headline, "Mansfield Is Cool on Vietnam War."

After returning to Washington, Mansfield presented two reports on Vietnam and Southeast Asia, a candid but guarded public report on behalf of all four senators on the trip and a confidential report by him alone to Kennedy. The public report created new concern in Washington and Saigon when it was released. According to Ambassador Nolting, the press coverage it generated constituted "the first nails in Diem's coffin." General Harkins thought Mansfield's visit the first "crucial turning point" against Diem. It was, however, the private report to a chosen audience of one that was more extensive and more powerful. Based on a stay of only two full days in Vietnam, without ever venturing outside Saigon, Mansfield managed to cut through the false hopes and bureaucratic optimism and to outline in prophetic terms the grave dangers that lay ahead. Mansfield wrote to Kennedy:

One thing is reasonably clear: From somewhere about 1956 or '57, the unusual combination of factors which had resulted in the establishment of the Republic under Ngo Dinh Diem began to lose its impulse. . . . It was distressing on this visit to hear the situation described in much the same terms as on my last visit although it is seven years and billions of dollars later. Viet Nam, outside the cities, is still an insecure place which is run at least at night largely by the Vietcong. The government in Saigon is still seeking acceptance by the ordinary people in large areas of the countryside. Out of fear or indifference or hostility the peasants still withhold acquiescence, let alone approval of the government. In short, it would be well to face the fact that we are once again at the beginning of the beginning. . . .

Ngo Dinh Diem remains a dedicated, sincere, hardworking, incorruptible and patriotic leader. But he is older and the problems which confront him are more complex than those which he faced when he pitted his genuine nationalism against first, the French and Bao Dai and then against the sects with such effectiveness. The energizing role which he played in the past appears to be passing to other members of his family, particularly to Ngo Dinh Nhu. . . . In a situation of this kind there is a great danger of the corruption of unbridled power. . . .

There is optimism that success will be achieved quickly. My own view is that the problems can be made to yield to present remedies, *provided* the problems and their magnitude do not change significantly and *provided* that the remedies are pursued by both Vietnamese and Americans (and particularly the former) with great vigor and self-dedication [emphasis in original].

Certainly, if these remedies do not work, it is difficult to conceive of alternatives, with the possible exception of a truly massive commitment of American military personnel and other resources—in short going to war fully ourselves against the guerrillas—and the establishment of some sort of neo-colonial rule in south Vietnam. That is an alternative which I most emphatically do not recommend. On the contrary, it seems to me most essential that we make crystal clear to the Vietnamese government and to our own people that while we will go to great lengths to help, the primary responsibility rests with the Vietnamese. Our role is and must remain secondary in present circumstances. It is their country, their future which is most at stake, not ours.

To ignore that reality will not only be immensely costly in terms of American lives and resources but it may also draw us inexorably into some variation of the unenviable position in Vietnam which was formerly occupied by the French. We are not, of course, at that point at this time. But the great increase in American military commitment this year has tended to point us in that general direction and we may well begin to slide rapidly toward it if any of the present remedies begin to falter in practice.

KENNEDY AND THE
PROSPECT OF WITHDRAWAL

The President received the report on December 18, the day after Mansfield and his party returned to Washington and as the city was emptying out in preparation for the Christmas–New Year holidays beginning the following week. Like the Kennedys, the Mansfields were escaping the capital to spend the vacation in Florida. To hear from the Majority Leader directly, Kennedy invited Mansfield to visit him at his vacation home in Palm Beach on the day after Christmas, December 26.

Kennedy, his wife, Jacqueline, their daughter, Caroline, two family dogs, and a few other family and friends were sailing on the presidential yacht. The yacht had been inherited from Presidents Truman and Eisenhower and renamed by Kennedy the *Honey Fitz* for his maternal grandfather, the former mayor of Boston John F. "Honey Fitz" Fitzgerald, for whom the President himself was named. The Mansfields, who had been delayed en route, caught up with the Kennedy party via a Secret Service speedboat on the Inland Waterway. It was a beautiful sunny afternoon. Kennedy, in a blue sport shirt and white slacks, guided the Majority Leader to a chair on the aft deck, his favorite spot, where he slowly read Mansfield's report, evidently for the first time, page by page. As he reached the critical assessment of conditions and potential dangers in Vietnam, the senator could see the President's neck and face reddening with anger. Kennedy objected, "This is not what my advisers are telling me." Mansfield would not back off, but pointed out, "You asked me to go to Vietnam" and that the report was the result.

Mansfield later recalled that in addition to his written observations, "I strongly advised a curb and then a withdrawal of U.S. troops. I pointed out that if the momentum of introduction of U.S. troops was not halted, it would create a desire—not necessarily a need—for more troops to be sent to beef up those who were there." This course eventually would lead, he said, to "a predominant American presence which would be counterproductive to this country's interests as well as Vietnam's." Kennedy did not comment on Mansfield's recommendations, although he did question his friend closely—Mansfield thought at times aggressively—on comments and conclusions in the report. Kenneth O'Donnell, who was not present at the conversation, said the President later told him about the discussion on the *Honey Fitz* and said, "I got angry at Mike for disagreeing with our policy so completely, and I got angry with myself because I found myself agreeing with him."

There the matter stood until sometime in the spring of 1963, when Mansfield spoke out during a congressional leadership breakfast at the White House against the continuing drift of U.S. policy in Vietnam. Kennedy, annoyed and embarrassed by the outburst, asked O'Donnell to bring Mansfield to the Oval Office for a private chat after the breakfast. The conversation that followed has stirred controversy among historians and touched off repeated bouts of speculation about Kennedy's plans and intentions regarding Vietnam in 1963.

According to O'Donnell, who sat in on part of the discussion,

The President told Mansfield that he had been having serious second thoughts about Mansfield's argument and that he now agreed with the senator's thinking on the need for a complete military withdrawal from Vietnam.

"But I can't do it until 1965—after I'm reelected," Kennedy told Mansfield.

President Kennedy felt, and Mansfield agreed with him, that if he announced a total withdrawal of American military personnel from Vietnam before the 1964 election, there would be a wild conservative outcry against returning him to the Presidency for a second term.

After Mansfield left the office, the President told me that he had made up his mind that after his reelection he would take the risk of unpopularity and make a complete withdrawal of American forces from Vietnam. "In 1965, I'll be damned everywhere as a Communist appeaser. But I don't care. If I tried to pull out completely now, we would have another Joe McCarthy red scare on our hands, but I can do it after I'm reelected. So we had better make damned sure that I *am* reelected."

The idea that Kennedy had decided to terminate the U.S. troop presence appeared to be given added credence by his decision, announced at the White House on October 2, 1963, to withdraw 1,000 troops from Vietnam by the end of that year. This cutback (out of a total at the time of about 16,000 U.S. military personnel) was cited by O'Donnell and other Kennedy loyalists as tangible evidence of JFK's intention to pull out of Vietnam, in stark contrast to the action of his successor, Lyndon Johnson, who sent more than half a million U.S. troops to the war zone. However, the preponderance of historical evidence is that this was intended to be a tactical adjustment, based on the optimistic conclusion by McNamara and Taylor, by then chairman of the Joint Chiefs of Staff, that "the major part of the U.S. military task can be completed by the end of 1965," rather than a strategic move toward withdrawal.

Mansfield, whose memory of people and events was remarkable throughout his long life, recalled the Oval Office conversation with Kennedy on numerous occasions from the time it was first raised with him by a writer on behalf of O'Donnell in 1969, six years after the event, until the last interview in which he and I discussed it in 1999. However, he remembered the details of Kennedy's statement in different terms on many of those occasions.

In his first rendition, in an October 1969 letter to freelance writer Joe McCarthy, who had queried him on behalf of O'Donnell, he recalled that Kennedy said "he was seriously considering the withdrawal of all U.S. troops from Viet Nam if he were elected to a second term." (McCarthy and O'Donnell evidently used Mansfield's letter as a guide to parts of their account.)

After the publication of the *Life* magazine account in August 1970, however, Mansfield answered two letters by saying he understood Kennedy was considering "a withdrawal" of troops, without specifying its extent. He also denied in one letter that the next presidential election was "even mentioned or thought of." A letter from Mansfield to a Kent State University professor in 1975 said Kennedy had been determined "to withdraw our forces from Vietnam," again suggesting a complete pullout. In a 1989 letter to another author Mansfield said Kennedy planned to begin the withdrawal of "some troops" following the next election. In my first discussion of the issue with him, in June 1998, he said Kennedy planned to begin after the 1964 election to begin withdrawing troops at the rate of 1,000 or so per month (which actually took place in October 1963). In his last discussion of the issue with me, in October 1999, he said Kennedy planned to perhaps make "some minor withdrawals" after the 1964 election.

Based in part on Mansfield's conversation with Kennedy, some commentators believe that Kennedy intended and even planned to terminate the U.S. military involvement in Vietnam during his presidency. Others have suggested that, even taking the conversation at maximum face value, Kennedy would have been forced to change his mind after the struggle between Diem and the Buddhists erupted in full force in Vietnam in the summer of 1963 and especially after Diem and Nhu were killed in November, only weeks before Kennedy's own death at the hands of an assassin. Still others, pointing to public statements by Kennedy, have expressed doubt that he ever intended to withdraw, suggesting that he might simply have been telling Mansfield what he knew the senator wanted to hear.

When I asked Mansfield if he believed that Kennedy would have withdrawn the troops from Vietnam had he lived, Mansfield replied, "Barring unforeseen circumstances, he might have. I can't say he would have."

Historians have used a great deal of paper and ink debating the question, which probably never will be settled.

Mansfield was in the habit from time to time of writing handwritten messages to himself, often headed with the word "Idea," to summarize and perhaps solidify his thinking. In the summer of 1963, as escalating conflict with the Saigon regime gave rise to grave doubts about the future of Diem and Vietnam and became a high-priority, day-to-day issue for American policymakers, he penned such a memorandum in sloping penmanship on six pages of a legal pad, headed "Idea: Viet Nam—Southeast Asia." It is evidence of his growing conviction that the United States had no vital interest that could justify the extensive expenditure of American lives and treasure in Southeast Asia.

"While it is probably true," he wrote, "that the fall of Viet Nam may mean the fall of Southeast Asia to hostile governments and forces, what does the survival of Viet Nam or, specifically, the Diem government in Viet Nam, mean? It means the continuance of the U.S. involvement at a high cost to the United States in Viet Nam for years on end. It means the continuance of or being subjected to blackmail demands by any government on the mainland on the grounds, too, that its fall would mean the loss of the entire area to hostile governments and forces." If Vietnam is vital to regional stability, he reasoned, the same might be said of Laos, Thailand, Malaya, or even Cambodia, Burma, or Nepal. The question is, however, whether maintaining the status quo in Southeast Asia is "*really* vital to our interests or is, in fact, peripheral to them." Answering his own question, Mansfield wrote that the great national interest in Southeast Asia as currently pursued appeared to be the negative one of "denial of that region to Chinese domination." But this was being pursued "not so much, it would seem from a rational evaluation of our interests, but from an essentially irrational fear of China and, perhaps even more pointedly, from a fear of domestic political consequences and, perhaps, on the basis of the fear of the bureaucracy for its function—since much of it is dependent on the maintenance of the present situation."

China, the central power in Asia, continued to be at the heart of his thinking about the region, as it had often been since he first went ashore as a U.S. Marine. In summary, he wrote to himself of U.S. policy:

Most significant is that the continuance in this present situation may well be at variance with our fundamental and, indeed, vital interest in Asia and may be inhibiting its pursuit. Historically that interest has centered on China. As evolved, that interest is defensible as the maintenance of friendly relations with the people of that country and, as far as possible, with their government and failing that, insuring that Chinese hostility is not greater toward us than it is toward any other leading power which may be involved. In the past decade and a half, however, not only have we failed to maintain friendly contact with the Chinese people and its government, but we have also been the number one target of their hostility. It may be that the break between Russia and China will now bring a change but it will not bring us any closer to the restoration of a system for defending our vital historic interest in the Far East so long as we persist in the present approach to policy in Southeast Asia.

His handwritten "idea" was the core of an eight-page private memorandum to Kennedy on August 19, which Kennedy had asked for as disorders continued in Saigon and sentiment was building in Congress and within the high councils of the administration for intensified pressure on Diem that might lead to his ouster. Mansfield's eight-page memorandum of "Observations on Viet Nam" in only two copies—his and Kennedy's—argued for lessening, rather than increasing, the U.S. stakes in the war. A notation with the carbon copy retained in Mansfield's files indicates that the senator personally handed the original copy to the President. This most likely took place when Mansfield attended a congressional leadership breakfast with Kennedy at the White House on August 20.

Mansfield's disenchantment with Diem, resulting from his visit to Saigon, was so great that in the opening paragraphs of the memo he described the issue of whether to continue to support Diem's government or replace it as a "secondary or tactical question" to be decided on the basis of what would be least costly in American lives and money—a far cry from his adamant and effective defense of Diem in the 1950s. Whatever happens with Diem, he wrote, "we are in for a very long haul to develop even a modicum of stability in Viet Nam. And, in the end, the costs in men and money could go at least as high as those in Korea." Before the die is finally cast, he continued, the fundamental questions should be addressed:

Is South Viet Nam as important to us as the premise on which we are now apparently operating indicates? Is it really as important to us as it is to the

Vietnamese themselves? Or have we, by our own repeated rhetorical flourishes on "corks in bottles" and "stopping Communism everywhere" and loose use of the phrase "vital interests of the nation" over the past few years given this situation a highly inflated importance and, hence, talked ourselves into the present bind? In short, have we, as in Laos, first over-extended ourselves in words and agency programs and, then, in search of a rationalization for the erroneous initial over-extension, moved what may be essentially a peripheral situation to the core of our policymaking consideration?

Holding the line in South Vietnam was far from essential for U.S. defense or the U.S. economy, Mansfield wrote. Following from his handwritten "idea," he stressed that the most compelling argument for a vast U.S. commitment in Southeast Asia was "the negative one of denying the resources of the region to Chinese domination." But in the absence of an international interest in this objective, he asked how great a cost in men and money could be justified by essentially unilateral action to block China. In this situation, he declared, "Viet Nam is not central to our defense interests or any other American interest but is, rather, peripheral to these interests." Therefore, he argued, the way out of the current bind in Saigon "is certainly not by the route of ever-deeper involvement."

To be sure it is desirable that South Viet Nam remain free of Communism but it is also desirable that we do not spend countless American lives and billions of dollars to maintain an illusion of freedom in a devastated South Viet Nam. And it is also desirable that we do not find ourselves, militarily, so bogged down in South Viet Nam or throughout Southeast Asia that we have few resources, short of nuclear, for deployment elsewhere in other critical peripheral situations.

Having warned about the consequences of growing U.S. intervention, Mansfield went on to propose ways to diminish, rather than to expand, the U.S. role. Several were changes in the rhetoric used to describe the U.S. stakes. One was practical, an abrupt and "symbolic" withdrawal of perhaps 10 percent of U.S. advisers in Vietnam as a demonstration to the Diem government that the U.S. commitment is not unlimited. Planning for the 1,000-troop withdrawal, which would be announced six weeks later, was already under way, although predominantly on a different premise, that the war was being won and these advisers could be spared.

As Kennedy was considering his advice, events moved rapidly toward a final showdown with Diem and Nhu. On August 21, Vietnamese special forces troops under orders from Nhu attacked Buddhist pagodas throughout Vietnam, arresting monks and sacking the sacred buildings. This dramatic action intensified the internal struggle in Vietnam and led to a cable from the Kennedy administration on August 24 that for the first time expressed active U.S. support for a military coup against Diem.

Mansfield, who in 1954 had publicly suggested that the United States should immediately suspend its aid to Vietnam if Diem were ousted, was silent nine years later as plans were made and implemented to overthrow him. On November 1, when the first word of the military coup against Diem was received—but before news that Diem had been killed—Mansfield issued a statement saying that the uprising "came as a complete surprise to me, and I am quite certain a surprise to the administration." In fact, the administration had approved and even promoted the coup. Unlike the situation in the mid-1950s when he was consulted at every turn, there is no indication that he was consulted about the coup plan this time. Nonetheless, it is difficult to believe that Mansfield, who read the newspapers closely and who was usually well informed about the government's plans, was so surprised and so ill-informed.

After news of Diem's death was received, Mansfield harked back to memories of earlier times, declaring in a Senate speech, "It is tragic that a leader who began by accomplishing so much that was constructive with so little, that a government which began with so much promise in the end crumbled in military coup and violent death, a situation which I deeply and personally regret." He went on to say that the events in Saigon were "a clarion call for a reassessment of U.S. policies with respect to Vietnam and southeast Asia," and that the outcome of the reassessment should be a reduction of U.S. involvement, rather than an increase. Dispirited by what had happened, he told Valeo, "I want to get out of this whole [Vietnam] thing. They'll get somebody else [in Saigon]. They'll go through this whole process all over again. Each time it will get worse." Beyond the Senate speech, however, it does not appear that Mansfield was active at this stage in promoting his point of view on either the past or the future in South Vietnam. When

Secretary of State Rusk appeared in closed session of the Foreign Relations Committee in the immediate aftermath of the coup, Mansfield attended but remained silent.

Perhaps remembering his hopes for Diem in the 1950s, Mansfield in later years had nothing but praise for Diem as the one person who might have led Vietnam to a secure and successful existence. When the subject of the Vietnamese leader came up for the first time in our conversations in July 1998, he declared emphatically, "I didn't have any respect for his brother, Nhu, nor for Nhu's wife, but I was for Ngo Dinh Diem *all the way*," swinging his arm into the air for emphasis. "Once he was assassinated, things went from bad—admittedly—to worse, and worse, and worse."

Differences over Vietnam, to the extent that they existed, did nothing to diminish the friendship between John Kennedy and Mike Mansfield. Less than a week after the contentious discussion on the *Honey Fitz* on December 26, 1962, Kennedy invited Mansfield to join him in the presidential helicopter to attend the Orange Bowl football game on New Year's Day in Miami. The two conferred intensively on the way down about the consequences of the recent death of Robert Kerr, the powerful Oklahoma senator.

When Kennedy was considering U.S. initiatives toward the Soviet Union in June 1963, he asked Mansfield to accompany him on a trip to Honolulu, during which they went over the plans. The key point was U.S.-Soviet negotiations for a treaty prohibiting nuclear weapons tests in the atmosphere. As Kennedy certainly anticipated, Mansfield heartily approved Kennedy's steps toward reducing cold war tensions, which were announced in JFK's speech at American University in Washington on June 10. When the treaty was completed and sent to the Senate for ratification, Mansfield helped to round up support. At a crucial moment in its consideration, Mansfield accompanied his Republican counterpart, Everett Dirksen, to an off-the-record meeting with the President, at which the three of them worked out final arrangements. Two days later, in an emotional speech that surprised and disappointed many conservatives, Dirksen announced his support for the treaty, saying "I should not like to have written on my tombstone, 'He knew what happened at Hiroshima, but he did not take a first step.'" With Republican support, the treaty was ratified on September 24 by an 80 to 19 margin.

Within hours after the Senate vote, Kennedy left Washington on a political fence-mending tour of eleven western states, including Montana. Earlier in the year, Mansfield had asked Kennedy to arrange a presidential visit in 1964, when Mansfield was up for reelection to the Senate, but this trip was a White House initiative. On September 25 Mansfield and his Senate colleague from Montana, Lee Metcalf, met Kennedy at Billings, the most populous city in the state but one considered normally Republican. Kennedy's earlier speeches about conservation, the designated theme of the tour, had been duds, in the opinion of almost everyone. At Billings, his praise for Mansfield and Dirksen for leading the way to ratification of the test ban treaty was greeted by enthusiastic and prolonged cheering and applause. Apparently surprised by the reaction, Kennedy launched further into a theme of easing tensions and dangers of the nuclear age. Stabbing his right forefinger in the air, his voice rising, he reviewed the recent nuclear confrontations over Berlin and Cuba. "What we hope to do," he declared, "is lessen the chance of a military collision between these two great nuclear powers which together have the power to kill 300 million people in the short space of a day. That is what we are seeking to avoid. That is why we support the test ban treaty. Not because things are going to be easier in our lives, but because we have a chance to avoid being burned." Almost by accident, according to the historian Arthur Schlesinger Jr., Kennedy had discovered a new and worthy theme that he continued to advance in the last two months of his life.

The following day Kennedy, accompanied by Mansfield and Metcalf, landed in Great Falls, but instead of going directly to the stadium for his speech, the President directed his traveling party to the small frame bungalow of Mansfield's father, Patrick. The ten-minute stop was Kennedy's idea, against the better judgment of the senator, who felt the modest house in a rundown section of town was unsuitable for a presidential visit. About 4,000 people were gathered in the neighborhood, perched on lawns, porches, and every available ladder, when the motorcade arrived. The Mansfield family, gathered at the house, waiting, was amazed at the preparations, especially the installation by White House officials of a red phone in the parlor in case of emergency when the President was there.

Patrick Mansfield had moved to Montana in 1925 to help operate his aunt Margaret's corner store. After she died and the store went out of business, he worked for the city, the city water department, and later the gas company in blue collar jobs, one of which was watering grass on the verge between sidewalks and the street. The senator also introduced his half-brothers, John, an accountant, and Joe, a captain in the Great Falls Fire Department. "What do you think of your son? I think he is doing a pretty good job," the President said to Patrick, who was eighty-seven years old and still vigorous. (He would live until eighty-nine, an unusually long life for a member of his generation.) "I think both of you are doing a good job. God bless you," was Patrick's reply. After they left, Kennedy commented to O'Donnell, "I wonder how many majority leaders in the United States Senate have had a brother still working in the hometown fire department."

Publicly, Mansfield praised the people of Montana, saying that the state "did itself proud" in the way it welcomed Kennedy with record-sized crowds. Privately he was relieved that the tour had ended without incident. "Thank God, he got out of this state without being harmed," he told Peggy DeMichele, his Washington secretary.

SAVING KENNEDY

In the autumn of 1963, a hidden scandal threatening the President was slowly rising toward the surface in Washington. Action by Mansfield and Dirksen averted a potential disaster for the popular President.

On July 3, FBI director J. Edgar Hoover, with whom the Kennedys had an uneasy relationship, informed Attorney General Robert Kennedy, his nominal boss, of an informant's claim that the President had had a sexual relationship with Ellen Rometsch, the twenty-seven-year-old wife of an airman attached to the West German military mission in Washington. Rometsch had grown up in East Germany and had become a member of communist youth groups before fleeing to West Germany at age seventeen. An attractive brunette, she became a part-time "party girl" in political circles, including at some events arranged by Bobby Baker, the Lyndon Johnson protégé who was secretary of the Senate majority. According to Baker, Bill Thompson, a lobbyist close to Senator George Smathers, on several occasions took Rometsch to the White House, where she had sexual relations with the President. Baker said Kennedy had called to thank him for helping to make the arrangements, saying that Rometsch had provided the best oral sex he had ever had.

Under investigation by the FBI, Rometsch denied spying for East Germany—an allegation that could have raised a scandal of international proportions, similar to the then-recent scandal involving the British defense minister, John Profumo. The FBI unearthed no evidence disproving her claim. She also denied having liaisons with the President, although there was information to the contrary on this point. Robert Kennedy, who was the defender and protector of his brother, took no chances. In August he arranged to have Rometsch suddenly sent back to Germany, accompanied by Lavern Duffy, one of the attorney general's closest friends and former aides. There the matter rested until one of the leading investigative reporters of the day, Clark Mollenhoff of the *Des Moines Register,* began looking into the case. On October 26, he reported Rometsch's sudden expulsion from the country and said her relationship with senators as well as "several high executive branch officials" was being investigated by the Senate Rules Committee as part of its investigation of Baker's financial and legislative activities. Mollenhoff often worked closely with Republican senator John Williams of Delaware, a hard-digging member of the committee, who frequently attended the daily breakfasts of Mansfield and Aiken.

With the Rometsch story breaking and a Senate committee preparing to investigate, Robert Kennedy called on Hoover for emergency help. Coming to the office of the FBI director, who in the past had been summoned by the attorney general to his supposedly superior office, Kennedy proposed on behalf of himself and the President that Hoover privately persuade Mansfield and Dirksen that no national security breach was involved in the Rometsch case, a conclusion that could permit them to suppress this aspect of the Senate inquiry. Hoover agreed. In the meantime Mansfield, alerted by the administration, invited the FBI director to his home, where a meeting with the two Senate leaders would not attract attention from reporters who were swarming around the story.

Hoover met Mansfield and Dirksen at 1:30 P.M. on October 28 at the Mansfield residence on Dexter Street, where Senate business was rarely conducted. Hoover read aloud an FBI memorandum on the case and said there had been no breach of national security in the Rometsch case. He reported Rometsch's denials and those of executive branch officials of any White House connection. However, he also laid out extensive details of liaisons between Baker's "party girls" and members of Congress, saying that such immorality had been "rather common in the Senate and the House." Reporting to Robert Kennedy that Mansfield was "particularly amazed and surprised" with what he had heard, Hoover said the senators were "perfectly satisfied and willing to keep quiet." They were in touch with the Rules Committee leadership and with Williams, who agreed to drop his inquiries into the sexual aspects of the Baker case. When another senator sought to bring up the sex angle of the Baker investigation, Chairman B. Everett Jordan of the Rules Committee ruled him out of order.

"Mike Mansfield by that meeting in his house in Wesley Heights saved the presidency of John Kennedy and probably the political future of Bobby Kennedy," Baker told me. "Had they not had that meeting and had the people who had relations with Ellen Rometsch been called to testify—because once you opened that box, I'm telling you, you guys in the press would have had the greatest field day in your history." Thus Mansfield and Dirksen played key roles in averting a scandal that would have destroyed Kennedy's reputation and severely damaged his presidency a month before it was to end in his assassination. Dirksen died in 1969, leaving no known record of the incident. When I asked Mansfield about it in April 1999 and again a year later, he said he had only "a very faint memory" of the meeting with Hoover, the only time he had ever met the FBI director, and could not remember details or why the meeting took place. Given his usually excellent memory, I suggested this might be one of the things he did not wish to remember because of its seamy nature. "No, I'm not usually shocked to that extent," he replied. He did recall he had discussed the incident with Maureen, but with no one else.

NEITHER A CIRCUS RING
MASTER NOR TAMER OF LIONS

The Baker scandal in the press brought to Capitol Hill swarms of reporters who rarely covered Congress and a harsh spotlight of press and public attention to the workings—and nonworkings—of the Senate. Many journalists with little familiarity with Senate procedures were dismayed by its slow-moving ways. In early November, approaching the end of the calendar year, the appropriations bills funding most of the government agencies after June 30 still had not been passed—a recurrent condition that subsequently led Congress to extend the government's fiscal year to September 30, which even then has not solved the problem to this day. Moreover, Kennedy's important tax bill and the civil rights bill were far from passage. Public and private comment increasingly compared Mansfield's style of leadership unfavorably with the high-visibility, high-pressure style of his predecessor, Lyndon Johnson.

In this atmosphere Democratic senator Thomas Dodd of Connecticut interrupted debate on another subject on the evening of November 6, in what one of the few journalists present remembered as a "boozy voice," to yearn for the days of Johnson and excoriate Mansfield's leadership. "One cannot be a leader and be every man's leader," he declared. "One must say No sometimes. One must say Yes even when it hurts to say Yes. I wish our leader would be more of a leader and lead the Senate as it should be led." Warming to his subject, Dodd said he wished Mansfield were present "because I know this will be construed as a criticism of him. It is meant to be. It is a criticism of him. I do not think he is leading the Senate as he should, and I believe we should have leadership." The Majority Whip, Hubert Humphrey, and others defended Mansfield, but the Dodd outburst touched off more criticism. Columnists Rowland Evans and Robert Novak, the latter especially close to Johnson, declared that "kindly well-meaning Senator Mike Mansfield has been a tragic mistake as Majority Leader."

For the first and only time since accepting the leadership at the request of both Kennedy and Johnson, Mansfield seriously considered resigning the post. He saw no reason, he told aides, for "shortening my life" in an exercise of futility. After further consideration he decided to respond to the public challenge with a counter-challenge of his own. He prepared a lengthy and pointed speech defending the record of the Senate but also declaring that he would not change his style of leadership:

> I confess freely to a lack of glamor. As for being "a tragic mistake," if that means, Mr. President, that I am neither a circus ring-master, the master of ceremonies of a Senate night club, a tamer of Senate lions, or a wheeler and dealer, then I must accept, too, that title. Indeed I must accept it, if I am expected as Majority Leader to be anything other than myself—a Senator from Montana who has had the good fortune to be trusted by his people for over two decades and done the best he knows how to represent them, and to do what he believes to be right for the nation.
>
> Insofar as I am personally concerned, these or any other labels can be borne. I achieved the height of my political ambitions when I was elected Senator from Montana. When the Senate saw fit to designate me as Majority

Leader, it was the Senate's choice not mine, and what the Senate has bestowed, it is always at liberty to revoke. . . .

I believe that I am, as are most Senators, an ordinary American with a normal complement of vices and, I hope, virtues, of weaknesses and, I hope, strengths. As such, I do my best to be courteous, decent and understanding of others and sometimes fail at it. But it is for the Senate to decide whether these characteristics are incompatible with the leadership.

I have tried to treat others as I would like to be treated and almost invariably have been. And it is for the Senate to decide, too, whether that characteristic is incompatible with the Senate leadership.

And, finally, within this body I believe that every member ought to be equal in fact no less than in theory, that they have a primary responsibility to the people whom they represent to face the legislative issues of the nation. And to the extent that the Senate may be inadequate in this connection, the remedy lies not in the seeking of short-cuts, not in the cracking of non-existent whips, not in wheeling and dealing, but in an honest facing of the situation and a resolution of it by the Senate itself, by accommodation, by respect for one another, by mutual restraint and, as necessary, adjustments in the procedures of this body.

Shortly after the Senate convened at noon on Friday, November 22, Mansfield interrupted an unseemly partisan argument about the Senate's difficulties in order to announce that he would deliver his long-awaited speech on his leadership the following Monday, and that he would insist that a quorum—at least half the senators—be on hand to hear his views. A few minutes after his announcement, however, shocking news bulletins began arriving from Dallas.

Richard Riddell, the Senate's press liaison officer, was the first to hear the news. He approached the dais and whispered to Senator Edward M. "Ted" Kennedy, who happened to be presiding over the Senate at the time, that his brother had been shot. "No," he said, as his body tensed involuntarily. He quickly gathered his papers and left the chamber. Senator Spessard Holland, a Florida Democrat, moved into the presiding officer's chair. As the news spread rapidly through the chamber, Mansfield, hastily conferring with Dirksen, moved that the Senate "stand in recess pending developments." Senators left the floor for the cloakroom behind the presiding officer's desk and crowded around the news tickers, awaiting further word from Dallas. As they, like other Americans, waited in shock and horror, Mansfield and Dirksen reconvened the Senate to hear a prayer by the chaplain, the Rev. Frederick Brown Harris, that the President's life might still be spared despite "this sudden, almost unbelievable news" and that the American people be "calm and steady and full of faith for the Republic in this tragic hour of our history." The Senate then adjourned until Monday. (When that day came, Mansfield placed the text of his speech, unspoken, into the *Congressional Record*, saying that "in the light of what has happened, I have no heart to read this report to the Senate.")

After Mansfield learned the dreaded news from the press association news tickers, he walked slowly back to his Capitol office a few feet from the Senate chamber. "Get—me—a—drink," he said to Oscar Morris for the only time in the memory of his staff, and then closeted himself in his inner office where he sat in silence, all alone, for a half hour before leaving for his Montana office in the Senate Office Building. Later Mansfield, joined by Maureen and Anne, rode in a motorcade with other congressional leaders to Andrews Air Force Base. There they awaited the return of Air Force One bringing the new President, Lyndon Johnson, who had been sworn into office aboard the plane before it left Dallas, and bearing the body of the slain President, attended by his widow, Jacqueline, the blood of her husband still visible on her coat.

A few hours later Jacqueline herself telephoned Mansfield to request that he and he alone present a eulogy at the televised national memorial service to be held Sunday in the rotunda of the Capitol. However, William "Fishbait" Miller, the doorkeeper of the House of Representatives, informed the Kennedy family that it would be unacceptable to the House for a senator alone to speak, whatever the circumstances. Eventually it was decided that House Speaker John McCormack and Chief Justice Earl Warren, representing the judicial branch of government, would also speak, but Mansfield's eulogy is the only one that was long remembered.

Taking their theme from a newspaper report that Jacqueline had slipped off her wedding ring and placed it in her dead husband's hand at Parkland Hospital in Dallas, Mansfield and his aide Frank Valeo wrote an appreciation of the slain President in poetic meter. Mansfield delivered it in the high rhetoric of his strong, spare senatorial voice, in direct and emotional words

that discomfited some listeners and greatly consoled others, among the latter, Jacqueline Kennedy.

There was a sound of laughter and, in a moment, it was no more. And so, she
took a ring from her finger and placed it in his hands.

There was a wit in a man neither young nor old, but a wit full of an old
man's wisdom and of a child's wisdom and, then, in a moment it was no more.
And so, she took a ring from her finger and placed it in his hands.

There was a man marked with the scars of his love of country, a body active
with the surge of a life far, far from spent and, in a moment, it was no more.
And so, she took a ring from her finger and placed it in his hands.

There was a father with a little boy and a little girl and the joy of each in
the other and, in a moment, it was no more. And so, she took a ring from her
finger and placed it in his hands.

There was a husband who asked much and gave much and, out of the giving and the asking, wove with a woman what could not be broken in life and,
in a moment, it was no more. And so, she took a ring from her finger and
placed it in his hands, and kissed him and closed the lid of a coffin.

A piece of each of us died at that moment. Yet, in death he gave of himself
to us. He gave us of a good heart from which the laughter came. He gave us of
a profound wit, from which a great leadership emerged. He gave us of a kindness and a strength fused into the human courage to seek peace without fear.

He gave us of his love that we, too, in turn might give. He gave that we
might give of ourselves, that we might give to one another until there would
be no room, no room at all, for the bigotry, the hatred, prejudice and the arrogance which converged in that moment of horror to strike him down.

In leaving us—these gifts, John Fitzgerald Kennedy, President of the
United States, leaves with us. Will we take them, Mr. President? Will we have,
now, the sense and responsibility and the courage to take them? I pray to God
that we shall and under God we will.

The eulogy over, he walked a few feet across the great rotunda and handed
Jacqueline the manuscript. "How did you know I wanted it?" she asked.
Mansfield bowed his head and replied, "I didn't. I just wanted you to have it."

Shortly after the service, Jacqueline telephoned Mansfield again to thank
him for his speech and for the manuscript. She said she had wanted only

him to speak at the service. Mansfield said he and Maureen planned to visit her, but knew of the strain she was under and hoped to see her later. "Oh yes, please do, let's get together," she replied. Then she said she had to try to get some sleep.

Several days later the Mansfields called on Jacqueline Kennedy at the White House, and a few days after that she responded with a handwritten note on black-bordered paper. "I do thank you and Maureen for coming to see me. The only time things are better is when I talk about Jack—and you and he were so close and built so much together. I will always care terribly about your happiness. Love, Jackie."

JOHNSON I

Years of Escalation

9 *Lyndon B. Johnson inherited a difficult struggle in Vietnam and transformed it into a full-blown American war. The tall Texan was determined to "win" or, at the very least, not to be "the first American President to lose a war." As Johnson grappled with decisions that would dramatically expand the military operations and commitments of the United States, Mansfield advised him repeatedly—but privately—against doing so at every turn. Mansfield also dissented with others present in top-level White House meetings, on three occasions the only person in the room to speak up in opposition to the President's plans. His efforts were in vain. If the war in Vietnam was the greatest tragedy to befall the United States, as he later declared, the failure of his extensive efforts to head off Johnson's escalation was Mansfield's greatest failure, which haunted him for the rest of his life.*

The first twenty months of Lyndon Johnson's presidency, from his ascent to power in November 1963 to his decision in July 1965 to dispatch hundreds of thousands of U.S. troops, fundamentally changed the American involvement and stakes in Vietnam. Informed by his previous experience, Mansfield clearly foresaw the consequences and quickly became the most insistent and articulate critic of Johnson's war policy from within the ranks of those with direct access to the President. On this score, only Undersecretary of State George Ball came close, and he did not contest the policy as long or as consistently. As Democratic leader of the Senate, Mansfield sought to persuade Johnson in private while continuing to support him publicly. In this uncomfortable situation, he was walking "a delicate line."

He had made some of the same arguments and adopted some of the same practices with his friend John F. Kennedy but with different results. Kennedy had listened carefully to his views on Laos and at the time of his death may have been poised to reconsider U.S. policy in Vietnam with the potential, at least, to shift it away from growing military intervention. Johnson, in contrast, tended to "handle" Mansfield as he had handled dissenters in the Senate, acknowledging their views and pretending to take them seriously while privately scorning and seeking to isolate them. This early and decisive period of the Johnson presidency was an agonizing time for Mansfield, who was torn between his belief in presidential supremacy in foreign policy and his clear-sighted understanding that the President's course would lead the nation to disaster.

The new era began, however, with hope and wonder on "a most remarkable evening," which he recorded immediately afterward in handwritten notes. Around 10 A.M. on December 5, 1963, Lady Bird Johnson telephoned to invite him and Maureen to dinner that night at The Elms, the chateaulike mansion that the Johnsons had bought from famed party-giver Perle Mesta, the model for the fictional heroine of Irving Berlin's Broadway musical *Call Me Madam*. Johnson had been president for two weeks but had not yet moved into the family quarters of the White House out of deference to Jacqueline Kennedy and her two young children, who were slowly adjusting to new circumstances. The new President and his wife had gathered three friendly and influential Senate Democrats, Majority Leader Mansfield, Majority Whip Hubert Humphrey, and Chairman J. William Fulbright of the Foreign Relations Committee and their wives, along with the new presidential aide Jack Valenti, a Texas publicist who had been drafted to the Johnson staff in Dallas on the day of John F. Kennedy's assassination.

Johnson, his pent-up energy bursting forth after his sudden release from the powerlessness of the vice presidency, was at his most frenetic. He asked his dinner companions to send him the names of people to be selected as ambassadors and to make lists of six to eight senators and three to four House members to meet over breakfasts with the administration's National Security Council. He invited Mansfield to have lunch with him and give him suggestions for appointments and legislation. He asked Mansfield and Fulbright to accompany him to New York three days later to the funeral of former senator Herbert Lehman. Three times during the evening, Johnson asked Mansfield to send him a memorandum of his views about Vietnam. "Wants to do his best & repeatedly expressed need for advice and counsel," Mansfield summed up in the notes he made immediately afterward.

Johnson already knew that Fulbright like Mansfield was deeply concerned about the U.S. direction in Vietnam. In a telephone conversation with Johnson three days earlier, Fulbright had told LBJ that "I'll be goddamned if I don't think it's hopeless." The only solution, Fulbright said, seemed to be "some kind of a semi-neutralized area" in which the Chinese would keep out. Johnson's Senate mentor, Richard B. Russell of Georgia, had also told LBJ repeatedly that he was opposed to the war. As recorded in Mansfield's notes, Johnson told his friends at The Elms dinner that "Russell wanted us to pull out."

Responding to Johnson's requests, Mansfield sent to the White House on December 7 copies of three private memoranda on Indochina that he had sent to Kennedy plus his seminal Michigan State speech of June 1962. A covering memo of his "thoughts on the present situation"—the first memorandum on the war he submitted to Johnson—succinctly presented two central ideas that would dominate his recommendations in the months to come: that U.S. commitments in Vietnam should not exceed the very limited U.S. national interests, and that a negotiated settlement should be the most important U.S. objective. In these pursuits, Mansfield offered three specific suggestions:

First, a shift in strategy inside Vietnam from military to nonmilitary means, "curtailing the present elusive and so far unsuccessful chase of the Viet Cong all over the land," and emphasizing instead the political and social actions Mansfield had long believed were fundamental in defeating the insurgency.

Second, "an astute diplomatic offensive" to work out a peaceful settlement between North and South Vietnam, involving France, Britain, India, and perhaps even Russia. "*France is the key country,*" he emphasized in italics, referring to the proposal by French President Charles de Gaulle four months earlier for a negotiated settlement in Southeast Asia. Such a settlement might reduce U.S. influence and U.S. costs but would also aim at inhibiting Chinese domination of the area, Mansfield wrote.

Third, "U.S. understanding, sympathy and sensible encouragement" for Prince Sihanouk's neutralist policies in Cambodia. Following the overthrow of Diem, the Cambodian leader had renounced further U.S. aid, fearing that Washington's opposition to his regime could end in his ouster. Encouraged by De Gaulle's proposal, he had called for an international conference to establish a neutral Cambodia and perhaps all of Indochina. Mansfield described Cambodia as "the principal prototype of any eventual peace for Southeast Asia, not dependent on a costly U.S. prop." Should Cambodia succumb to its rightist neighbors in Thailand and South Vietnam or come under Chinese domination, Mansfield maintained, "we may as well resign ourselves to an involvement of years in all of Southeast Asia at great cost in resources and, probably, lives. Or alternatively, we will be faced with an ignominious and dangerous abandonment of the Southeast Asian mainland to Chinese political domination."

In sum, Mansfield told the new President that the United States could not achieve its objective of halting the spread of communism by military means within Vietnam or even in a more costly regional war that might well extend to China. As in the Laotian settlement he had espoused, the Berlin settlement he had suggested, and the Cambodian situation he vigorously approved, Mansfield advocated negotiations for even a temporary accommodation rather than deepening U.S. support for armed conflict. The one senator who had served in all three military services in his youth had little faith in military solutions, a view intensified in the case of Indochina by his visits in the mid-1950s and in 1962.

Mansfield harbored no illusions that he would easily persuade Johnson to modify his course on the war, although he did believe that he had an opportunity and an obligation to try. He presented his views persistently, in his words, "pounding away," by memorandum after memorandum after he was fiercely rebuffed in person. In the end he realized that he had failed completely to avert the catastrophe he had foreseen. The tragedy of Vietnam was the one subject that brought forth an emotional reaction from this calm, unemotional figure in the many interviews I had with him in his final years. "It still haunts me," he said, his voice cracking and his eyes watering. "What a shame—55,000 dead, 305,000 wounded. Costs which we will be paying well into the middle of the next century. . . . A tragic mistake."

Despite Johnson's expressed eagerness to receive Mansfield's views in the first days of his presidency, he was already headed full speed in the opposite direction. As he assumed the office, Johnson faced a series of grave decisions about the war. Kennedy had sent to Vietnam 16,000 American troops, primarily as advisers, and had increasingly involved the United States in the affairs of South Vietnam. Less than a month before Kennedy was killed, Washington had encouraged the military coup in Saigon that led to the ouster and murder of President Ngo Dinh Diem and his brother, Ngo Dinh Nhu. By so doing, it had inherited great responsibility for the war, which was being waged ineffectively by the South Vietnamese Army (ARVN) under the leadership of unstable successor regimes in Saigon, of which there were many.

Johnson, in his first meeting on the war only forty-eight hours after becoming president, told the U.S. ambassador to Vietnam, Henry Cabot Lodge, and the top U.S. national security team that he "approached the situation with some misgivings," noting that some strong voices in Congress felt the United States should get out. He was particularly dubious about U.S. support for the overthrow of Diem and said he had "never been happy with our operations in Vietnam." Nonetheless, he had no intention of reducing the U.S. commitment or withdrawing from the field. He told Lodge, who was preparing to return to Saigon, "I am not going to lose Vietnam. . . . I am not going to be the President who saw Southeast Asia go the way China went."

Probably without giving it much thought, Johnson had already made a fundamentally important decision—to keep as his principal advisers the members of Kennedy's national security team headed by Secretary of State Dean Rusk, Secretary of Defense Robert McNamara, and National Security Adviser McGeorge Bundy. In his memoir, *The Vantage Point*, Johnson said that he had vowed even before arriving back in Washington from Dallas to pursue Kennedy's goals in Vietnam and elsewhere during the rest of Kennedy's elected term and that he shortly asked Kennedy's foreign policy team to stay on, "not just for a while, but for as long as I was president." This action projected continuity and enhanced public confidence in the new chief executive, but it contained the seeds of disaster. These were the people whose advice, often restrained and modified by Kennedy, had driven the United States more deeply into Indochina. With the same team remaining in place, the cards were stacked heavily against a serious reconsideration of existing policy.

Johnson, after retiring from the presidency, told his former aide Jack Valenti that he should have brought in his own advisers and taken a fresh look at the war, as he did much later with his old friends Clark Clifford and Abe Fortas after he finally lost confidence in the military advice he was getting. Over breakfast at the LBJ Ranch the summer after leaving the White House, Johnson told General William Westmoreland, the U.S. commander in Vietnam during most of his tenure, that he regretted not having asked for the resignations of the senior officials he had inherited from Kennedy, that he should have "fired the whole damn works," with the notable exception of Rusk, rather than proceed on the basis of their advice. It would have been difficult for Johnson to oust key personnel in the immediate aftermath of Kennedy's assassination, but he could have done so later, especially after his landslide victory in the 1964 election.

While retaining the personnel and general direction of Kennedy's war policy, Johnson in his early days in office began to shift toward a strictly military view of the problems in Southeast Asia and away from political-economic programs to deal with them. In other words, he was shifting in precisely the opposite direction from those Mansfield urged in his December 7 memorandum and his subsequent advice.

Johnson's most emphatic early expression of change came in the November 24 meeting on Vietnam with Lodge and the foreign policy advisers. According to the notes on the meeting drafted by CIA director John McCone, Johnson "wanted to make it abundantly clear that he did not think we had to reform every Asian into our own image. . . . He was anxious to get along, win the war—he didn't want as much effort placed on so-called social reforms." In a note to himself McCone contrasted the first "President Johnson tone" with the "Kennedy tone." He observed that "Johnson definitely feels that we place too much emphasis on social reforms; he has very little tolerance with our spending so much time being 'do-gooders.'"

Johnson and his new aides were even more emphatic in opposing proposals for international negotiations to seek a settlement, which in their minds would undercut the tenuous resolve of Saigon leaders and, they feared, would lead inevitably to communist victory. On December 10, three days after receiving Mansfield's memorandum, the White House heard from Lodge that the ruling generals in Saigon were "seriously concerned that the US secretly favors [a] neutral solution for South Viet Nam." In response, the State Department cabled Lodge, with White House approval by McGeorge Bundy, "You may categorically, and in a manner most likely to convince them, say to the Generals that USG [U.S. government] in no way favors neutral solution for SVN [South Vietnam]. As you know, powerful voices such as *NY Times* and [columnist Walter] Lippmann have been advocating some sort of neutral solution but this in no wise reflects US Government policy which has consistently been a win the war policy. . . . [T]his is US policy from the top down." On December 16, with concern still reported in Saigon, the State Department instructed Lodge to let the generals know that "nothing is further from USG mind than 'neutral solution' for Viet Nam. We intend to win."

DOWN THE SLIPPERY SLOPE

At the same time, Johnson continued to court Mansfield, who as Majority Leader would play a key role in the fortunes of his legislative program, domestic and foreign. In a telephone conversation shortly before Christmas, the President said he felt the need to sit down with Mansfield to discuss foreign policy, especially "what's happening in Vietnam that I don't think you know. . . . I don't think you know how serious it is." Johnson, who was preparing to travel to his Texas ranch, suggested that Mansfield travel to Texas on a military jet over the holidays from wherever he might be. Johnson said he wished to have "a quiet two or three hours with you to philosophize and see what you think about some of these hot spots, 'cause they're hotter than I think you think they are."

Mansfield did not go to the ranch, but on December 23 Johnson telephoned Frank Valeo, who had succeeded Bobby Baker as secretary to the Democratic majority, about the status of legislative business. He then went on to raise the possibility that Vietnam could be "another China"—that is, a communist victory politically damaging to Democrats. LBJ said, "We're going to look at that [Vietnam] war," suggesting a policy review of serious dimensions. Knowing that Valeo was an adviser and frequent wordsmith for Mansfield, Johnson asked for another memorandum on Vietnam.

On January 2, Johnson wired Mansfield in Los Angeles an invitation to the LBJ Ranch two days later so that the two could fly together back to Washington. This plan did not work out, but Johnson and Mansfield met at the White House for more than an hour on January 6. Mansfield gave the President another copy of his December 7 memorandum, along with a one-page covering note—his second memo to Johnson—arguing that the United States was becoming dangerously overcommitted.

> As you remarked to [Valeo] on the telephone, we do not want another China in Viet Nam. I would respectfully add to this observation: Neither do we want another Korea. It would seem that a key (but often overlooked) factor in both situations was a tendency to bite off more than we were prepared in the end to chew. We tended to talk ourselves out on a limb with overstatements of our purpose and commitment only to discover in the end that there were not sufficient American interests to support with blood and treasure a desperate final plunge. Then, the question followed invariably: "Who got us into this mess?" "Who lost China?" etc.
>
> We are close to the point of no return in Viet Nam. A way to avoid another Korea and, perhaps, another China may be found in the general policy approach suggested in the memo of December 7th. If so, there ought to be less official talk of our responsibility in Viet Nam and more emphasis on the responsibilities of the Vietnamese themselves and a great deal of thought on the possibilities for a peaceful solution through the efforts of other nations as well as our own.

What happened next was a revealing demonstration of Johnson's mind set and methods. Finally focusing on the fact that Mansfield was proposing a fundamentally different course, Johnson sent copies of the December 7 memorandum and the note that accompanied it to his top foreign policy aides, Rusk, McNamara, and Bundy—but not for their serious consideration. Instead, the documents were accompanied by a memo from Bundy to the other two, saying, "The President received the enclosed papers this morning from Senator Mansfield, and asks if each of you would write a personal memorandum of refutation" that he could use to rebut Mansfield at their next meeting. His aides needed no further prompting to perform as requested.

Ironically, Johnson and his three top advisers knew much less about Vietnam than Mansfield, who had been there four times and had dealt with its personalities and issues for more than a decade. Chester L. Cooper, a CIA official and later National Security Council staff member who was intimately involved in Vietnam policymaking during the Johnson era, explained, "Mansfield was regarded with respect but he was still an outsider and he was disagreeing with the party line. And the fact that he was an outsider with a helluva lot of knowledge didn't mean anything. . . . There was a tremendous amount of hubris. By December 1963 Johnson couldn't find Vietnam on an outline map of Asia. McNamara, who had a helluva lot of hubris about everything, knew nothing about Vietnam. Mac [Bundy] had never been there and wouldn't get there for another year. Rusk of course had been in Asia during the [Second World] war, but he had this mind set and he could not be moved from this mind set."

A contributing factor to the hubris was the prevalent view in both the White House and Congress that the executive branch had nearly exclusive possession of the legitimate authority in foreign affairs. "Johnson accepted the notion that members of Congress could bitch and moan, but for the most part they had to yield to the executive," according to Harry McPherson, who was an assistant to Johnson on Capitol Hill and later in the White House. McPherson recalled LBJ's reaction as vice president when he presided over a Senate debate on a Kennedy foreign policy issue. "I listen to them talk and it sounds so sensible," Johnson told McPherson, "but they'd shit if they had to decide." The members of Congress, including Mansfield and, at this stage even Fulbright, deferred to presidential power and responsibility in foreign affairs and considered the congressional role a secondary one.

The refutation of Mansfield's January 1964 memorandum that Johnson had requested from his advisers followed predictable lines of support for existing policy. Rusk told Johnson that the senator's advice added up to "neutralization" that the Soviet Union had rejected and the Chinese were unlikely to accept. Among the most unyielding, unquestioning, and unwavering civilian officials in support of the war, Rusk provided LBJ with an accompanying primer on "U.S. Policy On Viet-Nam" that declared "political and social acts of popular benefit" such as Mansfield proposed were essential in Vietnam but would only become possible after military successes provide greater confidence there. Rusk's policy paper held out the prospect of "victory" against the Vietcong (South Vietnamese communists) without major and direct U.S. involvement "*provided* the new South Vietnamese Government takes the proper political, economic and social actions to win the support of the rural people *and* uses its armed forces effectively [his emphasis]." He made this sound like an easy task for a wobbly government that had not undertaken those initiatives and, in any event, would be toppled before the end of the month.

McNamara, a true believer in the war in January 1964, advised Johnson, "The security situation is serious, but we can still win, even on the present ground rules." Any change in strategy toward "division" or "neutralization" would bring a communist-dominated government in Saigon, a U.S. complete withdrawal, and massive setbacks for the United States in Southeast Asia and even as far beyond as India, Japan, and Latin America, he wrote, repeating an extreme version of the domino theory, which was then the conventional wisdom among top U.S. civilian and military officials. Noting that Mansfield "is challenging what he regards as the gross imbalance between the extent of our involvement in Southeast Asia and our narrow self-interests in the area," McNamara insisted that "our important security interests . . . unquestionably call for holding the line against further Communist gains."

McGeorge Bundy also foresaw collapsing dominoes in Asia resulting from any moves in the direction of neutralization. At the same time, however, he appeared less confident than his colleagues of victory ahead. "We may have to move in these painful directions, but we should do so only when there is a much stronger demonstration that our present course cannot work," he wrote on January 6. After reading the comments of Rusk and McNamara, both of whom noted widespread U.S. public support for the present course, Bundy "as an ex-historian" sent Johnson an additional memo: "The political damage to Truman and Acheson from the fall of China arose because most Americans came to believe that we could and should have done more than we did to prevent it. This is exactly what would happen now if we should seem to be the first to quit in Saigon." Even so, he added, "*When* we are stronger, *then* we can face negotiations [his emphasis]."

The responses of Johnson's three most important aides failed to deal with Mansfield's central point, that the current course of deepening U.S. interven-

tion was leading to commitments and costs far in excess of U.S. interests—
with no likelihood of success at the end of the line. Instead of reevaluating the
growing military involvement in Vietnam, as Mansfield had hoped, the presidential advisers expounded on the risks and costs of changing course. Having
been in high office for the three turbulent years of the Kennedy administration, the advisers were cut off from outside reality to a greater extent than they
realized. Their daily contact with one another and with the government
bureaucracies, which served at their beck and call, made Rusk, McNamara,
and McGeorge Bundy victims of group think, in which countervailing ideas
from outsiders were no longer welcome.

How certain was Lyndon Johnson of his own position on the war? His
turning to his advisers for backing against Mansfield suggests that he was
testing them, and perhaps testing himself. In unguarded conversations
secretly recorded, he often agonized over the decisions facing him and
expressed doubts about the course being followed, especially to persons
whom he knew were skeptics or opponents.

Johnson was inexperienced in foreign affairs, but he was also a highly
intelligent man, especially sensitive to political consequences. That he never
wavered from the course of confrontation in Vietnam until it was too late
was in part due to a deep-seated fear of appearing to be weak, flowing from
his reading of the political lessons of contemporary history. After leaving
office, he told his assistant and later presidential historian Doris Kearns
Goodwin in a remarkably candid interview, "everything I knew about history told me that if I got out of Vietnam and let Ho Chi Minh run through
the streets of Saigon, then I'd be doing exactly what Chamberlain did in
World War II. . . . I knew that Harry Truman and Dean Acheson had lost
their effectiveness from the day that the Communists took over in China. I
believed that the loss of China had played a large role in the rise of Joe
McCarthy. And I knew that all these problems, taken together, were chick-
enshit compared with what might happen if we lost Vietnam." He went on
to reveal to Goodwin a deeper and more consuming fear. "Every night when
I fell asleep I would see myself tied to the ground in the middle of a long,
open space. In the distance, I could hear the voices of thousands of people.
They were all shouting at me and running toward me: 'Coward! Traitor!
Weakling!' They kept coming closer. They began throwing stones. At exactly
that moment I would generally wake up . . . terribly shaken."

During his presidency, Johnson did not reveal his nightmares, but his fear of weakness and defeat was plain to see. He told Valeo in his December 23 telephone call that "I don't want these people around the world worrying about us, and they are. . . . They're worried about whether we've got a weak president or a strong president." Later, erupting with passion against Mansfield's opposition to bombing North Vietnam, Johnson ripped into him, declaring that "cowardice has gotten us into more wars than response has." Mansfield, analyzing Johnson's dismissal of his early memoranda on the war, told me that the President "was a Texas Texan, sort of an Alamo man in his thinking . . . [who] didn't want to accept anything that bore the scent even of defeat. So he plugged on and on, and had a lot of people from the armed services and like the ones you mentioned [Rusk, McNamara, and McGeorge Bundy] and I think they made their reports not on the basis of what they knew—well perhaps they knew—of the facts, but because they knew what Johnson's attitude was and they complied with it. And he took it at face value."

In his 1995 memoir of Vietnam policymaking, McNamara quoted extensively from the memorandum he sent to Johnson rebutting Mansfield "to show how limited and shallow our analysis and discussion of the alternatives to our existing policy in Vietnam—i.e., neutralization or withdrawal—had been; and to illustrate that the consequences of Southeast Asia's loss to U.S. and Western security were now being presented to President Johnson with greater force and in more detail than on previous occasions." The upshot of the exchange, according to McNamara, was to harden Johnson's "preexisting attitude." He added:

> As the likely failure of our training strategy became more apparent in the months ahead, we tilted gradually—almost imperceptibly—toward approving the direct application of U.S. military force. We did so because of our increasing fear—and hindsight makes it clear it was an exaggerated fear—of what would happen if we did not. But we never carefully debated what U.S. force would ultimately be required, what our chances of success would be, or what the political, military, financial and human costs would be if we provided it. Indeed, these basic questions went unexamined.

Those, in fact, were the basic questions that Mansfield was raising in his memoranda to Lyndon Johnson. McNamara concluded his account of the

January 1964 exchange of memoranda between Mansfield and Johnson by recalling, "We were at the beginning of a slide down a tragic and slippery slope."

AN UNEASY RELATIONSHIP

The relationship of Lyndon Johnson and Mike Mansfield was a long and often very active one, but not an easy one. The two men were polar opposites in personality, Johnson a dominating, often domineering personality, and Mansfield a self-effacing loner who was quiet by preference and disposition. Jim Rowe, who introduced them and knew both men well, said that fundamentally "they didn't like each other much." Mansfield, who rarely spoke in negative terms about anyone, said of Johnson, "it was always an arm's length relationship. . . . We weren't close."

As noted earlier, their first contact was in 1942, when Mansfield asked Congressman Johnson for money to help finance his first successful race for the House. In their days together in the House, Johnson impressed Mansfield as "a man on the move who was full of energy and vigor, who had charted out his course as to where he was going." On arriving in the Senate, Mansfield backed Johnson for Democratic leader, and Johnson maneuvered to name Mansfield to a coveted place on the Foreign Relations Committee. Johnson later selected Mansfield to be majority whip, the number two post in the Democratic leadership. Mansfield backed Johnson for the 1960 Democratic presidential nomination, and after the election Vice President-elect Johnson helped persuade Mansfield to become his successor as Majority Leader. At Johnson's request, Mansfield sought unsuccessfully to arrange for Johnson as vice president to preside over the Senate Democratic Caucus.

Outwardly, the written exchanges between them, especially those from Johnson, who was a master of hyperbole, suggested a relationship more intimate than it was. When Johnson suffered a heart attack in 1955, two years before selecting Mansfield as his deputy, Mansfield wired him, "you are too valuable a man to your country to take any chances you may be down but not out." When Johnson was well enough to respond, he wrote Mansfield, "If I am a valuable man, it is for one reason and one reason only—because I have friends like Mike Mansfield who are always considerate, always helpful and always ready to throw their tremendous abilities into the breach." In early 1957, after Mansfield had been serving for two months as Majority

Whip, Johnson wired him that "I would rather have a quiet well done from Mike Mansfield than a ringing tribute from any other individual." Mansfield responded that LBJ's praise "caused me to blush as I read it." In September 1959, in an end-of-session letter, Johnson went so far as to write, "Dear Mike: If I were to die tomorrow, the most comforting thought would be that the future of my wife and my two daughters would be in your hands. In all my life, I have never known a man more selfless, more dedicated or more able than you."

There is evidence that as time went on Mansfield's truly close relationship with Kennedy was a sore point with Johnson. According to Bobby Baker, Johnson's protégé and close aide, Maureen Mansfield, whom he considered "the strong part" of the Mansfield family, "hated and detested Lyndon Johnson" even as she adored John Kennedy. Baker based his belief on comments from a Mansfield staff member as well as a personal episode in which he conducted a difficult negotiation between Maureen and Johnson about space for Mansfield's office in the Capitol.

In an early 1965 conversation with Hubert Humphrey, who had recently become Johnson's vice president, LBJ derisively referred to Mansfield and House Speaker John McCormack as "the Catholics" and claimed that Kennedy as President had told them to pay no attention to him as vice president. Humphrey wrote in his memoir, *The Education of a Public Man*, "While Mansfield and Johnson had a mutual respect, their personalities were not compatible." More vividly, Jim Rowe told of Humphrey's mimicking of conversations between the President and the Majority Leader. "Hubert would first get on one side of the table and imitate Johnson perfectly, and then he would run around to the other side. After Johnson would say, 'Now, Mike, you've got to do this, you've got to do that,' then he would imitate Mansfield, the pipe, 'No.' Then he'd run back and do Johnson, run back to Mansfield, Mansfield said, 'No.' They knew they were temperamentally two entirely different people."

Nonetheless, the Democratic President and the Democratic leader of the Senate did a great deal of business with one another. According to records at the Johnson Library, Johnson and Mansfield met 142 times at meetings of the legislative leaders during Johnson's presidency and spoke with each other in 207 telephone calls, about two-thirds of them initiated by Johnson. They also met on other occasions, including 59 bill signings at the White House and on 58 social occasions. Most important, they had 63 private meetings when only the two of them were present.

As they began to disagree sharply about Vietnam, LBJ made biting remarks about Mansfield and his views. He told a *Newsweek* reporter that "Mike is a cross between Jeanette Rankin and Burton K. Wheeler [famous isolationists from Montana] and I don't need advice from either of them." Mike Manatos, LBJ's White House liaison aide with the Senate, came across a copy of the *Newsweek* report in Mansfield's office, with the critical quotation underlined. In his secretly recorded telephone conversations, Johnson was much more derisive, treating with disdain, deliberate exaggeration, and occasional lack of comprehension Mansfield's memoranda on Indochina and describing its author as spineless and weak—damaging attributes in view of Johnson's self-image as courageous and strong. The President even suggested that Mansfield was cowardly because of his failure to accept Johnson's actions in expanding the war.

By February 1965 Johnson was so disrespectful of Mansfield that he sought to sexually engage his twenty-six-year-old daughter, Anne, when she came to the White House alone one evening to conduct an interview for *Visions,* a Latin American magazine for which she was working. Misinterpreting Johnson's repeated winks as friendly gestures rather than as an opening to flirtation, she winked back, whereupon he began moving to embrace her. She escaped Johnson's advances only by fleeing from him in the Oval Office. The astonished young woman did not tell her father about the incident, but her friends soon learned of it. With this background, it took unlimited gall for Johnson to describe Mansfield in a telephone conversation with Richard Russell ten days later as "a peculiar fellow."

For all this, when Johnson and Mansfield were speaking to one another, the tone of their recorded conversations was remarkably free of antagonism. Although five years younger than Mansfield, Johnson had been the senior and dominant figure organizationally in the Senate and as President. Mansfield deferred to him in many of the taped conversations, saying "Yes, sir" to Johnson's suggestions in domestic affairs, and even occasionally addressing Johnson as "boss." In conversations regarding Vietnam, Johnson was solicitous of Mansfield's views but often disingenuous, pretending that he was consulting the Majority Leader without the knowledge of his more hawkish advisers and claiming that moves of escalation were really intended to pave the way for diplomatic solutions.

The explanation for this complex relationship is that two leading Democratic figures, who shared many of the same political perspectives and aspirations for the nation, were required to work together on key legislation, despite differences of personality and a clash of views about Vietnam. Both Johnson and Mansfield were seasoned politicians who understood this necessity. An open break between them would have been damaging to both.

THE CIVIL RIGHTS BILL OF 1964

A high point of legislative-executive cooperation—and a landmark achievement—in the early days of the Johnson administration was the passage of the Civil Rights Act of 1964. Unlike the earlier efforts under Johnson's leadership of the Senate, it was not enacted under southern sufferance but by a strong majority over the unremitting opposition of the senators from Dixie. The 1964 act was one of the most far-reaching pieces of domestic legislation of the twentieth century. It went much further than ever before to enforce the right to vote; to ban racial discrimination in hotels, motels, restaurants, and other places of public accommodation; and to prohibit discrimination on the basis of race, creed, or gender in employment and throughout the land. Originally not intended to cover discrimination on the basis of sex, this provision was mischievously added in the House by opponents believing it would sink the bill—but it turned out to be an added strength, and the Magna Carta for female employment in the United States.

Shortly after noon on February 17, 1964, Mansfield rose in his front row aisle seat and paused expectantly as the Senate doorkeeper loudly announced the arrival of a messenger from the other side of the Capitol bearing the action copy of H.R. (House of Representatives bill) 7152, which had been passed by the House seven days earlier. The Majority Leader welcomed this long-awaited and bitterly divisive bill with an eloquent statement:

> Speaking for myself, let me say at the outset that I should have preferred it had the civil rights been resolved before my time as a senator or had it not come to the floor until afterward. The Senator from Montana has no lust for conflict in connection with this matter; yet this question is one which invites conflict, for it divides deeply. . . . But, Mr. President, great public issues are not subject to our personal timetables; they do not accommodate themselves to our individ-

ual preference or convenience. They emerge in their own way and in their own time. . . . The time is now. The crossroads is here in the Senate.

A western liberal loyal to the Democratic Party, Mansfield had never been known as a strong supporter of civil rights legislation, which threatened to split the party into northern and southern wings. African Americans, for whom the legislation was predominately crafted, made up only two-tenths of one percent of Montana's citizenry. In 1956, as noted earlier, Mansfield had joined three other western Democrats in voting to bottle up civil rights legislation in return for southern Democratic votes on a hydroelectric project in Idaho. In 1957 he voted for the first successful civil rights legislation since Reconstruction; however, despite the Herculean efforts of Johnson, then Senate majority leader, it was a relatively toothless bill that dealt only with voting rights, and those in very limited fashion. In 1962 Majority Leader Mansfield agreed to work for passage of a stronger voting rights bill sponsored by President Kennedy but abandoned the bill in the face of a southern filibuster after leading what Valeo later called "a halfhearted effort." Afterward Mansfield informed Attorney General Robert Kennedy that a Democratic president would never be able to enact such a bill because of the necessity of obtaining Republican votes to cut off debate in the Senate on this highly politicized issue.

By 1964, however, two crucial developments had transformed Mansfield's attitude and the legislative prospects. First, national sentiment toward the plight of the American Negro had changed dramatically. Thousands of black students had marched to obtain access to the lunch counters of Birmingham, Alabama, to be met by the fire hoses and police dogs of police commissioner Eugene "Bull" Connor; the Rev. Martin Luther King Jr. had been jailed in Birmingham, to the concern of President Kennedy in Washington; King and others had staged the impressive March on Washington at which King delivered his famous "I have a dream" speech. These and other powerful events, conveyed to the public via national television, had brought swiftly growing support for the civil rights cause. Second, Lyndon Johnson, immediately after John Kennedy's assassination, had made civil rights legislation a top priority of his administration, declaring to a joint session of Congress, "We have talked long enough in this country about equal rights. . . . It is time now to write the next chapter—and to write it in the books of law." And to do so in honor of the memory of the late President.

Johnson, whose early experiences and closest congressional ties arose from the segregationist South, was determined on becoming president to put the taint of racism behind him. His inclination was to dominate and manage everything within his grasp, but after the humiliation of the Democratic caucus of January 1961 he realized that overt and overwhelming intervention in senatorial affairs would be resented and probably counterproductive. Throughout the struggle for the 1964 civil rights bill he was a cheerleader in public speeches and interviews and worked assiduously behind the scenes with the key senatorial figures, discussing timing, procedure, and strategy with Mansfield and others. But even while giving the fight for civil rights legislation his prestige, power, and commitment, Johnson wrote in his memoirs, "I deliberately tried to tone down my personal involvement in the daily struggle so that my colleagues on the Hill would take tactical responsibility—and credit."

Mansfield had been in the Senate leadership in 1957 and 1960, when Johnson as Majority Leader had staged round-the-clock sessions on the issue, forcing pro–civil rights senators to sleep in their offices or the Capitol to answer quorum calls in post-midnight hours. The result was dramatic and sometimes hilarious, as senators shuffled into the well-lit chamber just awakened from sleep, their clothes in disarray. The failure to break the filibusters, however, required Johnson to water down the bills to the point that the southern bloc would accept them.

Early in 1963 as vice president, Johnson was eager to join the civil rights battle once more by taking advantage of the infirmity of its opponents. In a discussion with Eugene McCarthy and several other northern liberals, he ticked off the physical disabilities of prominent southerners—"Harry Byrd just got out of the hospital. Allen Ellender just went into the hospital. Dick Russell thinks he's got cancer of the throat. . . ."—and suggested a rigorous parliamentary challenge to take advantage of their weaknesses. However, as McCarthy later noted, this line of thinking was foreign to Mansfield. In 1964, despite prodding from LBJ and journalists, Mansfield refused to schedule round-the-clock sessions, which he considered dangerous to the health of elderly senators and demeaning to the Senate. "This is not a circus sideshow," he insisted. "We are not operating a pit with spectators coming into the galleries at night to see senators of the Republic come out in bedroom slippers without neckties, with their hair uncombed, and pajama tops sticking out of their necks." Johnson was unhappy with this decision but despite a close watch and frequent interjection into legislative affairs, could not overrule the Majority Leader.

As Mansfield saw it, there was little possibility of obtaining a face-saving compromise in 1964 by making deals with the southerners. The political momentum behind the legislation was too strong. Moreover, Johnson had pledged publicly and privately to civil rights leaders that the administration would not abandon the main features of the proposed legislation. This pledge was given despite the fact that the bill contained unprecedented provisions extending federal government power for the first time to discrimination in public accommodations and private employment.

Only one route to passage appeared open: obtaining the votes of the required two-thirds of senators present and voting to impose the cloture provision ending debate, which would permit a vote on the measure by majority rule. Since Mansfield assumed, correctly, that all of the 100 senators would be mobilized to vote on such a contentious measure, he would have to obtain 67 votes to cut off the debate. This cloture rule—opponents called it a "gag rule"—had been rarely imposed on a body that prided itself on unlimited debate. This was an arduous—many believed, impossible—task. Although the Democrats enjoyed a 67-to-33 majority, about 20 conservative Democrats from the South and elsewhere often joined most Republicans to weaken or oppose civil rights and government-spending measures. As the civil rights debate began, the influential news magazine *Time* put a portrait of a pensive Mansfield on its cover with a challenging headline, "Can Democrats Control a Democratic Senate?" The reality of existing voting patterns, the magazine observed, "brings into critical question the ability of a Democratic majority, no matter what its size, to achieve effective control of the Senate on some of the critical issues of the day."

Under normal procedures bills passed by the House would be routinely transferred to the appropriate Senate committee, in this case the Judiciary Committee headed by James O. Eastland of Mississippi, an inveterate and wily foe of civil rights legislation. This time, Mansfield announced that he would move to hold H.R. 7152 at the presiding officer's desk, bypassing the committee and asking that it become the legislative business of the entire Senate. Each of those procedural steps, as he knew, would be subject to lengthy debate, although southern strategists would later delay mounting their full-scale filibuster until the bill itself was being considered.

It was clear from the first that the only way to succeed was in close collaboration with his opposite number, Everett Dirksen, the minority leader, who held the key to Republican support for cloture. "Dirksen is the one who had to get the votes," Mansfield told me in looking back on the struggle. An unusual degree of trust and cooperation with leaders and members of the opposing party had been a hallmark of Mansfield's style from the beginning of his leadership, and here it served him well. "I think for a year or so [Dirksen] didn't know how to size me up," Mansfield recalled. "Never did anything behind his back. Neither did he with me. There would be no civil rights bill without Dirksen."

Mansfield had begun extensive discussions on civil rights with Dirksen even before President Kennedy submitted the original version of the civil rights bill to Congress in June 1963. Mansfield had also requested that the President and his brother, the attorney general, personally meet Dirksen and other Republican senators to make their case, which had been done. After Kennedy's assassination, President Johnson, who had close ties with Dirksen from his own days as Majority Leader, intensified his dialogue with the minority leader.

As he welcomed the bill, which had already passed in the House, on February 17, Mansfield asked the Senate to put aside expediency and political profit, passions, sectionalism, and inertia—a tall order for a highly political body. Turning to his opposite number across the narrow aisle that divides the desks of the parties in the chamber, he publicly appealed to Dirksen, "whose patriotism has always taken precedence over his partisanship, to join with me—and I know he will—in finding the Senate's best possible contribution at this time, to resolution of this grave national issue." Mansfield also appealed by name to George Aiken of Vermont, his customary breakfast companion and a progressive Republican who nevertheless was cool to cloture, and Bourke Hickenlooper of Iowa, a leader of the conservative wing of Senate Republicans, who was considered a firm opponent of cloture but who was on friendly terms with Mansfield and especially Valeo.

Well before the legislation came to the Senate, Mansfield decided that he would not act as Democratic floor manager for the bill. For that role, at Johnson's suggestion, he designated Hubert Humphrey, the Majority

Whip and an ardent advocate of civil rights going back to his earlier political career as mayor of Minneapolis. This arrangement put Humphrey in
the thick of the highly emotional struggle and left Mansfield above the
battle with lines out to senators of all points of view while still retaining a
role in strategic decisions.

Mansfield, on being designated as Majority Leader three years earlier, had
selected Humphrey over George Smathers to be majority whip (giving
Smathers the number three position as chairman of the Democratic
Conference). Although Humphrey and Mansfield denied it in later years,
their relationship was said by the Minnesotan's close friends and colleagues
to be difficult. Humphrey was as passionate and enthusiastic as Mansfield
was restrained and often uncommunicative. As floor leader for civil rights
Humphrey was an obvious and excellent choice. Due to his long experience,
he was intimately familiar with the details of the complex issues involved.
He was close to Johnson, who later selected him as his vice president. Equally
important, he enjoyed and retained the confidence of civil rights leaders,
black and white, and of the Justice Department operatives on the bill even
when tactical decisions were not to their liking.

A potential pitfall was Humphrey's tendency to become engaged simultaneously in a wide variety of subjects and causes, but this proved not the
case when he was given the lead responsibility for this historic bill. "Usually
[Humphrey] had three or four concentrations on different things going at
a time. Fine mind. But he seemed to have put everything else aside and concentrated on this bill," Mansfield recalled. It was Humphrey who met regularly and intensively with civil rights lobby groups and with administration
officials working on the bill. As the debate proceeded, key meetings often
took place in Dirksen's office in recognition of the crucial Republican role.
With few exceptions, Humphrey met Dirksen every day to discuss the politics and progress of the bill and urge him on.

Mansfield also sought to engage Richard Russell of Georgia, a valued
friend and a revered member of the Senate, who was the leader of the southern bloc and of the opposition to the bill. Mansfield, who credited Russell
with a central role in proposing him for the post of majority whip in 1957,
had enjoyed cordial relations with Russell dating from the days when
Russell's senior colleague from Georgia, Walter George, had been a mentor
to Mansfield in foreign affairs.

Shortly before the House bill arrived at the Senate door, Mansfield invited Russell to his Capitol office, where he outlined how he planned to proceed on the civil rights bill—bypassing the Judiciary Committee but with no duplicity, no attempts at end runs around the rules, of which Russell was a master, no all-night sessions or other attempts to coerce opponents of the bill. The rights of the southern minority as well as those of the majority would be fully protected, Mansfield said. Russell was astounded by Mansfield's candor and wondered if it were the prelude to some unpleasant surprise—perhaps a discovery of an obscure provision in the rules that had somehow eluded the master parliamentary experts from Dixie. Other than mounting an effort to win the day by obtaining 67 votes for cloture, which Russell considered unlikely, the Georgian could not understand how the Majority Leader hoped to succeed. This was only the beginning of Mansfield's candor with the leader of the opposition. "I kept Russell informed of every move that we made on the civil rights bill. I don't think he took me too seriously at first, but he did with the passage of time. [There were] no back strokes, no hidden areas," Mansfield told me.

On February 19, two days after welcoming the bill to the Senate, Mansfield and Humphrey convened a meeting with six western Democrats in the Majority Leader's office. Mansfield began by pointing out that there would be no civil rights bill of any consequence without imposing cloture to stop a filibuster, adding that the votes of western Democrats, who had traditionally been opposed to cloture, were essential to success. Humphrey brought up the politics of the situation: the Democratic Party "would take a beating" in urban areas if the Senate faltered on civil rights, with members of Congress rather than the President suffering the most. Humphrey reiterated Mansfield's frequently expressed view that 20 to 25 Republican votes were also required for cloture. "If we win, we will get credit along with the Republicans and if we lose we will get all the blame," Humphrey maintained.

Mansfield and Humphrey had counted on southern foot-dragging and opposition on procedural issues, but there was more of it than even they had expected. Debate on the bill began March 9, but it took until March 30 to establish it formally as the pending business of the Senate. In order to press for resolving the measure, Mansfield decreed that no other business would be transacted until consideration of the civil rights bill had been completed, and he barred committees from meeting during the hours—

most of the day—when the Senate was in session. Altogether the Senate met on the civil rights bill for eighty-three consecutive working days, involving 121 roll-call votes and more than 10 million words of oratory. This was the longest debate in Senate history, a record that still stands.

On April 9, in preparation for a strategy meeting to be chaired by Mansfield the following day with Attorney General Robert Kennedy, White House lobbyists, and key senators, Valeo presented his first detailed estimates of the votes available to cut off debate. Thirty-nine Democrats and nine Republicans were estimated to be certain to vote for cloture, with three more Republicans likely to do so. This added up to 51 votes, enough to pass a bill through the 100-member Senate but far short of the 67 votes needed for cloture. With twenty-two southern or border-state senators virtually certain to oppose cloture and only about a half-dozen additional Democrats amenable to possible persuasion, it was clear that most of the additional votes would have to come from Republicans, many of them from mid-western conservatives who had worked hand-in-glove with southern conservatives on controversial legislation for many years. The vote count dramatized anew that Dirksen and the conservative wing of his party held the balance of power.

While the talkfest on the Senate floor droned on, Dirksen conferred in private with the Republicans and began to position himself to make a deal. In a meeting on April 23, Mansfield, Humphrey, Kennedy, and others of the White House–Justice Department lobbying group decided to try to work with Dirksen to amend a controversial provision involving jury trials in contempt-of-court proceedings that arose from the bill. Mansfield picked up the phone and called the GOP leader, who walked into the Majority Leader's office to join the meeting minutes later. After a discussion of the issues he agreed to joint sponsorship with Mansfield of an administration-endorsed compromise. This was the beginning of serious negotiations with Dirksen, a development that suggested to Mansfield and the other participants that the end was approaching and victory was in sight.

Six days later Dirksen met in his office with Mansfield, Humphrey, Robert Kennedy, and a variety of senators and staff aides. To the surprise of his guests, Dirksen unveiled not just one but forty amendments to the bill, some technical but some substantive. Agreement on these amendments, most of which were acceptable or negotiable, brought Dirksen formally behind the bill. But further legislative jockeying, plus the necessity to sell the revised bill to Republicans and Democrats in both the House and Senate as well as the civil rights community, consumed most of May. By the beginning of June, the bill had won widespread approval, but senators were nearing exhaustion. The vote on a petition to shut off debate, co-sponsored by Mansfield and Dirksen, was scheduled for June 9, later changed to June 10. Fierce last-minute lobbying on all sides was quickly under way.

Mansfield, for whom arm-twisting or making unrelated political deals for votes was anathema, pursued the drive for cloture votes in his own way. While Humphrey and the White House pulled out the stops to win the balloting, Mansfield on June 3 quietly addressed personal letters to seven wavering western and border-state Democrats. Rather than engage them on the issue of civil rights, Mansfield cited his deep concern about the reputation of the Senate, which had been debating a set of critical issues of great public importance for more than two months without taking a single substantive vote. In a remarkably gentle appeal, a stark contrast from the muscular pressures that had been exerted by Johnson as Majority Leader and by Johnson now as President, Mansfield wrote:

> I can understand any position on the question of civil rights itself. I can understand and sympathize with your traditional viewpoint on cloture. Your people are not too different from mine. The situation in your state is not unlike mine. Yet, I can see no honorable way out of the present predicament for the Senate other than the course of cloture. I wish that it were otherwise but it is not.
>
> May I take the liberty to ask you, therefore, to consider again your position on the question of cloture. If you can see a way in good conscience to support the motion on next Tuesday, I would most respectfully ask you to take it. In the event that you cannot, it goes without saying that I shall understand it.

On the day of the vote the Democratic and Republican leaderships believed they had the votes to cut off debate, but nobody could be certain. The galleries were packed. On the Senate floor, nearly everyone was in his place. Mansfield rose and spoke first, declaring, "The Senate now stands at the crossroads of history, and the time for decision is at hand." Next was the turn of Russell, who charged that the bill violated both the spirit and the letter of the Constitution and "would destroy forever the doctrine of separation of powers." Humphrey spoke briefly, saying that senators voting for cloture would "make that dream of full freedom, full justice, and full citizenship for every American a reality." Finally it was the turn of Dirksen, who had been in poor health and whose peptic ulcer had recently flared anew. Those who expected his customary soaring oratory were disappointed. Speaking in a low voice, he cited one of his favorite quotations, by Victor Hugo: "Stronger than all the armies is an idea whose time has come." Dirksen declared, "The time has come for equality of opportunity in sharing in government, in education, in employment. It will not be stayed or denied. It is here." As Dirksen sat down in his front row seat, Humphrey crossed the aisle and shook his hand.

A hush fell over the chamber as the roll was called, leaving the Senate more silent, Mansfield said later, than he had ever heard it. In the end 44 Democrats and 27 Republicans, four more than the required 67 senators, cast their votes for cloture. Three of those who had received Mansfield's letter voted to cut off debate; four did not. The most dramatic vote was that of Democrat Clair Engle of California, near death from a brain tumor, who was wheeled into the chamber but, unable to speak, was barely able to point to his eye, which was registered as an "aye" vote before he was wheeled back out.

Following the victory, the Democratic and Republican leadership teams gathered in Mansfield's office for a joyous bout of handshaking, statements, and photographs for the press. True to his self-effacing nature, Mansfield avoided being included in any of the photographs.

Nine days of debate and voting followed the imposition of cloture, but everyone knew the die was cast. Final passage came on June 19 by a 73-27 vote. After a debate, the House agreed to accept the Senate-passed bill without amendment and sent it to the White House. Johnson signed the Civil Rights Act of 1964 into law in a grand ceremony in the East Room on July 2.

Most of the public acclaim went to Dirksen and Humphrey in the Senate, Democrat Emanuel Celler and Republican William McCulloch in the House, and Lyndon Johnson in the White House. Nonetheless, senators on all sides of the battle wrote letters of thanks and praise to Mansfield. "Much of the credit for the fact that [the bill] was disposed of without leaving large schisms was due to the good, calm, patient, magnanimous, long suffering, unselfish and much admired Mike Mansfield," wrote Smathers, who had opposed the bill. Pro–civil rights Republican Jacob Javits of New York wrote, "You knew when to speak and when to refrain from speaking. . . . Your hand on the controls was historic in its import, and your relations and confidence with Everett Dirksen were so strong as to bring within their influence Hubert Humphrey." Democrat Frank Lausche of Ohio, who had voted for cloture and the bill, wrote, "The credit . . . mainly belongs to you. If it had not been for your gracious and temperate consideration of the individuals who were deeply involved in the controversy, a split in the Senate might have occurred which would have been most damaging."

Passage of the Civil Rights Act of 1964 was the greatest legislative advance of the twentieth century in the battle against racial discrimination, but it did not solve all outstanding problems. With Johnson's backing, Congress later passed the Voting Rights Act of 1965, providing the assignment of federal officers to register voters in areas of the South where discrimination was rampant and, following the murder of Dr. Martin Luther King Jr., the Housing Rights Act of 1968, prohibiting discrimination in the sale and rental of housing. Having broken the southern filibuster in the first of the three historic civil rights acts, Dirksen led Senate Republicans into a bipartisan coalition that imposed cloture and permitted passage by majority vote in the two latter cases.

Perhaps the greatest immediate impact of the 1964 act was on employment opportunities for women, an issue that had not been considered by the original drafters of the measure but had been added by civil rights opponents in the House. At the time the act was passed, a little more than one in three American women over sixteen years of age was actively engaged in the labor force, but by the end of the century nearly two out of three women were so engaged. Although all discrimination had not been eliminated, millions of women had been raised to the supervisory or executive level, as the law was backed by a dramatic change in mores and ways of life.

MANSFIELD TRIES TO WORK FROM WITHIN

By early 1964, when Johnson had been in office a few weeks, Mansfield knew the drift of his thinking well enough to be apprehensive about his policies in Southeast Asia. Still, buoyed by his occasional success in intervening with Kennedy, Mansfield remained hopeful of influencing Johnson to move in different directions. Even while working in partnership with LBJ and the White House on the civil rights bill and other legislation, Mansfield carried on a private campaign to shift the emphasis and underlying principles of U.S. involvement in Vietnam. Mansfield understood "there would be no way that you could turn Johnson overnight on this question," Valeo recalled, "and that the best hope of doing it would be over a period of time in which you could gradually work from within on Johnson, as well as keeping a distance from him publicly" on the war. Valeo, however, had accompanied then-Vice President Johnson to Asia in 1961 and felt sure from Johnson's macho attitudes at that time that the current effort would be futile. "Let's keep trying," Mansfield insisted, and so Valeo continued to work on memoranda and speeches, with Mansfield providing the initiative and direction and Valeo doing most of the drafting.

On February 1, 1964, Mansfield sent Johnson his third memorandum on Indochina in the three months of Johnson's presidency. The four-page memo was prompted by a new de Gaulle statement calling for a negotiated transition to a neutral Vietnam and by a new military coup in Saigon. The de Gaulle approach, he said, "offers a faint glimmer of hope of a way to solution at a cost to us commensurate with our national interests." Mansfield recommended anew that the United States encourage and explore French-related neutrality policies in Laos and Cambodia as well as Vietnam.

He predicted accurately that the military coup in Saigon, this time against the plotters who overthrew Diem, was not likely to be the last one or to "produce any significant improvement in the situation," although it was being touted by officials as good news. On the contrary, he predicted, coup after coup of military leaders jockeying for control of U.S. aid could well produce Vietnamese governments "increasingly divorced from any real concern with the needs of the Vietnamese people." In that case, he foresaw, "we will find ourselves engaged merely in an indecisive, bloody and costly military involvement and the involvement will probably have to increase just to keep the situation as it is."

Referring to his earlier memoranda of December 7 and January 6 as background, Mansfield cautioned against expanding the U.S. role in Saigon. "We are already on the verge of turning a war in Vietnam which is still primarily a Vietnamese responsibility into an American war to be paid for primarily with American lives. I see no national interest at this time which would justify that plunge and I most emphatically do not recommend it." At that moment, however, the administration was asking General Nguyen Khanh, the new Saigon leader, to accept U.S. military advisers, previously resident only at the headquarters of Vietnamese provinces, at the level of districts within provinces in thirteen key areas. Khanh quickly approved, and 1,000 more U.S. advisers for Vietnamese districts and military units soon arrived, placing U.S. officers and men on the ground throughout nearly the entire South Vietnamese military hierarchy and diluting Vietnamese authority and responsibility.

Mansfield met Johnson to discuss this and other issues on the evening of February 10. Before the meeting Bundy suggested to the President that he tell Mansfield that "for the present any weakening of our support of anti-Communist forces in South Vietnam would give the signal for a wholesale collapse of anti-Communism all over Southeast Asia." In view of the tenuous situation in Saigon, Bundy also recommended that Johnson ask Mansfield "not to express his own doubts in public, at least for a while."

If such an appeal was made, it was not heeded. On February 19, two days after he welcomed the House-passed civil rights bill to the Senate, Mansfield delivered his first major address on Vietnam in the Senate since the Eisenhower administration. He gave no hint that he had sent a succession of private appeals to Johnson, but the key statement in his speech, repeated in many news stories, was a paraphrase of the February 1 memo: "We have teetered for far too long on the brink of turning the war in Vietnam which is still a Vietnamese war into an American war to be paid for primarily with American lives. There is no national interest at this time . . . which would appear to justify this conversion." As he often did, Mansfield softened his remarks with words of praise for Johnson, who he said "acted most appropriately" in trying to help the Vietnamese achieve stability and peace. The following day, Senator Jacob Javits, a New York Republican who was hawkish on the war, challenged Mansfield in a floor debate which, as the Majority Leader noted, broke "a long silence" in the Senate on Vietnam.

The President, while seemingly tolerant of Mansfield's private advice, was stung by this evidence of public dissent. Above all, Johnson wanted to avoid the opening of a debate in Congress on Vietnam that would challenge his decisions and damage the drive for the economic and social programs that were closest to his heart. The day after Mansfield's speech he asked McNamara to line up General David Shoup, the just-retired commandant of Mansfield's beloved U.S. Marine Corps, to try to "put a stop" to Mansfield's public remarks. Shortly thereafter syndicated columnist William S. White, a Texan so close to Johnson he was considered his unofficial spokesman, fiercely attacked Mansfield for his speech, declaring that "the bipartisan foreign policy of this nation is being undercut in an area of maximum crisis, Southeast Asia, by the Democratic leader of the Senate, Mike Mansfield of Montana." White wrote that neutralism as favored by de Gaulle [and endorsed by Mansfield] "is precisely what the Communists have always advocated as the first step to Communist conquest." Making clear the source of his concern, White said Johnson had remained silent on Mansfield's remarks because "a President needs a close relationship with the Senate leader of his own party, and the White House inevitably must walk softly in this embarrassing matter." As Johnson had feared, the Mansfield speech stirred a discussion in Congress and among columnists and editorial writers about U.S. policy in Vietnam—for the first time since LBJ became president—and about the responsibility of the Senate Democratic leader on questions of war and peace.

Twice more before mid-summer, Mansfield delivered his views directly to Johnson. On May 25 in his fourth memorandum, which he handed to the President at a White House breakfast, he appealed again for serious exploration of international negotiations to resolve the conflicts in Indochina peacefully, with special attention to the roles of the French and the United Nations. In telephone conversations, LBJ reacted scornfully, telling Richard Russell that Mansfield "just wants to pull up and get out," a proposition that the President subsequently repeated on numerous occasions, but which did not appear in any of Mansfield's memoranda or speeches to Johnson and was never expressed in his verbal advice. Reading parts of the most recent memo to Russell, the President declared that "conferences ain't gonna do a damn bit of good." To McGeorge Bundy, after acknowledging that the Indochina situation "worries the hell out of me," Johnson derided Mansfield's plea for a start of international negotiations to resolve the conflict, saying "it's just milquetoast as it can be" and that the Majority Leader "got no spine at all."

With Texas bravado, Johnson was proceeding unswervingly into the military morass. After an upsurge of fighting in Laos, U.S. warplanes in mid-May secretly began low-level reconnaissance flights over communist-occupied Laotian territory, the first direct and overt U.S. military action in Indochina. On June 9, the day before the hard-fought cloture vote on civil rights in the Senate, Mansfield was notified by a presidential telephone call that a U.S. reconnaissance plane had been shot down and that U.S. forces had bombed an antiaircraft site in retaliation. Despite his private contempt for international conferences and negotiations, Johnson sought to convince Mansfield that "we have told de Gaulle that we are very anxious to follow any conference route that we can, that we're very anxious to follow any plan of neutralization that we can." LBJ insisted that despite the need to show U.S. strength in Laos, "I don't want to get in a land war in Asia." Mansfield appeared to be mollified momentarily and said that so far as procedures with Congress were concerned, "I think you've done everything right." Nonetheless, within hours Mansfield delivered a new memorandum—his fifth—urging caution lest the reconnaissance flights and bombing of anti-aircraft sites in Laos involve the United States more deeply in war *even against our inclination or expectation*" (emphasis in original).

Mansfield repeated his consistent view that U.S. national interests were not served by "a deep military involvement in Southeast Asia." He urged that if Johnson continued along this line he should explain the basis for his decisions to the American people in a way "much clearer and more persuasive" than had been done. At the same time, he also made the point strongly—and repeatedly—that as President, "you alone can make the decisions. From the Senate, we can only give you, in the last analysis, our trust, our support and such independent thoughts as may occur to us from time to time in the hope that they may be constructive." Mansfield was torn between his opposition to the rapidly expanding U.S. military action and his continuing belief in presidential supremacy in matters of war and peace. He expressed both sides of this contradiction forthrightly in his memo.

The President, for his part, told Robert McNamara in a telephone conversation that the Mansfield memo was "interesting," and read parts of it to the defense secretary. McNamara said Mansfield was "absolutely right" that the American people should be alerted to the prospect of an "escalating chain" in Southeast Asia, although he added that "I'm not sure now is exactly the right time." Johnson, going into a presidential election campaign, did not think so. Continuing to distort and belittle Mansfield's advice, he told McNamara, "So what he comes out and says is he thinks we ought to get out of there. Which we can't and are not going to." No such statement existed in Mansfield's memorandum.

In spite of that dismissal, Mansfield's memo had touched a nerve with Johnson. When LBJ discussed it with his mentor, Richard Russell, the Georgia senator responded, "I in a way share some of [Mansfield's] fears" about the consequences of deepening involvement. The President replied, "I do too, but the fear the other way [failure to engage] is more." He added, "We're in here by treaty," referring to the SEATO treaty of 1954, "and our national honor's at stake. . . . And being there, we've got to conduct ourselves like men."

PHANTOM TORPEDOS IN TONKIN GULF

Until August 1964, most of Mansfield's advice to Johnson on Indochina had been volunteered and presented either in private or in rare Senate speeches and interviews, on a philosophical and political plane. On the evening of August 4, however, Mansfield for the first time dissented from Johnson's warlike actions in the presence of the senior congressional leadership and Johnson's top national security team. The event was a landmark in the political development of the war, and in the relations between the President and the Majority Leader.

On the early morning of August 2, the USS *Maddox,* a Navy destroyer on intelligence duty equipped with sophisticated listening devices, was attacked by three North Vietnamese torpedo boats near the North Vietnamese coast in the Gulf of Tonkin. The *Maddox,* which had intercepted a message ordering the attack, fired first and was not hit by any of the torpedoes. The Vietnamese boats were damaged by U.S. fire but, contrary to the confused early reports, none was sunk. On the night of August 4 (morning in the United States), the *Maddox* and a sister ship, the *Turner Joy,* reported being under renewed and continuous attack by torpedo boats. By lunchtime Johnson had decided on a retaliatory air strike, the first such overt attack by U.S. forces against North Vietnam. Even more important in the light of history, the State Department that afternoon put the finishing touches on a joint Senate-House resolution to be submitted to Congress citing the Tonkin Gulf attacks and authorizing the President "to take all necessary steps, including the use of armed force," to assist South Vietnam under the terms of the Southeast Asia Treaty of 1954. The combination of the first air strike against North Vietnam and passage of the Tonkin Gulf resolution crossed an important threshold, taking the United States closer than ever before to full-scale war in Indochina.

Johnson, a creature of Congress who was ever mindful of the need for legislative backing, called sixteen congressional leaders of both parties to the White House at 6:45 P.M. The meeting was couched as consultation about what to do, although Johnson actually had signed off shortly before the meeting on the retaliatory attacks—carried out within hours by fifty-nine U.S. warplanes from two aircraft carriers striking North Vietnamese patrol boat bases and an oil depot. The lawmakers and later the public were told that this was a necessary response to unprovoked attacks against U.S. vessels on the high seas and a daring challenge to the United States. The principal questions by the congressional leaders, according to White House notes of the meeting, were whether American warships in the area could protect themselves in case of further trouble and what targets had been chosen for retaliation. None of the leaders voiced objections—until Mansfield spoke up.

The news of the second attack had broken earlier in the day, giving Mansfield time to gather his thoughts about the likely reaction at the White House meeting. When asked for his opinion, he said he supposed Johnson wished him to be frank. "I don't know how much good it will do," he said, evidently referring to the statement of his position. The current situation, he noted, was in sharp contrast to the Cuban Missile Crisis, when the United States confronted the "principal enemy," the Soviet Union, and virtually ignored its minor partner, Cuba. This time, he said, "We may . . . be on the verge of getting ourselves into the trap of becoming inextricably and deeply involved with a minor, third rate enemy nation on its own terrain and by its provocation."

Not knowing that Johnson had already approved the order, he predicted accurately that the next step would be to bomb the torpedo boat bases, which could lead in turn to North Vietnamese ground action in the South. "Then what is to come in response if it is not another massive Korea-type involvement on our part, with not only the Soviet Union but China standing outside the fray at least at the outset?" This would be "the wrong confrontation" for the United States, he said. Unlike the Cuban crisis, it would not be quickly resolved but "promises a prolonged and massive military involvement by the United States throughout Vietnam." Assessing the intentions and determination of the North

Vietnamese in a fashion that proved to be extraordinarily accurate, he added, "The Communists are obviously, not going to be faced down. It now appears that they are not going to be stung down. That leaves only the possibility of mowing them down and that is going to take a lot of time and a great many lives."

Asked by Johnson to give him "a formula" for responding, Mansfield responded with four recommendations he had prepared before the meeting: (1) Place a moratorium on militant talk from General Khanh, the South Vietnamese leader and from all other sources; (2) Treat the incidents as "isolated acts of terror" and retaliate only in international waters; (3) Take the incident to the United Nations as a threat to the peace; and (4) Ask the Soviet Union and Britain, co-chairmen of the 1954 Geneva conference, to consider the problem "as a matter of urgency."

Mansfield's prediction that bombing North Vietnam could be the turning point toward greater war was accurate. Until the events of the Tonkin Gulf, North Vietnamese leaders, while working to strengthen communist-led insurgent forces in the South—known to Americans as Vietcong—had cautiously avoided authorizing actions that might incite the United States to expand its military role. According to William J. Duiker, a leading historian of the communist side of the war, the retaliatory air raids convinced North Vietnamese party leaders that the United States was preparing for major escalation, including the probable dispatch of U.S. ground troops. In the fall of 1964 the Politburo for the first time dispatched North Vietnamese Army (NVA) main force units to the South to join northern commanders and specialists in the growing Vietcong forces, hoping to topple the weak Saigon regime before the United States could intervene. Evidently seeking to impress Washington with the risks of greater involvement, Hanoi's leaders also reversed their previous caution and ordered terrorist attacks on U.S. installations in the South. The Tonkin Gulf bombing raids also reverberated in China, which immediately flew three dozen MiGs to an airfield near Hanoi to assist North Vietnamese air defenses. Mao Tse-tung, concerned that the United States was embarking on a general war, began moving the country's industrial factories away from vulnerable coastal areas into the interior to prepare for an American invasion.

The White House notes made by Johnson's aide Walter Jenkins do not record any response by the President to Mansfield's views or suggestions.

However, Secretary of State Rusk responded by saying that the "principal problem" was that China—always a major consideration in Rusk's mind—had not
committed itself to a course of action in Vietnam. He argued that the Cuban
Missile Crisis cited by Mansfield was "quite different in a number of respects"
and that limited retaliation, as proposed by the President, "gives the other side
a chance to pull away." Rusk had said earlier that the United States proposed
to take the attacks to the UN Security Council and to the Geneva Conference
co-chairmen, but *after* the U.S. retaliation had taken place.

Seeking to project a picture of congressional unity, the White House
sought to muffle Mansfield's objections to bombing North Vietnam and his
predictions of a much wider war. The *Washington Post*, evidently on the basis
of a White House briefing, reported the next morning that none of the congressional leaders in the meeting had raised objections. However, Johnson
himself acknowledged in a telephone call to Representative George Mahon
shortly after the meeting that Mansfield did not endorse the military strike.
As he had in May and June, he misstated Mansfield's position, claiming that
the Majority Leader "thought we ought to get out of there . . . just stay away
. . . he doesn't want to fight anybody." Yet in the account of the meeting published in his memoirs seven years later, Johnson ignored Mansfield's intervention and wrote erroneously, "Each [of the members of Congress in the
meeting] expressed his wholehearted endorsement of our course of action
and of the proposed resolution."

At the end of the meeting, Johnson made clear that his aim was to have
the resolution passed quickly. J. William Fulbright, chairman of the Senate
Foreign Relations Committee, responded with his support for the measure.
House Republican leader Charles Halleck did likewise and predicted it
would pass overwhelmingly. Reflecting the difficulty of failing to support a
president's response to an attack on U.S. forces, Mansfield's close friend
Senator George Aiken told LBJ insightfully, "By the time you send it up
there [to Capitol Hill] there won't be anything for us to do but support you."
At that point, Mansfield said only that he would send the resolution to the
Foreign Relations Committee.

Mansfield told me many years later that "we had our doubts" at the time
about what had actually happened in the Tonkin Gulf. Such doubts proved
to be well founded as further information eventually came to light about the
episode, which scholars have compared to the Japanese attack on Pearl

Harbor and the assassination of John F. Kennedy as among the most heavily contested episodes in contemporary American history. What Mansfield and the other congressional leaders did not know at the time, and what even most administration policymakers did not fully understand, was a host of facts that cast a different light on the incident:

Clandestine military raids on North Vietnam under CIA sponsorship had taken place for several years and had been stepped up in February 1964 in an effort to cope with growing infiltration to the South. On the night of July 30–31, precisely the time that the *Maddox,* whose mission was part of a separate intelligence-gathering operation known as a DeSoto patrol, was entering the Gulf of Tonkin, a CIA-backed raiding party shelled North Vietnamese radar and military installations. Even at this writing, it remains unclear whether someone in the U.S. chain of command deliberately arranged the juxtaposition of these events in hopes of provoking North Vietnam or whether there was simply a failure of coordination. In either case it appears entirely likely, as suspected by some senior officials in Washington, that the August 2 attack on the *Maddox* was a North Vietnamese response to the raids in the same area. The officials did not disclose this to the congressional leaders.

After the August 2 incident, instead of pulling back, Johnson signed off on new raids and assigned a second destroyer, the *Turner Joy,* to the sea patrol. He seemed to be anticipating a new attack on the destroyers and U.S. retaliation. Whatever provocation the renewed raids might have created, the weight of evidence now is that the "unprovoked" North Vietnamese attacks on the two destroyers on August 4, the basis for the U.S. retaliation and the joint resolution, never took place. Instead, the reports of attacks appear to have been the result of a dark, stormy night, jumpy crews, and a radar anomaly called "Tonkin Gulf Ghost" or "Tonkin Spook," found in that area and a few others, that generates false images on radar screens. Six weeks after the incident and the passage of the Tonkin Gulf resolution, Johnson privately expressed his own doubts, telling McNamara in a telephone call, "When we got through with all the firing, we concluded maybe they hadn't fired at all."

Plans for U.S. retaliatory bombing of North Vietnam, we now know, had been prepared months in advance in the executive branch, as had the joint congressional resolution authorizing unlimited U.S. military action in Vietnam. These needed only to be put in final form after the Tonkin Gulf events. This was unknown to the congressional leaders called to the White

House on August 4, although both Mansfield and Fulbright were suspicious that they did not know the whole story. An informant from the Pentagon told Democrat Wayne Morse of Oregon, the most outspoken senatorial opponent of the war, that the *Maddox* was not on a "routine patrol," as the administration had claimed, but was gathering intelligence in proximity to the CIA-backed raids in a way that added up to a provocation. Morse discussed the disclosure informally with other senators, but he did not pursue it forcefully and found nobody else willing to do so. On the basis of his inside information, Morse charged in the Senate floor debate that under the circumstances the United States was "a provocateur," but his views were ignored.

Why did Mansfield, Fulbright, and other Democrats leery of military involvement swallow their doubts? A large part of the answer was presidential politics. The Tonkin Gulf episode happened between the Republican National Convention in July that had nominated Senator Barry Goldwater of Arizona as its party's presidential candidate and the Democratic National Convention beginning August 24, which was set to nominate Johnson for a full four-year term. The tough-talking Goldwater, assailing Johnson from the right and calling for massive U.S. bombing of Vietnam, was considered by the Democrats as a dangerous warmonger, whereas the President was positioned in the center as a strong but prudent leader. According to Pat Holt, who was acting chief of staff of the Senate Foreign Relations Committee, the Democrats on the Foreign Relations and Armed Services Committees felt it necessary to support "a moderate Democratic President, or what looked like a moderate Democratic President, against the onslaughts of this bomb-them-out, shoot-them-up Republican." The Republicans on the committees, he added, "could scarcely refuse to support even this much."

Meeting in Mansfield's office on the afternoon of August 5, he and the Democratic and Republican leaders of the Senate Foreign Relations and Armed Services Committees and the House Foreign Affairs Committee decided on expedited procedures for the Tonkin Gulf resolution. In stark contrast to the lengthy consideration of the Taiwan and Middle East resolutions in the late 1950s, in which he had played a major role, Mansfield asked, as the administration had requested, that the resolution not be changed in any way but voted on as it had been submitted. Except for a single cosmetic amendment, that was done.

The hearing on the measure in the House Foreign Affairs Committee took only forty minutes, and the discussion on the House floor only another forty minutes before the House adopted the resolution by unanimous vote. The joint Senate hearing of the Foreign Relations and Armed Services Committees took only one hour, forty minutes, with Rusk and McNamara testifying that the *Maddox* had been on a "routine patrol in international waters." Mansfield, Fulbright, and Russell were present but asked no questions. Fulbright later called the proceedings "a tragic mistake" and explained, "At the time, I was not in a suspicious frame of mind. I was afraid of Goldwater."

On the afternoon of August 6, just hours after the joint committee hearing, Mansfield brought the resolution to the Senate floor. In a statement that is ironic in light of later disclosures, he opened the debate by saying, "The President has acted against repeated Communist provocations in the Tonkin Gulf. He has acted in the hope of preventing an expansion of the conflict in Asia, in the hope of minimizing the American involvement on that continent." Giving no public clue to his private objections to the retaliatory raids, he declared that Johnson "has acted with a cool head and a steady hand in a most critical situation." Signaling his backing for the resolution, Mansfield said, "the President has set a course for the best interests of the Nation, for Democrats and Republicans alike, for the Government and people of the United States. He asks for and will have, in this endeavor, the support of the Congress and the people of the United States."

Mansfield said in later years that he had been undecided how he would vote on the Tonkin Gulf resolution until Fulbright, in response to Gaylord Nelson, a Democratic senator from Wisconsin, declared during the debate that he interpreted the resolution as endorsing a continuation rather than a complete change in the limited U.S. role in Vietnam. "I took Fulbright's word at face value. What he said was his understanding, I'm sure, with the President," Mansfield told me in 1998. George Reedy, a close aide to Johnson and his press secretary at the time of the Tonkin Gulf events, later said that Fulbright "had very definite assurances from Johnson that the Tonkin Gulf Resolution was not going to be used for anything other than the Tonkin Gulf incident itself." Reedy added that "psychologically" Johnson had convinced himself that he had not given Fulbright these assurances, although Reedy was certain that he had.

Led by Mansfield and Fulbright, other skeptics about the war found it impossible to oppose or even cast doubt on U.S. military action in the face of what was described on nearly all sides as an unprovoked attack. For example, Democrat Albert Gore of Tennessee, a frequent critic of Johnson and a leading skeptic of U.S. policy in Vietnam, declared that "when U.S. forces have been attacked repeatedly upon the high seas, . . . whatever doubts one may have entertained are water over the dam. Freedom of the seas must be preserved. Aggression against our forces must be repulsed." Republican George Aiken, another leading skeptic, said he continued to oppose expanding the war and was "apprehensive" about Johnson's decision to retaliate but that after Johnson decided, "I feel that I, as an American citizen, can do no less than support the President in his capacity as leader of our nation."

The resolution passed the following day by a vote of 88 to 2, with only Morse and Democrat Ernest Gruening of Alaska voting against it. Johnson's popularity skyrocketed following the reprisal attacks. With one dramatic strike, he neutralized the Goldwater charge that he was a weak military leader and cleared the path for his landslide victory in the November election.

When Johnson began to escalate the war by ordering intensive bombing of North Vietnam and sending U.S. ground troops to South Vietnam in large numbers, he repeatedly used the Gulf of Tonkin resolution as his political and legal justification. Sometimes he waved a dog-eared copy in the face of reluctant lawmakers, insisting that the resolution gave him all the support he needed to prosecute a growing war in Vietnam as he saw fit. Mansfield deeply regretted his role in the passage of the resolution, calling it "the biggest mistake of my life." As the facts of the Tonkin Gulf incident began to surface, many members of Congress seethed with resentment at the way they had been misled and the use that Johnson had made of the legislation. In February 1966 Mansfield cooperated with Morse in the Senate debate on repealing the resolution but made the successful motion to kill Morse's legislation, saying "we are in too deep now." In 1969, however, with Johnson out of the White House, Mansfield concluded that the time was right for repeal and co-sponsored with Republican Charles M. "Mac" Mathias legislation to repeal the resolution. In mid-1970, the Senate voted to repeal it—not just once, but twice.

MANSFIELD'S 1964 CAMPAIGN

The presidential election year 1964 was the final year of Mansfield's second six-year term in the Senate. There was no question that Lyndon Johnson, having inherited the presidency after the assassination of John Kennedy the year before, would seek election in his own right. Nor was there any that Majority Leader Mansfield would ask the voters of Montana for another six-year term.

"It was a good year in the Senate for Mike Mansfield," reported Kenneth Scheibel, who covered the Montana delegation in Washington for several home state daily newspapers. In sharp contrast to 1963, when Mansfield was "catching brickbats almost every day," at the end of the 1964 legislative session "he walked out of the chamber with words of praise ringing in his ears."

"What did you do differently this year, Senator?" Scheibel asked.

Very little, he told the reporter with a toss of his head. "In 1963 we passed 72 percent of the recommendations of John F. Kennedy. This year, we passed 85 percent of the Kennedy-Johnson proposals." He said Johnson sent Congress fifty-two recommendations and the Senate passed all fifty-two, although six were still pending in the House. Among the highlights were the Civil Rights Act, a $11.6 billion tax cut, and education and conservation measures. Blowing a cloud of pipe smoke, he added, "It's a record which will compare with any one year in the history of the republic!"

Montana Republicans, in view of Mansfield's lopsided victory in 1958 and his continuing popularity in the state, knew they would have an uphill battle to give him a serious race. This time they recruited Alex Blewett Jr., the Majority Leader of the Republican-dominated state legislature and the son of a former legislator from Butte, to go up against Mansfield. Blewett easily won the Republican primary in June.

In late August the principal question about the Democratic National Convention was who Johnson would select as his vice presidential running mate, especially since there was no incumbent in the job. Once Johnson had eliminated Attorney General Robert Kennedy from the running in late July by saying he would not consider any current member of the cabinet—a transparent ploy to rule out Kennedy—speculation centered on Hubert Humphrey, the exuberant Majority Whip and quintessential mainstream liberal. LBJ had already indicated to Humphrey in the spring that he had the inside track for the job, but he kept the issue open publicly until the last minute, unsettling Humphrey and breathing some suspense and news interest into the Democratic political scene.

A few days before the convention opened, Johnson confided to Humphrey that "I think I'm going to drop Mike Mansfield's name into the hopper. He'll like it and it will give a lot of people something to talk about." Adding to the Johnson-initiated trial balloon for Mansfield, the President asked his close friend Jim Rowe, who was also an intimate adviser to both Humphrey and Mansfield, to "go to work on Mansfield" to be a candidate for the vice presidential nomination. On August 21, LBJ also telephoned Kenneth O'Donnell, a John F. Kennedy loyalist who had remained on the White House staff at Johnson's request, to discuss the idea of moving Mansfield to vice president while making Humphrey majority leader. Johnson mused that Humphrey would make a more effective majority leader. Johnson told O'Donnell, less than three weeks after Mansfield's opposition to the bombing of North Vietnam in connection with the Tonkin Gulf episode, that Mansfield was "a pretty judicious fella . . . a pretty careful fella . . . pretty strong on peace," and noted that his nomination as vice president would bring a Roman Catholic to the ticket.

Both Rowe and O'Donnell considered the suggestion to be one of LBJ's political games, and expressed grave doubt that Mansfield would be interested. Rowe also made the point that their differences on Vietnam policy would be a problem for a Johnson-Mansfield ticket. After hearing what was afoot, Mansfield himself told Johnson emphatically he would not consider it. To halt the rampant speculation that Johnson had launched, Mansfield issued a public statement on the first day of the convention declaring he would "most respectfully decline" a vice presidential offer. Humphrey was nominated.

With the Johnson-Humphrey campaign under way, the President asked Mansfield in a telephone conversation in late September if he could do anything in Montana to wrap up the Majority Leader's reelection "a million percent," to make the result so overwhelming that there "never will be any question" about Mansfield's political strength at home. Mansfield insisted despite all reports to the contrary that "it's going to be a tough race" and asked Johnson to make a campaign stop in Butte, the heart of Democratic strength in the state. Johnson did so on October 12 with a ringing presidential endorsement, asking the state's voters to return Mansfield to the Senate with "the largest majority per capita" of any senator that year. He declared, "Mike Mansfield, the pride of Montana and the nation, presided over the most productive session [of Congress] in this century. He possesses those two qualities that especially belong to a leader—reason and calm judgment."

Blewett, meanwhile, sought to turn Johnson's endorsement into a liability. In a campaign speech, he called Mansfield "a puppet politician who dances to the White House tune." At the same time he criticized Mansfield as a "namby pamby" figure who had been urging the Senate to consider the neutralization of Vietnam. Blewett charged that Mansfield had been "consistently wrong . . . consistently been an advocate of appeasement . . . opposed to any action that would take the initiative away from the Communists instead of playing into their hands."

As had been widely predicted, Blewett's attacks were no match for Mansfield's prestige and popularity and his consistent attention to his Montana constituents. Mansfield was back in the state ten times during the election year, despite the fact that Congress was almost continuously in session and he had major responsibilities as Senate majority leader. He tried to make a visit to every little Montana town, of which there are many, walking the streets or rounding up a few people for coffee at a local café. "It's a wonder he didn't drown in coffee," according to Peggy DeMichele, his longtime assistant. He would talk to the people about what was going on in Washington and ask what he might do for them. He'd write down their requests on the spot, sometimes on the back of a book of matches if that was all the paper he had, and send it back to his office in Washington for action. "He met a lot of everyday people" rather than concentrating on people in powerful positions, DeMichele said.

Mansfield claimed credit for a host of federal programs and projects, including the fact that one-fourth of the nuclear-tipped intercontinental Minuteman missiles on alert against the Soviet Union were emplaced in Montana. In the final paid radio broadcast of the campaign, he generously described his opponent as "a good man" but emphasized the difference in their stature by reporting that Maureen had taught Blewett in high school in Butte. The failure of the Blewett campaign to draw support from national Republicans was notable. Senate GOP leader Everett Dirksen, who had worked closely with Mansfield on civil rights and other issues, was quoted as saying he would go anywhere to campaign for Republican candidates for office, even to the moon, but "please, don't ask me to go to Montana."

On election day in November 1964 Johnson won 61 percent of the national vote against Goldwater, the largest margin in U.S. history, and he won 59 percent of the Montana vote. Mansfield did even better, winning 64 percent of the vote against Blewett and carrying all but five of the state's fifty-six counties.

VIETNAM: ADRIFT ON A SAGGING LIMB

The most lopsided presidential election victory in history provided Lyndon Johnson with a four-year term of his own, no longer as successor to martyred and now-idealized John Kennedy. It also provided him with a heavily Democratic Congress, encouraging Johnson to embark on his own massive program of domestic government expansion as well as a more intense phase of U.S. intervention in Vietnam. Mansfield assisted in passage of the domestic measures but redoubled his efforts to forestall the military steps.

Two days before the U.S. presidential election, a Vietcong unit wearing black peasant pajamas crept into the rice fields, palm groves, and villages surrounding the U.S.-built air base at Bien Hoa, only twelve miles north of Saigon. The local peasants knew the identity of the outsiders but did nothing to alert the U.S. or South Vietnamese authorities. Before dawn the guerrillas fired a hail of mortar shells into the base, where a squadron of U.S. B-57 jet bombers, recently flown to Vietnam, were lined up in the open. Six B-57s were destroyed and many others damaged; five Americans and two South Vietnamese were killed and nearly one hundred injured. With the U.S. vote looming, Johnson decided not to react, although he had earlier agreed to order strong reprisals against North Vietnam in case of further attacks on American units. He did agree, however, to establish a high-level working group, headed by Assistant Secretary of State William Bundy, the older brother of McGeorge Bundy, the presidential national security adviser, to take a broad-ranging look at the future course of U.S. action in Vietnam.

The discussions, which proved to be among the most important of the war, consumed the month of November and ended with cabinet-level consideration and final presentation to Johnson on December 1. The resulting recommendation was a two-phase program: In Phase I, heightened U.S. military pressures against North Vietnam, beginning with more air strikes in Laos and tit-for-tat bombing raids on North Vietnam in reprisal for Vietcong attacks in the South; in Phase II, "progressively mounting" air attacks on North Vietnam to persuade Hanoi's leadership to abandon the Vietcong and its military actions against the South; in essence, strategic bombing and the start of full-scale war.

George Ball, in a sixty-seven-page memorandum to Rusk, McNamara, and McGeorge Bundy in early October and in discussions with them in November, strongly dissented from the military approach, arguing for negotiations instead. But his efforts were considered a "devil's advocate" exercise and received no serious consideration. Careful to preserve his position within the administration, Ball voiced his strongest doubts when Johnson was not present. Ball's views were shared by several important mid-level officials, but none was ready to put his career at risk by dissenting in clear-cut terms.

The President accepted the rationale and general directions that emerged from the study but ordered the immediate implementation only of Phase I, while authorizing planning for Phase II. Little was said about the deployment of U.S. ground troops, although an appendix to the study contained Joint Chiefs of Staff documents calling for the deployment of divisions of U.S. ground troops in South Vietnam and Thailand to provide protection for the U.S. airfields.

At the start of the study, its drafters gave serious consideration to possible negotiations with the North, but this was downgraded in the course of the study. By the end, the cabinet-level officials adamantly opposed the convening of a new Geneva Conference on Vietnam and put little emphasis on early negotiations of any sort. When the report was presented to Johnson, he commented that stable government in South Vietnam was "most essential." According to the study, U.S. military measures were to be implemented only after such a government was created to replace the squabbling and shifting groups of generals and civilians who were in authority in Saigon. Everyone realized this was a precondition for success in South Vietnam, but as in the case of the Diem preconditions in 1954, it proved to be too difficult to accomplish and was quickly abandoned.

Responding to a suggestion from Johnson, Ambassador Maxwell Taylor briefed the Senate Foreign Relations Committee in closed session on December 3 before returning to Saigon. Taylor did not disclose the bulk of what had been discussed or decided but told the senators that most policymakers agreed on taking U.S. military action against the North at some point. Mansfield did not attend, but it is likely he was briefed by other senators or by Carl Marcy, the committee's staff director. Alone of the senators, Mansfield reacted with a private memorandum of warning to Johnson—his sixth to the President and one of his most prophetic and most specific:

> We remain on a course in Viet Nam which takes us further and further out on the sagging limb. That the Vietcong, a few weeks ago, pinpointed a major raid at Bien Hoa on an American installation and American personnel scarcely a dozen miles from Saigon may be indicative of a graver deterioration in the general military situation than has heretofore been apparent. It is also indicative of a growing boldness in the Vietcong. . . .
>
> If developments continue in the present pattern we are sooner or later going to have to face up to the fact that the preponderant responsibility for what transpires in South Viet Nam really rests with us even as it once had with the French. We will find ourselves saddled in South Viet Nam, no matter what we will, with a situation that is a cross between the present South Korean quasi-dependency and the pre-independence Philippine colony and at the 1964 level of cost in lives and resources. . . .
>
> Limited national interests point in the direction of an eventual negotiated settlement in Viet Nam as the basis for a sound United States policy and of actions now which create a situation in which bonafide negotiations are possible. Such negotiations are essential to the reduction of our present over-commitment and ultimate withdrawal. In the end they may also be essential to the preservation of the territorial integrity and independence of Viet Nam from Chinese domination.

Mansfield followed this assessment with specific suggestions to avoid U.S. military actions that would spread the war and to accommodate European and Asian countries that might wish to engage North Vietnam with commercial and other contacts. Above all, he emphasized the importance of developing a South Vietnamese government with enough authority to negotiate a settlement with the North, "perhaps on the basis of confederation." To be effective, such a government should begin speaking of peaceful unification of all of Vietnam, rather than of "liberating" the North or establishing "an isolated independence" as its goal, thus winning greater popular acceptance. For the longer run, he suggested, Washington should seek face-to-face contacts with Beijing to explore Chinese intentions in Vietnam and elsewhere. China's explosion two months earlier of its first atomic bomb made a new start at exploratory talks highly desirable, Mansfield wrote. If such things could not be done, Mansfield warned, "we had better begin now to face up to the likelihood of years and years of involvement and a vast increase in the commitment, and this should be spelled out in no uncertain terms to the people of the nation."

The military situation in the South continued to deteriorate, sometimes slowly, sometimes more rapidly. The government in Saigon, like that in Washington, was uninterested and even fearful of opening negotiations with the communists. Moreover; the North Vietnamese representative in Paris passed word after bombing raids against the North that Hanoi was no longer interested in negotiations. Mansfield's view of the limited U.S. interests in Vietnam and his suggestions for changes in policy or tactics were ignored. In retrospect, this was a moment when they could have had historic impact, if Johnson had given them serious consideration. Johnson later said that on the question of U.S. military action in Vietnam, he did "cross [the] bridge in my own mind" in December 1964. The "years and years" of U.S. involvement and the "vast increase" in the U.S. commitment took place, as Mansfield had feared, but this prospect was carefully hidden at the time rather than spelled out to the people of the United States.

Johnson met Mansfield for thirty minutes in the Oval Office on December 12, but there is no record of the discussion from either side. As was his practice, however, the President turned Mansfield's memo over to McGeorge Bundy for rebuttal. The security adviser, a former dean at Harvard, responded with sophistry. "There is a difference in emphasis between [Mansfield] and us but certainly no difference in fundamental purpose," he wrote in a memorandum intended to be sent on to Mansfield. Ignoring Johnson's secret decision just days earlier to accept the working group plans to expand the war, Bundy proceeded to rebut each of Mansfield's recommendations, sometimes expressing agreement in principle but going on to depict the suggestion as impractical due to existing circumstances. Johnson sent Bundy's memo to Mansfield on December 17 with a covering note that, according to internal secretarial notes, was also drafted by Bundy, telling the Majority Leader blandly that "I think we have the same basic view of this problem and the same sense of its difficulties." The note took issue only with Mansfield's description of the

U.S. "overcommitment" in Vietnam, saying, "Given the size of the stake, it seems to me we are doing only what we have to do." In a separate, more candid note to the President, Bundy reported that the response to Mansfield he had prepared was "designed to treat him gently. We could get into a stronger debate, but I doubt if it is worth it."

'KINDA SICK' OVER A VETERANS HOSPITAL

Vietnam was not the only topic of contention between Mansfield and Johnson as 1965 began. On January 11, Mansfield was notified by the Veterans Administration of a decision to close a VA hospital in the eastern Montana town of Miles City, one of fourteen hospitals being shut down around the country as an economy measure. The normally even-tempered Majority Leader made a passionate speech on the Senate floor describing the decision as "an outrage" and denouncing the failure to provide advance warning to members of Congress as "a ruthless, insensitive tactic." Correspondent Kenneth Scheibel wrote later that Mansfield's "face was white and his voice high-pitched and furious" in a speech that "raised the temperature of the Senate several degrees." Mansfield conferred with his friend, Jim Rowe, who was also a close political adviser to Johnson, and poured out his frustrations. "In forty years of friendship I have never seen him so angry, furious, mad and outraged," Rowe wrote in a memorandum to LBJ. "He appears to be seriously disaffected by what at first blush seems to be a relatively unimportant matter."

Always sensitive about matters affecting Montana, Mansfield had recently suffered a series of blows, the most damaging of which was the announced closing the previous month of Glasgow Air Force Base in northwestern Montana. It was among the newest in the country and the Air Force had recently spent $1 million lengthening the runways, but Mansfield told Defense Secretary McNamara he would go along with the decision without fuss. Another setback was the decision by the U.S. Treasury earlier in January not to mint more silver dollars for the time being, undercutting Montana's surviving mining industry as well as popular support for the dollar coins, despite the fact that Mansfield, on the basis of previous assurances from the Treasury, had promised constituents in his reelection campaign that silver dollars would be minted in 1965.

It was the decision to close the veterans hospital, however, that drew Mansfield's vehement protest. Based on his history in the Navy, Army, and Marines, he had always relied on the political backing of veterans. The Miles City hospital had been a special cause for him. Although it was far away from his western Montana congressional district, he had personally lobbied for construction of the hospital with President Truman in meetings in 1945 and 1948. The facility was opened in 1951, making it among the most recently completed in the country. Although the smallest hospital in the VA system, with only one hundred beds, it served veterans in a large area of eastern Montana, northern Wyoming, and the western part of North and South Dakota. If it closed, some veterans would have to travel hundreds of miles across the plains to the nearest VA facility.

Johnson, well aware that the closing of military and veterans facilities would stir a political storm, postponed the announcements until after the November election. Assistant Attorney General Ramsey Clark (later promoted to attorney general by LBJ) told the President that the small agricultural community at Miles City did not justify a VA hospital at all and that it had been constructed in "a political boondoggle." This could not have been a surprise to Johnson, who had freely used his influence over construction of federal facilities while in Congress and the White House. Clark also said, however, that if Johnson backed down in the face of Mansfield's protests, "it will be the last good economy move you make."

The President sought to placate Mansfield by proposing to pump more federal money into other projects in the Miles City area to compensate for the hospital closing. The Majority Leader flatly refused. Johnson sent Rowe to see him four times on the issue, but he was adamant. Johnson resented Mansfield's stubbornness, all the more so because he realized he was on weak political ground. When he informed House Speaker John McCormack that he planned to close the targeted VA hospitals no matter what Congress said about it, McCormack said that in that case Congress might pass legislation prohibiting him from closing any hospitals anywhere. Johnson said he'd veto that bill, but McCormack responded that, if so, Congress would override his veto and pass the bill into law anyway.

Johnson was not a good loser, especially at the hands of his former Senate whip. According to the Washington columnists Rowland Evans Jr. and Robert Novak, in meetings with his congressional leaders "the President repeatedly turned to Mansfield and, embarrassing other Democratic leaders, mercilessly needled him about his opposition to the hospital closings. But it was not a laughing matter to Mike Mansfield. Tense and white-faced, he sat silent, puffing on his pipe and seething inside." Privately, Johnson railed about Mansfield's attitude, telling Richard Russell that "he's got all of his chips on his hospital, and he's against everything else . . . he's an unusual fellow, a peculiar fellow." He told Attorney General Nicholas Katzenbach that "I just think he is a man that is kinda sick and problems at home and other places and he feels about the Veterans Hospital, and every time he reads, he reads where I was a leader and I was a dictator and he's not, and I think he gets upset."

To the irritation of Mansfield, the White House leaked stories suggesting that his opposition to Johnson's policies in Vietnam derived from pique over the closing of the veterans hospital, but this did Johnson no good on either issue. In April he was forced to suspend the plans to close the VA hospitals pending further study and in June to announce that Miles City and four of the other hospitals would remain open, after all. (At this writing the hospital is still open, serving veterans in a large area of eastern Montana and surrounding states.) Mansfield made certain that he reiterated his concern about Vietnam immediately after the order to close the hospital was rescinded, to demonstrate that his determination to keep the veterans facility open had nothing to do with his views on the war.

THE STREET CAR NAMED PLEIKU

The bombing raids in retaliation for the Tonkin Gulf attacks in August 1964 had made the United States for the first time an overt combatant in a war against North Vietnam. The response from the North had been to step up its backing for the war, sending main force units to the South for the first time and authorizing Vietcong forces to attack Americans and U.S. interests.

By the beginning of 1965, members of Congress were becoming apprehensive. An Associated Press poll of eighty-three senators published on January 6 reported that only eight senators favored the commitment of U.S. military force and only three favored immediate withdrawal. The largest group favored negotiations, either immediately (ten senators) or after the U.S. and South Vietnamese bargaining position was strengthened (thirty-one senators). Richard Russell told reporters, "We made a terrible mistake getting involved in Vietnam. I don't know how we can get out now, but the time is about at hand when we must re-evaluate our position." Unknown to them, the next step into the quagmire was being prepared—the beginning of intensive strategic bombing of the North. Mansfield would unsuccessfully seek to stave it off at a White House meeting in which he alone represented the Senate, and in which he alone objected to Johnson's course.

Around 2 A.M. on February 6, 1965, Vietcong guerrillas opened fire with mortars and automatic weapons at a lightly defended U.S. special forces encampment and air strip just outside Pleiku, a South Vietnamese provincial headquarters town in the Central Highlands. Eight Americans were killed, more than a hundred others were wounded and ten U.S. aircraft were destroyed. Johnson had decided not to respond militarily to two earlier attacks: the Vietcong attack at Bien Hoa, in which five Americans were killed, two days before the U.S. election in November; and a Christmas eve bombing of a U.S. billet in Saigon, in which two Americans died, that took place amid a South Vietnamese political crisis. This time, however, he responded with a massive air attack involving more than one hundred U.S. warplanes, which signaled the inception of a policy of systematic and increasingly heavy bombing of North Vietnam. The Pleiku attack was made all the more dramatic, and seemingly significant, because of the presence in Saigon of a visiting U.S. team headed by McGeorge Bundy—on his first trip to the country that had come to occupy so much of his time and attention. The situation was further complicated by the presence in Hanoi on an official mission of Soviet premier Aleksei Kosygin.

Only ten days earlier Bundy had joined McNamara in informing Johnson very confidentially that "our current policy can only lead to disastrous defeat" and recommending the application of much greater U.S. military power to change the prospects in Vietnam. After the December task force report and decisions, Johnson and the top ranks of the administration were ready to undertake Phase II, sustained strategic bombing of North Vietnam, as soon as there was sufficient provocation to justify it to Americans or the world, "something more than a potshot at a GI or some rather inconsequential bit of terrorism," in the words of Chester Cooper. In that respect, he said, Pleiku was "almost an ideal incident" to justify the planned bombing. McGeorge Bundy put it more colorfully when a reporter asked him a few days after the bombing to explain the difference between Pleiku and earlier incidents. "Pleikus are like street cars," Bundy replied—in other words, they come along with regularity when they are needed.

Word of the Pleiku attack was received in mid-afternoon on Saturday, February 6 (still early morning, Vietnam time). By that evening, all of Johnson's leading military and civilian advisers in Washington, joined by McGeorge Bundy, Ambassador Taylor, and General William Westmoreland in Saigon, recommended attacks on four sets of North Vietnamese military barracks by U.S. warplanes and, in a symbolic show of solidarity, by some South Vietnamese planes. Before formally approving the bombing, Johnson convened a National Security Council meeting at 7:45 P.M., to which Mansfield and House Speaker John McCormack were invited as the only outsiders. Sitting around the polished mahogany table in the Cabinet Room, "there was electric tension in the air," Johnson recalled.

Undersecretary of State George Ball, the most prominent in-house skeptic of the application of U.S. military power in Vietnam, was at the cabinet table in the absence of Secretary of State Rusk, who was out of town. When called upon for his opinion, Ball fell into line, saying the retaliatory attacks were necessary and the targets appropriate. (He later wrote that faced with unanimity among the other advisers, he felt his opposition would be "not only futile but tactically unwise.")

It was clear to Johnson's advisers that the President had made up his mind to launch the attacks. The targets had been specified in the meeting, complete with numbers of anticipated casualties among North Vietnamese military and civilians on the ground; the numbers of U.S. and South Vietnamese warplanes and the daylight nature of the attacks had been specified. A decision, the group was told, was needed within an hour.

Before making a final decision, Johnson's practice was to call on each person around the table to ask whether he agreed. Johnson may have seen this practice as a means of canvassing all opinions, but in fact it was a way of binding participants in a decision-making meeting to his chosen course. It would take a bold adviser to quarrel with a forceful and determined president in such circumstances.

Mansfield alone spoke up in opposition. "The North Vietnamese attack has opened many eyes," he said, looking straight at the President from a seat directly across the table. "We are not in a penny ante game. It appears that the local populace in South Vietnam is not behind us, else the Viet Cong could not have carried out their surprise attack." He pointed out that no solid government existed in Saigon, and he wondered with what government the United States had cleared this action. (At this point, Washington had requested but not received pro forma approval from the generals in Saigon.) Mansfield emphasized that the "implications and possible developments from this step" should be carefully analyzed before action was taken. He cited the possibility of a large-scale conflict with China, which had recently completed new roads and an airfield that could be used to provide supplies or troops, and the likelihood that the Soviet Union would resume major assistance to North Vietnam. He also expressed concern that U.S. bombing might help to heal the increasingly obvious and serious split between those two giants of international communism. In sum, Mansfield said, the situation as it was now developing in Vietnam could be worse for the United States than the one it had confronted in Korea.

Johnson responded with undisguised passion. "We have kept our gun over the mantle and our shells in the cupboard for a long time now. And what was the result? They are killing our men while they sleep in the night. I can't ask our American soldiers out there to continue to fight with one hand tied behind their backs." Johnson went on, charging that "cowardice has gotten us into more wars than response has." Applying to Southeast Asia the historical analogies closest to his mind, he said that if the United States had been courageous in the early stages, it would not have had to fight in World War I or World War II. He said he realized there was a risk of involving China and the Soviet Union but that neither of those powers was friendly to the United States and the answer was to face up to them.

William Bundy, who had led the task force that had recommended sustained bombing of the North and who had helped devise the U.S. military strikes at the Pentagon earlier in the day, was taken aback by Mansfield's statement—the only time he ever saw a member of Congress tell a president to his face that he was wrong on basic policy—and equally startled by Johnson's fierce reply, "terse and quite biting . . . not a rational attempt to persuade." Bundy later wrote, "My impression was that Mansfield would have given anything to be alone with the President; finding that he had to speak in front of others, he did so with typical courage and frankness." He suspected that Johnson could not imagine that even Mansfield would disagree with his gut reaction to strike back when American "boys" had been killed. Yet of greater significance for Mansfield lay the weighty consequences of the action Johnson proposed to take. Bundy realized that he had seen "nakedly revealed" a profound difference in policy between the President and the Majority Leader on a matter of grave import. Shortly after the meeting concluded, Johnson ordered the air strikes. U.S. warplanes, which were standing by in readiness, were launched within a few hours.

Mansfield joined the NSC again Sunday morning, February 7, to work on a press statement announcing U.S. actions and to discuss additional air strikes. Mansfield proposed that the White House announce a decision to take the evolving conflict to the United Nations or to a reconvened Geneva Conference on Vietnam. Johnson rejected both ideas, saying his advisers had told him it was hopeless to expect anything from the UN, and that he would not consider a renewal of the Geneva Conference at the present time. Ball chimed in that the United States should enter such a new international conference only from a position of greater strength. When Johnson went around the table asking for comments, Mansfield reminded the President that he had spoken frankly in response to Johnson's invitation to do so, but wished to assure him that "now the decision was made, that he would work to support him."

On Monday morning Johnson assembled his National Security Council once again, this time with Republican leaders Everett Dirksen and Gerald Ford as well as Mansfield and McCormack. Johnson told the group of his intention to go beyond retaliation for specific attacks to undertake strategic bombing "to deter, destroy and diminish the strength of the North Vietnamese aggressors and to try to convince them to leave South Vietnam alone." In a remark that may have been aimed at Mansfield, Johnson added gratuitously that he would not let "the views of a few senators" control his actions, and that the Tonkin Gulf resolution plus the legal authority of the presidency gave him the authority he needed. Mansfield said nothing, but after the meeting he presented Johnson with a new memorandum—his seventh.

Sticking by his positions, he repeated in writing his concern about where the retaliatory attacks would lead, especially with respect to the Soviet Union and China. He reiterated his trepidation about the "very unstable government" in South Vietnam, the "great majority" of whose people were war-weary and would provide no significant assistance. As for waging war against North Vietnam, he pointed out—as he had in the meeting—that General

Vo Nguyen Giap, "one of the best military tacticians in Asia," had an army of 350,000 well-trained men that could be engaged. Mansfield said he shared the President's feelings about the attack on U.S. servicemen in Pleiku and appreciated LBJ's repeated statements that it was not his desire to spread the war. "However, the prospect for enlargement now looms larger and I think it is only fair that I give you my honest opinions, as I did on Saturday and Sunday, because to do otherwise would be a disservice to you and to the Nation." At the end of his memorandum—as at the end of the meeting Sunday morning—Mansfield stated his willingness to assist in support of a policy he had sharply criticized. "You will recall," he wrote, "that I stated to you that the burden of decision was yours but that, regardless of my individual views, I would do whatever I could to support you in the exercise of your grave responsibility."

More than any that had come before, this was a moment of truth for Mansfield in his relationship with Johnson in connection with the war. Alone against the President's determined viewpoint and unanimous advice of other advisers present, Mansfield had spoken his mind in opposition to a course he was sure would lead to tragic conflict on a massive scale, far beyond anything justified by U.S. national interests. He had done what staff member Chester Cooper had only daydreamed about doing: declaring amid the pre-cooked consensus of Johnson NSC meetings, "Mr. President, gentlemen, I most definitely do *not* agree." Unlike Cooper, who was never bold enough to take such action, Vice President Humphrey openly dissented at an NSC meeting a few days later at which Mansfield was not present, and followed up with a lengthy memorandum to the President opposing U.S. bombing of the North. As a result Johnson barred him from Vietnam policy discussions for the rest of the year. Later in 1965, after Fulbright publicly criticized Johnson's policies in the Dominican Republic and Vietnam, the President virtually severed relations with the Foreign Relations Committee chairman, barring him from diplomatic dinners at the White House and snubbing him openly on many occasions. Johnson could not and did not sever relations with the Majority Leader responsible for pursuit of his legislative agenda, but he harshly rebutted his views on the war or, what was probably worse, simply ignored them.

In the context of today, Mansfield's statements of continuing support for implementation of war-and-peace decisions that he deeply disapproved of seems remarkable or even astounding. They were less so at the time. Humphrey, at the end of his memo of dissent that prompted Johnson to banish him from the decision-making counsels, declared that, "I intend to support the administration whatever the President's decisions." Ball repeatedly assured Johnson of his loyalty, telling him after objecting to the deployment of U.S. troops, "Let me make clear, if the decision is to go ahead, I'm committed."

I discussed with Mansfield on several occasions his reasons for keeping private his strong objections to Johnson's war policies, even backing the President publicly. "I was walking a tightrope. I wanted to be heard" within the administration's counsels, he said with anguish, and at the same time "to uphold the institution of the presidency" in matters of war and peace. "It was difficult. Maybe I walked that tight line incorrectly, but it was the best I could do under the circumstances at that time. I thought of it many times since. . . . I failed, but at least I was heard. . . . I think that I could have been more vigorous, I could have adopted another kind of procedure, but just don't know [his voice breaking here, in a rare show of emotion] what it was, and I did the best I could under extremely difficult and delicate circumstances because of the institutional relationship between the Senate and the White House. . . . It's something I'm not proud of, but something which I did to the best of my ability." He added, finally, "Let history speak for itself."

Despite the objections he had voiced, Mansfield continued to be invited to most top-level policy meetings on Vietnam whenever outsiders were present. After a Vietcong bomb in an enlisted men's billet at the coastal city of Qui Nhon on February 10 killed twenty-three Americans, the largest single toll until that point, Mansfield and eight other members of Congress were called to the White House to discuss the retaliatory strikes Johnson was prepared to order. Asked by Johnson if he wished to comment, Mansfield seemed about to speak, but according to White House legislative chief Larry O'Brien, who was sitting next to him, decided "at the last second" not to do so but to provide his views only in writing. As the meeting ended he handed Jack Valenti a memorandum to the President that he had written in advance. After Johnson's brutal rejoinder following the Pleiku attack, Mansfield followed this practice until the summer, sending more memos but avoiding a face-to-face challenge to the President in White House meetings.

In the February 10 memo—his eighth—Mansfield predicted, accurately, that in view of the air strikes North Vietnam would strengthen its air defenses and that rather than respond with warplanes of its own, the communists "are going to continue to play their strength against our weakness" by initiating further Vietcong attacks against American facilities in South Vietnam. As a result, he forecast, U.S. outposts "will have to be *vastly strengthened by American forces* or pulled into and consolidated in the Saigon area [emphasis in original]," a plan that Mansfield knew to be unlikely. Since Johnson had written off the United Nations as a venue for negotiations, Mansfield appealed again for U.S. efforts to reconvene the 1954 Geneva Conference on Vietnam and suggested that a cease-fire throughout Indochina should be its first initiative.

Johnson, undeterred, ordered retaliatory strikes against two North Vietnamese targets. Three days later he formally approved the policy of steadily increasing bombing raids aimed at punishing North Vietnam, no longer tied to specific Vietcong attacks but seeking to convince Hanoi's leaders to abandon the war in the South. Thus began the highly controversial bombing campaign known by its Pentagon code name as Rolling Thunder, which would last for years without achieving its purpose. The course was set, and the other side responded. The onset of strategic bombing was followed by intensified Vietcong attacks and the transit of greater numbers of soldiers and supplies from North Vietnam to the war in the South.

Publicly, Mansfield suppressed his opposition to the growing U.S. intervention and the bombing of the North. He told reporters that "in the circumstances, the President has had no choice but to respond as he did to the military developments in Vietnam." He wrote to a constituent, "I believe the President was acting with restraint in this matter." On March 1 he praised Johnson's policy in a Senate speech, saying, "He is trying to prevent a great war in Asia, and he is trying at the same time to meet a commitment to the people of South Vietnam of many years standing."

How might history have been different if the Democratic leader of the Senate, who was considered a leading expert on Asia, had publicly broken with the Democratic President on the pursuit of the war in early 1965? Robert Mann, a Senate staff member and author of a scholarly account of the role of American political leaders in the Vietnam War, wrote that Mansfield's refusal to challenge Johnson publicly had enormous consequences. "He might have taken to the Senate floor to denounce escalation in an effort to rally more senators, as well as the public, to his side. Had he done so, Congress would certainly have held more hearings. Fulbright and others might have been awakened from their post-election slumber. Johnson might have been forced to explain exactly what he hoped to achieve by taking the country into war in North Vietnam." Paul Kattenburg, a Foreign Service veteran who was director of Vietnam Affairs in the State Department in 1963–1964, later reflected that due to the decisive role of the presidents, the narrowness of their advisory circle and the failure of Congress to challenge executive policy, Vietnam decisions in the early and mid-1960s were taken and implemented in a "closed system" without necessary checks and balances. "When Congress does not fulfill the role of loyal opposition in foreign policy, this role does not seem to be fulfilled at all," Kattenburg observed.

Had Mansfield confronted Johnson's Indochina policy in a concerted public fashion, very likely he would have resigned as Majority Leader. Alben Barkley took this course in 1944 when he broke with President Franklin D. Roosevelt after unsuccessfully seeking to dissuade the President in private from vetoing a tax bill and from caustically condemning all who voted for it. The Senate backed Barkley in voting to override the veto, and Barkley was restored to leadership with greater prestige and authority than before. Republican William Knowland took a different tack when he differed with President Eisenhower over the Bricker amendment restricting the foreign policy prerogatives of the executive branch. To demonstrate the anomalous situation and his independence, Knowland left the Majority Leader's front row seat and delivered his speech at variance with Eisenhower's policy from a back row seat.

Mansfield, however, did neither of those things. He did not clearly separate himself in public from Johnson's war policy, although he raised doubts in general terms in several speeches while at the same time expressing support for the President. Instead, he continued to lead the Senate in passing the torrent of progressive social and economic legislation sponsored by the White House and did not object to the passage of legislative authority and appropriations to pursue a war that he deeply opposed. As he told me later, he was walking "a delicate line" between his leadership in the Senate and his personal opposition to Johnson's course in Indochina.

SENDING GROUND TROOPS TO FIGHT

In the spring of 1965 Johnson prepared to take another fateful step—the introduction of the first battalions of U.S. ground troops in a fighting mode. As he did at the inception of bombing raids against North Vietnam following the Tonkin Gulf episode in August 1964 and the start of sustained strategic bombing following the Vietcong attack on Pleiku in February 1965, Mansfield once again objected to the President's course in a White House meeting and tried to persuade Johnson that he was leading the nation to costly failure. He believed that sending U.S. ground troops was an irreversible action that would make the struggle in Vietnam fully an American war that, like the French war a decade earlier, foreigners would be unable to win.

Mansfield had predicted in his memorandum to Johnson on February 10 that communist forces would respond to regular bombing of the North by intensified attacks on U.S. facilities, requiring "vastly strengthened" American forces to protect them. Thus he could not have been surprised to receive a telephone call from McNamara on Saturday morning, March 6, saying that in view of the "very difficult" situation around the U.S. airfields at Danang, where many of the bombing raids on North Vietnam were launched, Johnson was considering sending in two battalions, or 3,500 Marines, for security duty. (Unknown to Mansfield, Johnson had already tentatively approved this deployment at least a week earlier.) Asked for his reaction, Mansfield replied that sending in Marines "would make a difficult situation more dangerous and tend to create the impression around the world that this was a preliminary to a stepped up escalation." He suggested instead that U.S. military advisers already in Saigon be sent to Danang for guard duty, but McNamara dismissed this as impractical.

According to Mansfield's record of the conversation, the defense secretary told him (inaccurately) that no decision had been made and asked if he "leaned against" sending in the Marines. Mansfield's terse answer was "yes," although the senator noted that the responsibility was that of the President and McNamara himself. Reporting to Johnson on the conversation by telephone three hours later, however, McNamara claimed that "I got [Mansfield] sort of half-agreed. But he'll fall off if anybody attacks him." The formal order was issued promptly, and the Marines splashed ashore at Danang on March 8 in full battle gear, met by pretty Vietnamese girls passing out leis of flowers. Years later the anonymous official authors of the Defense Department's secret history of the war, known as the Pentagon Papers, described the landing of the Marines at Danang as "a watershed event in the history of the U.S. involvement in Vietnam." The Pentagon historians noted:

> It represented a major decision made without much fanfare—and without much planning. Whereas the decision to begin bombing North Vietnam was the product of a year's discussion, debate, and a lot of paper, and whereas the consideration of pacification policies reached talmudic proportions over the years, this decision created less than a ripple. A mighty commandment of U.S. foreign policy—thou shall not engage in an Asian land war—had been breached. . . . The seeming ease with which the Marines were introduced and the mild reaction from Hanoi served to facilitate what was to come. It also weakened the position of those who were, a few scant months later, to oppose the landing of further U.S. ground troops.

For members of Congress and most Americans, the landing of the Marines at Danang did not seem as significant at the time as it appears in the light of history. Only a few lawmakers on Capitol Hill had been consulted, and as far as can be determined, only Mansfield took the matter up with Johnson in the aftermath. On March 18, in his ninth memo to LBJ, he asked that the number of American installations to be defended with U.S. ground troops be "strictly limited," that such installations be on the coast or otherwise readily accessible from the sea, and that Americans scattered elsewhere in Vietnam be pulled back into the American-defended installations. Otherwise, he told the President, "we will be drawn into deploying progressively larger numbers of United States ground troops throughout the country." This actually would strengthen the hand of the communist forces by supplying targets for guerrilla attack, he said. "The fewer the potential American targets in Viet Nam the better, unless, of course, we mean to take over the entire conflict in South Viet Nam."

Hearing nothing back from Johnson, Mansfield on March 24 sent the President his longest and most comprehensive appeal yet—his tenth—"out of a deep concern over the present trend of events in Viet Nam," and promised that it would be his last. Summarizing his disappointments, the Majority Leader declared that the direction of U.S. policy over the past few years had been directly opposite to the limitations and reductions he had urged. Now it appeared to him that it had been decided to "make whatever expenditure of American lives and resources" was needed to exercise "a primacy" over South Vietnam, including going into North Vietnam if necessary, and at the same time avoiding a search for the negotiated settlements Mansfield had so often and so ardently advocated. With Johnson moving rapidly in what he considered the wrong direction, Mansfield wrote that "I have no great hope that at this late date, these suggestions will be useful to you," but he presented them anyway "for what they may be worth."

He recommended, once again, that any ground forces sent to Vietnam should be concentrated in a few places close to the sea; that the United States should seek to arrange a cease-fire in place in both parts of the peninsula and that, once achieved, seek to reconvene the Geneva Conference for a negotiated solution to the war. "There will be risks to our national interests in a conference, but certainly, in my opinion, risks which are far smaller than those which we now run," he wrote. Mansfield conceded that the risks for the region included increased Chinese influence, which lay at the heart of the original justifications for American involvement in the war, but he took a less alarmist view than that of the administration. He argued (accurately, in retrospect) that China could not automatically expect to exert its control once a settlement was reached but would be confronted with historic Southeast Asian opposition growing out of fear and anxiety about its great neighbor.

"We are in very deep already and in most unfavorable circumstances," Mansfield wrote. Then, in another remarkable gesture to Johnson he added, "In my judgment we were in too deep long before you assumed office. But you know the whole situation on a day-to-day basis and I most certainly respect the decisions which you have felt compelled to make. . . . And I want you to know that you have my support on a personal as well as an official basis. If there is anything I can do to help you in this as in any other matter you have only to ask and I will try to the best of my ability."

On March 26, two days after receiving Mansfield's latest and longest memorandum the President expressed his frustration in a conversation with Senator George McGovern, who had come to the White House to express his own deepening concern about U.S. policy on the war. "Don't give me another goddamn history lesson," LBJ erupted. "I've got a drawerful of memos from Mansfield. I don't need a lecture on where we went wrong. I've got to deal with where we are now." On the same occasion Johnson, amplifying his real objectives in the rapidly escalating U.S. bombing attacks against the North, told McGovern, "I'm going up old Ho Chi Minh's leg an inch at a time. I'll have him by the balls before he realizes it."

Six days later, on April 1, Johnson agreed in a meeting with his closest national security advisers to send two more Marine battalions plus a Marine air squadron and logistical troops to Vietnam and to change the mission of the Marines from defense of the airfields to offensive combat operations as the need arose. Johnson admonished his aides to keep his decisions quiet. The secret was kept, and the shift to offensive combat in the mission of the Marines did not become public until two months later. It was one more giant step away from the policies that Mansfield had advocated and into the Vietnam swamp.

JOHNSON CONFRONTS HIS CRITICS

Having raised the military stakes, Johnson sought to placate the steadily increasing number of Americans—still a minority of the public—who were speaking, organizing, and even beginning to march in opposition to the war their government was waging. Members of the Senate led by Frank Church and George McGovern began openly criticizing U.S. over-involvement and calling for negotiations to settle the conflict. Although some newspaper editorial pages, including the *Washington Post*, backed Johnson's policies, opposition to expanded military action and calls for negotiations came from a large number of others, including the *New York Times* and the *Wall Street Journal*. University teach-ins to educate the public about growing dangers in Vietnam began on March 24, 1965, at the University of Michigan and quickly spread to scores of campuses. A "March on Washington," the largest antiwar event up to that time, was scheduled for April 17. The President attributed the protests to communist propaganda from abroad, but in fact most of the dissent was home grown, a result of the dramatic impact of American warplanes bombing North Vietnam and U.S. Marines landing in the South. In an attempt to quell the increasingly passionate opposition to the war, Johnson delivered a major address, broadcast in prime time by television networks, at Johns Hopkins University in Baltimore on the evening of April 7.

The Johns Hopkins speech was a skillful presidential display of both sword and the olive branch. Justifying the U.S. air attacks and ground action on the basis of defending "the independent nation of South Vietnam" from "total conquest" by the North, Johnson declared, "We will not be defeated. We will not grow tired. We will not withdraw, either openly or under the cloak of a meaningless agreement." At the same time, he proclaimed the goal of a peaceful settlement in Vietnam and announced that the United States was ready for "unconditional discussions" to that end, although within the administration he had been strongly opposed to negotiations until the military measures improved U.S. bargaining power. Finally, he proposed a $1 billion U.S. investment in a peaceful development program on the Mekong River in Southeast Asia, which he compared to the highly successful Tennessee Valley Authority (TVA) in the United States.

On the afternoon before the speech Johnson spent nearly ninety minutes going over it in detail with Mansfield and with Fulbright, who was becoming critical of the war but had not yet broken with Johnson. After they left, the President spent nearly half an hour with Church and McGovern, who had emerged as antiwar leaders in the Senate, and with Gale McGee, a prominent administration supporter. Despite the strong dissents he had voiced or written to Johnson in private, Mansfield praised the address publicly in a Senate speech as a "profound statement" that opened the door to a peaceful settlement. The Majority Leader placed in the *Congressional Record* editorials of praise for the speech from the *New York Times, Washington Post, Washington Star, Baltimore Sun,* and *Philadelphia Inquirer,* all of which expressed enthusiastic approval and hope for settlement of the war. In a letter to Mansfield, Johnson thanked the Majority Leader for his "eloquent statement" of support, saying, "I know how deeply troubled you have been about the situation in Vietnam, and for that reason your support is all the more welcome."

Immediately after Johnson's address at Johns Hopkins, North Vietnam issued an official declaration that the United States must stop its "acts of war" against the North and remove its troops from the South before talks could begin on settlement of the war. In internal deliberations, Johnson heard discussions of proposals for moving toward a political settlement, especially from Undersecretary of State George Ball, but none of the plans was adopted. In a telephone call to Mansfield on April 28, Johnson said he had been "trying every possible diplomatic angle and was looking for new ones and asked whether or not there were any suggestions." Despite his personal pique at Mansfield's attempts at written persuasion, he told the Majority Leader he would welcome additional memoranda and asked that the two of them sit down to discuss

Vietnam. Mansfield, perhaps discouraged by the fate of his previous interventions, did not take up Johnson's offer for more than a month.

By early May, Johnson was letting outsiders know that opposition to the bombing of North Vietnam by key Democrats in the Senate was "galling and embarrassing" to him. To force them to line up behind his war policy, Johnson on May 4 asked Congress for a $700 million appropriation to meet increasing military costs in Vietnam. In fact, the Defense Department did not need the money. Ever mindful of the opposition to President Truman in the Korean War, Johnson felt the need to shore up his congressional backing in the face of growing disaffection on Capitol Hill. Each member of Congress who approved the appropriation, Johnson said in his official request, "is saying that the Congress and the President stand united before the world in joint determination that the independence of South Vietnam shall be preserved and Communist attack will not succeed."

With increasing numbers of American troops committed in Vietnam, it became politically impossible for most members of Congress to deny funds to U.S. forces already committed to action overseas. Leverett Saltonstall, the ranking Republican on the Armed Services Committee, summed up the situation by saying, "We are faced with a realistic but a simple fact. Our troops are in South Vietnam and we must supply them." In a statement just before the vote, Mansfield regretted the need for the legislation but declared, "we will vote for this measure because there is not one member of this body who does not desire to uphold the President and those who are risking their lives in seeking to carry out the policies of the government." The bill passed 88 to 3 in the Senate after passing the House by the lopsided vote of 408 to 7 in only two days.

William Conrad Gibbons, the author of the Senate Foreign Relations Committee's authoritative historical series on the government and the Vietnam War, described the debate and action on the $700 million request as "the beginning of a profound qualitative change in political posture and political rhetoric." According to Gibbons, the requirement to provide support for U.S. forces already in the field was "probably the single most determinative factor in Congress' support throughout the war." As Representative Dante Fascell of Florida noted, the near-unanimous congressional support for troops already committed also became "the linchpin for greater involvement in Vietnam." Starting with Johnson's $700 million request, Congress found it impossible to deny the executive branch whatever funds it asked to pursue the war until the troops were withdrawn in 1973.

On the heels of the appropriation vote, Johnson ordered a temporary pause in the bombing of North Vietnam, which critics in Congress, the press, and the intellectual community had been demanding in hopes of creating an opening for peace talks. Discussing the resumption of bombing in a meeting with his advisers, Johnson said, "My judgment is the public has never wanted us to stop the bombing. We have stopped in deference to Mansfield and Fulbright, but we don't want to do it too long else we lose our base of support." The President also said, "To me it's a pure question of what happens in this country. . . . I would say to Mansfield, [Robert] Kennedy, Fulbright that we notified the other people [North Vietnamese and Russians]—and for six days we have held off bombing. Nothing happened. We had no illusions that anything would happen. But we were willing to be surprised." To which McNamara added, "Mansfield ought to know Hanoi spit on our face." However, seven months later, McNamara would refer to the May bombing halt merely as "a propaganda effort."

With the bombing of North Vietnam continuing daily, Johnson confided to Mansfield and other Democratic congressional leaders in the Oval Office on June 3 that the Joint Chiefs of Staff and others within his policy circle had advocated attacking the North Vietnamese capital of Hanoi, which had been off limits to U.S. warplanes since the start of the aerial bombardment. LBJ said he had "stalled them off" until he heard from Ambassador Taylor, who was soon to return to Washington, and because he feared this would bring China into the war. Russell Long, who had succeeded Hubert Humphrey as Senate majority whip, urged Johnson to "face up to the $64 question"—a reference to the top prize question on a popular television quiz show—and begin the bombing of China. This would initiate the war with China that the Majority Leader had always feared. Mansfield spoke up emphatically: "I disagree with you completely and absolutely."

Gravely concerned by this discussion, Mansfield abandoned his promise in March to send no more memos. On June 5 he told Johnson in a strongly worded memo—his eleventh—that attacks on Hanoi and the port of Haiphong would be "an irreversible extension" of the war and "a political act of the first magnitude." He foresaw that such bombing would "forestall indefinitely any prospects of discussions with the other side, unconditional or otherwise" and argued that it would have a negative impact on the positions of China, Russia, and the international community. Militarily, it would have no significant value, he wrote, since the North Vietnamese have expected and prepared for it. The danger, as he saw it, was that bombing Hanoi-Haiphong would "bring about an enlargement and acceleration of the ground war" and lead to the "rapid injection of more American forces on the ground, even to hold the situation in that region." Moreover he feared that the bombing would ensure that "the war eventually will have to be carried, in the search for decision, into North Vietnam, into other parts of Southeast Asia and probably into China itself."

In the ten months since the first U.S. bombing raids against North Vietnam after the Tonkin Gulf incident and the four months since regular and escalating bombing raids had begun, following the attack on Pleiku in February 1965, the situation on the ground in the South was still deteriorating and North Vietnam showed no signs of retreat. Instead of improving the U.S. position, the bombing appeared to have raised the ante on both sides. As the authors of the Pentagon Papers later wrote after extensive study, "Once set in motion . . . the bombing effort seemed to stiffen rather than soften Hanoi's backbone, as well as to lessen the willingness of Hanoi's allies, particularly the Soviet Union, to work toward compromise." Although Soviet leaders were not happy about the war in Indochina and hoped for a peaceful solution, they felt it necessary after the U.S. air attacks to begin supplying increasingly large amounts of arms and ammunition to the fraternal North Vietnamese. China, meanwhile, accepted a secret visit from Ho Chi Minh in May and June, and Mao Tse-tung agreed to provide him with substantial military and material support. This led to China's dispatch to Vietnam of 44,000 engineering and road-building troops. It also sent an eventual total of 150,000 antiaircraft troops, who downed large numbers of American warplanes over North Vietnam.

Mansfield, recognizing the failure of the bombing to deter North Vietnam or the Vietcong, summed up his June 5 memorandum with a rare condemnation of Johnson's advisers: "I think it is about time you got an accounting from those who have pressured you in the past to embark on this course and continue to pressure you to stay on it. It is time to ask, not only what immediate advantages it has in a narrow military sense, but where does it lead in the end: What was promised by the initial extension of the war in the air over the

North? And what, in fact, has it produced to date?" No such accounting took place, and the bombing continued.

THE GREAT ESCALATION

For the next seven weeks, from June 7 to July 27, Johnson and his close advisers—and Mansfield as well—were seized with the final decisions for the next great escalation of the war: the sending of American ground troops by the hundreds of thousands to fight in Vietnam. It was, the historian George C. Herring later wrote, "the closest thing to a formal decision for war in Vietnam," culminating eighteen months of deliberation in the presidency of Lyndon Johnson about America's policies. Mansfield fully understood the gravity of this decision and sought repeatedly to affect it, all in vain. Once the decision was made, there was no turning back.

On June 7, General Westmoreland, citing growing Vietcong strength, South Vietnamese army weakness, and North Vietnamese willingness to tip the balance in favor of the communists, asked for the deployment of U.S. troops in large numbers to provide a hard-hitting U.S. offensive capability and stave off what he insisted was potential military defeat. At the time, Westmoreland's forces in Vietnam consisted of nine U.S. maneuver battalions and one Australian battalion. The additions he requested, when modified by the Joint Chiefs of Staff, added up to thirty-four American battalions and ten foreign battalions, mostly from South Korea. Secretary McNamara estimated that this force would bring the total of U.S. troops up to 151,000, more than double the number either in Vietnam or authorized up to that date. The forty-four-battalion request, as Westmoreland's request was known, quickly transformed the policy debate among insiders in Washington. "Of the thousands of cables I received in my seven years in the Defense Department, this one disturbed me most," McNamara later recalled. "We could no longer postpone a choice about which path to take [in Vietnam]. The issue would hang over all of us like a menacing cloud for the next seven weeks."

Johnson, concerned about the potential reaction to such a massive increase, telephoned Mansfield at 5:05 P.M. on June 8 in a remarkable conversation that he used to test the waters. The President said he had been informed by his military advisers that roughly 75,000 American troops in Vietnam would be in great danger unless they were augmented by 75,000 more. "I'm no military man at all," said LBJ in a telephone call that he secretly recorded, but "if they get 150 [thousand], they'll have to have another 150. And then they'll have to have *another* 150. So, the big question then is: What does the Congress want to do about it?" Johnson was indirectly asking whether such a major change as he was contemplating would make it necessary to ask Congress for another expression of support similar to the Gulf of Tonkin resolution the previous August or, at a minimum, like the supplemental appropriation for Vietnam that Johnson had engineered in May. In Johnson's mind the necessity to send more troops was paramount and irrefutable, but once again Mansfield's perspective was entirely different. The veteran of the Navy, Army, and Marines saw such a further increase as futile and disastrous both on the personal level of the lives to be lost and the strategic level of potentially greater conflict in Asia. He sought yet again to persuade Johnson to change his mind or, at a minimum, to change his military strategy.

> Mansfield: "If you make another approach to Congress, I think really the roof will blow off this time, because people who have remained quiet will no longer remain silent. . . . I think you'd be in for some trouble. The debate would spread right out. . . . "
>
> Johnson: ". . . Do you think that we ought to send all these troops without a debate?"
>
> Mansfield: "No, sir. I think that we've got too many in there now. And we've been bombing the North without any appreciable results. . . ."
>
> Johnson: "What do we do about [Westmoreland's] request for more men? . . . If it assumes the proportions that I can see it assuming, shouldn't we say to the Congress, What do you want to do about it?"
>
> Mansfield: "I would hate to be the one to say it because, as you said earlier, it's 75,000, then it's 150,000, then it's 300,000. Where do you stop?"
>
> Johnson: "You don't. . . . To me, it's shaping up like this, Mike—you either get out or you get *in*. . . . We've tried all the neutral things. And we think they are winning. Now if *we* think they are winning, you can imagine what *they* think
>
> Mansfield: "They *know* they're winning."

Johnson: "And if they know that, you can see that they're not anxious to find any answer to it. . . . Therefore, where do you go?"

Mansfield: "You don't go ahead. . . . You don't pull out. You try to do something to consolidate your position in South Vietnam. And that may take more troops. It certainly will take more [South] Vietnamese [troops]."

Johnson: "They're getting more of them in, Mike, but . . . they're deserting just like flies!"

Mansfield: "When McNamara speaks about 300,000 American troops against Giap's 31 divisions in North Vietnam, that's the absolute minimum."

Johnson: "Yes, he knows that."

The conversation ended without resolving the issue of a new congressional endorsement, but the following day Mansfield was quick to supply the President with his own considered views. Referring to their telephone conversation the evening before, Mansfield sent Johnson a three-page memo—his twelfth to LBJ on the war—centered on what he called a crucial question: "In what direction are we going in Viet Nam?"

To begin, Mansfield made the fundamental point that "there is not a government to speak of in Saigon. . . . [W]e are now at the point where we are no longer dealing with anyone who represents anybody in a political sense. We are simply acting to prevent a collapse of the Vietnamese military forces which we pay for and supply in any event and who presumably are going in the same direction we are going." As if to underscore this observation, the existing four-month-old government of Phan Huy Quat, which had been in crisis for several weeks, was ousted by the military regime of Nguyen Van Thieu and Nguyen Cao Ky on June 12. Three days later Mansfield told the Senate that it was "the 19th coup or coup attempt or other change or attempted change in the Vietnamese government in which the people of Vietnam have had little if anything to say" since the overthrow of Diem less than two years earlier. (Although no one would have guessed it at the time, the Thieu-Ky regime would last for nearly the rest of the war.)

The Majority Leader then turned to the question of U.S. objectives and the probable military requirements to support them. If the objective was a holding operation to retain control of Saigon, the provincial capitals, larger towns, and coastal cities—and "at least tenuous lines of communication on the ground" between them—Mansfield said McNamara's estimate of 300,000 U.S. troops is too low, but "something in the range of 500,000 might do it, at least if Giap's army does not move in full and open force across the 17th parallel." This proved to be another of Mansfield's prescient estimates. Holding the main cities and towns and the lines of communications between them, even though most of the countryside remained insecure, was the practical U.S. objective for the rest of the war. The high point of American military deployments in Vietnam was 543,400 troops nearly four years later, in April 1969.

Regarding a new congressional resolution, Mansfield advised against it as he had in the telephone call. However one-sided the vote totals had been on the $700 million appropriation, support for the war rested on "grave doubts and much trepidation on the part of many senators," he wrote. Their support was taken "largely on faith, out of loyalty to you and on the basis of the general view that when the President has the responsibility and when he requests legislative support in a crisis, he should have it." Those words well described Mansfield's own position as he sought to support with his voice and votes Johnson's decisions on the war, even while privately opposing most of them.

Supporting the Mansfield position, Rusk warned Johnson against any submission to Congress that would touch off a full-fledged debate on the war because "the Commies would use their whole international apparatus to stir up trouble which might have serious international results." Nonetheless, Johnson continued to feel the need for additional congressional backing as he moved toward dispatching hundreds of thousands of troops to an expanded war. In a telephone conversation with McNamara, Johnson said that sending a new resolution to Congress would place the lawmakers on the spot either for approving his actions in Vietnam or "tucking tail and running." Exaggerating and distorting Mansfield's position, Johnson said the Majority Leader "came down with two memos in an hour [saying,] 'Oh, my God, don't send any resolution up here!' They don't want to *vote* against [sending more troops]. They just want to talk and *whine* about it. . . ." Then in a passage that, so far as records disclose, was purely imaginary, Johnson continued, "I just chucked it back to [Mansfield]. I said, . . . 'I don't want to do anything that doesn't represent the reasonable unanimity of this country. We ought to have these things settled at the water's edge. Then . . . we ought to be one nation united. I'm willing to let you write the ticket. If you'll write it. I thought you wrote it with the SEATO Treaty [which Mansfield had signed in 1954]. I thought you wrote it when you approved the [recent Vietnam-related] appropriation and the [Tonkin Gulf] action. But if you . . . want to tuck tail and run . . . you can just pass a joint resolution.' That jarred him, but it hasn't jarred him enough . . . to keep him from whining. He ran to [his regular breakfast companion, Republican Senator George] Aiken. . . . They had breakfast, and Aiken comes out . . . and says that Johnson is going to put us on the spot and get off the hook himself." Finally, however, Johnson told McNamara that in seeking a new congressional resolution supporting the war, "I think I'm just making more trouble for myself," a view remarkably close to the one that Mansfield had taken from the start.

While Johnson was privately sounding off against Mansfield, the Majority Leader was expressing a startling degree of sympathy and even support for Johnson in confidential discussions in the Senate. On June 25, in a closed-door luncheon of the Democratic Policy Committee, he urged the senior Senate Democrats to be aware of "the great pressures on the President" regarding Vietnam. "It will take an increased effort just to maintain our present position" in the war zone, he said, and therefore he anticipated "increases in the American forces in Vietnam in the next months." He added that "the President is trying in every way to find an honorable way out of the difficult circumstances he faces in Vietnam," and blamed North Vietnam for rebuffing a series of peace feelers. He said there was no doubt about his own views on the war either at the White House or in the Senate. Nonetheless, he asked that "all senators in speaking on this subject should recognize the President's position, ask ourselves what we would do if we were in his position, and if we must criticize, attempt to be constructive." Mansfield's appeal was backed by Humphrey, attending the meeting as vice president, who did not disclose that he had been excluded from virtually all Vietnam policymaking by Johnson because of his dovish beliefs.

On June 27 McGeorge Bundy, on behalf of Johnson, responded to Mansfield's memos of June 3 and June 9 and yet another memo (his thirteenth, dated June 14 but sent to Johnson on June 22) in which he proposed again that the United States move toward negotiations. Johnson had not completely ignored them, having read parts of the June 9 memo aloud to his national security team the day after it was received, to obtain their answers line by line. As in earlier correspondence with Mansfield, Bundy disputed some of his points and accepted some in broad generality while ignoring their specifics. In contradiction to Johnson's private disdain for Mansfield's views, Bundy wrote, "The President greatly values your counsel on this hard problem."

On July 17, Johnson secretly decided to approve the Westmoreland forty-four-battalion request but to keep the full dimensions of the troop increase hidden, so as not to arouse opposition. Johnson was advised by Bundy to wait for a formal report from McNamara, who had been dispatched to Saigon on a fact-finding trip and to delay a week after that before finally and officially informing Congress and the public. On July 21, the day McNamara returned, Mansfield rose in the Senate to make a rare formal speech on the situation in Vietnam. "It appears that the groundwork has been laid for a further intensification of the military effort in Vietnam," he declared. Mansfield said that there was talk on the U.S. side of a war lasting four or five or even ten years and that Ho Chi Minh, the North Vietnamese president, had stated that he was prepared for a war of twenty years duration. "The time for wishful thinking is past; the time for accepting the reality is now." Mansfield again suggested reconvening the Geneva Conference on Indochina, which was jointly chaired by the British and the Soviet Union. "Perhaps the hour is late," Mansfield concluded, "but the old saying, 'better later than never,' applies here and it applies with the greatest of force." The speech included a rare public acknowledgment by Mansfield that during the past ten or eleven years he had "as one Senator," made many suggestions, which he did not specify, to the executive branch on stabilizing the situation in Indochina. For Johnson's information, he sent a typescript of his speech to the White House complete with last-minute handwritten changes.

On the afternoon of July 23, with the final consultations among Johnson, his civilian advisers, and the Joint Chiefs of Staff under way, the President invited Mansfield and Republican leader Everett Dirksen to the family quarters of the White House. Mansfield brought to the meeting a new three-page memo of his views—his fourteenth—for Johnson's consideration, in which he asked for renewed emphasis on negotiations "between Saigon elements" and the Vietcong and opposed the large-scale U.S. troop increases being rumored. Once again Johnson raised the question of another congressional resolution backing the new phase of the war. Both the Senate leaders were against it. Mansfield said a new congressional resolution on Vietnam would produce "more opposition than heretofore" and "more difficulty ahead." Addressing Johnson's principal worry, he added, "The divisiveness, moreover, is likely to affect other aspects of the Great Society programs." This weighed heavily on the President, who was attempting to juggle his beloved domestic programs and the mushrooming war. In the end, armed with legal opinions from the State and Justice Departments that he did not need additional authority, Johnson decided against asking for a new resolution vote of congressional confidence.

Johnson was at his most persuasive when he described his plans as the sensible medium, the moderate course between collapse in Vietnam and giving in to powerful military pressures for escalation. In a subsequent telephone conversation with Mansfield, Johnson portrayed his stance as "taking the soft line of the deal" against those who urge him to "go all the way" in military measures. "I'm following more or less your memorandum," he claimed, by telling all those in and out of the administration opposed to a land war in Asia "to do all they can, around the clock . . . [to] try to find a way to get out." But while the President was taking this hopeful position on negotiations in conversation with Mansfield, the State Department at Johnson's direction was drafting a response to Mansfield—signed, ironically, by Undersecretary Ball—that threw cold water on his negotiation proposals. The demand that the National Liberation Front (NLF), the political side of the Vietcong, be included was described as the basic obstacle. "Any recognition of the NLF as a legitimate party would tilt the boat overwhelmingly in the direction of an immediate coalition government in Saigon that we believe could only result in Communist domination and, in effect, in defeat," the Ball reply to Mansfield said.

At his regular Tuesday morning breakfast with the Democratic leaders of the Senate and House on July 27, Johnson set forth the directions in which he planned to move. Early that afternoon Mansfield proposed, at the suggestion of Fulbright, that the President meet at the White House with a small group of senior senators concerned about the war: Russell, Aiken, Democrat John Sparkman, and Republican John Sherman Cooper, in addition to Fulbright and Mansfield. Johnson declined, but the meeting of concerned senators was convened at 3:30 P.M. in the Majority Leader's office. Mansfield began by reporting on the breakfast discussion, reassuring his col-

leagues that LBJ's objective "was not to get in deeply" and that Johnson said
he intended "to do only what was essential in the military line" for the rest
of the year while Rusk and Arthur Goldberg, ambassador to the UN, sought
a negotiated solution. A lengthy conversation followed, in which Mansfield
recorded nineteen points of concern, some in conflict with one another,
which he passed along to Johnson a short time later in a written memo, his
fifteenth to LBJ as President.

A fundamental point, which mirrored much that Mansfield had been
saying to Johnson since he became president, was observation number
seven: "The main perplexity in the Vietnamese situation is that even if you
win, totally, you still do not come out well. What have you achieved? It is
by no means a 'vital' area of U.S. concern as it was described by Lodge [the
soon-to-be reappointed U.S. ambassador to Vietnam] at a hearing this
morning." At Johnson's direction, this and other points were answered in
a memorandum by McNamara the following day. In a revealing assertion,
McNamara responded to this observation by saying, "South Vietnam *is*
vital to the United States in the significance that a demonstrable defeat
would have on the future effectiveness of the United States on the world
scene—especially in areas where people are depending upon our guarantee of their independence. It is a vital U.S. concern to maintain our honor
as an ally and or formidability as an opponent." It is likely that
McNamara's response was drafted by his assistant secretary for international security affairs, John McNaughton, who had described in an unusually candid official memo three months earlier his understanding of U.S.
war aims as they had evolved over time:

70%   To avoid a humiliating U.S. defeat (to our reputation as
      guarantor).
20%   To keep SVN (and then adjacent) territory from Chinese hands.
10%   To permit the people of SVN to enjoy a better, freer way of life.

The nineteenth and final point in Mansfield's memo on the meeting
reflected growing disquiet about the role of the secretary of defense in promoting as well as directing the war. "McNamara has been a disappointment
in his handling of this situation, probably because he is being used in a way
in which he ought not be used," Mansfield reported. LBJ did not ask

McNamara to comment on that view, but instead responded to Mansfield himself, "I consider Bob McNamara to be the best Secretary of Defense in the history of this country."

Johnson, now proceeding along a preset schedule toward announcing his decisions, convened the Democratic and Republican leaders of Congress in the Cabinet Room at 6:41 P.M. the same day. Joseph Califano, then a young White House aide attending his first top-level foreign policy meeting, was struck by the theatricality he saw in the room: "the President's riveting performance, even when he wasn't speaking . . . leaning back in his high-back black leather swivel chair . . . using his large weathered hands for punctuation." Johnson set the stage with a dire portrayal of the situation in Vietnam, which he described as "deteriorating," and outlined a variety of theoretical responses, such as massive bombing of North Vietnam, an abrupt U.S. pull-out, and remaining in Vietnam with forces at the present level. He then addressed the two that he said he was considering: (1) declaring a state of emergency, calling U.S. reserve units to active duty, deploying "thousands of men and billions of dollars," with the danger of provoking North Vietnam and causing China and the Soviet Union to increase their aid or (2) supplying Westmoreland with the men and materials he had requested on a less dramatic basis, increasing selective service calls, extending enlistments of naval officers and Marines, and asking Congress for $1 billion to $2 billion additional funds for the war.

Johnson then went around the table asking for comments from each of the leaders of Congress, including Mansfield, House Speaker John McCormack, House Minority Leader Gerald Ford, Senate Minority Leader Everett Dirksen and Senate Majority Whip Russell Long. Also sitting at the long table with the six Senate and five House leaders were Rusk, McNamara, Lodge, the Joint Chiefs of Staff chairman General Earle Wheeler, and the newly minted CIA director Admiral William Raborn. A bevy of White House aides, including McGeorge Bundy, sat around the sides of the room. Fulbright, who was a committee chairman but did not occupy a leadership position in the Senate as a whole, was not present, nor were others who had begun to voice objections to the deepening war. Most of the lawmakers present appeared to be relieved that Johnson had outlined what he depicted as a least-bad, moderate course. There was no opposition—until nearly everyone else had spoken and it was Mansfield's turn.

Mansfield had said nothing, looking on and puffing on his pipe, during the discussion of what he knew to be an irrevocable commitment to a wider war. As he had in recent meetings, he had brought with him a written statement, the distillation of much that he previously had told Johnson on the basis of his long experience with Indochina and his independent thought. Now he asked the President's indulgence to speak and proceeded to read his views aloud while others in the room listened in stunned silence.

Johnson sucked the stem of his eyeglasses as Mansfield began in that strong, spare voice, as lean and as bony as his physique. "The decision was yours to make and you have made it or will make it shortly," he said, reiterating his long-standing belief in executive supremacy in the execution of foreign policy. Mansfield said he would support the decision to the best of his ability as a senator and would do so even if "the additional requirement of circumspection" had not been imposed on him as a Senate leader. However, he went on, "I would not be true to my conscience, to the people I represent or to my oath, if I did not, now, in the confidence of this room, make known to you my feelings on this matter. I would not want it said that the opportunity to speak was offered and that it was met with silence on my part."

The decision Johnson was making appears "to have a certain inevitability" in light of other decisions over months and years to deepen U.S. military involvement. Nonetheless, he said, everyone should be clear on the following points:

1. Whatever unbreakable national pledge we may have had was to assist South Viet Nam in its own defense, not to take over its defense. And whatever the basic commitment, it was abrogated with the assassination of Diem. . . . We do not owe this present government in Saigon anything. . . . It has no verified claim on the loyalty or support of its own people.

2. We are going deeper into a war in which even a total victory would, in the end, be a loss to the nation. We cannot expect to win anything that can be called a total victory without a decimation of the Vietnamese people, friend and foe alike, communist and non-communist alike and

without massive destruction of their land. The survivors will thank us, not at all. Nor will the world think the more of us for it.

3. We cannot depend on any nation of consequence fighting with us in this situation.

4. We cannot expect our own people to support a limited war of 3 to 10 years duration without the severest tax on our inner unity, particularly as racial issues, the use of drafted manpower, and partisan politics may become involved.

5. In my opinion, we do not have tangible national interests in Viet Nam which justify the kind of involvement into which we are slipping and sliding more deeply every day.

6. We have offered too little, too late in the way of bringing about meaningful negotiations in this situation and we have not, to say the least, encouraged the French, who could have and may still be able to play the decisive role in this connection.

7. It is clear that escalation begets escalation as the experiment with this process in the past few months should make crystal-clear. If there is any assumption escalation will not continue to beget escalation for a long time to come, and up to and including a devastating wasting war in Southeast Asia, it is, in my judgment, an unwarranted assumption.

8. As we go more deeply into this conflict, in short, I think it is most advisable, at least, that we go in with our eyes open.

Johnson and the other participants were momentarily speechless as Mansfield finished. A heavy silence spread across the room. Finally it was broken by Bourke Hickenlooper, a mid-western conservative Republican, who said the U.S. goal should be to make Vietnam a "reliable buffer" against communism and who expressed suspicion of negotiations, having made prominent attacks on the Democratic presidents' negotiations at Yalta and Potsdam. After further conversation, with no reference to Mansfield's objections or his plea, House Speaker John McCormack closed the meeting by saying that the President would have united support of Congress and of "all true Americans" in whatever course of action he chose to follow.

Thinking back years later on the events of that evening, Jack Valenti, one of Johnson's closest aides, wondered what would have happened had Johnson listened to Mansfield's "remarkably prophetic" discontent and had given his views more weight. "Mansfield's assay of Indochina was probably closer to the mark than any other public men, with the possible exception of George Ball," Valenti wrote in a memoir of the Johnson presidency.In Valenti's mind Mansfield was "a quiet, untroubled man, with neither charisma nor electric charm; a man so clear in his purpose that he never hesitated in pursuit of his duty, and who saw with a dry, unclouded eye what needed to be done, and what ought not to be done . . . an honest man, with himself and with the public."

Mansfield had had his say and had succeeded in presenting his views in the National Security Council meetings he had attended and in the fifteen memoranda he had presented. Between February 6, when Johnson ordered the first bombing of North Vietnam, and the July 28 announcement of the large-scale U.S. troop commitment, Mansfield had also spoken with Johnson on the telephone 19 times, in many cases touching on Indochina. This seems a lot, but pales in comparison with Johnson's 331 telephone conversations with McGeorge Bundy in the same period of time, or the 171 conversations with McNamara, or the 87 conversations with Dean Rusk. Little of what Mansfield had been saying, so fervently and sometimes pleadingly, had made much of a dent in the President's thinking.

The following morning, Johnson summoned a much larger group of members of Congress to the State Dining Room, where he announced his plan to raise the U.S. troop strength in Vietnam from 75,000 to 125,000 men almost immediately, with more to be sent "as requested." Mansfield was present but did not speak. Johnson did not disclose that he had already secretly agreed to lift the total to 175,000 men by the end of the year and to send at least another 100,000 men in 1966. Minutes after the congressional meeting, he announced his decisions publicly in a televised press conference in the East Room.

Mansfield's persistent but futile efforts to prevent massive U.S. commitment in Vietnam were at an end. Shortly after the announcement, he rose in the Senate to praise Johnson's consultations with Congress, saying that he was among those who had been consulted three times within the past twenty-four hours. "The President is to be commended for the speech he made," the

Majority Leader declared. "I know of no one who is more interested personally in what is happening in Vietnam, no one who is more desirous of seeking an honorable settlement to a situation which is fraught with difficulties and imponderables. . . . I know of the hours that he spends on the problem. I know how it preys on his thinking. I know it is uppermost in his mind. He is open to suggestions from all sources. He is doing his very best; and that is all that any one man can do."

JOHNSON II

Years of Frustration

IO Lyndon Johnson's decision in mid-1965 to send hundreds of thousands of U.S. ground troops to Vietnam was answered by large-scale increases on the communist side. As both sides sent ever-greater numbers of troops to fight, Mansfield consistently opposed the policy of escalation in public and private and called for negotiations to end the conflict. At the same time he continued to uphold the primacy of presidential authority in decision making on the war. At a crucial moment in March 1968, the Majority Leader rejected the President's plea for support of a further major increase in American troop deployments but pleaded with him instead "to find a way out." Johnson took historic steps to do so, in ways Mansfield (and most other Americans) did not expect.

On the afternoon of December 2, 1965, Mike Mansfield, followed by four fellow senators, descended from a U.S. Air Force jet at Saigon's Tan Son Nhut airport. It was the first visit in three years by the tall, lean Senate leader to a country that had consumed much of his attention, and which was the subject of his grave concern. There were clear signs as he rode into town that the struggle in Vietnam was rapidly becoming an American war. Saigon was being transformed from a quiet backwater to a boom town with heavy and noisy traffic from automobiles, motorcycles, and motorized tri-lambrettas. The city was swollen with newly arriving Americans, military and civilian, hired contractors, and hangers-on and with new hotels, restaurants, bars, and prostitutes to serve them. Whole new military bases and airfields in the capital and the hinterland were being built. Beyond the port, fifty to sixty cargo ships were backed up, stretching for miles along the Saigon River, waiting to unload supplies of ammunition and equipment. Frank Valeo, who followed the senators off the plane, observed that the French colonial town he had known earlier had disappeared: "Saigon had become a total military city already. . . . It had become a war center."

In the six months since Johnson's decisions in May, the number of U.S. troops in Vietnam already had risen to 170,000, five times the earlier total. General William Westmoreland, the handsome, square-jawed U.S. commander, confided to Mansfield and his delegation shortly after they arrived that he planned at least to double that number "the quicker the better." In the past the Americans had been mostly advisers, but now their mission was combat, to search out and destroy the enemy, as the U.S. Command would later describe it. This was just what Mansfield had feared and warned against time after time in meetings at the White House and memos to Johnson.

Westmoreland spoke with pride in pointing out that in the month just passed, "American troops were involved to a much greater degree than at any previous time in the history of the war." Most of this action was against North Vietnamese regular forces in the desolate Ia Drang Valley, in the first big battle of the new war. As a result, 448 Americans had been killed in November alone, about one-third of all the U.S. combatants killed until that time. North Vietnamese and Vietcong casualties were estimated to be almost twelve times as great, a ratio considered by Western military experts to be very favorable. Mansfield, however, from his long experience in Asia, concentrated on the other side of the equation: the communists' almost unlimited manpower available in South Vietnam, in North Vietnam, and, if need be, in their giant ally, China, and their seemingly limitless willingness to suffer and die for their cause. Mansfield's nightmare—that American troops would be deployed and destroyed in large numbers in an endless war—was coming true before his eyes.

On the morning of their departure two days later, Mansfield and his delegation were awakened by a blast that shook central Saigon: a Vietcong terror
squad had detonated a truck packed with plastic explosives at the doorway of
a U.S. military hotel blocks away from where the senators were staying, blowing a hole in the hotel three stories high. A New Zealand soldier, 2 American
servicemen, and 8 Vietnamese were killed, and 134 people were wounded, half
of them Americans. Mansfield and his friend and colleague, George Aiken of
Vermont, toured the site two hours later with Ambassador Henry Cabot Lodge
and talked to some of the wounded. Mansfield was impressed that not even
the capital was secure against terrorism or sabotage. Underscoring the fragility
of the situation, the senators could hear explosions from clashes of arms with
Vietcong guerrillas on the outskirts throughout the night. As they flew out of
Saigon, they witnessed a napalm attack on communist forces only a short distance from the airport.

"Insofar as the United States is concerned, the war in Viet Nam is just
beginning," Mansfield wrote in his confidential written report to
Johnson—his sixteenth—later in the month. "In my judgment this struggle will go on, at least, as long as North Viet Nam wants it to go on and
has the means to pursue it. All indications, now, are that they are prepared
to stay with it for a long time." Therefore, he wrote, for the United States
"the realistic requirement had better be seen not as 170,000 men or
300,000 men or even double that figure but, rather, as an open-end requirement of unpredictable dimensions." All the choices open to the
United States are bad choices, Mansfield concluded. Under existing circumstances "we stand to lose in Viet Nam by restraint; but we stand to
lose far more at home and throughout the world by the pursuit of an elusive and ephemeral objective in Viet Nam."

"Open-end[ed]"—that was the key phrase, used in both the confidential report to Johnson and the less specific but still gloomy public report
issued in the Senate on behalf of all five senators of the Mansfield mission.
Claiborne Pell of Rhode Island, who did not participate in the mission but
who had been a Foreign Service officer earlier in his career, seized upon the
phrase when the Foreign Relations Committee discussed the public report.
This was, he said, "a thought that I have tried to express but could not find
a word for before." Such an open-ended need for American troops was
"almost unthinkable," he said, in view of the hordes that could be thrown

into the battle on the other side, and yet, "to pull out is unacceptable." Pell like others was searching, unsuccessfully, for another way.

The Mansfield report introduced to public debate the concept that much greater U.S. efforts on the ground might be matched by the other side and thus fail to be decisive. For most Americans, who had been paying little attention to Vietnam until the spring of 1965 and who initially supported the war, the phrase struck a cautionary note that grew as the months and years went by. In time the open-ended nature of the conflict consumed the American strategy in Vietnam; it increasingly became clear that the communist side could go on losing longer than the American side was willing to continue "winning." North Vietnam suffered massive losses in battle deaths, by some calculations about 3 percent of its population, a level rarely equaled in modern warfare, but its troops kept on fighting with fierce determination. The United States, whose casualties were grievous but far fewer, tired of the struggle and eventually gave up. The development of the war proved the truth of Ho Chi Minh's taunting challenge to the French decades earlier: "You can kill ten of my men for every one I kill of yours, but even at those odds you will lose and I will win." Mansfield recognized this from an early stage, but he was unable to persuade Johnson or his advisers.

In its realism about the essential problem and the likely course of the war, the Mansfield report was a milestone. Until that point, no one with the standing and authority of Mansfield and his colleagues had cast so much doubt on the future after a visit to the war zone. As a Washington reporter just beginning to write about Vietnam as national affairs correspondent for Knight Newspapers, I found the report to be "chilling," especially as it represented "the cheerless conclusions of men with greater recent access to the face-down cards on the table than any other citizens free from direct responsibility for the war." After discussing it in a background interview with the ever-cautious Senator Edmund Muskie of Maine, I wrote that "it seems to be saying that the war may be unwinnable, the peace unobtainable—and further escalation incalculable." After the release of the report, Valeo noted, "members of both parties began to question the direction of U.S. policy openly and with rising vehemence."

THE OPEN-ENDED WAR

His lifelong wanderlust firmly in place, Mansfield stoutly believed in traveling to trouble spots to see for himself, especially in his chosen realm of Asia. His 1944 trip to China for Franklin D. Roosevelt had built his self-confidence and his stature in Congress; his trips to Indochina in 1953, 1954, and 1955 had cemented his standing as an Asia expert and placed him in high-level policy deliberations with the executive branch; his Indochina visit as a personal representative of John F. Kennedy in 1962 had intensified his appreciation of the pitfalls of the U.S. presence and may have affected Kennedy's private view of the course ahead. In 1965, following his reelection the previous November, Mansfield decided to undertake an extensive new trip to examine international problems firsthand, especially those of Indochina.

Following his experience with Roosevelt, he had come to realize that presidential sponsorship of an overseas trip was extremely valuable. In 1962 Kennedy's sponsorship had provided him and the traveling companions he had chosen with an Air Force jet, State Department support, and access to top leaders in every country in his six-week journey around the world. Presidential sponsorship also had provided the opportunity to make a public report under the aegis of the Senate as well as a private, more candid report, which he delivered to Kennedy on his yacht in Florida. As the 1965 congressional session began to wind down, he broached the subject to Johnson of a new presidentially sponsored mission.

Mansfield's request presented a dilemma for the President. He could foresee that the on-the-spot examination was unlikely to provide anything but trouble for the administration's Vietnam policies, which Mansfield had consistently opposed, yet to deny the request would risk a serious rupture in a relationship of extraordinary importance. In a conversation with Mansfield in September, Johnson agreed to sponsor the trip. Mansfield selected as traveling companions Democrats Daniel Inouye of Hawaii and Muskie of Maine, and Republicans Aiken of Vermont and J. Caleb Boggs of Delaware, all of whom were centrists and well respected in the Senate. Except for Boggs, who had been on Mansfield's 1962 mission, none had ever been in Vietnam. As had been the case with his trip for Kennedy, Mansfield drafted the letter in which Johnson requested him to undertake the mission and promised "the full cooperation and assistance" of the executive branch.

In a telephone conversation with his appointments secretary, Marvin Watson, Johnson grumbled that Mansfield wanted the White House to publicize his mission but "we're not going to announce it, period." On the eve of the mission's departure, however, LBJ spoke cordially and effusively to Mansfield, instructing him, "Let me know anything you want. Whatever you want, you get."

The Mansfield mission took off from Washington on November 13, 1965, in an Air Force jet on a mind-boggling trip that took thirty-seven days and covered 30,000 miles. The group went sixteen capital cities, including Paris, Moscow, Riyadh, New Delhi, Rangoon, Vientiane, Bangkok, Phnom Penh, Saigon, Singapore, Manila, Pago Pago and points between.

The most important stops were Mansfield's return visits to the three Indochina states. In Laos, the officially neutralist government created by Kennedy's decision to negotiate rather than fight had turned quietly anti-communist. King Savang Vatthana complained about Chinese and North Vietnamese use of Laotian territory (the "Ho Chi Minh trail") to move men and equipment into South Vietnam and said that U.S. military action in Vietnam was "moral" and just. Prime Minister Souvanna Phouma, whom Mansfield had always respected but who had often been belittled in Washington, said the "firm stand" taken by the United States in Vietnam had reduced the communist military pressure on Laos. Mansfield concluded that the situation was much improved since his visit three years earlier but that the fate of Laos was "inextricably woven" with the outcome of the war in Vietnam. Mansfield made no mention in his report of the U.S. secret bombing of the Ho Chi Minh trail that had begun in 1964; much later, he said he knew nothing about it at the time.

The Cambodian leader, Prince Norodom Sihanouk, had broken relations with the United States in early May after heavy U.S. bombing of his border area with Vietnam. Despite the official rupture, Sihanouk turned out tens of thousands of people to greet the senatorial mission, the warmest welcome of any government on the trip. He persuaded the mission to extend the visit overnight for more talks and entertainment rather than leave in the afternoon as planned. Mansfield considered Sihanouk "the most able, hardworking and effective non-Communist leader in Southeast Asia" and urged Washington to work with him on an unofficial basis and to withdraw clandestine U.S. support from the Cambodia dissident movement.

Vietnam was the keystone, and the recent arrival of American troops in large numbers was the issue. What did it mean and where would it lead?

The U.S. Embassy briefing for the Mansfield mission on December 2 took place three years to the week after a similar session during the 1962 Mansfield mission. Four of those on the senator's side of the table had attended the earlier briefing: Mansfield, Boggs, and two aides, Valeo and Francis Meloy, a young Foreign Service officer (later killed in Lebanon) who often traveled with the Majority Leader. None of those on the embassy side of the table in 1962, junior or senior, civilian or military, was still around.

Ambassador Fritz Nolting and General Paul Harkins, who had seen light at the end of the tunnel and forecast a turning point toward rapid success in 1962, were long gone. Now a cautiously optimistic Henry Cabot Lodge, in his second tour as U.S. ambassador, presided while General Westmoreland etched out a different sort of future: "I foresee that the intensity of military actions will continue to increase. I foresee the need for a great number of additional U.S. forces. I foresee a protracted conflict. We cannot afford this time to underestimate the enemy. And, as I see it, this war is beginning to take on an attritional character." Commending Westmoreland for his frankness, Mansfield expressed agreement that "this is not a one-shot affair, that this is not going to be over in a year in my opinion, it is going to take a long time, it is going to cost a lot of money, and . . . the sooner the truth is told to the American people . . . the better off I think we will all be."

When Westmoreland was asked by Inouye what he meant by a war of attrition, the general responded with a bloodless, business school definition of victory. "It is a question, senator, of making it so expensive for the DRV [Democratic Republic of Vietnam, or North Vietnam] to send troops down here that this will not be a productive course of action—in other words, to inflict such heavy losses on the Viet Cong that we destroy his forces faster than he can destroy the ranks of the government forces and the forces that the U.S. is able to bring into the country." Westmoreland's response was in keeping with the thinking in the senior civilian echelons of Robert McNamara's Pentagon. Assistant Secretary of Defense John T. McNaughton, asked by McNamara in July 1965 to define victory in Vietnam, responded that the United States and its allies would "win" when "we succeed in demonstrating to the VC that they cannot win." The authors of the Pentagon's classified history of the war, the Pentagon Papers, later observed that this was "the assumption upon which the conduct of the war was to rest—that the VC could be convinced in some meaningful sense that they were not going to win and that they would then rationally choose less violent methods of seeking their goals."

As the United States and its South Vietnamese allies built up their forces, the communists were doing the same. Westmoreland informed the Mansfield mission that 73,000 troops were estimated to be on the other side, including 14,000 North Vietnamese army troops who had infiltrated South Vietnam. The total was three times the 23,000 enemy troops estimated to exist at the time of Mansfield's previous trip in 1962. Infiltration from the North had been minimal at that time, but now Westmoreland estimated that 1,500 troops per month were arriving from the North and forecast that this influx soon would rise to 4,500 per month. South Vietnamese regular forces had increased from 200,000 at the time of Mansfield's previous trip to Westmoreland's current estimate of 300,000. On the ground, the trends were not good. At the time of his earlier trip, Mansfield had been told that the South Vietnamese government controlled 70 to 75 percent of the country's population; now Westmoreland estimated that only 60 percent of the South Vietnamese were under "some form of government control." Mansfield concluded that despite all efforts to the contrary, "considerable ground has been lost" since his visit three years earlier.

The program to create "strategic hamlets" had died with Ngo Dinh Diem, the only Vietnamese anticommunist leader whom Mansfield had thought capable of competing successfully with Ho Chi Minh. Instead, the catchword in English for working in the countryside was "revolutionary development," a difficult concept for the status-quo Saigon regime. The new leaders of the fifth government since Diem had been overthrown only two years earlier were the flamboyant Air Force chief, General Nguyen Cao Ky, now the Prime Minister, and the diffident Army chief, General Nguyen Van Thieu, who had become chairman of the National Leadership Committee or ruling junta. Sparing in his enthusiasm, Lodge told the Mansfield mission that Ky and Thieu, who had taken over five months earlier, were "as good as you can reasonably expect to find in this country." Mansfield saw them both the following day and was favorably impressed by Ky, whom he thought "looks better than expected." He made no comment about Thieu.

Valeo had a more ominous opinion of the developments he observed. Decades before, as a soldier in China, he had been part of a rapid U.S. military buildup after the defeat of the Japanese. He understood what was under way in Vietnam to be relentless and unstoppable. His private view was, "I really don't want to be here. It's too late. We're really not going to do anything with this now. There's no way you can turn this around. It's already here."

Mansfield was discouraged by what he saw and heard but had not given up. He reported to Johnson that the 150,000 additional U.S. troops being publicly discussed were likely to be "only an installment" if the present patterns persisted. "Indeed, it is not too early to begin to contemplate the need for a total upwards of 700,000," Mansfield said in his confidential report, because "we are not confronted with an opposition whose strength is definable within fixed maximums" but one that can throw many more men into the battle.* "In sum, it may be said that the end, in the sense of a military victory, is not even remotely in sight in Viet Nam. And the social and economic changes which must follow, if the objectives of the present policy are to be achieved, are now, once again, only beginning to be perceived." Instead of going down that well-marked road, Mansfield appealed to LBJ to change course and seek a cease-fire and negotiations or, failing that, to reduce American military objectives in Vietnam to the protection of Saigon and major cities and military bases.

Mansfield and his traveling companions returned to Andrews Air Force Base outside Washington at midnight on Saturday, December 18. The following day Johnson invited him to the family quarters on the second floor of the White House for a talk. Mansfield presented a written copy of his report and summarized his conclusions. Like Kennedy before him, Johnson "didn't like the report," Mansfield told me. After half an hour they were joined by Lady Bird, the Johnsons' daughter Luci and her friend Bill Hitchcock for an informal luncheon. At the end of the meal, LBJ instructed his press secretary, Bill Moyers, to announce that Mansfield's observations and recommendations

---

*At that point talk of such a huge increase would have been shocking to Congress and the public, which had yet to absorb press speculation that the government was considering sending as many as 200,000 men. When presented with Mansfield's confidential report, Secretary of State Rusk ridiculed the 700,000 estimate. However, McNamara, who had left Saigon on a brief visit two days before Mansfield arrived, drafted a plan on his return to Washington for 400,000 U.S. troops by the end of 1966, and possibly 200,000 more in 1967. The U.S. Pacific military command (CINCPAC) shortly requested an even larger number, 443,000, by the end of 1966. As it turned out, the requests for additional forces were approved piece by piece, keeping the projected ceilings carefully hidden from the public. In the end, the maximum number of American troops in Vietnam was 543,000, reached in the early months of the Nixon administration.

would be "staffed out and thoroughly evaluated" within the executive branch. The President's own evaluation came three weeks later in his State of the Union address to a joint meeting of Congress. There were now 190,000 U.S. troops in Vietnam, he announced. He projected a course of full speed ahead, declaring, "We will stay until aggression has stopped."

FULBRIGHT AND MANSFIELD

J. William Fulbright of Arkansas and Mike Mansfield of Montana were the most prominent senatorial dissenters from the war in Vietnam during the Johnson administration, and they chose very different means to advance their views. As chairman of the Senate Foreign Relations Committee, Fulbright led an increasingly powerful public campaign of dissent beginning in 1966; Mansfield muted his differences with Johnson in public even though continuing to dissent in personal contacts and memoranda. Johnson cut Fulbright off from White House favor and, for a while, even contact. He continued to work closely with Mansfield on other subjects but gave little heed to his recommendations on the war.

Fulbright and Mansfield were men of the same generation, Fulbright being only two years younger. Unlike Mansfield, however, Fulbright was born to wealth and social prominence. While Mansfield was toiling in the copper mines of Butte after being the lowest enlisted rank in all three military services, Fulbright was a Rhodes Scholar at Oxford after attending the University of Arkansas. Later he traveled in Europe, attended law school at George Washington University in Washington, D.C., and taught law part-time at the University of Arkansas while living on his own 110-acre farm. In 1939 he was named the university's president—and the nation's youngest university president—before being fired two years later after a politically inspired turnover in the university Board of Trustees.

Fulbright and Mansfield were both elected to the House of Representatives as Democrats in 1942, and both immediately joined the Foreign Affairs Committee, whose activities were of the greatest interest to both. Fulbright quickly won fame as a forward-looking internationalist by introducing a resolution endorsing U.S. participation in a postwar international organization. The Fulbright resolution, as it was known, passed the House 360 to 29 and inspired a similar resolution in the Senate, paving the way for eventual U.S.

sponsorship of the United Nations. That success made Fulbright an instant national celebrity. After only two years in the House, he was elected to the Senate in 1944. In his second year as a senator, he cemented his national stardom by obtaining passage of the Fulbright program to provide government-paid scholarships for Americans to study overseas. He was a courageous and outspoken foe of the crude anticommunism of Senator Joseph R. McCarthy (who sneered at him as "Senator Halfbright") and played a leading role in McCarthy's censure by the Senate in 1954. During the Eisenhower administration, while Mansfield was emphasizing bipartisanship and working closely with Secretary of State John Foster Dulles, Fulbright was a severe and prominent critic of Dulles's reflexive anticommunism.

In 1959 Fulbright became chairman of the Senate Foreign Relations Committee, of which Mansfield was an active member. When Mansfield was elected majority leader two years later, his participation in the committee declined due to the pressure of time and his special status as a confidential adviser to Presidents Kennedy and Johnson. Although he attended few committee meetings, he was regularly briefed by the committee staff. Mansfield developed the Senate Democratic Policy Committee, which had rarely met under Johnson's leadership, into a body that periodically discussed foreign policy issues, especially Vietnam and U.S. troops abroad, but he was ever conscious of the Foreign Relations Committee's legislative prerogatives. True to form, Mansfield never sought the limelight at the expense of Fulbright or the committee. But neither did he inform Fulbright or others about his many personal interactions with Presidents Kennedy and Johnson on the war, considering them to be private and privileged.

Fulbright and Mansfield respected one another as foreign policy experts who shared many similar viewpoints, but they were not personally close. The affluent Fulbrights moved in different social circles and never set foot in Mansfield's private house. Fulbright, in an interview with Jeffrey Safford, a professor at Montana State University, said that his "first major get-together" with Mansfield was over Vietnam. Fulbright recalled that Mansfield had given him his proxy to vote in committee on all issues concerning Vietnam, which the Arkansas senator considered "extraordinary" and without precedent.

Fulbright, a southern progressive with national credentials, had been close to Johnson personally and politically. As Majority Leader, Johnson had frequently referred to Fulbright as "my secretary of state" and after the 1960 election urged President-elect Kennedy to appoint Fulbright to the post. (The opposition of blacks and liberals, based on Fulbright's voting record on civil rights legislation, and of Robert Kennedy denied him the appointment.) When Johnson became president, he initially continued his friendship with Fulbright and his wife, Betty, speaking warmly to them both in his first week, and a week after that hosting them, along with the Mansfields and the Humphreys, at the "most remarkable evening" at the Johnson residence recorded by Mansfield in his notes (see Chapter 9). With the cooperation of Mansfield, Fulbright served as floor leader for the Tonkin Gulf resolution in August 1964, an accommodation to Johnson both senators came deeply to regret.

With the Vietnam War escalating in early 1965, Fulbright became increasingly wary of LBJ's foreign policy, and Johnson became increasingly irritated with Fulbright's criticism. In February, Johnson complained to Douglas Cater, who was frequently a go-between with the Foreign Relations chairman, that Fulbright "is a cry baby—and I can't continue to kiss him every morning before breakfast." The following month Johnson told Richard Russell, "Fulbright's awful mean, and awful narrow, and awful little. . . . He's almost as tough to get along with as Mansfield."

The decisive break came in September 1965 when Fulbright in a Senate speech condemned Johnson's misleading comments and hasty actions during a crisis in the Dominican Republic several months earlier. In the aftermath of the speech and of Johnson's furious reaction, Fulbright began to speak publicly of his dissent from the policies being followed in Indochina. Johnson, who was highly sensitive to being challenged in public, severed personal relations with Fulbright and condemned him more sharply than ever. In a telephone conversation with Mansfield in late October, Johnson contrasted Fulbright's increasingly publicized opposition to the war with Mansfield's mostly private dissent. LBJ said of Fulbright, "I don't know why he didn't tell me [his views on Vietnam] instead of telling the *New York Times.* He ought to come and tell me. That's what you do. You sent me 50 memos here that haven't been in the newspaper. . . . And they have a helluva lot more effect than they do given [to] the *New York Times.*"

Johnson's estimate of the impact of the two men is most debatable. Although Fulbright (like Mansfield) refused to participate in protest marches or other antiwar demonstrations, his intellectual and political leadership was a factor in encouraging the public opposition that eventually brought down Johnson and his war policies. In contrast, Mansfield's dissents had little effect on the public or on Johnson, who grumpily tolerated them and continued to work with Mansfield on a variety of issues. When I asked Mansfield about the contrast between his and Fulbright's methods of opposition to the war, he responded, "I felt that as long as I was the Majority Leader, I was in a better position to state my views, not only on the [Senate] floor but to the White House directly. Otherwise I would just be talking to the wind." After a pause, he added that he was "talking to the wind anyway. But the wind was blowing less hard."

For all their different ways of working, Fulbright and Mansfield shared many viewpoints and were often linked together in Johnson's mind and voice. In December 1965 Johnson began a thirty-seven-day pause in the bombing of North Vietnam that was intended to test Hanoi's interest in negotiations but also to placate "Fulbright, Scotty Reston, Mansfield, Arthur Krock and the *New York Times*," the President explained to Averell Harriman. In Johnson's mind the two senators and the leading American newspaper comprised a cabal he was forever fighting. In 1966 he instructed Hubert Humphrey to rebut Mansfield's gloomy report with a hard-hitting trip report of his own that would "nail Fulbright, Mansfield and the *New York Times* editorial board to the wall."

When Johnson in early December was considering a temporary halt in the bombing, Mansfield—but not Fulbright—was among the congressional leaders he consulted. The Majority Leader, who had spoken to many world leaders and had just left Saigon on his long trip, responded by cable that a bombing pause "would likely be of doubtful utility" in bringing about negotiations unless coupled with broader U.S. initiatives. He recommended that Johnson propose a standstill cease-fire on all sides in Vietnam for about a month to thoroughly test the possibility of negotiations. However, the U.S. and Vietnamese military opposed a cease-fire on the ground even more passionately than they opposed the bombing pause, because of fears that the communist side would use it to reposition its forces and would cheat.

Johnson summoned Democratic congressional leaders on January 24 to discuss ending the pause, which was then thirty days old. After lengthy presentations from the President and McGeorge Bundy, only Mansfield opposed the immediate resumption of bombing. Afterward, Johnson told his aides that of the senior leaders of both parties, he believed "we'll lose only Fulbright and Mansfield" if the bombing were resumed. The President's forecast proved correct the following day, when he summoned the leaders of both parties in the House and Senate and the chairmen and ranking members of key committees. Told that Rusk, McNamara, and the Joint Chiefs of Staff all recommended resumption of the bombing, of nineteen members of Congress present, only Mansfield and Fulbright spoke against it.

"We have little to lose by [the] lull. Time is on the side of the enemy. [The] best chance of getting to [the] peace table is to minimize our military action," Mansfield declared. Reading from a statement he had prepared in advance, he urged Johnson to call for a complete cease-fire, followed by elections in Vietnam within three to six months, withdrawal of U.S. forces after amnesty for fighters on both sides, and internationally sponsored negotiations. Otherwise, Mansfield continued, U.S. casualties will rise, as will civilian deaths, possibly caused by the use of gas warfare or even atomic weapons in Vietnam. He forecast that the result would be increasing isolation of the United States and increasing conflict with China.

Fulbright said he agreed with Mansfield, and described the conflict in Vietnam as the residue of a colonial war, with the United States taking the place of the French. "If we win, what do we do? Do we stay there forever?" he asked. Instead, the United States should not resume bombing but try to find a way out. "After large casualties, we will come to a negotiation" in the end, he said. Johnson earlier had turned down proposals from Mansfield and members of the White House staff that he meet alone with Fulbright. Now as the Foreign Relations Committee chairman began to speak, the President turned to Rusk, who was seated on his immediate right, and pointedly engaged him in conversation until Fulbright had finished. Later, Johnson characterized the two dissenters in remarks to his aides: "If you understand Fulbright he wants us to get out. Mansfield wants us to hunker up."

The most passionate and influential plea to resume the bombing came from Russell, who declared, "This is the most frustrating experience of my life. I didn't want to get in there, but we are there. . . . I think we have gone too far in this lull, although I recognize the reason. This pause has cost you militarily. We are going to lose a lot of boys as a result—casualties of our care for peace." Russell, the Armed Services Committee chairman, long the most influential member of the Senate, then appealed with great emotion to Johnson, his former protégé, "For God's sake, don't start the bombing half way. Let them know they are in a war. We killed civilians in World War II and nobody opposed. I'd rather kill them than have American boys die. Please, Mr. President, don't get one foot back in it. Go all the way."

Mansfield's views about the impact on China were echoed then and thereafter by Undersecretary of State George Ball, who dissented in private from most of LBJ's escalatory moves, although he defended administration policy in public settings. On January 25, the same day as the meeting with congressional elders, Ball sent Johnson a lengthy memo arguing against further sustained bombing of North Vietnam, declaring his strong conviction that it "will more than likely lead us into war with Red China—probably in six to nine months."

Johnson, after new appeals from all sides and further meetings within the White House, ordered resumption of the bombing of North Vietnam on January 31 but authorized no major new targets to be struck for the time being. The President's announcement was greeted with speeches in and out of Congress, for and against his action, and rising protests against the action by religious and peace groups.

The Majority Leader rose on the Senate floor to express his sympathy and support for Johnson's efforts over the thirty-seven-day bombing halt to seek an avenue to negotiations, never revealing that the President had rejected his recommendations. "I think I probably know Lyndon Johnson as well as any other member of this body knows him. I have been closely associated with him for 24 years. I know how deeply concerned he is about Vietnam. I know the agonizing days and nights he goes through," Mansfield declared. Under the Constitution, he said, the President has the responsibility for military actions. "He cannot shove the buck to us. He knows that. He knows that, in the final analysis, there is only one man in this republic who can make the decision. . . . So far as the Senator from Montana is concerned, he will do his very best to give the President of the United States as much in the way of support as he possibly can." Mansfield's statement reflected not only his political and philosophical position about executive supremacy in foreign policy but also his personal feeling for Johnson, despite differences and disappointments. Shortly before he spoke in the Senate, Mansfield had sat with a few friends in his Capitol office to watch Johnson announce on television that he was resuming the aerial bombardment of North Vietnam. "I feel so sorry for him," Mansfield exclaimed. "I can imagine what he's going through."

THE MISERIES OF AMBIGUITY

Throughout 1966 and 1967, Mansfield was in an ambiguous position regarding the Vietnam War, which was increasingly the central issue in American politics and life. He continued to dissent energetically in private meetings and in memoranda to Johnson, but he refused to do anything to aid the growing number of senatorial or outside critics of the war. When he did express public criticism of administration policy, he never attacked Johnson directly and nearly always gave full credence to Johnson's gestures toward a negotiated settlement.

In late 1965 and early 1966 I spoke several members of the Senate Foreign Relations Committee in preparation for an article about the committee for the *New York Times Sunday Magazine,* for which I was a frequent contributor at the time. On February 18, I discussed my findings with a congressional affairs aide to LBJ, Henry Hall Wilson, an old friend of mine and a helpful White House source. "The Mansfield report was taken very seriously by many members of the Senate," I told Wilson, and "it stirred up a lot of people. . . . A lot of people were stirred up even more by the failure of the Administration to bother with answering the report."

For many years during and before Fulbright's chairmanship, the Foreign Relations Committee had been a quiet backwater of congressional influence on government policy. The committee met around a large table under a crystal chandelier in its ornate room on the first floor of the Capitol. Except when the committee voted on diplomatic nominations or foreign assistance legislation, most of its activity was closed to the press and it made little news. The small, unified staff responded to all members, Republican and Democratic. It was a striking departure from the usual for the committee to put on news-making public hearings, as it did in February 1966.

The committee began discussing the issue of hearings on Vietnam on January 11, when Mansfield and Aiken reported on their trip to Saigon and other capitals. After an hour of discussion of Vietnam issues, Frank Lausche of Ohio, a Democratic conservative, praised the hearing as "the most constructive hearing we have had in the whole time I have been a member of this committee." When Fulbright raised the possibility of further hearings, Mansfield approved but asked that they be held in executive (closed) session "because then you can feel freer to speak—just among our colleagues." As Fulbright continued to press for public hearings, Mansfield cautioned that "you do not know how the newspapers will play up public hearings or how they will whip up or interpret these things." Nevertheless, when the committee returned to the subject of open hearings on Vietnam three weeks later, Mansfield made the motion to proceed, which was carried unanimously. Yet, once agreed, he played virtually no role in the hearings. He attended only one session and asked no questions.

Neither Mansfield nor Fulbright anticipated the powerful effect of the public hearings. It was not the newspapers but the television networks that "whipped up" the public, as senators, war critics, and administration officials debated the wisdom of U.S. actions in Vietnam for the first time in high-profile fashion. The proceedings began on February 4, and all three major television networks, ABC, CBS, and NBC, covered the hearings live, gavel-to-gavel, preempting their entire weekday schedules. In the White House, Johnson, ever attuned to public opinion and appalled that his policy was being challenged so prominently, was quick to realize the potential damage to his policies. He suddenly announced at mid-morning on the first day of hearings that he was flying to Honolulu the following day to meet the Vietnamese leaders, Ky and Thieu, to discuss political, economic, and social matters in Vietnam. LBJ's trip was, as McGeorge Bundy said later, "a big farrago, meant to take the spotlight off the hearings," but the gambit did not succeed. The televised hearings introduced doubts about the war to the broad mass of the American public for the first time, shattering the nearly complete dominance of the White House over mainstream information and opinion regarding the war. As David Halberstam wrote later, before the Foreign Relations Committee hearings "the national media, in particular the television networks, had belonged exclusively to the executive branch." About 25,000 letters poured into the usually sparsely occupied mailboxes of the Foreign Relations Committee, more than 6 to 1 approving the committee's proceedings. Years after the hearings, it was revealed that Johnson, in a more sinister reaction, arranged to have the FBI monitor the hearings to compare the statements of senators, especially Fulbright and Vietnam war critic Wayne Morse of Oregon, with "the Communist Party line."

Mansfield's difficult position came into the open dramatically on March 1, when Morse offered an amendment on the Senate floor to repeal the Tonkin Gulf resolution, which Johnson continued to wave in his opponents' faces as justification for his military actions in Vietnam. Morse's amendment motivated Russell to propose a counter-amendment to reaffirm the Tonkin Gulf resolution, which authorized the President "to take all necessary steps, including the use of armed force," to assist South Vietnam. Twelve Democratic critics of the war, in one of the first strategy meetings of anti-war senators, were working on their own amendment, asking Johnson not to expand the war without coming to Congress for a declaration of war. To avoid votes on the substance of the issues, which opponents of the war were certain to lose but which could raise doubts all around about the position of the Senate, Mansfield, Fulbright, and Russell worked out a compromise arrangement to table the Morse amendment (put it aside without considering it) and drop the conflicting amendments by Russell and the main-stream Vietnam War critics without a vote.

When he heard about the tabling arrangement, Johnson implored Mansfield to make a statement in debate that the presidential authority to wage war would be unchanged and undiluted by what the Senate was about to do. Mansfield resisted, arguing that the President's authority and responsibility for the war did not depend on the Tonkin Gulf resolution, which Mansfield had come to regret deeply. When the moment of decision came, it was the Majority Leader who made the motion to table the Morse amendment, calling the measure "inappropriate and inadvisable in connection with this bill at this time." In a concession to Johnson's concern, he said the tabling of Morse's amendment would keep the Tonkin Gulf resolution "in effect with whatever constitutional force it may have." In a phrase that was much quoted, he argued against Morse's amendment, saying, "We are in too deep now. The situation is one of the utmost delicacy and the risk of misinterpretation is very great." His motion to table the Morse amendment carried 92 to 5, with Fulbright among those voting no. Eugene McCarthy of Minnesota, who was in the process of moving to an outspoken antiwar position, voted for the Morse resolution. He later wrote that Mansfield's maneuver was "a surprising move on Mansfield's part, since the move of Senator Morse was clearly within the range of Senate rights and responsibility, and the Mansfield motion was clearly in the service of the Johnson administration."

As public uneasiness spread and large-scale antiwar protests began, Mansfield's muffled dissent was displeasing to those who had begun to do battle on the home front. While the turbulence was rising outside, *Washington Post* reporter Andrew Glass observed a majority leader who continued publicly to defend the administration on Vietnam, "without quite agreeing with it." Glass reported that in private, "There is an ascetic, even priestly quality to Mansfield's manner as he chews reflectively on his pipe and drinks countless cups of hot black coffee with trusted friends around a marble table in his ornate Capitol retreat." In these days Glass found "a certain bleakness to the Mansfield landscape; his smile, while warm, is not quick in coming."

Mansfield's mail began to turn more critical of his posture than in the past. A letter from an Ohio woman cited the feeling of excitement she had felt on a visit to the Capitol nearly a decade earlier, when she discovered a Mansfield who reminded her of the young Lincoln, "long and spare, his face fierce, yet sensitive . . . [who] spoke with the words of the intellectual, the poet." She had always placed her faith in poets, writers, and artists, she wrote, because they pursue the truth, and it was wonderful to find a poet in such a position of public trust and power, knowing that he would recognize truth and fight for it. Now, however, she wrote in despair:

> What happened, Senator Mansfield, to you, the poet? I marched in New York with thousands of good and decent people who gathered to protest our involvement in Vietnam. Many times during the day my eyes filled with tears. These are people who are ashamed of our actions, people who love one another, and want only good things for mankind. They are not naïve children. They are well informed, educated people who know all about American politics, history, et cetera.
>
> They need a forceful champion. They do not have him. You might have been that man.

His antiwar colleagues in the Senate were also disappointed in him. Eugene McCarthy, in a retrospective interview with the historian Ross K. Baker, said, "I never thought that Mike did as much as he should have in challenging the involvement in Vietnam. The Senate failed pretty badly in taking the responsibility for challenging the escalation of the war. Mike had been chairman of that special committee that went to Vietnam in '65 and filed a very negative report, but that's sort of where he left it." George McGovern of South Dakota, who became a leading antiwar figure and a Democratic presidential candidate, told me that Mansfield's position in the late 1960s was a difficult one for opponents of the war: "It was frustrating because I knew, as did others in the Senate, that Mike shared our view about the tragic mistake this country made about going into Vietnam. . . . He had made it quite clear that he saw himself at least partially but importantly as the President's man in carrying out the administration's program in the Senate. . . . He had risen in the Senate in part because of Lyndon's friendship. I think we understood he was in a little different position from the rest of us who were opposed to the war."

From a different angle, Russell Long of Louisiana, who was Majority Whip to Mansfield in the late 1960s and a strong defender of the war, said in retrospect, "One thing about him that did disturb me a bit was during the Vietnam war that Mike should have backed the President more." Certainly Johnson himself felt that way, as indicated by numerous remarks to friends and associates. LBJ's close aide Harry McPherson wrote in his own memoir that when Mansfield's active support on Vietnam issues was needed, "his silence was almost as irritating to the White House as an exposed confrontation; it was not enough for a Democratic leader to look the other way as the line was being drawn in the dirt." Walt W. Rostow, Johnson's last national security adviser and a true believer in the justice and utility of the Vietnam War, even decades later, told me that, "at bottom, Johnson's view of Mansfield was that he didn't like the war and he wanted to get the hell out of it. Johnson wanted to get out of it too, but he wouldn't take defeat. . . . But on the other hand, Mansfield was loyal in the Senate and he expressed his view temperately, in moderate terms, even though it would end in accepting defeat. Johnson wanted this dialogue with him because he needed him for other purposes." As the Majority Leader's position on the war vexed Johnson in 1966 and 1967, according to Neil MacNeil, *Time*'s veteran Capitol Hill reporter, "Mansfield would be seated for White House state dinners at a table in one of the far corners of the dining room, and Dirksen would be seated at the President's table. Fulbright would not be invited to attend."

It was not Johnson's reproach but the ineffectiveness of his opposition to the war that weighed on Mansfield in later years. "I received kind of heavy criticism for not doing more, but I didn't know what more I could do," he told me in 1998. "I felt kind of helpless. But I wanted my position known.

That position never changed from the beginning to the end. I was never in any doubt that we were in the wrong."

LEADERSHIP IN A NEW SENATE

By the beginning of 1967, the midpoint in Johnson's four-year elected term of office as President, Mike Mansfield presided over a Senate that had dramatically changed from the one he had inherited. Gone was the Senate dominated and run by the Inner Club of southerners and elders that journalist William S. White had described in his 1956 book, *Citadel*. Robert Kerr of Oklahoma, the famed "king of the Senate," had died in 1963. Bobby Baker, the former Senate page who had facilitated the logrolling and deal making of the old Senate, had been forced out by scandal the same year. Richard Russell was still active and respected, but the bourbon and magnolia reign of the southern patriarchs had been degraded if not destroyed by Mansfield's decision to democratize Democratic policy decisions and committee assignments. The southern veto over civil rights legislation, enabled by use of the filibuster, had been broken by cloture votes in the legislative battles of 1964 and 1965. Most important, the central figure who had dominated the Senate and empowered the club in the 1950s, Johnson himself, had been removed to the White House, where he still sought industriously to manipulate votes and affect legislation, often successfully, but from which perch he was unable to affect the political and personal relationships that were at the core of the institution.

Mansfield was asked in a television interview early in 1967 about "the Senate establishment," much written and talked about even then, in which a small group was highly influential. "Oh, I think it's mostly newspaper talk," he replied. "There is no club in the Senate, unless you want to include all 100 members. . . . As far as the club idea goes, in my book, all senators are equal—I repeat—they are all considered the same, and all groups and factions within the Senate are kept fully aware of any developments which I might undertake in matters of great import." To the initial surprise of almost everyone, Mansfield meant what he said. Only in the most exceptional occasions did he actively lobby for legislation; as Majority Leader he never exerted political pressure on senators or made deals to swap a vote for a favor. Often he did not even inform senators of the administration's position on pending legislation but left this activity to White House lobbyists or

THIRTY-FIVE CENTS

MARCH 20, 1964

Can Democrats Control A Democratic Senate?

TIME

THE WEEKLY NEWSMAGAZINE

MAJORITY
LEADER
MANSFIELD

VOL. 83 NO. 12

A leadership challenge personified: Mansfield's way of gentle persuasion in the historic Senate struggle over the Civil Rights bill of 1964. *Time* drew the contrast with Lyndon Johnson's high-pressure tactics, which Mansfield rejected. (Courtesy Time Life Pictures/Getty Images)

Johnson and Mansfield in the Cabinet Room of the White House on March 27, 1968. When Budget Director Charles Zwick (back to camera) and Treasury Secretary Henry Fowler left a minute later, the President and Majority Leader began a lengthy test of wills at the turning point of Johnson's political future and the Vietnam War. Their conversation was secretly recorded by microphones placed in the underside of the table. (Photo by Yoichi Okamoto, Lyndon B. Johnson Library)

Richard Nixon and Mansfield often met alone for breakfast in the stately splendor of the Family Dining Room of the White House. In strictest confidence, they discussed plans for the U.S. opening to China and the future of the war in Vietnam. (File 5840.02, Nixon Materials, National Archives)

Mansfield and Cambodian leader Norodom Sihanouk after a performance of the Royal Ballet Corps in Phnom Penh in 1969. The visit, at the request of Nixon, reopened U.S. diplomatic relations with one of Mansfield's favorite countries and a leader he respected. Unknown to Mansfield, Nixon had already authorized secret U.S. bombing of Cambodia. (Photo 99-326, K. Ross Toole Archives, University of Montana)

After two years of support and forbearance, Mansfield turned sharply against Nixon's conduct of the war following the overthrow of Sihanouk and the U.S. invasion of Cambodia in 1970. Reversing his previous stand, he sponsored legislation that forced Nixon to end U.S. participation in the Indochina fighting. (Photo 99-573, K. Ross Toole Archives, University of Montana)

Chinese Premier Chou En-lai invited the Mansfields to visit Beijing before he invited Nixon. While outwardly endorsing Mansfield's trip Nixon secretly ordered Henry Kissinger to "screw it up any way you can." Here the Mansfields meet Chou for the last time in the hospital room where he was suffering from cancer. Maureen's expression of despair conveys her inner feelings. (Courtesy Anne Mansfield, family collection)

Gerald Ford's assumption of the presidency following Nixon's forced resignation in 1974 gave rise to a jubilant welcome from Mansfield, here with his arm around the shoulders of the new president. They are joined (on the left) by Senators Hugh Scott and James Eastland and (on the right) House Speaker Carl Albert and Senator Robert Byrd. (U.S. Senate Historical Office)

To my great friend Mike Mansfield –
Jimmy Carter
2-6-78

After retiring from the Senate in 1977, Mansfield accepted Jimmy Carter's appointment as ambassador to Japan. More independent-minded than most U.S. envoys, Mansfield supplied advice direct to Carter on controversial issues, including a civilian nuclear program in Japan. (Photo 99-4437, K. Ross Toole Archives, University of Montana)

Ronald Reagan surprised nearly everyone by retaining the former Senate Democratic leader as ambassador to Japan in his Republican administration—and keeping him on the job for his entire eight years in office. Sitting in on a Reagan-Mansfield meeting in 1985 are (on the left) Assistant Secretary of State Paul Wolfowitz and National Security Adviser John Poindexter and (on the right) Undersecretary of State Michael Armacost and National Security Council staff member Gaston Sigur. (Ronald Reagan Library)

After a U.S. nuclear submarine killed and injured Japanese fishermen in a collision at sea and then ran away, a public uproar threatened U.S.-Japan relations. Mansfield ended the furor by presenting the official naval report to Foreign Minister Sunao Sonoda with a very deep bow of apology, Japanese style, executed before the cameras of the Japanese press. (© Yomiuri Shimbun)

Prime Minister Yasuhiro Nakasone and his wife, Ivy, toast Mike and Maureen Mansfield with cups of sake at a private dinner. Mansfield's extensive dealings with Nakasone helped preserve and advance what the ambassador famously termed the world's "most important bilateral relationship, bar none." (Courtesy Anne Mansfield, family collection)

When Maureen died in September 2000, her husband delivered the heart-rending eulogy at her funeral at Fort Myer, Virginia, where his own funeral would be held a year later. After her death, he forbade his doctors to do anything further to prolong his own life. (Courtesy Fred Wilson, from videotape of Maureen Mansfield funeral)

COLONEL, U. S. AIR FORCE
1899 —— 1973

✠

MICHAEL
JOSEPH
MANSFIELD
PVT
US MARINE CORPS
MAR 16 1903
OCT 5 2001

Mansfield selected his own simple gravestone—the smallest available at Arlington National Cemetery—and chose to have inscribed only one of the earliest and simplest of his many accomplishments in the service of his nation. (Photo by Brian Barth) to the committee and subcommittee chairs, to whom he granted the chief responsibility for judging, shaping, and approving legislation and then managing the debate on their handiwork when it reached the Senate floor. "Mansfield simply did not view the Senate as an instrument of its leadership," said Muskie of Maine, who emerged as a major figure during Mansfield's tenure. "He felt that the way to make the Senate effective was simply to let it work its will. And he believed that the Senate would do just that. And he also believed that senators would rise to that responsibility if it was made clear to them that their responsibility was important."

The democratization of the Senate meant the dismantling of much of the power that Johnson and even earlier holders of the Majority Leader's post had managed to garner. When Humphrey, who had been majority whip, became vice president in 1965, Mansfield decided not to choose his successor as he easily could have done and was generally expected to do. Instead, he remained scrupulously neutral and permitted the Democratic membership of the Senate to decide between competing candidates. These included John Pastore of Rhode Island, who was personally close to Mansfield and shared his political philosophy, and Russell Long of Louisiana, who had neither attribute. Long won the balloting and served until January 1969 as Mansfield's deputy. It was a dysfunctional relationship. Long, who inherited the chairmanship of the Finance Committee shortly after becoming majority whip, clashed with Mansfield from time to time and occasionally even with Johnson and his aides.

Despite its drawbacks the Mansfield method, so harshly criticized toward the end of the Kennedy administration, worked effectively in the first years of the Johnson era. LBJ provided the initiative and impetus and lobbied hard from the White House; the committees stepped up to their responsibilities and produced a deluge of important national legislation; huge Democratic majorities after the 1964 election, often leavened by Republican cooperation, voted it into law. In 1965, according to Congressional Quarterly, "measures which taken alone would have crowned the achievements of any Congress were enacted in a seemingly endless stream."

The most celebrated and far-reaching legislation had long been contemplated but never enacted, especially Medicare, providing medical care for senior citizens, and the Elementary and Secondary Education Act, providing federal assistance to public schools. Both acts had been highly contentious. Among other historic measures passed were the Voting Rights Act and the Clean Air Act. Altogether the Johnson White House counted forty-four pieces of landmark legislation that became law in 1965. The deluge slackened in 1966 as budgetary pressures from the Vietnam War began to affect Congress and the domestic economy, yet the Teacher Corps, Model Cities program, and other domestic initiatives were passed. Most of the credit for passage of the Great Society legislation, as it was called, went to Johnson, but he could not have accomplished these goals without a cooperative Senate that was working creatively and well with the White House.

The congressional elections of 1966 saw Republican gains of three seats in the Senate and forty-seven seats in the House of Representatives. The gains were far from enough to endanger the heavy parliamentary majorities that had been piled up in the landslide election of 1964, but they were sufficient to make Congress more competitive. Mansfield, who had strongly supported Johnson's domestic social legislation, was also cautious about government spending, as he was about his own money. He felt it was now time to digest and to emphasize implementation rather than to pass a large number of additional programs. In the conference of Senate Democrats on the first day of the 1967 session, he called for "a careful retrospective look at what has emerged in administrative practice from the new federal programs which have been set in motion in the past three or four years . . . to see to it that these programs are off on the right foot and they are doing what they were designed to do, in effective and equitable fashion." Even before the Senate met, he asked the chairman of each of the legislative committees by letter to undertake a "top-to-bottom" evaluation of major federal programs. He added, "A complete restudy by the Senate could provide not only a basis for adjustment of legislation . . . but also a check on the equity and efficacy of the administrative interpretations and practices which have developed."

Johnson, who had been provided with a copy of Mansfield's letter, decided to resist even before the new Congress got down to work. Without mentioning Mansfield, he told a press conference he had no intention of slowing his requests "until we can provide each child with all the education that he can take; until we can see that our families have a decent income; until we can secure the measures that are necessary to improve our cities, to curb pollution, to reduce poverty." Privately he told Joseph Califano, his chief assistant for domestic policy, "If we don't keep them [members of

Congress] busy up there doing our work, they'll drive us crazy down here investigating and evaluating us." In the end, however, Johnson recognized that Mansfield's viewpoint was closer to political reality than his own. The President's requests were modest compared with those of the previous three congressional sessions. Even so, few of them emerged unscathed from an increasingly contentious legislative process, hemmed in by the fast-growing war in Vietnam, increasing budgetary difficulties, growing antiwar protests, and racial violence that had broken out in Newark and Detroit.

The most widely noted of Mansfield's legislative initiatives beginning in the mid-1960s was his effort to reduce the number of American troops stationed in Western Europe, which was opposed by the Johnson administration and the Nixon administration after it. As early as January 1961, even before being elected majority leader, he publicized his "personal opinion" that some of the American forces in Europe could safely be removed to ease the financial drain on the United States without harming Western security. He expressed the hope that the Soviet Union would make a corresponding withdrawal of its forces from Eastern Europe. If they did not and the Western Europeans felt weakened, they were financially able to strengthen their own forces, he pointed out. Instead, the West Europeans were periodically reducing their military budgets and their troop support for the North Atlantic alliance while the United States continued to carry a heavy burden.

Mansfield's views got nowhere until the summer of 1966, when France under Charles DeGaulle withdrew its forces from NATO, and the foreign currency drain of U.S. forces in Europe, combined with sharply rising costs in Vietnam, suggested to Senate conservatives and liberals alike that the United States had become seriously overextended. Beginning with a meeting on July 13, the Democratic Policy Committee, led by Mansfield, unanimously decided to exert its influence to bring about a "substantial" but unspecified cutback in the U.S. deployments. After a series of discussions involving Rusk, McNamara, Secretary of the Treasury Henry Fowler, and the ambassador to Germany, George McGhee, all of whom tried and failed to dissuade them, the thirteen leading Democratic senators agreed on August 30 to co-sponsor a resolution calling for reductions. At Mansfield's urging, the legislation was nonbinding rather than mandatory—but it gave the Europeans, Soviets, and the Johnson administration alike a jolting realization of the Senate Democratic position.

Johnson erupted in dismay on receiving the resolution, which the senators had decided not to provide to him in advance, knowing his opposition. The President knew better than to try to persuade Mansfield to disown his own handiwork but instead unsuccessfully sought to persuade Russell Long to abandon his support. With no advance notice, "this damn thing hit me in the face. . . .You've got to call me and let me know sometime that they are getting ready to be commander in chief for an hour or so," LBJ said sarcastically. Arguing that the action undercut negotiations for mutual cuts with the Soviet Union and U.S. demands on Western Europeans to increase their military support, Johnson insisted in his choice Texas vernacular that "a goddamned sense of Congress resolution ain't worth a shit unless this President has some respect for the sense of it." In a reference to Mansfield's Montana heritage, Johnson told Long that the resolution could "notify every enemy that we're just a bunch of un-unified folks running off like Bert Wheeler and Jeanette Rankin, in every god-damned direction." This, he said, would be dangerous because it would be interpreted as U.S. weakness. "Show a little weakness and if those sons of bitches think you're weak, they're like a country dog—you stand still, they'll chew you to death, if you run, they'll eat your ass out."

In deference to Johnson, Mansfield did not call up the resolution for action in the 1966 session but prepared to reintroduce it in January 1967. The administration sought to dissuade Mansfield by using the persuasiveness and prestige of John J. McCloy, the pillar of the foreign policy establishment who had been U.S. High Commissioner in Germany in the aftermath of World War II, but Mansfield retorted that conditions had changed since he was in Germany and that "we should change with them rather than remain chained to old ideas which were good 20 years ago." When Congress convened, Mansfield had the co-sponsorship of forty-one senators, nearly half the body, including Russell and Fulbright. The Johnson administration, which had initiated negotiations on troops and troop support with Germany and Britain as the congressional drive got under way the previous year, stepped up its negotiations, protesting all the time about pressure from Capitol Hill. In May 1967 the administration announced that it would return up to 35,000 of the 260,000 U.S. soldiers and airmen deployed in West Germany to bases in the United States, although they would be available for rotation back to Europe for maneuvers or when needed for operational reasons. Mansfield declared the action "an encouraging start" and "good enough for the time being." As everyone recognized, this token withdrawal was only a temporary fix. A year later, after the Soviet invasion of Czechoslovakia, the troops involved were sent back to Germany.

TUGGING AT JOHNSON'S COAT

By the spring of 1967 the U.S. war in Vietnam was ending its second year since Johnson had decided on all-out intervention in July 1965. U.S. troop strength in Vietnam had soared to 438,000, with presidential authorization in place to lift the total to 470,00 by the end of the year. U.S. casualties, U.S. bombing raids against North Vietnam, and public opposition at home to the course of the war had all risen sharply as well. In 1965 and 1966 up to 25,000 persons had joined protest marches against the war. On April 15, 1967, well over 100,000 and possibly as many as 400,000 antiwar protesters marched from Central Park to the United Nations in New York, led by the Rev. Martin Luther King Jr., recently the winner of the Nobel Peace Prize and the country's foremost civil rights leader, and Dr. Benjamin Spock, the country's most famous pediatrician. Whatever the accurate number of participants—that was much disputed—the march was described in retrospect as "by far the largest demonstration in American history up until that time." At the same time there was growing impatience and criticism from political figures on the right, including Richard Nixon, who was testing the waters for his return to presidential politics. Traveling to Saigon on April 17, Nixon accused Mansfield and Robert Kennedy of "prolonging the war" by giving comfort to the enemy.

On April 28, 1967, General Westmoreland, brought home from Vietnam to rebut the doubters and opponents, delivered a rousing address to a joint meeting of Congress, declaring that the forces he led would "prevail in Vietnam over the communist aggressor." The day before, in an unpublicized meeting at the White House, Westmoreland had asked Johnson to authorize a "minimum essential force" of at least 80,000 additional troops or an "optimum force" of nearly 200,000 additional troops. Asked how long the war would last, Westmoreland guessed at least five more years with the minimum force, three more years with the optimum force.* Although Westmoreland's recommendation was kept secret, Mansfield understood that his appearance in Washington was a harbinger of presidential decisions to send even more U.S. troops to Vietnam. "The war is going to get worse before it gets better. No doubt the number of men that will be sent to Vietnam will be above the quota set for this year," Mansfield told a reporter for the *New York Times* after Westmoreland's speech. Harking back to the fundamental judgment of his late 1965 mission to Saigon, a judgment validated as forces on all sides of the battlefield continued to grow, Mansfield said that sending more U.S. troops would "increase the chances of an open-ended conflict."

At 11:17 the following morning, a quiet Saturday, Mansfield entered the Oval Office bearing a five-page memorandum—his seventeenth—outlining three proposals to break the "steady escalation," as he called it, toward a wider war. In his deferential way, Mansfield apologized in advance for asking Johnson's consideration and justified his intervention in unusually personal terms, harking back to their long association. "You may recall that when you were the Majority Leader and I was your Deputy sitting next to you, that on occasion I would lean over and tug at the back of your coat to signal that it was either time to close the debate or to sit down. Most of the time but not all the time you would do what I was trying to suggest. Since you have been President I have been figuratively tugging at your coat, now and again, and the only purpose has been to be helpful and constructive." Mansfield expressed appreciation for Johnson's "courteous consideration" of his persistent views on the war. He added, "One last word—in my opinion, the hour is growing very, very late."

While Mansfield sat with him in the Oval Office, Johnson read the April 29 memorandum and said that in general, he was in accord with its contents. Shortly after Mansfield left, Johnson asked for "eyes only" comments on the memo from Walt Rostow, who had replaced McGeorge Bundy as his national security adviser in March 1966, and from Rusk and his deputy secretary of state, Nicholas Katzenbach.

---

*As Westmoreland noted in his memoir, *A Soldier Reports,* he eventually obtained close to his minimum force in the months after his prediction, and the American war ended five years later when the last U.S. troops departed Vietnam in 1972.

Mansfield made three basic recommendations, each of which had a history with him:

"An Approach Via China"

With his extensive interest in China, Mansfield had long been gravely concerned about the possible extension of the war to China and about the absence of meaningful U.S. contact with that communist regime. He had urged Johnson repeatedly since December 1964 to undertake face-to-face explorations with China at a high level, supplanting the sterile dialogue that had long existed between lower-level diplomats in Warsaw. The issue had come to the fore publicly in March 1967 when Fulbright conducted a series of Foreign Relations Committee hearings on U.S. relations with China, to the irritation of the administration.

On March 17, Mansfield had informed Johnson that he was considering trying to arrange a visit to Peking (as Beijing was then called) as well as to Moscow and Ulan Bator, Mongolia, to explore the possibilities for movement toward peace. He conceded that he did not know whether the Chinese would receive him but asked the President for his reaction. After consulting the State Department, Johnson did not object, responding the following day that "I frankly doubt that the Chinese would admit you," but that if they did, the trip could prove to be "most useful."

In the April 29 missive Mansfield deplored the bombing of North Vietnam, which, he argued, would make Hanoi increasingly dependent on China: "The road to settlement with Hanoi now very likely runs by way of Peking rather than Moscow." Mansfield resurrected his previous suggestion that he try to arrange a visit to "make a quiet and clearly conciliatory approach to China." In order to pave the way for official talks later, he would need at least "tacit Presidential approval" for his trip, during which he would hope to hear from Foreign Minister Chou En-lai the Chinese view of the requirements for a settlement in Vietnam and for the restoration of "more normal relations" throughout the Western Pacific.

Given Dean Rusk's unyielding antipathy to Communist China, it is unlikely that he had been personally involved in the positive presidential response to Mansfield's proposal of the previous month. This time he came down hard against a proposed trip in very revealing terms, in which he took a swipe at Mansfield for making the suggestion. Rostow reported to LBJ that "the Secretary of State is strongly opposed. It would be a major intervention in a troubled situation. The Soviet Union would be upset and suspicious. Above all, Senator Mansfield should remember that he is 'an officer of the United States Government,' as a member of the legislative branch. Therefore there would be great confusion among our friends in free Asia, including the fear that we were about to sell them out." The proper way to proceed with China, according to Rusk, would be to elevate the Warsaw talks to the foreign minister level (which Mansfield had been advocating publicly), but Rusk conceded that he had been "hesitant to propose this until the [Cultural Revolutionary] situation within Communist China has somewhat settled down." In fact, Rusk never did propose such a move.

"Border Barricade"

Like many others, Mansfield had become intrigued with the idea of stopping the flow of men and material from North Vietnam by erecting a physical barrier of fences, mine fields, and electronic sensors, backed by troops, across Vietnam and Laos. Mansfield had begun to advocate this plan publicly and would do so for many months to come. If it were successful, he argued in his April 29 memo, the bombing of North Vietnam would not be necessary.

This response to the infiltration problem was also fascinating to McNamara and some others in the Pentagon, although it was considered impractical by General Westmoreland and his command due to its static nature, the rugged terrain, and the long distances involved. According to a report from McNamara to Johnson, work on the project, sometimes dubbed "McNamara's Wall," had begun by mid-1966 at an estimated cost of $800 million and was scheduled to go into initial limited operation by the end of 1967. However, the project was preempted and the sensors diverted by the emergency buildup of U.S. defenses to protect the remote base at Khe Sanh from the North Vietnamese siege that began in January 1968. The barrier was never completed.

"An Approach Via United Nations"

Almost alone among those with good access to White House decision makers, Mansfield believed the United Nations had an important role to play.

In his April 29 memo, he called for taking the initiative on two resolutions in the Security Council:

1. An invitation for governments and political groups involved, including China, North Vietnam, South Vietnam, and the National Liberation Front, to present their views before the Security Council and discuss the possibilities of a solution.
2. The request for an advisory opinion from the International Court of Justice for a ruling on the applicability of the Geneva Accords to the current situation in Vietnam.

Rusk dismissed the International Court proposal in his response to Johnson, saying that the court "does not have jurisdiction" in this case and would be unlikely to take it up. However, he seemed mildly to favor taking the Vietnam issue to the UN Security Council, although he had opposed the idea at times in the past.

As early as the summer of 1964, UN Secretary General U Thant had sought to arrange secret negotiations between the United States and North Vietnam but had been stymied by Washington's refusal to participate because of its fear of the impact on the Saigon regime. Mansfield, as noted in the previous chapter, had advocated taking the issue to the UN in private meetings with Johnson in May and August 1964 and February 1965, and occasionally in public remarks. Johnson had privately dismissed the UN as ineffective and, at the same time, expressed fear that discussions there would limit U.S. freedom of military action in the war zone.

Mansfield had begun a more serious push for UN involvement with a speech at Johns Hopkins University on November 10, 1966, in which he had proposed that the UN Security Council sponsor face-to-face meetings of all the participants in the war, including North Vietnam, the National Liberation Front, and China. Following the speech, he spoke to Johnson, who expressed interest in the idea and suggested that he contact Goldberg and U Thant.

With this presidential go-ahead, he had traveled to New York on November 18, 1966, to discuss the proposal with them in a meeting in which Deputy Secretary of State Katzenbach also participated. The Secretary General was amenable to secret explorations of negotiations but not to public discussions in the Security Council as proposed by Mansfield, saying that such a confrontation would be "highly undesirable" and "could only lead to increased tensions between the Soviet Union and U.S." According to Mansfield's notes, "U Thant thinks only possibility for negotiations is thru private channels (himself)." U Thant, he said, "has personal contacts with Ho Chi Minh, whom he called a 'dove' but who faces conflicts in No. Vietnam. . . . He said Ho would deal with him but only on a strictly confidential basis and if any statement was made by anyone else about it he (Ho Chi Minh) would deny it." The Secretary General also told Mansfield, "China is real key and cannot be contacted; it will continue to encourage Hanoi and thereby increase its dependency on China." Johnson, in a letter drafted by Rostow coinciding with these events, had told Mansfield on November 19, "I should be delighted if the United Nations could serve as a channel and catalyst" for negotiations on the war. According to Mansfield, Johnson subsequently had directed Goldberg to present a letter to U Thant asking him "to exert every effort" to bring the Vietnamese situation to a solution—but despite travels by U Thant in Southeast Asia, nothing came of it in 1966.

When Mansfield resurrected his UN proposal in his April 29, 1967, memorandum, it had more appeal to Johnson. After barring U.S. bombing raids in and immediately around Hanoi for four months in a bid for negotiations, the President had recently approved strikes against the power-generating facilities near the center of the Vietnamese capital and attacks on other previously prohibited targets. Moreover, the President had in hand Westmoreland's requests for dispatch of many more troops to Vietnam, which had been endorsed by the Joint Chiefs of Staff. Johnson had no intention of changing his military policies but was amenable to some high-profile diplomacy at the UN, even if the ultimate results were dubious. Immediately after receiving Mansfield's April 29 proposal, Johnson ordered the wheels of government to begin turning rapidly on the UN issue.

Rostow met the same day with Goldberg and Katzenbach and reported to LBJ that both thought the idea to be "a gimmick," with Goldberg in favor of it and Katzenbach "leaning against" it. Rusk, although giving his reluctant approval of the idea on April 30, warned that U Thant and many members of the Security Council would oppose a UN initiative because Hanoi had made it clear it did not want the UN to be involved.

Johnson invited Mansfield and Wayne Morse, who also had long advocated a UN role, to breakfast May 1 in the family quarters of the White House with Rusk, Rostow, Katzenbach, Goldberg, and Califano. Katzenbach voiced the view of several officials that the proposal would be considered "a phony" by other nations. (Among the skeptical officials was Assistant Secretary of State William Bundy, who said in a memo to Rusk that the plan had no serious chance of success and would be regarded "as a rather cheap piece of theater that was really totally cynical in view of our bombing actions of these weeks.") Mansfield immediately disagreed with Katzenbach, saying it was "not a phony proposal but something that should be laid before the United Nations in good faith" and that this was the only way he would consider it. He also told Johnson, and reiterated the point in writing, that any official hints that the proposal was not serious would certainly doom it. If the administration undercut it by simultaneously taking additional new military measures in Vietnam or permitting leaks to the press expressing doubt about the proposal, he said, then it would be better not to pursue it. Mansfield and Morse participated in a second breakfast meeting with Johnson and administration officials to discuss the plan on May 3.

Johnson was concerned, he said at the initial breakfast meeting, about how the proposal would look in the eyes of the world. "Would it be a decline in our prestige? Would it make us look weaker and more foolish than we are? Would we keep on fighting while this was happening?" Everyone agreed that the answer to the last question was yes. Nevertheless, the more he thought about it, the more Johnson was worried that the UN discussion might take on a life of its own. According to a State Department memorandum a few days later, LBJ decided to defer the question of Security Council actions at least until June, and "expressed particular concern that any resort to the Security Council not interfere with our military operations in Vietnam."

It is unclear whether Mansfield was informed of Johnson's decision, but in any case he was not deterred. He spoke with fervor in the Senate on May 15 of the "vacuum" at the United Nations in dealing with Vietnam at a time when "the tendencies toward open-ended conflict are becoming more and more recognizable, whereas the alternatives toward a reasonable negotiation in seeking to bring about an honorable conclusion are becoming fewer and fewer all the time." Employing uncharacteristically emotional language Mansfield added, "If we remain silent, future generations will judge us as weaklings, as vacillators, and as cowards. It is to them, and to the generation now fighting in Vietnam, that we owe our chief responsibilities, because those who are over there are not there of their own free will. They are carrying out policy laid down here in Washington." For the United Nations, he declared, the time is "long past due" for it to make a contribution toward ending the conflict. He repeated his proposal that both Vietnam states as well as the NLF and China should take part in discussions organized there. As usual, he expressed sympathy and support for the President, who has to live with "this tragedy" twenty-four hours a day. Shortly after his speech, reports of military moves by Israeli and Egyptian forces in the Middle East and then the outbreak of war there distracted attention from further consideration.

Johnson had rejected a UN Security Council initiative only for the time being, not for all time, although his misgivings became increasingly well known. Mansfield, however, interpreted his several conversations with Johnson to be a green light to continue to put forward his idea. He made additional speeches on the subject in the Senate on May 18 and 24, and on May 30, at commencement exercises at Haverford University in Haverford, Pennsylvania, he told the new graduates that a Security Council invitation to the warring parties in Vietnam was "urgent." Whether it would succeed in initiating peace talks, he did not know, but "I will state, on my own responsibility, that the President would not look with disfavor on such a proposal." Rusk said publicly that the administration was considering the possibility of asking for a Security Council conference on Vietnam, but Johnson was publicly noncommittal.

CONFRONTING A WIDENING WAR

In mid-July, nearly three months after General Westmoreland had requested 80,000 to nearly 200,000 more troops in confidential discussions at the White House, Johnson had still not decided how to respond. The administration itself—like the political establishment in Congress and elsewhere and the U.S. citizenry at large—had become increasingly divided about the war. The shorthand for the protagonists in a host of disputes within and without the administration was "hawks"—those who wished to use more military power more forcefully to shorten or win the war— and "doves"—those who rejected the further enlargement of military power as too damaging or dangerous to U.S. national interests or too ineffective and who therefore favored increased emphasis on negotiations. By now, Mansfield was among the most prominent of doves and among the few doves on Capitol Hill who continued to have the ear of the President through frequent meetings and memoranda.

Johnson sent McNamara to Saigon in early July with instructions to work out a minimal version of the field commander's "minimum essential troop request." Washington was full of rumors of major new troop augmentation and approval of new bombing targets closer to North Vietnamese civilians or to the Chinese border. Mansfield did not know the details, but he knew that "once again, we are apparently approaching a fork in the road in Vietnam." He said so in a powerful speech in the Senate on July 11 before the results of McNamara's discussions were known. In an effort to introduce "a measure of historical perspective" based on his long experience, Mansfield tackled the claims of progress in the ever-deepening war:

> The fact is that reports of progress are strewn, like burned out tanks, all along the road which has led this nation ever more deeply into Vietnam and southeast Asia during the past decade and a half. They were present when the sole function of American military personnel in Vietnam was that of aid suppliers to the French-commanded Vietnamese loyalist forces. They were present when our military functions in Vietnam evolved into that of trainers and advisers of the South Vietnamese forces, to that of air transporters and supporters, to that of combat bulwarks and, finally, to that of combat substitutes for the South Vietnamese forces.
>
> The generalization on progress, in short, is the ever-present beat which is to be heard throughout the transition of the American military role from the most remote and invisible rear to the most forward and conspicuous front of the Vietnamese war. It has been present, this promise of progress, as the casualties in our forces in dead and wounded have increased from less than 10 a year, to 10 a month, to 10 a week, to 10 a day, to 10 an hour of every hour of every day. It has been present as the estimated expenditures of the federal government for Vietnam have increased from a few hundred million a year, to $2 billion, to $12 billion, to the current level of not less than $25 billion a year.

Shortly after his July 11 speech, Mansfield wrote a three-page explanation to the President of the concerns he had sought to address. He also repeated in his memo, his eighteenth to Johnson, his support for building a barrier to stop infiltration from North to South, and his interest in persuading the UN Security Council to sponsor a meeting of all participants in the war.

Johnson had told him more than a month earlier, Mansfield recounted in his memo, that he was rapidly running out of military targets in North Vietnam. "In my mind, that raised the question as to what might be the next step. Would it be escalation of the bombing and against what? De-escalation? Or would it be a cessation or a suspension of the bombing of the North?" Mansfield recommended a formula put forward by Senator John Sherman Cooper of Kentucky, limitation of the bombing to infiltration routes along the Ho Chi Minh trails and the area near the North-South dividing line at the seventeenth parallel. The bombing of sensitive targets, including Haiphong, Hanoi, and airfields close to the Chinese border "would raise the possibility of a confrontation with China and even the spectre of nuclear war," he wrote to Johnson. (In fact, all those targets eventually would be attacked without war with China, conventional or nuclear.)

When Johnson met Mansfield and the chairmen of Senate committees on July 25, he was faced with passionate objections to the war from Fulbright, which caused him to launch into an emotional counterattack in defense of the bombing of the North. Mansfield, true to his discomfort with open conflict between the Senate and the President, interrupted this heated argument to return the subject to government operations. Two days later, however, he joined a Senate debate led by Cooper to object to the intensified bombing. "You cannot bomb those people [North Vietnamese] into submission. You cannot return them to the stone age, because they are living in conditions not very far from it. They will dictate the kind of war which will be followed, whether it be conventional or guerilla. . . . They have fought it all too often at the time and place of their own choice."

On the level of principle, Mansfield defended the right—and the responsibility—of every senator to make his views known about the war. "When we speak out, it does not mean we are planning the strategy of the war in Vietnam. The President has that responsibility as Chief of State and as Commander in Chief."

The complexity of Mansfield's position is suggested by his handwritten notes on a carbon copy of the memo explaining his July 11 proposals for reversing the course of the war. He had evidently taken the copy to a later meeting with Johnson and used the back of it to make notes of marching orders from the President for measures to deal with the ballooning deficit: "(1) Get Approp[riations] Bills down . . . (2) Partic[ipation] Certif[icates, a means of raising funds for government], Call in all Demos . . . (3) See Dirksen about holding back on pay raise." Another document in the White House files for the same period is a report from Mike Manatos, LBJ's liaison officer with the Senate, on a status report by Mansfield on major legislation proposed by Johnson since Congress convened in January. As of July 24, the Senate had passed seventy administration measures, of which forty-seven had been signed into law and eighteen were awaiting action by the House, the rest being in conference committee of the two houses or similar status. Two other measures were awaiting Senate floor action and twenty-nine more were in Senate committees. Whatever their differences on Vietnam, the legislative partnership remained important and productive.

As the conflicts in the war zone and in U.S. public and political opinion continued to deepen in the second half of 1967, Mansfield concentrated on appealing for UN Security Council action to sponsor meetings of all the warring parties. On August 7 and August 10 he made speeches in the Senate calling for UN action and on August 28 led an organized Senate debate backing the idea, in which he was joined by a broad spectrum of senators of differing views on the war, Democrats Fulbright, John J. Sparkman, Frank Church, Philip A. Hart, and Morse, and Republicans Aiken, Cooper, Gordon Allott, and Frank Carlson, and subsequently also by Democrats Stuart Symington, Pell, Mondale, John O. Pastore, Lausche, and Edward V. Long of Missouri.

In the meantime Johnson, although he had received a report from Goldberg that there was absolutely "no possibility" of the United Nations coming to grips with the Vietnam problem, kept the Majority Leader's hopes alive by suggesting that Mansfield recruit John Sherman Cooper, a former U.S. ambassador to India, explore whether India would take the initiative in the Security Council. Mansfield spoke to Cooper, who met the Indian ambassador. The answer was no, unless the United States agreed in advance to stop the bombing of North Vietnam if called upon by the Security Council to do so. In the face of the broad congressional interest, however, Goldberg was authorized to explore possible sponsorship by Denmark of the Security Council initiative. It did not succeed.

Nonetheless, the initiative was very much alive on Capitol Hill. The Senate Foreign Relations Committee held hearings on resolutions by Mansfield and Morse, asking Johnson to request the Security Council to take up the Vietnam issue. Following letters that Mansfield sent to all members of the Senate explaining the action, his "Sense of the Senate" resolution was co-sponsored by fifty-nine members of the body. It was approved unanimously by the committee and adopted 82-0 by the full Senate on November 30.

Throughout discussions of the issue at the White House, in which Mansfield's name and views were cited frequently, Goldberg wavered on whether the Security Council could or should accept the Vietnam issue, finally coming down on the positive side. Rusk, who feared that a debate in the Security Council would alienate the Soviet Union, which was seen as the prime source of positive leverage on Hanoi, generally opposed the move, as did McNamara and Katzenbach. Johnson was concerned that to try but fail to persuade the Security Council to act would appear to be a defeat for the United States. His most serious misgivings, though, concerned what might occur if the effort succeeded. He told a meeting of his close Vietnam advisers at the White House on December 5, "I have feared that we would be asked to stop the bombing with nothing in return. We must anticipate the worst and prepare for it." Rusk pointed out to Johnson that no decision had been made to proceed. Despite the unanimous vote of the Senate, the Vietnam War issue was not taken to the Security Council, to the relief of the President and most of his senior advisers.

THE TET OFFENSIVE: A MOMENT OF CHANGE

Defense Secretary Robert McNamara's discussions with Westmoreland in July eventually produced an answer to the military commander's request in April for an increase in his combat forces. Westmoreland was promised 55,000 additional troops, considerably less than the "minimum essential" augmentation he had requested. Even so, this would bring the total U.S. deployment in Vietnam to 525,000, significantly above the politically important half-million mark and above the highest troop commitment of the Korean War. The additional commitment would also cost several billion dollars more in military expenditures at a time when the U.S. budget had already been running serious and, many economists believed, unsustainable deficits. It was the final blow to Johnson's fervent desire to finance both the war and the Great Society social programs without raising taxes.

On August 3 Johnson stood before a blackboard at a press conference in the White House and asked Congress to impose a 10 percent surcharge on all individual and corporate income tax returns. He also announced he was sending 45,000 to 50,000 additional U.S. troops to Vietnam. With that clear linkage of higher taxes and more troops, the nation's leading public opinion pollsters, George Gallup and Louis Harris, reported a sharp decline in public approval of Johnson's handling of the war. The drop in support by political elites in Congress and elsewhere was even more notable. A *Christian Science Monitor* survey of 205 members of the House of Representatives turned up 43 who said they had recently shifted from support of administration policy to more emphasis on finding a way out.

Antiwar protests, which had begun in major fashion two years earlier, grew powerfully from mid-1967. There were teach-ins and sit-ins on college campuses, petition drives and rallies, draft resistance and the public burning of selective service cards, intense political activity, and mass rallies and marches. Some protesters were violent, although most were peaceful. In late October, more than 100,000 people came to Washington by automobile, bus, train, and airplane to protest the war, and as many as 50,000 of them marched on the Pentagon, where U.S. Army troops surrounded the building to keep the marchers out. Shouting "Hey, hey, LBJ, how many kids did you kill today?" and other refrains, the crowds carried American flags—and a few Vietcong flags. Led by a group of protesters determined to stage acts of civil disobedience, 683 demonstrators were arrested when they violated previously agreed-upon rules and refused to leave. Although strongly opposed to the war, Mansfield was appalled by flag-burning, vulgarity, and violence. Above all, he believed in the democratic process, civility, and order. "I am all for dissent; provided it is constructive; provided it is reasonable; provided it is within constitutional bounds. But I am not for personal insults, rowdyism, harassment, violence, intolerance and disregard of the law," he told the Senate following the Pentagon march.

For the average person in mainstream America and for many of their political leaders, the gravest problem was not the morality of the war but the issue Mansfield had addressed consistently. Despite the rising costs and risks and all the official claims, it wasn't working. The war was not succeeding and the end was not in sight.

To stanch steadily growing impatience with and opposition to the war, the Johnson administration in the last months of 1967 energetically sought to convince the American people that, far from a stalemate, the war was on the verge of success. An interagency Psychological Strategy Group in the White House disseminated and celebrated the ever-positive official reports from the war zone and sought to rebut every speech in Congress critical of the course of battle. After a visit to Vietnam Vice President Humphrey returned to tell viewers of NBC's *Today* show, "We are beginning to win this struggle. We are on the offensive. Territory is being gained. We are making steady progress." On Veterans Day weekend in November, the President stood on the flight deck of the aircraft carrier USS *Enterprise* and promised that the war would continue "not many more nights . . . not while we stand as one family and one nation, united in one purpose." As the capstone of this drive, Johnson summoned Westmoreland to Washington with instructions to prepare for television appearances and a major speech. At his National Press Club address the normally cautious field commander declared his forces were preparing for a final phase of the war beginning in 1968: "We have reached an important point when the end begins to come into view."

Mansfield was not convinced. Amid Westmoreland's campaign, Mansfield told the Senate, "We should not delude ourselves by such phrases as 'phase down' on the level of American troops by 1969 to be matched by an increasing shift of responsibility to the South Vietnamese forces. Rather we should face up to the very strong possibility that the war in Vietnam may well take years and require, as it has heretofore, additional inputs of American forces unless a solution is found to bring it to a conclusion."

The communist forces, in fact, had begun to pull back from battle zones, but not because they were being beaten. In the spring, Ho Chi Minh and his Lao Dong Party leadership had concluded, as had many perceptive Americans, that the war was essentially at a stalemate. To transform the struggle, the Politburo decided the time had come for the General Offensive and General Uprising, the "once in a lifetime" all-out battle that, in Vietnamese communist theory, was the classic means of defeating the enemy. The order went down to military commands, probably in May, to make preparations for the battle. In July the Politburo approved the plans that had been drawn up. At the end of October, Hanoi's leaders decided that surprise attacks through the length of South Vietnam would take place three months later, in the midst of the Vietnamese New Year or Tet holiday.

The simultaneous Tet attacks on January 30 and 31, 1968, were bloody battles in the full view of American television cameras, and they wreaked havoc on nearly every city, town, and major military base in South Vietnam, including the symbolical battlefield of the U.S. Embassy in Saigon. The reports from the war zone shocked the American public, especially on the heels of the administration's misguided "success offensive." Although militarily ineffective and costly to the communist side in the war zone, the Tet Offensive was politically the turning point of the war in the United States. After a temporary "rally round the flag" support for the war, the events destroyed much of the remaining public confidence—and, even more, the confidence of the American leadership elites—in Johnson and his military strategy and actions in Vietnam. Reporting and analyses of this great historical anomaly and detailed accounts of the policy maneuvers it set in train can be found in dozens of books, including the account in my 1971 book, *Tet!* They will not be repeated here.

Unlike many members of Congress, Mansfield was not shocked by the development, since he had never doubted the capability and determination of the North Vietnamese and Vietcong to continue to prosecute the war. He commented publicly and gave his advice privately from time to time, but he did not seek to play a major role in the political and policy maneuvers in the wake of Tet. In a speech at Indiana University, he decried the fact that "the struggle in Vietnam has turned grim, pitiless and devastating" and said he did not wish to join the grisly parlor game of "who's winning in Vietnam?" He declared that "the basic military problem is as it has been from the outset. The war remains open-ended and escalation continues to rise with escalation."

On March 1, in an effort to defuse an increasingly acrimonious dispute between the Foreign Relations Committee and the administration, Mansfield suggested to Johnson that he meet privately with senior committee members "on an old colleague basis with no one else present." Johnson did so on March 6 with Mansfield, Fulbright, Sparkman, Aiken, and Hickenlooper. The President evidently disclosed that in the wake of the Tet Offensive Westmoreland had requested the large troop augmentation that he had been denied the previous year, because a discussion of the troops issue broke out the following day on the Senate floor. Fulbright, who led the discussion and was alarmed by the prospect of dispatching "200,000, 201,000, 206,000 or 250,000," was apparently well informed about Westmoreland's secret request for 206,000 additional troops, since that was one of the numbers he mentioned in speculative fashion in floor debate.

In his part of the colloquy, Mansfield declared, characteristically, that "it is my intention to uphold the hand of the President as much as I can in this particular matter, and at the same time stick to my own convictions." Almost alone among the senators, he gave full credit to Johnson's motives and his efforts to find a way to the negotiating table. "He has not gone as far as I would like; but he has done his best in a most difficult situation. . . ." Nonetheless, he continued, "We are in the wrong place, and we are fighting the wrong kind of war." He described the Tet Offensive as "neither a defeat nor a death rattle for our opponents. It was, if anything, a confirmation of a stalemate." Reiterating the viewpoint he had repeatedly expressed to Johnson, he insisted "we should not get in deeper, and that is what another addition of tens of thousands of men adds up to, because escalation only begets escalation." Rejecting the counsel of those who were advocating such measures as even more intensive bombing and an invasion of North Vietnam, Mansfield observed that "the war is in danger of becoming more open-ended than just Vietnam. If that takes place no one knows where or how it will end. We do know that there will be, in reality, no victory for anyone, only a legacy of distrust, suspicion, hatred and horror." Johnson, he said, should formally consult the Foreign Relations and Armed Services Committees before ordering any "sizable increase in American manpower in Southeast Asia."

Consulted privately about troop augmentations on March 2 by Clark Clifford, who had replaced McNamara as Secretary of Defense, Mansfield replied that the administration had "reached the end of the line on increases in American troop levels." On March 12, Johnson suffered a serious political blow at the hands of Senator Eugene McCarthy in New Hampshire's first-in-the-nation presidential primary election. The next day, at a White House meeting, after the *New York Times* revealed Westmoreland's request for 206,000 more troops, Mansfield handed the President a memorandum—his nineteenth—urging him to resist any substantial increase in the existing U.S. troop ceiling of 525,000 in Vietnam. "That does not mean we have to get out of Viet Nam. It does mean we have to concentrate and consolidate the already great commitment which we have there. It means the adoption of a patient strategy—less destructive of the country and of our forces and less voracious in the consumption of our resources . . . for purposes of negotiating a decent settlement of the conflict," Mansfield argued. In effect he was calling for the enclave strategy he had favored years earlier in Vietnam. Having had no response from Johnson, he made his views public, almost word for word, in his Senate speech of March 26, without mentioning the fact that he had previously submitted it to Johnson.

In early 1968, as political debate and upheaval took place all around him, Mansfield lived in the eye of the storm. In the Senate on March 7 he described the period as "the most troublous days in the entire history of the Republic, and I bar no period in making that statement." Personally, away from the Senate, he retreated into solitude. He was "quiet, very pensive," according to Sophie Engelhard, a Georgetown University student and an intern in the Majority Leader's office at the time. The daughter of the Mansfields' close personal friends Charles and Jane Engelhard, Sophie was a frequent visitor to the Mansfield residence and one of the few people who interacted with him frequently in both his private and public life. "He liked to sit on the side porch of the house, often by himself. At the Capitol, he liked to walk around the grounds from time to time with his pipe, in a space where he was not reachable. His reaction to stress was, he'd get more alone. He'd get very quiet and more alone," she recalled.

Charles Engelhard was a famed metals magnate with extensive holdings in gold, silver, and other precious metals and reputedly the inspiration for "Goldfinger," a James Bond antagonist dreamed up by Ian Fleming. Mansfield met Engelhard in the late 1950s through Johnson, who was then majority leader. Beginning in 1960 the Mansfields visited the Engelhards at "Pamplemousse," their palatial compound at Boca Grande, Florida, for a week or two almost every winter while Congress was out of session. Mike liked to sit outside in the sun and stare at the ocean, smoking his pipe and thinking. Maureen, a voracious reader, would bury herself in the newspapers or a book. It was a stress-free vacation in a grand style that the Mansfields could not afford on their own, complete with interesting visitors to the compound from the world of commerce or the arts. Because of their close relationship, Mansfield instructed the fund-raisers for his Senate campaigns not to accept money from Engelhard.

Johnson, who also continued to be close to Engelhard, tended to use him as a go-between in case of serious problems with Mansfield, according to George Christian, LBJ's last White House press secretary. It was through this connection that Mansfield was asked to visit Johnson early in the evening of March 27, 1968, as LBJ was pondering the future of the war and his own future as President. Documents in the LBJ Library indicate that Johnson's initial motivation had been to ensure that Mansfield would support him for the Democratic presidential nomination rather than Robert Kennedy, who had announced his candidacy eleven days earlier. With this prelude Mansfield appeared in the Cabinet Room of the White House at 6:01 P.M. as Johnson finished discussing budget cuts and the government's perilous financial situation with Secretary of the Treasury Henry Fowler and Budget Director Charles Zwick. The economics officials left, and for the next two hours the President and the Majority Leader, who had known each other's mind and way of thinking for many years, engaged in a surprising conversation.

CONVERSATION IN THE CABINET ROOM

"Mike, we're in a helluva shape, aren't we?"

"Sure as hell are."

The President, his hair turned to gray in high office, his eyelids heavy with exhaustion, the creases on his face deepening with worry, sat in his high-backed chair at the center of the cabinet table, his back to the fading light in the Rose Garden peeking from gaps in the drapery covering the French windows. Johnson seemed bone weary and beaten down, like a battered fighter picking himself up from the canvas one last time. Facing him in the chair to his left was Mansfield, his lean, angular face and steady gaze revealing little of the emotions beneath, a self-effacing, taciturn figure whose monosyllabic answers to questions from the Washington press corps belied his eloquence when his deep-seated convictions were engaged.

The two men sat alone at the long cabinet table—or so it appeared to the naked eye. Unseen were eight tiny microphones that had been secretly implanted in small holes drilled by military aides into the bottom of the table in January 1968 at Johnson's direction and connected by hidden wires to a recording system in a locked cabinet in the White House basement. The system was activated by a switch on a small table next to the President's armchair. On this day, Johnson had flipped the switch earlier to record a series of military and economic meetings in the Cabinet Room and either forgot or did not wish to turn it off when Mansfield appeared. Thus, most of this intimate debate over the future of U.S. policy in Indochina has been preserved on a slowly turning reel of audio tape; the tape ran out after one hour, fifteen minutes.

The conversation started with politics. "I had a very discouraging poll today," the President began, after ordering coffee for Mansfield and Fresca, a carbonated diet drink that was his favorite, for himself. Richard Nixon, the former vice president and likely Republican nominee, "leads us all" in popularity, LBJ told his visitor. Fixated on his political standings, Johnson called for a sheaf of public opinion poll results to be brought from his desk in the nearby Oval Office and read them to Mansfield. Shortly thereafter, the conversation was interrupted by the arrival of still more polling data, showing his standings in various cities and regions of Wisconsin compared with those of Eugene McCarthy, who was running on an antiwar platform, and Senator Robert Kennedy, who also was vocal against the war. The Wisconsin primary was scheduled to be on April 2, six days after this conversation. LBJ read off those results, which showed he was leading in some areas of the state, McCarthy leading in others, and Kennedy making strides—very mixed prospects for Johnson, at best, with the war the dominating issue in national politics.

"You are being pounded by Kennedy unmercifully, by McCarthy genteelly. He looks like Sir Galahad in comparison," Mansfield told Johnson. He added that Nixon, "isn't saying a word, just waiting for the opening and taking down every word that our own people say, to be used against us in the Fall. He has no pressures. The Republicans made it possible for him to just keep quiet and say practically nothing, gradually veer toward a position in the middle. I wouldn't be surprised if he moves a little bit to the left before he's through."

Although Johnson had not formally announced his candidacy for reelection, it was widely assumed that he was running again. With his approval, the Democratic political machinery had been mobilized to promote his candidacy. White House aides and cabinet members had been summoned to emergency political duties, and on the very morning of the meeting, former

governor Terry Sanford of North Carolina had agreed to be the official manager of LBJ's reelection campaign. "God bless you," resonded a greatful
Johnson. Primarily because of the impact of the developments in Vietnam,
Johnson's political operatives were deeply worried. Jim Rowe, the political
adviser to both Johnson and Mansfield, appealed to the President to do
"something dramatic" about the war before the Wisconsin primary, lest it
turn into a political rout. Johnson's chief political aide, Postmaster General
Larry O'Brien, had told him in a separate personal memorandum that the
American people would not continue to support an administration "rigidly
fixed into a position" on Vietnam but would support one that "lessened our
involvement." In conversation with military leaders, Johnson had outlined
the demands piling up on him from all sides and said, "I don't give a damn
about the election. I will be happy just to keep doing what is right and lose
the election. . . . I will have overwhelming disapproval in the polls and elections. I will go down the drain."

Over the past several years Johnson had confided to a few people, including Mansfield, the possibility that he would abandon his reelection bid in
1968 and retire from the presidency. He had told Mansfield around the
beginning of the year, but the Majority Leader didn't take him seriously. In
mid-January, shortly before the communist offensive at Tet, Johnson had
secretly prepared a dramatic announcement withdrawing from the presidential race as the climax of his State of the Union address to Congress but
decided against it at the last minute. Nonetheless, it remains a debatable historical question what he would have done in March 1968 had he been confident he could run again and win. His continuing fascination with the public opinion polls during the meeting with Mansfield suggests that on March
27, at least, he was actively assessing his election prospects and had not
decided to withdraw.

By the time Mansfield was ushered into the Cabinet Room the
President had presided over a long afternoon of meetings on the war, a
final stage in the decision-making process that had been precipitated by
Westmoreland's request for 206,000 more U.S. troops. In addition to the
525,000 already at war or authorized, Mansfield realized, this would bring
the total to more than 700,000 troops, the number he had projected in
his confidential report to Johnson after his 1965 visit to Vietnam and that
had been ridiculed by Rusk.

"We're going to send some extra troops, Mike. We've got to. It's a matter of how many, and what type, and over what period," the President confided. He complained about the leak of Westmoreland's request, saying that "the papers have hurt us very badly, and hurt me very badly." Johnson lamented, "We have some very disloyal people at State and Defense," by which he meant the leakers. He added that he was giving no consideration to sending such a large number of reinforcements and that even 100,000 more troops for the war had been ruled out. However, to fail to send more American men in view of the military requests would be a message to the military and the Vietnamese, said the President, that "we won't do it, and you just fight with what you've got."

In late March Johnson was under mounting pressure from all sides to abandon the status quo. He informed Mansfield that Senator Richard B. Russell of Georgia, chairman of the Armed Services Committee and long Johnson's mentor in the Senate, had opposed the 206,000 troop request but had privately urged Johnson two days earlier to "take out Haiphong" by heavy bombing of the North Vietnamese port. Several of Johnson's closest civilian leaders urged him not only to reject the troop request but also to halt the U.S. bombing of North Vietnam rather than step it up and to make a serious bid for peace talks. The previous day, a secret gathering at the White House of "Wise Men," respected former officials, including former Secretary of State Dean Acheson and future Secretary of State Cyrus Vance, who had endorsed the war policy two months before the Tet Offensive, had told Johnson that the war could not be sustained with the American public and recommended that he begin to disengage. Startled by their reversal of views, the President had summoned the government officials who had briefed the Wise Men to discover what they had imparted. "Everybody is recommending surrender," Johnson complained to the officials less than two hours before seeing Mansfield.

Now it was the Majority Leader's turn to make his case on the issues of troop reinforcements and bombing policy. On this occasion as often in the past, Mansfield had prepared a memorandum in advance covering the points he wished to make. Instead of handing it over, however, he expressed his views directly, clearly and succinctly, in stern and occasionally imploring tones.

"The feeling is built up in the Senate, I think, and among the people that 525,000 is *it*. I'm surprised at the emotion, some say panic . . . which is rapidly developing throughout the country. You've got to make the decision. I've always recognized that. It's not an easy one. . . . I don't know just what the hell we can do to get out of the box we are in. I just can't see the light at the end of the tunnel. . . . I just hope that in his wisdom, the Good Lord will do something which will give you an opening that you can seize and find a way out. You can't withdraw. You can't surrender. But there must be *some* way to bring this matter to a head."

Johnson had obtained air time from the television networks for a speech to the nation on Vietnam policy on March 31, four days after seeing Mansfield. The two central issues awaiting decision—troop reinforcements and bombing policy—were still on the table when Mansfield made his fervent plea on March 27 to find a way out of the morass.

Mansfield, by pleading for "an opening that you can seize and find a way out," may have unknowingly suggested a dramatic course of action that he did not know was available to Johnson or, alternatively, endorsed a dramatic course of action that already had been taking shape in Johnson's mind. That course was to couple important new decisions on the Vietnam War with a surprise announcement that he would not run for reelection, thus enhancing the credibility of his Vietnam actions by removing them from the context of political calculation or potential gain. On March 29 or 30, according to George Christian and James R. Jones, two of his closest White House advisers at the time, Johnson decided to combine the two initiatives.

Regarding troops for Vietnam, "I'm going to deploy whatever I think is absolutely required, and not one man more," the President told Mansfield. "Now the question of what is required is a matter that's open to a lot of judgments. The less I know about it, the more comfortable I feel. The more I know about it, the more problems I see." Referring to his forthcoming speech he said he would "make our best case in the next few days to get delivered in Vietnam enough troops to support our forces adequately . . . what allied commanders think they must have. Not what they want to have, but what they *must* have."

How many would that be? For starters, Johnson explained that in early February, immediately after the Tet attacks, he had dispatched 10,500 combat troops, paratroopers from the Army 82d Airborne Division and U.S. Marines, without the artillery, supply, and other support elements that go alongside to back them up. The additional troops to back them up would number 14,000 or 15,000, the President said. Mansfield said he could not object to this—"if you sent them without backup and they need backup, you'd have to send them"—but asked Johnson to minimize their number.

Westmoreland, the President continued, "would like for us to send him a minimum of another 40-odd thousand and call up the strategic reserves" to provide more forces ready for emergencies in Vietnam or elsewhere in the world. To justify these additions, Johnson read Mansfield extracts from a top secret cable received from Westmoreland earlier in the day projecting his "definitive minimum requirements" now that he had learned that the request for 206,000 was out of the question. In the midst of the meeting with Mansfield, Johnson telephoned Clifford to discuss the number of additional troops that should be supplied. The President and his new defense chief, old friends, bantered with each other and bargained over numbers. Johnson then asked Mansfield what his reaction would be if he were to send 40,000 more.

As Johnson must have known he would be, Mansfield was decisively negative about sending more troops. His voice rising with intensity and emphasis when the subject was raised, Mansfield declared, "Mr. President, if you send in [more troops] they will match you or more than match you." He cited many thousands of regular army troops under General Vo Nguyen Giap which still had not been deployed in the South.

"We've talked about that a long time this evening," LBJ responded, referring to earlier conversations with General Earle Wheeler, chairman of the Joint Chiefs of Staff, and General Creighton Abrams, Westmoreland's deputy in Saigon and later his successor. "Our people," he went on, think that it will be "very unsafe" for the North Vietnamese leader to continue to send large numbers of fresh troops to the South, because "he's got to have some protection for his people."

The President added, "We think if we can resist what he's trying to do this year, that we can bring him to the [negotiating] table. But we think now he is not trying to run us to the sea. He doesn't think he can. He thinks he can break us up here, like he did in Paris before [at the end of the first Indochina war in 1954], and we think he's done a pretty good job of it."

As an added element of persuasion, and perhaps to test the reaction of his Senate leader, Johnson called for the most recent draft of the "stay the course" speech to the nation he was preparing to deliver four days later. As if to reassure himself, he read large sections of it aloud to Mansfield in flat, expressionless cadences. LBJ began:

> I speak to you tonight in a time of grave challenge to our country. Our soldiers and allies on the battlefield are being challenged by an intensified military aggression. Our will is being challenged by the frustrations of a long war which we did not invite, and which we are anxious to conclude. Our economy is being challenged by the threat of inflation. And we are challenged at home— especially in our cities—a challenge that requires the best efforts of every level of government and every citizen. Such a multiple challenge tests the capacity of our nation and the confidence of our people.
>
> But this is America. This is the land that four times in this century has sent its men abroad to fight, not for love of combat or hope for material gain but for love of freedom, concern for human dignity, for a reliable peace and for our own security. None of these efforts has been easy. Yet each time, amid doubts and conflicting judgments, under stress and suffering, our people have said, "Yes, we'll see it through."
>
> This is a proud history. It gives us cause to believe that now, as in the past, America has the capacity—the intelligence, the resources and the will—to endure a distant struggle for freedom's sake.

As often happens in Washington, the question of what to say to the American people proved to be the focal point of internal argument and a vehicle for policymaking. In this case, the speech itself had a long history. The first draft of the speech had been written on February 5 while many Vietnamese cities were still smoldering after the eruption of the Tet Offensive and while heavy fighting continued in Hue and the isolated bastion of Khe Sanh. This draft had called for extending the tours of duty for U.S. military personnel in Vietnam from twelve months to eighteen months in order to provide more forces to Westmoreland. The Pentagon high command was extremely wary of the potential reaction. A handwritten comment from General Wheeler in the margin of this announcement read, "President shouldn't say this." (He didn't say it, and the tours were never extended.) In the end, Johnson decided to postpone the address.

The second draft was written on February 25 in anticipation of Wheeler's return from a visit to Vietnam with the new troop request. Its central feature was the announcement that "Tomorrow, the Secretary of Defense will announce a call-up of ____ reserves," with the blank to be filled in later. It also called on Congress to authorize the extension of all enlistments, appointments, periods of active duty and other periods of service of regular and reserve members of the armed forces. (This also was never done.)

The speech lay fallow for nearly a month, during which the 206,000 troop request was received, debated within the government, disclosed by the *New York Times,* and watered down in policy councils, and while a discussion of a proposal to halt the bombing gained ground. Drafting of the speech resumed on March 20, with the address to the nation planned for March 31. As drafted then, it announced the call to active duty of 48,000 reservists, an unspecified "substantial number" of whom would embark for Vietnam by late summer, with consideration of calling up an equal number of reservists later. One March 20 draft of the speech, which was quickly withdrawn for fear of leaks, also announced a halt in the bombing of Hanoi, Haiphong, and other targets near those cities.

The draft Johnson read to Mansfield on March 27 had been sent to the President three hours earlier by speechwriter Harry McPherson after being worked over by Clifford, Rusk, Rostow, and William Bundy. Still very much an appeal to the American people to "stay the course," it announced the call to active duty of 62,000 reservists, with 13,500 of them to be sent quickly to the war zone. Johnson's planned address repeated and gave new emphasis to his calls for higher taxes and severe budget cuts to make up for the costs of the war. There were no new diplomatic initiatives. The draft ended with an attack on those who opposed the war, declaring that such people "risk a far wider and more devastating conflict later."

When the President finished reading, he said, "I think most of the people ought to be with us" and then turned to Mansfield for his reaction. Mansfield paused to steel himself and clear his throat, and then he delivered his judgment in a firm, steady voice: "For what my opinion is worth, there will be a lot of criticism if you make that speech, in all likelihood. . . . To go to the people to accept [this policy] again . . . [there is] not too much there, laying it out hard and strong. . . ."

Johnson broke in, protesting that the people "don't want false hope." He said he could not speak in that fashion.

Mansfield replied: "I know, but I'm just explaining what I think the reaction will be. It will not be favorable in my opinion. That's your responsibility; you've got to face up to it. What the people are looking for in my opinion is not withdrawal, but a good deal of my mail indicates that, and I talked to other members [of Congress] and to their surprise they're getting a lot of that kind of thing—'withdraw right now'—you can't do it. . . .

"North Vietnam will be able to match you *and more* [his voice rising] because Giap has . . . 470,000 regular army, main force units. There's a militia, a type of organization which is fighting very well, and which numbers about 1,500,000, fighting in their own country. The more they are dragged in, the more they become dependent on China; the more Giap sends to the South, the more the Vietcong become dependent on Hanoi. . . .

"I would say that even yet the majority of people on our opponents' side in South Vietnam are South Vietnamese. And now they and the North Vietcong [*sic*] control a good deal more of the countryside since Tet. And with additional reinforcements coming down from the North to reinforce what's already down there. They can do it with less equipment, less logistics. They know the country better. They are willing to sacrifice their lives."

Earlier in the conversation Mansfield had expressed strong objection to increased bombing of the North, with emphasis on the Chinese factor, which was ever prominent in his considerations. Attacking the port of Haiphong as Russell and others recommended "will not achieve the objective, but will make things worse" by further involving China in overland supply; bombing the Red River dikes to flood much of the North, as some had recommended, would "just lay the groundwork for China to move in and *take over* (his emphasis) on a permanent basis." He recalled that Johnson had said some weeks ago that only about eighteen military targets of significance were left to be attacked in the North, "so what we're doing is bombing, rebombing and bombing again, cold targets."

Two hours before coming to the White House, Mansfield had appealed publicly for stopping the bombing of North Vietnam in an appearance on the twentieth anniversary program of the CBS Radio Network's *Capitol Cloakroom*. He declared that the bombing, which he had opposed from the first, had not achieved any of its military objectives and was an impediment to peace talks. He said he had been told by many friends and learned from reports from Hanoi that ending the bombing would be "a first step toward the negotiating table."

Now, face to face with the man who could decide, Mansfield spoke in an imploring, almost pleading tone: "Mr. President, *if* it wouldn't be possible, instead of carrying on the air war against the North, I repeat, you've said there are very few targets of real significance left. . . ."

Johnson interrupted before Mansfield could complete his plea. As early as March 4, Johnson had secretly signaled his willingness to consider ending the bombing, although he also knew that it would be highly controversial with military leaders and those civilian advisers who believed that more forceful action, not the opposite, was the solution to the Vietnam stalemate. Extremely secretive about all of his plans, LBJ was particularly guarded on this sensitive subject.

He first told Mansfield, "There are still a good many important storage areas that [the U.S. command] wants to hit very soon" but hasn't bombed yet. The President then detailed in rapid and scornful fashion previous short-term bombing halts that had failed to bring about the start of negotiations with the North Vietnamese. Nonetheless, he went on to tell Mansfield on a highly confidential basis that he was giving thought to a plan to stop U.S. bombing of North Vietnam except for the area immediately north of the Demilitarized Zone, where military movements threatened American forces—essentially the plan put forward by John Sherman Cooper that Mansfield had endorsed. Mansfield was pleased with that possibility but said the rest of the speech merely prescribed more of the same in Vietnam. To Mansfield, it appeared that the gulf between the two of them on the war was as wide as ever.

At 7:50 P.M., after almost two hours of the most intense face-to-face confrontation of their long relationship, Johnson rose from his chair in the Cabinet Room. As he prepared to return to the Oval Office, he put his hand on the doorknob, but then turned back to face Mansfield with a burst of candor and irritation, "Mike, I approve of your honesty but I only wish I had a Majority Leader who supported me." Mansfield was clear in his own mind: he was not Johnson's majority leader but the Senate's majority leader. He did not argue or respond but walked out of the White House alone.

The following morning Johnson's principal civilian advisers on the war—Rusk, Clifford, Rostow, William Bundy, and speechwriter McPherson—met in the Secretary of State's office to "polish the speech" before its presentation to the nation three days hence. Led by Clifford, who pronounced the tone and direction of the speech "a disaster," the group decided that McPherson should draft an entirely new speech—a speech about peace, including the partial bombing halt in North Vietnam—rather than a speech about staying the course and continuing the war. Rusk and Rostow, who had been the most steadfast believers in strong military action (although Rusk had also proposed a bombing halt) did not contest the far-reaching change in direction. Both versions of the speech were submitted to Johnson late that night. On the morning of March 29, he accepted the basic outline of the peace speech, which became the essence of what he said to the nation about the war.

No longer did the President begin with the "grave challenge to our country" and continue with sacrifice, reserve call-ups, and derogation of those who doubted the wisdom of the war. All that was eliminated and the bombing halt and a call for negotiations to end the war substituted instead. Although Johnson announced the dispatch of 13,500 backup troops to support the earlier deployment, that was the extent of the reinforcement. It was the last increment of U.S. troops authorized for the Vietnam War. As history has recorded, it was the beginning of the end, and the next (Nixon) administration began slowly but steadily withdrawing U.S. forces rather than augmenting them.

The start of the new speech characterized its content: "My fellow citizens: Tonight I want to speak to you of the prospects for peace in Vietnam and Southeast Asia." Five days later, in light of Johnson's actions, North Vietnam agreed to send officials to begin peace talks. It took nearly five more years for the United States fully to withdraw and seven more years for the end to come in Saigon, but Johnson's decisions in the final week of March 1968 proved to be the turning point of American involvement and of the war.

What Johnson did not tell the drafters of his speech was that by March 30 at the latest he had decided to add a startling peroration to his text, the announcement that "I shall not seek, and I will not accept, the nomination for another term as your President." He had given no hint to Mansfield in their latest conversation that he was considering such a momentous step; indeed, his preoccupation with the political polls during their meeting suggested otherwise. Yet he had spent no time in the lengthy meeting seeking

Mansfield's political support against Kennedy, which was an initial reason for summoning the Majority Leader.

Shortly before the broadcast on Sunday night, March 31, Johnson called Clifford, Rostow, and a few other close aides to the White House to tell them what he was going to do. At his direction a White House official imparted the news an hour before the speech by telephone to Mansfield, who was alone in a New York hotel room preparing to address a shoe-industry trade association the following morning. Mansfield absorbed the news in silence, then switched on the television and watched a speech that was nearly the opposite of the one he had heard from the President. Discarding his own prepared remarks, Mansfield told the shoemakers that Johnson's move was "a sacrifice" made out of a sincere desire to reunite the Democratic Party and the country. Without describing the substance of their meeting, he revealed that he had met with Johnson privately earlier in the week. "I recognized then as I had previously, the great strain that the President was under. I came away saddened," he said.

When the Senate met the day after the speech, Mansfield praised Johnson and his decision and defended him against his detractors. He cited the quotation from Isaiah that Johnson so often repeated as Majority Leader—"Come now and let us reason together"—and Mansfield declared, without giving details, that "he has reasoned with his advisers, with himself, and he has reasoned with some members of the Senate, both those who were for his policy in Vietnam and those who were against it. And he has done it on many occasions which were unpublicized. He has paid heed to what some of us had to say, and he has done his best to find a way to the negotiating table."

It is impossible to measure with certainty the impact on Johnson of the views Mansfield expressed in their lengthy meeting. The President could not have been surprised at Mansfield's opposition to sending additional U.S. troops to fight, nor at his opposition to continued extensive bombing of the North; this had been his consistent position both in advice to Johnson and in public statements. Was Johnson soliciting Mansfield's views at his moment of decision in order to use them, if necessary, against advisers from the opposite direction proposing that he send more troops and continue the bombing? Was he seeking to measure the depth of Mansfield's determination? In the past, the Majority Leader had expressed his opposition to

Johnson's war policies in many different settings, but he had remained aloof from congressional efforts to force a change through legislation. Would he now be ready to lead active resistance? Finally, it is impossible to know how Mansfield's almost desperate plea for "some opening that you can seize and find a way out . . . *some* way to bring this matter to a head" may have influenced Johnson's historic resolve to couple his Vietnam decisions with the announcement that he would not run again.

Thirty years later, with Johnson long dead and the war in Vietnam long since a matter for the history books, Mansfield vividly recalled the March 27, 1968, meeting. Before he or I knew that a secret tape recording existed, Mansfield described the discussion in extensive, almost entirely accurate detail, as among the most gripping of his many interactions with American presidents.

THE END OF THE JOHNSON ERA

Lyndon Johnson's surprise announcements of March 31 temporarily took much of the heat out of the Washington arguments about Vietnam. North Vietnam quickly announced it was willing to meet American representatives. In May, "preliminary discussions" about peace negotiations began in Paris. The negotiators were depressingly slow getting down to business, due to hesitation in both Saigon and Hanoi. It took eight more months, after Johnson halted all bombing of North Vietnam, after the obstacles were cleared for both the National Liberation Front and the South Vietnamese government to take their seats at the table, and days after the end of the Johnson administration, for formal peace talks to begin.

In mid-April Mansfield submitted to a television interview that was published in question-and-answer format by the *Honolulu Star Bulletin*. One of the readers was Mrs. Rose Hendricks of Hilo, Hawaii, who raised the issues that troubled Mansfield at the time about his role and plagued him later. The day the article appeared, she wrote Mansfield in a firm, clear hand:

> On Good Friday and with aching hearts, we buried my precious son—killed in Viet Nam. The first I have been able to read since getting the horrible news contains this statement by you: "we have no vital interest there and it is not necessary for the security of the United States." What in the name of God did

my son die for then? If it is your opinion and you do not approve (and I agree) are not then the leaders of this country responsible for his death, and was he not really murdered?

. . . He didn't die for his country but because of it, according to you. With all your power and influence, why did you not tell us of this? Armed with your statement, I would have defied the draft board. But, no, I thought he was doing something for the defense of his nation, and he thought so too.

How could your conscience let you see our boys get slaughtered if you really felt this way? I was not in favor of our being there, but then who was I to know? But you knew! . . . Can you answer my question: What did my son die for? I have to have some answer or I shall lose my mind.

Mansfield, who answered all letters from Montana and many others himself, did not do so on this occasion but asked Valeo to draft the response, which expressed "my deep regret if comments which I made in Hawaii may have added in any way to your sorrow." Although he had expressed disagreement over the years with many aspects of the nation's policy in Vietnam, he wrote, the commitment of military forces is a responsibility of "the Presidency" and is being lawfully discharged. "Your son died, Mrs. Hendricks, not in vain but in fulfillment of his obligations as a citizen of this nation. He carried out the terrible responsibilities which, for some, are entailed by citizenship in time of conflict. I honor him for his sacrifice on behalf of this nation, even as I regret profoundly his loss and the loss of thousands of other Americans in this tragic war."

Mrs. Hendricks wrote back a few weeks later: "You owe me no apology for your comments made in Honolulu. Every word is true. My regret is that you did not speak soon or loudly enough for me to hear."

Mansfield, who kept an updated card with the latest American casualty figures in his shirt pocket and was deeply anguished by the war and his role in it, did not respond.

In the meantime there was little peace at home. On April 4, Martin Luther King Jr. was murdered by a sniper in Memphis, touching off racial riots in many American cities, Washington being the site of one of the most serious. About midnight on June 4, Robert Kennedy was shot in Los Angeles while campaigning for the Democratic presidential nomination. Kennedy's death was deeply felt by Mansfield, who had been a friend to the Kennedy family and had suffered greatly at John F. Kennedy's assassination. Johnson called Mansfield to inform him of the shooting at 6:59 A.M. on June 5, before Robert Kennedy was pronounced dead but after the end was known. Mansfield arrived at the family quarters of the White House less than twenty minutes later to confer with the President. Lady Bird Johnson recalled seeing Mansfield "with a staring look in his eyes. He said, 'What is happening to the country?'"

Mansfield went from the White House to his office in the Capitol and wrote in longhand a statement of grief and anguish, which was later issued to the press:

> I grieve for my country and the Kennedys. What is wrong with our country that there can be an assassination of a President Kennedy, a Medger Evers, a Martin Luther King, and possibly a Senator Robert Kennedy?
>
> . . . What in the name of God has happened to us? Are we so blind that we cannot see? Are we so deaf that we cannot hear? Are we so dumb that we cannot understand? Are we so filled with hatred that we cannot love and appreciate one another? Are we so immersed in ourselves that we cannot live with one another in peace and amity? Are we so violent that we fail to comprehend the basic tenets of a democracy?

Sophie Engelhard, his young intern, remembered Mansfield as affected in a very profound way by Robert Kennedy's death, "maybe the most emotional I ever saw him." In the aftermath of the killing, he was determined to do something about control of firearms, although he knew this would be politically unpopular in Montana, where, as in other western states, hunters were prolific and guns were part of the traditional way of life. Rather than base his support for gun control on the assassinations of the Kennedys or King, Mansfield chose to highlight the case of Marine Second Lieutenant Thad Lesnick from the Montana town of Fishtail, population seventy, who was shot to death in a Washington, D.C., hamburger restaurant the week that Robert Kennedy died.

Seeking to take a politically acceptable stance, Mansfield opposed the bill introduced by the Johnson administration calling for the federal registration of all firearms. Instead he supported an alternative approach by Joseph Tydings of Maryland to encourage states to require registration of firearms, with the U.S. government involved only if states did not do so. On July 3, three weeks after becoming a co-sponsor of the Tydings bill, Mansfield told the Senate that his mail on the issue was the heaviest in his twenty-six years in Congress and overwhelmingly against his stand. He said he was not surprised at the unpopularity of his position in view of Montana traditions but that he did not expect the vehemence of the opposition. His old friend, "Scotty" James, editor of the *Great Falls Tribune,* wrote to him praising his courage but reporting that the gun legislation had unleashed a powerful wave of emotionalism, with Montana hunters signing petitions and telegrams of opposition and the newspaper's printers "convinced that any such legislation will take guns away from hunters." Mansfield wrote back, "It didn't take any courage to take my stand; I just felt that the time had arrived when something should be done to try to bring about a lessening of the violence which is so rampant in the country. . . . There comes a time when one has to make a difficult decision, and in all candor, there have been many such decisions to make down through the years."

Mansfield stood firm despite the overwhelming popular opinion in Montana to the contrary, quoting the British parliamentarian Edmund Burke, who said, "Your representative owes you not his industry only but his judgment." In an interview with Ken Scheibel, Washington correspondent for several Montana newspapers, he said, "I made my decision on the basis of my own conscience and my own responsibility." He added, "I am willing to take the consequences—whether they help me or hurt me." Mansfield's position helped the Tydings bill to pass the Senate, but it was blocked in the House and never became law. Later in the year, Mansfield supported the Gun Control Act of 1968, which contained less controversial provisions. As Mansfield anticipated, his gun control position was the principal issue in his next senatorial election two years later.

In the final months of the Johnson administration, Mansfield traveled to Czechoslovakia shortly before the Soviet invasion on August 20. The very day before the invasion, Mansfield had sent to Johnson his observations on his recently completed visit, including his judgment that "a Soviet military intervention in Czechoslovakia does not appear to be in the cards." Mansfield had been impressed with the reformist regime of Alexander Dubcek and, based on talks in Moscow, erroneously believed that pragmatism would outweigh ideological concerns in the Kremlin.

On the same trip Mansfield visited Paris and observed the stalled Vietnam peace talks, which he described as "two monologues proceeding separately, at the same time, without drawing the positions any closer." Before leaving for Paris, Mansfield had asked Johnson to press the Saigon government to accept the NLF as a negotiating partner, which it had been resisting. He also asked the President to "reduce the size of our military involvement in Vietnam," arguing that despite the silence in the Senate, the opposition to the war had grown rather than diminished. Should the war be intensified because of failure of the Paris talks, he predicted, "it would not only fail to serve a valid national purpose, it would increase, in my judgment, the public revulsion toward the war."

Johnson's efforts to bring the South Vietnamese government and the NLF into the Paris talks before the U.S. election were set back by the maneuverings of Anna Chennault (the widow of the wartime general whom Mansfield had met in China) on behalf of the Republican presidential candidate, Richard Nixon. On October 31 Johnson halted the bombing of all of North Vietnam in a move to expand the Paris talks, but it was too late to help the Democratic presidential candidate, Vice President Hubert Humphrey. On November 5, Nixon was elected president with a pledge to bring "peace with honor" in Vietnam.

In his farewell speech to Congress on January 14, 1969, Johnson went out of his way to praise "the wisdom of Senator Mansfield" among the mainstays that had contributed to his presidency. A week later, on Inauguration Day, Mansfield joined Johnson and President-elect Nixon at the White House for coffee in the Red Room before traveling to the Capitol in the official motorcade to Nixon's inauguration. Mansfield rode in car number three with Vice President Humphrey, Vice President–elect Spiro Agnew, and House Republican leader Gerald Ford, who was fated to be President himself in five years time.

Mansfield saw little of Johnson after the former President moved back to Texas. When Johnson died on January 22, 1973, Mansfield issued a brief public statement calling him "the greatest President in the area of social and domestic reform this nation has ever had" but omitting any mention of foreign affairs. The next day, in a fuller statement, Mansfield said more about Johnson's Great Society social legislation and about their close contacts beginning in the long-ago days when Johnson had chosen him as his majority whip, but made only a sketchy reference to their differences on Vietnam. "As might be expected, we did not always agree but at no time did our disagreements impair the civility of our relationship," said Mansfield. After a mix-up about the availability of a military plane, Mansfield decided not to attend the Johnson funeral in Texas. Told by Stan Kimmitt, his former student at the University of Montana who became secretary of the Senate Democratic majority, that the problems had been resolved and a plane made available, Mansfield adamantly refused to go. Kimmitt pleaded the case for the proprieties, but nothing could shake him. "Nope. I'm not going," was the final word.

Johnson "remembered his old friends in private and in public, but the longer he stayed in the White House, the more he became enamored of those officials who surrounded him and less close to his friends on the Hill," Mansfield wrote to a school principal in Texas who inquired about his estimate of Johnson two years after the former President's death. A decade later, following his retirement from public life, Mansfield told an interviewer, "Johnson was the ultimate politician but not the ultimate statesman. . . . He was a political person, first, last and always. He understood the rips and tides of politics. He could bring people toward his point of view until he assumed the presidency and stepped up the war in Vietnam. Then he lost it."

Even later, Mansfield told me in 1998 that Johnson was "a torn personality" due to Vietnam, where he was determined to win even though his doubts increased the longer he remained in office. As Majority Leader, Mansfield was also torn between his loyalty to the Democratic President, his belief in the predominance of the presidency in foreign affairs, and his opposition to the war in Indochina, which, from the start of American troop deployments, he believed would bring only tragic results to the United States. The delicate line he walked from 1963 to 1969 was the most difficult of his life.

WITH NIXON ON THE
ROAD TO CHINA

II *Richard M. Nixon won the presidency in 1968 by promising "peace with honor" to an American public that no longer predominantly supported the war in Indochina but, like Nixon, did not wish to leave the field in disgrace. As Democratic leader of the Senate, Mansfield gave the Republican President strong support until the invasion of Cambodia by U.S. and South Vietnamese forces in April 1970 persuaded him that Nixon was actually spreading the war rather than ending it. At that point Mansfield, abandoning his long-standing deference to the executive branch in foreign operations, sought to limit and eventually to end the U.S. role in the conflict through the exertion of legislative power. In the meantime he continued to see China as the key to peace and stability in Asia, and continued his efforts to establish direct contact with its leaders. Nixon had the same idea, which the two of them freely discussed in a series of intimate breakfast meetings. In the spring of 1971 the Chinese suddenly invited Mansfield to Beijing and then, within days, the U.S. President.*

With the inauguration of Richard Nixon in January 1969, the role of Mike Mansfield as Senate majority leader was transformed. No longer were the

Senate Democrats eclipsed by the power and predominance of a Democratic president in the White House, whether he was the popular and accommodating John F. Kennedy or the overbearing and exacting Lyndon B. Johnson. Now the foremost American political leader was a controversial and combative Republican president, although the voters had opted for divided government by leaving both houses of Congress in Democratic hands. The Senate, which surpassed the House of Representatives in public esteem and press attention, was the foremost bastion of the Democratic Party. The Majority Leader, freed from White House domination, was the party's leading spokesman and the nation's most important Democratic officeholder.

What did not change with the shift in the presidency was Mansfield's character and integrity, his ideas about the nation and the world, nor his high regard for the institution of the presidency. "I have a greater degree of flexibility and independence" in the new relationship with the White House, Mansfield told Harry Kelly of the Associated Press a few weeks after the Nixon era began. "But it also means that, so far as I'm concerned, I will do my best to uphold the hand of the President and help him become a good President. If we follow that policy and are successful his success will be the nation's success and his failures will hurt all of us in the long run. In other words, I don't intend to follow the concept of Bob Taft, Republican Senate leader who died in 1953 who said it was the duty of the opposition party to oppose. It is the duty of the opposition to oppose only if they find fault and they then come up with constructive alternatives."

Nixon and Mansfield had served together in the House of Representatives from 1947 to 1951, before going on to the Senate, Nixon arriving there two years prior to Mansfield. Beginning in 1953 Nixon served for eight years as vice president under Dwight Eisenhower, during which time one of Nixon's constitutional tasks was to preside over the Senate. Nonetheless, the two men rarely crossed paths. "Didn't know him" in the House; "didn't get to know him" as vice president "because he was seldom there," Mansfield told me. Politically, they were poles apart. Nixon had become famous for his strident anticommunism as a member of the House Un-American Activities Committee, which Mansfield had opposed, and especially for his charges (later validated in federal courts) against Alger Hiss. As Republican nominee for vice president, Nixon had campaigned briefly in Montana against

Mansfield in the ugly 1952 Senate race. Mansfield recalled that Nixon as vice president had urged Eisenhower to intervene militarily in Indochina in 1954 at the time of Dienbienphu, "and thank the Lord we didn't." The following year, Mansfield remembered, Nixon was among the advocates of U.S. bombing raids against China, which Mansfield had helped to block through his conversation with Secretary of State Dulles at Manila.

After his narrow victory over Vice President Hubert Humphrey in the 1968 presidential race, Nixon decided early on to attempt a close working relationship with the Democratic leader of the Senate. Two weeks after taking office, he telephoned Mansfield to present two goodwill offerings intended to smooth the way. He had decided, he said, to accept Mansfield's recommendation that he reappoint Jane Engelhard to the Board of Trustees of the Library of Congress and to the Commission for Preservation of the White House. Nixon certainly knew that she and her husband were prominent Democrats and that they were among the closest friends of the Mansfields. The President also gave his seal of approval to a pending bill that would raise the compensation of lawmakers, although he recognized that legislative pay "was their business and their responsibility." On February 19, a month after becoming president, Nixon began regular meetings with the House and Senate leaders of both political parties.

As a gesture of bipartisanship, Nixon invited Mansfield and Senate Minority Leader Everett Dirksen as well as other lawmakers from both parties to accompany him on a jaunt to the Kentucky Derby on May 3. Amid the mint juleps and pageantry, he asked John Sherman Cooper, the respected moderate Republican from Kentucky, if there was any Democratic senator whom he could really trust and who could help him in the Senate. Cooper strongly recommended Mansfield, but added that he would have to see him alone and frequently and that the relationship would have to be handled with complete confidentiality. Nixon took the advice. He told Mansfield he would like to meet privately at the White House once a month, and Mansfield said he would be delighted to accept. Available records from a variety of sources indicate that they met privately at least twenty-seven times in the fifty months between then and September 1973. Most of these were breakfast meetings of just the two of them, held at a small oval table under a crystal chandelier in the ornate, high-ceilinged Family Dining Room. On a few occasions they were joined at the table by National Security Adviser

Henry Kissinger, Secretary of State William Rogers or another senior official. For the most part these were one-way conversations, with Nixon presenting his ideas and proposals, and Mansfield saying little. "I feel it would be impertinent for me to break in unless I am asked a question or an opportunity arises," Mansfield said in a *Meet the Press* interview in March 1971, one of the few occasions when he discussed the breakfasts publicly. Asked on that program by *New York Times* correspondent John W. Finney if he spoke as forcefully and frankly to Nixon as he did in the television broadcast, Mansfield answered succinctly, "No." When Finney protested that Mansfield had a right to speak frankly, the Majority Leader responded, "Oh, I have a right, and I daresay he would listen to me, but I do not like to push myself personally."

These were two very different men, Mansfield taciturn but entirely secure in his own skin, Nixon driven and acutely insecure in his interaction with others, but they had extensive private dealings through their breakfasts and other meetings. No one else outside the executive branch of government had such intimate, continuous, and substantive contact with Nixon the President. Yet it is hard to say in retrospect that either had great impact on the other, personally or politically. Mansfield's recollection was that he and Nixon mostly talked about China policy in the confidential meetings. However, the notes of H. R. Haldeman, the White House Chief of Staff, who did not attend any of the meetings but often discussed them with Nixon, suggest that the President's purpose was often to obtain cooperation or at least acquiescence from Mansfield on a variety of domestic and foreign issues. Most of the meetings were not listed on Nixon's public schedule and Mansfield typically did not discuss them with fellow senators. Even his closest Senate aide, Frank Valeo, was told virtually nothing about their content.

According to Valeo, Mansfield modeled his relationship with Nixon on the confidential ties that Walter George, who was chairman of the Senate Foreign Relations Committee, had maintained with President Eisenhower and Secretary of State John Foster Dulles when Mansfield was a junior senator and something of a protégé of George's. Times had changed by the Nixon era, however, and so had the personalities involved. In retrospect, Mansfield said Nixon "felt insecure with me and I felt insecure with him. I think he was a very insecure man." Mansfield told me his personal and political relations with Nixon were "kind of close, based on the breakfast meetings," which sounds positive until measured against his characterization of his relations with other presidents: "close" relations with Kennedy and Johnson and "excellent" relations with Ford.

Nixon's private view of Mansfield varied with political circumstances, even before the Watergate investigation. In a conversation with Secretary of State Rogers, Nixon said, "Mike is a wonderful guy, a decent man." He highly valued Mansfield's personal integrity and often spoke to him in confidence on international questions. Speaking to an assistant about leaks to the press from members of Congress, Nixon declared, "Mansfield never does." In 1969, according to Valeo, Nixon requested that Mansfield be his primary point of contact with the Senate on foreign policy, supplanting the relationship with the more talkative and contentious Foreign Relations Committee. On one occasion in April 1971 Nixon informed Mansfield of plans to withdraw the next increment of U.S. troops from Vietnam before telling his own Republican congressional leaders. Mansfield agreed not to tell his Republican counterparts that the conversation had ever taken place.

When they clashed politically, however, Mansfield was a target of Nixon's malevolent instincts, the dark side of his personality that coexisted uneasily with his keen intelligence and political acumen. When Senate Democrats were investigating Nixon's shady dealing with the International Telephone and Telegraph Company and voting down his foreign aid bill in March 1972, the President complained to aides that Mansfield was "playing a ruthless game on everything" and ordered them to "let Mansfield squeal a little while" by interfering with the Majority Leader's planned trip to China. Kissinger responded that "I always thought that Mansfield was of upstanding quality," to which Nixon replied, "Sure, you're right. But that's the better him. There's two [Mansfields.]" A few minutes later, Nixon insisted that "Mansfield deserves a kick in the ass" and instructed Kissinger to "see if there's a way to screw Mansfield on this trip." In May, conversing with his politically combative aide Charles Colson, Nixon deplored Mansfield's continuing efforts to force an end to the Vietnam War through legislation. "Well, to hell with him. We've just got to fight him now. . . ." the President declared. In a display of his ambivalence he added, "Just because Mike is a nice guy, goddamnit, he's not for what we're trying to do, so hit him."

When Mansfield announced his retirement from Congress in 1976, two years after Nixon had been forced to resign as a result of the Watergate investigation, Nixon sent him a remarkable handwritten letter testifying to his "deep sense of respect and personal affection." He went on:

We have had our differences over the years—but on the great issues—like the opening to China and the new policy in the Mideast—we worked together for the more peaceful world which is our common goal.

Our breakfasts were particularly helpful to me—because you were one of those rare men in public life who never broke a confidence.

COOPERATING WITH NIXON

On February 4, 1969, two weeks after Nixon took office as President, Mansfield convened the first meeting in the new Congress of the Senate Democratic Policy Committee. The ambiance of the long, narrow, high-ceilinged conference room of the secretary of the Senate's office, with a big crystal chandelier and two tall windows looking out to the Capitol dome, the West front and the Mall, added to the solemnity of the occasion. After lunch was served at the conference table, the waiters were dismissed and nine Democratic elders, conservatives and liberals, from North, South, East, and West, began to consider how the Senate Democrats should deal with Richard Nixon.

We no longer have at the White House an automatically receptive ear to the views of the Democratic senators [Mansfield told his colleagues]. Conversely, I might add, we do not have an automatic party concern in seeking to cushion whatever difficulties the new administration may bring on itself. At the same time, public interest in the performance of Democrats as a party will no longer be fixed on the White House. . . .

With all due respect to the House a great deal of public interest is likely to concentrate on the performance of the Senate and its diverse personalities. It will be here, in my judgment, that much of the fate of the party will be determined during the next few years. If that is so, considerable significance attaches to what we do as Democrats in the Senate and when we do it—how we live among ourselves—how we live with the Republican minority in the Congress and with a Republican President in the White House.

He went on to express his personal view that "we must put, above all else, the interests of the nation and the President's unique role in safeguarding them as well as the demeanor and effective operation of the Senate as the Constitutional institution through which each of us serves those interests. These are the highest priorities."

Those around the table—Fulbright of Arkansas, Russell of Georgia, Ted Kennedy of Massachusetts, Pastore of Rhode Island, Symington of Missouri, Byrd of West Virginia, Hollings of South Carolina, and a new member, Hughes of Iowa—all agreed with Mansfield's sentiments. Russell, still the leader of the southerners and the most prestigious figure within the confines of the Senate, was especially emphatic. "We should play it by ear at the present" and "should give the White House a fair amount of time to make its proposals and thereby avoid being in the posture of opposing the new administration for the sake of opposition. . . . we must avoid getting in a position of opposing for its sake alone, but should be selective in taking our stand."

During the first year of the Nixon administration, Mansfield led the Democratic opposition to Nixon policies on taxes and on swift development of an antiballistic missile (ABM) system. More important, however, he accepted at face value Nixon's declarations that his objective in Vietnam was to terminate the war through negotiations. Despite his own impatience and growing public opposition to the war, Mansfield consistently argued for giving the President time to lead the nation out of the quagmire in Southeast Asia.

When George McGovern initiated senatorial criticism of Nixon's Vietnam policies in March 1969, Mansfield listened in silence and then told reporters outside the chamber, "I think the President would give his right arm for a settlement. I say, give him a chance." A few weeks later, speaking on *Meet the Press,* Mansfield said that discontent was growing with Nixon's war policy but that "I am sure that in his own way he is trying to bring this barbarous and tragic and futile war to what he has referred to as a responsible settlement." In May, he wrote a Montana constituent, "Insofar as the war in Vietnam is concerned, I have opposed our military involvement there from the onset. Nevertheless, we are deeply immersed in the conflict. I see the problem now as one of ending this cruel and barbaric struggle in an orderly fashion through negotiations. In that way our own participation is likely to be terminated at the soonest possible moment." After Nixon announced a new negotiating strategy at the ongoing Paris talks—proposals that the

North Vietnamese promptly rejected—Mansfield said on *Face the Nation* that the President was making "every reasonable effort" to achieve peace.

Opposition against the war on the part of the politicians, protesters, and the general public was rising as impatience began to spread. By the early weeks of Nixon's presidency, a substantial majority (52 percent against 39 percent, with the rest undecided) of those polled by Gallup said it had been a mistake to send U.S. troops to fight in Vietnam, although the public was sharply divided over what course to follow. Antiwar protests had peaked before Johnson's dramatic announcements of March 31, 1968, and diminished thereafter until the spring of 1969. Over Easter weekend in early April, 100,000 protesters marched in New York in spite of rain. In San Francisco, 40,000 marched, and in Chicago 30,000, the largest to date for that city. Mansfield, even while continuing to defend Nixon's intentions and decisions, became increasingly critical of the continuing heavy casualties and of U.S. tactics being employed in the war zone.

After a particularly bloody fight for control of Apbia Mountain near the Laotian border, which American troops dubbed "Hamburger Hill," Mansfield wrote a memo for his files on May 28 expressing his "feeling of futility and indignation over the continuing loss of human life in Vietnam. . . . Areas are won or lost many times on a temporary basis. Lives are lost always on a permanent basis." The memo became the basis for a Senate speech the following day in which he deplored the killing and defended the right of senators to criticize the war despite the opposition of the Nixon administration and its Republican backers. He warned, "When any senator speaks out of his mind and heart on any aspect of this struggle, his words are not to be dismissed as irrelevant or less by others in this government. Indeed, it would be the better part of wisdom to heed them carefully. They may be words which are not only in unison with the surge of sentiment throughout the nation; they may also contain a basis for a more effective policy of peace." The *New York Times* reported Mansfield's speech on its front page and printed excerpts from the text.

In the months that followed, two developments buoyed Mansfield's confidence in Nixon's policies and his ultimate intentions. Meeting South Vietnamese President Thieu at Midway Island on June 8, 1969, Nixon announced the decision to withdraw 25,000 of the 543,000 American troops in Vietnam and promised to make additional cutbacks as the United States turned over the fighting to South Vietnamese forces. This was the beginning of the gradual and unilateral withdrawal known as "Vietnamization" that was designed to mollify the restive U.S. public and extricate the United States without admitting defeat. Nixon pursued it, along with intermittent negotiations with the North Vietnamese in Paris, until the final pullout of U.S. troops in January 1973.

Mansfield had been publicly calling for reductions in U.S. forces since early April 1969, when he urged the withdrawal of 50,000 troops "as a starter." Although the initial cutback fell short of that, Mansfield recognized, as did an unhappy Thieu, that Nixon's decision would begin an irreversible process. In early July Mansfield told reporters that the United States should get out of Vietnam and Thailand "lock, stock and barrel," leaving only a peripheral presence, but he did not set a timetable. At some point in 1969 Nixon told Mansfield privately that the United States "would be out of Vietnam" by the end of his first term of office in January 1973.*

The second development that won Mansfield's approval was Nixon's declaration on his round-the-world trip in July that the United States would steer clear of future direct military involvement in Asia but would expect Asian nations to defend themselves. Nixon's headline-making statement came in a meeting with the accompanying press at a naval officers club during a brief stopover on Guam on the first leg of his trip. The journalists covering the event, including me, had no advance notice that important news was about to be made, but in the context of the time and place—the initial stop en route to Southeast Asia—Nixon's statements appeared to be, as I reported, "a new U.S. policy of decreasing military involvement in Asian conflicts."

Mansfield threw his strong support behind the declaration, which became known as the Guam Doctrine or the Nixon Doctrine, which the President embellished in later stops on the trip. "His intent, I believe, is to avoid future Vietnams but, at the same time, to render what assistance is feasible and possible to the nations of Asia. . . . We want him to know that he has our full support on the basis of what he has said in Guam and restated in the Philippines and Indonesia," Mansfield told the Senate. Warren Unna, a *Washington Post*

---

*Nixon's prediction was almost precisely accurate, as the last U.S. troops left Vietnam in March 1973. However, the slow pullout was more agonizing, more contentious, and more costly in U.S. lives than Mansfield had anticipated.

reporter who closely followed the politics of the war, observed, "It has been a long time since the Senate Majority Leader, a leading critic of the U.S. involvement in Vietnam and general U.S. military commitments abroad, has uttered such praise for administration foreign policy. It didn't occur when his own party was in the White House under President Johnson."

Mansfield's praise continued when congressional leaders from both parties were briefed by Nixon at the end of the trip. Sitting in the Cabinet Room, where he had uttered so many dissents from Johnson's policy, he told Nixon and the other leaders that he was "very much surprised and pleased" by Nixon's declaration. He added, "We have veered off into a new and more desirable path." Cautious about receiving so much praise from the dovish Majority Leader, Nixon told him privately at a breakfast meeting that the Nixon Doctrine "was not a formula for getting America *out* of Asia, but one that provided the only sound basis for America's staying *in*" to assist threatened Asian states. Mansfield continued his commendation in the hope that this would help Nixon to abide by the policy he had enunciated at Guam.

MISSION TO CAMBODIA

Norodom Sihanouk had been among the Asian leaders Mansfield most appreciated from the time they first met during the senator's 1954 trip to Indochina. Compared to chaotic, embattled Vietnam and weak, divided Laos, Cambodia stood out as a kingdom of relative peace, maintained by a precarious position of neutrality toward all sides, French and American, Thai and Vietnamese, communist and anticommunist. The key to its exceptional posture was an exceptional personality. Sihanouk, who had been crowned king at age eighteen, had abdicated the throne at age thirty-two to become prime minister and the leader of the dominant political party. A short, portly man with a high-pitched voice and an intense, mercurial manner, he was looked upon as a god-king by many of his subjects but regarded warily by officials in Western capitals, who were often put off by his maneuverings and unsure of his intentions.

"I was impressed with him, liked him, agreed with his ideals," Mansfield told me. "While he shifted here and there and everywhere else, he was always doing so because he wanted to keep Cambodia, Cambodia. As far as he was concerned, being king meant nothing. I think he willingly would have become a peasant if his country could have remained his country. . . . When I think of Sihanouk, I think of Cambodia; when I think of Cambodia, I think of Sihanouk."

The feeling was mutual. After Sihanouk rejected U.S. aid in 1963 in order to maintain his neutrality, his publication *Realities Cambodgiennes* described Mansfield as "a man who, in these difficult circumstances, forestalled us from doubting everything about his country. And if, some day, Khmer-American amity again flourishes, it will be due above all to Mr. Mansfield and other men of his caliber." In May 1965, Sihanouk formally broke diplomatic relations with the United States after U.S. bombing raids hit Cambodian villages in the thinly populated South Vietnamese border area, which was being used as a supply route and staging area by North Vietnamese military forces. Nonetheless, as noted earlier, Sihanouk six months later arranged an extraordinary welcome with full honors during Mansfield's 1965 tour of Asia. He told Mansfield he wished to rebuild relations with Washington but insisted there be no further bombings or incursions into Cambodian territory, a demand unacceptable to U.S. military forces faced with increasing North Vietnamese activity in the border region.

Both Sihanouk and the Johnson administration had seen Mansfield as a potential channel for improved relations. In late 1966 Secretary of State Rusk asked Mansfield to pass on anything he might hear from Sihanouk. The Cambodian leader in late 1967 suggested that Washington send a special envoy to find a solution to the growing conflict over the border area, and mentioned the possibility that it be Mansfield, "a just and courageous man whom we consider a friend."

Sihanouk told Stanley Karnow in December 1967, "We are a country caught between the hammer and the anvil, a country that would very much like to remain the last haven of peace in Southeast Asia," but he was finding peace increasingly difficult to maintain. In January 1968, as North Vietnamese forces in Cambodian territory were gearing up for the Tet Offensive in South Vietnam, the Communist Party of Cambodia decided to wage armed struggle against Sihanouk's rule. This decision was opposed, after the fact, by Chinese Premier Chou En-lai, who feared that conflict within Cambodia would push Sihanouk to the right and interfere with North Vietnamese use of the Cambodian border area. The war against the Americans should take priority, Chou insisted. The insurgency within

Cambodia, Sihanouk's attacks on the insurgents, and North Vietnamese use of the border area all continued.

It was in this context that Nixon in early 1969 decided to take a personal hand in the Cambodian question. On February 1, less than two weeks after being inaugurated as President, Nixon received the credentials of the new Singapore ambassador, E. S. Monteiro, who had been previously posted in Phnom Penh for four years and was an intimate friend of Sihanouk. He said the Cambodian leader had a very "warm feeling" toward Nixon based on a meeting in 1953, when the then–Vice President made a state visit to Cambodia, and a later meeting in Washington. Monteiro said Sihanouk "based a great number of his policies on purely personal attitudes." Nixon asked the ambassador to pass along a friendly message to Sihanouk, and instructed Kissinger to have a personal letter to Sihanouk drawn up "if that does not cross wires with something else."

In the letter, dated February 14, 1969, Nixon expressed "my sincere desire to see a genuine and lasting improvement in United States–Cambodian relations, and to work toward this objective." He also declared that "every effort must be made to localize the conflict in Vietnam" and assured Sihanouk of his commitment "to exercise the utmost restraint" in this connection. Sihanouk responded very positively but said further progress was conditional on "the cesssation of attacks from the air, and by military units based in neighboring territory upon the rural population in [Cambodian] frontier areas."

In mid-April the Australian ambassador to Cambodia delivered a formal U.S. declaration to Sihanouk declaring, "In conformity with the United Nations Charter, the United States of America recognizes and respects the sovereignty, independence and neutrality and territorial integrity of the kingdom of Cambodia within its present frontiers." Sihanouk expressed his great pleasure and responded that the resumption of normal relations should follow. On that basis U.S.-Cambodian relations officially resumed on June 11.

In the meantime Nixon, knowing of Mansfield's relationship with Sihanouk, had asked him in March to consider making a visit to Cambodia. Mansfield was interested but told the President he did not have time, in view of preparations for his reelection campaign in November 1970.

Even while Nixon was seeking to use Mansfield to restore relations with Cambodia, however, he was simultaneously initiating secret U.S. bombings of North Vietnamese base areas in Cambodia. This was partly a response to increasing North Vietnamese and Vietcong attacks in South Vietnam and partly an effort to penalize North Vietnam for lack of progress in the Paris talks, without risking the U.S. public uproar that would result from bombing raids against North Vietnam itself. On February 23, 1969, and later on March 4 Nixon ordered the secret bombing to begin, but both times he canceled the order after objections from, first, Secretary of Defense Melvin Laird and, second, Secretary of State William Rogers. On March 16, he once again ordered bombing to begin, and this time B-52 bombers of the Strategic Air Command dumped tons of explosives in the border area. This was the start of extensive raids that lasted for more than a year, involving 3,875 sorties and a total of 108,823 tons of bombs. The bombing was not publicly acknowledged, but it was not a secret to the American public following William Beecher's accurate revelations in the *New York Times* on May 9, and could hardly have been a secret to Sihanouk or to Mansfield.

Beyond Cambodia's relationship to the war, Mansfield, and Nixon as well, had a second—and potentially more powerful—reason to seek the personal cooperation of Sihanouk. Due to Mansfield's initiative, Sihanouk was a key intermediary in the effort to make high-level contact with the People's Republic of China.

Nixon, who had made political hay in the 1950s condemning the "appeasers" in the U.S. government who "lost" China, had begun to take a different tack by 1965 and 1967 when he traveled as a private citizen through Asia. In October 1967, in a thoughtful article in *Foreign Affairs* about American foreign policy after Vietnam, he wrote, "Taking the long view, we simply cannot afford to leave China forever outside the family of nations, there to nurture its fantasies, cherish its hates and threaten its neighbors. There is no place on this small planet for a billion of its potentially most able people to live in angry isolation." As an anticommunist politician, Nixon said little more about his ideas publicly, but immediately after taking office as President he began taking a series of small steps intended to pave the way toward a relationship with Beijing.

In an early private meeting with Mansfield, Nixon raised the topics of China and the Far East, which had had a magnetic attraction for the Majority Leader ever since his days as a U.S. Marine. Nixon told him that he too had "a lifelong interest in that part of the world—understandable for a California boy," Mansfield recalled in an interview for *U.S. News and World*

Report. The President proceeded to outline steps he planned to take: to lift the total U.S. boycott of Chinese goods that had been in effect for nearly two decades, since China's intervention in the Korean War; to ease restrictions on travel to China; and to resume the long-standing but interrupted talks between U.S. and Chinese diplomats at Warsaw. "You can't ignore China, it's too big. You have to live with it," he told Mansfield. The Majority Leader, who considered China the key to nearly everything in Southeast Asia, was pleased. At that initial stage, Mansfield recalled, "He never said anything about a trip to China, except that he would like to go. But then I don't think he expected to go."

In the summer of 1969 it was Mansfield—working through Sihanouk—who seemed likeliest to break the ice with a visit to Beijing. Among prominent American politicians, Mansfield was the most fascinated with China, the most sympathetic to the dramatic changes being made in the People's Republic and the most determined to make personal contact with the authorities in Beijing. He had been rebuffed by Dean Rusk during the Johnson administration when he proposed to seek a visa to China (see Chapter 10), but now with Nixon in the White House he renewed his efforts. Mansfield discussed with Nixon, possibly in their one-on-one breakfast meeting of June 11, his wish to go to China. Six days later he wrote to Sihanouk enclosing a letter to Chou En-lai requesting permission to visit Beijing. Expressing hope that "a new and informal exchange of views" could help initiate a change for the better, Mansfield asked for Sihanouk's help in overcoming the "formidable" problems of communicating with Chou. To keep the exchange confidential, the senator entrusted the letters to Huot Sambath, the Cambodian representative to the United Nations, for transmission to Sihanouk. Mansfield wrote to Sihanouk:

Among the requirements for a durable peace—and I stress the word durable—not only in Viet Nam but throughout Southeast Asia, as I see it, is a change in the climate between the United States and China. What is needed is not only a better understanding of mutual intentions in Southeast Asia but also a fresh examination of the issues which have existed directly between the two countries for so many years. At times, one has the feeling that the words which flow back and forth have lost relevance, if only because they have been spoken too often and at too great a distance. . . .

I have discussed this matter with the President of the United States. He understands fully my purpose in seeking this meeting in Peking. However, the arrangements are being pursued discreetly by me, on a personal and informal basis.

Enclosed in the same package was the letter, unsealed, that Mansfield asked Sihanouk to read and, if he approved, to forward to Chou:

Your Excellency:
The practice of exchanging animosities at long range—a practice which has persisted for two decades—has tended to keep alive a predisposition to conflict in Sino-U.S. relations. In my judgment, this prolonged enmity must be mitigated if there is to be a resolution of issues of direct concern between the United States and China. Furthermore, the durable termination of the tragic conflict in Viet Nam may well depend on the creation of a more amicable climate between our two countries.

The Chinese and American Ambassadors in Warsaw, to be sure, have been trying to bring about an improvement in the situation. It is only too apparent, however, that these formal meetings have been at an impasse for many years. In the circumstances, it is possible that an informal initiative might prove helpful.

I suggest most respectfully, therefore, the possibility of my meeting with you and, perhaps, with some of your associates in the government of the Chinese People's Republic. In this fashion, I would hope to develop a greater understanding of the position of the Chinese government on the issues which exist in Sino-U.S. relations. What might be learned would be conveyed to my country and, particularly, to my colleagues in the United States Senate.

May I say that the President of the United States is conversant with my intention of seeking this meeting and understands my purpose. If I were to call on you and your associates in Peking, however, I would do so in my individual capacity, as a member of the Senate. I would probably be accompanied to China only by my wife and a legislative aide.

It would be my hope that you share with me the belief that our countries might both benefit from a direct contact of this kind. I await a reply through the kindness of Prince Norodom Sihanouk which will indicate to me whether I might be received in Peking and, if so, on what dates.

Mansfield supplied a copy of both letters to Bryce Harlow, Nixon's senior contact with Congress, and asked him to bring them to Nixon's personal attention so that "the President knows every significant move I make in regard to this trip." Even by the relatively amicable standards of that day, this was a remarkable demonstration of the Democratic Majority Leader's trust in the Republican President and of Mansfield's determination to take significant initiatives overseas only with the full knowledge of the president in office, Democratic or Republican.

Nixon responded through Harlow that "he is most pleased with these initiatives." Kissinger, on his own, urged Harlow to suggest that Mansfield make his initiative public as a signal to China, but Mansfield wisely did not do so.

The letter through Sihanouk took a long time to reach Beijing. Mansfield had received no answer by the time Nixon returned in early August from his round-the-world trip during which he announced his new Asian doctrine in the stop in Guam. At that point, Nixon renewed his request for Mansfield to visit Cambodia. Mansfield agreed to do so and in discussion with Nixon, probably on August 9 when they met privately for forty minutes with Kissinger and Harlow also present, it was decided to add Burma and Laos, two other Southeast Asian countries that the President had not visited, as well as brief stops in Indonesia and the Philippines, which Nixon had visited. To pave the way for the journey, which was undertaken in an Air Force jet during the congressional recess in August, Nixon sent personal messages to the heads of state along Mansfield's route announcing the visit of "the distinguished Majority Leader of the U.S. Senate" and declaring that Nixon would be "very interested" in Mansfield's findings.

En route to see Sihanouk in Phnom Penh, which was the main objective of the trip, Mansfield saw two other controversial Asian leaders with whom he had forged unusually strong relationships, Ferdinand Marcos in the Philippines and Ne Win in Burma. James Lowenstein of the Senate Foreign Relations Committee staff, who along with Frank Valeo accompanied Mansfield and his wife, said in retrospect that Sihanouk, Marcos, and Ne Win were "his three boys out there" although all of them contradicted Mansfield's allegiance to democratic rule. In 1969 Marcos had been president only four years and was making economic and social progress. Three years later he imposed martial law and became increasingly corrupt and domineering, but Mansfield continued to have a very cordial relationship with him and his ambitious wife, Imelda. As for the reclusive Burmese

leader, Ne Win, who had come to power in a military coup in 1962 and created a declining one-party state, Mansfield was granted entrée that astonished the resident American ambassador, Arthur Hummel, who had not
been granted an audience with the Burmese leader since presenting his credentials nearly a year earlier. According to Lowenstein, Hummel strongly
objected when Mansfield announced on arrival in Rangoon that he was
going right over to see Ne Win at his residence. Mansfield insisted, and was
greeted enthusiastically by the Burmese leader and his wife, who threw their
arms around the senator and Maureen and invited the party to stay for an
intimate dinner, from which the ambassador was excluded. Hummel did not
know that Ne Win, who had met the Mansfields in Burma previously, had
sent a handwritten letter to "My dear friend" as soon as he learned of the
visit, proclaiming his happiness that "we are living at the same time" and his
eagerness to see the Mansfields again.

Moving on to Phnom Penh, Mansfield received a lavish ceremonial welcome, including hundreds of people waving Cambodian and American
flags, honor guards of troops with fixed bayonets and a necklace of scented
jasmine flowers hung around his neck by a young girl. Sihanouk hosted a
black tie dinner for the Mansfields and their party and key members of the
Phnom Penh diplomatic corps and arranged a ballet in their honor by the
Royal Ballet Corps, featuring Princess Bopha Devi, Sihanouk's daughter,
in the starring role. Mansfield also called on General Lon Nol, recently
installed as prime minister and defense minister, who would later overthrow Sihanouk. It was, as the newly arrived U.S. Chargé d'Affaires, Lloyd
Rives, reported to the State Department, "virtual Chief of State treatment
. . . the result of years of close association and friendship" between
Mansfield and Sihanouk. It was also a celebration, with cautious overtones,
of the newly reestablished relations between the United States and
Cambodia.

Clear-eyed about the eventual balance of forces in Southeast Asia,
Sihanouk told Mansfield privately that "a socialist Vietnam cannot be
avoided in the future" and predicted that "some day the United States will
withdraw from Vietnam." He maintained difficult relations with North
Vietnam and the recently created Provisional Revolutionary Government of
South Vietnam (the intended government entity of the National Liberation
Front, or Vietcong) but had no relations with the Saigon government.

Sichan Siv, who was a high school student in Phnom Penh at the time and much later a member of the White House staff, was surprised to see Vietcong flags for the visiting PRG chairman one day and the Stars and Stripes for Mansfield shortly thereafter. Two weeks after Mansfield's visit, Sihanouk declared a national day of mourning at the death of Ho Chi Minh and then flew to Hanoi for the funeral, where he was met with embraces from Premier Pham Van Dong, General Vo Nguyen Giap, and others.

The most important conversation, and one that eventually stirred controversy, took place between Sihanouk and Mansfield on August 22 under a massive painting of the temples at Ankor in an audience hall of the ornate Royal Palace, where the Mansfields were also staying. Mansfield, as was his style, asked few questions and said little. The voluble Sihanouk, as was *his* style, spoke almost without pause or interruption for more than two hours, on this occasion in English. The most difficult issue was continued use by the North Vietnamese and Vietcong of the thinly inhabited, heavily forested border area of Cambodia close to South Vietnam. The State Department, in a classified background paper delivered to Mansfield while he was en route to Cambodia, reported that "Communist pressure on Cambodia to continue providing sanctuary and supply lines [in the border area] has been intense, and has probably contributed to Sihanouk's reluctance to seek any close relationship with the U.S."

Speaking with great candor to Mansfield, Sihanouk said, "Some parts of Cambodia's frontiers are not controlled by Cambodia." He reported that the Vietcong had established more than thirty hospitals in one Cambodian border province alone. Noting that his forces were far inferior to those of the heavily armed Vietnamese, he said he had asked the communist forces to withdraw, but that they replied they would not do so until the United States withdraws. Sihanouk said he had protested to U.S. Ambassador to India Chester Bowles in an early 1968 visit to Phnom Penh for the Johnson administration against U.S. bombing in Cambodia, "but not against bombing sanctuaries in areas of Cambodia not inhabited by Cambodians." According to the very detailed memorandum of the conversation with Mansfield, written by Lowenstein, Sihanouk went on to say, "I never protest against such bombings." He said he learned of such bombings from *Time* or *Newsweek* and added, "It is in one's own interest, sometimes, to be bombed—in this case, the United States kills foreigners who occupy

Cambodian territory and does not kill Cambodians." However, Sihanouk continued, he did protest the bombings of Cambodian villages and the killing of Cambodian peasants, which sometimes occurred when the United States had faulty intelligence.

That part of the conversation became the subject of Washington debate four years later, in July 1973, in the post-mortem that followed the final withdrawal of U.S. forces from South Vietnam. When U.S. lawmakers harshly criticized what had been the "secret bombing" of Cambodia, the State Department cited Sihanouk's statements to Mansfield in justification of U.S. policy. The Majority Leader, asked to comment by the *New York Times,* responded that he did not recall Sihanouk accepting U.S. bombing "in any way, shape or form." The next day, after he had access to his records, Mansfield wrote in a memorandum for his files, "Insofar as I understood it then and now, there was not in his comment any agreement, actual, tacit or implied, by Sihanouk with the bombing. There was more the complaint that with a pitiful army and difficult terrain what could he do about violations of Cambodian neutrality in remote regions."

The item of greatest immediate interest to Mansfield, however, was Sihanouk's relationship with China and especially with Chou En-lai, to whom Mansfield had addressed the letter via Sihanouk two months earlier. As yet there had been no response from Beijing. For Mansfield's edification, Sihanouk described his recent interaction with China in detail, including his opposition to efforts by some Chinese to extend the ideology of the Cultural Revolution to Cambodian dissidents. When Sihanouk instructed his ambassador in Beijing to close his mission and withdraw, Chou had intervened to promise there would be no more interference in Cambodian affairs, which Sihanouk accepted. Cambodian relations with China had been "extremely cordial" before this recent discord, Sihanouk said. "Now they are just friendly but not too warm." Based on his knowledge of Beijing's attitudes, Sihanouk predicted that "unless the United States accepts the abandonment of Taiwan, friendship will not be restored between the U.S. and China."

His trip at an end, Mansfield stopped on the West Coast on his way home to brief Nixon privately for ninety minutes at the President's San Clemente, California, vacation compound on August 27. The Majority Leader handed Nixon a nineteen-page confidential report on his trip, full of concern about the absence of follow-through on the new policies of limited involvement in Asia that had been outlined at Guam. Persistent inquiries at U.S. embassies along the way "did not yield a single indication of anticipated change in current U.S. practices and programs," Mansfield reported. Still, he continued to express his faith in Nixon's "doctrine" of reduced U.S. involvement.

There was still no word from Beijing in response to Mansfield's request for a visa. Unknown to him and other outsiders, however, it was being given serious consideration by four Chinese marshals, all veteran military commanders, who had been assigned by Mao to study the People's Republic's foreign policy course. According to recently available documentation, they did not flatly reject the idea of using a Mansfield visit to begin an opening to the United States, but they advised that the time was not right for it and proposed to "let him wait for a while." However, Chou's response, dated August 24 and directed to Sihanouk, was unequivocal, although it did not mention Mansfield's name or the nature of his request:

I have received your letter of July 26.

In the relationship of China and the United States, the Nixon administration as well as previous American governments follows a policy of hostility to the Chinese people and occupying by force the province of Taiwan, which is the territory of China. It is the exclusive affair of the U.S. government that Chinese-U.S. relations are the way they are.

The people of China and Cambodia have a common struggle against colonialism, imperialism and neo-colonialism. Therefore I am sure you will understand the position above.

When Mansfield finally received Chou's letter via Phnom Penh, he sent Sihanouk a note of thanks for assisting his initiative.

While the response was not what I had hoped for, it was not unexpected. . . . However, in writing to the Chinese Premier I was persuaded that a point of beginning, a point of fresh contact, had to be found sooner or later if there was to be a peaceful solution respecting not only Taiwan but other issues between the United States and China. If it cannot be established at this time and in this fashion, I am hopeful that it will come in some other way and without too much delay. In any case, I am deeply grateful to you for your effort to be of assistance in this matter.

STICKING WITH NIXON

By the second half of 1969, Majority Leader Mansfield had come into his own as leader of the Democratic opposition to the Republican President. Citing his management of battles against the White House on the expansion of the Anti-Ballistic Missile program and on tax issues, John Finney of the *New York Times* observed that Mansfield, liberated from "the heavy L.B.J. hand" in the White House, "can finally be a leader in his own right and the role he is casting for himself is leader of the loyal but at times independent opposition." Finney added, "Mr. Mansfield is a loner, a man who strides between his front-row seat and his Senate office and seldom frequents the cloakroom for idle gossip. But at some point the Administration had better make his acquaintance if it wants some semblance of bipartisan cooperation over the next three and one-half years. The only difficulty is that Mr. Mansfield is enough of an Irishman to delight in his new role and he is incorruptible enough that the Administration probably has only one thing to 'buy him off'—namely peace in Vietnam."

As the majority leader who rides herd on the Senate, Mansfield "is sitting a lot taller in the saddle these days. The only question is whether he digs his spurs in hard enough," wrote Spencer Rich of the *Washington Post*. The crux of such criticism as there was revolved around Mansfield's "nonpartisan approach to most Senate business," Rich reported. A northern Democratic senator who did not wish to be identified told Rich, "We have not, in my judgment, really taken advantage of presenting a clear alternative to the inability of the administration to deal with current problems." A few senators, also unidentified, quarreled with Mansfield's accommodation with Nixon's Vietnam policy. Rich observed, "A long-time critic of the war—antedating many of those who are the most raucous now—Mansfield has repeatedly said in recent months that he believes the President is moving in the right direction and therefore he will refrain from sharp criticism on his Vietnam policies." However, despite criticism from a few, according to Rich, "a larger group believes he is doing an excellent job." Rich ended his report by quoting "a lobbyist, not altogether uncritical of Mansfield, [who] gave what is probably the best explanation for Mansfield's growing success and control: 'How can you dislike him? In a Senate where there are so many prima donnas, here is a guy who isn't and doesn't fake.'"

"By the usual standards of politics, Mansfield is as dynamic as a celery stick," wrote Saul Pett, the star feature writer of the Associated Press. "His clothes suggest an underpaid college professor of the '30s, which he was, and even when they aren't there actually, one imagines there are leather patches on his elbows. It took him years to get comfortable in the big black Cadillac that goes with the job of leader, frequently grumbling about being a 'limousine liberal.'" Pett quoted Minority Leader Hugh Scott, Mansfield's Republican counterpart and competitor after the death of Everett Dirksen, as saying that Mansfield was "the most decent man I've ever met in public life. . . . He's fair. His word rates in fineness above the gold at Fort Knox."

As he seemed to grow further in stature in the fall of 1969, Mansfield's anguish about the war in Vietnam continued. At one point he told colleagues he would "gladly give up his seat" in the Senate if it meant the solution of the war. He believed that Nixon was moving in the right direction but he was concerned that the movement was too slow. At the same time, he supported the right of antiwar groups to speak out against Nixon's policies and to demonstrate when they did so peacefully. When students returned to the campuses that fall, a nationwide antiwar ferment intensified, supported by many Democratic political figures who had remained silent while Lyndon Johnson was in the White House.

On October 15 massive rallies took place in cities and towns throughout the country in the largest numbers since the spring, under the title of a Vietnam Moratorium against the war: 100,000, mostly college students, heard McGovern speak in Boston; 20,000 gathered on Wall Street to hear former LBJ aide Bill Moyers; 30,000 listened in Washington to Coretta Scott King, the widow of the slain Martin Luther King Jr., before she led a candlelight procession that penetrated the darkness from the White House to the Washington Monument. Nearly everywhere the names of war dead from Vietnam were read in schools and churches amid the tolling of bells.

The event, almost completely without disorder or violence, touched nearly every community in what *Life* magazine called "the largest expression of public dissent ever seen in this country." The magazine's sister publication, *Time,* in a comment cited later by Kissinger, said the protests were "an unmistakable sign to Richard Nixon that he must do more to end the war and do it faster."

The administration's response was to announce that Nixon would address the nation on the war in two weeks and to encourage Republican congressional leaders to ask for a sixty-day halt to criticism in order to demonstrate to North Vietnam that American resolve was undiminished. Mansfield led the opposition to suspending dissent, telling the Senate, "I know of no basis for believing that the problem of Vietnam can be resolved now, any more than in the past, by a silence of acquiescence in the Senate or in the nation. . . . The Saigon officials will not be beguiled by silence. We will not confound Hanoi or confuse the N.L.F. by silence. . . . A silence in the Senate and in the nation will only add to our own bewilderment."

Mansfield continued to praise Nixon's reductions in U.S. forces, which had then reached 60,000 troops, and a shift of battlefield tactics that appeared to have brought about a lull in the fighting. On October 20, 1969, he told the Senate:

> I would like to see the country get behind President Nixon, not for the purpose of prolonging the war but for the purpose of bringing about a responsible settlement and a responsible peace at the earliest possible opportunity.
>
> I would like to see us encourage President Nixon in the efforts he has made in that direction.
>
> I would like to see him pull out our troops faster.
>
> I would like to see the war brought to an end sooner.
>
> I have made my position known on Vietnam for the past 6 years. But the President is the one at whose desk, in the words of Harry S Truman, "The buck stops." President Nixon is the one who will have to make the final decision. . . .
>
> I want to say, as a Democrat, that it would be my intention to support the President in every effort he would make toward a responsible and a peaceful departure from the quagmire in which we are caught, and I assure him that, so far as we are concerned, there will be no politics involved, because this is not a Republican responsibility, except that the President happens to be a

Republican. It is a responsibility which can be placed, if we go back far enough—and not too far—on the shoulders of Democrats and Republicans alike.

Mansfield's speech brought praise from editorialists such as those at the *Philadelphia Inquirer*, who called it an expression of "great wisdom as well as high statesmanship." But many liberal Democrats and peace advocates were dismayed. Mansfield received a personal letter from Tristram Coffin, a prominent Washington commentator who had been a longtime friend:

> I think, along with a lot of others, that you have, innocently, let yourself be used by Mr. Nixon in his game to discredit the peace movement. In fact, you have done more harm to dissent on Vietnam—hence to the process of democracy—than Vice President Agnew. This by seeming to endorse the President and his Plan at this very critical moment.
>
> This is surprising, because Mr. Nixon has not revealed his Plan, if indeed he has one, to anyone, not to you, not to George Aiken, not to Hubert Humphrey. My information is he has not yet made a final decision as to a number of proposals.
>
> I am sure you do not understand the impact of what was only a gesture of courtesy on your part. Protest, the only means of creating change, is rising along with the hopes of millions. Your apparent accepting of the President will mean more disillusion with democracy, more radicalization, and further destroy the faith of the young in the old.

Mansfield's expression of political support for Nixon's withdrawal policies was not mere Senate rhetoric. Amid the tumult of the antiwar demonstrations and widespread speculation about a Vietnam speech promised by Nixon in early November, Mansfield pursued an extraordinary secret initiative across party lines in an effort to influence the President. He first sought to persuade the Democratic Policy Committee to pass a resolution declaring that Democrats would not attack Nixon politically should he embark on major peace initiatives. When committee members balked at such a formal action, Mansfield proposed to call on the President secretly to transmit the message. On the afternoon of October 21, he convened the

Policy Committee to suggest that he tell Nixon orally and in strict confidence he would have "articulate public support" or, at the least, "no political criticism" from these senior Democrats should he take any or all of four dramatic steps to terminate the war rapidly: (1) a call for an immediate cease-fire; (2) accelerated troop reductions aimed at final withdrawal of all U.S. forces by the end of 1970; (3) U.S. disassociation from the Saigon government unless it moves toward an internal political settlement; and (4) direct U.S. negotiations with the National Liberation Front. These points, Mansfield said, represent his judgment of "what it will take to get our forces out of Vietnam without an insupportable delay in terms of the domestic urgencies of the nation."

In the discussion that followed, Richard Russell objected to naming an "arbitrary target date" for withdrawal, saying it would serve only to "harden Hanoi." Robert Byrd was fearful that cutting off the Saigon government and dealing with the NLF would subject Democrats to charges of betrayal and "selling out" to communists, as had happened after the fall of China. After nearly an hour, it was decided unanimously to approve a more general approach to Nixon "without pre-conditions or specific proposals" but stating "Democratic Policy Committee support for approaches leading to an end of U.S. involvement in the Vietnamese war."

The following morning, Mansfield telephoned the President and made an appointment to see him at 5 P.M. To make sure of his ground, Mansfield convened the committee again in the early afternoon to go over the points he would make orally to Nixon: that "the committee members are Americans before they are Democrats" and recognize Democratic as well as Republican responsibility for the evolution of the war; that if he moves toward its rapid termination, committee members would back him up with "such support and counsel as he may find useful and that they can, in good conscience, give him;" and that they will deal with him on this issue in strict confidence through Mansfield alone. His hope, the Majority Leader told his colleagues, was that the approach would be helpful "in dispelling the President's doubts about the political repercussions of his Vietnam policies." Once again, he called for absolute secrecy on this effort.

Mansfield went to the White House at 5 P.M. on October 22 to deliver the message. As he reported later to his senior Senate colleagues, he told Nixon that "we realize that the final responsibility was his, that his responsibility superseded ours but that we had a responsibility as well. We would hope to exercise it in the best interest of the nation *without* [Mansfield's emphasis] regard to political consequences and if he desires to make any moves which might engender criticism, we would do our best to protect his political flanks as far as the Democrats are concerned." The one area to which this assurance did not apply, he warned, would be a decision by the President to escalate the war. Mansfield noted Nixon's response as "friendly but guarded" in a memorandum for his files.

As Nixon's moment of decision approached, Mansfield decided to weigh in once more in his own voice, without the restraints of the consensus of other senior Democrats. On October 31 he sent Nixon a "private and confidential" memorandum declaring that "the continuance of the war in Viet Nam, in my judgment, endangers the future of this nation," not only because of the loss of life and waste of resources but most seriously because of the deep divisions to which "this conflict of dubious origin" had contributed within American society. Mansfield offered "my personal assurances . . . that, insofar as I am concerned, I will not criticize in any way, shape or form but, on the contrary, will give articulate public support" to presidential decisions to bring a rapid end to the war. Resurrecting the proposals he had taken to the Policy Committee ten days earlier, Mansfield suggested consolidation of U.S forces into enclaves, an immediate cease-fire in place, an accelerated program of troop reductions aimed at final U.S. withdrawal, pressure on the Saigon government to pursue new political policies, and negotiations with all Vietnamese parties, including the NLF. Such a settlement is not pleasant to contemplate, he wrote, "especially in view of the dug-in diplomatic and military positions which, unfortunately, were assumed over the past few years." Nevertheless, he continued, "we must ask ourselves not whether it is pleasant but, rather, what is the alternative? What shall we anticipate for this nation if the U.S. involvement in this conflict among Vietnamese is prolonged, even at a lower level of violence, for another four, five or more years."*

Mansfield's memo arrived as Nixon was in the midst of preparing his much-anticipated speech amid conflicting advice from Kissinger, his cabinet secretaries, the White House staff, political leaders, and the public. Mansfield had asked that Nixon read his memo before making any final decisions, and the

*The last U.S. troops left Vietnam three years and five months later, on March 29, 1973.

President took it with him to Camp David, where he spent a nearly sleepless night with pad and pen. Nixon considered that Mansfield's approach amounted to "a unilateral cease fire and withdrawal" from the war, which contradicted his own self-image and political instincts. Yet he also realized that with his memorandum Mansfield was offering "the last chance for me to end 'Johnson's and Kennedy's war,'" Nixon wrote in his memoirs. Without disclosing the secret Democratic initiative or Mansfield's private commitments, Nixon wrote that he interpreted Mansfield's words as "signals that he would even allow me to claim that I was making the best possible end of a bad war my Democratic predecessors had begun. I knew that the opponents of the war would irrevocably become my opponents if my speech took a hard line." In the end, Nixon wrote, "I could not escape the fact that I felt it would be wrong for me to end the Vietnam war on any terms I believed to be less than honorable."

In his November 3 address, one of the most important of his presidency, Nixon said he had adopted a plan for withdrawal of U.S. ground combat forces but refused to divulge the timetable. He unveiled several diplomatic initiatives with North Vietnam, including an exchange of correspondence with the recently deceased Ho Chi Minh, all of which had been unsuccessful. The main burden of the speech, however, was (as Nixon wrote in his memoirs) that "We were going to continue fighting until the Communists agreed to negotiate a fair and honorable peace or until the South Vietnamese were able to defend themselves." The high point was his combative call, in the face of antiwar protests, for "the great silent majority" of Americans to speak up in favor of his decisions. In highly emotional terms, he cast aspersions on the protesters, declaring, "North Vietnam cannot humiliate the United States. Only Americans can do that."

Those who had hoped for a reversal of U.S. policy were gravely disappointed. Fulbright called the speech "indistinguishable from Rusk and Johnson." Mansfield spoke up the day after the address, telling the Senate mildly that "there were no specifics" and that until they were provided "I am afraid the issue of Vietnam will remain as divisive as ever." He once again condemned the "cancerous and tragic war—in which we had no proper national purpose to become involved militarily in the first place." Asked by a radio interviewer about the "silent majority" that Nixon had cited, Mansfield responded, "We better think about the silent minority, about the dead and the wounded, about the casualties here at home, about the cost to this country and the need for us to face up to our own problems. . . . A lot of coffins have been coming back; a lot of hurt has been felt in the homes of the nation; a lot of problems have arisen out of this tragedy which is Vietnam; and I'm not very certain that there's a kind of majority which the President seems to think there is in this country. It could well be the opposite way."

Even so, Mansfield refrained from outright opposition, telling reporters that a "wait-and-see mood" had developed in the Senate following the speech. With Minority Leader Hugh Scott, he agreed to co-sponsor a Senate resolution endorsing Nixon's efforts to negotiate an end to the war, but he insisted that the measure be amended to call also for a mutual cease-fire. Nixon, seeking to keep his lines open to the Majority Leader, asked Mansfield to breakfast on November 13. When the President confided that he planned to visit the House of Representatives several hours later to thank lawmakers for their support, Mansfield invited him to be a guest for lunch in his office and then to speak in the Senate as well. The hastily arranged luncheon was attended by a bipartisan group of nine senators, including Mansfield's regular breakfast partner, Republican George Aiken of Vermont, Richard Russell, Ted Kennedy, and the Senate's only female member, Margaret Chase Smith of Maine. Fulbright and Scott joined the group after the meal. Nixon told the Senate that there were "dire predictions" when he took office that the nation would be divided on foreign affairs but that "I think the predictions have proved wrong."

In a statement to the Senate just before it adjourned for the year, Mansfield commended the President's efforts in Vietnam. "To be sure, peace has not been restored. Nevertheless, there have been changes for the better, the gears of war appear to have been reversed. We are moving out of, not into, the tragedy of Vietnam. The barbaric conflict is not expanding, it is contracting."

MANSFIELD REVERSES COURSE

The spring of 1970 was a time of testing for Americans on the war—especially for Mike Mansfield. Despite growing doubts, especially after the "silent majority" speech, he continued to back Nixon's direction if not all of his statements or actions in Indochina. Then, in the last days of April, Nixon sent 12,000 U.S. ground troops along with 8,000 ARVN troops into two

SENATOR MANSFIELD

Cambodian base areas that had been used by the North Vietnamese and Vietcong for many months. The invasion of Cambodia, which Nixon called an "incursion," touched off a firestorm of protest in the United States and dashed the remaining hopes of Mansfield and many others that the President was bent on progressively limiting and swiftly terminating the war. Until then, Mansfield had looked askance at congressional efforts to dictate war policy to the White House, accepting the view that executive branch authority was supreme in the case of ongoing military actions. But "Cambodia tore it," he said as he shifted his position. Beginning in the spring of 1970, he threw his full weight behind legislation that placed increasingly severe restrictions on prosecution of the war in Indochina and eventually forced U.S. withdrawal from the field—but not before many thousands more Americans were dead as a result of Nixon's policies. Overnight, Mansfield went from being a mere critic of the war to being one of the most powerful advocates of congressional coercion to bring it to an end.

Nixon's decision to invade Cambodia was precipitated by the overthrow of Norodom Sihanouk in March 1970 by General Lon Nol, the longtime Sihanouk aide whom Mansfield had seen as prime minister and minister of defense on his trip seven months earlier. The replacement of the neutralist Sihanouk by an avowedly anticommunist regime touched off new fighting in the Cambodian border area as North Vietnamese troops sought to expand their areas of operation and South Vietnamese forces sought to reduce or eliminate them. The U.S. command in Saigon and the Joint Chiefs of Staff in the Pentagon had recommended ground attacks against the Cambodian sanctuaries in 1967, but Lyndon Johnson had rejected the proposals. After the ouster of Sihanouk, the fighting in Cambodia had become fiercer despite the secret bombing in the border areas that Nixon had begun in March 1969.

Nixon was well aware that his decision to send U.S. and South Vietnamese troops into Cambodia would be bitterly opposed by Mansfield. Following the overthrow of Sihanouk, Mansfield had spoken repeatedly in the Senate to commend Nixon for staying out of Cambodia, which he called a Pandora's box. As Nixon was pondering his course, Mansfield had written the President on April 24 opposing any U.S. involvement, even the supply of U.S. arms or advisers to Lon Nol's government, citing his "long personal acquaintance with the Cambodian situation and many of its principals." In making his decision, Nixon had laboriously written down the pros and cons of the military operation and the political tactics involved on two sheets of yellow lined paper, including a scribbled instruction specifically directing his aides to withhold advance knowledge of the attack from Mansfield. As the moment for the announcement approached, Nixon instructed Kissinger and White House press secretary Ron Ziegler on ways to tailor their briefings to deal with adverse senatorial reactions, especially that of Mansfield.

On the evening of April 30 Nixon invited forty senior members of Congress to the White House to reveal that U.S. and South Vietnamese troops had moved into Cambodian territory and that he would announce this to the nation shortly. The President left the meeting to broadcast live to the nation from the Oval Office. Rogers and Laird, who had opposed the operation before it was ordered, were left in the White House theater to field the lawmakers' questions until the President delivered his speech, full of bravado and challenge. Nixon's chief of staff, H. R. Haldeman, recorded in his notes that Mansfield, Fulbright, Aiken, and Kennedy stood up and applauded when Nixon left the theater, a claim that Nixon repeated in his memoirs. Mansfield, however, recalled no such thing. When Nixon left the room, "I, of course, stood up with the others as a matter of courtesy and respect for the institution of the Presidency. I do not recall ever, under any circumstances, applauding," Mansfield told Gregory Olson.

Instead of minimizing the significance of the cross-border operation as some advisers had suggested, Nixon exaggerated it, dramatically declaring that "Tonight, American and South Vietnamese units will attack the headquarters of the entire communist military operation." (In fact, the forces found only deserted huts where a headquarters might once have been.) He announced that U.S. troops would not stay in Cambodia but would withdraw "once enemy forces are driven out of these sanctuaries and their military supplies are destroyed." Turning to a broader dimension, he declared that the United States would not act like "a pitiful, helpless giant" in the face of totalitarianism: "I would rather be a one-term president and do what I believe is right than to be a two-term president at the cost of seeing America become a second rate power and to see this nation accept the first defeat in its proud 190-year history." It was perhaps the most divisive speech of its time, with many Americans applauding Nixon's courage and decisiveness and many others passionately opposing the sudden expansion of a war they had hoped Nixon was ending.

Mansfield listened to the President's explanation and speech in silence sipping a cup of tea. After Nixon had left the Cabinet Room, "I just did a lot of thinking," he told Kenneth Scheibel of the *Billings Gazette*. Back at his house, he put pillows over the telephones to shut out calls from reporters, colleagues, and others while he tried to sort out his views in a sleepless night. Mansfield was in the habit of consulting Maureen, always his most important counselor, before taking any highly controversial or weighty action or making speeches of a crucial nature. This was no exception. With her assistance and advice he produced the makings of a speech and a position when morning came. Later in the day he gave a copy of the finished document to Maureen with his handwritten inscription atop the first page:

> To my darling wife Maureen
>   With love
>   Mike Mansfield

Beside his signature was a circle with "1X3" inside, a code in use among some couples of the period, including my own parents, to abbreviate "I love you." This is the only document I encountered among the 4,600 boxes of the Mansfield archive in Montana bearing such an inscription.

Shortly after noon on May 1, Mansfield rose in his front row seat in the Senate to speak with great forcefulness. The President, he said, "has exercised his responsibility, arrived at decisions after some days of consideration and, in announcing them to the American public, has laid his cards on the table." However, "we as individual senators and as a Senate, also have responsibilities to reach conclusions which may or may not coincide with the policy enunciated by the President of the United States. I must, therefore, as a senator from the state of Montana, and laying aside all political considerations, most respectfully disagree with the campaign into Cambodia . . . [which] can be regarded in no other light than as a widening of the war and an escalation of the conflict."

To oppose the incumbent President, Democrat or Republican, publicly on a matter of war and peace was a grave matter for Mansfield. He had never done so before in his role of majority leader. He told the Senate that Nixon had not made a decision on the basis of politics, nor is there politics in the Senate's reaction, "and insofar as I am concerned, there will not be."

Mansfield called for a revival of negotiations to neutralize Indochina, but otherwise did not outline a specific course of action.

Even as Mansfield was preparing his response to the invasion, campuses were erupting. The antiwar movement, which had been relatively dormant since the winter, came to life within hours of Nixon's speech as students and others became infuriated by what they saw as his startling reversal, from getting out of the war to expanding it. Hundreds of campuses joined the protests in strikes, marches, and other activities. In what was probably the most extensive antiwar action of the Vietnam era, more than 200 colleges closed, and students organized strikes in over 400 more. "It simply exploded with unprecedented force across the country, organized on each campus by whatever local activists there were," according to Fred Halsted, an antiwar organizer. The protests were propelled to ever-higher levels of passion by Nixon's spontaneous remarks the next day condemning "these bums, you know, blowing up the campuses" and by the tragic incident at Kent State University, where Ohio National Guard troops opened fire on protesters, killing four students. Public opinion polls showed that the nation was bitterly divided. Asked by pollster Lou Harris if they thought Nixon was right in ordering military operations in Cambodia, 50 percent of the respondents said "yes" but 43 percent said they had "serious doubts." At the epicenter of the debate, according to James Reston of the *New York Times*, the Cambodian decision was "dividing the capital of the United States as it has not been divided since the days of the late Senator Joseph R. McCarthy." Although many supported the invasion, groups of protesting students flooded into Washington. Letters arrived in huge numbers; mailbags were stacked in Senate corridors for want of a place to process them in senators' offices. Fulbright alone received 100,000 letters and telegrams in the first week.

Mansfield realized there was no possibility of successfully confronting a determined president on a partisan basis. He immediately sought to create a bipartisan rather than a partisan response. According to Valeo, he asked for and received instructions from the Democratic Conference to seek a meeting with Nixon for himself and his Republican counterpart, Hugh Scott, to ascertain where the President's Vietnam policy was headed, in or out. There is no record of a personal encounter of the two leaders with Nixon at that time, although Mansfield did attend a White House meeting of Nixon with the Senate and House Foreign Affairs Committees, convened in response to congressional requests, on May 5. The following day he and Scott, working together, addressed a joint letter calling for establishment of a high-level commission to investigate the unprecedented unrest on college campuses and the Kent State shooting in particular. (It was shortly done.) The day after that, May 7, Mansfield and Scott jointly asked Fulbright to give "the highest priority" in the Foreign Relations Committee to all measures related to Cambodia so they could be quickly moved toward full Senate action.

Over the following weekend Mansfield once again pondered what course he now should take. On Monday, May 11, he dictated a memorandum for his files that pointed him in new directions:

> I have reached the point in my thinking where, for the first time, I am giving the most serious consideration to a termination date after which no more funds will be appropriated for military operations in Indochina. This date should be set far enough ahead to avoid any perils in a precipitate withdrawal. It should reinforce an orderly and secure disengagement. It would reinforce the President's policy of ending the war. It would make it mandatory for the Thieu-Ky government to negotiate a political settlement in which all segments of the people of South Vietnam would be represented to be followed by an all-South Vietnam election to determine their own government and their own future.
>
> The American people feel let down, disappointed, concerned. They have appealed to the White House. They have appealed to the Congress. Their only hope, I think, is the Senate.

COOPER-CHURCH AND OTHER LIMITATIONS

Mansfield announced his backing for legislation to force the hand of the executive branch the following Sunday, May 17, on the CBS Television interview program *Face the Nation*. Less than a year earlier, he had opposed legislation setting a date for U.S. withdrawal, saying that it lacked flexibility. But now, he declared bluntly that he would back the Cooper-Church amendment (sponsored by Republican John Sherman Cooper and Democrat Frank Church) prohibiting U.S. military action in Cambodia after June 30, as well as the McGovern-Hatfield resolution (sponsored by Democrat George McGovern and Republican Mark Hatfield) requiring a halt to all U.S. combat activity in Vietnam by July 1, 1971. Mansfield became a prominent sponsor of these and other measures to end the war. The Majority Leader's turnabout provided greater impetus than ever before to antiwar legislation and was a significant factor in the domestic political battles over Indochina. The journalists on *Face the Nation,* knowing Mansfield's prior views, were startled by his position and his fierce determination.

When asked by moderator George Herman of CBS News why the Senate believed it had the right to interfere with the decisions of the commander-in-chief during a war, Mansfield responded, "I think we have a dual responsibility and the representatives of the people should and will be heard." Warren Weaver of the *New York Times* pointed out that the McGovern-Hatfield resolution laid out a timetable for withdrawal and asked if that could not be seen as an intrusion of the legislative branch into the rights of the executive branch. "I suppose it could be, and I went along with that thesis until Cambodia. But, as [far] as I was concerned, Cambodia tore it."

George Herman then asked: "Should the United States work to keep a stable pro-democratic or pro-western situation in Cambodia?" Mansfield responded, "No." Herman: "We should do nothing, if it goes Communist, for example?" Mansfield: "We should do nothing. Let the South Vietnamese handle it from their end; let the Thais handle it from the other, and let us not become involved, because all of Southeast Asia is not vital to the security of this Nation." When John Hart of CBS News interjected, "The Communists should be able to have all of Southeast Asia, if they want it," Mansfield showed just how far he had come from his early 1950s fear of a communist takeover. "That is up to the countries there to defend themselves," he replied. "We gave them plenty of help—Thailand, Laos, Vietnam. I don't know what more we could do. We have spent over $100 billion in that area. We have shed the blood of 325,000 Americans. Are we going to keep on going and going and going on?"

Mansfield's positions made headlines across the country the following morning. A delighted Prentiss Childs, co-producer of *Face the Nation,* wrote Mansfield that "I doubt that we have ever presented a better [interview]." He added, "You obviously were fired up more than ever for this one."

Not surprisingly, the reaction was very different in the White House. Nixon, at his Florida vacation spot at Key Biscayne as Mansfield spoke, told Haldeman the following day that "we now have to break it with Mansfield since he's really left the reservation on this whole deal." Two days later, still brooding about his political problems, Nixon reiterated to Haldeman his determination to "take on Mansfield, since he's now crossed us completely."

In the Senate, administration supporters decided to stall, which is easily done in that chamber, to prevent the Cooper-Church amendment from passing until June 30, the cutoff day for U.S. military involvement in Cambodia and the time when, according to Nixon's declarations, all American troops would be out of that country. Mansfield took a central role in the long debate, proposing cosmetic changes to win additional support for the amendment and leading the successful fight against changes that would have weakened the measure. From time to time he spoke clearly and strongly of the legislative power and responsibility in foreign policy that he previously had rejected. On June 9, at a crucial point in the debate, he declared:

Beyond military success or failure, the issue posed by Cooper-Church is fundamental. For too long, we have skated the thin ice of constitutional expediency in matters of war and peace. For too long, the Senate has shrouded its constitutional responsibilities in the skirts of Presidential authority. . . .

To be sure, the Senate's intentions have been of the best. For many years, we have seen our role in matters of war and peace largely as one of acquiescence in the acts of the executive branch. If we have had doubts, we have swallowed them. Since President Eisenhower's administration, at least, we have time and again deferred to the executive branch in international matters. The executive branch has presented us with decisions. We have gone along. We have rocked few boats. . . .

Six years of tragic aftermath to the Tonkin Gulf resolution flags the warning. We cannot consign the Senate's constitutional responsibilities in matters of war and peace. We cannot transfer them to the executive branch under this President or any other. We cannot take refuge from them without doing fundamental violence to the Constitution and endangering the stability of the Republic.

The Senate can work with a President within the constitutional framework in matters of war and peace. It can work with this President or another. But the Senate cannot and must not work for any President, regardless of party considerations, in matters of war and peace. It is not a question of supporting or opposing the President. It is a question of fulfilling our separate constitutional obligations.

On June 30 the Senate, after thirty-four days of debate and 288 speeches, passed the Cooper-Church amendment, 58 to 37. It was the first limitation ever voted on the president's powers as commander-in-chief during wartime. In retrospect, it was the tipping point in the 1970s between uncontested executive authority over war and the assertion of legislative authority. It was a moment of fundamental change for the Vietnam War and much else.

The amendment was initially defeated in the House, but it was passed by both houses in December and signed into law by Nixon in modified form that barred the introduction of U.S. ground troops into Laos or Thailand but, ironically, not into Cambodia, the invasion of which had given the major impetus for the measure. The Hatfield-McGovern resolution of 1970 and a similar measure the following year were defeated in the Senate in spite of Mansfield's support.

Despite his combative instincts and their political struggle over the war, Nixon found it impossible to "break it" (as he vowed to Haldeman) with the Majority Leader. On July 9 Nixon hosted another of their one-on-one breakfasts. A memorandum prepared for the meeting by William Timmons, a presidential aide, reported that "Mansfield was most concerned at not being informed in advance of Cambodian operations," which was a remarkably incomplete way of describing the depth of the Majority Leader's opposition. Timmons recommended that Nixon "indicate that the suddenness of the move into the sanctuary areas was in no way an indication of lack of trust in him—rather as Commander-in-Chief you had to take the harder, more difficult road in order to protect U.S. troops." Timmons might not have known that Nixon had gone out of his way to order that advance knowledge of the invasion be specifically withheld from Mansfield, or that Nixon had ordered that the time had come to "break it" with the Majority Leader.

CAMBODIAN AFTERMATH—ONE MAN'S STORY

John Bartlett, the son of a politically active Montanan from Whitefish, a small town near Glacier National Park and the Canadian border, was a U.S. Army helicopter pilot who flew into battle in Cambodia with the American attack force. After the massive protests at home, including the death of the student protesters at Kent State, Nixon halted the advance of Bartlett's unit twenty-one miles inside Cambodia and ordered it and all other U.S. troops to reverse course and depart the country by the end of June. "I was furious. I wrote a scathing letter to Senator Mansfield regarding political interference in my mission to destroy the enemy," Bartlett recalled. Two years later he left the Army for student life at the University of Montana. Three years after that, in 1975, he met Mansfield for the first time since his Army days in the receiving line of a Democratic Party dinner.

As he shook Mansfield's hand, introducing himself, the senator held his hand in a strong grip and looked squarely into his eyes.

"You're the helicopter pilot, right?"

"Yes, sir."

"You wrote me a letter."

"Yes, sir."

"Who was right, you or me?"

"You were, sir."

"I thought so."

With that, Mansfield released his grip and dropped the young man's hand, and Bartlett was dismissed.

THE ELECTION OF 1970

In November 1970 Mansfield went before the voters of Montana to ask for another six-year term in the Senate. He had been Senate Majority Leader for a decade and was renowned for his attentiveness to his Montana constituents, regardless of party affiliation. Reelection would have been an easy hurdle except for one thing: his advocacy and votes for gun control (see Chapter 10), a position that was highly unpopular among the many hunters and ranchers in the state.

The Republican candidate was Harold E. "Bud" Wallace, a former swimming coach at the University of Montana and a sporting goods salesman. He campaigned wearing a tan jacket with the stars and stripes prominently displayed on the front. Following a line of attack from earlier GOP campaigns, he charged that Mansfield was "soft on communism." His most potent weapon, though, was Mansfield's position on gun control, which, he charged, "made many people realize that Mr. Mansfield did not care about the people of Montana."

Ray Dockstader, a longtime Mansfield aide, reported to the senator after a two-week tour of the state in July that "generally the campaign looks good." He added, however, that the gun question "has been and will undoubtedly be a very loud, nasty issue promoted by a small group associated with the [John] Birch Society, ultra conservative groups, some gun clubs and Republicans interested in making it uncomfortable for the Senator. . . ." In mid-campaign, attack posters appeared sponsored by "Citizens against Mansfield":

WANTED
Mike Mansfield!!
Removed from the U.S. Senate
For violations of the second amendment in supporting gun registration and licensing—and—breaking his trust with the good citizens of Montana (picture of bullets) For the price of a box of ammunition we can retire Mike Mansfield to pasture

Mansfield's administrative assistant, Peggy DeMichele, who had spent most of her life in Montana before joining his congressional staff, began receiving threatening telephone calls in Billings from a gun dealer demanding to speak to the senator. DeMichele advised Mansfield to get out of town. Montana authorities became so concerned for his safety that a deputy sheriff was assigned to accompany him on the streets. Late in the campaign, Mansfield made a statewide television address to defend his position, declaring that his controversial vote had been "against guns in the hands of the drug addict, the felon, the fugitive." Wallace's only substantial asset, according to an Associated Press political analyst writing before the election, was the gun registration issue and "the support it has brought him from gun buffs."

In 1970 Mansfield was especially popular with young people because of his effective work in lowering the voting age from twenty-one to eighteen. In notes for his files two years earlier, he had written that "with the responsibilities which 18-year-old's now have in regard to marriage, contracts, the draft and so forth, it is ridiculous, with all these rights and obligations, they still have to wait three years, in most states, before they can exercise the most important function of all in a Democratic society." Mansfield had the opportunity to redress the omission in March 1970 when he led the way by attaching an amendment to lower the voting age to another pending measure. The

Senate and the House passed the voting provision for eighteen-year-olds and Nixon signed it into law. The Supreme Court upheld it in a 5 to 4 decision for federal elections only, but a constitutional amendment the following year lowered the voting age to eighteen for all elections.

Mansfield campaigned in 1970 in the folksy, low-key fashion of his typical visits from Washington, which had become short and increasingly rare as his Senate responsibilities increased. He would be driven from town to town and walk the streets, shaking hands and saying hello. He would stop in a favorite restaurant or hotel lobby, smoke his pipe, and converse with whoever turned up before moving on to another town. If pressed for time on a weekend trip, he would fly into Billings on a Friday night, have a Saturday-morning interview with the *Billings Gazette,* be driven to Great Falls and an interview with the *Great Falls Tribune,* then go on to Missoula and the *Missoulian.* On Sunday he would stop at newspaper offices in Butte and Helena before returning to Great Falls to fly back to Washington. There would be little or no warning that he was coming, but he would make front page news with a different national story in the leading paper of each of Montana's five largest cities.

Mansfield's unheralded weekend visits became legendary among the state's journalists. Charles S. Johnson, a veteran state capital reporter who was then a twenty-four-year-old rookie on the *Missoulian,* recalled being summoned to work on a Saturday in the early 1970s to interview Mansfield. When the fledgling journalist asked how the Vietnam peace talks in Paris were progressing, Mansfield asked to use a telephone and returned in a few minutes with authoritative word from Henry Kissinger. The reporter was stunned. Another journalist, Roger Clawson of the *Billings Gazette,* always kept a clip-on tie (unfortunately marred with gravy stains) in his desk drawer in case he was called to interview Mansfield. One weekend afternoon the senator telephoned Clawson from his room at the Northern Hotel and said "he had time to talk if I cared to listen." Hastily attaching his tie, Clawson hurried to the hotel to find Mansfield sitting in his suite, reading a newspaper in his underwear. "Skivvies, of course. Mike was a Navy man."

Fortunately for Mansfield, who lived off his Senate salary and a few paid speeches a year and who disliked raising political funds, running for office in Montana in 1970 required an incredibly small amount of money even by the standards of that day. Contributions to his primary campaign, when he faced only a minor opposition candidate, came to $7,465. His expenditures were reported to be $1,745, including the $425 filing fee and one round-trip air fare from Washington. General election contributions came to $96,745, of which he spent all but $368, but he sent $30,000 of it to the Democratic State Central Committee and amounts of up to $1,000 each to many Democratic county committees.

It is questionable whether Mansfield could have survived in the era of big money politics that has pervaded Montana and the nation since then. Democrat Max Baucus spent $3.7 million in his 1996 campaign for reelection to the Senate seat once held by Mansfield. In 2002 Baucus spent $6.1 million on his reelection drive. Even these are modest sums compared with the huge amount of money being spent for contemporary elections in more populous states.

If Mansfield's reelection in 1970 was ever in doubt, it was virtually guaranteed in the final weeks of the campaign when Nixon sent a U.S. Air Force jet to fly the Majority Leader to Washington to accompany him on Air Force One for a presidential address at the United Nations. With Mansfield and Senate Minority Leader Hugh Scott, who was also up for reelection, by his side, the President told a gathering at the U.S. Mission across the street from the UN that both senators would win their races and that "I'm endorsing them both." The White House promulgated the unlikely story that Nixon, always extremely conscious of the press, did not know reporters were present when he made his statement. Whether inadvertent or deliberate, Nixon's comments embarrassed Montana Republicans. Presidential press secretary Ron Ziegler sought to soften the blow by saying Nixon's remarks were merely "an expression of courtesy" to the Majority Leader. Three days later the President sent a telegram to Wallace announcing "my wholehearted support" for his campaign, but nobody believed it and the damage was done. On election day, Mansfield won 60 percent of the vote and carried all but six of Montana's fifty-six counties.

THE CLASH OVER TROOPS IN EUROPE

For fully a decade, since 1961, Mansfield had been almost a lone voice in the Senate advocating the reduction of U.S. troops in Europe, arguing that the increasingly prosperous European countries should bear most of the burden of their own defense instead of relying on Americans to protect them. Mansfield's leadership on this issue in 1966 had precipitated a battle with Lyndon Johnson, forcing the administration to announce a limited cutback in the European deployments (see Chapter 10).

On May 11, 1971, Mansfield rose in the Senate to propose a new troop-reduction measure that quickly brought on the most dramatic, intense, and highly publicized battle of his career against the massed forces of the executive branch. What was new, and very timely, was the method—a proposal to require a meat-axe cut of 50 percent in U.S. forces in Europe as a matter of law rather than as a "sense of the Senate" recommendation—and the moment—when the costs of the deployment and the economic policies of prosperous European nations were eroding the value of the dollar.

Although Mansfield had announced the previous December that he was planning to offer binding legislation to force U.S. troop cuts in Europe, its introduction on May 11 caught the administration by surprise. The shock was all the greater when vote counters from both parties reported that it was likely to pass the Senate easily, although its fate in the House was uncertain. Kissinger, in his memoirs, explained that Mansfield's amendment to the Selective Service bill then before the Senate was "a formidable challenge" because its author was not just any senator but "the Majority Leader, widely respected for his fairness, universally liked for his decency . . . one of that small band of patriots who have made our maddeningly delicate system of checks and balances actually work."

Kissinger went on in the memoir to state his often-expressed view that "at heart Mansfield was an isolationist, eager to reduce all American overseas commitments, reflecting the historical nostalgia that sought to maintain America's moral values uncontaminated by exposure to calculations of power and the petty quarrels of shortsighted foreigners." In addition to Mansfield's leadership and a balance-of-payments crisis, Kissinger wrote, the strong backing for the amendment "was symptomatic of the bitter and destructive mood of the period and of the substantial breakdown of national consensus."

Nixon and Kissinger decided to pull out all stops to combat the Mansfield amendment. At noon on May 12, Kissinger convened officials of the White House, State, Defense, and Treasury Departments in the White House Situation Room, traditionally the site of deliberations on international crises.

Taking personal charge despite Nixon's wish that Secretary of State Rogers lead the administration fight, Kissinger cast the battle in cosmic terms, saying that the amendment would "strike at our whole foreign policy without even consulting our allies and with no idea of where this might be taking us." Nixon was determined, he said, there would be no compromise, ruling out the softening amendments that were already being proposed by both friends and foes of the Mansfield measure.

By the end of the Situation Room session, the uncompromising administration strategy had been set: to organize senior officials of the administration, including the President, to lobby senators of both parties; to launch attacks on the amendment by prominent newspapers such as the *New York Times* and the *Washington Post;* to seek a statement from the West German government suggesting additional support for the U.S. troops; and to line up prestigious former officials, headed by former Secretary of State Dean Acheson and former Deputy Secretary of State George Ball, to conduct a high-profile campaign of opposition.

The following afternoon, Nixon played host in the Cabinet Room to eleven former high officials, including Acheson and Ball, Nicholas Katzenbach, Henry Cabot Lodge, John J. McCloy, and Cyrus Vance, and retired generals Lucius Clay, Andrew Goodpaster, Alfred Gruenther, Lyman Lemnitzer, and Lauris Norstad. Nixon said he had never asked them for support on Vietnam, where many disagreed, but that they had always been united on NATO. Referring to the title of Acheson's autobiography, the President said he too had been "present at the creation" of U.S. containment policy in Europe. All agreed to sign a statement of opposition to the Mansfield amendment and to solicit other prominent signers. Some agreed to lobby senators. The gathering was reminiscent of Lyndon Johnson's convening of the Wise Men, including some of the same prestigious former officials, at crucial moments in the Vietnam War. Kissinger and others called the 1971 gathering "the final meeting of the Old Guard." The former officials were soon joined in opposition to Mansfield's proposal by Johnson himself, who issued a statement at the suggestion of the Nixon White House.

Acheson, who had been attacked viciously by Nixon in the 1952 presidential campaign as proprietor of "Dean Acheson's Cowardly College of Communist Containment," was selected to speak to the press on the steps of Nixon's White House. It would be "asinine" and "sheer nonsense," he said, to reduce U.S. forces without a reciprocal cut in Soviet forces. His pungent remarks delighted those on the President's side but angered some of the senators weighing the arguments on Capitol Hill.

Mansfield took the hoopla with considerable calm and some amusement. At one point in the debate he told the Senate, "For the past week we have heard the wailing of Cassandra from downtown, uptown, on this floor and from overseas. We have read it in the press. We have heard it from the mouths of horses, so that we should be shaking in our boots, and we should be fearful that if we do anything, the foundations of NATO will not only be shaken, but, loosened, and finally will crumble." He did not importune any of his colleagues to vote for the measure, taking his accustomed stance that the Senate is made up of mature people who can make their own decisions. He also refused to endorse any of five compromise amendments; all were voted down by a coalition of senators who followed his wish for a record vote on the strongest possible version, and by administration supporters who believed that softening Mansfield's proposal would make it more difficult to defeat.

Had he wished to win the vote to force a mandatory cutback of U.S. forces, aides said, there were many ways to compromise. "A reduction of 25 percent rather than 50 percent in troops in Europe would have carried—and he knew it," according to James Lowenstein, the Foreign Relations Committee staff member who worked on the issue for Mansfield. Lowenstein's theory then and since is that "he didn't want it to carry; he wanted to hold it out there to give the executive branch a weapon [to bring about increased European efforts or American cutbacks] and to give himself a good talking point with the Europeans." In private conversation Mansfield referred to his efforts as "an educational exercise." Six months later, he said that had the amendment passed in May, "I would have fallen through the floor of the Senate because it was too much of a cut, too quickly, and too soon. The purpose was, after a decade of trying by way of a sense of the Senate resolution, to make a dent in the situation, to bring the matter to the attention of the administration downtown, to bring it to the attention of our allies, and to get away from ignoring it, as we so easily do in the country on subjects which are discomforting."

As it turned out, the coup de grâce for the Mansfield cutback of May 1971 and his subsequent efforts at unilateral reductions came not from the White House but from the Kremlin. On May 14, amidst the most intense phase of the lobbying campaign, Soviet leader Leonid Brezhnev declared his readiness to begin negotiations on mutual troop reductions in Europe. This powerful argument against unilateral U.S. cutbacks was "like manna from heaven" for administration supporters as well as senators who were uneasily backing Mansfield, Kissinger later wrote. The State Department quickly conferred with the Soviets about starting the negotiations, which became the long-running (and frustrating) talks on Mutual and Balanced Force Reductions (MBFR). These were eventually followed by the Conventional Forces in Europe (CFE) negotiations, which finally produced an East-West arms reduction treaty in 1990, nearly twenty years later.

Mansfield welcomed the Brezhnev statement and the Nixon administration's response, even though it was clear that it doomed his initiative. As the Senate prepared to call the roll on his proposal on the evening of May 19, he told the body:

Sometimes it takes a sledge hammer to make an imprint and place an issue on the table. I did raise this issue. I have been raising it for 11 years. . . . [R]egardless of the outcome of the vote tonight, it will not disappear. It will not return to the cobwebs where it has rested so peacefully for the past two decades and one year. . . .

What I have endeavored to do is to move from the past into the present and to look to the future. What I have tried to do is not to look over my shoulder in order to hang onto policies which were good two decades ago and think that despite the changing world, those policies are just as good and just as effective today.

When the roll was called, the Mansfield amendment was defeated 36 to 61. The following year Mansfield kept the initiative alive by proposing a 40 percent cut in U.S. forces in Europe, which narrowly passed the Senate before being reversed six hours later after renewed administration lobbying. Mansfield kept trying, but his cutbacks never again obtained a majority vote in the Senate.

DOUBLE-DEALING ON THE ROAD TO CHINA

The most important business between Mansfield and Nixon in 1971 arose from the determination by each of them to end the two decades of hostile separation between the United States and the People's Republic of China. When the Chinese moved to break the ice with stunning suddenness in April, Mansfield received an unexpected invitation to visit Beijing. Nixon encouraged him and promised strong support—until his own invitation suddenly arrived. Then he reversed field. Without Mansfield's knowledge, he secretly sought to postpone or even scuttle the Majority Leader's trip. Many of these maneuverings were secretly recorded in the extensive taping system that Nixon had had installed in February 1971 and that ultimately proved to be his undoing in the Watergate scandal.

Five microphones were built into Nixon's desk in the Oval Office, two more were placed in wall lamps on either side of the fireplace near a grouping of chairs and sofas where he often sat, two were placed in the Cabinet Room under the table near the President's chair, and four more were placed in his private office in the Executive Office Building. White House telephones were also wired, and later the recording was extended to the Lincoln Sitting Room in the family quarters and several locations at Camp David. Unlike Lyndon Johnson's secret taping system, most of these devices were voice-activated. They picked up virtually everything that was said. Some of this electronic lode was as mundane as the comments of cleaning personnel chatting with one another, but much was central to the workings of government. This was the case in Nixon's conversations with Henry Kissinger, who did not know of the taping system, as they grappled with the prospect that Mike Mansfield might visit the People's Republic of China before they were able to do so.

Despite Chou En-lai's rejection in August 1969 of his request sent through Norodom Sihanouk, Mansfield persisted in his desire to visit China and to play a role in U.S. rapprochement with the People's Republic. He repeatedly discussed the topic with Nixon in their private breakfasts. The President continued to encourage the Majority Leader in his quest, and early in 1970 told him that if he succeeded, he should be the first to go to China, and would go as the President's envoy. Mansfield said from the beginning, "No, you should. The President of the United States should be the first one." At the time, without telling Mansfield, Nixon was already making efforts of his own to contact the Chinese through a variety of diplomatic channels. In December 1970 Chou had proposed secretly through the Pakistanis that a U.S. "special envoy" come to Beijing for talks, but he appeared to limit the subject to be discussed to Taiwan. Nixon sent back a message proposing talks on issues broader than Taiwan. A similar exchange took place in January 1971 through the Romanians. There the high-level dialogue stopped.

The overthrow of Sihanouk and the U.S. invasion of Cambodia had generated Mansfield's legislative activism on the war. After his ouster, Sihanouk took refuge in Beijing, from which he directed a series of letters and appeals on his own behalf to Mansfield, his closest friend and most prominent supporter in the United States. The exiled Cambodian, who was in close contact with the Chinese leadership, did not forget his friend's 1969 bid to visit the People's Republic, but pursued it in the Chinese capital. On April 11, 1971, he addressed a letter to Mansfield:

> Mr. Senator:
>
> Two years ago you expressed a desire to meet the Prime Minister of the People's Republic of China.
>
> I have the honor to inform you that his excellency Prime Minister Chou En-lai is very willing to meet you in Peking along with Madame Mansfield.
>
> You are free to choose the date at your convenience.
>
> I am happy to have carried out an affair that you gave me the honor of undertaking regarding China two years ago.

Mansfield received the message with great anticipation. Rather than making a public statement or proceeding on his own to accept the invitation, he immediately informed the White House. Nixon sent word back through Kissinger that he appreciated Mansfield's confidential handling of the message, and he arranged a meeting for the following day.

In discussion among themselves, Nixon and Kissinger were wary of involvement with Sihanouk, a deposed leader for whom they had little regard. Going through Sihanouk is "a lousy way," said Kissinger. "I think [a China visit] should be under our auspices across the board rather than Sihanouk's auspices. . . . Sihanouk, I think would be a bad—the wrong auspices," Nixon agreed.

Yet, when Mansfield arrived at the Oval Office a little after 11 A.M. on April 17, a Saturday, Nixon raised no objection to pursuing Sihanouk's invitation. "In the line of our China policy, a direct visit to China would be in our interest," Nixon said. He urged Mansfield to keep the invitation confidential for fear that publicity might cause the Chinese to turn down the visit, leaving the impression that U.S. contacts with the People's Republic were cooling. His problem, Nixon said, was that "we're nurturing a very fragile flower" in the overall initiative toward China.

Kissinger, seeking to steer the invitation into a channel that he and Nixon could control, told Mansfield it would be "ideal" for the White House to dispatch his response to China via Romania. The President confided that following his trip to Romania in 1969, Romanian leader Nicholae Ceausescu had traveled to Beijing and talked to Chou on his behalf. Kissinger volunteered to ask the Romanian ambassador to pass the word to China of Nixon's support for a visit from "the opposition, the Senate Majority Leader." The President agreed, "Mike is the best man to go. It's ideal because he's—first, he's in the other party than the President. He's not only interested in Asia. He has, he keeps his mouth shut, you know. He will be highly responsible. [To Mansfield] You are the perfect man to go."

Mansfield had brought with him a letter to Nixon, which said in part, "Unless you think some other approach more desirable, I would make clear . . . that while you are aware of my intentions to seek the talks, I ask for them in my individual capacity as a senator and Majority Leader of the Senate. That approach would give the visit a status neither as unofficial as that of say, a U.S. journalist nor as official as that of a presidential representative. If need be, either side could back off gracefully from its consequences." He added verbally to Nixon, "That would protect you in case there was any bad reaction."

"As far as I'm concerned, I approve it completely," Nixon said. "I think it's an excellent idea. So, there's no concern about that because you're going over there to talk and see what's going on. Let me ask Henry, what does this do, uh, what does this do in terms of the other matter, the Russians?"

Kissinger: "Well if we send the senator as an official emissary—"

Nixon: "Then that sticks it to the Russians."

Kissinger: "That would be really tough medicine."

Nixon: "You see, Mike, let me say . . . well, the Russians, naturally, are watching this. . . . I don't want to do something which is a direct kick at the Russians. Where they could then say, well, it's SALT [the Strategic Arms talks], the Mideast and the rest. They're going to cool off. See we want to play poker, that's the game we're playing."

Three days earlier, shortly before Mansfield received Sihanouk's letter, the White House had taken the latest in a series of small unilateral steps to diminish official U.S. hostility toward Beijing, in this case a partial lifting of the U.S. embargo on trade, relaxing currency restrictions, and agreeing to expedite visas for Chinese wishing to visit the United States. Knowing his interest, Kissinger had called Mansfield to advise him of these actions. The Majority Leader responded that Nixon was making "a historic contribution" and told Kissinger, "Whatever our differences, I'm with him 100 percent." Showing that he meant it, Mansfield had praised Nixon for these actions in a Senate speech the following day.

In their Oval Office discussion, Nixon confided to Mansfield that the recent moves had been only the first step, a "pretty little package," with two more "packages" on trade already planned for coming months. He was determined, the President said, not to appear overanxious, thus courting a Chinese rebuff, but to proceed cautiously. "Our long-range goal is normalization of relations with China but that will come over a period of time, so I'm not going to cross those bridges yet."

Mansfield expressed concern that one of the perhaps dozen other members of Congress who had made requests to China for visits might be chosen to make the trip ahead of him. "I would hope that [the Chinese] would take yours and, frankly, not the others," Nixon said. "I would rather have them take one responsible man." Otherwise you would have "a lot of . . . unsophisticated congressmen and senators running around over there, Mike. That isn't going to help. . . . They'll come back, write books, make speeches and all that. You will go . . . you'll come back, you'll give us your report, you'll make your own statement or whatever you want to do. I just don't like amateurs getting involved in this business."

Earlier in the conversation Mansfield proposed to send a telegram of acceptance direct to Chou En-lai, and permit the White House to work through Ceausescu at the same time. "If we get it, fine; if we don't, well, we tried."

Although not overtly opposing this, Kissinger continued to suggest that the White House should utilize the Romanian channel on Mansfield's behalf. The Romanians would be told, he proposed, that "from the point of view of advancing relations, the senator would be the best member of the legislative branch."

"Good, we'll say that," Nixon responded.

Before the conversation ended, the President, perhaps not entirely in jest, suggested that he and Mansfield should trade places. He didn't want Mansfield's job, he said, but he would be interested in the journey to Beijing that seemed to be in prospect. "There's nothing I'd rather do than go to China," Nixon said, not knowing that the possibility would soon arise.

Mansfield, true to form, told Nixon that "I wouldn't take your job under *any* circumstances," and repeated the statement.

"Good luck," said Nixon as Mansfield prepared to depart after the twenty-two-minute conversation. Then, in a reference to the recent and surprising Chinese overture to the United States of inviting an American table tennis team to visit, the President added, "Take the Ping-Pong table." Mansfield laughed as he departed.

Within hours, after a break for lunch, Nixon quickly began backing away from the idea that the scholarly majority leader—or any Democrat—might be the first prominent official to visit the People's Republic. The Democrats want to "be part of breaking the ice with China," Nixon complained to Kissinger and Haldeman. "Enormous, it's an enormous story. . . . And they didn't have anything to do with the goddamned event, not one goddamned thing."

Haldeman asked, "Do we have to let Mike be the guy to go?" Nixon responded it was probably inevitable under the circumstances, suggesting craftily that "we should cooperate so that it looks like our move rather than that he did it on his own."

Seemingly resigned to having Mansfield go first, Haldeman suggested that Senate Minority Leader Hugh Scott, a collector of Chinese pottery, be added to the Mansfield delegation to "bipartisan it." Nixon thought this a good idea but cautioned that "it's got to be handled very subtly" lest Mansfield think the White House was trifling with him. The Majority Leader would be "the first person of consequence" to visit China, he said. "He has been very tempered, considering. You know, considering the fact that he totally opposes our war, Henry, and has always opposed it and has never been for it, he's been pretty good, right?"

"Oh, yes indeed," Kissinger responded.

The more they thought about it, the more Haldeman and Kissinger expressed caution about bringing Scott into the mission. The President considered Mansfield "responsible" but Scott to be "untrustworthy," and Haldeman considered Scott "slimy" and "totally unprincipled." Kissinger added, "Scott leaks, as we know, like a sieve." Nonetheless, Kissinger won Nixon's approval to ask the Romanian ambassador, Corneliu Bogdan, to send word to the Chinese leaders that if they want to have "serious, measured progress" they should expand the invitation to also invite Scott, "who is an expert in Chinese art and who we know would be happy to go." Kissinger said, "I'll also tell Bogdan . . . that if they start playing around with [presidential] candidates, this thing will become a political football and they'll never get anywhere." At that point, Nixon brought up his worst fear: that "what's next after Mansfield [would be] Muskie, Ted Kennedy, Humphrey"—his potential opponents in the 1972 race—who would share the glory.

An advantage of the senatorial trip, Kissinger interjected, is that it "would really drive the Russians up the wall." As he mused about the development, Kissinger said he had previously thought a China breakthrough might come in Nixon's second term but now "I don't absolutely exclude that it could happen next year," the presidential election year of 1972. Nevertheless, he told Nixon, "We shouldn't even begin to think about it yet. It's a little premature."

Kissinger's concern about Scott's willingness to keep secrets was not misplaced. Covering the Nixon White House as well as writing a weekly op-ed column for the *Post* on the presidency, I kept in touch with the Minority Leader as a good source of information. In remarkably few days after the April 17 meeting, Scott told me confidentially that something big regarding China was being discussed at the White House, although he said he did not know exactly what. I immediately requested and obtained a meeting with Kissinger, who briefed me on a long list of small steps toward Beijing that had been taken since Nixon came to office. Although ignorant of the Chinese decision to invite Mansfield and of the White House wish to add Scott, I devoted my op-ed column of April 23 (as the headline announced) to "Nixon's Swing on China." Reciting the record of Nixon's change in direction since his condemnation in the 1950s of "appeasers" in the U.S. government who "lost" China, I wrote that "the emerging turn in China policy may prove to be one of his historic moves as President."

Although they did not know the origin of my interest, Nixon and Kissinger were pleased with the column, according to their private comments recorded on a White House tape. The President, who was forever gauging the impact of press reporting, tempered Kissinger's enthusiasm.

"That's just one article," Nixon said. "If it's not television, it's gone . . . that's what really matters in terms of the public thing."

After speaking to Nixon and Kissinger, Mansfield decided to move ahead promptly. He discovered he could not send a cable to Chou En-lai from the United States, so he took a letter to the U.S. Post Office and sent it as registered mail to Chou in China. To his irritation, it came back to him seven days later marked "Return to Sender" with the notation, "No Registry Service to This Country." With approval from Nixon and Kissinger, he dispatched the letter again via the French Embassy for delivery to Sihanouk in Beijing and through him to Chou.

The more Nixon and Kissinger thought about Mansfield's invitation to China, the more it irked them. "We don't want any senators over there, by God. . . . It's not to our advantage to have Mansfield or anybody else go. We want our own representative to go. This has got to be our initiative," Nixon told Kissinger on April 20.

On April 23, in another conversation, the President's partisanship emerged again. "The problem is . . . I kind of hate to see, I just don't want to see Mansfield be the first American to be invited." He then asked Kissinger, "what about having . . . the first man going to China, the public man, being Mansfield? Doesn't that bother you?"

Kissinger responded, "Well, it bothers me. It bothers me." He proposed sending a message to the Chinese through the Romanians that "this is a very delicate place and time in our relationship, and the official contacts, we strongly recommend, would be with the government. I won't even mention Mansfield."

Nixon reiterated: "I just hate to see Mansfield go over because Mansfield, by the time we get reports back, it's through State [which Nixon mistrusts] and everything else. You see, we've got to have this directly under us. We've got to control this situation with the Chinese." On the other hand, the President said cautiously, "We can't indicate that we're blocking Mansfield's visit. . . . 'We believe that political visits should require a bipartisan basis.' Why don't you put it that way?"

Kissinger responded: "Yeah, but I'll make clear to Bogdan that we really don't want any political visits." The national security adviser recalled what he had been able to accomplish in January by making a "delicate request" to Soviet leaders through Ambassador Anatoly Dobrynin in Washington that they make no proposals on international issues to Senator Edmund Muskie, at that stage the most likely Democratic opponent of Nixon in the 1972 presidential race, who was soon to visit Moscow. As it turned out, Muskie had meetings in the Soviet capital with Alexei Kosygin, chairman of the Council of Ministers, and with Foreign Minister Andrei Gromyko but was not able to see the top official, General Secretary Leonid Brezhnev, and heard little beyond the standard Soviet line. "If [Mansfield] goes, we may be able to set it up as we did with Muskie," Kissinger remarked. "After all, it's obvious now that they didn't tell Muskie a damn thing but they did play our game. They saw him for a long time but he got absolutely no mileage out of it."

Nixon was more attuned to the public impact of the race to China than was his foreign policy aide. Remembering the most exciting event of his first year in office, the landing of American astronauts on another mysterious and fabled place, Nixon observed that if Mansfield or anybody went to China, it would be "an enormous story. It's like going to the moon. It really is. . . . Goddamnit, there's no reason to screw around on this thing. We're playing for very big stakes now."

Summing up what had been decided, Haldeman wrote in his notes for April 23 that Nixon "feels we've got to control this [Mansfield's invitation to China], and so K's [Kissinger's] going to try to make contact via Romania and get the invitation cut off, even though we have to appear tonight to be endorsing it."

Unknown to Nixon and Kissinger, while they were fretting over the invitation to Mansfield, Chinese leaders were making a new—and bold—bid for direct talks with the top-level of the U.S. administration. On April 21 Chou En-lai had dispatched a handwritten message to Nixon via Pakistani President Yahya Khan, still another intermediary who had been employed by the White House. Chou insisted that for Sino-American relations to be "restored fundamentally," the United States must withdraw its forces from Taiwan and the Taiwan Strait. But to find a solution to the issue, Chou proposed "direct discussions between high level responsible persons of the two countries" in Beijing. This time he pointedly did not limit the discussions to Taiwan as he had in earlier exchanges. And this time he was more specific about the American interlocutor, who could be a "special envoy" of Nixon, "for instance, Mr. Kissinger," the U.S. Secretary of State, or even the

President himself. Chou proposed that arrangements be made through Pakistan. The letter had arrived in Pakistan on April 23 and had been sent by courier to Washington, which took several more days.

Chou's message arrived at Kissinger's office via Pakistani ambassador Aghi Hilaly shortly after 6 P.M. on April 27. Kissinger immediately took it to Nixon in the Lincoln Sitting Room of the presidential residence. Almost immediately the two began to discuss who should be the emissary to Beijing. Initially they thought of David K. E. Bruce, a veteran diplomat who had served as ambassador to London under Presidents Kennedy and Johnson and since July 1970 had been chief of the U.S. delegation to the Vietnam peace talks in Paris. He was ruled out because his involvement in the Vietnam talks might put off the Chinese. Henry Cabot Lodge was briefly considered but also rejected as too closely associated with the Vietnam problem. When Nixon raised the name of Secretary of State Rogers, Kissinger opposed the idea and he was dropped from consideration.

A little later, Nixon telephoned Kissinger with more suggestions: Nelson Rockefeller, Kissinger's former boss and sponsor, whom the Chinese would consider "important" and who would absolutely "do in" the liberals in the United States? Kissinger's first impression: "He wouldn't be disciplined enough." Later in the conversation he conceded that to the Chinese "a Rockefeller is a tremendous thing" and opined that "I think Nelson might be able to do it," particularly if accompanied by Kissinger's senior deputy, Alexander Haig.

Nixon then suggested George H. W. Bush, at the time U.S. ambassador to the United Nations. Kissinger: "Absolutely not, he is too soft and not sophisticated enough." Nixon: "I thought of that myself." Later in the conversation, Kissinger described Bush as "too weak," and Nixon agreed but said he was "trying to think of anybody with a title."

If Thomas E. Dewey, the former New York governor and unsuccessful GOP presidential candidate in 1944 and 1948, were alive, Nixon suggested, "he could do it." Kissinger said he thought "Nelson [Rockefeller] actually would be a little better." And besides, Nixon chimed in helpfully, "Dewey's not alive." (He had died the previous month.)

Nixon and Kissinger were keeping the new breakthrough secret from the State Department and, indeed, from everyone except a few of their closest White House associates. Yet, as demonstrated by the tape recordings of their discussions, their elation and their expectations were soaring. At one point in their conversation of the evening of April 27, Kissinger said he had never given their carefully nurtured China connection more than a one-in-three chance of coming to fruition, but now, "if we get this thing working, we'll end [the] Vietnam [War] this year."

There was still one nagging question: what to do about the invitation to Mansfield? "We've got to get the Mansfield thing turned off somehow," Nixon insisted. "I don't know how we can do it, but one way we could do it would be to—if we get this game going, is to, you could invite him to go along."

Kissinger: "No. Why give this to him?"

Nixon: "I know, I know."

Kissinger: "Take him along with you when you go—"

Nixon: "That's what I mean."

Kissinger: "Oh, but not when your emissary goes."

Nixon: "Oh Christ, no, no, no. That is, invite him and maybe Scott, see. See my point?"

Kissinger: "If you want to share it with the Democrats—"

Nixon: "You know the meaning of share—it doesn't mean a thing. The Chinese will treat them very well but they'll know where the power is. We know that."

The President continued to be worried, though, that the Chinese leaders could schedule a visit by Mansfield before receiving a formal reply from the White House of its plans for dispatching an emissary to prepare an eventual presidential visit. It was estimated (and did) take two weeks to make these preparations. Nixon suggested that Kissinger inform Beijing through the Pakistani channel that pending the formal reply, "other visits by political people, by representatives of this government or the Congress and so forth should be held in abeyance." Kissinger sent this message the following morning through Hilaly, the Pakistani ambassador but requested that Yahya Khan, the Pakistani president, describe it as his own "personal assessment" rather than a White House request. This was done.

By the evening of April 28, the issue of a Mansfield visit was still unsettled, but Nixon was moving closer to deciding to send Kissinger rather than anyone else as his emissary to China and to make the first contact secretly.

The possibility of sending Nelson Rockefeller was raised again by Kissinger, but Nixon was unenthusiastic: "Goddamnit, he's got money but he's an amateur. Jesus Christ, I could wrap Rockefeller around my finger. He's fine, he's tough but if he didn't have that billion dollars. . . . The point is, he doesn't have the subtlety. He's the kind of guy also who wants to make a quick shot, dramatic, you know, let's do something bold but goddamnit, we don't want something bold. You can do it."

Kissinger was not shy in accepting the task. He told Nixon, "I don't want to toot my own horn but I happen to be the only one who knows all the negotiations."

"Believe me, it's a bigger bang for you to go than Rockefeller," Nixon observed. "Jesus Christ. I mean sure, it's a lot of cosmetics but [the Chinese] know where the power is."

The best idea, Nixon decided, was for Kissinger to engage the Chinese as his emissary to arrange the agenda and other details for a presidential visit. "It keeps Rockefeller out of it, keeps Bruce out of the middle and I don't have to tell the State Department anything and I think that's the way it ought to be handled," he said.

What were the Chinese hoping to achieve from this breakthrough in the first place? "Scaring the Russians, that's got to be it," Nixon concluded. For his side, he had great hopes that a China connection would open the way to end the Vietnam War on U.S. terms. "Let me say that before I get there, the war has to be pretty well settled. . . . The fact must be known in the United States that the war is settled. I won't come to China before that," Nixon declared, although he soon would change his mind. He noted, however, that none of the Chinese messages had even mentioned Vietnam. As it turned out, there would be much discussion of Vietnam in the Kissinger and Nixon trips to China but no resolution of the issues.

Even though Kissinger had initiated a request that Beijing refrain from inviting any prominent U.S. political figures in the immediate future, Nixon was still worried that "we may have a slight problem on our hands. They may take Mansfield and all those other clowns." Kissinger agreed that the Beijing leaders "may take him and give him a tour of China."

That possibility "doesn't seem to bother" Kissinger, Haldeman pointed out in a discussion with Nixon in the late afternoon. "Yes, who the hell cares?" Nixon responded. Alexander Butterfield, Haldeman's deputy (and the person who later revealed the existence of the Nixon taping system), observed, however, that "if any political figure goes in there [to China], it doesn't matter if he doesn't see anybody, just walking in the gates" would be an enormous story. Nixon agreed.

Following these discussions in April 1971, little or nothing more was said on the subject between the President and the Majority Leader, despite the fact that they had another of their private breakfasts on June 23, as Kissinger was making his final preparations for his historic mission. On July 9, feigning a stomachache in Pakistan during a lengthy overseas trip, the national security adviser flew in a Pakistani airliner to Beijing, where he met Chou En-lai and worked out the arrangements for Nixon's forthcoming visit. On July 15 Nixon announced the Kissinger trip and unveiled the dramatic new relationship with China in a sensational seven-minute broadcast to the nation from Los Angeles, near the President's vacation home in San Clemente.

Mansfield was given no advance notice of the developments or the announcement, but he approved of both the Kissinger trip and the secrecy that surrounded it. He never spoke a word of criticism to me or, as far as I have been able to determine, to anyone else about Nixon's dissembling and double-dealing on the China visits.

On July 19, Nixon's first day back in Washington after Kissinger's trip to China, he met Mansfield privately for fifty-two minutes over breakfast, accompanied by Kissinger and Rogers, before briefing the rest of the Senate and House leadership. As was often the case, the Majority Leader was the last to speak among the congressional leaders who were gathered in the Cabinet Room. Turning to Nixon, who was sitting on his immediate left, Mansfield summed up, "On our side, Mr. President, you're walking on eggshells. On the other side, Chou is walking on eggshells. Anything we in Congress say may jeopardize further talks. We're moving out of an old era and into a new one. This will take a great deal of understanding. . . . We've taken a long step; the PRC has taken a long step. I'm hopeful that the prospects for world peace will be enhanced."

VIETNAM, CHINA, WATERGATE, AND BEYOND

12

The early 1970s was a time for the culmination of things:

- The long war in Indochina flared fiercely toward its end. A final deal negotiated in Paris brought the withdrawal of all U.S. troops and the return of American prisoners of war. The agreement permitted North Vietnamese troops in the South to remain in their positions, from which they rolled into Saigon two years later as the last Americans executed an ignominious evacuation from the roof of the U.S. Embassy.
- President Nixon made his historic opening to the People's Republic of China in a dramatic and highly publicized visit to Beijing. Mansfield was not far behind in the first of three visits to China in a period of five years.
- Nixon won reelection by a landslide in the 1972 presidential election, but he later was ensnared in the botched illegal break-in at Democratic National Committee headquarters at the Watergate office building. A secret tape-recording system he had authorized finally established his guilt in seeking to cover up the crime. Nixon was forced to resign the presi-

dency, giving way to the two-year administration of the former House Minority Leader Gerald Ford.

Mansfield played important roles in all these episodes, opposing the war, pursuing the dialogue with China, and establishing the Senate inquiry that uncovered Nixon's abuses. In 1977 Mansfield retired from the Senate, ending the sixteen years of his leadership, the longest such tenure in American history and one of the most eventful.

In March 1971 *National Journal,* a respected independent publication focusing on official Washington, published a fourteen-page report on the leadership of Mike Mansfield after a decade as Senate majority leader. The first paragraph and central message of correspondent Andrew J. Glass was that Mansfield had presided over "a quiet revolution in the Senate." His fundamental reform, the article reported, was to resuscitate little-known and little-used institutions, especially the Senate Democratic Policy Committee and the Democratic Conference, or caucus, to bring both greater democracy and a voice with collective authority to the majority party. The Policy Committee, which was established by law in 1947, was little more than a coffee klatch under most of Mansfield's predecessors and had declined into virtual disuse under the one-man rule of Lyndon Johnson. The Texan had diminished the previously unchallenged powers of the barons of the Senate, the seniority-enshrined committee chairmen, but had not created workable leadership structures that would survive him.

When Johnson moved on to the executive branch as vice president and then president, Mansfield and his colleagues subordinated their collective voice on most issues to that of the Democratic President. From the beginning of the Nixon era, however, the fourteen-member Policy Committee, composed of an ideologically and geographically diverse group, had come to life, debating and deciding on seventeen policy positions, ranging from tax and economic issues to foreign affairs questions and issues regarding Senate rules. The policy positions were not binding and were subject to reconsideration by the Democratic Conference, the caucus of all Senate Democrats, but they were regarded on all sides as influential. It was also agreed, on the basis of a reform committee named by Mansfield, that the

Conference could vote by secret ballot at the beginning of each Congress to approve or disapprove the appointees to committee chairmanships.

Philip Hart, the respected liberal senator from Michigan, told *National Journal,* "We've shifted our way of doing things in a bloodless coup, and outsiders have hardly noticed." Another veteran Democratic senator, who spoke without attribution, ascribed the changes to "Mansfield's uncanny ability to take really precedent-smashing moves without appearing in the least to threaten entrenched interests." Mansfield himself told *National Journal,* "One reason I'm Leader is maybe I can keep the party together and prevent us from breaking up into argumentative fragments." Ironically, his comment was published less than two weeks after the most divisive stand that the Policy Committee had ever taken, one that led to an impassioned debate when taken to the Democratic Conference. According to *National Journal,* it was the first time in the history of the caucus that a leadership initiative had split party ranks.

The subject was the war in Indochina. From early in the Nixon era, the majority of Senate Democrats had concluded that the Republican President was bent on continuing the war, not ending it, even while slowly withdrawing American ground troops. Even Mansfield, who had given Nixon the benefit of the doubt much longer than most of his colleagues, had become an outspoken opponent of the President's war policies after the invasion of Cambodia in April 1970.

In February 1971 a new challenge had arisen to test the mettle of the senatorial opponents of the war. Nixon, seeking to forestall an expected communist offensive in Vietnam, decided on a major attack on North Vietnamese supply lines in neighboring Laos. Once again the war seemed to be spreading geographically even as the number of American troops engaged was slowly diminishing. The problem for Nixon was that the final version of the Cooper-Church amendment the previous year had barred the introduction of U.S. ground troops into Laos. In light of this prohibition, the U.S. Command in Saigon arranged for South Vietnamese forces to do the job, backed by U.S. air power. North Vietnam threw five divisions into the fight, producing heavy casualties and a disorderly rout of the untested South Vietnamese, who fled along roads littered with corpses and ruined vehicles or sought to escape by dangling desperately from the skids of U.S. medical evacuation helicopters.

On February 22, with the fighting in Laos under way, Mansfield took the issue of the war to the Democratic Policy Committee, which agreed 6 to 1 on a "Resolution of Purpose" calling for "an end to the involvement in Indochina and a withdrawal of all U.S. forces from that tragic conflict and a release of the prisoners of war by a time certain." The following morning, Mansfield convened the Democratic caucus to consider the proposal. The frank but intense discussion of nearly two hours, all behind closed doors in a Senate conference room, revealed the deep fissures among Democrats about their posture on the war.

The first to object to the Indochina provision—on grounds that it should have been considered by legislative committees first—was Henry "Scoop" Jackson of Washington, a strong supporter of military action abroad. He was followed by John Stennis of Mississippi, chairman of the Armed Services Committee, who bluntly and passionately objected to the proposal to call for total U.S. withdrawal by a fixed date. "What better message can we give to the enemy? He can just wait us out." He added, "If you pass this, how do we send a man into battle? Are you going to tell him we have already thrown in the towel? . . . I think we are making a terrible mistake. It will boomerang on us. I won't be a party to running up the flag of surrender, then sending our boys to fight. I ask that this matter be deferred."

In response Mansfield stated his strong belief, which until then he had usually spoken only in private, that "in my opinion, they are going to wait us out anyway." Increasingly certain that the war was doomed, Mansfield had become convinced that the only acceptable U.S. course was to get out as quickly as possible with as little additional carnage as possible. "As far as the flag is concerned," he told Stennis, "I don't doubt the patriotism of any member of the United States Senate."

Mansfield, referring to the updated casualty figures he carried every day on a card in his breast pocket, told the caucus that as of February 13, 53,479 Americans had been killed in Indochina and 294,946 wounded. In a rare personal appeal, he continued, "I feel this very deeply. I know something about war. I was a seaman second class in the Navy, a private in the Army and a Pfc. in the Marines. I want to see the Democrats do something—try to accelerate our withdrawal, help the President, act as responsibly as we can. While the President's responsibility is greater [than] ours, we must never forget our own individual responsibility as senators and collectively as a Senate."

In the spirited but respectful debate that continued, the proposal was backed by Humphrey of Minnesota, who had defended the war as vice president and had returned to the Senate the previous month. Humphrey declared, "I wholeheartedly support this resolution. It is not easy for me to get up here and do this. I know what the war did to President Johnson. I have never seen a man wrestle so with this problem. It broke his heart, it broke his spirit, and it broke him politically." Humphrey did not add, but his fellow senators certainly understood, that his own inability to break decisively with Johnson on the war had probably cost him the presidency in his race against Nixon in 1968. "It is true that I have changed my mind," he said. "Ten years of Vietnam have gone by, and we can be in the jungle another ten years. I am glad the Policy Committee has taken this initiative. We are not the commander-in-chief but we do have influence. That is what the Policy Committee is for, and it is time we came down hard on the issues."

After further debate Mansfield called for a roll-call vote, which was 30 in favor of the Indochina provision and 8 opposed. After polling absent members who cared to vote, the count was 35 in favor and 12 (of whom 9 were southerners) opposed. Two senators, Byrd of West Virginia and Talmadge of Georgia, supported the statement except for the words, "by a time certain."

At the White House, Nixon's reaction was entirely political. He told Haldeman in a conversation recorded on his secret taping system, "We have got to develop a line with regard to how we handle the Democratic attacks on the war." His central question was "how do you exploit the differences" within the Democratic ranks, noting that there were ten to thirteen Democratic "hard-liners" who opposed the majority position on the war. He was especially anxious to put Edmund Muskie, a potential challenger, "on the spot." As to the substance of the Democratic position, which was widely interpreted as mandating a final withdrawal by the end of Nixon's first term in January 1973, the President remarked, "I don't want to say we're going to get out in '73 either, but we are—everybody knows that—if they give us the [American] prisoners."

THE MANSFIELD AMENDMENTS

The passage of the Democratic Policy Committee resolution on Indochina in February 1971 opened the way to a new phase of Mansfield's legislative activism against the war. In the year that followed, he sponsored a series of three amendments to pending legislation, in June and September 1971 and

January 1972, expressing the sense of Congress that hostilities should be ended and U.S. forces withdrawn within a shifting set of increasingly short timetables. Although not binding with the force of law, each of them represented his determined view that the war had to be ended quickly and on almost any terms as long as American prisoners of war were permitted to come home. Each of the amendments passed the Senate and was the focus of congressional and public attention, but all of them were watered down or abandoned in the legislative process as a result of presidential persuasion. Their passage, however, paved the way for the eventual binding congressional action that forced Nixon to end U.S. military action, including bombing, in Indochina.

Especially after the debacle in Laos early in the year, public support for the war was sinking rapidly. Beginning in mid-April, 1971, antiwar protesters in large numbers converged on Washington. More than seven hundred veterans gathered at the Capitol on April 23 to throw away their war medals as a gesture of protest. The following day hundreds of thousands of people marched against the war, filling Pennsylvania Avenue from the White House to the Capitol, many carrying blue-and-white placards to petition Congress, "ENOUGH—OUT NOW!" Pollster Louis Harris reported in the *Washington Post* on May 3, "The tide of American public opinion has now turned decisively against the war in Indochina," triggered, he said, by the belief that the U.S.-backed invasion of Laos had been a failure. Even Nixon realized that a major shift had taken place. "Trust is like a thin thread," he confided to Kissinger and Haldeman on May 26. "We had broken our thin thread with the American people as to the winding down of the war when we moved into Laos, and it's going to be very hard to put that together again."

On June 22 Mansfield proposed his first amendment, which he placed on the Draft Extension bill, calling on Nixon to withdraw U.S. forces from Vietnam within nine months if American prisoners of war were released. The most prominent and successful of seventeen congressional antiwar efforts that spring, it passed the Senate 57 to 42, with twelve Republicans voting in favor. Publicly the President called the Mansfield amendment "the least irresponsible of the irresponsible resolutions" because it was a sense-of-Congress measure that did not carry the force of law. Privately, however, he felt pushed into a corner by the amendment, which commanded widespread support and was commended editorially by both the *New York Times* and the *Washington Post*. Speaking to his aides in the privacy of the Oval Office, but with the tape machine rolling, Nixon called it a "horrible, irresponsible thing" for Mansfield to do because of its potential impact on the secret negotiations with North Vietnam, which had been restarted by Kissinger in Paris three weeks earlier. "How possibly can you negotiate when you tell the enemy we're going to get out in nine months . . . [in that circumstance] the enemy won't negotiate about cease-fire and POWs. What the hell. . . . This may destroy the negotiations."

The morning after the Mansfield amendment passed, Nixon had breakfast with its author at the White House. Afterward he "rather happily" described to his senior aides H. R. Haldeman and John Ehrlichman how he had given Mansfield "a basic ultimatum regarding the harm that the Senate did." If the Paris negotiations fail, Nixon told his guest, he "will have to go on to the people and explain that the reason for the collapse was the action of the Senate, and that Mansfield will have to take that blame." He went on to say that "if we do get to the point where we have to withdraw because the negotiations failed," it would be accomplished with "a total bombing of the North to eliminate their capability of attacking; so in order to get out, we escalate to accelerate our withdrawal."

Ever suspicious of political motives, Nixon asserted that some of the lawmakers calling for an end to the war voted for it "because they knew it would destroy the negotiations. . . . They don't want to see us succeed." Instead, they want to "see us go down." Nixon vowed, "Well, we're not going to, by God. We're going to fight it. And if we go out, we're going to go out with a bang. . . . That's for damn sure."

Henry Kissinger was in and out of the Oval Office several times that morning, preparing to leave for a round of secret talks in Paris with Le Duc Tho, a key member of the North Vietnamese Politburo. With the presidential campaign of 1972 in prospect, Nixon took a different tack in his instructions to his undercover negotiator. He told Kissinger that "this is it" regarding the talks—he had to get a settlement promptly because "from here on everything is based on the domestic political outlook." He also made the point that if the talks should fail, "with the Mansfield resolution, now maybe we have the excuse for flushing the whole deal. We had to make that decision last year, either to stand up or to flush, and we made the decision to stand up, feeling that we'd never have the chance to decide it again. But now we probably do have that chance, because of the Senate resolution; and if the negotiations fail, that may be exactly what we do."

The House of Representatives, heavily lobbied by the White House, refused to accept this first Mansfield amendment, leading to a lengthy stand-off between the two houses of Congress on the issue. In the end the Senate agreed to accept a watered-down version of the amendment, which was signed into law by Nixon. The final version declared it to be "the sense of Congress" that U.S. military action in Indochina terminate "at the earliest possible date" and that all U.S. forces withdraw at an unspecified "date certain" subject to the release of POWs and accounting for the missing in action. The nine-month deadline for withdrawal in Mansfield's original amendment had been dropped.

The second Mansfield amendment was attached by Senate vote on September 20 to the Defense Procurement bill, another essential piece of national security legislation. This time the sense-of-Congress measure called for the withdrawal of all U.S. troops within six months if POWs were returned, shaving the time allowed because three months had passed since the original amendment was offered. In an effort to court Republican votes, Mansfield argued that "the purpose of the amendment is not to undermine the President but to help him, to extend a hand of cooperation, and to become involved with him as coequal branches of this government" in exiting Vietnam.

Nixon did not appreciate such "help" and sought to kill the measure in the House. On October 19 the House voted down the measure, but by a smaller margin than on similar amendments before. On the same day, Mansfield, frustrated by the roadblock in the House and by a resumption of U.S. air operations in Cambodia, told the Senate in an unusually bitter speech that "we have tried everything we can to confine this war, to limit it, to get us out, and it seems we are thwarted at every turn." Part of his frustration was due to a close Senate vote to delete an antiwar provision from the Foreign Aid Authorization bill. Mansfield told the Senate that consequently he had decided to vote against the entire authorization bill and the appropriations bill that would follow. "The intention of Congress has been overridden too many times and too consistently and it is about time to stand up and be counted. I am sorry I am so late, but there is an old saying, 'Better later than never.'"

Ten days later the Senate followed Mansfield's lead, voting down the Foreign Aid Authorization, 41 to 27. It was the first time the Senate had rejected the aid measure since its inception in the aftermath of World War II. The surprise vote sent shock waves through the administration and political Washington. Joseph Alsop, whom Mansfield had distrusted since their first meeting in China in 1944 and who later had become among the most hawkish of the nationally syndicated columnists, wrote that it was now clear that Mansfield and Foreign Relations Committee chairman J. W. Fulbright "are actively, unashamedly eager to see the United States defeated in war." Alsop leveled a venomous personal attack on Fulbright for "astonishing vanity and basic laziness." Mansfield, he wrote, "with his sweetness, and his refusal to face this world's realities, is like a very good, religious man who believes that the world is flat as an article of faith."

Meanwhile, the Senate-House conference committee on the Defense Procurement bill agreed to emasculate the second Mansfield amendment, dropping the six-month withdrawal deadline and simply calling for "prompt withdrawal from Indochina" of U.S. forces subject to the release of American POWs and accounting for the missing in action. Unknown to the lawmakers, Kissinger had already secretly offered in Paris in August 1971 to withdraw all U.S. forces by August of 1972 simultaneously with release of the prisoners held by both sides. The hang-up continued to be political issues, especially the North Vietnamese demand for the ouster of the Thieu government in South Vietnam and the counter-demand of North Vietnamese withdrawal from the South.

When the bill reached the White House for Nixon's signature, he announced he would ignore the Vietnam provision, describing it as "without binding force or effect." Informed of the President's statement, Mansfield told reporters, "It may be ignored, but it will be in the back of his mind." Noting that the Senate had approved an end-the-war amendment in one form or another four times and that the language was becoming ever stronger, Mansfield made clear his determination: "They talk about the cat having nine lives. This bill will have more than nine lives if necessary."

When Congress reconvened in January 1972, Mansfield told reporters he planned to attach his third Vietnam amendment to the first appropriate bill that reached the Senate floor. The amendment, adopted as Democratic policy by the caucus on January 25, called for U.S. military withdrawal within six months, subject to the return of prisoners and "recoverable missing in action." The caucus vote was 28 to 8, with fourteen more senators joining the majority when they were polled after the meeting.

Within hours after the Democratic caucus, Nixon spoke to the nation via television in one of his most memorable statements on the war. Stripping away some of the secrecy that had enveloped Kissinger's activities, the President revealed that his aide had been negotiating secretly with the North Vietnamese since August 1969 but that negotiations were deadlocked, which he blamed on Hanoi's intransigence. In an effort to break the deadlock, he unveiled a U.S. position remarkably similar to the one that Mansfield had advocated: the United States would withdraw all forces within six months of an agreement, all prisoners of war would be exchanged, and a cease-fire in place (no longer requiring North Vietnamese withdrawal) would take effect. As for the future of the South, Nixon stated a position that had been secretly transmitted to the North Vietnamese on October 11: that internationally supervised elections would be held in South Vietnam five months after a peace agreement, and that President Nguyen Van Thieu would step down one month before the election.

Mansfield watched Nixon's broadcast with Secretary of State Rogers and immediately described it as "a great step forward," adding that "I don't think you could go any farther than you've gone." Rogers informed Nixon, who was pleased by Mansfield's reaction, calling it "a very significant thing" and expressing the hope that the senator would repeat these views publicly. His hope was realized when Mansfield, addressing the Senate the following day, called Nixon's proposals "a long step forward," representing "a degree of flexibility which has been absent up to this time." The President and Congress, he said, "are coming closer together."

Although Mansfield was nonpartisan, Nixon was not. In the Oval Office on January 27, he urged his aides to attack the Democrats hard as "the party of surrender." At the same time, though, his aides recognized and hoped to build on the Majority Leader's positive reaction to the new U.S. negotiating positions. "Mansfield is good," Haldeman told Nixon. Kissinger seconded the view: "He was good."

Several hours later, Nixon placed a telephone call to Mansfield, recorded by his secret taping system, to say, "I'm very grateful for your statement that you made on our proposal the other night, and I can assure you that we'll keep hammering away at it and do everything we can to try to get it. It ought to make some progress." His opinion, the President said, was that the communist side would launch another offensive in February or March [they did so on March 30, Easter weekend, in the largest attack of the war, committing nearly twice as many troops on the Tet Offensive of 1968], but then "they have to make a very big decision," whether to negotiate or to continue to fight. "We want to have on the table a very forthcoming offer that . . . they will in good conscience be able to accept. . . . So our intention is to keep it on the front burner, in front center, and do just as well as we possibly can."

"I'm delighted, Mr. President," Mansfield responded.

Nixon then confided that the White House was in "very close touch " with the Chinese on this situation but would deny it if asserted publicly. "Oh, good," Mansfield said. Nixon continued, "We are in *very* close touch with the Russians on it. Now I am of course praying that it will not be an issue by the time we get to Russia" for the summit meeting planned for Moscow in the spring. "We're going down that road" with the Chinese and Russians "as hard as we can," Nixon asserted. "Let's keep going," Mansfield replied.

In a demonstration of good faith, Mansfield withdrew the Vietnam amendment that he had attached to pending legislation in the Senate, in view of Nixon's peace proposals. This delighted Nixon, especially because— partisan as always—he calculated that it put Mansfield at odds with Democratic presidential front-runner Edmund Muskie. "It's amazing that Mansfield would do that," Nixon commented to Haldeman.

On the morning of February 3, Mansfield was invited to the White House for another breakfast with the President, who was accompanied this time at the table in the family dining room by Kissinger. The national security adviser discussed the negotiations he had been pursuing in Paris and a new proposal from the National Liberation Front, the political arm of the South Vietnamese communist (Vietcong) movement. Kissinger told Mansfield that "our cease-fire is almost verbatim the same as their [NLF] cease-fire proposal." The developments in the Paris talks filled Kissinger with optimism. "My smell of the whole thing all along," he told Nixon, "was that when they didn't turn down our first proposal in October and kept it open and when they didn't turn it down last week—this is the year in which they're going to have a settlement."

MANSFIELD'S 1972 MISSION TO CHINA

One subject on which Nixon and Mansfield agreed unconditionally was the importance of establishing relations between the United States and the People's Republic of China. It had been a principal subject of most of their intimate breakfast meetings. In public as well as privately, Mansfield had consistently backed Nixon's efforts to shift U.S. policy on this politically sensitive issue. Moreover, Mansfield had been patient and supportive in his willingness to see the President go to Beijing first, even though his invitation from Chou En-lai had predated Nixon's. Despite their differences on Vietnam and other subjects, the President was indebted to Mansfield for his unwavering assistance on China policy.

On the third day of his ground-breaking trip to China in February 1972, Nixon began to repay Mansfield for his support and forbearance. In a conversation with Premier Chou En-lai on February 23, the President raised the issue of a joint visit by Mansfield and his Republican counterpart Hugh Scott later in the year. Although Mansfield "is, of course, of the other party and has disagreed with us on some policies, as he should, on our China initiative he has been a strong supporter," Nixon said. The President said he was proposing a joint mission by the two Senate leaders "because they asked me," not disclosing it was he who originated the idea in order to neutralize any acclaim that Democrats might garner.

Chou had not forgotten the earlier invitation to Mansfield and did not let Nixon forget what he had done in putting it aside: "We have abided by our promise to Dr. Kissinger, and even though . . . we felt it would be difficult" to postpone visits from political people until after the President came. Nixon responded with appreciation for Chou's decision, then quickly returned to the idea of a bipartisan visit from the two Senate leaders.

Kissinger, concerned by the prospect that Scott might obtain confidences from Chinese leaders, interjected, "It's fair to tell the Prime Minister that Senator Scott sometimes has the same tendency of our Japanese friends—anything you say to him is likely to find its way into the press." Nixon added, "But Mansfield does not leak. Now to show how fair I am I'll say that the Democrat does not leak but the Republican does leak." This drew knowing laughter from the Chinese participants." Chou approved the Mansfield-Scott visit in this initial conversation, and he did so again in a conversation in Shanghai on the final morning of Nixon's visit.

On his return to Washington, as congressional leaders of both parties began to gather in the Cabinet Room to be briefed about Nixon's trip, the President summoned Mansfield and Scott to the Oval Office to tell them of Chou's approval of a joint mission by the two of them. At this point,

Mansfield and Scott had not actually agreed to go together, but the President reported that he had told Chou they would like to do so. "I'd be delighted if Mike were willing to make it a joint venture," Scott volunteered, adding, "Our wives are very fond of each other." Mansfield responded, "I'm delighted. I couldn't think of a better traveling companion than you."

Seeking to gain maximum credit from Mansfield and Scott, Nixon exaggerated his achievement in obtaining Chinese agreement. In truth, Chou had readily approved the leaders' visit in an initial exchange with Nixon that took no more than two or three minutes and had confirmed his approval in a second, even briefer, exchange. The President told the leaders, however, that he had discussed it in Beijing three times and that only on the morning of his departure did Chou extend the invitation. To Clark MacGregor, his chief congressional relations aide, Nixon said, "I worked that out after tortuous negotiations." In a subsequent telephone conversation, Nixon told Scott, "I think you should know that this took me about three hours with Chou En-lai to work this out. Don't tell Mike this, but . . . I just said, 'These are the guys that ought to go,' and he agreed."

The first hitch developed within minutes after Nixon revealed the joint mission to the rest of the bi-partisan congressional leadership. The two leading members of the House of Representatives, Speaker Carl Albert, a Democrat, and Minority Leader Gerald Ford, a Republican, were irked that they had sat in the Cabinet Room while Nixon met privately with the Senate leaders. When Albert and Ford returned to the Capitol, they summoned White House liaison officer Richard Cook to the Speaker's office to voice their resentment.

The traditional preeminence of the Senate in foreign affairs is "an anachronism" not consistent with its role in recent challenges to the executive branch, they insisted. The House rather than the Senate has "carried the water" for the White House on foreign policy issues for the three years of Nixon's presidency and should be treated on "at least a co-equal basis," they said. Moreover, they argued that Mansfield and Scott had not shown loyalty to Nixon on "gut" votes and could not accurately convey congressional attitudes to the Chinese. Albert, in a veiled threat of future non-cooperation, speculated that he might be unable to fend off Mansfield's future antiwar amendments after being embarrassed in his relationship to the President.

The following day Albert, still angry, threatened publicly that the House would take "appropriate action" if its leaders were left out of future invitations to China.

Albert made it clear to the White House that he had no wish to visit Beijing but suggested that Ford team up with Majority Leader Hale Boggs, the number two Democrat in the House. Kissinger quickly began working with the Chinese to set up their visit, which the House leaders suggested take place in early July, about two months after the mid-April to early May timetable that had been established for the trip of Mansfield and Scott.

The second hitch, which seemed more serious for a time, was a stark illustration of the fierce passions that lay just beneath the surface of the President's impressive intellect. Angered by Mansfield's approval of a Senate investigation of the Nixon administration's dealings with a giant American corporation, the President on March 29 demanded that Kissinger "see if there's a way to screw Mansfield on this trip."

The issue was the high-profile Senate Judiciary Committee hearings into the relationship between the International Telephone and Telegraph Corporation's secret pledge of $400,000 to support the Republican National Convention, which was to be held in San Diego, California, and the settlement of the Justice Department's antitrust suit against ITT, which was announced nine days after the secret pledge. ITT was then among the largest conglomerates in the United States, and its president, Harold Geneen, was close to the Nixon administration and the Republican Party. Since early March, the committee hearings—ostensibly on the confirmation of Richard Kleindienst to be attorney general but actually on the ITT affair—had been front page news and a political embarrassment to the White House in a presidential election year.

Clark MacGregor had been in touch with Mansfield in the hope that he would find a way to terminate the sensational Judiciary Committee hearings. On March 28, Senate Republicans led by Scott went public with a partisan demand for an end to the hearings, declaring them to be "a frantic exercise in continuing irrelevancy" and evidence of Democratic "jackassery." Mansfield deflated the White House hopes by telling reporters that the inquiry should continue "until all the legitimate witnesses are heard." Nixon had become increasingly emotional, even close to panic, about the Democratic charges.

On the morning of March 29, Kissinger informed Nixon that a formal invitation had been received from Beijing to receive the House leaders, Hale Boggs and Gerald Ford, in the early summer, well after the Mansfield-Scott trip was expected to take place. At that point Nixon turned his ire on Mansfield.

First, Nixon proposed to send the House leaders, Boggs and Ford, at the same time that Mansfield went to complicate and downgrade his trip. When Kissinger expressed doubt that the Chinese would agree, Nixon ordered Kissinger to arrange for the House leaders to go first. "Have them go before Mansfield and Scott, Henry. That would be better. Now that's very important, Henry. Very important. You've got to put it to Mansfield, you've got to put it to him. . . . He's playing a ruthless game on everything. On foreign aid. He's playing a ruthless game on Kleindienst. . . . And we just give things to him and that's not fair."

Kissinger interjected, "I have always thought that Mansfield was of upstanding quality."

Nixon: "Well, you're right . . . that's the better him. There's two [Mansfields]." He went on to instruct Kissinger about the Majority Leader's trip, "Screw it up any way you can." Later he added, "I don't know how you're going to work it out, but just put your mind to it. . . . See if there's a way to screw Mansfield on this trip."

Finally Kissinger agreed with his boss's characterization of the Majority Leader: "I think Mansfield has been nothing but trouble for us. He will probably stop short of an all-out onslaught until he's been in China."

Later in the morning, immediately after discussion of the ITT hearings, Nixon spoke to Haldeman about his plan to postpone Mansfield's trip until after the House leaders broke the ice in China.

Nixon: "Mansfield deserves a kick in the ass."

Haldeman: "It would be a beautiful thing. Put the congressmen in there ahead of him. It would be a good kick in the ass for Mansfield."

Nixon: ". . . Shove them both, particularly Mansfield. He's got to be shoved back as far as possible. . . . The main consideration is to get Mansfield shoved back as far as possible."

When Kissinger rejoined the conversation shortly before noon, Nixon's demeanor was calmer but his determination had not diminished. "Number one priority is to push [the Mansfield-Scott trip] back, their visit back, as far as you can. . . . Second point is, as far as the Boggs-Ford thing is concerned, the Chinese may object to the order of visits. But in any event, the closer you can put Boggs and Ford [to Mansfield-Scott], the better. . . . I'd really like Boggs and Ford to go for a much shorter time—four days—and go before."

Boggs is "partisan," Nixon continued, "but on the other hand, he's voted with us on every national security issue. . . . Mansfield has voted against us on every national security issue and there hasn't been an exception."

Kissinger suggested that the "paramount thing" to obtain from the Chinese on the Mansfield trip was a commitment not to "try to use Mansfield" by dangling potential concessions on Vietnam.

Otherwise, Nixon picked up, "he will want to come back and then go to the Democratic National Convention and say, 'I went to China and [the U.S. administration] should have settled Vietnam and all that sort of thing."

Kissinger: "But of course we may settle Vietnam."

Nixon: "You're damn right."

The President went on to suggest that Kissinger inform the Chinese that "we would consider it a breach of every understanding, if they were to discuss any substantive issues, particularly the Vietnam issue, with any senators. Now goddamnit, that's true too. It violates our law."

Within hours of these White House discussions, before Kissinger was able to seek postponement of the Mansfield-Scott trip, the Chinese notified American officials through the confidential channel that had been set up in Paris that they would receive the two Senate leaders starting April 16. U.S. diplomats in Paris immediately informed Mansfield and Scott. When Kissinger told Nixon, the President was furious at "the little shit asses in the State Department" who permitted the trip arrangements to go forward that way.

It is unlikely that Kissinger did anything more to postpone the Mansfield-Scott trip. Within a week Kissinger's senior aide, Alexander Haig, informed Cook, the White House liaison with the House of Representatives, that "we believe the congressmen [Boggs and Ford] should wait until Senators Mansfield and Scott return before proposing specific dates and itinerary to the Chinese."

The senatorial trip began in mid-April as planned.

Mansfield knew nothing of Nixon's flare-up. On the morning when Nixon was instructing Kissinger to "screw up" his trip to China, the Majority Leader was meeting *New York Times* columnist C. L. Sulzberger at the

Capitol. Praising Nixon, Kissinger, and Rogers for the China opening and other foreign policy achievements, Mansfield told the columnist, "We must learn a lesson from the Chinese—to be patient and not to be impetuous, shooting from the hip. You must have time to think things through."

On April 4 the Majority Leader publicly stated that critics of Kleindienst had not made a case against his confirmation as attorney general and called for speeding up the consideration of his nomination, although Mansfield also said the Judiciary Committee should continue its investigation of ITT issues. The committee did so intermittently until June, when Kleindienst was finally confirmed, with Mansfield's vote among others. Reporting the outcome to Nixon, John Mitchell, who had resigned as attorney general to head the Committee to Re-elect the President, Nixon's reelection campaign, said Mansfield's was "the big vote" for Kleindienst. "Mike is a fellow that doesn't always go the political way. He sometimes does what's right," Mitchell said. With Kleindienst confirmed, the hearings on ITT and the Republican National Convention limped to a close without clear-cut resolution.

On the afternoon of April 11 Nixon and Kissinger met with Mansfield and Scott for a final discussion of their impending journey. By this time Nixon's anger at Mansfield had diminished and all thoughts of interfering with his trip had been abandoned. Suddenly the Majority Leader had become, once more, a person to be wooed and accommodated where possible. Nixon instructed Press Secretary Ron Ziegler to announce that the bipartisan mission to China "has the approval of the President." Mansfield, Scott, their wives and aides took off in an Air Force special mission plane on April 15 and arrived in China on April 18 after stops in Honolulu and Guam. For Mansfield, it was the return to a country of great fascination to him since his visit as a Marine in 1922, half a century earlier, and especially since his wartime mission to China in 1944 and his brief postwar visit in 1946.

The visit was also special for Scott, who had traveled to pre-revolutionary China as a tourist in 1947 and thereafter had become a devotee and prominent collector of Chinese art, especially ancient bronze and ceramic pieces. He had even written a book in the mid-1960s on the subject, *The Golden Age of Chinese Art: The Lively T'ang Dynasty.* The two men worked well together in the Senate and on the trip. "There was a mutual respect," recalled William Hildenbrand, who went along as Scott's principal staff assistant. "They were both very low key. They were both Asian experts. . . . Mansfield had been a Marine, Scott had been a Navy lieutenant. They just got along from a personality standpoint. They were both genteel men. . . . They were honorable men." Nonetheless, Mansfield insisted that the Democrats should keep their own counsel on the trip, with no sharing of notes with Scott and the Republicans. Mansfield made it clear to Chou En-lai and everyone else that he hoped to return to China alone, or at least without Republican companions.

Met at the airport in Shanghai by members of the local Revolutionary Committee, the U.S. delegation then boarded a waiting Chinese aircraft, which flew them to Beijing and stayed with them through the rest of their sixteen-day visit. "We were totally at the mercy of the People's Republic. We had no idea what we were going to do. We had no idea where we were going to go. We had no idea what we were going to see. We just got off the airplane and they took over and we went wherever they told us to go," Hildenbrand recalled.

On their second day in Beijing, the visitors were summoned to the Great Hall of the People for meetings and a dinner in their honor with Premier Chou En-lai, the urbane government leader and revolutionary acolyte of Chairman Mao Tse-tung. Chou's first remark after shaking hands was that Chinese leaders thought they had invited Mansfield a year and a half earlier and had expected him, but then Nixon's trip developed and they decided they had better allow the President to come first so he could "win the race." (In fact, it had been April 11, 1971, just over a year, since Norodom Sihanouk had written to Mansfield that he was invited to visit Beijing.) Mansfield expressed his thanks for the invitation and said the delay was probably due to "a misunderstanding" on his part. Both senators said the U.S. opening to China had strong bipartisan support—evidenced by their joint mission to open the official legislative contacts between the two countries.

Eight hours of conversations with Chou, before and after the dinner in the Great Hall and on a second occasion two days later, revolved around the issues of Indochina, where the war had been recently intensified, and touched on the Soviet Union, Korea, Japan, and Taiwan as well as bilateral U.S.-China relations. Evidently responding to White House appeals not to say much to Mansfield and Scott, Chou spoke in predictable terms of China's positions on Vietnam and other issues. In connection with the especially sensitive Taiwan question, Chou took refuge in an agreement with Nixon that "we should not discuss any specific issues discussed between the two sides" during the presidential trip. "The foremost issue is the Indochina war, no matter what form in which it continues, either directly by the United States or by puppets," Chou maintained. He said it would be "comparatively easy to relax tensions and solve issues relating to Taiwan, Korea and Japan if only the war could be settled."

It was China itself rather than the Chinese position on international issues that captivated Mansfield, Scott, and their traveling companions. After five days in Beijing, they returned to Shanghai for two days and then visited the lake city of Hangzhou; the historical and agricultural center of Xian; Changsha in Mao Tse-tung's home province of Hunan, where Mao had begun his revolutionary activities; and Guangzhou (Canton), the commercial hub of South China. Everywhere they saw great masses of people, walking or riding bicycles, with few automobiles in sight except for the boxy locally built limousines provided to the official visitors. The people were a study in monochrome: virtually everyone in the cities wore high-necked Mao suits in various qualities of cloth and various shades of blue or, occasionally, gray. Whenever the Americans moved from place to place, crowds of curious people gathered instantly, as if by magic, to stand silently and gape at this latest curiosity in their lives. When the visitors and their official guides headed into the masses, the crowds would part to let them through. Salpee Sahagian, Mansfield's administrative assistant, was reminded of the biblical parting of the Red Sea.

Mansfield was deeply impressed by the contrast between what he was shown of the "New China," as he called it, and the widespread poverty, misery, and disease of the China he had visited as a Marine and as a fledgling congressman. If measured by American standards, China is a bottle half empty, he reported to the Senate when he returned. But "if China is viewed in the light of its own past, the bottle is half full and rapidly filling." He continued:

> Today's China is highly organized and self-disciplined. It is a hard-working, early-to-bed, early-to-rise society. The Chinese people are well fed, adequately clothed and, from all outward signs, contented with a government in which Mao Tse-tung is a revered teacher and whose major leaders are, for the most part, old revolutionaries.

There has not been a major flood, pestilence, or famine for many years. The cities are clean, orderly and safe; the shops are well stocked with food, clothing and other consumer items; policemen are evident only for controlling traffic and very few carry weapons. Soldiers are rarely seen. The housing is of a subsistence type, but is now sufficient to end the spectacle of millions of the homeless and dispossessed who, in the past, walked the tracks and roads or anchored their sampans in the rivers of China and lived out their lives in a space little larger than a rowboat. Crime, begging, drug addiction, alcoholism, delinquency are conspicuous in their absence. Personal integrity is scrupulous. In Canton, for example, a display case for lost and found articles in the lobby of the People's Hotel contained, among other items, a half-empty package of cigarettes and a pencil. . . . In every aspect of society, there is evidence of China being rebuilt on the basis of Chairman Mao's dictum, "serve the people."

In the final dinner, given by the Americans in Canton the night before crossing over to the British colony of Hong Kong to end the visit, Mansfield spoke "with appreciation for what the Chinese people have done; with a true regard to the dedication of the Chinese people towards their outstanding leader, Chairman Mao Tse-tung; [and] with great admiration for Premier Chou En-lai."

Beyond his immediate field of vision China was still deeply affected by the turmoil and radical dislocation of Mao's Cultural Revolution, during which millions of Chinese were killed or imprisoned. It had begun in 1966, had reached its limits in 1969, and had begun to wane after the abortive coup attempt and death of Mao's chosen successor, Lin Biao, in September 1971. Mansfield, in a personal and private report to Nixon following his trip, said that China had "emerged" from the Cultural Revolution, which he naively seemed to approve. He described it as "a vast revolutionary purification" with its effects "felt particularly in the civilian and military bureaucracies." He added, "It appears also to have elevated the concept of economic self-reliance, intensified national unity, consolidated revolutionary supremacy in outlying provinces and forestalled the alienation of the first post-revolutionary generation of Chinese youth."

Such uncritical estimates were not unusual in the early 1970s among Americans who were visitors to the People's Republic for the first time. The prominent journalist James Reston of the *New York Times*, for example, described the efforts at mass mobilization as "one vast cooperative barn-raising," guided by "many aspects of the old faiths the West has dropped along the way." Mansfield, with his scholarly background and bent and his previous experience in China, might have been expected to be more discerning.

Mansfield and Scott had spent sixteen days in China, longer than almost any other American visitor at the time (Nixon's visit was eight days), but they were entirely in the hands of Chinese officials. "No discernible signs of personal oppression were encountered," Mansfield wrote in his private report to Nixon. "Nor are there in the places visited, notable indications of discontent with the present political leadership, notwithstanding the upheaval of the recent cultural revolution. Indeed, the almost total absence of armed guards, police and soldiers from the streets is a striking measure of change from the past."

Mansfield's staff sought to balance such views by inserting a note of skepticism in the draft of his report to the Senate, saying that China as he found it "is a classless, controlled society; there is as yet, no real intellectual freedom. And the free enterprise system, as we know it, does not exist." Mansfield, however, deleted that statement from the final report. Five months later he continued to praise the accomplishments of Mao's China in a speech to a trade association in Arizona. Nonetheless, he also said that "the Chinese People's Republic is more closely controlled and highly organized than ever before. Intellectual and artistic freedom are non-existent. Nor is there representative government and free enterprise as we know them. However, if we have learned one truth from our experience in Asia, it should be that American values are not necessarily adaptable wholesale in Asia."

In his private report to Nixon, Mansfield declared that within China, "whatever transpires is a Chinese affair. That is the one cardinal principle with which we should enter into the rapprochement. Our involvement with China should stop at the water's edge of the Chinese mainland. . . . To immerse ourselves once again in the inner affairs of the Chinese people, in my judgment, would be to court a new disaster."

VIETNAM: THE FINAL STRUGGLE

On Easter weekend 1972, as Mansfield and Scott were making preparations for their mission to China, North Vietnam launched its biggest military offensive of the war, throwing the equivalent of nearly twenty divisions, virtually every combat unit in the North Vietnamese army, into a three-pronged invasion of the South. Nearly all U.S. ground forces had been withdrawn, leaving only two combat brigades in South Vietnam. Nixon responded by temporarily halting the Paris talks and dispatching additional U.S. air and naval forces to support the beleaguered South Vietnamese. As the battles raged, he resumed heavy bombing of North Vietnam, first in the area close to the DMZ and then farther north.

When Mansfield and Scott arrived at Hickam Air Force Base in Honolulu on April 16 on the first leg of their trip, they were met by Admiral John McCain, the commander of U.S. forces in the Pacific (and father of the future senator, who was then a prisoner of war in Hanoi). McCain informed them that B-52 bombers had attacked Hanoi and Haiphong for the first time since Johnson had halted the bombing in November 1968. "Mansfield was convinced that the Chinese would withdraw their invitation, and almost turned us around and brought us back," recalled Hildenbrand. For the Chinese, however, the budding relationship with the United States was far more important than solidarity with Vietnam. As it turned out, according to Hildenbrand, "they welcomed us with open arms and treated us exceptionally well. While we talked about Vietnam, they sort of understood our position as well."

On the morning of May 8, Mansfield's first business day back in Washington, the fighting was still flaring in Vietnam and an emergency meeting of the National Security Council was reported to be under way at the White House. At this juncture Mansfield convened the Senate Democratic Caucus to consider the escalating situation. In two hours of discussion, the senators were unable to reach a consensus about what to do, other than to instruct Mansfield to ask Nixon to meet with a bipartisan leadership group from Congress. Mansfield placed the request orally with the White House at 12:30 P.M., and in writing at 1:30 P.M. In fact, Nixon had decided well before the National Security Council meeting, which ended at 12:20 P.M., to order the mining of Haiphong and six other ports and still-greater bombing of North Vietnamese rail and supply lines in a massive effort to roll back the enemy's Easter Offensive. He signed the formal order at 2:00 P.M. The congressional leaders were summoned at 5:00 P.M. to a meeting at 8:00. The President spoke to them for about fifteen minutes about the actions he was taking and then departed to prepare for a televised announcement to the nation at 9:00, leaving senior aides behind.

William Safire, then a member of the White House staff and the note-taker for the occasion, considered Nixon's meeting the congressional leaders merely "a Constitutional courtesy" and found the meeting "as tense a session as I attended in four years." Kissinger did not attend, but his deputy, Alexander Haig, observed that both Democrats and Republicans received Nixon's request for support in "stony silence" and with a "display of cold indifference."

Led by Mansfield, the lawmakers showed their displeasure to the officials whom the President left behind, Admiral Thomas Moorer, chairman of the Joint Chiefs of Staff, and Secretaries Rogers and Laird. As soon as Moorer began his presentation, Mansfield interrupted, his voice trembling: "How long ago were those orders issued?" Told that the orders had been issued that afternoon, Mansfield continued, "What it means is that the war is enlarged. It appears to me that we are embarking on a dangerous course. We are courting danger here that could extend the war, increase the number of war prisoners and make peace more difficult to achieve."

Coming to the rescue of the startled Moorer, who was momentarily unable to answer, Laird responded, "As far as the extension is concerned, Mike, it was extended by the enemy. It's not a fair charge to charge us with that responsibility." Mansfield's friend and breakfast companion, Republican George Aiken, who also attended the briefing, wrote in his diary that Mansfield "was mad and made no bones about it." Aiken sympathized, believing there was "only an outside chance" that the bombing and mining would be successful.

On Capitol Hill the following day Mansfield once again convened the Democratic caucus, this time amid widespread opposition to Nixon's actions and fierce indignation on the part of many about his failure to consult Congress in advance. Fulbright offered a resolution of "no confidence" in Nixon. He was rebutted by Sam Ervin of North Carolina, who declared that the President had the constitutional authority to act as commander-in-chief of the armed forces, and that, even if he was misguided, to repudiate him in wartime would be "a catastrophe for our party." Some agreed with Ervin and others sharply disagreed, saying Nixon lacked authority to make war in Vietnam after the repeal of the Tonkin Gulf resolution.

By this time the sentiment in the Senate had turned definitively against the war. Now the argument was about tactics—how best to reassert what had been, to the regret of many, the nearly unchallenged domination of the presidency and the disregard of the role of Congress, especially of the Senate. During the caucus meeting Mansfield said little in nearly three hours of intense discussion, and spoke up only to bring the debate to a close. He had listened with interest, he said, and although his feelings against the war were known to all, he was persuaded that votes on any of the several proposals that had been offered might only show the division within the party. In the absence of overwhelming support for any of them, the results could become "a political issue" which the Democrats could not win.

Despite Mansfield's cautionary words, the caucus voted 29 to 14 (Mansfield agreeing) to "go on record as disapproving the escalation of the war in Vietnam as announced by the President on May 8th." The caucus then voted 35 to 8 to cut off funds for any military activity in Indochina four months after an agreement to release U.S. prisoners and account for the missing in action. Mansfield noted in discussion with reporters that this was the first time the caucus had voted to back a fund cutoff for the war. Hours later on the Senate floor, the Majority Leader criticized the new military actions as likely to lengthen and expand the war, noting that "we were told about it after the fact, not before." Nevertheless, he did not criticize Nixon directly or even mention him. Instead, he offered a powerful statement of his views:

As far as I am concerned personally, the sooner this horrible, tragic war is brought to a close and every American is brought home, the better off I will feel, because to me 358,918 U.S. casualties in a 12-year period is 358,918 too many in a war in which we have no business and which is not vital to the security of this Nation, a war which, in my opinion, is the greatest tragedy which has ever befallen this Republic.

Mr. President [addressing the Senate's presiding officer], it does no great nation any harm to admit that a mistake has been made. And sometimes when nations and men will do so, they will be the bigger and the better for it.

On May 16, Mansfield proposed an amendment requiring the withdrawal of U.S. troops from Indochina four months after North Vietnam agreed to release American prisoners, even without the internationally supervised cease-fire which the President had proposed as a withdrawal condition. Nixon, once again exasperated with the Majority Leader, saw Mansfield's actions in personal terms. He told his aide Charles Colson the following day, "Son of a bitch just wants everything and gives nothing in return." To Haldeman, Nixon insisted, "We've just got to quit this babying of Mansfield. . . . We sent him to China, for God's sake. We've given him planes. We've done everything and all he does is kick us in the ass." Again, to Colson: "To hell with him. We've just got to fight him now. . . . Just because Mike is a nice guy, goddamnit, he's not for what we're trying to do, so hit him." There is no evidence that Nixon's attack order was carried out. Two days later the Majority Leader was at the White House for the bipartisan leadership briefing on the impending Moscow summit, which had Mansfield's strong and important support.

Nixon's orders had unleashed the most extensive U.S. air, naval, and artillery bombardment of the war, in addition to the mining of harbors, which virtually stopped the sea traffic of supplies to North Vietnam. By July the Easter Offensive had been stopped and turned back by the combination of devastating American firepower against targets in both North and South Vietnam, South Vietnamese army tenacity, and North Vietnamese army mistakes. The North Vietnamese army took more than 100,000 casualties in its 200,000-man invasion force and lost more than 50 percent of its tanks and heavy artillery. As a result, its strategist and senior commander, the legendary General Vo Nguyen Giap, was eased out of power and replaced by General Van Tien Dung, who was to lead the final offensive against South Vietnam. But due in part to the failure of the Easter Offensive, it took three years to mount it.

In mid-July, with the battles in Vietnam subsiding, the Senate debated end-the-war amendments on the Foreign Military Assistance authorization bill, including one requiring the removal of all U.S. troops from Vietnam by September 1, which Mansfield agreed during floor debate to extend to October 1. In a complex series of parliamentary motions and votes, the Senate adopted an even stricter end-the-war measure sponsored by Republican Edward Brooke of Massachusetts, only to see the overall bill defeated by a combination of pro-administration Republicans and anti-assistance Democrats. Despite all the debate on a variety of competing measures, no legally binding antiwar legislation made its way to final passage in 1972.

The final months of the presidential election year brought a flurry of developments as Nixon and Kissinger sought to end the war through negotiations. Mutual concessions in the Paris talks, especially the U.S. acceptance of North Vietnamese troops in South Vietnam and Hanoi's acceptance that South Vietnam's President Thieu would remain in office, made possible a tentative agreement in October and a declaration by Kissinger that "peace is at hand." Thieu, however, balked at the U.S. concessions, which he believed would doom his regime. After Nixon's landslide victory in the November 7 presidential election, when he won forty-nine of the fifty states, he sought to make adjustments to the previous tentative deal, but North Vietnam refused to budge. Nixon then ordered heavy bombing of Hanoi and Haiphong in mid-December in an attempt to force Hanoi to make concessions.

Congressional opponents of the war harshly condemned the "Christmas bombing," as it was dubbed, and some suggested that Nixon was losing his mind. Mansfield called the bombing a "stone age strategy being used in a war almost unanimously recognized in this nation as a mistaken one." He predicted it would prolong the war rather than bring it to an end. Following the bombing, however, North Vietnam and the United States returned to the talks in Paris, where on January 27 they, the South Vietnamese government, and the Provisional Revolutionary Government (the diplomatic arm of the Vietcong) signed the Agreement on Ending the War and Restoring Peace in Vietnam, commonly known as the Paris Accords. It called for U.S. troops to be withdrawn from Vietnam and U.S. prisoners of war to be returned within sixty days but permitted North Vietnamese troops to remain in the South under a stand-still cease-fire.

Mansfield was invited to fly to Paris for the signing ceremony and stood behind Secretary of State Rogers as the deed was done. Later, Rogers sent Mansfield a pen with which he had signed the agreement. After the signing Mansfield praised Kissinger and Nixon in the Senate for ending "the tragic war in Vietnam." His overarching priority was to stop the killing of Americans in a disastrous and unnecessary war, never mind the practicality of the agreement. He recited the grisly figures of U.S. casualties—56,000 dead and 303,000 wounded, at the latest report—and declared, "Let us hope that never again will another Vietnam or Indochina occur. . . . Let us admit our mistakes—and that applies to nations as well as to individuals—and learn from the past so that, in remembering, we will never again repeat the mistakes of this tragedy ever again."

THE WATERGATE INVESTIGATION

The presidential election year of 1972 was a political disaster for the Democratic Party, but in the long run it germinated the seeds of an even greater disaster for Richard Nixon. At 2:30 A.M. on June 17, five members of the secret White House "plumbers" unit, formed for political intelligence and espionage, were arrested planting listening devices in the offices of the Democratic National Committee at the Watergate office complex in Washington. The Watergate burglary and especially the attempt to cover it up would eventually bring Nixon down.

Early in the year Edmund Muskie appeared to be the front-running candidate for the Democratic presidential nomination and a formidable challenger to Nixon's reelection. Political mistakes—some of them instigated by a "dirty tricks" team reporting to the White House—severely damaged Muskie's campaign. During the Florida primary campaign, the same Nixon operatives wrote scurrilous letters on Muskie stationery accusing Hubert Humphrey and Scoop Jackson of sexual misconduct and drunkenness. When Muskie dropped out of the race after poor showings in primary elections, George McGovern rose steadily to win the Democratic presidential nomination in mid-July. After two other senators declined, McGovern selected Thomas Eagleton of Missouri as his vice presidential running mate. Mansfield told McGovern that "he couldn't have made a better choice." In late July, however, Eagleton confirmed a news report that earlier in his life he had undergone electroshock therapy for depression, a fact unknown to McGovern.

On Sunday night, July 30, with his campaign tottering under sensational media coverage of Eagleton's medical history, McGovern slipped out of his house in Washington through the back door and scurried down a steep embankment, avoiding the press. With the help of the Secret Service detail assigned to him as Democratic presidential nominee, he made his way unnoticed to Mansfield's house. It was about 10 P.M., and the Majority Leader, who usually retired early and rose early, came to the door in his pajamas, looking as though he had been awakened by his unexpected visitor. Inside,

McGovern confided that he had decided to drop Eagleton from the ticket. He begged Mansfield to take his place as his vice presidential running mate. "You know, Mike, we are in trouble now . . . deep trouble, but I think that as a strong, admired person [you] would quickly pull us out of this hole. Beyond that, you'd make a wonderful president. If I get elected and anything ever happens to me, we couldn't have a better president of the United States."

The reply was instantaneous and unequivocal: "Well, George, I don't want that job. I don't want to be vice president, I don't want to be president, I want to be a senator from Montana. That's all I've ever been and all I ever want to be." Mansfield repeated, "I don't want that job" and recalled that Lyndon Johnson had initiated suggestions that he seek the vice presidential nomination in 1964 "and I told him the same thing." Mansfield advised McGovern to keep Eagleton, who in his view had made a "terrific" defense of himself earlier in the day on a television interview program. McGovern thought otherwise and went on unsuccessfully to ask Ted Kennedy, Abraham Ribicoff, Hubert Humphrey, Reubin Askew, and Edmund Muskie to accept the vice presidential nomination before finally recruiting Sargent Shriver, John Kennedy's brother-in-law and former Peace Corps director. When the Democratic National Committee met in a televised meeting on August 8 to nominate Shriver officially, Mansfield placed his name in nomination. Unlike the other potential candidates, Mansfield never told the press that he had been asked and declined the vice presidential nomination.

Throughout the summer and fall, the *Washington Post* and at times other news organizations reported on the increasingly clear connections between the Watergate break-in and the White House. Early on, Mansfield had been quick to exonerate the President from responsibility for the scandal—too quick, in the opinion of McGovern. As more information came to light, Mansfield found the scandal disturbing and distasteful. "When Watergate jokes were going around, he wouldn't listen to one, or repeat one, for love nor money," according to Peggy DeMichele, his longtime administrative assistant. Adding to his dismay was a *Post* report a month before the election of "a massive campaign of political spying and sabotage" directed by officials of the White House and the Committee for the Re-election of the President. To this champion of openness and political rectitude, bugging, spying, and sabotage were abhorrent and far beyond the boundaries of acceptable polit-ical competition.

Campaigning in Montana on behalf of his Senate colleague, Lee Metcalf, and other Democrats, Mansfield declared in Helena on October 29, nine days before the election, that it was "mandatory" for the Senate thoroughly to investigate the Watergate affair "and all its ramifications." Beyond the illegal break-in itself, he was also alarmed by spurious letters aimed at Democratic contenders in the Florida Democratic presidential primary. "If a political candidate for the presidency can be maligned and slandered and reputations are torn to shreds, then this practice can also be applied to other individuals," he told reporters.

By the time Mansfield returned to Washington after the election, he had settled on the idea of a single committee to conduct the Senate's investigations into all aspects of Watergate and campaign dirty tricks, and on Sam Ervin of North Carolina as the most appropriate leader. A former North Carolina Supreme Court Justice, Ervin "was a constitutionalist, and I wanted to stick to the Constitution pretty closely," Mansfield told me. "I knew he'd be fair minded." He did not realize, he added, that the deliberate and folksy Ervin would become a highly popular national figure in televised hearings into the scandal. To get Ervin as the committee chair, however, he had to persuade James Eastland of Mississippi, chairman of the full Judiciary Committee, who was close to Nixon and an arch-segregationist, and Ted Kennedy, who chaired a Judiciary subcommittee on administrative practices, to give up their claims to the investigation. Mansfield first went privately to Kennedy, who agreed to give up jurisdiction, and then to Eastland, who did the same. He finally persuaded Ervin, who took the assignment reluctantly.

Mansfield made another decision, which, in retrospect, was a crucial factor in all that would come later: that the struggle with the Republican White House over illegality and dirty tricks would be waged not on the expectable partisan basis, but on as bipartisan a basis as possible. In following this course, Mansfield avoided the bitter fiasco a quarter century later of the Bill Clinton impeachment process, which turned into a partisan wrangle that ultimately united the Democrats and saved the President. In the Watergate proceedings Mansfield appointed the right people to the Democratic side of the investigating committee and then kept his hands off, letting the committee uncover the story bit by bit in a way that also educated the public. In the end it was senior Republicans rather than Democrats who faced Nixon in a climactic meeting and told him his support in Congress had vanished. He knew then he would have to resign or be impeached.

Mansfield, in personally selecting the Democrats to serve on the Senate Watergate Committee, ruled out anyone who was seen as highly partisan or who was reputed to have presidential or vice presidential aspirations. He was determined that the committee would not only be nonpartisan but that it would be seen by senators and the public to be so. Mansfield did not permit the ones he chose to turn down the assignment, despite its controversial and taxing nature. Daniel Inouye of Hawaii said no to Mansfield's invitation twice but finally succumbed. Herman Talmadge of Georgia, who was chairman of the Agriculture Committee, listed six committees on which he served and pleaded that this workload was about as much as he could handle, but Mansfield simply kept repeating, "Herman, I want you to serve on the Watergate Committee." Talmadge complied.

As a result of Mansfield's decisions and the esteem in which he was held by Republicans as well as Democrats, the Watergate Committee was created by a unanimous vote of the Senate, 77-0, on February 7. Probably no other leader in the contemporary history of the Senate could have obtained such a result.

Nixon, however, was unimpressed by either Ervin's fairness or Mansfield's nonpartisanship. "Ervin, for all his affected distraction and homely manner, was a sharp, resourceful and intensely partisan political animal," Nixon claimed in his memoirs. As for Mansfield, Nixon considered his sponsorship of the Watergate investigation "a purposeful ploy in the congressional campaign to put the presidency on the defensive." Nixon wrote in his diary that it suggests "a very hard four years" ahead. With no recognition that there was anything serious to be investigated, he wrote that "Mansfield is going to be deeply and bitterly partisan without question. The Democrats actually are starting four years early in their run for the White House."

Once he conceived the Watergate Committee and set it in motion, Mansfield took no part in the investigation and commented only occasionally on the issues before it. In April, Mansfield commended Nixon for his action in forcing the resignations of Haldeman, Ehrlichman, and Kleindienst. In June, at his initiative, while Soviet leader Leonid Brezhnev was in the country conferring with Nixon, he and Scott arranged for a week's recess in the hearings, because former White House Counsel John Dean was about to deliver sensational testimony.

In July, following the revelation that Nixon had been secretly tape-recording official meetings since 1971, Mansfield commented mildly, "I am not surprised but I don't like it. I wouldn't have minded if they told me." Throughout, he was respectful of Nixon, even when praising the work of the committee and defending it against attack. "I have long believed in the principle—and this applies to the President as well as any other citizen—that a man is innocent until his guilt is proven," he said in August 1973, despite mounting evidence of Nixon's involvement in the cover-up.

NIXON'S FINAL MONTHS

As the Watergate scandal exploded with resounding impact in 1973–1974, and a weakened Richard Nixon struggled to keep his presidency alive and its powers strong, the political balance between Congress and the White House was shifting at home and abroad. Coincident with the domestic judicial and political conflict over Watergate issues, the legislative and executive were battling over the power to undertake military action beyond the nation's shores. Under the U.S. Constitution, the President is commander-in-chief of military forces, but Congress declares war and holds the power of the purse. Preceding Nixon's presidency, in the cold war era of nuclear weapons and potential split-second decisions, Congress had rarely successfully challenged the executive branch. But as Richard Nixon continued to pursue an unpopular war in his first term of office, Congress became increasingly resistant, as reflected in the Senate approval of the series of Mansfield amendments in 1971–1972. All the same, no legislation that limited the President's power to wage war actually became law until Nixon was weakened by Watergate and U.S. troops had left Vietnam under the terms of the Paris Accords. With American forces no longer at risk, Congress was free to express the nation's dominant antiwar sentiment without endangering U.S. troops in the field. The result was the assertion of legislative power in foreign policy that began with Indochina issues of the day and continued in the 1970s with such actions as the War Powers Resolution and restrictions on U.S. intelligence operations.

Mansfield, who had been notable for his acceptance of executive supremacy in foreign relations earlier in his career, increasingly cast off these inhibitions after Nixon's invasion of Cambodia in 1970. By Nixon's second term, he was, as he told a *New Yorker* writer in 1973, deeply concerned that "the balance of power is dangerously tilted in the direction of the executive." He understood that "Congress has only itself to blame" for the abdication of its powers, but declared that because of the war "it's waking up to the fact." Mansfield himself was becoming one of the most important advocates of creating and enforcing legislative restrictions, especially on further U.S. engagement in Cambodia, a country that had long been of special interest and concern to him.

In early February, two weeks after the Paris signing, the government-in-exile of Prince Sihanouk, who had become a figurehead leader for forces dominated by the homegrown Khmer Rouge, announced that fighting against the U.S.-backed Lon Nol regime would continue. Nixon then authorized U.S. bombing in Cambodia with greater intensity than before to assist Lon Nol. According to Arnold Isaacs, a historian of the post-Paris period, more than 250,000 tons of bombs were dropped by U.S. warplanes in Cambodia in the next six months, exceeding the tonnage of bombs that fell on Japan in all of World War II.

Mansfield initially urged forbearance about the bombing in the hope that the administration could negotiate the return of his old friend Sihanouk, whom he believed would be able to pacify and unify the country. When the bombing and fighting continued, the Democratic caucus in early May adopted a resolution calling for legislation to ban further use of U.S. funds for any military activity in Cambodia.

Led this time by the House, where antiwar sentiment had risen sharply after the withdrawal of U.S. troops from Vietnam, both houses of Congress voted a ban on bombing in Cambodia. In late June, Nixon vetoed the legislation, which had been placed on an important appropriations bill. Mansfield was by then so disaffected that he responded with uncharacteristically bitter rhetoric. The veto, he told the Senate, "can lead only to a constitutional impasse over the issue of war and peace and the ability of the American people to affect those issues as never before witnessed in the history of this Republic." The bombing ban represented "the loud and clear will of the American people," he declared. "What Congress has attempted to do is to stop an ill-advised, illegal, unconstitutional slaughter of Cambodians by American bombing. . . . The United States does not belong in Indochina and never has, and of all the places we do not belong in, Cambodia is the most outstanding. We are supporting a corrupt dictator. We have created a client state and we are keeping it in power through bombings."

Mansfield vowed that if the veto was upheld, he intended to attach similar riders to every possible piece of legislation "because under the Constitution only the Congress has been given the war-making power, not the President, and Congress has spoken." After the veto was narrowly sustained, Mansfield announced that he would not permit passage of any major appropriation bill for the next fiscal year, which would virtually close down the government, unless Nixon agreed to a bombing ban.

In the face of rising antiwar sentiment in Congress and weakened by Watergate, Nixon capitulated. He agreed to accept a prohibition on further military action in or over Cambodia, even after Congress extended the ban on U.S. bombing to include North and South Vietnam and Laos, if the lawmakers would put off the deadline until August 15. For the first time in the Indochina war, Congress had foreclosed military options that the President as commander-in-chief had declared to be essential to U.S. objectives.

Before signing the final restrictions, Nixon wrote Mansfield and House Speaker Albert on August 3 that although the administration would obey the law, "this abandonment of a friend will have a profound impact in other countries, such as Thailand, which have relied on the constancy and determination of the United States, and I want the Congress to be fully aware of the consequences of this action." He did obey the law, and the bombing stopped on August 15.

As the legislation to halt the bombing was moving through the House and Senate, so was a broader measure of less immediate impact but greater permanence: the War Powers Resolution, which requires presidents to notify Congress promptly if U.S. forces are introduced into hostilities or hostile situations, and mandates that the forces be withdrawn within sixty days unless Congress approves. Mansfield took little part in its passage, leaving this to Fulbright and others, but he heartily approved. Passed over Nixon's veto, it has never been fully accepted by the executive branch, which has made only half-hearted attempts to comply with it.

In many respects the most multifaceted crisis month of Nixon's presidency was October 1973. On October 6, during the Jewish holiday of Yom Kippur, Egypt and Syria attacked Israel, setting the Middle East aflame. The United

States responded with an airlift of war material to the Jewish state, anger-
ing the Arabs and triggering the Arab oil embargo that devastated the world
economy. On the morning of October 10, Nixon summoned congressional
leaders to tell them what was happening and to declare that he was attempting to maintain good relations with both Israelis and Arabs and to avoid a
confrontation with the Soviet Union. Mansfield, who was nearly always
helpful to presidents in moments of international crisis, said only that "we
want no more Vietnams." Neither Nixon nor Kissinger, who had replaced
Rogers as Secretary of State in September and had taken charge of the crisis, had any intention of sending U.S. ground troops.

At home, two historic actions were taking place in the legal arena. The
U.S. Court of Appeals for the District of Columbia was preparing to rule
that the President must hand over nine of his secretly made tapes to
Archibald Cox, the special Watergate prosecutor whom Nixon had been
forced to accept at the Justice Department. After the court made its 5 to 2
ruling on October 12, Nixon issued orders to fire Cox rather than hand over
the tapes, and Attorney General Eliot Richardson and Deputy Attorney
General William Ruckelshaus resigned rather than take part in implement-
ing Nixon's order. This touched off the greatest political uproar of the
Watergate saga.

Also on October 12 in a federal courtroom in Baltimore, Vice President
Spiro Agnew pleaded no contest to a charge of income tax evasion in connection with kickbacks he had received earlier in his career. As part of the
plea agreement that spared him a prison sentence, he resigned his high office.
That afternoon, Nixon called Mansfield and House Speaker Carl Albert to
the White House to hear their views on Agnew's successor. Under the
Twenty-fifth Amendment to the Constitution, which had been passed in
1967, the new vice president would have to be confirmed by both houses of
Congress. The person selected would have an excellent chance of becoming the Republican presidential nominee in 1976, when Nixon would be
barred from running again. Once more, under dramatic circumstances, the
President was confronted with the requirement to accommodate congressional power, which was predominantly in the hands of the Democrats.

Nixon's favorite for the job was John Connally, the decisive former
Democrat from Texas, but many Democrats disliked and feared him.
Evidently referring to Connally, Mansfield told Nixon that "there is one fel-

low we're going to go over with a fine-tooth comb if his name is sent up."
As for Nelson Rockefeller or Ronald Reagan, whom Nixon was also con-
sidering for the post, Mansfield forecast strong congressional opposition.
The Majority Leader preferred a "caretaker" vice president, such as Senator
John Sherman Cooper of Kentucky or former Secretary of State William
Rogers, who were unlikely to run for president in 1976. The crucial sugges-
tion in the discussion came from the Speaker: Why not select Jerry Ford, the
House Republican leader since 1965, who had advanced his party's positions
but who also had worked well with Democrats? Albert said Ford could be
easily and quickly confirmed. Nixon turned to Mansfield, who agreed that
Ford would be a good choice.

After surveying the practicalities, Nixon complied with the suggestion
of the lawmakers. With all the problems he was having with Watergate—
problems that were soon about to deepen sharply—he was in no position to
have a pitched battle within the Republican Party or with Congress over the
vice presidency. Nixon felt satisfied with the choice, since he saw Ford as ideologically compatible, loyal, and, above all, confirmable. Ironically, the
knowledge that Ford was in place to succeed Nixon—rather than the highly
partisan Agnew—made it much easier for Democrats to contemplate
Nixon's impeachment.

The final months of Nixon's presidency was a difficult time in the relationship of Congress and the White House. On January 24, 1973, in the first
month of the new Congress, Mansfield had breakfast with the increasingly
embattled President, who told him he would fight any attempt at impeachment and had no intention of resigning. The Majority Leader took him at
his word. Knowing that a trial in the Senate would be the last phase of the
impeachment process if the House chose to act, Mansfield scrupulously
refrained from taking a position on impeachment of the President and refused
to discuss resignation, saying that was an issue for the President alone. Two
weeks later, in a crushing blow to Nixon's hopes for help from Congress, the
House voted 410 to 4 to proceed with an impeachment investigation and to
grant full subpoena powers to the House Judiciary Committee.

Little by little throughout the spring and summer, Nixon was forced by
the Senate and House investigating committees, the courts, and his own
Justice Department to yield the tapes and transcripts that would prove his
guilt in the cover-up of the Watergate break-in. Amid the start of House

Judiciary hearings on impeachment and mounting public and political pressures for Nixon to resign, Mansfield spoke up in the Senate on May 13. "Resignation is not the answer, because the cries for the President's resignation can echo and reecho throughout the land, but the only one who can decide that question is the President himself." As for impeachment, he said, "the Senate has not arrived at any hard and fast conclusion any more than the House has. So far as this body is concerned, there will be not only the appearance of fair play but there will be the reality of fair play and impartiality. . . . this matter is going to be carried through to a final conclusion. There is no other way."

The next three months brought a rapid series of developments that ultimately doomed Nixon's presidency: guilty pleas or convictions on Watergate-related charges of important Nixon aides, including Erhlichman, Colson, John Dean, and Attorney General Kleindienst; the 8 to 0 ruling by the Supreme Court that Nixon must turn over sixty-four tapes of Watergate discussions; and House Judiciary Committee votes in favor of three articles of impeachment of the President. Finally on August 5, the White House was forced to release transcripts of three conversations between Nixon and Haldeman six days after the break-in. They conclusively proved that Nixon had personally ordered that investigations be stymied and the White House connection covered up. Much that Nixon, his lawyers, and defenders had said about his conduct in the wake of the break-in was shown to be lies. With the publication of the "smoking gun" tapes, virtually all of his remaining Republican congressional support fell away. On August 7, Senator Barry Goldwater, the patriarch of the party, and Hugh Scott and John Rhodes, leaders of the Senate and House Republicans, went to the White House and told Nixon that his cause in Congress was hopeless.

Nixon, who had already been working on a resignation speech, made a final decision to resign rather than be impeached, but there was no confirmation of widespread rumors to that effect. On August 7, Mansfield told reporters that he believed the Senate should proceed with an impeachment trial even if the President resigned. "The constitutional process should be carried through one way or another. It has gone on so long we have no choice," he said. That afternoon, Mansfield rose in the Senate to state publicly as Majority Leader "that despite our domestic difficulties, we will continue, as Democrats, to work with our Republican counterparts to make certain and make known to all countries that our foreign policy will continue to be conducted on a bipartisan basis, that the moves made by the Nixon administration to normalize relations with the People's Republic of China, to further détente with the Soviet Union, and to use our efforts to stabilize the situation in the Middle East, all will be continued." Hugh Scott then rose to endorse the statement from the Republican side and say that he would show copies of their exchange to foreign visitors who had "expressed their concern" about the United States. In fact, the two leaders had been meeting frequently to assess Nixon's situation and prepare for a possible trial in the Senate. Together they asked the Rules Committee to review the Senate's rules and precedents in connection with impeachment trials to see what revisions might be required. The last such trial had been held in the impeachment of President Andrew Johnson in 1868, more than a century before.

At 8:00 A.M. on August 8, Mansfield met with the House Democratic leadership in the Speaker's office, to learn that a vote of impeachment would probably come by August 22, with the issue then being transferred to the Senate for trial. At 9:30 A.M. Mansfield convened the Senate Democratic caucus, reporting that the House was "moving very rapidly" toward impeachment. "These are wrenching and difficult times for all involved," he said, but the Senate's responsibility is clear—to be prepared for a trial under the impeachment clause of the Constitution. "Can we avoid facing this responsibility? Would not a Presidential resignation spare us the necessity?" Mansfield asked. Answering his own question, he continued, "As I have said many times, the question of a Presidential resignation is solely one for the President. If he does reach that decision, then we will face a new situation. But in my view, it would be an abuse for the Senate itself to stimulate resignation so as to avoid a judgment under the regular Constitutional procedures. I am not sure whose purposes would be served thereby." Unknown to Mansfield, Nixon had already made his decision to resign, and preparations to announce it were well advanced.

As Nixon went through the painful ritual of preparing his speech to the nation and informing Vice President Ford and others, he summoned congressional leaders of both parties to the Executive Office Building office on the evening of August 8. "I told them that I appreciated their support on many issues through the years, and that I was especially grateful for their support during the last Soviet summit, when I knew that partisan pressures had been very great," Nixon wrote in his memoirs. "I said that I had always respected them when they had opposed my policies. I was looking directly at Mike Mansfield when I said this, but he did not react at all. He just sat there in a more dour mood than usual, puffing on his pipe. I said, 'Mike, I will miss our breakfasts together,' and he nodded, but without much responsiveness." That was Mansfield's last direct contact with Nixon as President. Ninety minutes later, Nixon announced his resignation. He vacated the White House the following day.

THE FORD PRESIDENCY

Mansfield felt more comfortable personally with Gerald Ford than with any other president of his time in Congress, except for his great friend John F. Kennedy. After a complex relationship with Lyndon Johnson and difficult times with Richard Nixon, Mansfield was delighted to see the arrival at the White House of a straightforward, unpretentious, and relatively uncomplicated personality. "Ford was himself while President," Mansfield told me. "We were lucky to have him."

The two men became friends in the House of Representatives during Ford's first term in 1949–1950, before Mansfield moved to the Senate in 1953. Ford found Mansfield to be "a loyal Democrat but he was also fair and broad-minded in his relationship with Republicans. My wife also got to know Mike's wife very well, and they struck it off as good friends." When Mansfield became leader of the Senate Democrats in 1961 and Ford the leader of House Republicans in 1965, they had many opportunities to interact. In private life, Mansfield arranged for Ford's oldest son, Mike, to serve as a Senate page. Like Mansfield, Ford was a man steeped in the collegial affairs of the Congress of that day, and like Mansfield, he had never sought the presidency. As noted earlier, Mansfield had played a role in Nixon's selection of Ford to be vice president.

On August 20, 1974, when Ford had been President less than two weeks, he made the unusual gesture of traveling to the Capitol to participate in a surprise party in honor of Mansfield's record-breaking tenure of 13 years and 225 days as Majority Leader. In a photograph from that occasion, the new President is standing in a circle of friends of both parties from the Senate and House; Ford and Mansfield, in the center, have their arms around each others' shoulders, with big grins on their faces. A month later Mansfield reciprocated by hosting a breakfast for Ford at his house with three other senators and the Mansfields' friend Jane Engelhard attending. The breakfast, a symbol of Democratic good will toward Ford, appears to be the only occasion when Mansfield invited a president to his private residence.

In Ford's twenty-nine months in office as President, Mansfield attended thirty-four bipartisan leadership meetings with Ford, had nine private meetings with him and forty-two telephone conversations, and attended twenty-nine White House social events, according to records in the Ford Library. William Hildenbrand, the senior assistant to Senate Minority Leader Hugh Scott, observed that Ford treated Mansfield "with the respect that someone who is majority leader deserved to be treated, unlike the Nixon operation. And Mansfield responded in kind."

Ford and Mansfield had their differences on numerous issues, including the residual questions regarding Indochina after the withdrawal of U.S. forces, but they were able to work with one another in friendly fashion. Ford created the greatest political uproar of his presidency a month after taking office when he issued a presidential pardon for Nixon, an action that contributed to his defeat at the polls two years later. Leading Democrats harshly condemned the pardon, but Mansfield announced that he would not do so. Although he raised questions about the need for a pardon and its implications for other Watergate figures, Mansfield said Ford had "faced up to his responsibility [and] made a decision which he thought was right." As he had stated earlier, Mansfield expressed regret that Nixon's resignation had cut short the constitutional process of impeachment.

THE END OF THE INDOCHINA WAR

The most important business between the Majority Leader and the President in Ford's first year was the end of the war in Indochina. The American public and Congress had ended the war in their minds and hearts with the Paris Accords, the withdrawal of U.S. forces, and the return of American prisoners of war in early 1973, but in Southeast Asia the fighting went on. Administration attempts to continue the bombing in Cambodia and potentially elsewhere had been foreclosed by the congressional ban that Nixon had reluctantly accepted in August that year. In the spring and summer of 1974, Congress slashed the administration's request for $1.45 billion in military assistance for Vietnam to $1 billion. Then, on August 6, the House voted overwhelmingly to limit actual spending to $700 million, half of the administration's initial request. Two days later, in perhaps the biggest blow yet to the aid package, Richard Nixon announced his resignation, removing the most important U.S. advocate of continued support for South Vietnam's war effort.

In January 1975 Ford, overruling the White House staff and others who saw the effort as futile, asked Congress for a $300 million supplemental appropriation to make up for some of the earlier cuts. Even before his request officially reached the Senate, Mansfield spoke up in opposition. "I had thought that we had left Vietnam two years ago next month. I had thought we were finished with that misadventure. I had thought that the price we paid was high—55,000 dead Americans, 303,000 wounded, $140 billion in treasure. . . ." The supplemental negotiation went nowhere, to the shock and dismay of the South Vietnamese.

I was in South Vietnam as a *Washington Post* correspondent that spring as the country's army was collapsing under North Vietnam's final offensive. With war material in increasingly short supply and confidence even scarcer, South Vietnamese defenses crumbled, often without a fight. Ford sent a fact-finding group to Saigon headed by General Fred Weyand, the Army Chief of Staff and a seasoned Vietnam commander, who recommended an infusion of U.S. funds to resuscitate the South Vietnamese defenses. It was abundantly clear to all of us who had seen Vietnam at earlier stages, however, that the curtain was coming down on the prolonged drama.

Ford appeared at a Joint Session of Congress on April 10 to request $700 million in emergency military aid for South Vietnam. Mansfield convened the Democratic caucus and told his colleagues that, in his opinion, the Senate would find it "extremely difficult" to furnish funds quickly in view of the "massive military collapse" in Vietnam. He also took offense at the beginnings of a campaign—later advanced by Kissinger and others—to blame Congress for the failure of the war. Mansfield would have none of it. "At this late date to see the cyclonic change in the military situation in South Vietnam as something that could have been withstood if only Congress had put up a few hundred million dollars more in military aid during the past few weeks is a distortion so immense that it borders on—I choose the word carefully—it borders on the irrational," he told the Senate on April 15. The Democrats sent Ford's request to committees, from which it never emerged.

In the final days of April, Congress was pushing the administration to proceed with the evacuation from Vietnam of Americans and such Vietnamese as could be quickly extricated. On April 30, hours after the evacuation, North Vietnamese forces rolled into Saigon effortlessly, as what was left of the government capitulated. Later that day, Mansfield praised the collaboration between the President and Congress in the evacuation. "A tragic episode in our history has now come to a close in Vietnam," he declared in the Senate.

Cambodia, rather than Vietnam, dominated Mansfield's concerns in the dramatic spring days of 1975. As in the case of Vietnam, he opposed emergency military aid to the Phnom Penh government and its rapidly failing military forces but backed humanitarian assistance. He continued to hope that a negotiated settlement could bring the return to power of his friend Norodom Sihanouk, who was still in exile in Beijing. Encouraged by the Chinese and in his fury against those who had overthrown him, Sihanouk had agreed to act as the nominal head of the forces battling the Phnom Penh government, even though the insurgents were predominantly Cambodian communists, the Khmer Rouge, a group of anti-establishment radicals that he had opposed for most of his life. Against all odds, Mansfield hoped that Sihanouk could restore orderly government and inner peace to that tormented country. Mansfield told the Senate on March 10 that although Sihanouk would not negotiate with the senior leaders who had overthrown him in 1970, he was willing to negotiate an end to the fighting with lesser figures. "In this he has the concurrence of the premier of the rebel movement Khieu Samphan, who is also the leader of the forces in the field," said Mansfield, oblivious to the dominating figure of Pol Pot in the rebel movement and Sihanouk's powerlessness.

In handwritten preliminary notes as he prepared for the speech, Mansfield wrote, "10% of Cambodians killed since 1970. Millions homeless. . . . Let leaders leave Cambodia" and added a one-word description, "Messy."

The following day Mansfield met Um Sim, the ambassador of the Phnom Penh government, who said its senior leaders were prepared to leave and that "Phnom Penh is more than anxious to have Sihanouk come back; more so than the Khmer Rouge." He appealed to the Majority Leader to make contact with Sihanouk on the government's behalf to arrange a peaceful transition of power. Mansfield said he would do so only at the request of Ford or Secretary of State Kissinger. As a precaution, Frank Valeo drew up preconditions for such a mission, including its initiation by Ford and its acceptance in advance by both Cambodian sides.

Mansfield heard nothing from the executive branch, which had made several abortive efforts of its own to arrange a transition involving Sihanouk, and the idea was dropped. Just before Phnom Penh fell to the Khmer Rouge on April 12, Washington made a final unsuccessful effort to engage Sihanouk in the takeover. In victory, the Khmer Rouge sent the populace of Phnom Penh out to the countryside and quickly began to fasten their horrific rule on the country. Sihanouk returned to Cambodia on December 31 as a symbol of Khmer Rouge legitimacy and their virtual prisoner.

A month after the Khmer Rouge takeover, Ford ordered U.S. military forces into action after Cambodian troops seized the *Mayaguez*, a U.S.-registered container ship, which had sailed into an island area that, unknown to the crew, was being hotly disputed between the Cambodian and Vietnamese victors in the Indochina war. Acting amid considerable misinformation, confusion, and a desire to show Asia and the world that the United States remained a strong power, Ford landed troops on the ship, which had been abandoned, and dispatched a heavily armed rescue force to an island where it was mistakenly believed the crew had been taken. He also ordered bombing of a naval base and airfield on the nearby Cambodian mainland.

With the War Powers Resolution having become law over Nixon's veto and the post-Vietnam Congress very sensitive to U.S. military action in Southeast Asia, Ford ordered telephone calls to twenty-one senior members of Congress, beginning with Mansfield, on the second day of the four-day crisis. The leaders were called again on the morning of the third day, May 14, to inform them that three Cambodian patrol craft had been sunk. At 6:30 P.M. that day, as the major U.S. actions were to begin within an hour, Ford and his senior military and diplomatic advisers briefed seventeen congressional leaders in the Cabinet Room. The President said the briefing was "to comply with the War Powers Act and in order to keep you abreast of developments."

After Ford outlined his military plans, Mansfield was among the first to respond. "Why are we going into the mainland of Asia again [referring to the planned bombing] when we practically have the boat in our custody?" he asked. Ford said the actions were designed to prevent Cambodian forces from interfering with the U.S. operations. Toward the end of the briefing, during which most of the lawmakers present appeared to be supportive, Mansfield found himself in a familiar dissenting role in the Cabinet Room discussions of the impending use of military force. "I have to express my concern that we are once again invading by air the Asian mainland. We have plenty of force and I think it will not have a salubrious outcome," he said. When Minority Whip Robert Byrd asked the President why Congress had not been consulted as required by the War Powers Act rather than merely informed, Ford said, "We have a separation of powers. The President is the commander-in-chief so long as he is within the law." He had complied with the law by notifying Congress and had exercised his presidential powers, he declared.

Several hours later, after hearing on the radio that U.S. forces had taken the *Mayaguez* under control, Mansfield telephoned Ford from his home to urge him to call off further military action. Ford responded that it was "too late," as the landings and bombings were already under way. Fifteen Marines were killed in action during the brief occupation of the island where the crew was mistakenly believed to be held, and twenty-three more servicemen were killed in a helicopter crash on the way to Cambodia. The ship and its entire crew were rescued safely, however. The domestic elation at the success of the operation immediately boosted Ford's popularity, as measured by the Gallup Poll, from negative to positive territory. The *New York Times* called the incident "a domestic and foreign triumph."

LAST MISSIONS TO CHINA

In December 1974 and October 1976, Mansfield fulfilled his undiminished determination to return to what he called "the new China." Following his and Scott's 1972 visit, he had immediately set in motion plans to return. He brought up the subject with Kissinger barely two months after this trip. Kissinger urged the Chinese to cooperate in four separate conversations with Huang Hua, then PRC ambassador to the United Nations, but without results. In March 1973 Mansfield wrote Nixon formally proposing that he undertake a new mission to China as "a most emphatic demonstration of the collaboration of the Senate's Democrats with a Republican Administration's initiatives of policy." In a one-on-one breakfast meeting the following month, Nixon said he "would do his best" to work it out, but the return visit did not materialize during the Nixon administration.

In October 1974, two months after Ford entered the White House, the Chinese issued an invitation for Mansfield and a party of chosen companions to make a three-week visit in December. When Mansfield asked Ford to make an official request for him to go as the basis for providing an Air Force plane—standard practice for Mansfield on his trips—the President immediately agreed. Similarly, Ford readily authorized another three-week mission in October 1976.

Mansfield's visits came during a hiatus in Sino-American relations caused by Nixon's political weakness and eventual resignation; by turmoil in the Chinese leadership brought on by the failing health of Chairman Mao Tsetung and Premier Chou En-lai, his urbane messenger to the rest of the world; and by U.S. unwillingness to end its ties to the Nationalist regime on Taiwan. Chou, the official who had authorized Mansfield's initial visit even before Nixon was invited, and in whom Mansfield reposed great confidence, had been in and out of the special leadership hospital in Beijing since the spring of 1974, suffering from heart attacks and the cancer that eventually would kill him. In deference to his illness, Mansfield did not ask to see him on his visit that December. Chou, however, requested a visit from the Mansfields, who were whisked to the hospital on short notice to see the ailing premier. At the door was a red carpet for the distinguished visitors; inside, Chou rose to greet them wearing a dark high-necked tunic and slacks but looking pale and gaunt, his skin stretched tight over his high cheekbones.

In what all of them knew was likely to be their last meeting, they spoke about old times, of Mansfield's visit to China in 1944 when Chou was negotiating with Chiang Kai-shek; and of the Nixon visit in 1972. Chou said that Mao had read Nixon's pre-presidential *Foreign Affairs* article about the need to deal with China and had made the decision then to move toward rapprochement. Mansfield assured Chou that the opening executed by Nixon was irreversible in the United States. When Mansfield asked for his counsel about current Sino-American relations, Chou declined to engage, saying that it was up to Foreign Minister Qiao Guanhua, who had been named to his post only the previous month and with whom Mansfield had been meeting, and to Qiao's associates. A photograph taken by an official

Chinese photographer shows Maureen looking sadly, almost despairingly, at the ailing Chinese leader. As the meeting came to a close, Chou invited the Mansfields to return to China again. Then he struggled to his feet and accompanied them to the door of the room. "The door between our two countries should never have been closed," he said in farewell. Outside Maureen broke down in tears. It was "a buoyant but a sad meeting," her husband wrote in his notes.

The illness and later the death of the premier gave an opening to Jiang Qing, Mao's ambitious and highly political wife, who led three other high officials in seeking power and advancing their radical agenda for Chinese life. The Gang of Four, as it was known, was emerging as a powerful force behind the scenes during Mansfield's 1974 visit, although Chou had managed to bring the pragmatic Deng Xiaoping back to power as deputy premier. In that post he was effectively the number one government official in Chou's absence, against the wishes of the radicals. Deng had been purged during the height of the Cultural Revolution and would be purged again shortly after Chou's death.

I was part of the U.S. press contingent that accompanied Kissinger in China in late November 1974, just days before Mansfield arrived, in my first visit to the Middle Kingdom. I found it to be a "a vast nation marching to a strange and different tune," where people were reluctant to say anything beyond the current Communist Party line, where nearly everyone of both sexes wore the high-necked Mao suits, and where hordes of people on bicycles (but in few cars) moved through the streets of Beijing and other cities. I also had my first glimpse of Deng, the short, tough, outspoken veteran of the Long March, whom I later got to know much better when I accompanied him in 1979 on his tour of the United States.

Mansfield's most important substantive meeting in his 1974 trip was with Deng, at a luncheon for the senator and his party in the Great Hall of the People. With developing countries suffering from the fourfold rise in oil prices arising from the Middle East war and the Arab oil embargo of the previous fall, Mansfield appealed to China, as a growing producer of oil and "leader of the third world," to assume some responsibility for less-developed countries. Deng rejected the idea of any such leadership, and said that China had learned from the United States the expense of economic assistance. "Don't call on us," he insisted. When Mansfield raised the subject of U.S.

troops in Asia, Deng responded that they were spread too thinly and over too great an area to be effective. "If you try to use your ten fingers to catch ten fleas, you will never succeed," he said. Deng's most astute remark came on the subject of Cambodia. Better briefed than Mansfield on the nature of the Khmer Rouge, which was then supported by China, Deng said that in Cambodia a previously peaceful people had been turned into the opposite by oppression. Mansfield disputed this remark, saying that in his view the Cambodian and Laotian peoples were "the most peace-loving in the world." He would soon be proven wrong by the locally grown Khmer Rouge.

In his twenty-two days in China in 1974, Mansfield traveled 6,000 miles by plane, train, and car. In his report to the Senate, Mansfield concluded that "China's political system is no longer an experiment. . . . It is a way of life for China's 800 million people. Chinese society, today, is based on the communist theories of Chairman Mao Tse-tung which, to the Western ear, can sound not only like Marxism but also common sense and a mixture of understanding and severity in confronting the frailties of human nature." He predicted that the system would survive Mao, who was already sinking into senility, but that there also would be "political turmoil" of a periodic nature within the framework of Maoism. In his private notes, Mansfield found the Chinese "More confident than ever,—More self-contained: economically—oil; politically—less concern of USSR; socially—*their* system working; financially—very little debt." Regarding the United States, Mansfield found the Chinese "still friendly but less patient" and "more outspoken." Mansfield's assistant Salpee Sahagian noticed that no one had smiled at her during the 1972 visit, but that "I got smiles on the second and third trips."

The wholly positive nature of Mansfield's report brought criticism from Taiwan and from some Western experts on the People's Republic. Lord Michael Lindsay, an Englishman with long experience in China, objected to "the absence of any critical analysis or thought" in Mansfield's report. "Other visitors who have published favorable reports have at least noted the elaborate apparatus of indoctrination, the tremendous pressure for conformity and the repression of intellectual and cultural life to fit the party line. . . . Senator Mansfield simply ignores the repressive aspects of life in the 'People's Republic,'" he wrote.

By all indications, Mansfield was measuring what he was shown in China as a distinguished visitor against his memory of its oppressive and destitute past. When I asked him in 1999 to account for his uncritical attitude toward the China of the 1970s, he cited that reason, along with a "greater degree of knowledge than the usual visitor, a greater degree of interest in China and that part of the world in our future." This may fall well short of a satisfactory explanation in light of current knowledge of the Cultural Revolution, but it is the only one I obtained.

In the fall of 1976, before retiring from the Senate, Mansfield made his final official visit to China, his third following the Nixon breakthrough four years earlier. The death of Chou En-lai in January 1976 had touched off mass demonstrations in Tiananmen Square by people who approved of his and Deng's pragmatism and feared the ascendancy of Jiang Qing and her radical friends. In April the ever-suspicious Mao, now sinking into his final months, had approved his wife's entreaties to purge Deng. Five months later, on September 9, Mao had died.

The Chinese leadership, which had agreed many weeks earlier to begin Mansfield's visit on September 21, did not seek to postpone the visit but reversed the order of his planned activities, sending his party to Nanjing near Shanghai and on a Yangtze River cruise and then to the Xinjiang autonomous region in the far west before bringing the visitors finally to Beijing for meetings with officials. The reason given was that the capital was still in mourning for Mao, as, indeed, Mansfield found the entire country to be, with most people wearing black armbands and buildings hung with black and white crepe balls. But there was another, more compelling reason hidden from view: the leadership was racked with fierce political maneuvering, plots and counterplots, which ended with the secret arrest of Jiang Qing and her three comrades in the Politburo, "the Gang of Four," on the night of October 6, the same night that Mansfield and his party arrived in Beijing for their meetings.

Mansfield met the following afternoon with Wang Hairong, a vice minister of foreign affairs, who was Mao's niece and who probably knew of the arrests, and on October 9 with Vice Premier Li Xiannian, who certainly knew, since he was a full member of the Politburo. Neither official gave a clue that anything unusual was taking place. As the party prepared to leave China from Shanghai on October 12, U.S. Consul Donald Anderson told Mansfield of a report that Jiang Qing and others had been ousted in a Politburo showdown, but according to Anderson the senator was not inclined to believe it.

One subject discussed in detail with both the vice minister and vice premier was Taiwan. The Chinese officials were unhappy that the United States had not moved quickly to end its military and diplomatic relationship with the Republic of China on Taiwan. Mansfield was sympathetic to their view. In his confidential report to President Ford, sent to the White House on October 26, Mansfield wrote that "it would appear that we remain enmeshed in Taiwan on the basis of past policies and because of developments in our own political situation. . . . The longer the Taiwan issue remains in limbo, the more pressure seems to be building for continuing indecision as a substitute for policy. The more tortured become the proposals for evasion of the issue."

From Ford's standpoint 1976 was not a good time to take the dramatic steps of severing diplomatic and military relations with Taiwan, as promised by Nixon and demanded by China as the price of establishing full U.S.-PRC relations. The President had been opposed in the Republican primary elections in the spring by Ronald Reagan, who took a strongly pro-Taiwan stand, and Taiwan remained an issue with Republican conservatives such as Barry Goldwater. The Democratic presidential nominee, Jimmy Carter, was also cautious about severing ties to Taiwan but, Mansfield hoped, amenable to persuasion.

The senator's public report to the Senate, issued three weeks after Carter's election, was more forceful and explicit on the subject than had been his confidential report to Ford. "The national interest is deeply involved, in my judgment, in moving without further delay to settle the Taiwan problem. Gambling for more time? For what? Further delay could well prove to be another in the long series of disastrous miscalculations which have afflicted U.S. foreign policy in Asia since World War II." Mansfield said the United States should "act now" to sever the Taiwan ties on the basis of American interests in the Pacific. Carter, however, decided to go slowly. It would take him two years to cut official ties with Taiwan and establish full diplomatic relations with the People's Republic.

"A TIME TO GO"

In March 1976, Mansfield was entering his seventy-third year. He would be up for reelection in November and if he won, as universally expected, he would be seventy-nine years old by the time his term ended. Although he had been hospitalized for viral pneumonia in 1959 and for urinary tract infections in 1966 and 1972 and again for a severe virus in 1975, he was strong and physically self-reliant, and his health was good for a man of his age. Following his early experiences in the Navy, in the Army, and in the Marine Corps, as a copper miner in Butte, and as a student and professor at the University of Montana, he had spent nearly half his life in Congress. In January he had entered the thirty-fourth year since his arrival in the House of Representatives, his twenty-fourth year in the Senate and his sixteenth year as Majority Leader, setting a record for longevity in office and for the respect and affection of his colleagues that was unlikely ever to be equaled. He and Maureen decided it was time to go.

He did the deed in characteristically modest fashion. He sent an announcement of his decision not to seek reelection to the Montana state capitol at Helena, with instructions that it be released at noon on March 4. At 11:00 A.M. he walked down the corridor to the office of Minority Leader Hugh Scott to impart the decision. "The place won't be the same, Mike," said his Republican counterpart, who was seventy-five and who had previously announced his own retirement. "There will always be others to take our place," Mansfield replied. He arranged for a personal letter to Ford announcing his decision to be delivered to a White House liaison official at 11:40 A.M. with instructions to deliver it to the President at noon.

Immediately after the Senate convened at noon, Mansfield rose in his front row seat to deliver his speech, drafted, as often the case on important occasions, by Frank Valeo. Summarizing his long years in Congress, he noted that they encompassed "one-sixth of the nation's history since independence; the administrations of seven presidents; the assassination of a president and other extreme outrages against human dignity; able political leadership and seamy politics and chicanery; the dawn of the nuclear age and men on the moon; a great war and a prelude to two more wars and an uneasy peace; and a dim perception of world order and an uncertain hope for international peace."

"Through this and more," he continued, "the Senate, together with the House, has been the people's institution. In all this and more, I have believed and believe it still, that the Federal Government will not atrophy and the people's liberties will be safe from tyranny if the Senate remains vigorous, independent, and vigilant. The Senate is stronger, more responsive, more alive, more innovative today, than it was at the time of my entry so many years ago."

Alerted by aides and a premature wire service report from Montana, the chamber began rapidly to fill up with senators. He continued with his brief speech, emphasizing that the decision had been made jointly with his wife, Maureen, and asking the people of Montana to tap a new source within the state to represent them in the Senate.

"There is a time to stay and a time to go," he said, reprising the words that his beloved friend, John F. Kennedy, had written on the photograph depicting the Majority Leader turning away from Lyndon Johnson and other members of the congressional leadership group. "Thirty-four years is not a long time but it is time enough." Finally, "I will not be a candidate for election to the Senate of the 95th Congress."

When Mansfield was finished, Scott rose just across the aisle to begin a spontaneous outpouring of emotion and affection from a political tribe whose public remarks were often impersonal. Mansfield had told him that he hoped nothing would be said following his announcement, Scott reported, "but this imposes too great an obligation on all of us who love him so dearly." He then spoke—as close to fifty of his colleagues did one after another, Democrats and Republicans, liberals and conservatives, senators from every section of the country—of a man "distinguished by his complete fairness and his total integrity [who] has in every instance put the interests of the country above any other consideration." Moreover, said Scott, "he has never stooped to anything which would demean his conduct or lower the respect for the institutions of government." Some went on at length about Mansfield's contributions, but one of the most moving tributes came from Mark Hatfield, a liberal Republican from Oregon, who spoke, in the spirit of a man of few words, only a few sentences: "As the father of two sons, I wish they could be the mirror of Mike Mansfield. I think any father knows that this says it all."

The news media, for whom Mansfield was always an accessible and respected figure but never the source of leaks, scoops, or self-glorification, chimed in enthusiastically. "Other majority leaders, like Mansfield's predecessor, Lyndon Johnson, bullied, threatened and arm-twisted recalcitrant colleagues. The Montanan soothed, persuaded with calm reason and took the quiet way," reported *Time.* "Seldom has a less flamboyant figure graced

the Senate, much less held the powerful position of Majority Leader . . .
Mansfield's strength lay in his integrity and his genuine lack of ambition
beyond representing Montana and serving the Senate," wrote Sam Shaffer
of *Newsweek,* dean of Senate correspondents. Columnist James Reston,
under the headline, "Say It Ain't So, Mike" wrote in the *New York Times,*
"This is not primarily a political loss, like the departure of Lyndon Johnson
or Robert Taft from Capitol Hill, but a personal loss. Mike has been not so
much the majority leader of the Senate as the moral leader of the Senate,
whose personal integrity and fidelity to the nation crossed all party and personal controversies."

Although his personal qualities won universal acclaim, serious assessments
of Mansfield's leadership abilities were mixed in their conclusions. A
Washington Post editorial expressed a longing for Lyndon Johnson's "more
effective virtuoso style" and suggested Mansfield was so popular with his colleagues because he demanded so little of them. The Senate under Mansfield,
the *Post* editors said, "has been managed, steered and steadied, but it has not
been consistently led—either by Mr. Mansfield or by anyone else—in a way
that communicates vision and coherence to a nation seeking just those elements in politics." Under Mansfield, *National Journal* observed as he retired,
the Senate had become "increasingly democratized in the way it operates"
but, at the same time, "the increased responsibilities of each senator have
detracted from the capability of the Senate as a whole to grapple with overriding national policy issues."

Writing fifteen years after Mansfield's retirement, the political scientist
Ross K. Baker noted, "Much criticism of the modern Senate is in effect, a
commentary on institutional features that emerged during Mansfield's
term as Majority Leader. The hyperindividualism, the ability of willful or
obstructionist members to hold the institution hostage at times to their
own petty interests, the hypertrophy of Senate staff and their assumption
of unprecedented, even unwarranted, authority, are all developments of
the Mansfield era."

At the same time, Baker observed that the Mansfield Senate and those
that followed it were shaped by larger forces in American politics, especially
the decline of the party system and the rise of individualism in political campaigns. My own list of centrifugal forces that changed the Senate would start
with the rise of big money politics and the growing dominance of the media,

paid and unpaid, in American political life and would also include the growth of bureaucratic and impersonal decision making throughout government, which began in Mansfield's time and has expanded greatly since then. Mansfield's insistence on working for a Senate of equals spelled the demise of the predominance of an inner club of entrenched and often elderly men. The democratization and decentralization of the Senate, however, also forestalled the emergence of towering figures to match the Lyndon Johnsons, Everett Dirksens, Richard Russells, and other renowned senators of the earlier day. Mansfield, whose long reign brought so much change to the institution, was himself one of the last of the Senate greats in the estimation of his peers and of the American press and public.

American political life was dominated by the presidential election of 1976 in the final months of Mansfield's Senate service. For the first time since the Kennedy-Nixon race of 1960, no senator or former senator was the nominee of either major political party. The public reactions to Watergate, to Ford's pardon of Richard Nixon, and to the collapse of the costly U.S. effort in Indochina were dominant factors in the race between Ford and Jimmy Carter, who was personally unknown to most Democratic senators. In June, Mansfield introduced the former Georgia governor to the Senate Democratic caucus, predicting he would be a "builder of bridges" if elected in November.

As the Senate prepared to adjourn for the year in mid-September, Mansfield rose once more to say goodbye. Before he could do so, his colleagues mounted another extraordinary display of praise and affection for the departing leader. Always uncomfortable with such acclaim, he walked from the chamber when the round of tributes began. When he returned, he took a rear seat, head bowed, his face a mask, shuffling papers on his lap. When it was announced that the Rules Committee had unanimously resolved that Room 207, the conference room where he had often presided over the Democratic caucus, be designated the "Mike Mansfield Room," Majority Whip Robert Byrd asked for unanimous consent to proceed to immediate consideration. "I object," said Mansfield, softly but firmly. But when an aide called him off the floor briefly, the Senate swiftly and unanimously adopted the renaming measure.

Toward evening, when all the tributes were done, Mansfield delivered his closing remarks. "I do not leave this place in sadness," he declared in his clear, strong orator's voice. "I leave as one who has lived as a part of it and loved it deeply. I leave personally fulfilled and contented to have been here, one senator of the over 1,700 men and women who have served their states and the Republic in the Senate of the United States." After expressing thanks to a host of people, beginning as always with Maureen and including the Republican as well as Democratic leaderships and the younger members of the Senate, he concluded by saying he did not know whether those gathered in the chamber that day would meet again before this session of Congress was over or, as this group, ever again. "To you who are my friends—to all of you—I can only say thank you and goodbye." With that, he gathered the papers from his desk and walked briskly up the center aisle and out of the chamber, while his colleagues stood and applauded. He did not look back.

AMBASSADOR TO JAPAN

13

By the mid-1970s, Japan had reemerged as one of the world's great powers, yet the U.S.-Japan political relationship seemed little changed since the aftermath of World War II. In the postwar years, Japan's economy had grown twice as fast as that of West Germany or France, and three times as fast as that of the United States to become the capitalist world's second largest economy. Japan's trade surplus with the United States was beginning to rise rapidly, causing growing consternation in Washington. Mansfield, recruited by President Carter and reappointed by President Reagan, worked as U.S. ambassador to Japan in a record-breaking span of eleven and a half years to stabilize and improve what he famously called America's "most important bilateral relationship, bar none."

Preparing to retire from the Senate in late 1976, Mike Mansfield was getting ready to "loaf, think and read," he told a Montana newspaper. "We will be free for the first time in our lives," added Maureen. They planned to build a house on property they had acquired near Missoula, the university town where they were wed, and to spend their summers there. Winters, which are cruel in Montana, would be spent in Florida. Those who knew and admired the retiring Majority Leader had different ideas. A *Baltimore Sun* editorial proposed that incoming President Jimmy Carter move to normalize the still-unofficial relationship with China and name Mansfield the first U.S. ambassador. His successor as Majority Leader, Robert Byrd, recommended to Carter that he send Mansfield to Beijing to be chief U.S. representative there or, failing that, appoint him ambassador to the Soviet Union.

Shortly after taking office, Carter asked Mansfield to serve as ambassador to Mexico, believing that he needed a strong person to deal with problems on the U.S. southern border. Although Mansfield had given courses in Latin American history as well as Far Eastern history in his teaching days and had been longtime chairman of the U.S.-Mexico Parliamentary Group, he turned down the job on the grounds that Mexico City's climate would not be good for Maureen, who was already experiencing heart trouble. Nevertheless, after putting down the phone declining the appointment, he wrote in longhand to Carter, "As I said to you, you do not owe me anything; rather, I owe you a great deal for your kindness and consideration. If I can ever be of service to you, I am at your disposal." He did not have long to wait.

In February, Carter asked Mansfield to go to Hanoi in a delegation headed by Leonard Woodcock, president of the United Auto Workers (UAW) union, to discuss the problem of Americans missing in action (MIAs) and the potential for improved relations with Vietnam. When the mission returned, a Mansfield posting to China loomed as a possibility in the internal discussions of the new administration.

Richard Holbrooke, the incoming Assistant Secretary of State for East Asia and the Pacific, saw a serious problem in a Mansfield assignment to Beijing. Mansfield's final report to the Senate as a result of his 1976 trip to China advocated immediate and unconditional U.S. recognition of the People's Republic, but Carter as a candidate had said he would take no such action before obtaining assurances that China would not attack Taiwan—assurances that China refused to supply. To send Mansfield to Beijing under those circumstances, Holbrooke argued in discussions with Secretary of State Cyrus Vance, "would weaken if not undermine completely our negotiating position" with China on this central issue. Impressed with Woodcock's performance in Hanoi, Holbrooke proposed that the UAW chief, who was among the few people to whom Carter was politically indebted, be sent to Beijing as chief of the U.S. Liaison Office with a charter to negotiate normalization of Sino-American relations, and Mansfield be appointed ambassador to Japan, the most important U.S. ally in Asia. Vance presented the plan to Carter, who greeted it with enthusiasm. Both Woodcock and Mansfield accepted the offers they were given.

Carter did not know Mansfield well but was aware of the nearly universal admiration in which he was held and of his extensive experience in Asia. Knowing that Mansfield had a much greater background in the area than Holbrooke, the President considered him a senior counselor about all of Asia, not just Japan, and instructed U.S. ambassadors in the region to regard him in that light. The word was passed that Carter was prepared to name Mansfield "Ambassador to Asia" as well as ambassador to Japan, a prospect that horrified Holbrooke and the East Asia bureau of the State Department and struck Mansfield himself as impractical. Nonetheless, Carter did ask Mansfield for advice on other countries, sending him to Australia, New Zealand, and Singapore on reporting missions.

Mansfield's experience in Asia included Japan as well as China and Indochina. His ship had stopped in Nagasaki briefly on his way home from the Philippines as a Marine in 1922. In the 1930s he had learned about Japan during summer sessions at UCLA from Kazuo Kawai, a Japanese-born professor who had come to the United States as a child. Based on what he learned from Kawai and extensive reading, Mansfield assigned Japan a large role in the Far Eastern history courses he taught at the University of Montana. In 1942 Mansfield served briefly as a member of an Enemy Alien Hearing Board in Missoula to ascertain the loyalty of Japanese residents who had been rounded up after the Japanese attack on Pearl Harbor. Later, many of those interviewed were sent to internment camps for the rest of the war, whether or not they were judged to be potentially disloyal. Mansfield told me he remembered little of the episode except that his board had given "a clean bill of health" to the Japanese it interviewed.

After being elected to Congress in November 1942, Mansfield spoke often about Japan as a ruthless and determined enemy in World War II. In the postwar years he spoke supportively of the democratization of Japan, especially after witnessing the devastation of Hiroshima and visiting General Douglas MacArthur in 1946. As early as March 1955 he called for much more attention to Japan, the "key to war or peace in the Far East," and charged in a Senate speech that the Eisenhower administration acted "as though these 90 million people in the core of the Western Pacific had sunk into a hole in the sea." In another Senate speech the following year he called for actions by the United States and other free nations to head off a potential realignment of Japan with the Soviet Union or China. Mansfield observed that Japan "must literally fish and trade on a vast scale to survive in peace" but was increasingly running into "the political reality of the adjustments which free nations have to make in their own economies if they are to accommodate Japanese trade." In a foretaste of controversies to come, Mansfield asked, "To put the problem bluntly, how far are the free nations prepared to go in admitting imports from Japan?" In the crisis year of 1960, when the U.S.-Japan Security Treaty was revised and student demonstrations forced cancellation of President Eisenhower's visit to Tokyo, Mansfield made an extensive visit to Japan and issued a comprehensive analysis of U.S.-Japan relations, in which he took Japan seriously as a major world player.

In September 1967 Mansfield was the keynote speaker at the Shimoda Conference in Japan, the first substantial policy dialogue of unofficial leaders of the United States and Japan. He took the occasion to suggest the return to Japan of the Bonin Islands, which had been occupied by U.S. forces since World War II. He also proposed that the greater problem of the return of Okinawa could benefit from consultations on Pacific security between the United States, Japan, and the Soviet Union, leaving out China because of the Cultural Revolution turmoil that had recently begun. Mansfield had been told confidentially by the State Department in advance of his trip that the military importance of the Bonin (Ogasawara) Islands was "small" but was asked not to bring up the issue and to wait for a Japanese appeal. Although he disregarded this advice, Mansfield sent an advance copy of his text to the State Department. Asked by reporters to comment after Mansfield's speech, Secretary of State Dean Rusk threw cold water on the suggestion for three-way discussions involving the Soviets, and told reporters only that the return of the Bonins was under discussion. Johnson returned the Bonin Islands to Japan by executive order the following year. As for Okinawa, it remained for the Nixon administration to work out the complicated and politically sensitive issues regarding its reversion to Japan. When agreement was reached and sent to the Senate, Mansfield learned that the vote had been scheduled for a day when few senators would be in town, thus leading to a skimpy vote and little oratory on the issue. He postponed the vote and alerted senators, resulting in an 84 to 6 tally that resoundingly endorsed the return of Okinawa and the importance of U.S.-Japan relations more broadly.

From then until his retirement from the Senate, Mansfield's office was an important port of call for prominent Japanese political figures on visits to Washington, and he was nearly always ready and willing to see them. Mansfield made a total of six trips to Japan as a member of Congress and commented frequently on Japan-related topics. The last trip, lasting eight days, was in July 1976, several months before he left the Senate. As usual, he saw the prime minister, then Takeo Miki, and other principal officials of the government. His report to the Senate Foreign Relations Committee concluded, "U.S.-Japan relations are good but they could be better. The era of patron-client is over. A new relationship on the basis of equality and a mutuality of interests has begun."

THE BATTLE OF TOKAI MURA

Jimmy Carter met Mansfield in the Oval Office on May 24, 1977, to give him private instructions as his ambassador. Preparing for the conversation, he wrote down seven brief notes in longhand as guidelines for his policy. The first was, "No Shokus" referring to the shock to Japan of President Nixon's opening to China and lesser shocks from other uncoordinated U.S. moves. Of the other six points Carter noted, two dealt with trade and four dealt with security or international political issues. The most urgent was identified by Carter's note, "Tokai—next week." What arose from that item would underscore Mansfield's unusual status as an American diplomat and send his prestige soaring within Japan.

The issue was Carter's opposition to a Japanese pilot plant for the reprocessing of nuclear fuel at Tokai-mura [Tokai village] northeast of Tokyo, which was nearing completion after an expenditure of $200 million and which embodied fervent Japanese hopes for greater energy independence. Carter was well acquainted with nuclear issues since serving as a young naval officer under Admiral Hyman Rickover, the godfather of the U.S. nuclear navy. In his presidential campaign Carter spoke passionately against the spread of nuclear weapons, and in his inaugural address he declared that his ultimate goal was "the elimination of all nuclear weapons from this earth."

As President, he began a high-visibility national and international fight against reprocessing, an industrial operation that separates out plutonium from irradiated nuclear fuel. Plutonium is useful as fuel in civilian power reactors, which is what the Japanese had in mind, but it is also the raw material of nuclear weapons. Having suffered the only atomic attacks in history—the U.S. strikes against Hiroshima and Nagasaki in 1945 at the end of World War II—the Japanese government and public had always been strongly opposed to nuclear weapons. Carter and his administration were not concerned that Japan would make weapons from the plutonium but considered the fate of the Tokai plant the first test of their global drive against reprocessing and thus an issue of great importance in the fight against nuclear proliferation.

When Prime Minister Takeo Fukuda visited the White House in March, only two months after Carter took office, the U.S. President called reprocessing "uneconomical" and said he wanted all nations, including the United States, to halt it. Nevertheless, energy-short Japan was determined to go ahead. Fukuda asked a series of specific questions on the issue, whereupon Carter tossed a copy of a reprocessing report sponsored by the Ford Foundation across the table while startled officials looked on. Fukuda promised to study the document, which recommended an end to reprocessing. In early April, Carter announced that the United States would defer indefinitely its own reprocessing of nuclear fuel as encouragement to others to do so.

As Mansfield prepared to travel to Japan, the White House was considering plans to eliminate or drastically alter the production of plutonium at the nearly completed Tokai plant or even to prevent it from operating. Washington had leverage to make such demands because the enriched uranium materials to be used in the plant originated in the United States, and therefore Japan was required to obtain U.S. permission to reprocess them. The United States had made no objection while the Japanese were building the plant and preparing to operate it. Japan was therefore reacting sharply to the well-publicized White House deliberations, especially because U.S. allies in Britain, France, and West Germany were all operating reprocessing plants. The United States was powerless to stop these operations because they did not use U.S.-supplied materials. To stop Japan from reprocessing while others went ahead was seen in Tokyo as unequal treatment and gross discrimination.

"We are in a genuine bind," wrote Michael Armacost, then an Asian affairs specialist on Carter's National Security Council staff in a secret memorandum on the problem. "The Japanese need to avoid the appearance of submitting to unilateral U.S. decisions which, whatever the intent, have a discriminatory result. We need to avoid actions on Tokai that would compromise the broader principles of the President's nonproliferation policy." Zbigniew Brzezinski, Armacost's boss, passed on these concerns to Carter, adding that any clear indication of discrimination would "enormously weaken" the domestic political position of Japanese Prime Minister Takeo Fukuda, "generate anti-American nationalistic reactions on the Right and Left, precipitate Japanese efforts to diversify their sources of enriched uranium supplies, and complicate our talks of eliciting Japanese cooperation on a broad range of multilateral issues." Nonetheless, as Armacost and Brzezinski realized, Carter remained dedicated in his intense opposition to reprocessing, which he considered a worldwide danger, and few in the new administration were willing to take him on.

By the time Mansfield arrived in Tokyo on June 7, Carter had secretly given tentative approval to a U.S. demand that Japan modify the Tokai plant to produce a mixture of radioactive products rather than the much-feared pure plutonium that could be used in nuclear weapons. A joint technical study team of U.S. and Japanese officials estimated that the changes would cost more than $240 million and would delay the operation of the facility by at least five years. Administration officials agreed that the Japanese were likely to resist such changes but disagreed about how hard to push for them.

In his first weeks in Japan, Mansfield quickly grasped the gravity of the nuclear production dispute for the Japanese, who are entirely dependent on imported energy and who had been alarmed by energy shortages in the aftermath of the 1973 Middle East war. Prime Minister Fukuda and his aides depicted nuclear energy as a "matter of life or death" for the nation. With the Carter administration moving to a hard line against reprocessing at the Tokai plant, Mansfield decided to intervene.

On July 12, he sent a lengthy confidential cable addressed personally to Secretary of State Vance urging Washington to seek a compromise, with a request that his views be made known to Carter. As ambassador, Mansfield did his own thinking but delegated most of the execution and almost all of the details to his staff, more like a chairman of the board than a chief operating officer. In this case, the cable and many of the arguments behind it were products of the Tokyo embassy's Science Counselor, Justin Bloom, an experienced official in whom Mansfield reposed great confidence. "Justin, should I sign it?" the ambassador asked when presented with the finished product, which made a strong case against Carter's inclination and the existing White House consensus. Bloom sat in silence for half a minute, understanding that the cable would be committing the ambassador to a potential clash with the President. "Yes, sir I think you should," he said finally. Mansfield reached for the pen on his desk and affixed his signature.

"I have been at this post only a few weeks but it is now clear to me that there is one political issue between US and Japan that warrants my sending you a direct message. I refer to the nuclear fuel reprocessing problem that lies before both governments," the cable began. Unless the two sides urgently seek a compromise, he continued, it could have "profoundly adverse effects on our future relations." After stressing the importance of the issue to Japan and reciting some of the misunderstandings with Washington, Mansfield wrote:

> I am not in a position to offer to you the technical basis for a compromise; I leave that to the experts on both sides. However, I am of the strongest possible opinion that, first, a compromise is mandatory if the bilateral alliance is to be preserved in a form that is free of lingering Japanese suspicions and best encourages positive Japanese support. Second, the compromise must be reached expeditiously—within a very few months at the most; to procrastinate longer will act to harden each side's position. Third, the compromise must include permission for the Tokai plant to operate in some fashion at the earliest possible time. And fourth, the Japanese must be permitted to retain the option of operating the plant for commercial reprocessing purposes in the event that the U.S. is unsuccessful in stopping plutonium reprocessing throughout the world.

Mansfield's cable was relayed to the White House, where Carter read it and was persuaded. He wrote in its upper-right margin in a firm, clear hand, "To Cy [Cyrus Vance]—Inform Mansfield that I will personally expedite the compromise decision. He can tell Fukuda. Give me options without delay[.] JC." The cable and the President's reaction were quickly made known to top decision makers. Brzezinski sent a copy of Carter's comments to Vance with the admonition, "The President feels this is very urgent." According to Armacost, who was working on the issue at the National Security Council, Mansfield's cable was "a very critical element" in shaping the U.S. willingness to work out a compromise acceptable to Japan. "It seemed mind-boggling at the time. It was a 180-degree shift" from earlier thinking.

On July 15, Carter signed a letter to Fukuda officially informing him that "I believe we can find a compromise that will accommodate both our interests, and I will work hard to achieve it." One copy was sent to Fukuda via a little-known direct and private telecommunications link (oddly named "the Batman channel") that had been set up in 1972 but which had been used only twice before. The original copy was delivered in person by Mansfield in his first official meeting with Fukuda since arriving a month before. The prime minister said Carter's assurances established "a good direction" for both sides to settle the vexing and, by now, highly publicized problem.

Mansfield's intervention and Carter's commitment to seek a compromise established the outlines of the eventual settlement of the issue. After negotiations with the Japanese, Carter agreed to permit the Tokai plant to begin operating on schedule to produce plutonium, but the settlement also required it to convert to production of mixed elements in later years if this were found to be technically feasible and effective.

The struggle over Tokai-mura was the first international test of Carter's anti-plutonium policy. The outcome was seen by Jessica Tuchman Mathews, a leading nonproliferation proponent on the White House staff, as a "very serious blow" to the policy under formation. The American press called it a "turnabout" by the administration that averted a serious clash with Japan. Veteran Tokyo correspondent Sam Jameson said, "Fukuda and the entire government would have been in a state of revolution if the United States had said no" to operation of the plant.

News of Mansfield's role slowly emerged as a result of leaks to the press in Washington and Tokyo. Without knowing the details—some of which have been highly classified until now—an editorial in *Mainichi Shimbun,* a major Japanese daily, commented on Mansfield's part in the Tokai saga under the headline, "A Giant Walks among Us." From that time on, the Japanese were never in doubt that Mansfield had a direct and unencumbered pipeline to the president, whether Carter or Reagan, whatever the true facts of the matter. When a visiting journalist, David Broder of the *Washington Post,* mentioned *Mainichi's* evaluation during a 1977 visit to Tokyo, a "distinctly nervous" Mansfield responded, "Sometimes I think they expect too much of me and they build me up too much. That's what scares me. I'm no giant. I'm just a fellow embarking on a new career."

THE NEW BOY ON THE BLOCK

Mansfield's life in Tokyo was very different from what he had known in Washington. His responsibilities, while great, were narrowly focused on a relatively small set of issues concerning the United States and Japan rather than on all the issues, foreign and domestic, that come before the U.S. Senate. In his personal life, he and Maureen had gone from taking care of themselves in a modest brick house in Washington to living in a palatial residence staffed by Japanese servants and American aides intent on providing them with every possible comfort and assistance. The residence, built in 1929 on the crest of a hill overlooking a prestigious section of downtown Tokyo, had been occupied from 1932 to 1942 by Joseph C. Grew, the celebrated ambassador who experienced a precipitous decline of U.S.-Japan relations down to the final blow of the Japanese attack on Pearl Harbor. "Big bushes, smooth green lawns, flowers, tessellated pools . . . a real oasis in the more or less ugly surroundings of the new-grown city," wrote Grew of the residential compound where he was interned for seven months after the outbreak of the war before being repatriated in a prisoner exchange.

After the defeat of Japan, the residence was home for six years to General Douglas MacArthur, the American proconsul who remade the Japanese government and, to some extent, Japanese society. It was here in September 1945 that Emperor Hirohito, in cutaway and top hat, called on the conquering general, who was wearing khakis with an open collar, and posed for a famous photograph of vanquished and victor that symbolized the Japanese world turned upside down. From 1961 to 1965 the residence was occupied by another celebrated ambassador, the noted Japan scholar Edwin O. Reischauer, who spoke the language fluently, knew the history and culture intimately, and whose wife, Haru, had been born in Japan.

Mansfield was familiar with Japan from his university days and his long service in Congress, but as ambassador he made no effort to learn the language or to become deeply engaged in Japanese culture. At that stage of his life, however, he and Japan were a perfect fit: he was a senior and respected person who said little and understood much about politics and human nature. "He was an American with Japanese habits," said Thomas Foley, who visited Tokyo often as a member and, later, Speaker of the House of Representatives and who was among Mansfield's successors as U.S. ambassador to Japan. "Senior Japanese do not talk a lot. The tradition is to let the subordinates do the discussion, offer the options and carry on the debate and then the senior person decides. Mike's famous taciturn behavior fit right into the Japanese tradition."

Based on his reputation as Senate Majority Leader and his initial success in the Tokai case, Mansfield's prestige in Japan was sky-high from the beginning of his ambassadorship. He was universally considered an *omono*—a very important person. "He didn't hesitate to tell the Japanese what he thought. Neither did he spare his own countrymen," observed Kimpei Shiba, a columnist for Japan's influential *Asahi Shimbun* in 1980. "He has become one of the very few ambassadors here (perhaps the only one) of 60, whose name the average Japanese knows." Even amid the depths of bilateral trade disputes his voice was heard if not always heeded by Japanese leaders. "If Lee Iacocca [then chairman of Chrysler Corporation and an outspoken critic of Japan] says it, Japanese become defensive," observed SONY chairman Akio Morita in 1986. "But if Mike says it, in his way, he gets listened to."

Asked by a radio reporter in 1980 how the ambassadorship compared to his expectations, Mansfield said there was not much difference except that the job was "not quite as difficult as I anticipated." Every indication is that he found the post less taxing and more satisfying than his later years in the Senate and that Maureen found it one of the happiest times of her life. To a far greater degree than in Washington, he was able to be home for lunch and dinner. Maureen was part of his official life inside and outside of the residence, and with a staff that made everything much easier. A venturesome and outgoing person, she made friends with Japanese artists and intellectuals. Always eager to please her, Mike was known to cancel diplomatic meetings to accompany Maureen to fashion shows and cultural events in which she had an interest.

Their early social activities presented a worrisome problem. Ambassador and Mrs. James Hodgson, who immediately preceded them to Tokyo, briefed the Mansfields before they left Washington about what to expect. Hodgson, a former vice president of Lockheed Aircraft Company, spent a great deal of personal money on entertainment, including as much as $1,000 monthly on flowers. Maureen, like Mike, a veteran of the Great Depression and a person with limited financial resources, was shocked and dismayed, according to William Sherman, who was the State Department's country director for Japan at the time and later deputy chief of mission in Tokyo. "Maureen had no intention of spending 10 cents on flowers," Sherman recalled. "In early days, when she saw a flower, she wanted to know who bought it and who was paying for it."

For U.S. ambassadors, a principal means of interacting with the Japanese and important foreigners in Japan is embassy receptions. Terrified by the potential drain on their limited financial resources, Maureen insisted on keeping the books herself on entertainment and household expenses, rather than leaving the task to embassy administrative officers as is usual. "Maureen spends all her time keeping the household accounts. Like a CPA," her husband complained four months after their arrival. Initially she insisted that no more than forty people be invited to receptions at the residence. Seeing this limitation as impractical in view of official and social obligations, she gradually relaxed the restrictions. In his second year in Tokyo, Mansfield personally appealed to Carter in a White House meeting for more representational (social) funds, on grounds that costs in Tokyo were much higher than even those in New York. The request was granted from State Department special funds.

Dan Russel, a young Japanese-speaking Foreign Service officer who was Mansfield's staff aide in 1985, recalled the ambiance of the first reception he attended on the spacious first floor of the residence:

We went through the very formidable cast iron doors into the very elegant and dramatic foyer of the mansion. There was Mansfield, standing all alone in the entryway of a big hall, a sight that I would see again and again over the next two years—Mansfield alone, quiet, comfortable. We all walked up and I introduced my wife to him. He said in typical Mansfield style, "Dan, why don't you take your wife here and go and look around the joint?" My wife was about six months pregnant and he was very solicitous of her— frequently cautioned me at events to make sure she didn't have to stand too much, to find her a chair to relax. I got my first glimpse then of Mrs. Mansfield, coming down the long, sweeping Hollywood style marble stairs. I thought she was very, very handsome—exquisitely dressed. She gave off an aura of warmth and kindness.

The ambassador was comfortable standing in the reception line even if no guests were there, and rarely left his post to mingle. He often kept a shot glass of bourbon and a glass of water on a table within reach. According to Russel, the receptions were notorious even in the late 1980s for having little quality and sparse food. If the invitation was for 6:00 to 7:30 P.M., as was often the case, the bar and food service would shut down sharply at the appointed end time, and Russel would round up the guests and herd them toward the exits.

The other half of Mansfield's life in Tokyo centered on the ambassadorial office on the ninth floor of the glass-and-steel embassy office building just down the hill from the residential compound. As he had done throughout his congressional career, Mansfield rose very early in the morning. By 7:30 A.M. at the latest, he had dressed, had breakfast with Maureen, and walked alone past the back garden of the residence down a steep set of stone steps to the office building, where a U.S. Marine guard was waiting to let him in. At a landing on the steps he passed the marker of the grave of Ambassador Grew's beloved dog Sambo, whose rescue from the icy waters of the Imperial moat attracted great press and public attention.

Mansfield prided himself, as he had in Washington, on being the first to arrive at his office, and his personal staff was wise enough not to show up ahead of him. He spent the first hour or so reading cables, mail, the English language newspapers, and embassy translations of the Japanese press. With a pair of shears, he cut out items of interest and studied them carefully, often passing them with a note to an embassy official asking for explanation or corroboration.

As always, press reports were a prime source of information for him and were taken as seriously—sometimes more seriously—than official reports. He considered relations with journalists important and in Tokyo, as in Washington, always spoke to reporters on the record, even in private conversation, never taking refuge in "background" or "off the record" comments that could not be attributed to him by name. At his first formal press conference, only a week after his arrival, he skipped the usual introductory niceties and simply began, "Ladies and gentleman, I'm the new boy on the block. . . . Shoot!" More than one hundred Japanese reporters and members of camera crews were momentarily stunned, even after the translation, partly in confusion over his admonition to "shoot." Reporters became accustomed to his short but often pithy answers. Asked during a controversy over the proper exchange rates between dollars and yen what he thought a dollar was worth, Mansfield avoided a possible diplomatic gaffe by replying without hesitation, "100 cents."

The U.S. Embassy in Tokyo with its seven consulates in major cities was America's largest overseas diplomatic establishment, with 700 officials and employees, American and Japanese, representing twenty-two different U.S. government agencies. From time to time the embassy's senior staff gathered in Mansfield's conference room for meetings, which were often remarkably short, sometimes only five or ten minutes. "He liked people to speak in the way that he spoke, in a very concise way," according to Rust Deming, who was a political officer in the embassy in the early 1980s and later political minister. On one occasion an embassy official pleaded that "it would take me several hours to adequately outline the full detailed ramifications of this policy," to which Mansfield responded, "I don't think you could do it if you had several years." Recounting the incident to a reporter, a Mansfield aide explained, "He has a very low tolerance for, uh, how can I say it politely, barnyard bunk." If someone was inclined to ramble on, Mansfield was known to walk out of the meeting.

His same terse and yet impressive ways were evident in his meetings with the parade of visitors to his office nearly every working day. He would agree to at least a brief meeting with almost anybody who asked to see him unless a senior aide objected, and sometimes even then. "To anyone from Montana or who had lived in Montana, or had a close relative in Montana or had even stopped in Montana, he invariably said yes," according to Dan Russel. Improving the back-home ambiance were paintings and prints by Charles M. Russell, the famous western artist who Mansfield had admired as a boy, and copies of the *Hungry Horse News* on the table.

Whether from Montana or elsewhere, whether American or Japanese, Mansfield's welcome for visitors was always the same and nearly always their most vivid memory of the occasion. After greeting them at the doorway, he would escort them to the sofa and ask if they would like a cup of coffee. "He would then go around to the back of his office where there was a little kitchenette and a pot of hot water and some cups," recalled Russel. "He would place a spoonful of Tasters Choice instant coffee in each cup and fill each one with water. He'd carry the cups out. Once I stood up, feeling awkward doing nothing, and I met Mansfield halfway and took the cups from him. I got such a dirty look from the visitor that I realized I had denied him the singular pleasure of being handed a cup of coffee personally prepared by Ambassador Mansfield. From that point on, I just watched." Mansfield's coffee routine was impressive to Americans and astounding to Japanese, who were accustomed to the invariable service of tea by secretaries or other women attendants known as "office ladies." A Japanese academic who had paid a call on the ambassador before an extended trip to the United States confided to Mansfield during a return call that he had told his wife about the ambassadorial coffee service. "What did she say?" Mansfield asked. "She fainted," was the reply. Mansfield told me that he had begun the practice, which he continued at his Washington office after his retirement as ambassador, in an effort to break down the "office lady" habit, which he found demeaning to the servers. "I hoped that by my pouring coffee, I would not only show personal friendship but alleviate somewhat the position of the ladies who served tea," he said. It wasn't successful in breaking the Japanese habit, but it succeeded in making a visit to Mansfield memorable to a generation of Japanese and Americans.

Beyond seeing Japanese in his office, Mansfield made it a personal project to visit each of the country's forty-seven prefectures, which he accomplished by September 1980. In nearly all cases, the visits were substantial, including meetings and speeches. He often insisted on staying in an ordinary and modest hotel room, to the discomfort of his hosts, who always wanted to put him in the most elegant suite available. Maureen frequently traveled with him and sometimes traveled separately. When she went to the famous snow festival in Sapporo, the principal city of the northern Japanese island of Hokkaido, Maureen insisted on going down the ice slide. The U.S. Consulate personnel were terrified that she would be hurt, but were powerless to stop her. "She enjoyed it with childlike glee," according to Donald Westmore, then the consul general.

His relationship of trust and confidence with Japanese of particular interest or importance to him was extraordinary. Sunao Sonoda, who was foreign minister from September 1977 to November 1979 and again from May to November 1981, had been an officer in the Japanese *kamikaze* (suicide) corps during World War II and had voted against the U.S.-Japan Security Treaty. He had not been notably friendly to Americans and had never set foot in the U.S. Embassy. When he became foreign minister for the first time, Mansfield immediately called on him and persuaded him to make an early trip to Washington, with Mansfield paving the way by contacting his friends in the Senate. They became such good friends that Sonoda often sent texts of his speeches to Mansfield for comment, sometimes before they were delivered. When Mansfield approved, Sonoda considered it "a heartwarming gesture to me." Sonoda wrote in his memoirs, which were intended for a Japanese audience and published only in that language, "Ambassador Mansfield loved the United States more than anything else. At the same time, he never lost a calm and objective perspective either toward his own country or toward Japan. Responding to necessity, he was even equipped with the courage to state his personal opinion on both. I consider that a true statesman is this type of person."

Although it was not widely known during his service in Japan, Mansfield forged close ties with members of the Imperial family. Among these was his relationship with Crown Prince Akihito, who succeeded to the Chrysanthemum Throne on the death of his father, Hirohito, in 1989, shortly after Mansfield left Japan. Akihito usually spent the month of August at the mountain resort of Karuizawa, where the romance between the royal couple had originally blossomed. He invited the Mansfields six or seven times to a small private luncheon there in which he and the other guests—all the rest being Japanese—were casually dressed. After lunch Akihito, who by postwar practice was required to remain aloof from substantive issues of Japanese or international life, usually took a walk with Mansfield, during which he quizzed the ambassador about such questions as the U.S.-Japan relationship, China, Korea, and the division of Europe. Akihito never expressed an opinion and Mansfield kept their relationship confidential. When the Crown Prince and Princess visited the United States in 1987, Mansfield took the unusual step of accompanying them across the Pacific on their Japan Air Lines jet and at every step on their tour of Boston, Washington, and New York. Shortly before leaving Japan the Mansfields hosted an intimate and informal dinner at the embassy residence for the royal couple, who rarely came to diplomatic or private residences. There were no photographs, no publicity, and nothing appeared in the society columns.

As ambassador, Mansfield joined few organizations, an exception being Kibokai, a society of people born in the year 1903, which was the Year of the Rabbit in the Oriental zodiac. On his birthday in 1983, Mansfield wrote his thoughts on the occasion in Japanese style on a *shikishi*, a square paper card usually used for calligraphy. Mansfield's contribution to the society was in his clear, firm hand in English:

> On reaching 80 years
> I've been fortunate
>> A good wife
>> good health
>> good friends
> To be in a country like Japan
> On life—no complaints but
> pleased at the way it has treated
> me
>> Mike Mansfield
>> U.S. Ambassador
>> Tokyo—3/16/83

NEGOTIATING FOR CARTER

In his formal letter to Mansfield setting forth his ambassadorial authorities and responsibilities, President Carter declared that as "my personal representative," he expected Mansfield "to report with directness and candor" on the situation in Japan. He added, "The Secretary of State and I will always welcome the opportunity to consider your recommendations for alternative courses of action and policy proposals." The letter was a standard missive sent to new ambassadors, but Mansfield took Carter at his word. He considered himself authorized to communicate personally with the President, which most U.S. ambassadors are never able to do. Based on his long experience in dealing with presidents from Franklin D. Roosevelt to Gerald Ford, Mansfield understood the vital importance of such direct communications rather than indirect ties in which his views could be muffled or lost in the bureaucracy below.

Mansfield accepted the fact that for the first time in his career, he was serving "under" a president as a subordinate rather that serving "with" a president as an independent member of Congress. Yet he also knew that Carter—and Reagan after him—expected him to use and to express his own judgment to a greater degree than most career diplomats or other government aides. Unlike other U.S. ambassadors, for example, he never cleared his public speeches or remarks to the press with the State Department before delivering them but sent them to Washington after the fact.

Although he was careful not to dilute the impact by overdoing it, he seized the opportunity on numerous occasions to communicate personally with Carter, as when he wrote to him in longhand after turning down the ambassadorship to Mexico. After receiving the White House Christmas card in mid-December 1977, Mansfield penned a substantial letter in the guise of a thank-you note, discussing recent U.S.-Japan trade talks and the challenges of the North Pacific. "My prayers and my hopes for our country ride with you. May the Lord continue to watch over you and guide you," he wrote to the notably religious president.

A remarkable example of Mansfield's direct approach is a four-paragraph message of advice on unmarked stationery that he handed to Carter in the White House in March 1978 as planning was under way for the Washington summit in May with Prime Minister Takeo Fukuda. "It is important that we not treat the visit of Prime Minister Fukuda as an occasion for 'turning up the heat' on the Japanese with respect to trade issues," Mansfield's note began. Mansfield explained that a Japanese prime minister is not an independent decision maker in the American sense but that his stature and ability to "coordinate" policy would be affected by how the public at home views the summit. "In Japan, appearance is everything," he wrote. "If Fukuda's meeting with the President looks like confrontation or even lack of agreement, we will inexorably move into that mode and the progress we both desire will not take place." Despite growing concern in Washington regarding trade issues, Carter received Fukuda in a cordial and cooperative spirit without notable clashes.

These examples should not suggest that Mansfield always succeeded in presenting his ideas undiluted. In November 1977, for example, he cabled a lengthy report on the "state of the relationship" with Japan, addressed to

Vance and Holbrooke, with a request that it also be presented to Carter. He found the "increasingly contentious atmosphere" between the two countries to be disturbing. Although acknowledging that the problems were serious and that "Japanese performance in some areas leaves much to be desired," he urged that Washington should "assign responsibility carefully, recognize limitations on Japanese government's ability to influence situation, and avoid bearing down so hard on specific problems that we cause others to emerge." In sum, he wrote, "We have our difficulties with Japan; we need to keep in mind that Japanese have good many with us as well."

At the White House, Brzezinski asked Armacost to summarize the Mansfield cable in a brief memorandum for Carter. Armacost's draft of the memo said that Mansfield's general appraisal "as usual . . . registers some eminently sensible points," which he briefly mentioned. Armacost added, "The message, however, also bears the unmistakable traces of the embassy's traditional 'Cherry Blossom Protection Association' mentality," referring to an image used to deride those believed to be overprotective of Japan, "and therefore tends to obscure other important considerations that we should bear in mind over the coming months." Armacost urged that "we push hard for equitable access to Japan's markets" despite the adverse effect it would have on the bilateral political relationship. In sum, he wrote, "the Embassy assessment is only part of the picture. Mansfield has indicated his hope that his message will be brought to the President's attention. I think it is a bit discursive for that purpose."

Brzezinski, mindful of the relationship between Carter and Mansfield, edited Armacost's memo, omitting his criticism of the embassy's "Cherry Blossom Protection Association" mentality, and his conclusion that it did not merit presentation to Carter. The final result summarized for Carter Mansfield's eleven pages of "eminently sensible points" in one paragraph but went on to state, "They are not the only considerations, however, that should guide us in the weeks ahead." The memo advocated "strong external pressure" on Japan to be applied "adroitly, yet persistently," declaring that the political fallout in Japan "should be manageable." Mansfield has been instructed to make a strong presentation to Fukuda on the trade issue shortly, the memo said.

Mansfield did make such a presentation, as did a special emissary from Washington, Richard Rivers of the Special Trade Representative's office. The sudden toughening of the U.S. stand generated headlines in Washington as well as Tokyo. Two weeks later, Mansfield reported optimistically that he believed "we have basically accomplished our major task—that of convincing the GOJ [Government of Japan] that we are dealing with a serious problem." Henry Owen, the White House coordinator for international economic policy, quoted Mansfield's report as well as a U.S. intelligence report on a private conversation between Fukuda and Foreign Minister Sonoda in telling Carter, "It is barely possible that a foreign economic policy success of some importance may be in the offing." Nonetheless, the fast-rising bilateral trade imbalance in Japan's favor continued its upward spiral in 1978. The imbalance was reduced temporarily in 1979 owing to U.S. pressure and economic developments but rose sharply again in 1980 and throughout the rest of Mansfield's ambassadorship.

A surer way to get his views across, Mansfield understood, was to present them to the President in person, as difficult as that is for most ambassadors. In his letter in response to the White House Christmas card in December 1977, Mansfield expressed his desire to see Carter in person when he returned to Washington on leave in early February. Carter responded by telling Mansfield—and the presidential appointment secretary, Tim Kraft—that he looked forward to a private meeting when the ambassador was in town. On the morning of February 7, 1978, accompanied by Vance, Brzezinski, Holbrooke, and Armacost, Mansfield met Carter in the Oval Office for twenty-five minutes. After Mansfield briefly expressed satisfaction with the resolution of the Tokai nuclear issue and with recent trade negotiations, he encouraged Carter to boost Fukuda's sagging political standing at home by inviting him to a Washington summit in May (which took place as he suggested). Mansfield then turned to an issue that was much on his mind, U.S. military deployments in Asia and the Pacific.

In this meeting and another face-to-face meeting with the President in October 1978, the man who had proposed to bring half the U.S. troops home from Europe and who had fought strenuously against U.S. military action in Southeast Asia urged Carter to beef up American naval and air forces in Asia and the Pacific. When I asked him years later about the apparent contradiction between his wish to reduce troops in Europe and his wish to increase forces in Asia and the Pacific, he responded that he saw these as "two separate issues—no connection." Others thought differently. Brent Scowcroft, who had dealt frequently with Mansfield as Henry Kissinger's aide in the Nixon administration and national security adviser for President Ford, told me he had "never seen such a transformation" as had taken place when Mansfield went to Japan. As a member of Congress "he thought we ought to come home and tend to our own knitting and to hell with the rest of the world," Scowcroft said, but as ambassador "he just turned around completely" and became "one of the leading advocates for American involvement . . . reaching out and participating [in the world]."

Following the anguishing U.S. retreat and defeat in Vietnam, Carter had come into office vowing to remove American ground troops from South Korea. This position was endorsed by Mansfield until a re-evaluation of North Korean troop strength caused him to change his mind and forced Carter to drop his plans. Before this happened, in the February 7, 1978, meeting Mansfield expressed his strong support for the Korean troop withdrawals but also said "it would be helpful to our regional position if we simultaneously augmented and strengthened our naval and air forces in the Pacific."

He was more emphatic in a lengthy cable he addressed directly to Carter after the meeting to reiterate his views. Thoughtful people in Japan and perhaps throughout the region, he said, "understand that the attention we paid East Asia in the Vietnam war years was artificial and unsustainably intense. But they nevertheless feel now that we may have swung too far in the other direction." Faced with a rising Soviet naval presence in the region, Mansfield urged that "we ought to strengthen the Seventh Fleet and the Air Force in the Pacific" in an "appropriate and prudent response." In his view this would contribute to maintaining "strategic equilibrium" in the area. "No less important," he added, "it would be a psychological shot in the arm to all of Asia, demonstrating that we mean it when we say we are in the Pacific and along the rim of Asia to stay."

Eight months later, in another meeting with Carter at the White House, this one arranged through Vice President Fritz Mondale, Mansfield continued his appeal while drawing a sharp contrast between the deployment of troops on the Asian mainland and naval power stationed offshore, an appealing distinction for Carter as a former naval officer. "Mr. President, we are a Pacific power," he began in a forty-minute meeting on October 27. "I have been concerned about the disparity between our fleets in the Atlantic and in the Pacific. We are not a mainland Asia power, and we have only run into trouble there. We should stay out militarily. But we are interested in the rim of Asia." Once more Mansfield urged adding to the Seventh Fleet, which patrols the Pacific and Indian Oceans, and beefing up the U.S. Air Force in the area. He also reported, with approval, that the Japanese "are increasing their military establishment but gradually and not in a way that will alarm their neighbors and provoke bad memories of the past."

Carter, who was sparing in his praise of subordinates or associates, expressed himself as "quite pleased with your service in Japan," which he described as "both constructive and stabilizing." Both he and Fukuda have "absolute confidence in you," the President continued. "You have helped avoid economic disturbances. Knowing that you are in Tokyo and having the benefit of your sound observations and candid comments has helped our relationship." Carter went on to concede that in the two years of his presidency, "we have not adequately emphasized Asia, which is natural as a result of the sensitivities over Vietnam and the Taiwan question." But more recently U.S. attention has grown, he said, as evidenced by "an escalating series of visits" by senior officials to Japan, Southeast Asia, and the People's Republic of China. He did not tell Mansfield that Brzezinski, who was present at the meeting, had secretly informed Deng Xiaoping in May that Carter had "made up his mind" to normalize relations with China and that intense planning to solve the remaining issues—from which Vance and the State Department were excluded—had been held in the White House only two weeks earlier.

"The North Pacific is the most strategic region in the world" in view of the presence of the United States as well as the Soviet Union, China, and Japan," Mansfield continued. "Everything is there if we'll only grab the opportunity. I've felt this since my service in the Marines in the 1920s and in Congress and my time at the University of Montana."

Although Carter praised Mansfield's role and views, he was not happy with the Asia policies of his own administration. "What can we do to capitalize on what Mike has said? I need some specific recommendations" he said, turning to Vance, who was accompanied by two other State Department officials.

"OK, and then we'll come up with a list of specifics," the Secretary of State replied.

"Now our approach is haphazard. We have no clear-cut agenda," Carter complained.

"OK, we'll provide an agenda," Vance responded lamely.

Three months later the idea of intensified activity in Asia was cut short by dramatic events in another part of the world. In mid-January the Shah of Iran left Tehran for exile following massive riots. Two weeks after that, the Ayatollah Khomeini arrived to take power. This led to the redoubling of international oil prices and eventually to the seizure of U.S. diplomats in Tehran as hostages. These events brought on the greatest crises of the Carter presidency.

KEEPING TIES TO CAPITOL HILL

Even while performing the role of a diplomat, Mansfield retained his ties to Congress. His appointment as ambassador to Japan had brought an outpouring of support from lawmakers. His swearing-in ceremony at the Capitol had been attended by 85 of the 100 senators as well as many friends from the House of Representatives and elsewhere. Knowing the crucial importance of congressional support for foreign policy—something on which the Carter administration was notably deficient—he was determined to use these relationships to good advantage.

In his private office in Tokyo, he placed framed and autographed photographs of the leaders of the House and Senate of both parties alongside the traditional pictures of the president and vice president that appear in every embassy. His first major speech as ambassador dwelt heavily on the role of Congress in contemporary foreign affairs. He backed this up with stern lectures on the danger that excessive exports would trigger protectionist reactions in Congress, where "the first rule is political survival." Speaking to Japanese audiences, who, like other non-Americans, tend to think of the U.S. government only in terms of the executive branch, he rarely failed to emphasize the role of the legislative branch that he knew so well.

When senior members of Congress visited Japan, Mansfield usually met them at Narita Airport, an hour away from downtown Tokyo by car, even when they pleaded that meeting them there was a waste of his time. During office meetings with members of Congress, an aide would often appear with a message after about half an hour only to be waved off with the admonition, "Tell them I am busy, seeing a congressional delegation," emphasizing that for him this was top priority. He also made it a point to meet U.S. state governors who came through Tokyo; by 1986 he had met the governors of forty-seven of the fifty states as they toured Japan.

In correspondence to members of congressional committees and their study groups, Mansfield continually urged lawmakers to visit Japan to obtain clearer ideas about the nature of the problems between the two nations. He was also quick to respond to charges from members of Congress that the embassy was less than vigilant in promoting U.S. economic interests, as when he answered a letter to that effect from a congressional task force on Japan in 1978. "I am satisfied that my staff is vigorously at work to help American businessmen in this complicated market and that they bring to their jobs a sensitive understanding of how best to accomplish our aims. Sometimes they can accomplish more in a non-confrontational atmosphere than they can in a head-on clash. I think we should look at the results and not at the methods," he wrote to Representative James R. Jones of Oklahoma, the Japan Task Force chairman.

A highly publicized contact between Mansfield and a representative of Congress occurred in mid-1978 when Michael Pillsbury, a Republican staff member of the Senate Budget Committee, visited Tokyo. Pillsbury, according to an embassy staff member who accompanied him as an interpreter, downgraded Mansfield's views in talks with Japanese officials, saying that the ambassador was "out of touch" with Capitol Hill. When this was reported up the line, Mansfield wrote a four-page cable to Edmund Muskie, the Budget Committee chairman, complaining of this and other statements Pillsbury had made in Tokyo. Pointing out that he had been among those who created the Budget Committee and that he had followed its recent deliberations, rather than being out of touch, "it strikes me as a bit out of order that he should go around Tokyo talking this way," Mansfield wrote.

As soon as Mansfield's cable was received, Muskie and the ranking Republican on the committee, Henry Bellmon, summoned Pillsbury back to Washington, where he was fired. When the story hit the press, I called Pillsbury to get his side of it. He came to the *Washington Post* to protest that he had been misquoted, but the documents that he brought with him indicated otherwise. Mansfield told me that a year or two later he had met

Pillsbury, who apologized to him for what he had said. Never one to hold a grudge, Mansfield said he viewed Pillsbury as "a nice enough fellow" but unfortunately "full of himself."

REAPPOINTMENT BY REAGAN

As Carter's four-year term of office was winding down in 1980 and his campaign for reelection getting under way, Mansfield was thinking once more of retirement. In May he told his old friend William D. James, editor of the *Great Falls Tribune*, who was visiting Japan, that he would not accept another appointment as ambassador from Carter or another president. At age seventy-seven "I would like to have a few years surcease," he said. In June he told the embassy staff that he would retire after the presidential inauguration in January, whether Carter won or lost. At his direction, his decision was made public by the embassy's spokesman.

After Ronald Reagan defeated Carter, however, Mansfield changed his mind. It was a stunning surprise that a lifelong Democrat, the former Democratic leader of the U.S. Senate, went to work for a conservative Republican president—and continued in the job for eight more years. Admiration and support for Mike Mansfield were among the very few things that Carter and Reagan had in common.

Reagan and Mansfield had never met until April 1978, when the former governor of California stopped in Tokyo on his way to Taiwan, but each was wary of the other. Reagan had been outspokenly critical in radio speeches and in print of the Mansfield amendments to bring U.S. troops out of Europe and told aides that he doubted he and Mansfield would agree on much. Mansfield knew Reagan only from the press and seemed uncomfortable meeting the man described as a fire-breathing rightist politician. When they met on Sunday afternoon, April 16, the preconceptions on both sides quickly fell away.

Reagan had not asked the State Department for any assistance regarding his trip to Tokyo but had notified the department of his planned itinerary. Reagan's foreign policy aide Richard V. Allen contacted the embassy after arriving in Tokyo to suggest that the governor—and potential Republican presidential candidate—call on the ambassador as a courtesy before beginning his round of meetings with Japanese business and political leaders. In typical self-effacing manner Mansfield responded that he would rather call on Reagan instead. The meeting was arranged at Reagan's suite at the Hotel Okura, one of Tokyo's best, which is directly across the street from the U.S. ambassador's residence.

According to Peter Hannaford, a longtime Reagan aide who was present, "Governor Reagan seemed to sense that Mansfield might be expecting him to match old stereotyped descriptions and began discussing—in well-informed detail—the current issues worrying the Japanese. . . . Mansfield's reserve began to melt as he realized that he and Reagan saw eye-to-eye on these issues. Indeed, the atmosphere was so cordial after an hour that both seemed to genuinely regret having to end the visit." Allen then accompanied Mansfield to the hotel's front door. When he returned, he found Reagan standing at a window that looks across to the embassy residence and a taxicab line outside. Before Allen could speak, Reagan said, "I take it all back. That's a *fine* man." Shortly thereafter, Mansfield telephoned the suite and invited the Reagan party to join a reception that had already been scheduled for that evening. Reagan, his aides, and their wives did so. By the time the group got to Taiwan, according to Allen, Reagan was "waxing enthusiastic [about] a great man, nice man, obviously very intelligent, surprising how much we agreed on."

In mid-August 1980, a month after Reagan won the Republican presidential nomination, he sent his vice presidential running mate, George H. W. Bush, to Beijing in an unsuccessful effort to calm the waters with Chinese leaders, who were outraged by Reagan's pro-Taiwan rhetoric. With Allen at his side, Bush stopped en route to see Prime Minister Fukuda in Tokyo. While there, Bush and his party were the honored guests at a reception given for them by Mansfield at the embassy residence. Returning from Beijing, Bush and his party stopped for nearly an hour to change planes at Narita Airport, where Mansfield came to meet them once again. While Bush was occupied in another conversation, Allen took Mansfield aside and asked him "a purely hypothetical question"—what if Reagan were to win and what if he were to ask you to serve in his administration, what would you say? According to Allen, he responded, "Well, Dick, if the president asked me to serve I would certainly listen very carefully." He didn't say yes, but Allen told him, "That's all you have to say."

The first outward sign that Mansfield was changing his mind about retirement came in an interview with the *Washington Post* managing editor

Howard Simons and Tokyo correspondent William Chapman in late November, three weeks after Reagan's electoral victory over Carter. Simons had heard hints from Reagan's foreign policy team that Mansfield might be asked to continue "a little while longer" in Tokyo. Noting that Mansfield had previously said he would leave when Carter's term was over, the journalists asked if he would stay if Reagan wanted him. "Mansfield replied with uncharacteristic coyness, 'I'd give it serious consideration.'" Simons and Chapman went on to say that "the big Montana smile shows he would be delighted to remain."

Mansfield's newfound desire to remain was not passive. He telephoned former President Gerald Ford and contacted Democratic Senators John Glenn, Henry Jackson, and Sam Nunn to ask that they recommend to Reagan that he be retained as ambassador. All of them passed along their recommendations to the Reagan team. "I did so because he had done a fine job under Carter and was highly respected by the Japanese officials and the public," Ford told me. When I asked Mansfield why he had sought to remain, he said it was because "I wanted about six months more to finish up what I thought should be finished up." This did not seem entirely candid. None of the approvals suggested such a minimal extension of his duty.

As Reagan prepared to take office, several members of his transition team discussed the possibility of asking Mansfield to stay on. According to Tom Korologos, who had worked closely with Mansfield as a White House liaison to the Senate in the Nixon administration, a principal motivation of these advisers was the desire to speed the Senate confirmation of Alexander M. Haig Jr. as Reagan's first Secretary of State. Korologos said he, Edwin Meese, and Richard Perle as well as Richard Allen believed that a Mansfield reappointment would create enough goodwill among Senate Democrats to make a difference in the confirmation of Haig, who was blamed by some Democrats for his role in arranging the controversial pardon of Nixon by Ford.

On January 7, just short of two weeks before inauguration day, Reagan was preparing to travel from his temporary quarters at Blair House, across from the White House, to Capitol Hill for a luncheon meeting, his first with Senate Democrats. Allen broached the subject of a Mansfield reappointment and told Reagan he felt sure Mansfield would accept. Reagan decided on the spot to ask Mansfield to serve and authorized Allen to get him on the phone. Due to the time difference it was after midnight in Tokyo. The U.S. Marine guard at the embassy was reluctant to wake Mansfield, who typically retired early but was persuaded on the grounds that this was an emergency. A sleepy Mansfield finally came to the phone and was connected to Reagan, who asked him to stay on. Mansfield said he would be honored, and the deed was done.

A few minutes later Reagan appeared at a luncheon with the Senate Democrats that, as luck would have it, was held in the Mike Mansfield Room under a large painting of the revered former leader. The Democrats were in a testy mood, having lost their majority in the Senate in the November election for the first time since 1955. The President-elect led off with a few of his standard Hollywood jokes, which had limited appeal to his audience, before getting to his surprise. With a gesture toward the portrait on the wall behind him, he broke the news, attributing the idea to Haig, that he had asked Mansfield to stay on as his ambassador and that the former Democratic leader had accepted. The Democrats responded with a standing ovation and prolonged applause. Breaking into French, Robert Byrd, recently demoted to minority leader from the majority post, told Reagan he had just "delivered the *coup de maître* (master stroke) when you told us about your intentions with respect to Ambassador Mansfield." Minority Whip Alan Cranston said the same thing in English and told reporters, "It was Haig's idea, so it helps Haig." Haig was closely questioned in several days of committee hearings but was confirmed the day after Reagan's inauguration. The decision to retain Mansfield was widely hailed in Japan, where he was given a standing ovation at a company reception with 2,000 business and government officials in a Tokyo hotel.

The reappointed ambassador was immediately confronted with one important and delicate piece of business that remained unsettled after Reagan succeeded Carter—the plight of the U.S. auto industry, which had lost over $4 billion and laid off more than 300,000 auto workers in 1980. The central problem for the American industry was the massive shift in consumer demand, resulting from the rapid rise in gasoline prices and long lines at U.S. service stations following the Iranian revolution in 1979. Forswearing the big, gas-guzzling cars that had previously been in favor, many American consumers opted for the smaller, more fuel-efficient cars produced and exported by Japanese automakers. The U.S. industry, unable to modernize and retool their factories quickly, looked for government relief against the Tokyo tide. In November 1979 Douglas A. Fraser, president of the United

Auto Workers, whose membership had declined by more than 40 percent, called on the U.S. government to "get tough" with Japanese automakers and threatened to launch a boycott of Japanese cars in the United States.

Mansfield was among the first officials to call for Japanese restraint. In a speech to the Japan National Press Club on January 28, 1980, he warned that in the face of massive layoffs in the United States, "the trade questions could turn into a political issue that will do neither country any good." He urged Toyota and Nissan to build auto factories in the United States, as Honda was doing. "I hope the big Japanese companies are giving some thought to the seriousness of the situation because if something is not done—and I do not utter these words lightly—you are going to find in this campaign year a great swell for protectionist legislation which will be directed against those who import too much, too quickly." The major companies, while sensitive to the growing U.S. concern, were initially cautious about moving into the unfamiliar U.S. manufacturing environment.

Mansfield's concern that the Japanese auto imports could become a political issue was validated in September when Reagan, who was normally a strong advocate of freer trade, campaigned at a Chrysler factory in Detroit and declared that "government has a role it has shirked so far"—to persuade the Japanese "in their own best interests" to slow the deluge of cars into the United State. When he won the election and moved into the White House, however, his administration was sharply divided on the question of restraining imports.

In his initial cable as ambassador to Reagan and Secretary of State Haig, Mansfield expressed confidence that "Japan will play its part [in solving the auto problem], possibly though voluntary restraints, possibly through negotiating an orderly marketing agreement with us" if the administration was able to work out a policy on the issue and speak with one voice. That was easier said than done amid conflicting counsels, but in a climactic meeting on March 19, 1981, Reagan decided on a face-saving solution that had been suggested by Vice President Bush. Mansfield was instructed to warn Foreign Minister Masayoshi Ito that "a firestorm" was building in Congress against the rising auto imports and suggest that the way to head off protectionist legislation was for Japan to adopt "voluntary" limits. In a sop to his battered free trade principles, Reagan ruled that no specific numbers for such limits should be conveyed to the Japanese. According to Reagan biographer Lou

Cannon, Haig nonetheless provided to Mansfield a range of acceptable numbers of Japanese imports, 1.6 to 1.8 million cars per year. As Mansfield had suggested they would, the Japanese accepted the plan, and agreed to a "voluntary" limit of 1.68 million cars for the year to come. Although the numbers were adjusted from time to time, Japan continued the voluntary quota arrangement from year to year for the rest of the Reagan administration either in agreement with the United States or on its own volition.

Although Mansfield was willing, perhaps even eager, to ameliorate the conflicts with Japan, he was unwilling to use his prestige and political influence on unrelated issues. When the Reagan administration in October 1981 was embroiled in its first major struggle with the Senate, over the issue of selling AWACS surveillance aircraft to Saudi Arabia, Haig asked Mansfield to sign a personal endorsement of the sale, written in Washington, and to pressure six wavering Democratic senators via telephone calls from Tokyo. Mansfield refused. He wrote in the margin of a cable from the State Department on the issue, "Bad policy. They would never change if I called." He considered parts of the message "an insult" to senators. He had never pressed his fellow senators to vote his way as Majority Leader, and he was not willing to start doing so, even though he was now serving "under" a president rather than being an independent legislator. His standard answer to the many such appeals from Washington to use his clout with members of Congress was that "if the senator or representative wants to ask my views, I will be happy to give it." However, he would not take any such initiative.

MILITARY MISSIONS

Japan came out of its defeat in World War II a disarmed and dispirited nation with a "Peace Constitution" drafted by General Douglas MacArthur's political section in which the Japanese people "forever renounce war as a sovereign right" and declared that it would never maintain "land, sea and air forces." MacArthur changed his mind after the start of the Korean War in 1950 and authorized formation of a "National Police Reserve," which grew in time into a new Japanese Army, Navy, and Air Force under the label of "Self-Defense Forces." Still, due to strong pacifist sentiments following the militaristic disaster of World War II and in view of continued reliance on U.S. forces for its protection, Japan's forces were much smaller and more restricted in their operations than would be expected of an increasingly important global economic power. As Japan's economy continued to expand rapidly in the 1960s and 1970s, there was growing criticism in Washington of its military weakness and charges that it was getting a "free ride" from the U.S. defense of its home islands and protection of the region in which it lived and prospered.

In his report to the Senate on his 1976 visit to Japan, Mansfield had expressed his approval of the existing defense arrangements and relationship with the United States. He noted that Japan was spending 0.089 percent of its gross national product (GNP) on defense compared with 5.5 percent of GNP spent by the United States. Nonetheless, he wrote, "It behooves us to be very cautious in taking any step that could be interpreted by Asians, or by the Japanese people, as pressing the Japanese government to make a quantitative increase in the size of its defense force or to change its defense posture in a significant way." In preparation for President Carter's initial meeting with Mansfield as ambassador to Japan in May 1977, Zbigniew Brzezinski informed the President that "we do not envision an expanded Japanese military role in the Western Pacific" but that the administration did favor improved Japanese air defense and anti-submarine capabilities, and hoped for increased Japanese contributions to the costs of maintaining the 50,000 U.S. troops still stationed in Japan. Brzezinski added, underlining the admonition to give it emphasis, *"It is important to cover these defense points with Mansfield, since his own inclination would be to neglect this dimension of our relationship."*

In fact, once in office Mansfield proved to be extremely attentive to security issues, although his initial emphasis was on calling for an increase in U.S. military forces in the Pacific, as he did in the private White House meetings in February and October 1978. Little emphasis was given, by either Carter or Mansfield in their early meetings, to Japanese defense efforts. The climate changed dramatically in 1980, the final year of the Carter administration, following the Soviet invasion of Afghanistan, when cold war tensions and U.S. military budgets expanded rapidly. In each of the three ministerial-level U.S.-Japan meetings in that year, the United States asked Japan to raise its defense spending. American officials were increasingly critical of Japan's unofficial but politically important limit of 1 percent of GNP.

In a press conference with Japanese reporters on March 14, 1980, Mansfield said he was satisfied with Japan's steady increases in military spending, which had averaged 8 percent yearly over the preceding ten years. He said the "free ride" charges were not deeply rooted in U.S. opinion. His remarks were particularly annoying to officials of the Pentagon, who were calling for further increases in Japanese defense efforts. "There was a sense that Mansfield was unwilling to push [the Japanese] hard," according to Nicholas Platt, who was the Asia specialist on the staff of Secretary of Defense Harold Brown. Responding to Robert Komer, the activist official who was Undersecretary of Defense for policy, Platt did a statistical analysis of Mansfield's press conference statements and found that most of them were in line with data available at the time he spoke. However, a new Pentagon analysis that had not then been sent to Mansfield downgraded the Japanese effort. "We, of course, agree with neither the data (with the new analysis in hand) nor the tenor of Mansfield's remarks," Platt reported to Komer. Platt, who had been State Department country director for Japan from mid-1977 to mid-1978 and had worked closely with Mansfield, expressed the hope that he could get Mansfield "on board" or that Carter would bring up the issue in a forthcoming meeting with his ambassador. Komer, a much more incendiary personality, sent Platt's report to Secretary of Defense Harold Brown. "Amb. Mansfield's defensiveness on this matter is not only contrary to USG [U.S. government] policy as I understand it, but confuses the Japanese," he wrote. "However, Nick Platt says that only the President would be able to turn Mansfield around. Therefore we will propose you send a memo to the President just before Mansfield returns for the [Prime Minister Masayoshi] Ohira visit urging he do so." There is no indication that such a memo was written or that such a Carter-Mansfield discussion took place.

Four months later, however, Brown himself reacted negatively to another statement by Mansfield in Tokyo, this one praising Japan's decision to increase defense spending by 9.7 percent, less than the Pentagon wanted. "Are we sending confusing signals?" Brown asked Komer in a marginal comment on a wire service report of Mansfield's statement. Komer replied, "Yes, we *are* sending confusing signals, and I've been raising a little cain about it. Once again, Mansfield has gone off the reservation, and I've asked Platt how best to set the record straight. . . . But State runs for cover where Mansfield is concerned, saying he's a close friend of the President."

The Reagan administration was even more concerned about security in the Pacific and about Japan's contribution than the Carter administration had been. At the start of the Reagan years, a well-timed Mansfield cable once again played a direct and unusual role in formulation of official policy. On January 26, 1981, six days after Reagan's inauguration, Mansfield dispatched a lengthy cable "For the President and the Secretary [of State]" summarizing his views on policy toward Japan. One of his most specific recommendations was to "re-focus our defense discussions on our respective security requirements and how we propose to attain them jointly." With his recent battles with the Pentagon in mind, he wrote, "This would enable us to back away gracefully from an essentially unproductive debate over the percent of Japan's GNP or national budget devoted to defense and allow the Japanese to elaborate to its own people as well as to us just what it has in mind in terms of comprehensive security. It would also permit us to define much more precisely not only respective roles and missions and perceived deficiencies but also our view of how the security burden might be more equitably shared."

Mansfield's cable landed amid a debate on the issue within the new administration. Secretary of Defense Caspar Weinberger had been advocating an early and private approach to the Japanese, emphasizing roles and missions that Japan could accept and de-emphasizing the percentages that had been given so much attention in the past. Weinberger found that the State Department bureaucracy opposed the idea, arguing that Japan had to set its own pace in this sensitive area without U.S. involvement. Reagan, however, approved Mansfield's suggestion, which was then sent to the relevant officials with the President's endorsement. Giving credit to Mansfield, Weinberger wrote in his memoir that due to his intervention "the approach that I favored became United States national policy the next week." This proved to be more successful with the Japanese, although Congress continued to focus on percentages.

Mansfield's most dramatic intervention in the military field came after the U.S. nuclear-powered and nuclear-armed submarine, the *George Washington*, collided with a Japanese cargo vessel, the *Nissho Maru*, when the sub came to the surface in stormy seas on the morning of April 9, 1981. Rather than investigate what had happened or assist the crew of the sinking freighter, the U.S. submarine submerged again and left the scene. The captain of the sub later said he did so in order that his vessel not be identified as a ballistic missile submarine. The Japanese vessel sank within fifteen minutes after the collision, but the *George Washington* did not report the collision to anyone until ninety-two minutes later nor request an aircraft search of the area, which was fruitless, until almost two hours later. The captain and first mate of the Japanese ship drowned, and the other thirteen members of the crew floated in two life rafts at sea for eighteen hours before being rescued by a Japanese destroyer.

News of the deadly accident and especially survivors' reports of the "hit and run tactics" of the U.S. submarine caused a storm of protest and anger in Japan. At the Foreign Ministry, Minoru Tamba, who was chief of the security bureau that dealt extensively with the United States, wept when he was informed, believing that this event would be extremely destructive to a crucial relationship. Tokyo correspondent William Chapman reported in the *Washington Post* that the sinking and the crew's accounts "have become a major public issue and have provided some of the sharpest anti-American press commentary in several years. It has given critics of the U.S.-Japanese security relationship a new platform . . . [and] provided a new cause for Japan's vociferous antinuclear organizations, which staged a protest march to the American Embassy here."

As soon as he learned the news, Mansfield insisted that "we have to apologize for this." He quickly contacted the Japanese Foreign Ministry, although initially he had to offer his personal apology rather than that of the United States. Seeking to calm Japanese anger, Reagan sent an "expression of regret" about the accident to Japanese Prime Minister Zenko Suzuki. Meanwhile, Mansfield pressed the Navy to make a speedy and candid report, but with little success. A preliminary report saying that the *George Washington* did not know the freighter had sunk was not given to Japanese officials until nearly a month after the accident and was widely denounced in Japan. Despite Mansfield's appeal for urgency, the final investigative report was not sent to the embassy for transmission to the Japanese government until August 31, nearly five months after the accident. In the report, the Navy took full responsibility for the accident and said "inadequate command supervision" and "less than professional watch-standing procedures" as well as a combination of coincidences had caused the accident. The report also sharply criticized the submarine crew's "disregard of one of the mariner's historic, and primary, responsibilities," to render assistance to vessels in distress.

As soon as he received the seventy-page report and the instruction to present the official U.S. apology, Mansfield knew what he was going to do. He told his deputy chief of mission, William Clark, that he was going to present the report in person to Foreign Minister Sunao Sonoda, and he wanted to be accompanied by his naval attaché in full dress uniform. "There will be a lot of press around and I am going to bow . . . because for all of our talk about Japanese literacy, the Japanese are a lot like the Americans: they skip the front page and probably read the sports page, but they see the pictures. And that picture will be on every newspaper in Japan." Clark said that was true, but the picture of an ambassador bowing down would also appear in the United States "and you'll probably be criticized for it." Mansfield responded with his characteristic "Yup."

Mansfield took the report to the foreign minister's office where, as he expected, still and video cameramen from the Japanese press had been summoned for a photo opportunity. After a minute or two of pleasantries, Sonoda's aides gave the signal for the press to depart but Mansfield surprisingly said, "Let them stay please." With that he rose from his seat, walked over to Sonoda and expressed "the sincere apologies" of the U.S. government with the report in one hand, the other stiffly by his side. Then he bowed deeply from the waist to nearly a 45-degree angle, more deeply than Japanese bow to one another on almost any occasion. "The cameras got it. I wanted them to. I wanted the Japanese people to know it," Mansfield told me in recalling the occasion. When I asked him how he decided how low to bow, he responded that he just bowed as deeply as he could. As predicted, Mansfield's bow of apology was featured prominently in every Japanese newspaper and television news program, and it abruptly diminished the ill will over the accident. "He is a rare diplomat in that he understands the Japanese mentality very well," a Japanese journalist told *Newsweek*. "Instead of merely passing the message he always tries to present it in a form that is easy for us to take." As also predicted, Mansfield was criticized in the United States when the photograph appeared. Some Americans complained he had "kowtowed" to the Japanese and cited it as a prime example of a tendency

to favor the Japanese viewpoint over that of his own country. He was prepared for that and unconcerned. "I thought it was the least and the most I
could do," he said later.

THE NAKASONE ERA

During his eleven and a half years in Japan, Mike Mansfield dealt with five
prime ministers: Takeo Fukuda, Masayoshi Ohira, Zenko Suzuki, Yasuhiro
Nakasone, and Noboru Takeshita. All were members of the misnamed
Liberal Democratic Party—actually the conservative party that had ruled
Japan nearly continuously since the end of the U.S. postwar occupation—
and all of the prime ministers were very different personalities. Suzuki, who
was a caretaker minister following the death in office of Ohira, lasted twenty-
eight months. Mansfield dealt with the others for much shorter periods of
time, with one exception, Nakasone, who was in office for five years and
made the greatest impression on Mansfield and the greatest impact on Japan.
In Mansfield's view Nakasone's longevity in office—as well as his character
and abilities—made him an outstanding leader in Japan and East Asia.

Yasuhiro Nakasone, born in 1918, was a junior naval officer in World War
II and an elected member of the Japanese Diet from 1947. Before becoming
prime minister he had two decades of experience in a variety of ministerial
posts, including a stint as minister in charge of the Defense Agency, a job that
most prominent politicians of that era shunned. I remember him as a very
active and articulate minister of International Trade and Industry during my
time as a correspondent in Tokyo in the early 1970s. My publisher, Katharine
Graham, recalled meeting him in 1965, when she was on a world tour, and
including him on an informal list of "sexy men" she had met along the way.
(Nakasone was stunned and delighted when I told him of Kay's recollection,
which she had mentioned in her Pulitzer Prize–winning memoir, *Personal
History.* He immediately sent an aide out to buy a copy.)

Nakasone's priorities in international affairs became evident on November
27, 1982, the day after he was elected to the post by the Diet. The first international figure he spoke to by telephone was President Reagan, whom he later
dealt with extensively as "Ron," while the U.S. President called him "Yasu."

Two days later, at 6 P.M. on November 29, Mansfield made the first of
many visits to Nakasone as prime minister. According to Kazutoshi

Hasegawa, a veteran diplomat who served as Nakasone's Foreign Ministry secretary, it was rare for Japanese prime ministers to see ambassadors, usually sending them to the Foreign Ministry instead. Mansfield was different: "He was the only U.S. ambassador after the war who could meet the prime minister at any time on short notice. I arranged such meetings many times."

Nakasone, one of the few Japanese politicians of his generation who could understand and speak passably well in English, began by conversing in English with Mansfield in the presence of Japanese reporters and photographers before the press was ushered out of the room. When the two got down to business, Mansfield expressed concern that the coming year promised to be "the most difficult in our recent history." He laid heavy emphasis on "storm signals" of rising protectionist sentiments in the U.S. Congress, where legislation requiring "local content" from domestic manufacturers in imports from Japan was a serious threat. "While the President and his administration support free trade, the difficulties are not only economic but are political and psychological," Mansfield added. He suggested that "a bulwark of friendly senators" from states producing tobacco, beef, and citrus—all products whose importation to Japan was severely limited, to the ire of the U.S. producers—would be needed to sustain presidential vetoes of protectionist measures. Turning to defense, Mansfield asked that Japan substantially increase its military budget. He stressed that the United States was "not asking that Japan do more so that we can do less, but rather so we can both improve our defense posture."

Nakasone commented on each item in positive fashion. He had been prime minister only a few days and could still be considered "a tenderfoot," he said, but even so he acknowledged that trade and defense were the most important issues between the two countries. He promised "full discussions" with his new cabinet and then with the ambassador to resolve them. Mansfield reported to Washington, "I found the Prime Minister to be very confident, both in his manner and in his treatment of the issues raised. He did not in any way become defensive when discussing either trade or defense, but showed a very positive outlook in terms of attempting to seek solutions. I had the strong impression that we will indeed be able to engage in frank discussions with this prime minister." For his part, Nakasone found Mansfield's initial presentation "very straightforward, in a strong voice, telling me what he thought without reservation." In a normal situation, Nakasone told me,

"I would have been offended" by Mansfield's bluntness, but in this case he was impressed instead with his frankness and honesty. The ambassador's lack of all pretensions on this and other occasions made a lasting impression: "A statesman of his caliber could behave more arrogantly. But on the contrary, he never pretended that he was a big man."

Within weeks Nakasone began to show that although the powers of a Japanese prime minister are limited, he would stretch them to the maximum. Toward the end of December he was visited by Matsuhide Yamaguchi, director general of the Ministry of Finance's Budget Bureau, who told him that in the existing financial situation, it was impossible to add to the previously scheduled appropriation for defense, which was about 5 percent more than the year before. Nakasone told him, "Japan-U.S. relations are cardinal for the security of the country. Increased budget expenditures are very important." The hapless director general agreed but said he had no money. Masaharu Gotoda, the chief cabinet secretary, berated the bureaucrat, demanding to know how he could come to the prime minister "with your pockets empty." As Yamaguchi turned pale, Nakasone reiterated the importance of the Japan-U.S. relationship and the Japanese security commitment. Yamaguchi reluctantly promised to find the money somewhere—and he did. The defense account was increased first by 6 percent and eventually, under further prodding, by 6.5 percent. This brought defense spending to 0.98 percent of GNP, just short of the 1 percent ceiling that was a political limit at that time.

Nakasone was even more forthcoming on roles and missions. His predecessor, Zenko Suzuki, had agreed in principle to extend Japanese protection of its sea lanes, through which its crucial oil supplies and commerce flowed, out to 1,000 nautical miles from the main islands, although Japan did not yet have the capability to do this. Nakasone, in the first appointment of his first official visit to Washington on January 18, 1983, told *Washington Post* editors and reporters at a breakfast meeting and subsequently told Reagan at a White House meeting that he would seek to make even more dramatic changes in the security policies of hitherto-pacifistic Japan. Specifically, he volunteered that Japan would block the flight of Soviet Backfire bombers through Japanese air space and would blockade the strategic straits controlling the Sea of Japan to bottle up Soviet vessels there in time of emergency. These major changes in Japan's intentions were made all the more controversial at home by the prime minister's remark that Japan should become "an unsinkable aircraft carrier" in the service of free world defense—a phrase reminiscent of a hollow wartime boast by the militaristic World War II Japanese government.

I had done the questioning of Nakasone on the defense issues at the *Post* breakfast and wrote the resulting story, only to learn later that the "unsinkable aircraft carrier" was an exaggerated translation by his official interpreter rather than the prime minister's original phrase. Nakasone's statements generated a stern warning from Moscow and inquiries from Beijing, but he was unperturbed by the furor. It was a "blitzkrieg shock" in Japan, he told me later, and he believed it helped Reagan "to understand me better."

Nakasone did not ignore Mansfield's requests in the economic field, but his efforts were less dramatic. Insisting that Japan lower its tariff on imported cigarettes, he personally met with the relevant members of the Diet to advance this request. Nakasone "steam-rollered" several hard-headed representatives of tobacco constituencies, according to Hasegawa, who sat in on the meetings. "There was some enmity on the part of these representatives, but he said, 'What is at stake is the interest of the state—not one particular industry,'" his secretary recalled. In many industrial and agricultural areas, however, his efforts to open Japan's markets ran into massive political and economic difficulties.

During Mansfield's ambassadorship, Japan developed into an economic superpower that increasingly challenged and often aggravated the United States. The last U.S. trade surplus with Japan was registered in 1964; by 1977, Mansfield's first year in Tokyo, the U.S. deficit in merchandise trade was more than $8 billion and climbing toward the $10 billion mark, which was then seen as a catastrophic figure. In the 1980s the deficit grew by leaps and bounds to $52 billion in 1988, Mansfield's final year. By the end of the decade, Japan's share of the world's output of goods and services had grown to 16 percent (from 5 percent in 1950), one of the largest such shifts ever accomplished by any nation in a comparable period. In the 1980s, Japan's huge international surpluses, the growing strength of the yen against the dollar, and the country's high savings rate made it the world's leading creditor nation, whereas the United States became the world's leading debtor. "Japan is fast becoming the leading economic power in the world," the international financier George Soros wrote in 1987.

Beginning late in 1981 Mansfield sought to dramatize the importance of the U.S.-Japan relationship by calling it "the most important bilateral relationship in the world, bar none." From that time on, he repeated this phrase in almost every speech, to the point that members of his staff began to call the embassy the "Bar None Ranch," although not within the ambassador's earshot. "At first nobody believed it, but after some years when he continued to say that, many Japanese began to believe it," according to Takakazu Kuriyama, a senior Japanese diplomat and eventually ambassador to the United States. "This had a great impact on Japanese psychology, and may have been his greatest contribution."

When I asked Mansfield in 1999 to sum up his thoughts about his years as ambassador, he replied unhesitatingly, "That a greater degree of understanding developed in Japan about the United States at the same time as an increasing degree of dissatisfaction was occurring in this country based on trade, which was the single most important factor in my eleven and a half years in Japan, and which seemed to start with the year I went there. Their surpluses with us increased and we were gradually able to bring about an agreement or agreements covering various discrepancies in our trade. But unfortunately we did it by a single issue to issue basis instead of facing up to the whole problem and kept alive a system which I think will take us well beyond the year 2000 and be a perennial source of trouble."

As ambassador, Mansfield was always careful to say publicly and privately that both sides were to blame for deepening economic difficulties and that both sides needed to take remedial actions. "It's easy to blame the Japanese for all our problems—they don't yell back," he told the Tokyo correspondent of the *Chicago Tribune*, Ronald E. Yates. In a typical private statement, he told Foreign Minister Shintaro Abe in September 1985 that "Japan must open its markets to rectify the enormous trade deficit" and should accelerate implementation of agreements on the importation of telecommunications, electronics, and medical/pharmaceutical supplies, as well as promised tariff cuts on forest products. "On our side, we must deal with problems which Japan cannot manage for us—the budget deficit, high interest rates, the high dollar. Perhaps the greater burden rests with us, for which we cannot avoid responsibility. In the meantime, we look to Japan for help," he said. Mansfield was clear-eyed about the chances for success. "The odds are against us. But we must do our best, for the sake of our relations. We have no choice," he told Abe.

His even-handedness and basic fairness were prized and praised in Japan but criticized in economic and political circles in the United States. As was the case with his leadership in the Senate, critics said Mansfield was not tough enough in his methods of persuasion. John Duncan, a ranking Republican member of the House Ways and Means Committee, publicly urged Reagan to fire Mansfield in late 1985 because his stance toward Japan was not strong enough. Late in his tenure in Japan, Mansfield became a target of those who believed Japan was moving steadily and deliberately to a dominant economic position over the United States. In a biting critique of the U.S. Embassy in Tokyo under Mansfield, Clyde V. Prestowitz Jr., a former Commerce Department official, wrote in a much-quoted book that in Japan "neither the ambassador nor most of his staff see penetration of the Japanese market as an important matter. . . . The embassy always opposes any firm attitude toward Japan."

During the Reagan administration there were recurrent rumors and even published reports that Mansfield would soon be replaced. In January 1983 the *New York Times* reported that David M. Abshire, president of the Center for Strategic and International Studies (CSIS), had been chosen to succeed Mansfield in Tokyo. In April 1985 *Newsweek* reported that Gaston Sigur, then the Asia specialist on the National Security Council staff, would replace Mansfield. In August 1985 the *New York Times* reported that Mansfield had told the White House he would like to retire and that Robert C. McFarlane, Reagan's national security adviser, had expressed interest in the job. In July 1987 the *Washington Times* reported that U.S. business leaders were campaigning to draft Lee Iacocca, the tough-talking chairman of Chrysler Corporation, to take Mansfield's place.

The trouble with all these reports—and manifold additional rumors—was that Mansfield retained the confidence of Secretary of State George P. Shultz and of Reagan, and he had no intention of retiring. Shultz's predecessors, especially Kissinger and Haig, were principally oriented to strategic and military issues in which China was of intense fascination and high priority and Japan of lesser interest. Shultz, in contrast, was a professional economist for whom the countries of greatest interest were reversed. "For me, the centerpiece has always been Japan," Shultz wrote in his memoirs. "By far the largest economy in Asia, Japan is a key strategic partner and a dramatic example of successful democratic governance in an area where that is scarce."

With the postwar assistance of the United States, he wrote, "Japan has achieved a new kind of status as a world power, based on its strong economic accomplishments."

Shultz had great confidence in Mansfield as an experienced and mature public official whom he had met many times in his three cabinet posts in the Nixon administration. Shultz often told the story of his first meeting with Mansfield in Washington after becoming secretary of state. It was Shultz's practice on sending out new ambassadors to take them over to the big globe in his formal office at the State Department and ask them to "show me your country." Apologetically, he asked Mansfield to take his little test to see if he could locate Japan. "He went to the globe. Mike put his hand on the United States and said, 'Here's my country.'" In inaugurating the new campus of the Foreign Service Institute, named for Shultz in 2002, the former secretary implored American diplomats to "always remember Mike's words. Be proud to be a citizen, let alone a representative, of the greatest country ever, the United States of America."

Mansfield, although seven years older than the President, was closer to his generation than most others in the administration. As had been his practice with Carter, Mansfield sent numerous personal and handwritten notes of thanks and encouragement to Reagan on appropriate occasions. His calm, clear way of thinking and speaking was appreciated by the President, who reportedly waved away all suggestions that Mansfield be replaced, saying "I like the old guy." In January 1982, a year into the Reagan administration, amid grumbles in the U.S. bureaucracy that Reagan had done his bit for Mansfield and should retire him, the President invited Mansfield to attend a meeting of top-level officials concerned with U.S. policy toward Japan. At the start of the meeting, Reagan called on the ambassador for introductory comments. According to Undersecretary of Commerce Lionel Olmer, who was present, "Mansfield gave one of those amazing, coherent, fact-packed but down to earth statements, which left everyone incredibly impressed. I could see the light in Reagan's eyes, fascination and appreciation for what Mansfield was saying." Mansfield then sat quietly, puffing on his pipe, as the meeting proceeded, its members deeply affected by what he had said.

In a similar situation in April 1987, as top officials met in the Oval Office to prepare for a visit by Nakasone, Mansfield was called upon by Reagan to make initial comments on the situation in Japan, although he had not been scheduled originally to participate in the meeting. Without a single note, he cited facts and figures with a sure and clear perspective—"a virtuoso performance, like a teacher instructing a group of students, which changed the nature and atmosphere of the meeting," according to Jim Kelly, who was the Asia expert on the National Security Council and later would become assistant secretary of state for East Asia and the Pacific in the George W. Bush administration. "There had been rumors that Mansfield was losing it, and out of touch. This pretty well proved that was by no means the case," said Kelly. Two months later, Mansfield celebrated a full ten years as U.S. ambassador of Japan. The previous December, he had broken the 3,465-day record in the job previously held by Joseph C. Grew, the pre–World War II ambassador.

In November 1987 Nakasone left the prime ministership after five years in office. On the eve of his departure from office, Mansfield hailed him as "an unusual type of leader for Japan who has finally brought Japan onto the world stage, front and center." Nakasone's predecessor, Zenko Suzuki, had been forced to fire his foreign minister for even using the word *alliance* to describe Japan's relationship with the United States. Nakasone openly declared that the U.S. and Japan were linked by a "common fate" and forged a closer alliance between them than that between the United States and several Western European countries. Nakasone undertook the massive task of reshaping Japan's economy to bring it more in tune with the outside world but found this an imposing and difficult task. As the U.S.-Japan trade imbalance continued to widen, protectionist pressures and trade frictions with Washington increased. With his usual candor, Mansfield declared that "Nakasone has issued a number of statements, declarations and proposals to open up the market, but in my opinion they've been mostly bone and little meat."

After leaving office, Nakasone told me that in his view the United States had sent three remarkable figures of the highest rank as ambassadors to Japan—Grew, Reischauer, and Mansfield, and that "of the three, I would rate Mansfield at the top." In appreciation of their relationship, Nakasone planted a dogwood tree in Mansfield's honor at his country retreat in the mountains west of Tokyo, commemorating a visit that the ambassador had made. He also planted two other flowering trees, another dogwood to celebrate a visit by Reagan, and a cherry in honor of a visit from Soviet President

Mikhail Gorbachev. When I last saw Nakasone in Tokyo in November 1998, he told me all three trees were growing tall.

SAYONARA TO TOKYO

In late December 1987 Maureen noticed that her husband was slipping physically and insisted that he go to the U.S. Naval Hospital at Yokosuka for a checkup. He tried to ignore the condition and her advice, but she "practically forced" him, saying, "No, you're going to go, you're going to go." The Yokosuka doctors diagnosed heart and prostate problems but because of his age, eighty-four, sent him off to a more advanced facility, Tripler Army Hospital in Honolulu. After a brief examination, he was hustled aboard the admiral's plane nonstop to Washington and the Army's top medical facility, Walter Reed Army Hospital. There on January 2 he underwent triple bypass surgery and, after that, a prostate operation. As usual, he credited his new lease on life to Maureen, who stayed with him each step of the way and pulled him "back from the brink" just by being there. "There was an awful lot of feeling on my part if I was just around Maureen," he told me in recounting the episode. "Just knew she was there."

At the end of February, before leaving Washington following his convalescence, he received a certificate at a White House ceremony for beginning his fiftieth year of service to the U.S. government: four and a half years of service in the Navy, Army, and Marine Corps, thirty-four years in Congress, and ten years, nine months as ambassador to Japan. After he returned to Tokyo, *New York Times* correspondent Clyde Haberman found him physically changed, his spare frame bordering on gauntness after losing weight from the ordeal. "But the opinions remain clear as glass and, as ever, they are stripped clean of oratorical frills and expressed in a powder-dry voice," Haberman reported. When asked about a rumor he was about to retire, Mansfield responded, "Never thought of it," and closed that part of the discussion. Haberman noted wryly after Mansfield served him the usual cup of instant coffee that "Illness, it seemed, had not damaged, nor improved, his coffee-making skills."

It was clear to everyone, including Mansfield, that his service in Tokyo would end with the inauguration of a new U.S. president. Shortly after

George H. W. Bush won the November election, Mansfield notified
Shultz by cable that he and Maureen had concluded "it is time for us to
go." On November 14, he summoned the U.S. and Japanese press to the
embassy auditorium. After describing the current state of U.S.-Japan relations in some detail, he announced that he had resigned "subject to the
will of the President" and that he and Maureen would leave Japan before
the first of the year. "We do so with regret because it has been an exhila-
rating experience, because we have learned so much, given so little and
gotten a great deal in return, and because we think that the situation is
now stable enough so that we can leave with our heads high and our arms
swinging." When he turned to questions, Mike Tharp of *U.S. News and
World Report* began simply, "It is not a question. Thank you, Mr.
Ambassador." The press corps exploded with prolonged applause, which
is rarely bestowed on public officials by journalists at any time. In an
extraordinary display, some of the correspondents, including Tharp and
Sam Jameson of the *Los Angeles Times,* burst into tears. "It was such a wonderful, glorious expression of happiness, satisfaction and confidence,"
Jameson explained later. "What he said was just so moving . . . you knew
that this was his last job. The summing up was an emotional setting and
his confidence, to be that alert and mentally on-line at that age. . . . It was
just a very moving [experience]"

Composure restored, Jameson asked how Japan had changed on his
watch. Mansfield replied:

> The Japanese have come upon the world scene because of their tremendous
> ability to recover like a phoenix from the ashes and to make something of
> their country which has so little in the way of resources and so much in the
> way of people. What they have done has been, in my opinion, almost
> miraculous. They have achieved maturity. They no longer stand in the cor-
> ner and bow their heads and remain silent. They stand on their own feet—
> as an equal. They express their views candidly as they should and they have
> been recognized as a superpower economically and a great power generally
> speaking. . . .
>
> And it is this nation and our own which will work together in the next
> century which will be the Century of the Pacific. Our two nations working

together will be able to complement and guide the rest of the world as it moves into this area, into the [Pacific] Basin, because we both realize that it is in that Basin where it all is, what it is all about, and where our joint future lies.

When all the questions had been asked and all the answers given, Mansfield asked if he might make a final remark. He then thanked the press for "the courtesy and consideration" shown to him and Maureen during their stay in Japan. "I am deeply appreciative of all you have done and I thank you very, very much," he said in closing. The journalists rose from their seats in another lengthy ovation.

After a long series of farewell observances and editorial praise in Japan and the United States, the Mansfields boarded a plane for Washington on December 22. On January 19, the last full day of the Reagan presidency, Reagan presented the Presidential Medal of Freedom, the nation's highest civilian award, to two members of his administration, George Shultz and Mike Mansfield. "Through 34 years in Congress—including 16 as Senate majority leader—and with more than a decade as U.S. ambassador to Japan, Mike Mansfield has set his indelible mark upon American foreign policy and distinguished himself as a dedicated public servant and loyal American," the citation for Mansfield read. Two weeks later Prime Minister Noboru Takeshita, in another Washington ceremony, presented Mansfield with Japan's highest civilian award, the Grand Cordon of the order of the Rising Sun with Paulownia Flowers, which had been given to only two other non-Japanese, former West German Chancellor Konrad Adenauer and General Douglas MacArthur.

THE FINAL YEARS

14 When Mike Mansfield left government service in January
1989 he was eighty-five years old and expecting to go at
last into full retirement. Before he left Tokyo, however, a
representative of Goldman, Sachs, the international investment banking
firm, asked him to consider accepting a post as a senior adviser to the firm.
"I thought he was crazy, just kidding. . . . I never heard of hiring anybody
at eighty-five," Mansfield told me. But the offer turned out to be real, and
after brief negotiations, he joined Goldman, Sachs in its Washington office
in March 1989 for the modest salary of $75,000 per year plus the exclusive
use of a car and driver. He had not driven since being furnished with a chauf-
feured limousine as Majority Leader nearly three decades earlier.

According to Henry James, former president of Goldman, Sachs (Japan),
who originated the proposal, the firm had been unsuccessfully seeking a
recently retired high-ranking Japanese official to be a senior adviser, to
smooth the way for its contacts and activities in Tokyo. When James learned
of Mansfield's impending retirement, he obtained the enthusiastic approval
of New York headquarters to approach Mansfield, who was held in greater

esteem by the Japanese than any other living American. "It was the rough equivalent of hiring General [Douglas] MacArthur as an adviser in Japan," James recalled. Mansfield made it clear from the first discussion that he would do no lobbying for the firm on any subject. Stan Kimmitt, his former student at the University of Montana and later secretary to the Senate majority and secretary of the Senate, who negotiated the agreement with Goldman, Sachs, said Mansfield had only one simple question, "Are they good people?"

During the Mansfields' later years in Japan, they had bought a large apartment on Watson Place in Northwest Washington, D.C., into which they moved after leaving Tokyo. For most of the last twelve years of his life, Mansfield took a long walk almost every morning, often six or seven miles, before being driven to the Goldman, Sachs office on Pennsylvania Avenue, about halfway between the Capitol and the White House. In a private office decorated with photographs and artworks from his congressional and ambassadorial careers and a big wall map of Asia, he met visitors, including virtually all prominent Japanese who traveled to the U.S. capital. He never made a sales pitch for Goldman, Sachs, but he did introduce members of the firm to high-ranking Japanese, some of whom they had been seeking to meet for many years. On his one return trip to Tokyo, in May 1992, the cream of Japanese business and society lined up to meet him at a reception sponsored by the firm.

Asked by a Montana journalist in 1995 what the job entailed, Mansfield answered, "Not too much, to be honest about it. I have access to newspapers, the English language dailies in Japan, periodicals, studies, and reports. I meet with a lot of Japanese. If Goldman, Sachs wants me to address some of their clients, some of their partners, I'll be glad to answer questions. The job is [to be] an advisor about Asia and the Pacific—primarily, Japan. I don't know why they hired me in the first place. In the second place I don't know why they're keeping me. I do no lobbying. I still don't know why the hell they hired me."

Mansfield was determined not to be perceived as a lobbyist or a has-been seeking to preserve his former powers. "I've seen too many retired senators go back too often," he told an interviewer in his early months back in Washington. Although his office was an easy walk from the Capitol, he ventured there only when invited to participate in special occasions, or for the biweekly prayer breakfasts, a nonpolitical and nonpartisan event that he enjoyed.

On his ninetieth birthday, in 1993, Senate Democrats honored him at a luncheon and Senate Republicans at a tea, in keeping with the bipartisanship he had practiced. The previous day, David Broder and I teamed up to interview him for a *Washington Post* article that appeared on his birthday. "I'm not going to celebrate it. I'm going to endure it," he told us when we inquired about his thoughts on reaching that age. Asked if he had any laws of life to offer others, he responded, "Not exactly, except you should never take yourself too seriously. If you win in politics, you don't win on the basis of your charm, or your education, or your good looks. There are a thousand people out there who know more than you do, who could probably do a better job, but they didn't get the breaks. And recognize there are two sides to almost every issue. Sometimes, the other side is right—it doesn't do any harm to listen."

A periodic task he enjoyed in this era of his life was a send-off talk each year to "Mike Mansfield fellows." They were U.S. civil servants who had been designated to receive a year of Japanese language training and a year of full-time work in Japanese ministries in Tokyo, with the objective of building a corps of Japanese specialists within the U.S. government. The Mansfield fellows program, established by Congress in 1994, was an outgrowth of the Maureen and Mike Mansfield Foundation, which Congress had established in 1983 with a $5 million appropriation to promote understanding and cooperation between the United States and Asia. The foundation was well on its way to enactment before Mansfield learned of it. Had he been consulted, he said later, he probably would have opposed it. He kept himself at arm's length from the foundation while he was ambassador and insisted that it not seek any funds in Japan as long as he was there on grounds of possible conflict of interest.

From time to time he commented on contemporary affairs in substantive and insightful fashion. In an address at West Point in 1990 on receiving an award for unselfish public service, he lamented the shift in national views after the moral clarity of the cold war. "Just as other nations were becoming more prosperous and more assertive, we began to turn from internationalism to unilateralism," he declared. "Therein lies the great irony. When we were at our most powerful, in the first two decades after the [Second World] War, we were also in our most cooperative and international mode, showing a decent respect for the opinions of others, and seeking their cooperation and support. But as others became stronger relative to us—economically, politically and militarily—we *started* to try to change the world on our own, or blame others for our problems." In an interview with Jim Ludwick of the *Missoulian* in 1995 he expressed unhappiness with the shifts he saw in political life, including in the Senate, from the days of relative collegiality and understanding among colleagues of both parties to an era when "the feeling of friendliness is gone . . . [when] a little hate is getting into it" on Capitol Hill. A serious problem, he was sure, was the prohibitive cost of running for office. His last senatorial campaign, in 1970, cost less than $100,000, but "when you figure that you need a million, or a million-and-a-half, to run for senator in a state like Montana, you spend too much time collecting money, and in collecting the money you collect obligations." Despite his excellent grasp of political reality, he underestimated the costs. Democrat Max Baucus in Montana spent $3.7 million in his 1996 reelection campaign.

Mansfield's most prominent return to the Capitol came in March 1998, shortly after his ninety-fifth birthday, when Senate Majority Leader Trent Lott, a Mississippi Republican, asked him to address the Senate and invited guests as the first speaker in a Senate-sponsored lecture series on leadership. His address took place in the Old Senate Chamber, which had been home to that body from 1810 until it moved to the present chamber in 1859 on the eve of the Civil War. After being vacated by the Senate, it became the home of the U.S. Supreme Court until the imposing Supreme Court building was constructed across the street in 1935. Mansfield as Majority Leader in the mid-1970s sponsored the drive to restore the historic room.

Rather than make a major pronouncement on the issues of the late 1990s, Mansfield chose to read the speech on leadership in the Senate he had expected to make on the tragic afternoon of November 22, 1963, when President Kennedy was assassinated. He had never delivered the speech, only placing it in the *Congressional Record* a few days later, Before the assembled senators of a generation later, he began, first, with a tribute to Maureen, who was already in the throes of illness, and to his other two "great loves," Montana and the United States Senate. Before reading the speech he established his philosophy by quoting the ancient Chinese sage Lao Tzu, "A leader is best when the people hardly know he exists. And of that leader the people will say when his work is done, 'We did this ourselves.'"

His hair turned white, his shoulders now slightly stooped, he spoke for thirty-eight minutes in his strong, unadorned, almost toneless yet powerful senatorial voice. At its end he was greeted with a standing ovation and the individual congratulations of one senator after another, those few with whom he had served, including Robert Byrd of West Virginia, Strom Thurmond of South Carolina, and Ted Kennedy of Massachusetts, and many who were not yet in political life when the speech had been written thirty-five years earlier.

It was shortly before the Senate leadership event that I first approached Mansfield with the idea for a biographical work—which he immediately rejected—and a month after the event that I went back to him and began the series of conversations, which turned into interviews, that lasted until shortly before his death. Despite his advanced age his memory was excellent and his mind was keen about current affairs as well as past history.

Beginning with his ninetieth birthday, several reporters who had covered his activities in Washington joined him each year for an informal birthday luncheon organized by his friend, Charles Ferris. I was invited into the group starting in 1999. It was on that occasion that Broder wrote an op-ed column for the *Washington Post* describing Mansfield as perhaps "the greatest living American." For the most part at that luncheon and others, he preferred to hear others talk while he carefully listened. But when asked a question about China's policy toward its neighbors, he succinctly described the state of conflicting territorial claims and other issues with every contiguous country, down to China's occupation of a tiny reef off Palawan, which most of the journalists had never heard of but which he accurately described as "the westernmost of the Philippines." As the journalists tried to absorb the well-organized presentation, made entirely without notes or known preparation, Mansfield stopped abruptly and said quietly of his amazing performance, "Lot of wind."

During this period he was increasingly concerned about the health of his wife, to whom he always insisted he owed everything. By 1995 she had begun to show signs of memory loss, a worrisome precursor of Alzheimer's disease, which had afflicted her late sister, Anne. On his ninety-fifth birthday, just short of her ninety-third, however, she rose to the occasion by penning a letter to "My darling Mike" in a sloping scrawl unlike her previously elegant schoolteacher's penmanship. "I have never loved you more and I really want to be with you for your 100th birthday. Wouldn't it be wonderful if we could celebrate our 100-year anniversary together?" she wrote. He told an interviewer a few hours later, "The nicest thing that happened today was that my wife wrote me a love letter last night, which I picked up this morning when I woke up."

With the assistance only of a day worker four or five days a week, he cared for her lovingly as she slowly declined. In December 1998 she was admitted to a nursing home with worsening memory loss and periods of angry outbursts described by the doctors as "dementia." She was released weeks later, then admitted again. When a committee of the Montana legislature proposed in March 1999 to authorize a statue of Mansfield to be placed in the state capitol—only the second in those hallowed halls, after his predecessor in the House, the antiwar heroine Jeannette Rankin—his response was immediate. "If me alone, no—with Maureen, yes." A statue of the two of them, with Maureen looking adoringly at her husband, was commissioned and eventually placed in the capitol.

"She is living in the past," he told me around that time. Toward the end she confused her husband with her father, and thought she was a girl again back in Butte. Through it all, he loyally went to see her twice each day, on his way to the office and on his way home.

When she died on September 20, 2000, he decided to deliver the eulogy at her funeral in the chapel at Fort Myer, on the perimeter of Arlington National Cemetery, where a prestigious plot had been long reserved for them both. "She sat in the shadow," he declared in his strong senatorial voice, "I stood in the limelight. . . . She literally remade me in her mold, her own outlook, her own honest beliefs. What she was, I became. Without her—I would have been little or nothing." The final lines were delivered with uncharacteristic emotion, which caused him momentarily to choke up, "I will not say good-bye to Maureen, my love, but only 'so long' because I hope the good Lord will make it possible that we will meet at another place in another time and we will then be together again forever."

By 1999, the year before Maureen died, his circulatory system that had been rescued by the triple bypass operation in 1988 had begun to wear out. Following a medical calculation in June 1999 that he was getting only about 40 percent of the oxygen he needed, a procedure was performed in which thin balloons were inserted across his aortic valve to improve the flow of blood. At age ninety-six, "nobody thought he'd be a candidate for this operation, but he decided to go ahead," according to Lieutenant Colonel William Gilliland, his lead physician at Walter Reed Army Medical Center. Mansfield's main concern, said Gilliland, was to be sure to outlive Maureen so he could care for her. Once she died, he refused to permit his doctors to do anything more to prolong his life. He was persuaded to have a pacemaker inserted in his chest in September 2001, but on grounds it would improve his quality of life rather than extend it.

When I saw him in his office after Maureen's death, he had a newspaper picture from her obituary taped to a piece of poster board by his desk. "I'm with Maureen most of the time now," he told me. When I asked what he meant, he responded, "She's in my mind all the time. . . . When I think of the things I should have done for her and didn't, think of the things she did for me, and did. A terrible loss." His gray and white hair had receded, leaving an expanse of mottled forehead.

The surgeons estimated that the 1999 procedure would sustain his blood flow for a year, possibly two years. When that time had passed, he began to have increasing difficulty doing anything that put a strain on his heart, including walking for very short distances. In fact, his heart valve was slowly failing. He took it philosophically. He told his doctor that he did not look forward to death but that he did not fear it.

My final meeting with Mike Mansfield was on the evening of September 25, 2001, when I visited his apartment to take his daughter, Anne, and his granddaughter, Caroline Marris, to dinner. He retired very early those days, so I came at six o'clock in order to see him and give him a copy of his mother's death certificate, which I had ordered months before from the Municipal Archives of New York City. He was fascinated, as he had never been sure when (November 24, 1910) or why (nephritis, a kidney disease) she had died, a death which launched him to Montana and a very different life from the one he would have had in New York. He appeared gaunt, as he had in recent meetings, but his color was good and he was completely engaged in our brief conversation. I thought to myself how amazing he was at age ninety-eight, and began to believe that he actually might be alive when my biography was finished.

When it was time for me to leave, he said good-bye and walked unaided toward his bedroom. As he crossed the room, I called out the miner's admonition that he often repeated to end meetings with me and others, "Tap 'er light." He turned and responded with a clear, strong voice, "Tap 'er light." Those were the last words I heard from the former copper miner from Montana. He entered Walter Reed Army Hospital the following day and died peacefully nine days later.

ACKNOWLEDGMENTS

Mike Mansfield lived such a long, varied, and historic life that collecting the diverse elements of his story and assembling them into a narrative was the work of many hands. I am grateful to the dozens of people who helped me in this voyage of discovery and re-creation.

My first and most important debt is to Mansfield himself, who never sought to sit for this biographical portrait and never formally agreed to it. When David Broder and I interviewed him for the Washington Post in connection with his ninetieth birthday in 1993, he told us he would not write his memoirs or cooperate in any oral history project on his life and times. "I think historians will tell the truth fifty years, one hundred years from now, when they write. And if you write too soon, you make too many mistakes, writing your own stuff." He made similar statements on many other occasions and, as noted in the preface, rejected my initial entreaty. He had refused to entertain proposals from more than a dozen publishing houses to write his memoirs after leaving Japan, some of which he described as lucrative. Why he nevertheless proceeded to talk to me at length, I do not know. A mutual interest in Asia certainly helped. He had less to do in his last years and seemed to welcome our periodic discussions, to which I contributed my impressions of people and events in the Asian scene. The thirty-two interviews, from our first biographical conversation in February 1998 until September 25, 2001, just ten days before his death, were essential for my understanding of his life and works.

I am greatly indebted to his daughter, Anne, who provided valuable insights into her parents' lives and who made available to me important personal and official papers that remained in her father's apartment after his death. Like her father, she never asked for my conclusions or access to any part of what I was writing. I am also grateful to Sophie Engelhard Craighead, a family friend who provided personal insights not available elsewhere. Mansfield's half-brother, the late John Mansfield, was also welcoming and helpful, as were Sheila Miller, John's daughter, and her husband, Bill.

Among those who worked closely with Mansfield in his congressional years I am particularly grateful to Francis R. "Frank" Valeo, his foreign policy associate for many years, who answered my questions in four interviews and innumerable telephone calls. Others who were especially helpful were Mansfield's former student, Senate associate, and friend, Stan Kimmitt; Mansfield's former legislative assistant Ray Dockstader; and Mansfield's longtime secretary, the late Peggy DeMichele. His former administrative assistant Salpee Sahagian and former Senate Foreign Relations Committee staff member Norvill Jones, who accompanied Mansfield on trips to China, provided not only recollections but also important documentation I did not find elsewhere. Charles Ferris, Mansfield's former Senate aide and his closest friend at the end of his life, was an important source of information and, I believe, even more important as a source of encouragement to his former boss to continue discussions with me.

Many of Mansfield's close associates in the U.S. Embassy, Tokyo, were of great assistance. I am indebted to his deputy chiefs of mission, Thomas Shoesmith, Bill Sherman, Bill Clark, and Desaix Anderson, and to others who worked with him on affairs of Japan, especially Richard Allen, Justin Bloom, Bill Breer, Rust Deming, Richard Holbrooke, Charles Kartman, Roy Mlynarchik, Nicholas Platt, and Albert Seligmann. I am especially indebted to Dan Russel, who was Mansfield's staff aide beginning in 1985 and who provided important recollections. Many distinguished Japanese assisted me, including former prime minister Yasuhiro Nakasone and his close associate, Kazutoshi Hasegawa; former ambassadors Takakazu Kuriyama and Yukio Satoh; and my old friend Yasuo Takeyama. I am especially grateful to Sam Jameson, long the dean of Tokyo foreign correspondents, for his insights and assistance.

At Goldman, Sachs, I am particularly indebted to Barbara Hickey, Mansfield's personal secretary there, who arranged my many interviews with him, and to Judah C. "Judd" Sommer, chief of the Washington office, and Henry James, former president of Goldman, Sachs (Japan).

Interviews are of great importance, but so also is documentary material, which was extensive in the case of Mansfield—much more so than he ever acknowledged. For reasons that I do not know, he stated on several occasions that he had never taken notes on his many White House meetings, but fortunately this was not true. His detailed and perceptive notes illuminated many of his conversations with U.S. presidents from Franklin D. Roosevelt to Gerald R. Ford. Moreover, the files of his many private memoranda to presidents were essential in re-creating his valiant efforts to prevent or limit the tragic war in Indochina.

A historian by training and early profession, Mansfield rarely threw away anything of importance that crossed his desk. These materials have been catalogued and carefully preserved in 4,600 archival boxes and associated audio, film, and memorabilia record in the Mansfield Archive, part of the K. Ross Toole Archives in the Maureen and Mike Mansfield Library at his alma mater, the University of Montana. I am grateful to the helpful and efficient staff there, especially archivists Jodi Allison-Bunnell, Teresa Hamann, and Chris Mullen and my research assistant in Missoula, Amanda Johnson. This archive is a treasure trove for researchers on the role of Congress in foreign affairs as well as on the life of Mike Mansfield. I intend to add to it by donating to the archive the tape recordings of all my interviews with Mansfield as well as the documents I collected for this book, so that most of the materials on Mansfield's life will be available to scholars in one place.

Others in Montana added to my knowledge and documentation of Mansfield's life. I am especially grateful to Jeffrey Safford of Montana State University, who made available his files for a hoped-for biography of Mansfield, and to Jim Ludwick, currently at the Albuquerque Journal, who gave me access to the research he had done for his special coverage by the

Missoulian. Tom Kotynski of the Great Falls Tribune; Judy Ellinghausen, archivist of the Cascade County Historical Society, and Ellen Crain, archivist of the Butte–Silver Bow archives, were also helpful.

I am grateful to Norodom Sihanouk, the Cambodian head of state and friend of Mansfield, for seeing me in Phnom Penh and especially to Julio Jendres, Sihanouk's official biographer and archivist, who provided me with valuable documents of Mansfield's correspondence with Chou En-lai.

Also in Asia, I wish to thank Professor Luo Shu-wei, former chief of the historical office of the Academy of Social Sciences of Tianjin, China, and his son, Stephen Law, for helping me explore Tientsin as Mansfield knew it during his seminal service there as a Marine in 1922.

Many presidential archives and officials thereof were of great importance. These included the Franklin D. Roosevelt Library in Hyde Park, New York, and archivist John Ferris; the John F. Kennedy Library in Columbia Point, Boston, Massachusetts, and archivist Megan F. Desnoyers; the Lyndon B. Johnson Library in Austin, Texas, its former director Harry Middleton, and archivists Ted Gittinger, Regina Greenwell, and Linda Seelke; the Gerald R. Ford Library in Ann Arbor, Michigan, and archivist Karen Holzhausen; the Ronald Reagan Library in Simi Valley, California, and archivists Greg Cumming and Steve Branch; and the Jimmy Carter Library in Atlanta, Georgia, its assistant director Martin Elzy, and archivist James Yancey. I am especially grateful to former president Carter for an interview during a visit to the archive and his personal interest in my work there.

During his Senate years Mansfield himself had taken a leading role in generating some of the most valuable official resources I tapped. His personal initiative in which he enlisted Minority Leader Hugh Scott brought about the creation of the Senate Historical Office in 1975. Typically, he kept hands off its operations once it was established. The oral histories it recorded, its other extensive files, and especially the insights of Associate Historian Donald Ritchie were extremely helpful.

Mansfield also played an important and unheralded role in preserving the secret tape recordings made by President Nixon, which made it possible to obtain authoritative details on their interaction. Seventeen hundred hours of secret tape recordings from February 1971, when Nixon began taping, through June 1972 have been released by the National Archives, which obtained possession of the tapes as a result of the Presidential Records and Materials Preservation Act of 1974. Mansfield was the first to insist in letters to government agencies and offices in January 1973 that all documents or other records with a bearing on Watergate be preserved intact rather than be destroyed or turned over to the Nixon White House. That action saved some key documents. In September 1974 he sponsored a resolution insisting that the tapes (whose existence had then been revealed) be maintained as public property rather than be turned over to Nixon after three years time as had been planned. This resolution passed the Senate unanimously and paved the way for the law cited above.

The Nixon tapes so far released include 302 conversations with Mansfield or conversations between the President and Henry Kissinger, H. R. Haldeman, or other aides in which he is mentioned. Listening to each of these conversations and transcribing the substantial ones was a rewarding but laborious and time-consuming task. I wish to express my thanks to my research assistants, Bonnie Bokenyi, Vicky Cheung, Richard Daniel Ewing, Allison Lin, and Abigail Somma, at the Paul H. Nitze School of Advanced International Studies (SAIS), Johns Hopkins University, for this and other research work and for Yukiko Ko for her assistance. I am also grateful to archivists Ron Sodano and Steve Glenn of the Nixon Presidential Materials Project at the National Archives and to Bill Burr of the National Security Archive, George Washington University, for his advice and guidance.

Among the documentary sources on various phases of Mansfield's career, two books stand out: Francis R. Valeo's *Mike Mansfield: Majority Leader* (Armonk, N.Y.: M.E. Sharpe, 1999) and Gregory A. Olson's *Mansfield and Vietnam* (East Lansing: Michigan State University Press, 1995). Several academic works were especially helpful. These include Charles Eugene Hood Jr.'s "'China Mike' Mansfield: The Making of a Congressional Authority on the Far East" (Ph.D. diss., Washington State University, 1980), which has unmatched information on his early life; David R. Turner's "Mike Mansfield and Vietnam" (Ph.D. diss., University of Kentucky, 1984); James Edward Schwartz's "Michael J. Mansfield and U.S. Military Disengagement from Europe" (Ph.D. diss., University of North Carolina, 1977); William D. Miller's "Montana and the Specter of McCarthyism 1952–1954" (Master's thesis, Montana State University 1969); a paper by Eugene J. Kraszewski, "Senator Mike Mansfield and the

Origins of American Involvement in the Second Indochina War" (Cornell University, 1973); and a paper by Mansfield's former student John A. Buzzetti, "The Honorable Mike Mansfield, Representative, First District Montana" (University of Wisconsin, 1948). Copies of these documents can be found in the Mansfield Archives at the University of Montana.

Regarding the interaction of Congress and the executive branch during the Vietnam War, nothing comes close in detail and authenticity to the four volumes of William Conrad Gibbons's *The U.S. Government and the Vietnam War* (Washington, D.C.: Government Printing Office), issued as Committee Prints by the Senate Foreign Relations Committee in April 1984, December 1984, December 1988, and June 1994. They were extremely useful, as was yet-unpublished material for a future volume that Gibbons generously made available. Published historical works on Indochina, on U.S. policy in China and Japan, and on various congressional actions were also important and are cited in the notes.

Numerous friends read all or parts of the manuscript and made valuable suggestions. Fred Greenstein, Fred Logevall, Jim Ludwick, Greg Olson, and Donald Ritchie read virtually the entire manuscript. Parts of the manuscript were read by a long list of people, including Sam Jameson, Paul Kattenburg, Mike Lampton, Bob Mann, Harry McPherson, Paul Miles, Ed Miller, and Nathaniel Thayer. I wish to express my appreciation to them all.

Guiding my manuscript into a book was also the product of many hands. I especially wish to thank Joy Harris, my longtime literary agent and guide; Don Fehr, the director of Smithsonian Books; my editor Jeff Hardwick and all his colleagues; and Joanne S. Ainsworth, a meticulous copy editor.

I am very grateful to Johns Hopkins University's Paul H. Nitze School of Advanced International Studies for continuing to give me an ideal academic perch as journalist-in-residence; to Zhaojin Ji, who protected me from many visitors and phone calls while this work was under way; and to Linda Carlson and all her colleagues on the SAIS library staff, who did so much to facilitate my research.

The greatest thanks of all go to my first and finest editor and closest friend, my wife, Laura K. Oberdorfer. And to Lily, our English cocker spaniel, who knew when I had been sitting at the computer terminal long enough, and placed her head in my lap to tell me to rise and shine.

NOTES

Abbreviations and Short Forms Used in the Notes

AP	Associated Press
Brzezinski Materials	Materials from the Zbigniew Brzezinski files, National Security Council, Jimmy Carter Library, Atlanta, Ga.
China Mike	Charles Eugene Hood Jr. "'China Mike' Mansfield: The Making of a Congressional Authority on the Far East." Ph.D. dissertation, Washington State University, 1980
CR	Congressional Record. Washington, D.C., Government Printing Office, various dates
DOS	Department of State
FDRL	Rranklin D. Roosevelt Library, Hyde Park, N.Y.
FOIA	Freedom of Information Act
FRUS	Foreign Relations of the United States. Prepared by the Office of Historian, Department of State. Washington, D.C.: Government Printing Office, various dates
Gibbons	William Conrad Gibbons. The U.S. Government and the Vietnam War: Executive and Legislative Roles and Relationships. 4 parts. Prepared for the Committee on Foreign Relations, U.S. Senate. Washington, D.C.: Government Printing Office, 1984–1994
JCL	Jimmy Carter Library, Atlanta, Ga.
Jendres Archives	Archives of Julio Jendres, biographer of Norodom Sihanouk
JFKL	John F. Kennedy Library, Boston, Mass.
LBJL	Lyndon B. Johnson Library, Austin, Tex.

LBJ tapes   Telephone tape recordings, Lyndon B. Johnson Library
MMA   Mike Mansfield Archives, part of the K. Ross Toole Archives in the Mike and
                Maureen Mansfield Library, University of Montana, Missoula
NA   National Archives, Washington, D.C., and College Park, Md.
Nixon   Text documents in Nixon Presidential Materials, National Archives
Materials
Nixon tapes   Tape recordings in the Nixon Presidential Materials, National Archives
NSC   National Security Council
NYT   *New York Times*
Time interview Interviews with Mansfield by *Time* magazine in March 1957 (text in the pos-
                session of the author)
UNGA   United Nations General Assembly
USVNR   *United States–Vietnam Relations, 1945–1967* (commonly known as the
                Pentagon Papers). This edition printed for the use of the House Armed
                Services Committee. Washington, D.C.: Government Printing Office, 1971
WHCF   White House Central File
WP   *Washington Post*

I. GOOD-BYE TO PRIVATE MIKE

4   "In an age of alarums . . .": Saul Pett, "Mansfield of Montana," *CR,* 6/10/70, p. S8711.
"the Navy's police force" and "a propaganda machine": Quoted in Allen R. Millett,
Semper Fidelis: The History of the United States Marine Corps (New York: Macmillan,
1980), pp. 469–508.

5   "understood that in this body . . .": Quoted in Robert G. Kaiser, "The Smiling
Majority," *WP,* 6/6/01.
"It is true . . ." : Mansfield to Helms, MMA, Series 22, Box 136.

6   Stevens story: Marc C. Johnson, "Mike Mansfield," *Montana Magazine,* Mar.–Apr. 2002.
Biden story: Joseph Biden, telephone interview, 5/16/02. All interviews were conducted
by the author, except where otherwise noted.

8   "Mike came to the door . . .": George McGovern, interview, 2/7/02.

9   "I had lunch last week . . .": David S. Broder, "Mr. America," *WP,* 3/21/99.

10   The texts of all eulogies are in the possession of the author.

12   Mansfield on Dirksen and civil rights legislation: Mansfield interview, 11/10/00.

2. THE EARLY YEARS

16   Incidence of nephritis in the early twentieth century: Dr. Adrienne Noe, Director of
the National Museum of Health and Medicine, telephone interview, 11/20/01.

17   Montana visits: Jim Ludwick, "Mansfield: The Senator from Montana," special section of the *Missoulian* [1988], p. 5.
Tossed out of bar: Jim Murry, former chairman of the Montana AFL-CIO, interview,
3/13/02.
"There has always been something held back . . .": Stan Kimmitt, interview, 6/7/99.
"sort of a loner . . .": Mansfield interview, 4/20/00.

18   Grandchild offered share of property: Sheila Mansfield Miller, granddaughter of
Patrick Mansfield, interview, 6/17/99.
Patrick's appeal to take children: Details of Patrick's life are extremely sketchy; he
rarely spoke of them. Virtually nothing is known of Josephine. I have relied on informa-
tion from Patrick's son John, the half-brother of Mike; John's daughter, Sheila Mansfield
Miller; an interview that Patrick gave to a *Time* correspondent in 1957; and "Kennedy's
Call on Mike's Parents Is One of Many Proud Moments in Distinguished Career of

Senator," an article in the *Great Falls Tribune*'s Sunday supplement, *Montana Parade*, 9/27/63, in which the reporter apparently gleaned biographical information directly from Patrick Mansfield.

19 "Wooden sidewalks . . .": Mansfield interview, 9/19/98.

Richard Mansfield's life: Obituary in the *Great Falls Tribune*, 8/24/12, plus materials in the Cascade County Historical Society Archives, Great Falls.

Mansfield grocery: Mansfield, *Time* interview.

Description of the store and many other details of Mansfield's early life: *China Mike*. Charles E. Hood Jr., the author, interviewed many of Mansfield's family members and schoolmates who are no longer alive.

20 Mansfield and Russell: *China Mike*, p. 61, and "Mansfield South Side Boys' Hero," *Great Falls Tribune*, 3/25/84.

"At the drop of a hat . . .": Mike Mansfield, "Sen. Mansfield Relates Lesson Learned as Boy," *Lewistown (Mont.) Daily News*, 12/13/60.

Mansfield's early youth, recollections, and attitudes were covered several times in our many interviews, especially on 7/9 and 9/10/88, and 11/26/99.

Committed to state home: *China Mike*, pp. 65–66, 72.

21 Dreams of adventures and faraway places: Mansfield interview, 6/10/98.

"I had quite an imagination . . .": Mansfield, *Time* interview.

Details of the 1917–1918 events: Mansfield interview, 4/20/00.

Smuggled aboard troop train to Long Island: Mansfield, *Time* interview.

22 "quiet, homelike accommodations, . . .": Advertising brochure for Van Rensselaer Hotel, 1912, in files of New-York Historical Society.

Change of birth certificate: Mansfield, interview by the Montana Children's Theatre, 10/26/89.

Official documents on Mansfield's Navy, Army, and Marine Corps service: National Personnel Records Center, St. Louis, Missouri, 2/22/00.

23 "I am not asking you . . ." and "appeals to me . . .": Mansfield to Walsh, and Walsh to Daniels, respectively, Thomas J. Walsh Papers, Subject File A (Montana), Box 91, "Military Discharges," Library of Congress.

25 For information on Jardine Matheson: Robert Blake, *Jardine Matheson* (London: Weidenfeld and Nicolson, 1999).

The sights of Tientsin: I am indebted to Professor Luo Shu-wei, former chief of the historical office of the Academy of Social Sciences of Tianjin (the name of Tientsin in *pinyin*, the new Chinese transliteration) and his son, Stephen Law, for a personal exploration of the history and remains of early-twentieth-century Tientsin during my visit to the city in April 2000.

Population data and other information on Tientsin: O. D. Rasmussen, *Tientsin* (Tientsin Press, 1925).

26 On the Fifteenth Infantry and its history: Edward M. Coffman, "The American 15th Infantry Regiment in China, 1912–1938," *Journal of Military History* 58 (January 1994).

Guarding outposts: U.S. Marine Corps archives, Report of Operations, "A" Company Marine Battalion, U.S. Asiatic Fleet, 5/11/22.

27 On barracks living: Mansfield interviews, 7/8/98 and 2/18/00, Further details on Fifteenth Infantry from *China Mike*, pp. 110–111.

"absolute debacle" and "men of the type . . .": *Peking and Tientsin Times*, Tientsin, 3/6/22.

Disappearance of warlord armies: Mansfield interview, 6/6/98.

"for my developing an intense personal interest in China . . .": Mansfield to James E. Schwartz, 6/6/76, MMA, Series 19, Box 591.

28 Promotion to private first class: Mansfield's service records show that he remained a private during his entire Marine Corps active duty service, and the Marine Historical Center was unable to find a record that he had been promoted to private first class, the rank he claimed in later life. However, Senator George Smathers said in his oral history

NOTES TO PAGES 29-36

NOTES TO PAGES 29–36

for the Senate Historical Office (8/1 to 10/24/89) that he had been suddenly promoted from captain to major after coming to Congress and that Mansfield had told him he had received a promotion too.

3. TO THE MINES AND THE LOVE OF HIS LIFE

29   "the Japanese might be . . .": Paul Chumrau, a former student of Mansfield, quoted in *China Mike,* p. 187.
30   "My ten years in Butte . . .": Mansfield, Labor Day speech, Butte, Sept. 1939, MMA, Series 21, Box 36.Voting data: Ellis Waldron and Paul B. Wilson, *Atlas of Montana Elections, 1889–1976* (Missoula: University of Montana, 1978), p. 202.
Wage as mucker: *Time* interview.
"I thought I was on the road to riches . . .": Labor Day speech, 1939.
31   "huge, sprawling . . .": Kinsey Howard, "Boisterous Butte," *Survey Graphic,* May 1939.
"a city of paradox . . .": Workers of the Writers' Program of the Work Projects Administration in the State of Montana, comps., *Copper Camp: Stories of the World's Greatest Mining Town, Butte, Montana* (New York: Hastings House, 1943), p. 1.
Ratio of bars to churches: Howard, "Boisterous Butte."
Transportation figures: *A Short History of Butte* (Butte: Chamber of Commerce, 1925).
Daly's Anaconda Copper Mining Company: Mary Murphy, *Mining Cultures* (Champaign: University of Illinois Press, 1997), p. 3.
32   Butte population figures: *Fourteenth Census of the United States,* 1920, vol. 2, *Population: General Report and Analytical Tables* (Washington, D.C.: Government Printing Office, 1922), 952–953. I have included the figures for Silver Bow County outside the city of Butte as part of the overall population total.
Butte history: See Murphy, *Mining Cultures,* and Michael P. Malone and Richard B. Roeder, *Montana: A History of Two Centuries* (Seattle: University of Washington Press, 1976).
When Mike Mansfield arrived in Butte: Chronology compiled by Teresa Jordan at Butte-Silver Bow Public Archives, Butte, Montana.
Mansfield's career in mines: *China Mike,* pp. 121–122.
"It was no trouble . . .": Mansfield, address to Silver Bow Council, Aug. 1939, MMA, Series 21, Box 36,
Data on mining hazards: Murphy, *Mining Cultures,* p. 18.
33   Death of miner: *Butte Miner,* 12/5/22.
"Once you got on that cage . . .": Quoted in Murphy, *Mining Cultures,* p. 19.
"Gus Erickson . . .": Mike Mansfield, "Mansfield Credits Education to His Wife," *Hungry Horse News,* 12/28/62.
34   Engineering education and advancement: Mansfield to J. B. Speer, registrar of State University of Montana, 6/16/34, Mansfield personnel file, University of Montana.
Description of Maureen: Mansfield, "Mansfield Credits Education."
Maureen's schooling: Mansfield interview, 7/20/2001, and UCLA records in the possession of the author.
35   "I had always been a loner . . .": Mansfield, "Mansfield Credits Education."
"She literally remade me . . .": Mansfield's eulogy for Maureen, 9/26/00, copy in the possession of the author.
"Maureen doubled . . .": Mansfield interview, 6/1/01.
"He always consulted her. . . .": Salpee Sahagian, interview, 11/4/99.
"They were co-dependent . . .": Sophie Engelhard Craighead, interview, 4/24/02.
"had taken the place of the mother . . .": Mansfield interview, 11/1/00.
36   On Mansfield's "failure" to give his wife credit: Mansfield's eulogy for Maureen.
Social register: Federal Writers' Project, *Copper Camp,* p. 24.
"There isn't a man . . .": Federal Writers' Project, *Copper Camp,* p. 23.

36   Attitude of Maureen's father: A close associate of Mansfield's who prefers to remain anonymous, interview, 11/4/99.

37   "He was always dabbling . . .": Frank Hayes, telephone interview, 7/29/99.

Maureen's mother: Maureen Shea, telephone interview, 7/29/99.

Mansfield's social life in Butte: *China Mike,* and Joan Shannon Scanlon, interview, 6/1/00.

38   "I thank God . . .": Handwritten letter, Maureen to Mike Mansfield, 3/16/83, copy in the possession of the author.

Dating: Mansfield interview, 11/20/00.

Told Maureen of early life: Mansfield, "Mansfield Credits Education."

Data on Mansfield's academic career: Mansfield's academic file, Human Resources office, University of Montana.

Application for work in Chile: Documented in a letter to the Navy Department from the Anglo-Chilean Consolidated Nitrate Corporation, 7/3/29, in his Navy personnel file.

39   Conversation about university education: Mansfield, "Mansfield Credits Education."

"absurd" remark: Mansfield, "Mansfield Credits Education."

"Mr. Mansfield in some respects . . .": Prof. Walter Scott to Mabel M. Murchison, 8/31/31, Mansfield's personnel file, University of Montana.

40   "A sense of quiet . . .": Mike Mansfield, "The Montana Campus," essay for journalism test, Mansfield's academic file, University of Montana.

Academic grades: Mansfield's academic file, University of Montana.

Professor's comment: Mansfield's academic file, University of Montana.

"Be sensible . . ." and hamburger story: Mansfield, "Mansfield Credits Education."

On economic circumstances in 1933: See H. G. Merriam, *The University of Montana* (Missoula: University of Montana Press, 1970), pp. 62ff.

41   Graduate instructor offer, "Here was the goal . . . ," and "Tonight, Mrs. Mansfield . . .": Mansfield, "Mansfield Credits Education." I have relied on his university personnel record for some details.

Master of arts thesis: Michael Joseph Mansfield, "American Diplomatic Relations with Korea (1866–1910)" (M.A. thesis, University of Montana, 1934), held in library of University of Montana, Missoula.

"After all, . . .": Mansfield, "American Diplomatic Relations," p. 81.

42   No teaching prospects: *China Mike,* pp. 172–173.

Academic record at UCLA: Office of the Registrar, UCLA. See also letter from Mansfield to President Simmons of University of Montana, 8/3/37, Mansfield's academic file, University of Montana.

"I've never before . . .": Quoted in *China Mike,* p. 179.

"I took a minor in history . . .": Wayne Petersen, former student, telephone interview, 7/14/95.

4. INTO THE POLITICAL WORLD

44   "sort of a loner": Mansfield interviews, 10/20/99, 4/20/00.

"who pushed me . . .": Mansfield, interview by Jim Ludwick of the *Missoulian,* 6/23/95, p. 17, manuscript in the possession of the author.

45   Advice on run for office: Peter G. Meloy to Mansfield [1996], in the possession of the author.

On Meloy's political record, Waldron and Wilson, *Atlas of Montana Elections,* p. 327.

Discussion with Roberts: Philip M. Roberts to Mansfield, 7/28/42, MMA, Series 14, Box 3, File 1.

"I felt that if I did . . .": Mansfield to J. A. Buzzetti, 12/4/47, p. 3, MMA, Series 19, Box 591.

45   Trip to Washington, D.C.: Mansfield to President George F. Simmons of Montana
       State University, 8/3/37, Mansfield's personnel file, University of Montana.
       On the bus ticket: *Time* interview.
       On the whole trip: See *China Mike*, p. 190.
       On O'Connell: See Michael P. Malone and Dianne G. Dougherty, "Montana's
       Political Culture," *Montana, the Magazine of Western History,* Winter 1981, p. 53.
       Already considering a run: *China Mike*, p. 190.
46   Participation in different sort of politics: *China Mike*, p. 189.
       O'Connell-Thorkelson race: Richard T. Ruetten, "Showdown in Montana, 1939,"
       Pacific Northwest Quarterly, Jan. 1963.
       "Everybody who knows him . . .": Quoted in *China Mike*, p. 191.
47   "very excellent likelihood . . ." and "I think he has got the intelligence . . .": Quoted
       in *China Mike*, p. 194.
       "friendly interest" and "my entry into the race . . .": Mansfield to Wheeler, 3/23/40,
       Burton K. Wheeler Papers, MC 34, Box 3, File 12, Montana Historical Society.
       "no part in the primary campaign . . .": Quoted in *China Mike*, p. 195.
       "I was not in his classes . . .": Robert Pantzer, telephone interview, 6/12/00.
48   "I want to see . . .": Mansfield, interview by Jim Ludwick, 6/23/95, p. 17, in the pos-
       session of the author.
       "I was in a certain sense . . .": "An Interview with Michael J. Mansfield," *American
       Society during World War II,* Oral History Series, vol. 1, Center for American Studies,
       University of Tokyo, in MMA, Series 33, Box 2, File 2-5.
       "I feel that we are now engaged . . .": Letter to voters [spring 1942], MMA, Series 21,
       Box 36.
       Meeting of Mansfield and Rowe: Mansfield, interview by Sam Kernell, 3/28/90, in
       the possession of the author.
50   "in a sense . . ." and "a man of great honesty . . .": Mansfield, interview by Kernell.
       "is a very poor man . . .": Rowe to Flynn, 8/11/42, J. H. Rowe Jr. file, Assistant to the
       Attorney General, 1941–1943, Container 38, File: "Mansfield, Mike," FDRL.
       "private individuals . . .": Rowe to Mansfield, 9/1/42, MMA, Series 19, Box 603, File 5.
       On Rowe and labor funds: Robert A. Caro, *The Path to Power* (New York: Knopf,
       1982), p. 716, and Caro, *Means of Ascent* (New York: Knopf, 1990), p. 225.
       On campaign finance: "Reports on State Campaign Filed in House, Senate,"
       Associated Press, 11/7/42, MMA, Series 24, Scrapbook 1.
       Johnson and Rowe relationship in 1940 campaign: Robert Dallek, *Lone Star Rising*
       (New York: Oxford University Press, 1991), pp. 199–205.
       First contact between Johnson and Mansfield: Mansfield to Rowe, 9/9/42, J. H. Rowe
       Jr. file, Container 38, File: "Mansfield, Mike," FDRL.
51   "Mansfield has a lot of common sense . . .": Rowe to Rayburn, 8/31/42, MMA, Series
       19, Box 903, Folder 5.
       "an intelligent New Dealer . . .": Rowe to Roosevelt, 9/16/42, J. H. Rowe Jr. file,
       Container 38, File: "Mansfield, Mike," FDRL. See also Rowe to Roosevelt, 10/29/42,
       same file.
       "I have tried to meet . . .": Mansfield, radio speech, 10/26/42, MMA, Oral History
       tape, OH 022-308.
       "I AM DELIGHTED. . . .": Telegram, Rowe to Mansfield, 11/4/42, MMA, Series 14,
       Box 2, File 2.
       "From 'Mucker' to 'Congressman' . . .": Floyd J. Hughes to Mansfield, 11/11/42,
       MMA, Series 14, Box 3, File 2.
52   On the Dec. 1942 trip: *Time* interview.
       On newcomers' search for housing: David Brinkley, *Washington Goes to War* (New
       York: Knopf, 1998), pp. 231–232.

52   First to serve on committee: *Missoulian,* 1/23/43, MMA, 24, Scrapbook 1.
        Spoke up confidently about Asia: *China Mike,* pp. 205ff.
        "The Chinese are being starved . . ." and "this war . . .": Quoted in "Insist Lend-Lease
        Keep China in War," *New York Times,* 3/9/43.

53   "Today Japan holds . . .": "What Are We Going to Do about the Pacific?" radio
        address, 4/30/43, MMA, Phonograph Record Collection, Box 1.
        "The defeat of Japan . . .": Radio speech, 8/26, 27, 28/43 over three Montana stations,
        MMA, Series 19, Box 36, Folder: "June 1943."

55   Anaconda's role in Montana: See K. Ross Toole, *Twentieth-Century Montana*
        (Norman: University of Oklahoma Press, 1972).
        "They never went after me . . .": Mansfield interview, 10/26/99. For his backing of
        copper tariffs, see Chapter 6.

56   On responses to constituents: Ray Dockstader, telephone interview, 3/28/02.
        "he believed the reason . . ." and "So, we packed up some snow . . .": Quoted in Rick
        Foote, "Peggy Never Saw 'The Boss' Angry," *Montana Standard,* 10/26/77.

57   Christmas cards: MMA, Series 19, Boxes 150–228.
        "Whenever a Montanan . . .": Steve Doherty, "Maureen and Mike Mansfield," in 100
        Montanans (Missoula, Mont.: *Missoulian,* 2000), p. 5.
        Recollections of DeMichele: Peggy DeMichele, interview, 7/26/99.
        Buzzetti story: John A. Buzzetti, "The Honorable Mike Mansfield," University of
        Wisconsin student paper, Jan. 1948, MMA, Series 19, Box 591.
        Greeting Norma Keil by name: Norma Keil to the author, June 2000.
        Morgan and Bartlett stories: Hearing on a Mansfield statue before the State
        Administration Committee, Montana Senate, 3/8/99.

58   Tokyo story: Embassy official who wishes to remain anonymous, interview, 1/7/00.
        "a hardworking guardian . . .": Michael P. Malone and Pierce C. Mullen, "Mansfield
        of Montana," unpublished manuscript, Autumn 1971, in possession of author.
        "He has declined": Quoted in Malone and Mullen, "Mansfield of Montana," p. 9.
        "Mansfield deliberately . . .": H. L. Maury to Sen. James Murray, 2/2/46, Murray
        Papers, University of Montana Archives.
        "I never get . . .": Quoted in Robert Sherrill, "The Invisible Senator," *Nation,* 5/10/71.

59   "individuals who are neither . . .": Mansfield to Arthur Lamey, 3/19/47, MMA, Series
        14, Box 8, File 10.
        "a conservative-liberal . . .": Mansfield to Eric Goldman, 1/25/55, MMA, Series 19,
        Box 453, File 1.
        "saving Flathead Lake": Mansfield interview, 4/9/99.
        "do everything in your power . . .": Mansfield to FDR, 7/8/43, MMA, Series 3, Box 15, File 1.

60   Power destined for plutonium production: According to the U.S. Army history of the
        Manhattan Project (responsible for building the first atomic bomb), Vincent C. Jones,
        Manhattan: The Army and the Atomic Bomb (Washington, D.C.: Center of Military
        History, 1985), the War Production Board was informed in January 1943 that the
        Manhattan Project would be seeking a large block of additional electric power some-
        where in the Pacific Coast and was told in February that it would be at Hanford.
        According to Vera Springer, *Power and the Pacific Northwest* (Washington, D.C.:
        Bonneville Power Administration, U.S. Department of the Interior, 1976), cited to me
        by the Bonneville Power Administration, BPA and the Corps of Engineers were asked in
        1943 "to look for sources of electric energy that might be developed rapidly for the war
        effort without the excessive use of scarce resources." Studies identified Flathead Lake as
        a promising upstream dam site that could provide additional power as well as storage to
        regulate river flow, according to the book. The overwhelming opposition in June 1943
        caused the plan to be withdrawn.
        Attacks on Montana Power Company: MMA, Series 3, Box 17, File 5.

60   "I noticed Judge Latta . . .": Mansfield memorandum for files, MMA, Series 19, Box 604, File 16.

5. MISSION TO CHINA

63   "which might be of value . . . ": Mansfield to Ambassador Wei Tao-ming, 3/2/43, MMA, Series 4, Box 19, File 11.

Mansfield-Vorys effort to visit China: Vorys to Wei, 6/17/44; Wei to Vorys, 6/20/44; Stettinius to Mansfield, 7/11/44, all in MMA, Series 19, Box 511, File 1.

"bring the matter . . .": Wei to Mansfield, 7/18/44, MMA, Series 19, Box 511, File 1.

"I brought the matter . . .": Memorandum of meeting with FDR, 10/2/44, MMA, Series 19, Box 511, File 1.

64   "China, the Philippines . . .": Radio broadcast, 10/26/42, MMA, Oral History tape, OH 022-308.

On the six weeks in Siberia: "Professor! Acquainting You with the Faculty of Montana State University," *Great Falls Tribune,* 12/11/37. "That was a lie": Mansfield interview, 9/9/99.

"Mike, I have asked you . . .": Reported by Drew Pearson and by *Time,* among others. It is told in Mansfield's own words in an answer to questions by his former student, John Buzzetti, "The Honorable Mike Mansfield."

"fair enough": Mansfield interview, 4/9/99.

65   President's agreement to Stilwell's ouster: See Barbara Tuchman, *Stilwell and the American Experience in China* (New York: Macmillan, 1970), p. 498. Roosevelt was still trying to save a place for Stilwell in the Burma campaign, but he had given in on the central issues of placing a U.S. commander in charge of all Chinese armed forces and on Stilwell's continuance as Chiang's chief of staff. See Roosevelt to Chiang Kai-shek, 10/5/44, *FRUS, 1944,* vol. 6 (China), pp. 165–166.

"will plow under . . ." and "the most untruthful . . .": Wheeler and FDR quoted in Basil Rauch, *Roosevelt: From Munich to Pearl Harbor* (New York: Creative Age Press, 1950), p. 304.

66   "if somebody kidnaps Wheeler . . .": Quoted in *Roosevelt and Frankfurter,* annotated by Max Freedman (Boston: Little, Brown, 1967), p. 611.

Mansfield selected to run against Wheeler: Dan Whetstone, "Mike Had Eyes on Orient," *Cut Bank Pioneer Press,* 10/4/46.

"too much of a novice": Mansfield interviews, 8/18/99, 6/30/00.

Guests and seating at Kung luncheon: Mansfield, memorandum for files, 10/4/44, MMA, Series 19, Box 511, File 1.

67n   For information on Lauchlin Currie: See Allen Weinstein and Alexander Vassilev, *The Haunted Wood* (New York: Random House, 1999).

67   Meeting between John Carter Vincent and Mansfield: Mansfield, memorandum for files, undated, MMA, Series 19, Box 511, File 1.

Black market: Memorandum on Vincent luncheon and meetings with other officials, 10/6/44, MMA, Series 19, Box 511, File 1.

Visit of Lt. Sidney Wald: Mansfield, memorandum for files, 11/13/44, MMA, Series 19, Box 511, File "China Mission."

68   Details of Mansfield's journey to and in China: Except as noted all are taken from his remarkably detailed trip diary or his report to Roosevelt, which is published in *FRUS, 1945,* vol. 7 (China), pp. 2–26. A typewritten copy of his diary is in his papers, MMA, Series 8, Box 35, File 9. The handwritten copy is in the possession of Anne Mansfield.

68   On Merrill and Merrill's Marauders: See Tuchman, *Stilwell,* pp. 272, 432ff.
72n   Alsop description of Mansfield: Joseph Alsop, "The Cambodian 'Cover-Up,'"
        Washington Post, 8/8/73.
72   Unmilitary fashion of Alsop: Mansfield interview, 9/10/98.
        "quite democratic . . .": Report to Roosevelt, *FRUS,* 1945, 7:2–26; Report to House,
        CR, 1/16/45, pp. 289–296.
        "nearer to Soviet Russia . . ." and "Beware of Russian reports. . . .: Mansfield's notes
        titled "History and Organization of Communist Party," MMA, Series 19, Box 512, File 2.
73   Stalin's comments to Harriman in 1944: Tang Tsou, *America's Failure in China*
        (Chicago: University of Chicago Press, 1963), p. 163.
        Moscow's secret connections with China's Communists: John W. Garver, *Chinese-
        Soviet Relations, 1937–1945* (New York: Oxford University Press, 1988), p. 255.
        "Mao and his comrades . . .": Michael M. Sheng, *Battling Western Imperialism* (Princeton, N.J.:
        Princeton University Press, 1997), p. 56. For differing views see Garver, *Chinese-Soviet Relations,*
        and Odd Arne Westad, *Cold War and Revolution* (New York: Columbia University Press, 1993).
74   "it was a tough job . . .": Mansfield, "Memo: November 26, 1945," MMA, Series 19, Box 511, File 2.
75   On evacuation plans and a new capital: George Atcheson (chargé d'affaires in
        Chungking) to SecState, 12/5/44, *FRUS,* 1944, vol. 4 (China), pp. 199–200. For a vivid
        description of the situation in Chungking at the time see Theodore H. White and
        Annalee Jacoby, *Thunder Out of China* (New York: William Sloane, 1946), pp. 193–198.
76   The shift in U.S. perspective: See Theodore H. White, *In Search of History* (New
        York: Harper and Row, 1978).
77   "The Japanese are a disease . . .": Quoted in White and Jacoby, *Thunder Out of China,* p. 129.
78   "First over . . ." and "'First [to accomplish] . . .": These observations are in the hand-
        written diary but not in the typewritten version.
        Mansfield's meeting with FDR: Mansfield, memorandum for files, MMA, Series 19,
        Box 604, File 16.
79   "the French have gotten . . .": Quoted in Mansfield, memorandum for files, MMA,
        Series 19, Box 604, File 16.
        FDR's refusal to authorize U.S. participation: For Roosevelt's attitude and the
        wartime situation regarding Vietnam, see Mark Philip Bradley, *Imaging Vietnam and
        America* (Chapel Hill: University of North Carolina Press, 2000), esp. chap. 3,
        "Trusteeship and the American Vision of Postcolonial Vietnam."
80   No notes or markings on report: Original copy obtained from FDRL.
        FDR's condition in January 1945: See Robert H. Ferrell, *The Dying President*
        (Columbia: University of Missouri Press, 1998).
81   "one of a handful . . .": Drew Pearson, "Washington Merry-Go Round," *Washington
        Post,* 11/1/44.

6. THE TRUMAN YEARS

83   Military police returned to White House: Bertram D. Hulen, "Work in Capital Goes
        on Fitfully," *NYT,* 8/11/45.
        Japan's Kwangtung Army: MMA, Series 19, Box 604, File 16. There is no explicit state-
        ment in either Mansfield's or Truman's notes from 8/10/45 of discussion of the emperor
        issue, although Mansfield's notes say they discussed "the terms of surrender the Japanese
        had offered," of which the future of the emperor was the central issue. On several occasions
        Mansfield recalled discussing the issue with Truman, although the dates and precise circum-
        stances of this discussion are unclear. See Mansfield interviews, 9/10/98, and 9/9/99.
84   Truman was "keenly aware" of the problem: "Surrender Offer Is Made by Japan,"
        NYT, 8/11/45; also, AP, 8/10/45, MMA, Series 24, Scrapbook 2.

84   "I told [Truman] I wasn't . . .": Mansfield memorandum for files, undated, MMA,
      Series 19, Box 604, File 16.
85   President's commitment to see Mansfield: Mansfield to Connally, 7/4/45 and 8/6/45,
      Papers of Harry S. Truman, Official File, Truman Library, Independence, Missouri
      (hereafter, Truman Papers).
      Report sent to Margaret Truman: Mansfield raised the possibility of sending his
      report to Margaret Truman when he saw the president on 5/23/45. See the Mansfield
      memorandum of that meeting, MMA, Series 19, Box 604, File 16. The letter to
      Margaret Truman is at MMA, Series 19, Box 511, File 2.
      "the White House like[s] me . . .": Mansfield memorandum for files, 7/23/45, MMA,
      Series 19, Box 604, File 16.
      "someone on our side . . ." and "I wanted to go as . . .": Mansfield, memorandum for
      files: 8/10/45, MMA, Series 19, Box 604, File 16.
86   "they would understand far better . . .": CR, 10/11/45, p. 9780.
87   "gunboat policy" and "unwarranted interference": Mansfield, speeches in the House,
      CR, 10/11/45 and 10/30/45.
      "most unwise": Memorandum, Director of the Office of Far Eastern Affairs
      (Vincent) to the Undersecretary of State (Acheson), 10/16/45, FRUS, 1945, 7:580–581.
      Enclosing speeches and requesting a meeting: Mansfield to Truman, 11/7/45, Truman
      Papers.
      "terrible discontent" and other quotations from discussion: Mansfield memorandum
      for files, 11/27/45, MMA, Series 19, Box 604, File 16.
88   "Mike Mansfield . . .": Buzzetti, "The Honorable Mike Mansfield."
      Mansfield description: Francis R. Valeo, interview, 8/26/98.
      On Rankin campaign: Time interview.
89   Missoula barber, bartender, and customer quotations: Buzzetti, "The Honorable
      Mike Mansfield."
      Montanans' visit to Mansfield in Washington: Mansfield, answers to questions from
      Buzzetti on 12/4/47, in Buzzetti, "The Honorable Mike Mansfield."
      Post of majority whip: Mansfield to Rayburn and McCormick, 11/16/48, MMA,
      Series 19, Box 450, Folder: "Democratic Whip Position, 1948."
90   "If you took half as good care of my business . . .": Corcoran to Rowe, 11/24/48,
      MMA, Series 19, Box 450, Folder: "Democratic Whip's Position, 1948."
      "Many of them wonder . . . ": Sullivan to Mansfield, 10/27/49, MMA, Series 19, Box
      604, Folder 2.
      "I believe that it is my first duty . . .": Statement of Congressman Mike Mansfield,
      10/31/49, Press release, MMA, Series 4, Box 17, Office files.
      Interior Department and University of Montana posts: Mansfield to Rt. Rev. Msgr. Emmet
      J. Riley, 9/6/50, MMA, Series 19, Box 450, Folder: "Offer of Presidency of State Univ."
91   Luncheon with MacArthur: Mansfield, Travel Diary from his 1946 trip, quoted in
      China Mike, pp. 13–15. The diary could not be located in his archives, despite diligent
      searches by members of the library staff. Mansfield also made a more circumspect report
      to the House on 2/3/47, which can be found in CR, pp. 764–770. The MacArthur
      lunch was also described in Mansfield interview, 6/1/01.
      "Devastation over a large area . . .": Mansfield, Travel Diary, quoted in China Mike.
92   "The B-29 . . .": Mansfield, statement on surrender of Japan, undated typescript,
      MMA, Series 19, Box 604, File 16.
      "the formula . . .": Mansfield, speech headed "My Fellow Montanans," undated type-
      script, MMA, Series 4, Box 10, Folder: "Atomic Bomb."
      "an atomic armaments race": Mansfield, "My Fellow Montanans."
      Support for intervention in Korea: Mansfield, handwritten statement on hostilities in
      Korea (undated), MMA, Series 19, Box 511, Folder 4.

93   "No matter what we do . . .": Mansfield, Travel Diary, quoted in *China Mike*, p. 14.
"as long as we . . .": Mansfield, "Report on Conditions in the Far East," House
speech, *CR*, 2/3/47, pp. 764ff.
"I must admit . . .": Mansfield to Marshall, 10/22/47, DOS files, Microfiche 711.93/11-
347, CS/A, NA. "close relations" and "in general . . .": Memorandum, (W. Walton)
Butterworth to General Carter, 11/3/47, DOS files, NA.

94   Address in New York: "The Chinese Policy of the United States" (paper presented at
the annual meeting of the Academy of Political Science, New York, 11/12/47), Salpee
Sahagian materials, in the possession of the author.
"A man thinks of a lot of things . . .": Mansfield, Journal of official trip, Sept.–Oct.
1947, Anne Mansfield Papers.

95   Views of situation with Maureen: Mansfield, Journal of official trip, 1947.
House travels 1947–1952: "Biography of Mike Mansfield," sent to the *Washington Post*
by Mansfield's office, 1/8/53, in the possession of the author.
"the most beautiful women . . .": Mansfield, Journal of official trip, Sept.–Oct. 1947.

96   Assassination of Gaitán: See CNN Perspective Series, "Soldiers of Peace, Educational
Guide," www.Turnerlearning.com, 1999.
"the Red tide . . .": Rep. Donald L. Jackson, "Report on Bogotá," speech, 4/15/48,
CR-Appendix, 4/20/48.
"tremendously" overestimated danger: Mansfield, Diary of Bogotá conference, MMA,
Series 4, Box 2.

97   "would be followed by . . .": *CR*, 8/18/49, pp. 11781–11782.
"due to the incredible ineptitude . . .": Mansfield, "What Should United States Policy
in China Be?" Extension of remarks, *CR*, 2/9/50, pp. A1010–1011.
"under present circumstances . . .": Mansfield, "The Foreign Policy of the United
States," Extension of remarks, *CR*, 7/10/51, p. A4254.

98   "We felt, as did everybody . . .": Valeo, interview, 8/26/98.

99   "to try to connect . . .": Jimmy Sullivan, Notebook on prospects for the 1952 race,
MMA, Series 14, Box 14.
"as a younger member . . ." and "Keep punching . . .": Mansfield to Truman, 1/17/47,
Truman Papers.

100 "copper miner . . .": UNGA, Press Release No. 1300 add 1, MMA, Series 4, Box 21,
Folder: "Letters to Mike as UN Rep."
"talking like a lumberjack . . .": Quoted in "Mansfield to Run for Seat in Senate,"
NYT, 2/9/52.
"as calm and as cool . . .": Eleanor Roosevelt, "It's Slow Work Trying to Convince
Russians," *Washington Daily News*, 12/27/51.
"arrogant man . . .": Mansfield, campaign speech, Great Falls, 10/20/52, MMA, Series
14, Box 23, File 3.
"he stood right up . . .": Truman, campaign speech in Havre, Montana, 9/30/52,
MMA, Series 4, Box 14, File 2.

101 On the 1952 campaign: William D. Miller, "Montana and the Specter of McCarthyism,
1952–1954" (Ph.D. diss., Montana State University, 1969), MMA, Series 19, Box 591.
Another good depiction of the 1952 race is in Gregory A. Olson, *Mansfield and Vietnam*
(East Lansing: Michigan State University Press, 1995), pp. 13–16. See also Mansfield, mem-
orandum for files on the 1952 campaign, undated, MMA, Series 14, Box 23, File 13.
Ecton campaign slurs: Scrapbook on the 1952 campaign, MMA, Series 24, Scrapbook 3.
Great Falls woman blamed Mansfield: Mrs. John Brockes, radio broadcast, tape in
MMA Oral History record, OH22-196.
Anonymous phone calls and whispering campaigns: Miller, "Montana and the
Specter of McCarthyism"; Olson, *Mansfield and Vietnam;* Mansfield, memorandum for
files on the 1952 campaign; and Scrapbook on the 1952 campaign.

101   "The Senate is not worth losing . . .": *China Mike,* p. 346.
       McCarthy and smear campaign: Robert Griffith, *The Politics of Fear* (Lexington: University Press of Kentucky, 1970), p. 195. Griffith points out that in fact McCarthy's influence in the 1952 elections was overrated, but the legend of power pervaded American politics at the time.
102   "either stupid or a dupe" and "you don't hunt skunks . . .": "McCarthy Lauds Sen. Ecton, Hits Mansfield," *Daily Missoulian,* 10/15/52.
       "McCarthy had a violent hatred . . .": Harvey Matusow, *False Witness* (New York: Cameron and Kahn, 1955), p. 166.
       Matusow broadcast: Harvey Matusow, broadcast speech in 1952 campaign, tape recording in MMA, OH22-11.
       People avoided meeting him: Mansfield interviews, 9/10/98, 11/26/99, 11/10/00, 6/1/01.
103   "If I win this election . . .": Mansfield, radio broadcast, "Final Speeches in Senatorial Campaign," 11/3/52, typed transcript in MMA, Series 19, Box 593, File 11.
       1952 election victory: Mansfield interviews, 11/26/99, 11/10/00.
104   Postelection encounter with McCarthy: Mansfield interview, 9/10/98.
       Matusow's attempted apology: Memorandum of telephone call, Matusow to Sullivan, 11/20/53, MMA, Series 14, Box 23, File 10; also Memorandum of telephone call, from Harry Kelly of Associated Press, 2/15/55, MMA, Series 14, Box 23, File 11.
       "Some things . . .": Quoted in "Matusow Declares He Apologized," *Great Falls Tribune,* 2/16/55, cited in Olson, *Mansfield and Vietnam,* p. 16.
       "We know, of course, . . .": Quoted in *CR,* 5/6/57, p. 6350.

7. INTRODUCTION TO INDOCHINA

105   Stalin's death leading to a decision by his successors: Kathryn Weathersby, "Stalin, Mao, and the End of the Korean War," in *Brothers in Arms: The Rise and Fall of the Sino-Soviet Alliance,* ed. Odd Arne Wested (Stanford, Calif.: Stanford University Press; Washington, D.C.: Woodrow Wilson Center Press, 2000), pp. 90–116.
106   Description of the Navarre briefing for Mansfield: Francis R. Valeo, Oral History interview, 7/3/85–3/11/86, available for inspection at the Senate Historical Office, Washington, D.C., p. 88 (hereafter cited as Valeo Oral History), and Valeo, interview, 8/26/98.
       "really brilliant . . .": *Executive Sessions of the Senate Foreign Relations Committee,* Historical Series, 1/19/54 (Washington, D.C.: Government Printing Office, 1977), 6:48–49.
       "The French control . . .": Graham Greene, *The Quiet American* (New York: Bantam Books, 1956), p. 17.
       "On the one hand . . .": Lucien Bodard, *The Quicksand War: Prelude to Vietnam* (Boston: Atlantic Monthly Press, 1967), p. 81.
108   Public backing of Johnson wrecked rebellion: Jim Rowe cited in John Bartlow Martin, *Adlai Stevenson and the World* (New York: Doubleday 1977), p. 28.
       Story of the Mansfield-Humphrey assignments to Foreign Relations: Robert A. Caro, *Master of the Senate* (New York: Knopf, 2002), pp. 492–499.
       "Dear Lyndon . . .": Thank-you note, Rowe to Johnson, 1/13/53, LBJL, LBJA, File: "Selected Names," Box 32, "Rowe, James H. (1939–55)."
       Purchase of house: Mansfield interview.
109   "the bloodier, the better": *Time* interview.

109   Purchase of statue in 1949: FBI file of Michael J. Mansfield, HQ 46-51453, copy in the
        possession of the author.
            "a rock of integrity, . . .": Memorandum, Jack Anderson to Drew Pearson, 12/28/56,
        Pearson Papers, Box G265, LBJL. I am grateful to Senate historian Donald Ritchie for
        calling my attention to this memo.
110   "probably the Senate's leading authority . . .": Robert Albright, "Front-Runners Fill
        the 'Back Row,'" *WP,* 11/25/54.
            "Indo-China is at this time . . .": Memorandum for the files, "Memo: 2/19/53,"
        MMA, Series 12, Box 7, File 5. See also, *NYT,* 2/21/53.
111   "under present conditions . . .": *The Pentagon Papers, NYT* ed. (New York: Bantam
        Books, 1971), p. 10.
            "essentially is a struggle . . .": "Some Notes on the Political Situation in Indochina,"
        briefing paper supplied to Mansfield by U.S. Embassy Saigon in Sept. 1953, MMA,
        Series 13, Box 7, File 5.
            Valeo and Mansfield trip to Indochina: Valeo Oral History, p. 86.
            Valeo background: Valeo Oral History, preface.
112   On drafting speeches and memoranda: Valeo, interview, 2/6//02.
            "first-hand knowledge. . .": Draft of cable, Mansfiled to Department of State,
        undated, MMA, Series 22, Box 95, File 1.
            "an ardent interventionist": Denis Warner, *Certain Victory: How Hanoi Won the War*
        (Kansas City: Sheed Andrews and McMeel, 1978), pp. 95–96.
            "I'm sure you can't be right . . .": Quoted in Warner, *Certain Victory,* pp. 95.
113   Meeting between Mansfield and Souvanna: Valeo Oral History, p. 104.
            "we have two battalions . . .": Quoted in Valeo Oral History, p. 90.
114   "meaningless if it was won . . ." and "Cambodia should join . . .": Quoted by Donald
        Heath, *FRUS,* 1952–1954, vol. 13, part 1, pp. 809–810.
            "whatever military steps" and "get tough": Quoted in *FRUS,* 1952–1954, vol. 13, part 1, p. 825.
            "only an outright invasion . . .": Mansfield, *Indochina,* report prepared for the Senate
        Foreign Relations Committee of his mission to Vietnam, Cambodia, and Laos
        (Washington, D.C.: Government Printing Office, 1953), p. 7. Hereafter cited as
        Mansfield report to Senate Foreign Relations Committee, 1953.
            "in my opinion . . .": Quoted in *CR,* 2/8/54, p. 1506.
            "a logical extension . . .": Quoted in *CR,* 2/9/54, pp. 1550–1552.
            "When I taught . . .": Mansfield to William B. Ellis, 2/19/54, MMA, Series 13, Box 6,
        File 2.
115   "I am very glad . . .": *Executive Sessions of the Senate Foreign Relations Committee,*
        Historical Series, 2/16/54 (Washington, D.C.: Government Printing Office, 1977), 6:142.
            "I think our policy . . .": *Executive Sessions of Senate Foreign Relations Committee,*
        2/24/54, 6:183.
            "The war in Indo-China . . .": "Indo-China, Memo: 3/18/54," MMA, Series 13, Box 7,
        File 5.
            "it is not going to be won . . .": CBS transcript, "Man of the Week," 4/25/54, MMA,
        Series 19, Box 593, File 16.
117   Appeal from Diem for U.S. aid: Edna F. Kelly to Mansfield, 7/20/51, MMA, Series 4,
        Box 21, Folder 14.
            "nothing less than . . ." and "no rallying point . . .": Quoted in Memorandum of conversa-
        tion, by Edmund A. Gullion of the Policy Planning Staff, 5/7/53, *FRUS,* 1952–1954, 13:553–554.
            "left with the feeling . . .": Mansfield interview, 8/28/98. Mansfield undoubtedly
        mean "Vietnam," as South Vietnam did not yet exist in 1953.
118   Diem and his Catholic connections: For a thorough account see Seth Jacobs, "'Our
        System Demands the Supreme Being': The U.S. Religious Revival and the 'Diem

Experiment,' 1954–55," *Diplomatic History*, fall 2001. See also John Cooney, *The American Pope: The Life and Times of Francis Cardinal Spellman* (New York: Times Books, 1984), pp. 240–245.

118   "Not at all. . . .": Mansfield interview, 8/28/98.

"had already taken on . . .": Mandfield, *Report on Indochina,* report prepared for the Senate Foreign Relations Committee of his mission to Vietnam, Cambodia, and Loas (Washington, D.C.: Government Printing Ofiice, 1954), p. 7. Hereafter cited as Mansfield report to Senate Foreign Relations Committee, 1954.

On the situation in Hanoi: See Mansfield report to Senate Foreign Relations Committee, 1954, and Valeo Oral History, p. 98. Also Valeo, interview, 8/26/98.

119   Lansdale's activities: See the *Pentagon Papers,* pp. 58–60.

Mansfield knew nothing: Mansfield interview, 7/20/01.

Evacuation figure: Mansfield report to Senate Foreign Relations Committee, 1954.

Navy ships ferried refugees: Robert Shaplen, *Lost Revolution* (New York: Harper and Row, 1966), p. 114.

"they had chosen . . .": Mansfield, "American Foreign Policy in the Far East," commencement address at Carroll College, 5/22/55, Salpee Sahagian Papers.

"lacks what it takes . . .": Mansfield memorandum for files (unsigned; apparently written by Valeo), "Ambassador Dillon, Paris, 8/28/54," MMA, Series 22, Box 95, File 2.

"the drive or capacity": Mansfield memorandum for files (unsigned; apparently written by Valeo), "Conversation: Jim Lucas (Scripps-Howard)," 8/30/54, MMA, Series 22, Box 95, File 2.

"have written off Viet Nam . . .": Mansfield, memorandum for files (unsigned; apparently written by Valeo), "Parsons (in charge of Embassy at Bangkok)," 8/31/54, MMA, Series 22, Box 95, File 2.

120   "the chances are poor" and "The situation is more likely . . .": "Post-Geneva Outlook in Indochina," National Intelligence Estimate 63-5-54, 8/3/54, *FRUS,* 1952–1954, 13:1905–1906.

"Diem does not have control . . .": "Political Conditions in Indochina," CIA report from Saigon, 8/23/54, *FRUS,* 1952–1954, 13:1976.

"in order that the Senator . . .": Cable, Heath to DOS, 9/3/54, *FRUS,* 1952–1954, 13:2001–2002.

"the political plotting . . .": Mansfield report to Senate Foreign Relations Committee, 1954.

121   "utterly honest . . .": Mansfield memorandum for files, "Ambassador Heath. Saigon, 9/2/54," MMA, Series 22, Box 95, File 2.

"with his eyes opened . . .": Mansfield, memorandum for files, "Wesley Fischel *[sic]* (Adv. to Diem) Saigon, September 4, 1954 (Valeo only)," MMA, Series 22, Box 95, File 2.

"Our only chance . . .": Mansfield, memorandum for files, "Paul E. Everett. Saigon, 9/4/54," MMA, Series 22, Box 95, File 2.

"We do not have a good chance . . .": Mansfield, memorandum for files, "Wesley Fischel *[sic]* (Adv. to Diem) Saigon, September 4, 1954 (Valeo only),"

122   "ability, energy . . .": Letter, Mansfield to Dulles, 3/28/52, John Foster Dulles Papers, Box 62, Mudd Manuscript Library, Princeton University.

"I always had the feeling . . .": Dulles to Mansfield, 4/4/52, Dulles Papers, Box 62.

"bluster and retreat . . .": Quoted in Rose McKee, "Mansfield Blasts GOP's Diplomacy," *WP,* 7/9/54.

Mansfield's criticism of Dulles: Speech, "Geneva: Failure of a Policy," *CR,* 7/8/54, pp. 9997–10011.

Dulles's unused answer: Quoted in *America in Vietnam: A Documentary History* (New York: Anchor Press, 1985), pp. 166–168.

SEATO treaty: For details on the treaty and its meaning, see Gibbons, Part I, pp. 271–276.

Signators to treaty: Gibbons, Part 1, p. 273.

123n   "the SEATO Treaty . . .": *Public Papers of the Presidents of the United States: Lyndon B. Johnson,* 1967 (Washington, D.C.: Government Printing Office), p. 972. This quotation is one example of many statements.

"no justification whatever": Mansfield, statement on SEATO treaty (undated), MMA, Series 22, Box 52, File 2.

123n   "not merely an inconsequential relic . . .": Mansfield, address at Paul H. Nitze School of Advanced International Studies (SAIS), Johns Hopkins University, *CR,* 3/19/73, p. 8408.

123   "would be good . . .": Olson, *Mansfield and Vietnam,* p. 33.

124   "It is time to stop . . .": Mansfield, Senate speech, "After Geneva: American Policy—Germany and Japan," 8/14/54, copy in the possession of the author.
"Why did the Administration . . .": Quoted in Edward T. Folliard, "GOP Sees Uphill Battle for D'Ewart," *WP,* 9/20/54.
Reception in Manila: Mansfield interview, 7/24/98.
Eisenhower administration's assistance to Nationalist Chinese: Nancy Bernkopf Tucker, "John Foster Dulles and the Taiwan Roots of the 'Two China' Policy," in *John Foster Dulles and the Diplomacy of the Cold War,* ed. Richard H. Immerman (Princeton, N.J.: Princeton University Press, 1990).

125   Mao Tse-tung's increased pressure on Nationalists: Chen Jian, *Mao's China and the Cold War* (Chapel Hill: University of North Carolina Press, 2001), pp. 167–170.
"would have grave psychological repercussions" and all other quotations and information in this paragraph: Cable, Dulles to DOS, 9/4/54, *FRUS,* 1952–1954, 14:560.

126   Mansfield's position on military intervention: Mansfield interview, 7/24/98. See also, Mansfield Oral History for John Foster Dulles Oral History Project, Princeton University, Princeton, N.J., 5/10/66, pp. 5–7; and Marvin Kalb and Elie Abel, *Roots of Involvement* (New York: Norton, 1971), pp. 92–93, based in part on an interview with Mansfield.
Transmission of Mansfield's views: Cable, Dulles to Smith, National Archives, DOS records, RG 793.5/9-454. Mansfield's views were also summarized, along with the plan to inform Eisenhower, in footnote 4 to Smith to Manila, 9/4/54. *FRUS,* 1952–1954, 14:561.
Signing of treaty: A photograph of Mansfield's signing and the pen he used are in MMA, Series 24, Scrapbook 14.
"It is doubtful . . .": Memorandum prepared by Dulles, 9/12/54, *FRUS,* 1952–1954, 14:611–613.
"If we act without Congress . . .": Memorandum of discussion at NSC meeting, Denver, 9/12/54, *FRUS,* 1952–1954, 14:613–624.

127   "effective service": Cable, Dulles to James C. Hagerty, 9/10/54, Dulles Papers, Box 84.
Gift of elephant tray: Maureen Mansfield–Dulles correspondence, Nov. 1954, Box 84, Dulles Papers.

128   Views of La Chambre and Dulles: Memorandum of conversation, Dulles and La Chambre, 9/6/54, *FRUS,* 1952–1954, 13:2007–2010.
Conversation of La Chambre and Mansfield: Quoted in Dulles to DOS, 9/8/54, *FRUS,* 1952–1954, 13:2012–2013.
"We realized we had to proceed . . .": Quoted in Shaplen, *Lost Revolution,* p. 118.
Dulles's personal message to Mansfield: "Rough Draft" of message, MMA, Series 12, Box 95, File 2.

129   "The political crisis in south Vietnam . . .": Cable, Mansfield to Dulles, Berlin, 9/24/54, *FRUS,* 1952–1954, 13:2055–2056.
"is in support . . .": Quoted in Summary Minutes of DOS Meeting, 9/25/54, *FRUS,* 1952–1954, 13:2069.
"would have great influence . . .": Smith to U.S. Embassy Saigon, 9/25/54, *FRUS,* 1952–1954, 13:2070.
"stunned the French": Quoted in Shaplen, *Lost Revolution,* p. 118.

130   "acute crisis," "a military dictatorship," and "In the event that the Diem government falls . . .": Mansfield report to Senate Foreign Relations Committee, 1954, p. 14.
On the 100,000 copies: Cable, Undersecretary of State Herbert Hoover Jr. to U.S. Embassy Saigon, 12/15/54, *FRUS,* 1952–1954, 13:2379.
Far East Bureau reaction: *FRUS,* 1952–1954, 13:2141–2142.
Cutler's suggestion of Vietnam as topic: Memorandum attached to Comments on Mansfield's Report, 10/15/54, National Archives, DOS, FE/SEA files, Lot 58 D207, Vietnam: Senator Mansfield.

131   "the US will have to reconsider . . .": Cable, Hoover to Dulles, 10/22/54, *FRUS,* 1952–1954, 13:2159–2160.

131   "and the importance . . .": Quoted in cable, Dillon to DOS, 10/23/54, *FRUS*, 1952–1954, 13:2165–2166.

Mendes-France was "aghast": Memorandum of Conference at Dulles Residence, 10/31/54, *FRUS*, 1952–1954, 13:2198–2199.

New instructions to representatives: Cable, Dillon to DOS, 10/23/54.

"developing and maintaining . . .": Letter, Eisenhower to Diem, undated, *FRUS*, 1952–1954, 13:2166–2167.

On citation of Eisenhower letter: See Chester L. Cooper, *The Lost Crusade* (New York: Dodd Mead, 1970), p. 134.

"lack of personality . . .": Cable, Heath to DOS, 10/22/54, *FRUS*, 1952–1954, 13:2151–2153.

132   "deserves serious cpnsideration": "Memprandum of Conference," 10/31/54, *FRUS*, *1952–1954*, 13:2199.

Collins's initial conclusions: Cable, Randolph A. Kidder, chargé d'affaires at U.S. Embassy Saigon, to DOS, 12/6/54, *FRUS*, 1952–1954, 13:2341–2344.

Mansfield's reaction to Collins's cable: Memorandum of conversation with Mansfield, 12/7/54, *FRUS*, 1952–1954, 13:2350–2352.

Possibility raised by Collins of withdrawing from Vietnam: Cable, Kidder to DOS, 12/13/54, *FRUS*, 1952–1954, 13:2362–2366.

134   Mansfield's views on Diem and endorsement of Quat: Hoover to U.S. Embassy Saigon, 12/15/54, *FRUS*, 1952–1954, 13:2378–2379.

On timing of Diem's rejection and Mansfield's endorsement: Kidder to DOS, 12/17/54, *FRUS*, 1952–1954, 13:2398.

"the final development . . ." and bringing Bao Dai to Saigon: Cable, Kidder to DOS, 12/16/54, *FRUS*, 1952–1954, 13:2379–2382.

"on basis of facts. . .": Hoover to U.S. embassy Paris, 12/17/54, *FRUS*, *1952–1954*, 13:2392–2394.

135   "strong feelings": Dillon to DOS, 12/19/54, *FRUS*, *1952–1954*, 13:2400–2405.

Collins's insistence on replacing Diem: Cable, Collins to State Department, 3/31/55, *FRUS*, 1955–1957, 1:168–171.

"we ought to talk to Mansfield . . .": Telephone conversation between Eisenhower and Dulles, 4/1/55, *FRUS*, 1955–1957, 1:175–176.

"getting progressively worse" and "were worse than . . .": Mansfield, memorandum for files, 4/1/55, *FRUS*, 1955–1957, 1:176–177.

Congress not likely to authorize more money: Cable, Dulles to Collins, 4/4/55, *FRUS*, 1955–1957, 1:196–197.

136   Decision of General Ely: Cable, Collins to Dulles, 4/7/55, *FRUS*, 1955–1957, 1:215–218.

Collins's own judgment: Cable, Collins to DOS (Dulles) 4/17/55, *FRUS*, 1955–1957, 1:218–220.

"The US should stick to its guns . . .": Memorandum of conversation, Young and Mansfield, 4/8/55, *FRUS*, 1955–1957, 1:221–222.

"we are disposed . . .": Cable, Dulles to Collins, 4/9/55, *FRUS*, 1955–1957, 1:229–231.

"I have no way of judging . . .": Cable, Collins to Dulles, 4/10/55, *FRUS*, 1955–1957, 1:231–235.

Mansfield's days in Vietnam: Based on Mansfield's schedules and notes from his archives.

137   Eisenhower's undiminished confidence in deputy: Memorandum of telephone conversation between John Foster Dulles and Allen W. Dulles, 4/11/55, *FRUS*, 1955–1957, 1:235.

"Vietnam is perhaps only days away . . .": Quoted in Russell Brines, "Mansfield Fears 'Crisis Diplomacy' May Cost Free World Japan, Vietnam," *WP*, 4/10/55.

Pleas and pressures: Mansfield, memorandum of meeting with French Embassy minister Pierre Millet, 4/21/55, *FRUS*, 1955–1957, 1:277; summary of remarks of General Lawton Collins, 4/27/55 [from Mansfield's files], *FRUS*, 1955–1957, 1:292–293; Valeo memorandum in regard to conversation with Wesley Fishel, 4/25/55, *FRUS*, 1955–1957, 1:288–289.

Mansfield's observations on visit by Millet: Mansfield memorandum of meeting with Millet, *FRUS*, 1955–1957, 1:277.

137   On proposed ouster of Diem: Cable, Dulles to Dillon, 4/27/55—6:11 P.M., *FRUS,*
        1955–1957, 1:297–298. Several historical accounts of these events say that Mansfield
        agreed and even participated in the policymaking leading to the decision to oust Diem,
        but there is no documentary evidence for this and I doubt it was the case. This assertion
        apparently began with Robert Shaplen's account in his 1966 book, *The Lost Revolution,*
        which relied heavily on an interview with Kenneth Young of the State Department, and
        has been repeated in various places. I strongly believe this was mistaken or perhaps mis-
        understood. Mansfield adamantly denied to me and others, including Gregory Olson
        (*Mansfield and Vietnam,* p. 58), that he ever agreed to ousting Diem or making him a
        mere figurehead. Paul Kattenburg, who was Vietnam desk officer at the State
        Department at the time, told me in a letter dated 8/18/01 that he would "completely
        agree" that Mansfield never wavered in his support of Diem.
138   "Lansdale may have tipped off Diem . . .": See Anderson, *Trapped by Success,* pp. 111–113.
        Mansfield statement backing Diem: "Conditions in South Vietnam," *CR,* 5/2/55, pp.
        5288–5289. Mansfield released the text of his speech on Friday, April 29, because of the
        developments. See also John Scali, "U.S. Differs with France, Decides to Stand by
        Diem," *WP,* 4/30/55; Elie Abel, "U.S. Reiterates Vietnam Backing," *NYT,* 4/30/55, p. 1.
        Humphrey statement backing Diem: Quoted in Gibbons, Part 1, p. 297.
139   "Since your departure . . .": Cable, Dulles to Collins, 5/1/55, *FRUS,* 1955–1957, 1:344–345.
        "at a time when we were facing . . .": Diem to Mansfield, 5/4/55, MMA, Series 12, Box
        95, File 5.
        "you have stood steady . . .": Mansfield to Diem, 5/17/55, MMA, Series 12, Box 95, File 5.
        "the predominant factor . . .": Mansfield, *Viet Nam, Cambodia, and Laos,* Report to
        Senate Foreign Relations Committee (Washington, D.C.: Government Printing Office,
        1955). Hereafter cited as Mansfield report to Senate Foreign Relations Committee, 1955.
140   "exuded an air of self-confidence . . .": Mansfield, "Reprieve in Viet Nam," *Harper's
        Magazine,* Jan. 1956.
        Vietnam Lobby: For a full and careful account of the organization and its activities,
        see Joseph G. Morgan, *The Vietnam Lobby* (Chapel Hill: University of North Carolina
        Press, 1997).
        Buttinger organizes support for Vietnam: Buttinger to Mansfield, 2/21/75, MMA,
        Series 22, Box 55, File 1.
        Public relations firm hired by Diem: Gilbert Jonas, former executive secretary and
        later secretary of AFV, telephone interview, 8/4/01.
        Mansfield asked to give keynote address: Angier Biddle Duke to Mansfield, 4/17/56,
        American Friends of Vietnam files, Box 4, Folder 20, Vietnam Archive, Texas Tech
        University, Lubbock, Texas.
        Kennedy AFV address: John F. Kennedy, "America's Stake in Vietnam," *Vital Speeches,* 8/1/56.
        Mansfield on letterhead: 1959 AFV letterhead, American Friends of Vietnam files,
        Box 4, Folder 20, Vietnam Archive.
141   "is not only the savior . . .": Mansfield tribute to Diem, *CR,* 5/13/57, pp. 6759ff.
142   "leaned a little bit too heavily . . .": Mansfield, interview by Richard D. Challener,
        5/10/66, Dulles Oral History Project, Princeton University Library, Princeton, N.J.
        Dulles's suggestion of Mansfield as informal liaison: Dulles Papers, Eisenhower
        Library, Abilene, Kansas.
        Dulles's proposal and Eisenhower's response: Memorandum of conversation between
        Eisenhower and Dulles, 8/8/56, *FRUS,* 1955–1957, 16:164.
        "had more urgent business . . .": Arthur Steinberg, *Sam Johnson's Boy* (New York:
        Macmillan, 1968), p. 460.
143   "I have to look after . . .": Quoted in Olson, *Mansfield and Vietnam,* pp. 76–77.
        Mini-crisis in Syria: Handwritten notes on Mansfield's draft statements on Syria
        [September 1957], MMA, Series 19, Box 603, File 1.

143   "because circumstances . . .": *CR*, 1/28/55, p. 975.
144   "a major triumph": "The Congress: The Word for the Middle East," *Time*, 2/25/57,
        pp. 17–18.
        "Under the guidance . . .": Quoted in *Congressional Digest*, Mar. 1957, from a Senate
        speech by Mansfield, 2/29/57.
        "most powerful" and "He is critical. . .": *New York Times Sunday Magazine*, 3/3/57.
145   "an urgent need exists. . .":Quoted in "Establish a Joint committee on Centeral
        Intelligence," Press release, 3/10/54, salpee Sahagian Papers.
        "we might obtain information . . .": Quoted in John Ranelagh, *The Agency* (New
        York: Simon and Schuster, Touchstone Books, 1987), p. 284.
        "not a single member . . .": Grant Dillman, "Mansfield Asks Strong Cabinet," *WP*,
        6/24/60.
        Proposal stymied by Russell: Gilbert C. Fite, *Richard B. Russell Jr., Senator from
        Georgia* (Chapel Hill: University of North Carolina Press, 1991), pp. 589–591.
        "If we had accepted . . .": Quoted in *CR*, 5/19/56, p. 14673.
146   Mansfield's trips abroad: *Time* interview.
        "of impressive . . .": Benjamin DeMott, "Looking for Intelligence in Washington,"
        Commentary, Oct. 1960.
        "he thought . . .": Valeo, Oral History, Senate Historical Office, p. 334.
147   Lobby of Johnson: Letter, Rowe to Johnson, 11/15/56, LBJL, LBJA, "Selected Names
        (1955–57)," Box 32, Folder: "Rowe, James H."
        Smathers vetoed by Rayburn: Ross K. Baker, "Mike Mansfield and the Birth of the
        Modern Senate," in *First among Equals: Outstanding Senate Leaders of the Twentieth
        Century*, ed. Richard A. Baker and Roger H. Davidson, (Washington, D.C.:
        Congressional Quarterly Press, 1991), pp. 269–270.
        "Johnson really worked . . .": George A. Smathers, Oral History for Senate Historical
        Office, 8/1 to 10/24/89, pp. 47–48.
        "Lyndon insisted . . .": Quoted in Steinberg, *Sam Johnson's Boy*, p. 450.
        Russell proposed Mansfield: Mansfield interviews, 10/8/98 and 11/10/00.
148   Hell's Canyon dam: Good coverage of the Hell's Canyon deal can be found in
        Donald E. Spritzer, *Senator James E. Murray and the Limits of Post-War Liberalism* (New
        York: Garland, 1985), pp. 230–233.
        Asking senators to delay voting: Donald A. Ritchie, associate historian of the Senate,
        "Advice and Dissent: Mike Mansfield and the Vietnam War," manuscript, p. 10.
        "I was really . . .": Mansfield, interview by Jim Ludwick, 6/23/95, in the possession of
        the author.
149   Story of small business provision to aid lumbermen: Robert E. Wolf, e-mail to author,
        10/16/01.
        Mansfield's behavior during congressional recesses: Peggy DeMichele, interview,
        7/26/99.
150   "He's learning": Quoted by Robert E. Wolf, e-mail to author, 10/15/01.
        "stubborn insistence": DuBerrier to R. J. Scanian, 8/27/58, MMA, Series 14, Box 40,
        File 16.
        "I certainly have no apologies . . .": Quoted in Olson, *Mansfield and Vietnam*,
        p. 77.

8. INTO THE LEADERSHIP FOR KENNEDY

151   "the cork in the bottle": Fred I. Greenstein and Richard H. Zimmerman, "What Did
        Eisenhower Tell Kennedy about Indochina? The Politics of Misperception," *Journal of
        American History*, Sept. 1992, p. 576.

152   Kennedy on Mansfield: *Robert Kennedy in His Own Words,* ed. Edwin O. Guthman
       and Jeffrey Shulman (New York: Bantam Books, 1988), p. 421.
          Relationship with Kennedy: "Retiring Mansfield Calls for Carter Fireside Chats,"
       Baltimore Sun, 11/15/76.
153   Kennedy's complaints about hospital costs: Mansfield interview, 10/8/98; also,
       "Retiring Mansfield Calls for Carter Fireside Chats."
          Kennedy's wealth: See Theodore C. Sorensen, *Kennedy* (New York: Harper and Row,
       1965), p. 16.
          Maureen worked part time: *Time* interview.
          Collier's story: John Newhouse, telephone interview, 8/13/01.
          Johnson's request that Mansfield enter the vice presidential race: Mansfield to Jim
       Ludwick, 8/3/88, in the possession of the author.
          "the tremendous showing . . .": Mansfield to Kennedy, 8/24/56, MMA, Series 18, Box
       18, File 7.
          "Your letter explains . . .": Kennedy to Mansfield, undated, MMA, Series 18, Box 18,
       File 7.
154   Johnson a "long shot": Mansfield, interview on Voice of America, 5/18/60, MMA,
       Oral History transcript, OH 22-34.
          Montana's convention votes: Mansfield, Oral History for JFKL, 6/23/64, p. 2.
          Conversation with JFK about majority leader post: Mansfield, confidential memoran-
       dum for files, 11/11/60, MMA, Series 22, Box 103, File 1.
          Conversation with LBJ about majority leader post: Mansfield, confidential memoran-
       dum for files, 11/11/60, MMA, Series 22, Box 103, File 1.
155   "I'm 43 years old . . .": Kenneth P. O'Donnell and David F. Powers, *Johnny, We Hardly
       Knew Ye* (Boston: Little, Brown, 1972), pp. 192–193.
156   "and that would be . . .": *Robert Kennedy in His Own Words,* p. 421.
          Baker's urging Mansfield to take job: Telephone call, Baker to Mansfield, 11/14/60,
       MMA, Series 22, Box 103, File 1.
          Johnson's unorthodox plan: Johnson's meeting with his Senate friends and other
       aspects of the scheme are presented in colorful detail in Robert A. Caro, *Master of the
       Senate* (New York: Knopf, 2002), pp. 1035–1040. Caro evidently did not know about
       Mansfield's conversation with Kennedy on January 15 about the scheme. I believe Caro
       is incorrect in reporting that Mansfield threatened to resign if the motion to permit
       Johnson to preside was defeated. According to the records of the Democratic
       Conference, Mansfield's resignation threat came the following day, 1/4/61, on another
       issue.
          "gonna be just the way . . .": Quoted in Bobby Baker, *Wheeling and Dealing* (New
       York: Norton 1978), p. 134.
          Conversation in advance of meeting: Memorandum, "Luncheon Conversation with
       President-elect Kennedy," 12/15/60, MMA, Series 22, Box 105, File 20.
157   "pro forma" position: Mansfield interview, 10/8/98.
          Initial meeting of Democrats: I relied first and foremost on the official record of the
       meeting, "Minutes of the Democratic Conference, Tuesday, January 3, 1961," MMA,
       Series 22, Box 90, File 1.
          "a crescendo . . .": Francis R. Valeo, *Mike Mansfield: Majority Leader* (Armonk,
       N.Y.: M.E. Sharpe, 1999), p. 13. Valeo was present at the meeting and described it in
       detail in his book.
          "We might as well ask . . .": Baker, *Wheeling and Dealing,* p. 135.
          Mansfield quickly assured Conference: "Minutes of the Democratic Conference"; see
       also Rowland Evans and Robert Novak, *Lyndon B. Johnson: The Exercise of Power* (New
       York: New American Library, 1966), pp. 305–308.

158   "I now know the difference . . .": Robert Dallek, *Flawed Giant* (New York: Oxford University Press, 1998), p. 8.
       Top of list: "Possible Points of Discussion on Foreign Policy," 12/15/60, MMA, Series 22, Box 105, File 20.
159   "for him alone": "Luncheon Conversation with President-elect Kennedy."
       "the only question . . .": Valeo, interview, 9/10/98.
       Joining committee: Stanley D. Bachrack, *The Committee of One Million* (New York: Columbia University Press, 1976), table 5.2.
       Fulbright-Mansfield letter to Eisenhower and letter of rejection from Acting Secretary of State Douglas Dillon: Dated 6/26/59 and 7/28/59, respectively, MMA, Series 13, Box 35, File 8.
       Call for "new approaches: "Outer Mongolia and Newsmen to China, Suggested New Approaches," *CR*, 4/19/60, pp. 8136–8144.
       Kennedy reactions: "Luncheon Conversation with President-elect Kennedy."
160   Chinese journalists: Leonard A. Kusnitz, *Public Opinion and American Policy* (Westport, Conn.: Greenwood Press, 1984), p. 97
       Possibility of relations with Mongolia: See Kusnitz, *Public Opinion*, p. 97ff.
       No major changes in China policy: Dean Rusk, *As I Saw It* (New York: Penguin Books, 1991), pp. 282–283.
       "China is for the second term": Quoted in Charles Cogan, "Lost Opportunity or Mission Impossible? De Gaulle's Initiatives in China and Vietnam, 1963–1964," *French Politics and Society*, Winter 1995, p. 60.
       On December 19: My account of the Palm Beach interlude is taken from a handwritten memorandum by Mansfield, 12/19/60, Anne Mansfield Papers.
161   Kennedy and Laos: Sorensen, *Kennedy*, p. 640.
162   "sparsely populated, . . .": Mansfield, *Viet Nam, Cambodia, and Laos,* report prepared for the Senate Foreign Relations Committee (Washington, D.C.: Government Printing Office, 1955), p. 18.
       "pretty lousy": "Memo: Telephone call from Florida from John Kennedy 9:55 a.m.," MMA, Series 22, Box 103, File 9.
       Memorandum on Laos: Mansfield to the President-Elect, "Observations on the Laotian Situation" (undated), MMA, Series 22, Box 103, File 9.
163   "I came away . . .": Quoted in Fred I. Greenstein and Richard H. Immerman, "What Did Eisenhower Tell Kennedy about Indochina? The Politics of Misperception," *Journal of American History*, Sept. 1992.
       Souvanna lament: Souvanna Phouma to Mansfield, personal and confidential, 1/7/61, MMA, Series 22, Box 102, File 9.
       Recommendations on Laos: Memorandum, Mansfield to Kennedy, "The Laotian Situation," 1/21/61, MMA, Series 22, Box 102, File 9.
       Proposal for neutral commission: Memorandum, Mansfield to Kennedy, "Supplementary memo on the proposal for a neutral commission in Laos composed of India, Pakistan and Afghanistan," 1/23/61, MMA, Series 22, Box 103, File 16.
164   "take whatever steps . . .": Wallace Carroll, "U.S. Ready to Face All Risks to Bar Red Rule of Laos," *NYT,* 3/21/61, p. 1A.
       On Rostow's role in background interview: David Kaiser, *American Tragedy* (Cambridge: Harvard University Press, 2000), p. 43.
       New memorandum "on the highly dangerous . . .": Mansfield to Rusk, "The Laotian Question," 3/22/61, MMA Series 22, Box 103, File 9.
       "the domino theory . . .": Confidential memoranda, Mansfield to Kennedy, 3/22/61, MMA, Series 22, Box 103, File 9.

165   "probably followed up . . .": Cable, Brown to DOS, 4/26/61, *FRUS*, 1961–1963, 24:139–140.

Kennedy's meeting with advisers: Memorandum of meeting, 4/26/61, *FRUS*, 1961–1963, 24:142–143.

NSC meeting: Details of the meeting are still classified. A good account, based on oral histories and other data, is in Herbert S. Parmet, *JFK* (New York: Dial Press, 1983), pp. 148–151.

166   Meeting with congressional leaders: The meeting is described in detail in notes made by Kennedy's military attaché, General Chester V. "Ted" Clifton and Deputy Undersecretary of State U. Alexis Johnson. Their notes, which remained classified until 1993, are in the National Security Files, Chester V. Clifton, Conferences with the President, Congressional Leaders, 1961–1962, Box 345, JFKL.

167   "we have to be prepared . . .": Burke's comments on nuclear weapons were stricken from the record when the minutes of the meeting were declassified thirty-two years later, but the subject is clear from the context. In his oral history in 1965, Robert Kennedy said the Joint Chiefs plan involved "using atomic weapons" if conventional operations in Laos ran into trouble. See *Robert Kennedy in His Own Words*, p. 248.

168   Private meeting with Kennedy: Memorandum, Mansfield to Kennedy, "The Laotian Situation," 5/1/61, MMA, Series 22, Box 102, File 9.

169   Pathet Lao delegation discussing cease-fire: Memorandum, "pay" to General Clifton, 5/1/61, 4:45, President's Office Files, Box 121, Folder 12, "Countries: Laos Security, 5/61–6/61," JFKL.

"a definite transition . . .": Arthur J. Dommen, *Conflict in Laos*, rev. ed. (New York: Praeger, 1971), p. 200.

Mansfield's views played significant role: Examination by the author of President's Office Files, "Laos—General, 1961–63," Oct. 1999, JFKL.

170   "Thank God the Bay of Pigs . . .": Quoted in Sorensen, *Kennedy*, p. 644.

Position of majority leader not mentioned in Constitution: See Floyd M. Riddick, *Majority and Minority Leaders of the Senate*, Senate Doc. 100-29, 100th Cong., 2d sess., 3/22/88.

Origins of majority leader post and "the most significant . . .": Richard A. Baker and Roger H. Davidson, eds., *First among Equals* (Washington, D.C.: Congressional Quarterly Press, 1991), p. 2.

"set for himself . . .": John G. Stewart, "Two Strategies of Leadership: Johnson and Mansfield," in *Congressional Behavior*, ed. Nelson W. Polsby (New York: Random House, 1971), p. 61.

171   The "Taj Mahal": For a description, see Robert Dallek, *Lone Star Rising* (New York: Oxford University Press, 1991), p. 540.

Johnson's refusal of Mansfield's request to vacate the Taj Mahal: Steinberg, *Sam Johnson's Boy*, p. 548.

Lunch alone: Tom Korologos, interview, 3/5/02.

"No, that's all right. . . .": Quoted by Salpee Sahagian, interview, 11/4/99.

"He is slightly built. . . .": Frederic W. Collins, "How to Be a Leader without Leading," *NYT Magazine*, 7/30/61, p. 50.

172   "I could not stand . . .": Quoted by William Sherman, telephone interview, 5/2/02. Johnson's manipulations are well described in Caro, *Master of the Senate*.

"I don't collect any IOUs. . . .": Quoted by Robert C. Byrd, "Mike Mansfield's Senate: The Great Society Years," *CR*, 9/8/86, p. S12049.

"working for Mike Mansfield . . .": Baker, *Wheeling and Dealing*, p. 140.

"like going home . . .": Harry McPherson, *A Political Education* (Boston: Houghton Mifflin, 1985), p. 182.

172   "was what one might expect . . .": McPherson, *A Political Education,* p. 45.
       "Yes": Quoted in Stewart Alsop, *The Center* (New York: Harper and Row, 1968), p. 297.
173   "as representative as possible . . .": Quoted in "Minutes of the Democratic
       Conference," 1/4/61, MMA, Series 22, Box 90, File 1.
       Leadership of committees: Stewart, "Two Strategies of Leadership," pp. 74–75.
       "He would sit back . . .": Joseph R. L. Sterne, interview, 11/18/99.
       "a conventional leader . . .": George A. Smathers, Oral History, Senate Historical
       Office, pp. 120–121.
174   On George Aiken: Mansfield interview, 11/10/00. Mansfield said his Democratic col-
       league from Montana, Lee Metcalf, was ahead of even Aiken, but I believe this state-
       ment was merely a matter of form, as he saw much less of Metcalf, who was at times
       critical of Mansfield's politically cautious stands.
       Breakfast with Aiken and "when I got into . . .": Mansfield interview, 11/10/00.
       Pro-administration Democrats less than 50 percent of votes: Sorensen, *Kennedy,* p. 342.
175   "did a good deal of acting . . .": Byron C. Hulsey, *Everett Dirksen and His Presidents*
       (Lawrence: University Press of Kansas, 2000), p. 145.
       "immeasurable damage": Douglas to Kenneth O'Donnell and Douglas to Larry
       O'Brien, 8/29/62, General file: "Congressional," JFKL.
       "you've got [the election] . . .": Quoted in Hulsey, *Everett Dirksen,* p. 171.
       "final blow" to campaign: Paul H. Douglas, *In the Fullness of Time* (New York:
       Harcourt Brace Jovanovich, 1971), p. 574.
       On presidential meetings: Data from card files of presidential meetings, JFKL.
176   Legislative request figures: Sorensen, *Kennedy,* p. 352.
       "an introspective . . .": Walter Jenkins, Oral History II, p. 4, Oral History Interviews, LBJL.
       "didn't lead, really lead. . . .": Gerald Siegel, Oral History III, p. 9, Oral History
       Interviews, LBJL.
       "excessive pessimism . . .": Sorensen, *Kennedy,* p. 356.
       "despite the dispersal . . .": Stewart, "Two Strategies," p. 87.
177   "After a few minutes . . .": James Grady to author, 10/14/01.
178   "is to bring home . . .": Don Spritzer, interview, 7/15/99.
       1960 data: Ray Dockstader, "Federal Expenditures in Montana," newsletter from
       Mansfield's office, 10/20/60, MMA, Series 21, Box 66, File 7.
       For 1969 data: Paula Wilmot, "IRS' Take in Montana Less Than U.S. Spends," *Great
       Falls Tribune,* 12/26/69, MMA, Series 21, Box 61, File 1.
179   "This is one senator . . .": Memorandum, Daly to O'Brien, 3/5/63, White House Staff
       File "Lawrence P. O'Brien," Senate File: "Mike Mansfield," File 2, JFKL.
       Chairmanship of Africa Subcommittee: Carl Marcy, Oral History, Senate Historical
       Office, p. 52.
180   "The problem for us . . .": Memorandum, Mansfield to Kennedy, "The Cuban
       Aftermath," 5/1/61, Cuban Missile Crisis files, National Security Archive, George
       Washington University, Washington, D.C.
       Mansfield and Smathers flown to Washington: On Mansfield's movements, Mansfield
       Oral History, pp. 18–22, JFKL.
       On briefing about Cuban Missile Crisis: Ernest R. May and Philip D. Zelikow, *The
       Kennedy Tapes* (Cambridge: Harvard University Press, 1997), pp. 245ff.
       Mansfield comments after Kennedy's speech: "Cuban Situation," 10/22/62, MMA,
       Series 21, Box 41.
181   Mansfield's frequent speeches on East-West confrontation: Memorandum, Salpee
       Sahagian to Mansfield, "List of Statements pertaining to Germany-Berlin," 9/12/61,
       MMA, Series 23, Box 38, File 4.
       "a very hard . . .": Conversation between Sorensen and Mansfield, 5/24/61, MMA,
       Series 22, Box 103, File 1.
       "an older man . . .": Memorandum, Mansfield to Kennedy, "Observations on the
       Forthcoming Talks in Vienna," 5/26/61, MMA, Series 22, Box 102.

182   Mansfield's 1959 proposal: See his speech, "Policies Respecting Germany," *CR*, 2/26/59, pp. 3036–3039.

      1961 proposal: Speech made in the Senate, "A Third Way on Berlin," *CR*, 6/14/61, pp. 9598–9604.

      West German diplomatic reaction: Memorandum, Foy Kohler to Dean Rusk, 6/22/61, "Your Meeting with Ambassador Grewe," Berlin crisis file, National Security Archive.

      Public and newspaper reactions to Mansfield's 1961 speech and Mansfield's reaction: *CR*, 4/20/61, pp. 9992–10003, also Mansfield's reaction.

183   Invitation to be interviewed on national television: The invitation from commentator George Fielding Elliott of NBC is in a conversation with Elliott, 6/16/61, transcribed by Mansfield's office, MMA, Series 22, Box 103, File 1.

      Invitation to meet Menshikov: Memorandum regarding the invitation from Menshikov, 6/29/61, MMA, Series 19, Box 609, File 9.

184   On the September crises: "The Kennedy Program and Commitments, 1961," *USVNR*, Book 2, IV.B.1, p. iv.

      Guerrillas occupying provincial capital: Associated Press, "Vietnam Rebels Burn City in Raid," *NYT*, 9/19/61.

      "Washington will face . . .": "Aggression in Vietnam," *NYT*, Editorial, 9/20/61.

      "The Vietnamese problem . . .": Confidential memorandum, Mansfield to Kennedy, "Laos and Vietnam," 9/20/61, MMA, Series 22, Box 102, File 9.

184n   "and Vietnam looks . . .": The most detailed account of this part of Kennedy's conversation with Reston is in David Halberstam's book *The Best and the Brightest* (New York: Random House, 1969), p. 76. Reston also discussed it in the *NYT*, 6/10/79, and in more explicit terms in his memoir, *Deadline* (New York: Random House, 1991), pp. 291–292. Having known Reston, I am confident he reported accurately what Kennedy told him, although it seems to me to be likely that this was an off-the-cuff reaction by the President that he later reconsidered.

      Robert Johnson's comments: Johnson, interview, 10/1/01. For more on this issue, see Kaiser, *American Tragedy*, pp. 101–102.

185   "on this most important, . . .": Confidential memorandum, Mansfield to Kennedy, 11/2/61, *FRUS*, 1961–1963, 1:467–470.

187   "he didn't seem to have any expert knowledge . . .": William Bundy, interview, 3/25/99.

      Kennedy meeting with advisers: Notes of Meeting (handwritten notes of General Lyman Lemnitzer), White House, 11/11/61, *FRUS*, 1961–1963, 1:577–578.

      Approval of other measures "apparently taken for granted": "Kennedy Program and Commitments: 1961," *USVNR*, Book 2, IV.B.1, p. 115.

188   U.S. troop figures: Harry G. Summers Jr., *Vietnam War Almanac* (Washington, D.C.: Facts on File, 1985).

      Michigan State/Fishel relationship: See Edward Miller, "The Professor and the President" (paper presented at the annual meeting of the Society for Historians of American Foreign Relations, Washington, D.C., 6/14/01).

      "a man for whom I have the highest respect . . .": Mansfield, address at Michigan State University, 6/10/62; manuscript in the possession of the author.

189   Reaction to Michigan State speech: John Mecklin, *Mission in Torment* (New York: Doubleday, 1965), p. 130.

      "the instability in Viet Nam . . .": Madame Tran Van Chuong to Mansfield, 6/14/62, MMA, Series 22, Box 105, File 19.

      "the Diem government . . .": Chuong, quoted by Valeo in memorandum to Mansfield, "Meeting with the Vietnamese Ambassador," 6/15/62, MMA, Box 105, File 19.

190   "there was not one chance . . . ," "absolutely drunk . . . ," and "didn't date": Chuong, quoted by Valeo in memorandum to Mansfield, "Meeting with the Ambassador of Viet Nam and Madame Tran Van Chuong," 10/30/62. MMA, Series 22, Box 105, File 19.

      "she's crazy . . ." Valeo, quoting Chuong, interview, 11/29/99. "because I really don't think . . .": Valeo, interview, 9/10/98.

190   On the Khiem case: Michael York, "Judge Frees Son Held in Parents' Deaths: Man
       Ruled Unfit for Trial in '86 Case," *WP,* 10/22/93.
       "we can see the light . . .": Nolting quoted in Summary Record of Meeting, American
       Embassy Saigon, 11/30/62, MMA, Series 22, Box 96, Folder 12.
       Navarre's phrase: See Olson, *Mansfield and Vietnam,* p. 285n9.

191   "President Diem is a depressed man . . .": Mansfield, memorandum for files, 12/2/62,
       MMA, Series 22, Box 102, File 10.
       "Diem seemed to have turned into a recluse . . .": Mansfield, interview by British
       Broadcasting Company, 12/3/76, p. 4; interview in the possession of the author.
       Nhu's claim about strategic hamlets: Ellen J. Hammer, *A Death in November: America
       in Vietnam,* 1963 (New York: Dutton, 1987), p. 82.
       "The Nhus are very aggressive . . .": Mansfield, memorandum for files, 12/2/62.
       Mansfield meeting with reporters: William Prochnau, *Once upon a Distant War* (New
       York: Times Books, 1995), p. 209.
       "We were quite pessimistic . . .": David Halberstam, quoted in Gibbons, Part 2, p. 131.
       Proposed embassy statement: MMA, Series 22, Box 53, File 6.

192   "I came away . . .": Mansfield, memorandum for files, 12/2/62.
       Report of refusal to accept departure statement: David Halberstam, "Mansfield Is
       Cool on Vietnam War," *NYT,* 12/3/62.
       "the first nails in Diem's coffin" and "crucial turning point": Quoted in Olson,
       Mansfield and Vietnam, p. 110.
       "One thing is reasonably clear . . .": Report, Mansfield to Kennedy, 12/18/62, *FRUS,*
       1961–1963, 2:779–787.

194   Mansfield caught up: United Press International (UPI), "Mansfield Didn't Miss the
       Boat," *WP,* 12/27/62.
       "This is not what my advisers": Mansfield interview, 6/10/98.
       Kennedy questioned Mansfield: Mansfield to Joe McCarthy (researcher-writer for
       Kenneth O'Donnell), 10/6/69, MMA, Series 22, Box 136.
       "I got angry at Mike . . .": Kenneth O'Donnell, "LBJ and the Kennedys," *Life,*
       8/7/70, and O'Donnell and Powers, *Johnny, We Hardly Knew Ye,* p. 16.
       Mansfield spoke out: Diligent efforts to establish the date of this incident have so far
       failed. Records indicate Mansfield participated in nineteen congressional leadership
       breakfasts at the White House during the first half of 1963. Mansfield had no record or
       recollection of the precise date. It would be helpful to know the context in which this
       meeting took place, especially whether it was before or after May 8, when nationwide
       Buddhist protests erupted after South Vietnamese government troops shot and killed
       Buddhist demonstrators on the Buddha's birthday in Hue.

195   "The President told Mansfield . . .": O'Donnell, "LBJ and the Kennedys." The
       account in O'Donnell and Powers, *Johnny, We Hardly Knew Ye,* differs slightly but not
       significantly, evidently because of changes by the book editor.

196   "he was seriously considering . . .": Mansfield to McCarthy, MMA, Series 22, Box 136.
       "a withdrawal": Mansfield to Robert Hurley, 8/19/70, MMA, Series 19, Box 587, File
       31, and Mansfield to Esther McGuire (election not "even mentioned . . ."), 9/28/70,
       Olson, *Mansfield and Vietnam,* p. 112.
       "to withdraw . . .": Mansfield to James B. Sidney, 12/8/75, MMA Series 19, Box 587, File 31.
       "some troops": Mansfield to Francis X. Winters, 10/24/89, quoted in Kai Bird, *The
       Color of Truth* (New York: Simon and Schuster, 1998), p. 260.
       Kennedy planned to begin after 1964 election: Mansfield interview, 6/10/98.
       "some minor withdrawals": Mansfield interview, 10/20/99.
       "Barring unforeseen circumstances, . . .": Mansfield interview, 6/10/98.

197   "Idea: Viet Nam—Southeast Asia": Memorandum to self, MMA, Series 22, Box 54,
       File 1. The memo is undated but the substance and similarity to some thoughts and
       phrases strongly suggest it was written shortly before the August 19 memorandum to

Kennedy. For policymakers' increasing focus on Vietnam, see Fredrik Logevall, *Choosing War* (Berkeley: University of California Press, 1999), p. 4.

198 Kennedy's request for memorandum: Richard Reeves, *President Kennedy: Profile of Power* (New York: Simon and Schuster, 1993), p. 556.

"Observations on Viet Nam": Memorandum, Mansfield to Kennedy, 8/19/63, MMA, Series 22, Box 103, File 14.

200 "came as a complete surprise . . .": Gibbons, Part 2, p. 206.

"It is tragic that a leader . . .": *CR,* 11/5/63, pp. 21060–21061.

"I want to get out . . .": Valeo, interview, 2/6/02.

201 Attended but remained silent: Olson, *Mansfield and Vietnam,* p. 119.

"I didn't have any respect . . .": Mansfield interview, 7/24/98.

Death of Kerr: Admiral George W. Anderson, Oral History, 4/25/67, JFKL.

On the test ban treaty: Telegram, Kennedy to Mansfield, 6/5/63, File TR 61, JFKL; also, Mansfield, Oral History, pp. 29–32, JFKL.

Dirksen and the test ban treaty: Hulsey, *Everett Dirksen and His Presidents,* pp. 179–180.

202 On Mansfield's request: Lawrence O'Brien to Mansfield, 7/11/63, Ivi/1964/St26, JFKL.

On White House initiative: Mansfield Oral History, p. 46, JFKL.

"What we hope to do . . .": For a description of the Billings speech and the western tour, Sander Vanocur, "Kennedy's Voyage of Discovery," *Harper's Magazine,* Apr. 1964. Also Arthur M. Schlesinger, *A Thousand Days* (Boston: Houghton Mifflin, 1965), p. 979.

Family amazed at preparations: John Mansfield, interview, 7/2/99.

203 "What do you think . . .": Quoted in "'He's Doing a Good Job,' President Kennedy Tells Mansfield's Father on Visit to Home," *Great Falls Tribune,* 9/27/63.

"I wonder how many . . .": Quoted in O'Donnell and Powers, *Johnny, We Hardly Knew Ye,* p. 379.

"Thank God, he got out of this state . . .": Peggy DeMichele, interview by Missoula Children's Theatre, Missoula, Mont., 10/24/89.

Rometsch story: Basic facts about the story come from Evan Thomas, *Robert Kennedy: His Life* (New York: Simon and Schuster, 2000); Taylor Branch, *Parting the Waters* (New York: Simon and Schuster, 1989); and Michael Beschloss, *The Crisis Years* (New York: Harper Collins, 1991). Confirmation of President Kennedy's liaisons with Rometsch came from a telephone interview with Bobby Baker, 10/3/01, and a personal interview, 12/31/01. I also used Hoover memoranda about the case, most of which were severely redacted. These were available under the Freedom of Information Act at the FBI.

Kennedy thanks: Bobby Baker, interview, 12/31/01.

205 "Mike Mansfield by that meeting . . .": Bobby Baker, interview, 12/31/01.

"a very faint memory" and "I'm not usually shocked . . .": Mansfield interviews, 4/9/99 and 4/20/00.

206 "Boozy voice": Joseph R. L. Sterne, interview, 11/18/99.

"One cannot be a leader . . .": *CR,* 11/6/63, pp. 21246–21249.

"kindly, well-meaning . . .": Rowland Evans and Robert Novak, "The Senate's Scandal," *WP,* 11/11/63.

"shortening my life": Valeo, *Mike Mansfield,* p. 82.

"I confess freely . . .": Senate speech, *CR,* 11/27/63; manuscript in the possession of the author.

207 News of assassination: "Stunned Senate Adjourns As Chaplain Offers Prayer," *Washington Evening Star,* 11/22/63; "Edward Kennedy Presiding As Word Reaches Senate," *WP,* 11/23/63.

Senate proceedings on 11/22: *CR,* 11/22/63, p. 22693.

208 Mansfield's initial reaction to dreaded news: Salpee Sahagian, interview, 11/4/99.

"William 'Fishbait' Miller, . . .": William Manchester, *The Death of a President* (New York: Harper and Row, 1967), p. 508.

209 "There was a sound of laughter . . .": Mansfield recalled on several occasions his post-midnight work composing the eulogy; Valeo in interviews with me and others said he

did the essential drafting from an idea supplied by Mansfield, and that Senator John Pastore of Rhode Island and others were also participants in that much-acclaimed speech. I never cleared up the contradiction.

209   The eulogy over: Manchester, *Death of a President*, p. 541.

Telephone call from Jacqueline: Mansfield, memorandum for files, 11/24/63, MMA, Series 22, Box 103, File 10.

210   "I do thank you . . .": Note, Jacqueline Kennedy to the Mansfields, MMA, Series 19, Box 602, File 15.

9. JOHNSON I: YEARS OF ESCALATION

211   "the first American . . .": John P. Burke and Fred I. Greenstein, *How Presidents Test Reality* (New York: Russell Sage Foundation, 1989), p. 191.

Greatest tragedy: Mansfield, "The Situation in Vietnam," *CR,* 5/9/72, p. 16355.

212   "a delicate line": Mansfield interview, 6/10/98.

213   "Wants to do his best . . .": Mansfield, handwritten memorandum for files, "12/5/63, The Elms," MMA, Series 19, Box 603, File 15.

"I'll be goddamned . . .": Quoted in Michael Beschloss, *Taking Charge* (New York: Simon and Schuster, Touchstone, 1997), p. 88.

Recommendations on Vietnam: Memorandum, Mansfield to Johnson, "Southeast Asia and Vietnam," *FRUS, 1961–1963,* 4:691–692.

215   "It still haunts me": Mansfield interview, 7/24/98.

First meeting on the war: Memorandum of meeting, 11/24/63, "South Vietnam Situation," *FRUS, 1961–1963,* 4:635–637.

"I am not going to lose Vietnam . . .": Quoted by the *New York Times* White House correspondent Tom Wicker in his book *JFK and LBJ* (New York: Morrow 1968), p. 205, attributed to "one who was present" at the meeting with Lodge.

Vowed to pursue Kennedy's goals: Lyndon Baines Johnson, *The Vantage Point* (New York: Holt, Rinehart and Winston, 1971), pp. 19, 42.

216   Should have brought in own advisers: Jack Valenti, interview, 10/7/00.

Should have "fired the whole damn works": Paul Miles, former military assistant to Westmoreland, who witnessed the Johnson-Westmoreland conversation, e-mail to author, 1/2/02.

McCone's notes on meeting: Memorandum of meeting, 11/24/63, "South Vietnam Situation," *FRUS, 1961–1963,* 4:635–637.

Opposition to international negotiations: The issue of neutralism and the Johnson administration's opposition to it is well covered in Logevall, *Choosing War,* pp. 82–90.

217   "seriously concerned . . .": Telegram, Lodge to DOS, 12/10/63, *FRUS, 1961–1963,* 4:695n2.

"You may categorically . . .": Cable, State Department to Saigon Embassy, 12/10/63, *FRUS, 1961–1963,* 4:695–696.

"nothing is further . . .": Cable, State Department to Saigon Embassy, 12/16/63, *FRUS, 1961–1963,* 4:710.

Need to sit down to discuss foreign policy: Beschloss, *Taking Charge,* p. 115.

Johnson call to Valeo: Quoted in Beschloss, *Taking Charge,* pp. 123–124.

218   Meeting at White House: President's Daily Diary cards, Drawer 53, LBJL.

"As you remarked . . .": Memorandum, Mansfield to Johnson, "Viet Namese Situation," 1/6/64, *FRUS, 1964–1968,* 1:2–3.

"The President received. . .": Note, Bundy to Rusk and McNamare, 1/6/64, *FRUS, 1964–1968,* 1:2–1.

219   "Mansfield was regarded . . .": Chester L. Cooper, interview, 11/24/99.

"Johnson accepted the notion . . .": Harry McPherson, telephone interview,5/10/02.

"I listen to them talk . . .": Johnson, quoted by McPherson, interview, 5/10/02.

Deference to presidential power: For Fulbright's views on presidential supremacy, see

William C. Berman, *William Fulbright and the Vietnam War* (Kent, Ohio: Kent State University Press, 1988), p. 12.

219   Rusk, McNamara, and Bundy responses: Printed in *FRUS*, 1964–1968, 1:8–15.

221   "everything I knew about history . . .": Doris Kearns Goodwin, *Lyndon Johnson and the American Dream* (New York: St. Martin's Press, 1991), pp. 252–253.

222   "I don't want these people . . .": Cited in Beschloss, *Taking Charge*, pp. 124.

"cowardice has gotten us into more wars . . .": Memorandum of White House Meeting on Vietnam, 2/6/65, *FRUS*, 1964–1968, 2:160.

"was a Texas Texan, . . .": Mansfield interview, 11/26/99.

"to show how limited and shallow . . .": Robert McNamara, *In Retrospect* (New York: Times Books, 1995), pp. 106–107.

223   "they didn't like each other much": James Rowe, Oral History, 11/9/69, Part IV, p. 4, LBJL.

"it was always an arm's length relationship . . .": Quoted in "Retiring Mansfield Calls for Carter Fireside Chats," *Baltimore Sun*, 11/15/76.

"a man on the move . . .": Mansfield to Jakie L. Pruett, 3/11/76, MMA, Series 22, Box 136.

"you are too valuable a man . . .": Telegram, Mansfield to Johnson, 7/6/55, Congressional File: "Mike Mansfield," LBJL.

"If I am a valuable man, . . .": Johnson to Mansfield, 9/27/55, MMA, Series 18, Box 18, File 1.

224   "I would rather have a quiet well done . . .": Telegram, Johnson to Mansfield, 3/15/57, Congressional File: "Mike Mansfield," LBJL.

"caused me to blush . . .": Mansfield to Johnson, 3/15/57, Congressional File: "Mike Mansfield," LBJL.

"Dear Mike . . .": Johnson to Mansfield, 9/15/59, MMA, Series 18, Box 18, File 1.

"hated and detested Lyndon Johnson": Bobby Baker, interview, 12/31/01.

LBJ conversation with Humphrey: Michael Beschloss, ed., *Reaching for Glory:Lyndon Johnson's Secret White House Tapes, 1964–1965* (New York: Simon and Schuster, 2001), p. 207.

"While Mansfield and Johnson . . .": Hubert H. Humphrey, *The Education of a Public Man* (New York: Doubleday, 1976), p. 297.

"Hubert would first get on one side . . .": Rowe, Oral History, 11/9/69, Part IV, p. 4, LBJL.

Business between Mansfield and Johnson: Data from LBJL records compiled from the President's Daily Diary and summarized by Yukiko Ko.

225   "Mike is a cross . . .":*Newsweek*, 2/14/66

Newsweek report in Mansfield's office: Memorandum, Manatos to Johnson, 2/10/66, Mansfield file, WHCF, LBJL.

Johnson's advances: Anne Mansfield, interview, 3/27/02. According to LBJL records, she was in the Oval Office with Johnson from 7:11 P.M. to 8:25 P.M. on 2/24/65.

"peculiar fellow": Russell to Johnson, LBJ tapes, conversation WH6503.03, PNO 2, 3/6/65, 12:05 P.M.

"Boss" comments in telephone calls: Johnson to Mansfield, LBJ tapes, conversation K6312.15, PNO 10, 12/23/63, 1:10 P.M., and Mansfield to Johnson, LBJ tapes, conversation WH6405.02, PNO 22, 5/5/64, 7:10 P.M.

Johnson solicitous but disingenuous: See Beschloss, *Reaching for Glory*, pp. 344–348, 373–374, 411–413.

226   Civil rights: In researching and writing this section, I benefited greatly from the extensive account in Valeo, *Mike Mansfield*; from two studies of the Civil Rights Act of 1964 by Robert D. Loevy, *To End All Segregation* (Lanham, Md.: University Press of America, 1990), and *The Civil Rights Act of 1964*, which he edited (Albany: State University of New York Press, 1997); from Charles and Barbara Whalen's *The Longest Debate* (Santa Ana, Calif.: Seven Locks Press, 1985); and from Robert Mann's account of the civil rights protagonists in the Senate, *The Walls of Jericho* (Orlando, Fla.: Harcourt Brace, 1996).

226   "Speaking for myself . . .": Senate speech, *CR,* 2/17/64, p. 2774.
227   "a halfhearted effort": Valeo, *Mike Mansfield,* p. 112.
        President would never be able to enact such a bill: Burke Marshall, Oral History,
        LBJL; *Robert Kennedy in His Own Words,* p. 202ff.
228   "I deliberately tried . . .": Johnson, *The Vantage Point,* p. 159. For an excellent account
        of Johnson's role in the battle, see Dallek, *Flawed Giant,* pp. 111–121.
        This thinking foreign to Mansfield: Eugene McCarthy, quoted in Ross K. Baker,
        "Mike Mansfield and the Birth of the Modern Senate," in Baker and Davidson, *First
        among Equals,* pp. 283–284.
        "This is not a circus sideshow . . .": Quoted in Mann, *The Walls of Jericho,*p. 394.
229   "brings into critical question . . .": "The Congress—When Is a Majority a Majority?"
        Time, 3/20/64.
230   "Dirksen is the one . . ." and "I think for a year or so [Dirksen] didn't know . . .":
        Mansfield interview, 11/20/00.
        LBJ's role in Humphrey's selection: See Humphrey, *The Education of a Public Man,* p. 274.
231   Selection of Humphrey over Smathers: Valeo, *Mike Mansfield,* p. 127.
        Humphrey-Mansfield relationship: Carl Solberg, *Hubert Humphrey* (New York:
        Norton, 1984), p. 185. I also benefited from the comments of Thomas L. Hughes, a for-
        mer aide and close friend of Humphrey.
        "Usually [Humphrey] had three or four concentrations . . .": Mansfield interview,
        11/20/00.
        Humphrey's meetings: Hubert H. Humphrey, "Memorandum on Senate Consideration
        of the Civil Rights Act of 1964," in Loevy, *The Civil Rights Act of* 1964, p. 87.
        Mansfield-Russell meeting and Russell's reaction: Valeo, *Mike Mansfield,* pp. 131–136.
232   "I kept Russell informed . . .": Mansfield interview, 11/20/00.
        Meeting with western Democrats: "Meeting on Civil Rights in S-208, The Capitol,
        February 19, 1964," MMA, Series 22, Box 105, File 1.
        Data on civil rights bill in Senate: Loevy, *To End All Segregation,* pp. 1, 315.
233   Estimate of votes: Memorandum, Valeo to Mansfield, 4/9/64, MMA, Series 22, Box
        105, File 1.
234   "I can understand any position . . .": Mansfield to Alan Bible, 6/3/64, MMA, Series
        22, Box 105, File 1. Identical letters went to Senators Edmondson, Cannon, Walters,
        Yarborough, Gore, and Hayden.
        "On the day of the vote. . .":*CR,* 6/10/64, pp. 13307–13327.
235   Senators cast votes for cloture: E. W. Kenworthy, "Senate Invokes Closure on Rights
        Bill," *NYT,* 6/11/64.
        Avoided being photographed: John G. Stewart, "Independence and Control," in
        Loevy, *The Civil Rights Act of* 1964, p. 321.
        Letters from senators: MMA, Series 18, Box 32, File 3.
236   Women in the workforce: In 1960, 23,240,000 women were working or looking for
        work, which made up 37.7 percent of all women of working age at that time. In 1999,
        the last year for which figures are available, 64,855,000, or 60 percent, of all working-age
        women were working or looking for work, according to the U.S. Bureau of the Census,
        Statistical Abstract of the United States (Washington, D.C.: Government Printing Office,
        2000), p. 408.
237   Valeo quotations and Mansfield's and Valeo's attitudes in early 1964: Valeo, Oral
        History, Senate Historical Office, pp. 375–376 and 439.
        Third memo in three months: Memorandum, Mansfield to Johnson, "The
        Vietnamese Situation," 2/1/64, MMA, Series 22, Box 102, File 12.
238   The advisory buildup: See "The Advisory Buildup, 1961–67," *USVNR,* Book 3, IV.B.3.
        "for the present . . .": Bundy to Johnson, "Notes for your meeting with Senator
        Mansfield today at 6:00," 2/10/64, *FRUS,* 1964–1968, 1:67.

238   First major address on Vietnam: Olson, *Mansfield and Vietnam*, p. 130.
"We have teetered . . .": Senate speech, *CR*, 2/19/64, pp. 2993–2994.
Javits challenged Mansfield: *CR*, 2/20/64, pp. 3277–3281.
Johnson wants to avoid debate: Beschloss, *Taking Charge*, p. 250.

239   "the bipartisan foreign policy . . .": William White, "Sees Mansfield Hurting Viet-Nam," *Cleveland Press*, 2/26/64.
Stirred discussion in Congress: Olson, *Mansfield and Vietnam*, pp. 130–131.
Fourth appeal for negotiations: Memorandum, Mansfield to Johnson, 5/26/64, MMA, Series 22, Box 102, File 12.
LBJ telephone conversations following memo: Beschloss, *Taking Charge*, pp. 363–373. The May memorandum was preceded by a Senate speech along the same lines. See *CR*, 5/21/64, pp. 11552–11557.
Secret reconnaissance flights: Gibbons, Part 2, p. 252.

240   U.S. forces bombed antiaircraft site: There is some doubt about this story. Edwin E. Moise, in his book *Tonkin Gulf and the Escalation of the Vietnam War* (Chapel Hill: University of North Carolina Press, 1996), p. 44, quotes McGeorge Bundy as saying in a White House meeting on June 10 that it was "not true" that a U.S. plane in Laos was fired upon and that the story should not have been disseminated.
"I don't want . . ." and "I think you've done . . .": Johnson and Mansfield quoted, respectively, in Beschloss, *Taking Charge*, pp. 394–395.
Urging caution about U.S. involvement in war: Mansfield to Johnson, 6/9/64, MMA, Series 22, Box 102, File 12.
"absolutely right . . ." and "So what he comes out and says . . .": McNamara and Johnson, respectively, quoted in Beschloss, *Taking Charge*, pp. 397–399.

241   "I in a way share . . ." and "I do too, . . .": Russell and Johnson, respectively, quoted in Beschloss, *Taking Charge*, p. 403.
Tonkin Gulf episode: My account relies principally on the excellent account of the administration and congressional maneuvering in Gibbons, Part 2, esp. pp. 280–342, and the very detailed and authoritative account of the military action in Moise, *Tonkin Gulf.*

242   Johnson meeting with congressional leaders: Logevall, *Choosing War*, p. 470n10.
No objections by leaders except Mansfield: "Notes Taken at Leadership Meeting on August 4, 1964," *FRUS*, 1964–1968, 1:615–621.
"Then what is to come . . .": Mansfield memorandum for his files, 8/4/64, MMA, Series 22, Box 103, File 13.

243   Results of U.S. retaliatory raids: William J. Duiker, *The Communist Road to Power in Vietnam*, 2d ed. (Boulder, Colo.: Westview Press, 1996), pp. 249–250; also Duiker, *Ho Chi Minh* (New York: Hyperion, 2000), pp. 540–543.
Chinese assistance to North Vietnam: Logevall, *Choosing War*, p. 207.
Mao moves factories and Rusk's responses: Chen Jian, *Mao's China and the Cold War* (Chapel Hill: University of North Carolina Press, 2001), pp. 214–215.

244   "thought we ought to get . . .": Telephone call, Johnson to Representative George Mahon, 8/24/64, conversation WH6408.06, LBJL.
"Each expressed . . .": Johnson, *The Vantage Point*, p. 117.
"we had our doubts": Mansfield interview, 7/24/98.
Comparison of Tonkin Gulf with Pearl Harbor and the Kennedy assassination: See the remarks of David Kaiser in Ronnie E. Ford, "Shedding New Light on the Gulf of Tonkin Incident," *Vietnam*, Aug. 1997.

245   "When we got through . . .": Beschloss, *Reaching for Glory*, p. 39.
Fulbright's suspicions: Dallek, *Flawed Giant*, p. 148.
Morse's reaction to information: Gibbons, Part 2, p. 304.

246   Morse's charge that United States was "provocateur": *CR*, 8/6/64, pp. 18423–18430.

246   "a moderate Democratic . . .": Quoted in Gibbons, Part 2, pp. 314–315.
247   "The hearing on the measure. . .": Gibbons, Part 2, pp. 305, 308.
       Joint Senate hearing: Gibbons, Part 2, pp. 310, 313.
       "The president has acted . . .": Senate speech, *CR,* 8/6/64, p. 18399.
       Fulbright's response to Nelson: See *CR,* 8/6/64, p. 18407.
       "I took Fulbright's word . . .": Mansfield interview, 7/24/98.
       "had very definite assurances . . .": Quoted in Gibbons, Part 2, pp. 334–335.
248   "when U.S. forces have been attacked . . ." and "I feel that I, . . .": Gore and Aiken,
       respectively, quoted in Gibbons, Part 2, pp. 319–320.
       Johnson's skyrocketing popularity: George C. Herring, *America's Longest War: The
       United States and Vietnam, 1950–1975,* 3d ed. (New York: McGraw-Hill, 1996), p. 137.
       "the biggest mistake . . .": Mansfield interview, 10/20/00.
       "we are in too deep now": Quoted in Stanley Karnow, *Vietnam* (New York: Viking,
       1983), p. 491.
249   "In 1963 we passed 72 percent . . .": Quoted in Kenneth Scheibel, "Good Year for
       Mansfield," *Missoulian,* 19/11/64.
       "I think I'm going to . . .": Quoted in Humphrey, *The Education of a Public Man,* p.
       297.
250   "a pretty judicious fella . . .": Telephone call, Johnson to O'Donnell, LBJ tapes, tran-
       scripts, conversation WH6408.30, 8/21/64. O'Donnell tells a much more colorful version
       of the conversation and offer in his and Powers's memoir, *"Johnny, We Hardly Knew Ye."*
       One of LBJ's political games: Rowe, Oral History, 9/9/69, Part II, pp. 41–42, LBJL.
       Differences would be a problem: Jenkins, telephone transcript, 8/21/64.
       "a million percent": Johnson to Mansfield, LBJ tapes, transcript, conversation
       WH6409.16, 9/28/64.
       "Mike Mansfield, the pride of Montana . . .": *Public Papers of the Presidents of the
       United States:Lyndon B. Johnson, 1963–64* (Washington, D.C.: Government Printing
       Office, 1965), 2:1310.
251   "a puppet politician . . .": "Blewett Assails Foreign Policy of Administration,"
       Missoulian, 10/14/64, MMA, Series 24, Scrapbook 117.
       "It's a wonder he didn't drown . . .": Peggy DeMichele, interview, 7/26/99.
       Final broadcast: Mansfield final campaign speech, 1964, MMA, Oral History, tape
       OH22-48.
       "please, don't ask me . . .": Dirksen, quoted in Olson, *Mansfield and Vietnam,* p. 137.
252   Vietcong attack on air base: Karnow, *Vietnam,* p. 402.
253   Ball's dissent: See Logevall, *Choosing War,* pp. 266–267.
       For discussion of the November study: See *USVNR,* Book 4, VI.C.2., (C) "Military
       Pressures against North Vietnam, November–December 1964," Part 3. For the attitude
       on negotiations, see esp. pp. 53–54.
       Stable government "most essential": Quoted in Gibbons, Part 2, p. 376.
       Taylor briefing of senators: Gibbons, Part 2, pp. 376–377.
254   "We remain on a course . . .": Memorandum, Mansfield to Johnson, "Developments
       in Viet Nam," 12/9/64, National Security file, Box 6, Name File: "Mansfield, Mike,"
       LBJL.
       On the North Vietnamese position: See Duiker, *The Communist Road to Power,* p. 262.
       "cross [the] bridge . . .": Quoted in Gibbons, Part 3, p. 156.
       Thirty-minute meeting: Daily Diary cards, Drawer 53, LBJL.
       "There is a difference in emphasis . . ." Bundy to Johnson, 12/16/64, *FRUS,*
       1964–1968, 1:1009–1012.
       "I think we have the same basic view . . .": Johnson to Mansfield, 12/17/1964, *FRUS,*
       1964–1968, 1:1009–1012. The copy of Johnson's note to Mansfield with the secretarial
       markings is from National Security File, Box 6, Name File: "Mansfield, Mike," LBJL.

256   "designed to treat him gently. . . .": Memorandum, Bundy to Johnson, quoted in Gibbons, Part 2, p. 379.

Closure of VA hospital: *CR,* 1/16/65, pp. 773–782.

"face was white . . .": Kenneth Scheibel, "When Mike Blows His Top . . . Duck!" *Billings Gazette,* 4/30/67.

"In forty years of friendship . . .": Memorandum, Rowe to Johnson, "Mansfield and Miles City Veterans Hospital," 1/14/65, White House Central File, Box 307, Name File: "Rowe, James H. (1/1/65–12/31/66)," LBJL.

257   "a political boondoggle" and "it will be . . .": Clark to Johnson, Oval Office, LBJ tapes, conversation WH6501.05, PNO 4, 1/28/65, 4:00 P.M.

Mansfield refusal of Johnson's offer: Rowe to Johnson, "Veterans Hospital—Miles City," 4/5/65, White House Central File, Box 307, Name File: "Rowe, James H. (1/1/65–12/31/66)," LBJL.

The McCormack-Johnson exchange and Johnson anger at Mansfield: Evans and Novak, *Lyndon B. Johnson: The Exercise of Power,* p. 499.

258   "he's got all of his chips . . .": Johnson to Russell, LBJ tapes, conversation WH6505.03, PNO 2, 3/6/65, 12:05 P.M.

"I just think he is a man that is kinda sick . . .": Johnson to Katzenbach, LBJ tapes, conversation WH6503.06, PNO 4, 3/11/65, 10:35 P.M.

Reiterated concern about Vietnam: Valeo, *Mike Mansfield,* p. 202–203.

"We made a terrible mistake . . .": Quoted in Burke and Greenstein, *How Presidents Test Reality,* p. 148.

259   Vietcong attack on 2/6/65: Karnow, *Vietnam,* p. 412.

"our current policy . . .": McGeorge Bundy to Johnson, 1/27/64, *FRUS,* 1964–1968, 2:95–97.

"something more than a potshot" and "almost an ideal incident": Cooper, quoted in Gibbons, Part 3, p. 61.

260   "Pleikus are like street cars, . . .": Quoted in David Halberstam, *The Best and the Brightest* (New York: Fawcett Crest, 1973), p. 646.

Account of the February 6 NSC meeting: Except as noted, based on notes kept by Bromley Smith, executive director of the NSC (*FRUS,* 1964–1968, 2:155–157), and a memorandum by William Colby, then chief of the Far East Division, CIA (*FRUS,* 1964–1968, 2:158–160); on Mansfield's memorandum to Johnson, 2/8/64 (*FRUS,* 1964–1968, 2:203–206), and on Johnson's memoir, *The Vantage Point,* pp. 124–125.

"not only futile . . .": George W. Ball, *The Past Has Another Pattern* (New York: Norton, 1982), p. 390.

For Johnson's decision-making methods, with special reference to the 2/7/64 meeting: See Burke and Greenstein, *How Presidents Test Reality,* esp. pp. 144–146.

261   "We have kept our gun over the mantle . . .": Johnson, *The Vantage Point,* p. 125. The rest of his comments are from Colby's memorandum on February 6 NSC meeting.

"terse and quite biting . . .": Quoted in Gibbons, Part 3, pp. 63–64. See also William Bundy, Oral History, pp. 11–15, LBJL.

262   "now the decision was made, . . .": Memorandum for the Record, "NSC Meeting, 7 February 1965," *FRUS,* 1964–1968, 2:169–172.

"to deter, destroy and diminish . . .": "Summary Notes of the 547th Meeting of the NSC," 2/8/65, *FRUS,* 1964–1968, 2:188–192.

"very unstable government" and rest of quotations in paragraph: Memorandum, Mansfield to Johnson, 2/8/65, *FRUS,* 1964–1968, 2:203–206.

263   "Mr. President . . .": Chester Cooper, *The Lost Crusade* (New York: Dodd, Mead, 1970), p. 223.

Humphrey, *The Education of a Public Man,* pp. 320–325. See also, Memorandum for the Record, 2/10/65, *FRUS,* 1964–1968, 2:220–25.

264   "I intend to support . . .": Quoted in Burke and Greenstein, *How Presidents Test Reality*, p. 167.
        "Let me make clear, . . .": Quoted in Burke and Greenstein, *How Presidents Test Reality*, p. 219.
        "I was walking a tightrope. . . .": Mansfield interview, 10/20/99.
        Memorandum he had written in advance: "Notes on the Congressional Leadership Meeting," 2/10/65, *FRUS*, 1964–1968, 2:225–226. For Mansfield's hesitation, Burke and Greenstein, *How Presidents Test Reality*, p. 169.
265   "will have to be *vastly strengthened* . . .": Memorandum, Mansfield to Johnson, "Further Observations on Viet Nam," 2/10/65, *FRUS*, 1964–1968, 2:226–227.
        Bombing campaign known as Rolling Thunder: *USVNR*, Book 4, IV.C.3, "The Rolling Thunder Campaign Begins," pp. 48ff.
        "in the circumstances, . . ." and "I believe . . .": Quoted in Olson, *Mansfield and Vietnam*, pp. 145–146.
        "He is trying to prevent . . .": Senate speech, *CR*, 3/1/65, p. 3776.
        "He might have taken . . .": Robert Mann, *A Grand Delusion* (New York: Basic Books, 2001), p. 396.
266   "When Congress does not fulfill the role . . .": Paul M. Kattenburg, *The Vietnam Trauma in American Foreign Policy*, 1945–75 (New Brunswick, N.J.: Transaction Books, 1980), pp. 234–237.
        Barkley seeking to dissuade Roosevelt: Donald A. Ritchie, "Alben W. Barkley," in Baker and Davidson, *First among Equals*.
        Knowland delivered speech from back row: Duane Tananbaum, *The Bricker Amendment Controversy* (Ithaca, N.Y.: Cornell University Press, 1988), p. 178.
        Walking "a delicate line": Mansfield interview, 6/10/98.
267   Predicted that communist forces would intensify attacks: Memorandum, Mansfield to Johnson, "Further Observations on Viet Nam," 2/10/65, *FRUS*, 1964–1968, 2:226–227.
        Telephone call from McNamara: "Telephone Conversation between Secretary of Defense McNamara and Senator Mansfield—March 6, 1965, 11:15 P.M." MMA, Series 22, Box 103, File 1.
        Johnson's tentative approval: Memorandum, Wheeler to Sharp, 2/27/65, *FRUS*, 1964–1968, 2:380–381; also, *USVNR*, Book 4, IV.C.4, "Marine Combat Units Go to Danang," p. 5.
        "I got [Mansfield] . . .": Quoted in Beschloss, *Reaching for Glory*, pp. 213–216.
        Description of the Marine landing: William C. Westmoreland, *A Soldier Reports* (Garden City, N.J.: Doubleday, 1976), p. 124.
        "a watershed event . . .": *USVNR*, Book 4, IV.C.4, "Marine Combat Units Go to Danang," p. 22.
268   Reaction to landing of Marines at Danang: Gibbons, Part 3, p. 125.
        March 18 memorandum: Quoted in Gibbons, Part 3, pp. 125–126.
        Tenth appeal: Memorandum, Mansfield to Johnson, 3/24/65, *FRUS*, 1964–1968, 2:477–481.
269   "Don't give me . . .": Quoted in George McGovern, *Grassroots* (New York: Random House, 1977), pp. 104–105. According to the LBJL, the meeting with McGovern was on 3/26.
270   "I'm going up old Ho Chi Minh's leg . . .": Johnson, quoted by McGovern, interview, 2/7/02.
        Shift to offensive combat: *USVNR*, Book 4, IV.C.5., "Phase I in the Build-up of U.S. Forces," p. 59.
        Broad public opinion: See John E. Mueller, *War, Presidents, and Public Opinion* (New York: Wiley, 1973), p. 54.
        Opposition to expanded military action: Logevall, *Choosing War*, p. 361.
        University teach-ins: Thomas Powers, *The War at Home* (New York: Grossman, 1973), p. 56.

270 Johnson's Johns Hopkins speech: Quoted in Logevall, *Choosing War,* pp. 355–357.
271 Afternoon before the speech: Gibbons, Part 3, p. 218n5.
"profound statement": Senate speech, *CR,* 4/8/65, pp. 7490–7498.
Editorials in praise of speech: *CR,* 4/9/65, pp. 7735–7736.
"I know how deeply troubled . . .": Johnson to Mansfield, 4/12/65, *FRUS,* 1964–1968, 2:547–548.
"trying every possible diplomatic angle . . .": Mansfield, memorandum for files, 4/28/65, MMA, Series 22, Box 102, File 13.
272 "galling and embarrassing": *WP,* 5/4/65.
"is saying that the Congress . . .": *CR,* 5/6/65, p 9729.
"We are faced with . . .": Quoted in Gibbons, Part 3, p. 246.
"we will vote for this measure . . .": Quoted in Gibbons, Part 3, p. 245.
Gibbons's description of debate and action on funding request, including Fascell quotation: Gibbons, Part 3, p. 250.
273 Johnson and McNamara quotations: Notes of meeting of Johnson and advisers, 5/16/65, 6:45 P.M. *FRUS,* 1964–1968, 2:665–668.
"a propaganda effort": Quoted in Gibbons, Part 3, p. 255.
"face up to the $64 question" and "I disagree . . .": Long and Mansfield, respectively, quoted in "Memorandum of Senator Mike Mansfield," 6/3/65, confidential, MMA, Series 22, Box 102, File 13.
Eleventh memo to Johnson: Mansfield to Johnson, "Viet Nam," 6/5/65, *FRUS,* 1964–1968, 2:725–727.
274 "Once set in motion . . .": *USVNR,* Book 4, IV.C.3, "The Rolling Thunder Program Begins," p. i.
Soviet leaders felt it necessary to supply arms: Ilya V. Gaiduk, *The Soviet Union and the Vietnam War* (Chicago: Ivan R. Dee, 1996), p. 37.
China's assistance to North Vietnam: Chen Jian, *Mao's China and the Cold War,* pp. 219–229.
"I think it is about time . . .": Memorandum, Mansfield to Johnson, "Viet Nam," 6/5/65.
275 "the closest thing . . .": Herring, *America's Longest War,* p. 155.
Westmoreland's request: Westmoreland to Joint Chiefs of Staff, 6/7/65, *FRUS,* 1964–1968, 2:733–736. See also Westmoreland, *A Soldier Reports,* pp. 138–143.
McNamara's estimate: "Memorandum for the Record," 6/8/65, *FRUS,* 1964–1968, 2:739.
"Of the thousands of cables . . .": McNamara, *In Retrospect,* p. 188.
Johnson's telephone call to Mansfield: Beschloss, *Reaching for Glory,* pp. 344–348.
277 Twelfth memo: Mansfield to Johnson, "Viet Nam," 6/9/65, *FRUS,* 1964–1968, 2:741–744.
"the 19th coup . . .": Senate speech, "Vietnam Chronology," *CR,* 6/15/65, pp. 13577–13579.
278 "the Commies would use . . .": McGeorge Bundy, "Personal Notes of a Meeting with President Johnson," 6/10/65, *FRUS,* 1964–1968, p. 748.
Johnson's telephone conversation with McNamara: Beschloss, *Reaching for Glory,* p. 351.
279 "the great pressures . . .": Speech, Meeting of Democratic Policy Committee, 7/15/65, MMA, Series 22, Box 89, File 8.
Thirteenth memo: Mansfield to Johnson, "Suggestions on the Vietnamese Situation," 6/14/65, National Security File, Name File: "Vietnam, Mansfield Memo and Reply," LBJL.
June 9 memo read aloud: Gibbons, Part 3, p. 288.
280 "The President greatly values . . .": M. Bundy to Mansfield, 6/17/65, National Security File, Name File: "Vietnam, Mansfield Memo and Reply," LBJL.
"It appears that the groundwork . . .": Senate speech, "The Situation in Vietnam," *CR,* 11/21/65, pp. 17144–17146.

280   Mansfield and Dirksen invited to White House: Daily Diary cards, 7/23/65.
       Fourteenth memo: Mansfield to Johnson, "Viet Nam," 7/23/65, MMA, Series 22, Box
       103, File 13.
281   "I'm following more or less . . .": Beschloss, *Reaching for Glory,* pp. 411–413.
       "Any recognition of the NLF . . .": Ball to Johnson, 7/24/64, National Security File,
       Name File: "Mansfield Memo and Reply," LBJL.
       Mansfield proposed meeting: Beschloss, *Reaching for Glory,* pp. 411–413.
282   Mansfield report on breakfast discussion: Mansfield to Johnson, 7/27/65, "Meeting
       on Viet Nam," MMA, Series 22, Box 102, File 13.
       "South Vietnam *is* vital . . .": Memorandum, McNamara to Johnson, enclosed in
       Johnson to Mansfield, 7/28/65, MMA, Series 22, Box 102, File 13.
       McNaughton's understanding of war aims: Gibbons, Part 3, p. 157.
283   "I consider Bob McNamara . . .": Johnson to Mansfield, 7/28/65.
       "the President's riveting performance, . . .": Joseph A. Califano Jr., *The Triumph and
       Tragedy of Lyndon Johnson* (New York: Simon and Schuster, 1991), p. 41. The description
       of the meeting is also based on the notes of McGeorge Bundy, *FRUS,* 1964–1968,
       3:264–269.
       Mansfield's views read aloud: "Notes on Viet Nam," 7/26/65, MMA, Series 22, Box
       102, File 13. Mansfield's handwritten addition mistakenly says, "Given 7/28/65 at White
       House," but the statement was actually given 7/27.
286   "Mansfield's assay . . .": Jack Valenti, *A Very Human President* (New York: Norton,
       1975), p. 355.
       Nineteen telephone conversations with Johnson: President's Daily Diary
       cards, LBJL.
       Telephone conversations with M. Bundy, McNamara, Rusk: Burke and Greenstein,
       How Presidents Test Reality, p. 140.
       "The president is to be commended . . .": Senate speech, *CR,* 7/28/65, p. 18507.

10. JOHNSON II: YEARS OF FRUSTRATION

289   "Saigon had become . . .": Valeo, Oral History, Senate Historical Office, 1985–1986,
       pp. 390–391.
       "U.S. Mission Council Briefing for Codel Mansfield," 12/2/65, Top Secret
       (cited hereafter as 12/2/65 Mission Briefing), pp. 5, 15, MMA, Series 22, Box
       99, File 4.
290   Explosion at military hotel: Charles Mohr, "Saigon G.I. Billet Bombed in Vietcong
       Terror Attack," *NYT,* 12/4/65.
       Tour of blast site: Cable, American Embassy Saigon to DOS, "Codel Mansfield,"
       12/8/65, National Security File, International Meetings and Travel File, "Senator
       Mansfield's Trip (SE Asia), November 1965," Box 32, LBJL.
       Napalm attack: Confidential report, Mansfield to Johnson, "Vietnam: The Situation
       and Outlook, December 17, 1965," published in 1973 in *Two Reports on Vietnam and
       Southeast Asia to the President of the United States by Senator Mike Mansfield,* 93d
       Congress, 1st sess., Doc. 93-11 (cited hereafter as *Mansfield 1965 Report*), p. 19; see also,
       Valeo, *Mike Mansfield,* p. 205.
       "Insofar as the United States is concerned, . . .": *Mansfield 1965 Report,* pp.
       30, 33.
       "a thought that I have tried to express . . .": *Executive Sessions of the Senate
       Foreign Relations Committee,* 1966, 89th Cong., 2d sess. (printed by the
       Government Printing Office for the use of the committee; made public February
       1993), pp. 27–28.

291   North Vietnam casualties and the Ho Chi Minh quote: Glen Gendzel, "Attrition Strategy,"
        in *Encyclopedia of the Vietnam War*, ed. Stanley I. Kutler (New York: Scribner's, 1996), p. 76.
            "the cheerless conclusions . . .": Don Oberdorfer,"Chilling Mansfield Report Holds
        Little Hope," *Miami Herald*, 1/9/66.
            "members of both parties . . .": Valeo, *Mike Mansfield*, p. 207.
292   Johnson agreed to sponsor trip: In a telephone conversation with Johnson the day
        before his departure, Mansfield recalled that Johnson had promised to provide the Air
        Force plane for his mission two months earlier, Mansfield to Johnson, LBJ tapes, con-
        versation WH6511.05, Program 12, 11/12/65, 11:22 A.M.
            "the full cooperation . . .": Johnson to Mansfield, MMA, Series 22, Box 94, File 9.
            "we're not going to . . .": Watson to Johnson, LBJ tapes, conversation WH6511.04,
        Program 9, 1/9/65, 11:22 A.M.
293   "Let me know anything you want. . . .": Mansfield to Johnson, LBJ tapes, conversa-
        tion WH6511.05, Program 12, 11/12/65, 11:22 A.M.
            Vatthana's and Phouma's comments on U.S. action in Vietnam: American Embassy
        Vientiene to DOS, "Codel Mansfield," 12/9/65, Secret, "Senator Mansfield's Trip, Nov. 1965."
            Mansfield's reaction to Vatthana's and Phouma's comments: Memorandum, Mansfield
        to Johnson, "Brief Impressions, listed country-by-country," 12/18/65, "Senator
        Mansfield's Trip, Nov. 1965."
            Bombing of Ho Chi Minh trail: See Kenneth Conboy, *Shadow War* (Boulder, Colo.:
        Paladin Press, 1995).
            Mansfield's lack of knowledge of bombing: Mansfield to Prof. Jeffrey Safford, 8/2/77,
        copy in the possession of the author.
            "the most able, . . .": Memorandum, Mansfield to Johnson, "Brief impressions." pp. 7-8.
294   "I foresee that the intensity . . .": 12/2/65 Mission Briefing, p. 37.
            "It is a question, . . .": 12/2/65 Mission Briefing, p. 13.
            "the assumption upon which . . .": *USVNR*, Book 4, C.6(a), "U.S. Ground Strategy
        and Force Deployments, 1965–1967," 1:4–5.
295   "considerable ground has been lost": *Mansfield 1965 Report*, p. 20.
            "as good as you can reasonably expect . . .": 12/2/65 Mission Briefing, p. 3.
            "looks better than expected": Memorandum, Mansfield to Johnson, "Brief impres-
        sions," p. 8.
296n   Rusk ridiculed estimate: Francis Valeo, interview by William Gibbons, Patricia
        McAdams, Anna Nelson, 10/29/78, p. 16, on file at Senate Historical Office.
            McNamara drafted plan for troops: *USVNR*, Book 4, C.6(a), p. 27.
            CINCPAC requested 443,000: *USVNR*, Book 4, C.6(a), , p. 28.
296   "I really don't want to be here. . . .": Valeo Oral History, Senate Historical Office,
        1985–1986, pp. 390–391.
            Mansfield discouraged: Valeo Oral History, Senate Historical Office, 1985–1986, p. 392.
            "In sum, it may be said . . .": *Mansfield 1965 Report*, pp. 23, 24, 30.
            Johnson invited Mansfield to quarters: President's Daily Diary cards for 12/17/65 and
        12/19/65, LBJL.
            "didn't like the report": Mansfield interview, 10/8/98.
297   "staffed out and thoroughly evaluated": President's Daily Diary for 12/19/65, LBJL.
            "We will stay . . .": Johnson, *Public Papers*, 1966, 1:9.
298   Fulbright not told of Mansfield's interactions with presidents: Norvill Jones, interview, 8/17/99.
            Different social circles: Jeffrey Safford, interview, 5/25/00.
            "first major get-together": Fulbright, interview by Jeffrey Safford, 8/18/76, notes in the
        possession of the author.
299   Speaking warmly to them both: Initial Johnson-Fulbright conversation from
        Beschloss, *Taking Charge*, pp. 65–66.

299   "remarkable evening": Mansfield, handwritten memo, "12/5/63, The Elms," MMA, Series 19, Box 603, File 15.

"is a cry baby . . .": Dallek, *Flawed Giant*, p. 289.

"Fulbright's awful mean, . . .": Johnson to Russell, LBJ tapes, conversation WH6505.03, Program 2, 3/6/65, 12:05 P.M.

"I don't know why he didn't tell me . . .": Mansfield to Johnson, LBJ tapes, conversation WH6510.02, Program 6, 10/22/65, 3:05 P.M.

300   "I felt that as long as I was the Majority Leader, . . .": Mansfield interview, 7/24/98.

"Fulbright, Scotty Reston, . . .": Johnson to Harriman, 12/28/65, *FRUS*, 1964–1968, 3:720.

"nail Fulbright, . . .": Quoted in David Halberstam, *The Best and the Brightest* (New York: Random House, 1972), p. 649.

Johnson consulted Mansfield but not Fulbright: Gibbons, Part 4, p. 120.

"would likely be of doubtful utility": Telegram, Bundy to Johnson, 12/10/65, *FRUS*, 1964–1968, 3:635–637.

301   "we'll lose only Fulbright and Mansfield": Gibbons, Part 4, p. 145.

Only Mansfield and Fulbright spoke against bombing: David M. Barrett, *Lyndon B. Johnson's Vietnam Papers* (College Station: Texas A&M University Press, 1997), p. 320.

"We have little to lose . . .": Notes of Meeting of Johnson with bipartisan congressional leaders (hereafter cited as Notes of Meeting), 1/25/66, *FRUS*, 1964–1968, 3:141–145.

"If we win, . . .": Notes of Meeting, 1/25/66.

President engaged Rusk in conversation: Gibbons, Part 4, p. 147.

"If you understand Fulbright . . .": Gibbons, Part 4, p. 155.

302   "For God's sake, . . .": Notes of Meeting, 1/25/66.

"will more than likely lead us into war . . .": *USVNR*, Book 4.C.7(a), 1:47.

No major new targets: *USVNR*, Book 4, C.7(a), 1:75.

"I think I probably know Lyndon Johnson . . .": Quoted in Louis Baldwin, *Hon. Politician: Mike Mansfield of Montana* (Missoula, Mont.: Mountain Press, 1979), pp. 152–153.

303   "I feel so sorry . . .": Quoted in Andrew J. Glass, "Power-Shy Mansfield Soft-Sells in Tough Job," *WP,* 9/25/66.

"The Mansfield report was taken very seriously . . .": Henry Hall Wilson to Johnson, 2/18/66, FG431/Foreign Relations, 11/23/63–2/18/66, LBJL. I had no idea until coming across this document in the Johnson archives that Wilson wrote a lengthy report to the President on our conversation the day I saw him. The article I was preparing for the *NYT Sunday Magazine* was overtaken by events, but some of the material contributed to a later article for the same publication.

304   "because then you can feel freer to speak . . .": *Executive Sessions of the Senate Foreign Relations Committee*, 1966, 89th Cong., 2d sess. (printed by the Government Printing Office for the use of the committee; made public February 1993), pp. 33, 37.

Motion to proceed: *Executive Sessions of the Senate Foreign Relations Committee*, 1966, p. 234.

"a big farrago, . . .": Quoted in Randall Bennett Woods, *J. William Fulbright, Vietnam, and the Search for a Cold War Foreign Policy* (Cambridge: Cambridge University Press, 1998), p. 115.

"the national media, . . .": David Halberstam, *The Powers That Be* (New York: Knopf, 1979), p. 492.

Letters to Foreign Relations Committee: Gibbons, Part 4, p. 249.

"the Communist Party line": Gibbons, Part 4, p. 228.

305   Disagreement in committee about Tonkin Gulf resolution: For good coverage of this dispute see Gibbons, Part 4, pp. 254–259.

Compromise to drop amendments: Gibbons, Part 4, p. 257.

Johnson implored Mansfield to make statement: Telephone conversation between Johnson and Mansfield, 3/1/66, *FRUS*, 1964–1968, 4:267–268.

"in effect with whatever constitutional force . . .": Quoted in Mann, *A Grand Delusion*, p. 505.

305   "a surprising move on Mansfield's part, . . .": Eugene McCarthy, *Up Until Now* (New York: Harcourt Brace Jovanovich, 1982), p. 184.

306   "without quite agreeing . . .": Glass, "Power-Shy Mansfield Soft-Sells in Tough Job."

"long and spare, . . .": Evelyn Goldstein to Mansfield, undated but postmarked 4/29/67, MMA, Series 13, Box 75, File 4. My thanks to Gregory Olson for pointing out this letter.

"I never thought that Mike . . .": Baker, "Mike Mansfield," pp. 287–288.

307   "It was frustrating . . .": George McGovern, interview, 2/7/02.

"One thing about him . . .": Baker, "Mike Mansfield," p. 288.

"his silence was almost as irritating . . .": McPherson, *A Political Education,* pp. 74–75.

"at bottom, . . .": Walt W. Rostow, interview, 1/13/99.

"Mansfield would be seated . . .": Gibbons, Part 3, p. 129.

"I received kind of heavy criticism . . .": Mansfield interview, 7/24/98.

308   Inner Club: William S. White, *Citadel: The Story of the U.S. Senate* (New York: Harper and Row, 1956).

"Oh, I think it's mostly . . .": "Men of the Senate, No. 6—Senator Mike Mansfield," National Educational Television broadcast with Paul Niven, transcript, *CR,* 2/3/67, p. S1422.

309   "Mansfield simply did not view the Senate . . .": Quoted in Baker, "Mike Mansfield," p. 276.

Long clashed with Mansfield: Baker, "Mike Mansfield," pp. 279–280.

"measures which taken alone . . .": *Congress and the Nation,* vol. 2, 1965–1968 (Washington, D.C.: Congressional Quarterly, 1969), p. 3.

310   "a careful retrospective look . . .": Memorandum of remarks to the Democratic Conference, 1/10/67, MMA, Series 22, Box 90, File 9.

"until we can provide each child . . ." and "If we don't keep them . . .": Quoted in Califano, *Triumph and Tragedy,* pp. 180–181.

311   Racial violence that had broken out: *Congress and the Nation,* pp. 8–12.

Removal of forces: "Personal Opinion of Senator Mike Mansfield," Press release, 1/2/61, MMA, Series 21, Box 41, File 1/2/61.

Democratic senators agreed to co-sponsor a resolution: See Senate Democratic Policy Committee minutes of 7/13, 7/18, 7/20, 7/22, and 7/30/66, MMA, Series 22, Box 89, File 9.

312   "this damn thing . . .": "Telephone conversation between President Johnson and Senator Russell Long," 9/1/66, *FRUS,* 1964–1968, 15:398–404.

"conditions had changed . . .": Senate Democratic Policy Committee, minutes of 1/9/67, MMA, Series 22, Box 89, File 10.

313   "an encouraging start" and "good enough . . .": Quoted in Chalmers M. Roberts, "U.S. to Recall 35,000 GIs From Europe," *WP,* 5/3/67.

Protest marches: Thomas Powers, *The War at Home* (New York: Grossman, 1973), pp. 183, 195.

Nixon accused Mansfield and Kennedy: Gibbons, Part 4, p. 698.

In an unpublicized meeting: Don Oberdorfer, *Tet!* (New York: Doubleday, 1971; reprinted, Baltimore: Johns Hopkins University Press, 2001), p. 79; Westmoreland, *A Soldier Reports,* p. 228.

314   "The war is going to get worse . . .": Quoted in Tom Wicker, "Westmoreland Tells Congress U.S. Will Prevail," *NYT,* 4/29/67.

"You may recall . . .": Mansfield to Johnson, "Subject: Vietnam," 4/29/67, National Security File, Box 6, Name File: "Senator Mansfield," LBJL.

Johnson read the memorandum: Memorandum (marked "draft"), Mansfield to Johnson, 5/1/67, MMA, Series 22, Box 105, File 12 (hereafter cited as Mansfield Memorandum 5/1/67).

315   Trying to arrange visit: Mansfield to Johnson, 3/17/67, National Security File, Box 6, Name File: "Senator Mansfield," LBJL.

315   "I frankly doubt . . .": Johnson to Mansfield, 3/18/67, and back-up papers, National Security File, Box 6, Name File: "Senator Mansfield," LBJL.

Rusk's responses as relayed by Rostow to Mansfield's proposal: Rostow to Johnson, 4/30/67, National Security File, Box 6, Name File: "Senator Mansfield," LBJL.

316   McNamara's Wall: McNamara to Johnson, 8/7/67, Confidential File, Box 148, Name File: "Man," LBJL; Westmoreland, *A Soldier Reports,* p. 200.

317   Rusk's responses as relayed by Rostow: Rostow to Johnson, 4/30/67, National Security File, Box 6, Name File: "Senator Mansfield," LBJL.

318   "highly undesirable" and "could only lead . . .": Quoted in Gibbons, Part 4, p. 403. Gibbons has an excellent account of the maneuverings over a UN role. However, he evidently did not have access to Mansfield materials, which were only in the senator's files and not sent on to the White House.

"U Thant thinks . . .": Mansfield, "Memo on Meeting with U Thant, November 18, 1966," National Security File, Box 6, Name File: "Senator Mansfield," LBJL.

"I should be delighted . . .": Johnson to Mansfield, 11/19/66, with attachment from Rostow, National Security File, Box 6, Name File: "Senator Mansfield," LBJL.

Johnson directed Goldberg to present letter: Mansfield Memorandum 5/1/67. In the LBJL NSF file, cited in previous note, is a copy of a letter from Mansfield to Goldberg dated 11/11/66, the day after Mansfield's Johns Hopkins speech explaining the proposal in more detail. Mansfield called Johnson that morning at 9:28 A.M. at the LBJ Ranch, according to White House records. Mansfield gave the President a copy of the letter to Goldberg on November 25, when he and Maureen were overnight guests of the Johnsons at the ranch.

Johnson's ban on Hanoi bombing: John M. Hightower, "4-Month U.S. Bid Ignored by Hanoi," *NYT,* 5/9/87.

Request for more troops: *USVNR,* Book 4, C.7(b), "The Air War in North Vietnam," 2:15–21.

"a gimmick": Rostow to Johnson, 4/30/67, National Security File, Box 6, Name File: "Senator Mansfield," LBJL.

319   "as a rather cheap piece of theater . . ." Quoted in Gibbons, Part 4, p. 679n21.

"not a phony proposal . . .": Mansfield Memorandum 5/1/67.

Reiterated point: Mansfield to Johnson, "Additional Comments on U.N. Approach to a Solution in Viet Nam," 5/3/67, National Security File, Box 6, Name File: "Vietnam, Mansfield memo and reply," LBJL.

"Would it be a decline . . .": Mansfield Memorandum 5/1/67.

"expressed particular concern . . .": Quoted in Gibbons, Part 4, p. 679.

"the tendencies toward open-ended conflict . . .": Senate speech, *CR,* 5/15/67, pp. S6861–S6863.

320   "I will state, . . .": Mansfield commencement address, 5/30/67 (erroneously printed as 1937), *CR,* 6/1/67, pp. S7572– S7574.

Administration asking for conference on Vietnam: Gibbons, Part 4, p. 680.

321   "once again, . . ." and "The fact is that reports of progress . . .": Senate speech, *CR,* 7/11/67, pp. S9353–S9354.

322   Seventeenth memo to Johnson: Memorandum, Mansfield to Johnson, undated but apparently written July 13, MMA, Series 22, Box 114, File 5.

Mansfield interrupted argument: Barrett, *Vietnam Papers,* pp. 451–453.

"You cannot bomb those people . . .": Mansfield, Senate debate, *CR,* 7/27/67, p. S10329.

323   "(1) Get Approp[riations] Bills down . . .": Carbon copy of notes, MMA, Series 22, Box 114, File 4.

Report on status report: Manatos to Johnson, 7/24/67, WHCF, Box 73, Name File: "Mansfield, Mike 7/1/67–12/31/67," LBJL.

323   Account of the maneuverings over the UN Security Council issue in late 1967: Except where otherwise noted, based on Gibbons's excellent and detailed account in Gibbons, Part 4, pp. 915–922.
Call for UN action: Senate speeches, *CR*, 8/7/67, S11017; *CR*, 8/10/67, S11286–S11287. Senate debate, *CR*, 8/28/67, S12286–S12290.
Goldberg report: Gibbons, Part 4, p. 916.
The suggestion about India: Manatos to Johnson, 8/15/67 and 8/19/67, WHCF, Box 73, Name File: "Mansfield, Mike 7/1/67–12/31/67," LBJL. Copy of correspondence on Cooper-Nehru meeting in the possession of the author from MMA, but location not found.

324   "I have feared . . .": Gibbons, Part 4, p. 922.
Mid-1967 troop increase and its repercussions: Oberdorfer, *Tet!*, pp. 78–81.

325   On August 3: Oberdorfer, *Tet!*, pp. 83–84.
Nancy Zaroulis and Gerald Sullivan, *Who Spoke Up?* (New York: Doubleday, 1984), p. 142.
"I am all for dissent . . .": Senate speech, *CR*, 11/16/67, p. 32779. See also Mansfield's remarks on protesters burning draft cards and evading the draft, *CR*, 10/18/65, pp. 27251–27252.

326   Political situation in late 1967: Oberdorfer, *Tet!*, pp. 81–86, and Oberdorfer, "The 'Wobble' on the War on Capitol Hill," *New York Times Sunday Magazine*, 12/17/67.
"We are beginning to win this struggle. . . ."; "not many more nights . . ."; and "We have reached an important point . . .": Humphrey, Johnson, and Westmoreland, respectively, quoted in Oberdorfer, *Tet!*, pp. 98–106, which see for details on the Psychological Strategy Group's offensive drive.
"We should not delude ourselves . . .": Senate speech, *CR*, 11/20/67, p. S16755.
The General Offensive and General Uprising: On the basis of information then available from captured documents and prisoners, I wrote in *Tet!* that the Tet Offensive was ordered in July 1967 by the Lao Dong Politburo. That was correct, but John M. Carland, a U.S. Army historian has traced the decision in more detail based on documentary materials from North Vietnam that have subsequently become available. Carland, "The Tet Offensive of 1968: Desperate Gamble or Calculated Risk?" in the possession of the author.

327   "the struggle in Vietnam has turned grim, . . .": Speech at Indiana University Convocation, 2/23/68, in the possession of the author.
"on an old colleague basis . . .": Manatos to Johnson, 3/1/68, WHCF, Name File: "Mansfield, Senator Mike," LBJL.

328   "it is my intention . . .": Mansfield, meeting with Johnson and committee members, 3/6/68, *CR*, 3/7/68, pp. 5644–5661.
"reached the end of the line . . .": Quoted in Clark Clifford, *Counsel to the President* (New York: Random House, 1991), p. 498.

329   "That does not mean . . .": Memorandum, Mansfield to Johnson, "Subject: Reports of requests for an additional 200,000 men in Viet Nam," 3/13/68, Meeting Notes, Box 2, LBJL.
Made his views public: Senate speech, *CR*, 3/26/68, p. 7661.
"the most troublous days . . .": Senate speech, *CR*, 3/7/68, p. 5659.
"He liked to sit on the side porch . . .": Sophie Engelhard Craighead, telephone interview, 7/16/02.
Description of stress-free vacation: Craighead, telephone interview, 7/16/02.
Money not accepted from Engelhard: Rowe to Mansfield, 7/1/70, MMA, Series 14, Box 87, File 4.

330   Engelhard used as go-between: George Christian, interview, 1/13/99.
Mansfield asked to visit Johnson: Jim Jones to LBJ, 3/25/68, 6:20 P.M. Marvin Watson to LBJ, 3/26/68, 8:50 P.M. both from Diary backup for 3/27/68, LBJL. In this instance

Johnson used Arthur Krim, President of United Artists and a fund-raiser and confidant of LBJ, as a go-between with Engelhard. Krim reported on March 25 that Mansfield had told Engelhard "he was for the President and definitely not for Bobby." When Johnson continued to be uncertain on 3/26, Engelhard (primed by Krim) repeatedly called Mansfield to suggest he come to the White House.

331   Johnson-Mansfield meeting: The meeting of 3/27/68 took one hour, forty-nine minutes according to White House records. The tape recording covers one hour, fifteen minutes of the meeting, after which the tape evidently ran out. The recording of the meeting was made available to Mansfield at his request by the LBJL. Mansfield, who was delighted to learn that the meeting had secretly been taped, shared it with the author. All direct quotations from their dialogue, except as noted, were taken directly from the tape recording.

332   "God bless you": Quoted by Terry Sauford to author, 4/7/71.

"something dramatic": Rowe to Johnson, "Peace with Honor in Vietnam," 3/19/68, WHCF, Box 307, Name File: "Rowe, James H.," LBJL.

"rigidly fixed . . .": Memorandum, O'Brien to Johnson, 3/21/68, quoted in David M. Barrett, ed., *Lyndon B. Johnson's Vietnam* Papers (College Station: Texas A&M University Press, 1997), p. 698.

"I don't give a damn . . .": Meeting with General Wheeler and General Abrams, 3/26/68, Tom Johnson's Notes, Box 2, LBJL.

Didn't take him seriously: Kenneth Scheibel, "Mansfield Says LBJ 'Sacrificed' for Nation," *Billings Gazette,* 4/2/68.

700,000 troops projection ridiculed by Rusk: For Mansfield's comment on this, see Mansfield interview with the BBC, 12/13/76. Transcript in the possession of the author.

333   "Everybody is recommending surrender": CIA-DOD Briefing by General Dupuy and George Carver, 3/27/68, Tom Johnson's Notes, Box 2, LBJL..

334   Johnson combined the two initiatives: George Christian, "The Night Lyndon Quit," *Texas Monthly,* Apr. 1988; and James R. Jones, "Behind L.B.J.'s Decision Not to Run in '68," *NYT,* 4/16/88.

335   Mansfield's reaction to the backup force: Mansfield interviews, 2/2/98 and 6/10/98.

LBJ telephone call with Clifford and Mansfield's reaction to the 40,000: Mansfield interviews, 2/2/98, 7/24/98, 2/16/99.

336   "I speak to you tonight . . .": Successive drafts of the 3/31 speech can be found in Statements file, Boxes 270 and 273, LBJL. See also Larry Berman, *Lyndon Johnson's War* (New York: Norton, 1989), pp. 235–236, for an analysis written by Rostow.

338   "a first step . . .": MMA, Oral History collection, *Capitol Cloakroom,* twentieth anniversary broadcast, 3/27/68.

339   Mansfield-Johnson discussion: The tape ran out as Johnson was reacting to Mansfield's plea to halt the bombing, before he mentioned the possibility that he would partially do so. That part of the exchange and Mansfield's reaction is from Mansfield interview, 6/10/98.

"Mike, I approve of your honesty . . .": There have been several versions of Johnson's last words to Mansfield on 3/27/68 and of Mansfield's response. This version is based on Mansfield interviews, 2/2/98 and 6/10/98. He told me he made no response to Johnson's complaint about his role as Majority Leader.

341   White House official imparted news to Mansfield: Scheibel, "Mansfield Says LBJ 'Sacrificed' for Nation," *Billings Gazette,* 2/2/68.

"I recognized then . . .": "Mansfield Sees Possibility of Draft," *Washington Evening Star,* 4/1/68.

"he has reasoned with his advisers, . . .": *CR,* 4/1/68, pp. S3669–S3673.

342   Television interview: "Viewpoint," *Honolulu Star-Bulletin,* 4/18/68.

Hendricks-Mansfield correspondence: MMA, Series 13, Box 81, File 1. My thanks to Jim Ludwick for bringing it to my attention.

344 "with a staring look . . .": Lady Bird Johnson, *A White House Diary* (New York: Holt, Rinehart and Winston, 1970), p. 386.

"I grieve for my country . . .": "Statement of Senator Mike Mansfield—June 5, 1968," MMA, Series 22, File 6.

"maybe the most emotional . . .": Craighead, telephone interview, 7/16/02.

Reaction to Tydings bill: *CR,* 7/3/68, pp. 19891–19894.

345 "convinced that any such legislation . . .": William "Scotty" James to Mansfield, 6/24/68, MMA, Series 22, Box 116, File 6.

"It didn't take any courage . . .": Mansfield to James, 6/28/68, MMA, Series 22, Box 116, File 6.

Mansfield stood firm: Senate speech, *CR,* 7/3/68, pp. 19891–19894.

"I made my decision . . .": Quoted in Kenneth Scheibel, "Montana Blistering Mike for Gun Stand," *Billings Gazette,* 6/20/68.

"a Soviet military intervention . . .": Memorandum, Mansfield to Johnson, "Observations on a Recent Visit to Europe—East and West," 8/19/68, National Security File, Files of Walt Rostow, Box 5, Name file: "Mansfield, Senator Mike," LBJL.

346 "two monologues . . .": Memorandum, Mansfield to Johnson, "Observations on a Recent Visit to Europe—East and West," 8/19/68.

"reduce the size of our military involvement . . .": Mansfield to Johnson, "Viet Nam and the Paris Negotiations," 7/16/68, National Security File, Files of Walt Rostow, Box 2, "Meetings with the President, July–December 1968," LBJL.

"the wisdom of Senator Mansfield": Johnson, *Public Papers,* 1968–69, p. 1270.

Inauguration Day, President's Daily Diary for 1/20/69, LBJL.

"the greatest President . . ." and "As might be expected, . . .": Mansfield, Press releases, 1/22 and 1/23/73.

347 "Nope. I'm not going": Quoted by Stan Kimmitt, interview, 6/10/02.

"remembered his old friends . . .": Mansfield to Jakie L. Pruett, 10/9/75, MMA, Series 22, Box 136.

"Johnson was the ultimate politician . . .": Mansfield, interview by Jim Ludwick, 6/23/95, manuscript in the possession of the author.

"a torn personality": Mansfield interview, 10/19/98.

II. WITH NIXON ON THE ROAD TO CHINA

349 "I have a greater degree of flexibility . . .": Quoted in Harry Kelly, "Mansfield Enjoys New Lease on Life," *WP,* 3/13/69.

"Didn't know him": Mansfield interview, 9/10/98.

350 "and thank the Lord . . .": Mansfield interview, 8/28/98.

Bombing raids against China: Mansfield interview, 7/24/98.

"was their business . . .": Nixon quoted in Mansfield, memorandum for files, 2/4/69, MMA, Series 22, Box 103, File 5.

Kentucky Derby trip: Don Oberdorfer, "Nixon Cheers California Colt Home," *WP,* 5/4/69.

Cooper recommended Mansfield: Rowland Evans and Robert Novak, *Nixon in the White House* (New York: Random House, 1971), p. 106.

Meeting privately at White House: Mansfield interview, 9/10/98.

351 "Oh, I have a right . . .": Mansfield Says He's Not So Blunt Talking to Nixon," *WP,* 3/29/71.

President's purpose was to obtain cooperation: H. R. Haldeman, *The Haldeman Diaries* (New York: Putnam, 1994) and the CD-ROM made available with the book.

Told virtually nothing: Frank Valeo, interview, 9/10/98.

Mansfield modeled his relationship: Valeo to Professor Jeffrey Safford, 7/21/77, letter in the possession of the author.

351   "felt insecure with me . . .": Ernest B. Furgurson, "Retiring Mansfield Calls for Carter Fireside Chats," *Baltimore Sun,* 11/15/76.
       "kind of close, . . .": Mansfield interview, 10/8/98.
352   "Mike is a wonderful guy, . . .": Nixon tapes, telephone conversation 19-77, 1/25/72.
       "Mansfield never does": Nixon tapes, conversation 476-7, 4/9/71.
       His primary point of contact: Valeo, *Mike Mansfield,* p. 225.
       Mansfield agreed not to tell: Nixon tapes, telephone conversation 42-6, 4/6/71.
       "playing a ruthless game . . .": Nixon tapes, conversation 696-1, 3/29/72.
       "Well, to hell with him. . . .": Nixon tapes, conversation 131-19, 5/17/72.
353   "deep sense of respect . . .": Nixon to Mansfield, 3/7/76, MMA, Series 22, Scrapbook 280.
354   "We no longer have at the White House . . .": Senate Democratic Policy Committee Luncheon, minutes, 2/4/69, MMA, Series 22, Box 89, File 11.
       "I think the President would give his right arm . . .": Richard L. Lyons, "Senate Is Cool to McGovern Attack on War," *WP,* 3/18/69.
       "I am sure that in his own way . . .": "Senator Mansfield Interviewed on *Meet the Press,*" *CR,* 4/1/69, p. S3410.
       "Insofar as the war in Vietnam is concerned, . . .": Mansfield to Vera L. Praast, 5/6/69, MMA, Series 13, Box 53.
355   "every reasonable effort": "Senator Mansfield's Comments on the CBS program *Face the Nation,*" *CR,* 5/26/69, p. S5630.
       A substantial majority of those polled: John E. Mueller, *War, Presidents, and Public Opinion* (New York: Wiley, 1973), pp. 54ff. Public opinion regarding the Vietnam War is a complex subject because of the public uncertainty and the difficulty of comparing answers to different questions asked. Mueller's outstanding study, which is considered authoritative by many researchers and historians, uses the Gallup "mistake" question as a principal index of public support because it is worded in neutral fashion and was asked in the same way from 1964 to 1971.
       Over Easter weekend: Fred Halstead, *Out Now!* (New York: Monad Press 1978), p. 451.
       "feeling of futility and indignation . . .": "Memorandum on Viet Nam and Hamburger Hill," 5/28/69, MMA, Series 22, Box 103, File 5.
       "When any senator speaks out . . .": Quoted in Robert B. Semple Jr., "Mansfield Urges Dialogue on War," *NYT,* 5/30/69.
356   Urged the withdrawal of 50,000 troops "as a starter": George C. Wilson, "Mansfield Urges GI Cutback in Vietnam," *WP,* 4/10/69.
       "lock, stock and barrel": Quoted in Don Oberdorfer, "Mansfield Asks Pullout in S.E. Asia," *WP,* 7/19/69.
       "would be out of Vietnam": Quoted in Richard Harwood, "JFK Decided in '63 to Order Viet Pullout after Election," *WP,* 8/3/70.
       "a new U.S. policy . . .": Don Oberdorfer, "U.S. Bars New Asia War Role," *WP,* 7/26/69.
       "His intent, . . .": Quoted in Warren Unna, "Mansfield Supports Nixon's Asia Stand," *WP,* 7/29/69.
357   "It has been a long time . . .": Unna, "Mansfield Supports Nixon's Asia Stand."
       "very much surprised . . .": Quoted in memorandum, Patrick J. Buchanan to Nixon, 8/5/69, "One Observor's [*sic*] Notes of Legislative Leadership Meeting held Monday, 8/4/69, 8:30 A.M." Folder: "Memoranda for the President," Box 79 (8/3/69–12/28/69), White House Special Files, Nixon Materials.
       "was not a formula . . .": Richard Nixon, *The Memoirs of Richard Nixon* (New York: Grosset and Dunlap, 1978), p. 395.
       "I was impressed with him, . . .": Mansfield interview, 8/28/98.
358   "a man who, . . .": "The Greatest Homage," *Realities Cambodgiennes,* 12/6/63, MMA, Series 22, Box 115, File 2.

358   Unacceptable to U.S. military forces: Cable, American Embassy Bangkok to Secretary of State, "For President and Secretary from Senator Mansfield," 12/1/65, Manuscript Division, LBJ National Security File, Asia and Pacific, Roll 14-0889, Library of Congress.
       Rusk asked Mansfield: Mansfield, handwritten note, "Rusk-4:13—12/21/66," MMA, Series 22, Box 115, File 2.
       "a just and courageous man . . .": Quoted in Stanley Karnow, *Vietnam: A History* (New York: Viking, 1983), p. 590. Karnow's account of Sihanouk's attitude toward incursions into Cambodian territory does not square with Bowles's letter to Mansfield after his mission or with Sihanouk's correspondence with Mansfield at the time, both found in MMA, Series 22, Box 115, File 2.
       "We are a country . . .": Karnow, *Vietnam*, p. 590.
       War against Americans should take priority: Qiang Zhai, *China and the Vietnam Wars* (Chapel Hill: University of North Carolina Press, 2000), pp. 184–185.
359   "based a great number . . ." and "if that does not cross wires . . .": Memorandum, Nixon to Kissinger, 2/1/69, Folder CO 26: "Cambodia (1969–1970)", White House Special Files, Subject Files: "Confidential Files 1969–1974," Box 5 (hereafter cited as Cambodia 1969–1970), Nixon Materials.
       "my sincere desire . . .": Draft letter, Nixon to Sihanouk, 2/12/69, "Cambodia 1969–1970," Nixon Materials.
       "the cesssation of attacks . . .": Sihanouk to Nixon, 2/24/69, "Cambodia 1969–1970," Nixon Materials.
       "In conformity with the United Nations Charter, . . .": Memorandum, Kissinger to Nixon, "Next Steps in Cambodia," 4/21/69, "Cambodia 1969–1970," Nixon Materials.
       Mansfield was interested but did not have time: Olson, *Mansfield and Vietnam*, p. 206.
360   He once again ordered bombing: Henry A. Kissinger, *White House Years* (Boston: Little, Brown, 1979), pp. 239–254.
       Raids that lasted for more than a year: Tad Szulc, *The Illusion of Peace* (New York: Viking, 1978), p. 54.
       Nixon's quote on "losing" China: Don Oberdorfer, "Nixon's Swing on China," *WP,* 4/23/71, based largely on a background interview with Henry Kissinger. Details of Nixon's statements in his 1965 and 1967 trips can be found in Jim Mann, *About Face* (New York: Knopf, 1999), pp. 17–18.
       "a lifelong interest . . .": "A Size-Up of President Nixon" [interview with Mansfield], *U.S. News and World Report,* 12/6/71.
361   "Among the requirements . . .": Mansfield to Sihanouk, 6/17/69, WHCF, Confidential Files, Box 6, Nixon Materials.
       "Your Excellency:": Mansfield to Chou En-lai, undated, WHCF, Confidential Files, Box 6, Nixon Materials.
363   "the President knows every significant move . . .": Memorandum, Mansfield, quoted by Harlow to Nixon, 6/23/69, WHCF, Confidential Files, Box 6, Nixon Materials.
       "he is most pleased . . .": Memorandum, Alexander Butterfield to Kissinger and Harlow, 6/26/69, WHCF, Confidential Files, Box 6, Nixon Materials.
       Urged Harlow to suggest that Mansfield make initiative public: Kissinger, *White House Years,* p. 179.
       August 9 meeting: WHCF, President's Daily Diary for 8/9/69, Nixon Materials.
       "the distinguished Majority Leader . . .": Nixon to heads of state 8/13/69, WHCF, EX FO (Foreign Affairs), Box 1.
       "his three boys . . .": James Lowenstein, interview, 10/4/99.
364   "My dear friend": Ne Win to Mansfield, 8/13/69, Anne Mansfield Papers.
       "virtual Chief of State treatment . . .": "CODEL Mansfield Visit, August 21 through 23, 1969," State Department Airgram from Embassy Phnom Penh, 9/8/69, Jendres Archives.

365   Vietcong flags one day and the Stars and Stripes thereafter: Sichan Siv, interview, 9/26/99.
       Sihanouk declared a national day of mourning: *Kambuja,* Sept. 1969, in the posses-
       sion of the author.
       Conversation that stirred controversy: Memorandum of conversation, Sihanouk and
       Mansfield, 8/22/69, MMA, Series 22, Box 115, File 1.
       "Communist pressure on Cambodia . . .": DOS to Amembassy Rangoon,
       "Background Paper" (declassified), 8/15/69, Jendres Archives.
366   "in any way, . . .": Quoted in Bernard Gwertzman, "State Department Asserts
       Sihanouk Solicited Raids," *NYT,* 7/26/73.
       "Insofar as I understood it . . .": Mansfield, memorandum for files, 7/26/73, MMA,
       Series 22, Box 115, File 1.
       "extremely cordial": Memorandum of conversation, Sihanouk and Mansfield,
       8/22/69, MMA, Series 22, Box 115, File 1.
367   "did not yield a single indication of anticipated change . . .": Mansfield, "The New
       Policies in Asia," report to the President of the United States, 8/27/69, Anne Mansfield
       Papers.
       "let him wait . . .": Chen Jian, *Mao's China and the Cold War,* 247–248.
       "I have received your letter . . .": Chou En-lai to Sihanouk, 8/24/69 (in French; trans.
       Laura Oberdorfer), Jendres Archives.
       "While the response was not what I had hoped . . .": Mansfield to Sihanouk, 9/24/69,
       MMA, Series 22, Box 113, File 7.
368   "the heavy L.B.J. hand": John W. Finney, "Congress: Mansfield More and More the
       Leader," *NYT,* 7/27/69.
       "is sitting a lot taller . . .": Spencer Rich, "Mansfield Leadership Stature Grows," *WP,*
       12/28/69.
369   "By the usual standards of politics, . . .": "Mansfield of Montana," *CR,* 6/10/70, p.
       S8711.
       "gladly give up his seat": Minutes of the Democratic Policy Committee, 10/21/69,
       Anne Mansfield Papers.
370   "the largest expression of public dissent . . .": Nancy Zaroulis and Gerald Sullivan,
       Who Spoke Up? (New York: Doubleday, 1984), p. 269; Halstead, *Out Now!,* p. 488.
       "an unmistakable sign . . .": Quoted in Kissinger, *White House Years,* pp. 291–292.
       "I know of no basis . . .": "Senators Reject War Silence," *WP,* 10/16/69.
       "I would like to see the country . . .": Senate speech, *CR,* 10/20/69, p. S12779.
371   "I think, along with a lot of others, . . .": Coffin to Mansfield, 10/22/69, MMA,
       Collection SC-295, File 6.
       Mansfield's support for Nixon's withdrawal policies: Valeo, *Mike Mansfield,* p. 223.
372   Four steps to terminate war: Remarks made at Democratic Policy Committee meet-
       ing, 10/21/69, Anne Mansfield Papers.
       Discussion that followed Mansfield's remarks: Minutes of Democratic Policy
       Committee meeting, 10/21/69, Anne Mansfield Papers.
       "the committee members are Americans . . .": Remarks made at Democratic Policy
       Committee meeting, 10/22/69, Anne Mansfield Papers.
       "in dispelling the President's doubts . . .": Minutes of Democratic Policy Committee
       meeting, 10/22/69, Anne Mansfield Papers.
       "we realize that the final responsibility . . .": Mansfield memorandum for files,
       10/23/69, Anne Mansfield Papers.
373   "the continuance of the war in Viet Nam, . . .": Mansfield to Nixon, 10/31/69,
       President's Personal Files, Name/Subject File: "Mansfield, Mike," Box 11, Nixon
       Materials.
374   "a unilateral cease fire . . .": Nixon, *Memoirs,* pp. 407–409.

374   "indistinguishable from Rusk . . .": Quoted in *CQ Weekly Report,* 11/7/69, p. 2217.
        "there were no specifics": Senate speech, "President Nixon's Vietnam Address," *CR,*
        11/4/69.
        "We better think about the silent minority, . . .": Mansfield, radio broadcast, *Capital
        Cloakroom,* 11/5/69, transcript of tape, MMA, Oral History 22-70.

375   "wait-and-see mood": Quoted in Murrey Marder, "Viet March Worrying Hill
        Doves," *WP,* 11/9/69.
        Luncheon attended by a bipartisan group: President's Daily Diary for 11/13/69, Nixon
        Materials.
        "dire predictions": Quoted in Carroll Kilpatrick, "Nixon Thanks Congress," *WP,*
        11/14/69.
        "To be sure, peace has not been restored. . . .": Quoted in Spencer Rich, "Hill Ends
        Session in Harmony," *WP,* 12/24/69.

376   "Cambodia tore it": Mansfield on *Face the Nation,* 5/17/70, MMA, Series 24,
        Scrapbook 225.
        Mansfield commended Nixon: "The Situation in Cambodia," *CR,* 4/16/70, p. 12137.
        "long personal acquaintance . . .": Mansfield to Nixon, 4/24/70, MMA, Series 22,
        Box 115, File 2.

377   Scribbled instruction specifically directing aides: Robert W. Merry, *Taking on the
        World* (New York: Viking, 1996), p. 487.
        Nixon instructed Kissinger: Haldeman, *Diaries,* p. 157.
        Stood up and applauded: Haldeman, *Diaries,* p. 158; Nixon, *Memoirs,* p. 451.
        "I, of course, stood up . . .": Olson, *Mansfield and Vietnam,* p. 218.
        "Tonight, American and South Vietnamese units . . .": Richard Nixon, "Address to
        the Nation on the Situation in Southeast Asia," 4/30/70, *Public Papers of the Presidents of
        the United States: Richard Nixon, 1970* (Washington, D.C.: Government Printing Office,
        1971), pp. 405–410.

378   "I just did a lot of thinking": Quoted in Kenneth Scheibel, "Mike Was Stunned,"
        Billings Gazette, 5/3/70, MMA, Series 24, Scrapbook 225.
        "1X3": Statement of Senator Mike Mansfield, 5/1/70, MMA, Series 24, Scrapbook 235B, p. 7.
        "has exercised his responsibility, . . .": Senate speech, "Cambodia," *CR,* 5/1/70, pp.
        S6515–S6517.

379   "It simply exploded . . .": Halstead, *Out Now!,* p. 537.
        Military operations in Cambodia: Louis Harris Poll, *WP,* 5/5/70.
        "dividing the capital of the United States . . .": James Reston, "A Confused Capital,"
        NYT, 5/4/70.
        Fulbright received 100,000 letters: Randall Bennett Woods, *Fulbright: A Biography*
        (Cambridge: Cambridge University Press, 1995), pp. 567–568.
        Mansfield asked for and received instructions: Valeo, *Mike Mansfield,* p. 228.

380   "the highest priority": Mansfield and Scott to Fulbright, 5/7/70, in the possession of
        the author.
        "I have reached the point . . .": Mansfield, memorandum for files, "Cambodia and a
        New China," 5/11/70, MMA, Series 22, Box 103, File 5.
        "I think we have a dual responsibility . . ." and rest of interview: *Face the Nation,*
        5/17/70, transcript, MMA, Series 24, Scrapbook 225.

381   Childs to Mansfield, 5/19/70, MMA, Series 19, Box 541, File 1.
        "we now have to break it . . ." and "take on Mansfield, . . .": Quoted in Haldeman
        notes, 5/18 and 5/20/70, respectively, in Haldeman, *Diaries,* CD-ROM.

382   "Beyond military success or failure, . . .": Senate speech, *CR,* 6/9/70, pp. 18904–18906.

383   "Mansfield was most concerned . . .": Memorandum, Timmons to Nixon, "Breakfast
        Meeting with Senator Mansfield," 7/8/70, Folder: "Memoranda for the President," Box
        81 (6/7/70–8/9/70), White House Special Files, Nixon Materials.

384   "You're the helicopter pilot, . . .": Quoted by John Bartlett, testimony before Montana
       Senate-House Committee Hearing on authorization of the Mansfield statue, 3/8/99.
       "made many people realize . . .": Harold Wallace, brochure for 1970 senatorial race.
385   "generally the campaign looks good": Ray Dockstader, "Mansfield Campaign—
       Summer 1970," 7/28/70, MMA, Series 24, Box 87, File 1.
       Threatening telephone calls: Peggy DeMichele, interview, 7/26/99.
       "the support it has brought . . .": J. D. Holmes, "Mansfield-Wallace Race: What Will
       Be the Vote Margin?" *Great Falls Tribune*, 11/1/70.
       "with the responsibilities . . .": Memorandum, "Notes on Voting Rights for 18 Year
       Olds," 5/1/68, MMA, Series 32, Box 5, File 1.
386   Mansfield returned with word from Kissinger: Charles S. Johnson, interview, 3/13/02.
       "Skivvies, of course. . . .": Roger Clawson, "Whatever His Height, Mike Mansfield
       Stood Tall," *Billings Outpost*, 10/10/01.
387   Finances of 1970 campaign: Judy Turner and Robert Fullmeth, "Mike Mansfield,"
       Ralph Nader Congress Project, Aug. 1972.
       Baucus campaign expenses: Federal Election Commission, as of 12/11/02.
       "I'm endorsing them both": Quoted in Haldeman notes, 10/23/70, in Haldeman,
       Diaries, CD-ROM.
       "my wholehearted support": Quoted in "President Endorses Wallace," *Great Falls
       Tribune*, 10/27/70, MMA, Series 24, Scrapbook 232.
       Proposal of troop-reduction measure: Except as noted this section is based on two
       excellent accounts of the struggle over troops in Europe: James Edmond Schwartz,
       "Senator Michael J. Mansfield and United States Military Disengagement from Europe"
       (Ph.D. diss., University of North Carolina, 1977); and Phil Williams, *The Senate and
       U.S. Troops in Europe* (New York: St. Martin's Press, 1985).
388   "a formidable challenge": Kissinger, *White House Years*, p. 939.
389   Nixon's wish that Rogers lead: Haldeman notes, 5/12/71, in Haldeman, *Diaries*, CD-ROM.
       "strike at our whole foreign policy . . .": Memorandum, "LIG [Legislative
       Interdepartmental Group] Meeting, May 12, 12:00 Noon," 5/12/71, NSC Files, Name
       Files, Box 824, "Mansfield Amendment," Nixon Materials.
       Description of the Situation Room meeting and strategy: Kissinger, *White House
       Years*, pp. 944–945.
       Johnson's opposition to proposal: Ken W. Clawson, "Johnson Joins Nixon Attack on
       Troop Cut," *WP*, 5/16/71.
390   "For the past week . . .": Senate speech, *CR*, 5/19/71, p. 15903.
       "A reduction of 25 percent . . .": James Lowenstein, interview, 10/4/99.
       "an educational exercise" and "I would have fallen through the floor . . .": Schwartz,
       "Senator Michael J. Mansfield," pp. 123–124.
391   "Sometimes it takes a sledge hammer . . .": Senate speech, *CR*, 5/19/71.
392   Microphones and wire taps: William Doyle, *Inside the Oval Office* (New York:
       Kodansha International, 1999), p. 168.
       Discussion of a China trip with Nixon: "Memo to file by Senator Mansfield re:
       Breakfast with President, August 13, 1970," MMA, Series 22, Box 103, File 5. In conver-
       sation with Kissinger on 4/23/71, Nixon said, "I suggested to [Mansfield] over a year ago
       that if he goes . . . he'll be our envoy," Nixon tapes, conversation 487-1.
       "No, you should. . . .": Mansfield interview, 6/1/01.
       Nixon making efforts to contact the Chinese: For Nixon's maneuvering on China in
       1969–1971, see two well-documented books by American journalists: *About Face* by Jim
       Mann and *A Great Wall* by Patrick Tyler (New York: Public Affairs, 1999). Basic sources
       are *The Memoirs of Richard Nixon* and Kissinger's *White House Years*.
       The Pakistan and Romanian-based exchanges: Reported in Kissinger, *White House
       Years*, pp. 700–704.

393   "Mr. Senator: . . .": Sihanouk to Mansfield, 4/11/71 (in French; trans. Laura
         Oberdorfer), Jendres Archives.
         Nixon and Kissinger discussion: Nixon tapes, conversation 250-5, 4/16/71.
         "In the line of our China policy, . . .": Except as otherwise noted, all quotes regarding
         this meeting are from Nixon tapes, conversation 481-5, 4/17/71.
395   "a historic contribution": Nixon tapes, conversation 479-1, 4/14/71.
         Mansfield praised Nixon: Senate speech, "Reopening of Trade with the Chinese
         People's Republic," *CR*, 4/15/71, pp. 10470–10471.
         Two more packages: For the content of the other two packages, see Kissinger, *White
         House Years*, p. 712.
396   "Enormous, it's an enormous story. . . ." and the comments that followed between
         Nixon, Kissinger, and Haldeman: Nixon tapes, conversation 581-7, 4/17/71.
397   "the emerging turn in China . . .": Don Oberdorfer, "Nixon's Swing on China," *WP*, 4/23/71.
398   "That's just one article": Nixon tapes, conversation 487-7, 4/23/71.
         Mansfield letter to Chou En-lai: Mansfield, memorandum for files, 4/26/71, MMA,
         Series 22, Box 115, File 2.
         "We don't want any senators over there, . . .": Nixon tapes, conversation 483-4, 4/20/71.
         "The problem is . . .": Except as noted, the April 23 conversation is from Nixon
         tapes, conversation 487-1, 4/23/71.
         On "delicate request" regarding Muskie: Anatoly Dobrynin, *In Confidence* (New York:
         Times Books, 1995), p. 211, and Don Nicoll, telephone interview, 11/19/02.
399   "feels we've got to control this . . .": Haldeman notes, 4/23/71, in Haldeman, *Diaries*,
         CD-ROM.
         Chou's proposal of discussions: The text of Chou's message is in Kissinger, *White
         House Years*, p. 714.
400   Nixon-Kissinger discussion about emissary to China: Nixon, *Memoirs*, p. 550.
         Nixon-Kissinger telephone discussion: Nixon tapes, conversation 2-52, 4/27/71. The por-
         tions about Bush were withdrawn from the tape released by the National Archives but
         appeared in a transcript produced by Kissinger's secretary; in the possession of the author.
401   Nixon's instructions: Nixon tapes, conversation 2-52, 4/27/71.
         Kissinger's message: Described in Kissinger, *White House Years*, p. 718.
         "Goddamnit, he's got money . . .": Nixon tapes, conversation 252-20, 4/28/71.
403   Mansfield given no advance notice of trip: Mansfield interview, 3/16/99.
         Met with Mansfield privately: President's Daily Diary for 7/19/71, WHCF, Box FC-
         26, Nixon Materials.
         "On our side, Mr. President, . . .": Quoted in memorandum from Clark MacGregor
         for the President's file, 7/19/71, President's Office files, Memoranda for the President,
         5/2/71-8/15/71, Box 85, Nixon Materials.

12. VIETNAM, CHINA, WATERGATE, AND BEYOND

405   "a quiet revolution . . .": Andrew J. Glass, "Congressional Report/Mansfield Reforms
         Spark 'Quiet Revolution' in Senate," *National Journal*, 3/6/71.
         Conference could vote by secret ballot: Fred R. Harris, *Deadlock or Decision* (New
         York: Oxford University Press, 1993), p. 123.
406   South Vietnamese forces in Laos: What happened in the 1971 invasion of Laos, code-
         named Lamson 719, is still controversial. I have drawn my brief account from Harry G.
         Summers Jr., *Vietnam War Almanac* (New York: Facts on File, 1985), p. 224, and
         Karnow, *Vietnam*, pp. 629–631.
407   "an end to the involvement in Indochina . . .": "Statement of Senator Mike Mansfield
         on a Resolution of Majority Purpose Adopted by the Majority Policy Committee, U.S.
         Senate," 2/22/71, MMA, Series 22, Box 89, File 13.

407   "What better message . . ." and other quotations that follow: Minutes of the Senate Democratic Conference, 2/23/71, MMA, Series 22, Box 90, File 12.

408   Vote on Indochina provision: Memorandum, Kimmitt to Mansfield, 3/4/71, MMA, Series 22, Box 90, File 12.

409   "We have got to develop a line . . .": Nixon tapes, conversation 457-5, 2/24/71, Nixon Materials.
        March against the war: Zaroulis and Sullivan, *Who Spoke Up?*, pp. 358–359.
        "The tide of American public opinion . . .": Louis Harris, "Tide of Public Opinion Turns Decisively against the War," *WP,* 5/5/71.
        "Trust is like a thin thread": Quoted in Haldeman, *Diaries,* pp. 292–293.

410   "How possibly can you negotiate . . .": Nixon tapes, conversation 528-1, 6/23/71, Nixon Materials.
        "a basic ultimatum . . ." Quoted in Haldeman notes, 6/23/71, in Haldeman, *Diaries,* CD-ROM.
        "because they knew . . .": Nixon tapes, conversation 528-1, 6/23/71, Nixon Materials.
        "from here on . . .": Quoted in Haldeman notes, 6/23/71, in Haldeman, *Diaries,* CD-ROM.

411   "the purpose of the amendment . . .": Quoted in Olson, *Mansfield and Vietnam,* p. 227.
        "we have tried everything . . .": Senate speech, "Cambodia," *CR,* 10/19/71, p. S16388.

412   "are actively, unashamedly eager . . .": Joseph Alsop, "Undercutting the War," *WP,* 11/5/71.
        Second Mansfield amendment: Larry Berman, *No Peace, No Honor* (New York: Free Press, 2001), p. 83.
        Kissinger's secret offer to withdraw troops: Kissinger, *White House Years,* pp. 1034–1035.
        "It may be ignored, . . .": Quoted in Carroll Kilpatrick, "President to Ignore Viet Rider," *WP,* 11/18/71.
        U.S. military withdrawal within six months: Minutes of the Senate Democratic Conference, 1/25/72, MMA, Series 22, Box 90, File 12.

413   Mansfield's and Rogers's responses to Nixon broadcast: Nixon tapes, conversation 19-77, 1/25/72, Nixon Materials.
        "a long step forward": Senate speech, "The President's Proposals on Indochina," *CR,* 1/26/72, p. 1316.
        "Mansfield is good": Nixon tapes, conversation 658-3, 1/27/72, Nixon Materials.
        Mansfield-Nixon telephone conversation: Nixon tapes, conversation 19-134, 1/27/72, Nixon Materials.

414   "It's amazing . . .": Nixon tapes, conversation 318-39, 2/2/72, Nixon Materials.
        "our cease-fire is almost verbatim . . .": Nixon tapes, conversation 665-8, 2/3/72, Nixon Materials.

415   Nixon-Chou conversation: Memorandum of conversation, 2/23/72. Top Secret/Sensitive/Exclusively Eyes Only (declassified 1999), National Security Archive, copy in the possession of the author.

416   "I'd be delighted . . .": Nixon tapes, conversation 675-8, 2/29/72, Nixon Materials.
        President told leaders of invitation: Mansfield notes of meeting with Nixon, 2/29/72, Anne Mansfield Papers.
        "I worked that out . . .": Nixon tapes, conversation 20-117, 2/29/72, Nixon Materials.
        "I think you should know . . .": Nixon tapes, conversation 20-131, 2/29/72, Nixon Materials.
        "carried the water": Memorandum, Richard Cook to Nixon, "House Resentment over Mansfield-Scott Trip to PRC," 2/29/72, WHCF, EX FO 8, Box 71, 2/19/72, Nixon Materials.

417   "appropriate action": Quoted in "Albert Vexed by Lack of China Bid," *WP,* 3/2/72.
        "see if there's a way to screw Mansfield . . .": Nixon tapes, conversation 698-1, 2/29/72, Nixon Materials.

417   "a frantic exercise . . ." and "until all the legitimate witnesses . . ." Scott and
        Mansfield, respectively, quoted in Fred P. Graham, "Republican Senators Urge End to
        I.T.T. Hearings," *NYT,* 3/29/72.
        Nixon increasingly emotional: Nixon, *Memoirs,* p. 583; see also, Haldeman notes,
        3/29/72, in Haldeman, *Diaries,* CD-ROM.
418   Morning of March 29: The Nixon-Kissinger conversations that day concerning
        Mansfield's trip, Nixon tapes, conversation 696-1, 3/29/72, Nixon Materials.
419   "the little shit asses": Nixon tapes, conversation 697-2, 3/30/72, Nixon Materials.
        "we believe the congressmen . . .": Memorandum, Haig to Cook, "The Boggs-Ford
        Trip to China," 4/5/72, WHCF, EX FO 8 Box 71, 2/19/72, Nixon Materials.
420   "We must learn a lesson . . .": Quoted in C. L. Sulzberger, *Postscript with a Chinese
        Accent* (New York: Macmillan, 1974), p. 74.
        Nomination of Kleindienst: Spencer Rich, "Mansfield Says Kleindienst Foes Fail to
        Make Case, Asks Speedup," *WP,* 4/5/72.
        "Mike is a fellow . . .": Nixon tapes, conversation 133-26, 6/9/72.
        "has the approval . . .": Nixon tapes, conversation 329-26, 4/11/72, Nixon Materials.
        "There was a mutual respect": William Hildenbrand, Oral History, Senate Historical
        Office, pp. 132–133.
421   Democrats should keep their own counsel: Norvill Jones, interview, 8/17/99.
        Mansfield hoped to return alone: Memorandum of second substantive conversation
        with Premier Chou En-lai, 4/22/72, Salpee Sahagian Papers.
        "We were totally at the mercy . . .": Hildenbrand, Oral History, p. 162.
        Conversation at Great Hall: "Memorandum of Conversation with Chou En-lai prior
        to a Banquet Given in Their Honor by the Premier," 4/20/72, Salpee Sahagian Papers.
        Eight hours of conversation: "Memorandum of Second Substantive Conversation
        with Premier Chou En-lai," 4/22/72, Salpee Sahagian Papers.
422   Parting of the Red Sea: Salpee Sahagian, interview, 11/4/99.
        "if China is viewed . . .": Senate speech, "Journey to the New China," *CR,* 5/11/72, pp.
        17054–17059.
423   "with appreciation . . .": "Remarks of Senator Mike Mansfield at the Pan Chi
        Restaurant," 5/2/72, Salpee Sahagian Papers.
        "a vast revolutionary purification": Mansfield, "The People's Republic of China—
        1972: Transmitted for the Consideration of the President of the United States," report to
        the President, 5/8/72, p. 6 (declassified 2002), Nixon Materials.
424   "one vast cooperative barn-raising": James Reston, quoted in Harry Harding, *A
        Fragile Relationship* (Washington, D.C.: Brookings Institution, 1992), pp. 60–61.
        "No discernible signs of personal oppression . . .": Mansfield, "The People's Republic
        of China—1972," p. 3.
        "is a classless, controlled society; . . .": "Draft Report—Journey to the New China,"
        undated, Norvill Jones Papers.
        "the Chinese People's Republic . . .": "China Revisited: A New Era in Asia," remarks
        to the Glass Container Manufacturers Institute, Phoenix, Arizona, 10/26/72.
        "whatever transpires . . .": "The People's Republic of China—1972," pp. 24–25.
        North Vietnam's biggest military offensive: Harry G. Summers Jr., *Historical Atlas of
        the Vietnam War* (Boston: Houghton Mifflin, 1995), p. 174.
425   "Mansfield was convinced . . .": Hildenbrand, Oral History, p. 152.
        Nixon had decided: Kissinger, *White House Years,* pp. 1133–1136.
426   "a Constitutional . . .": William Safire, *Before the Fall* (New York: Doubleday, 1975), p. 422.
        "stony silence": Alexander M. Haig Jr., *Inner Circles* (New York: Warner Books,
        1992), p. 287.
        "How long ago . . ." and "As far as the extension is concerned, . . .": Mansfield and
        Laird quoted, respectively, in Safire, *Before the Fall,* p. 425.

426   "was mad . . .": George Aiken, *Senate Diary: January* 1972–*January* 1975 (Brattleboro, Vt.: Stephen Greene Press, 1976), p. 56.
        Discussion in Democratic caucus meeting: Minutes of Senate Democratic Conference, 5/9/72, MMA, Series 22, Box 90, File 12.
427   Mansfield discussion with reporters on caucus vote: *Facts on File* 32 (5/7–13/72): 342.
        "As far as I am concerned . . .": Senate speech, "The Situation in Vietnam," *CR,* 5/9/72, p. 16355.
428   "Son of a bitch . . .": Nixon tapes, conversation 189-1, 5/17/72, Nixon Materials.
        "We've just got to quit . . .": Nixon tapes, conversation 189-10, 5/17/72, Nixon Materials.
        "To hell with him. . . .": Nixon tapes, conversation 131-19, 5/17/72, Nixon Materials.
        Easter Offensive: Philip B. Davidson, *Vietnam at War* (Novato, Calif.: Presidio Press, 1988), pp. 701–705; Summers, *Historical Atlas of the Vietnam War,* p. 178.
429   "stone age strategy . . .": Senate speech, "Vietnam," *CR,* 1/6/73, p. 412.
        A pen from Rogers: Mansfield to Rogers, 4/9/73, MMA, Series 22, Box 12, File 57.
        "Let us hope . . .": Senate speech, "Peace in Vietnam," *CR,* 1/29/73, p. S1141.
430   "he couldn't have made . . .": Olson, *Mansfield and Vietnam,* p. 232.
        Mansfield-McGovern conversation: George McGovern, interview, 2/7/02; see also, McGovern, *Grassroots* (New York: Random House, 1977), pp. 212–213, 222.
431   "When Watergate jokes were going around, . . .": Quoted in Ludwick, "Mansfield: The Senator from Montana," special section of the *Missoulian,* 10/14/01, p. 26.
        "a massive campaign . . .": Carl Bernstein and Bob Woodward, "FBI Finds Nixon Aides Sabotaged Democrats," *WP,* 10/10/72.
432   "mandatory" for Senate to investigate Watergate affair: AP, "Mike Predicts Probe of Watergate," *Missoulian,* 10/30/72. Mansfield's recollection to me and to others was that he first made public his decision to mount an investigation in a speech in Missoula, rather than Helena, but, if so, it was not reported in the press.
        Spurious letters aimed at Democratic contenders: Mansfield interview, 10/8/98. In the interview, he mentioned only the campaigns of Humphrey and Jackson, but his 11/17/72 letter to Eastland mentioned Muskie, Jackson, "and others."
        "If a political candidate . . .": AP, "Mike Predicts Probe of Watergate."
        "was a constitutionalist, . . .": Mansfield interview, 10/8/98.
        Assignment of members to Watergate Committee: *Tributes to the Honorable Mike Mansfield of Montana in the United States Senate,* 94th Cong., 2d sess., S. Doc. 94-270, 9/16/76. Inouye's remarks appear on pp. 67–70; Talmadge's remarks on pp. 70–71.
433   "Ervin, for all his affected distraction . . ." and quotations from diary: Nixon, *Memoirs,* pp. 772–773.
        Mansfield commended Nixon: Senate speech, *CR,* 4/30/73, pp. 13466–13467.
        A week's recess: *CR,* 6/18/73, p. S11395.
434   "I am not surprised . . .": Quoted in Stanley I. Kutler, *The Wars of Watergate* (New York: Knopf, 1990), p. 386.
        "I have long believed . . .": Quoted in Don Schwennesen, "Mansfield Believes Nixon's Reassurances," *Missoulian,* 8/19/73.
435   "the balance of power is dangerously tilted . . .": "Notes and Comment," *New Yorker,* 4/23/73.
        Bombs dropped on Cambodia by U.S. warplanes: Arnold R. Isaacs, *Without Honor* (New York: Vintage Books, 1984), p. 217.
        Mansfield urged forbearance about bombing: "The Deteriorating Situation in Cambodia," *CR,* 4/18/73, p. 7682.
        Democratic caucus calls for ban on funds: "Action of Democratic Conference on May 2, 1973," *CR,* 5/3/73, pp. S8232–S8234.
        "a constitutional impasse . . .": Senate speech, "The President's Veto of the Urgent Second Supplemental Appropriation," *CR,* 6/27/73, pp. 21618–21619.

436   Mansfield would close down the government: William Bundy, *A Tangled Web* (New York: Hill and Wang, 1998), p. 389.
        "this abandonment of a friend . . .": Nixon to Mansfield, 8/3/73, WHCF, Subject Files, CO, EX CO 26—Cambodia, Nixon Materials.
437   "we want no more Vietnams": Quoted in Nixon, *Memoirs,* p. 924.
        "there is one fellow . . .": Quoted in Haig, *Inner Circles,* p. 367.
438   Choice of Ford: There are conflicting versions of this exchange. Nixon in his memoir (p. 925) said he proposed Ford as a possible vice president and Mansfield did not object but merely puffed on his pipe. The version here, which appears to me to be more believable, is from Jimmy Cannon, who was a senior aide to Ford and Nelson Rockefeller, in a broadcast and an essay on the Web site of Public Broadcasting's *News Hour,* www.pbs.org/newshour/character/essays/ford/html.
        President would fight impeachment and not resign: Minutes of Senate Democratic Conference, 1/24/74, MMA, Series 22, Box 91, File 1.
439   "Resignation is not the answer, . . .": Senate speech, *CR,* 5/13/74, pp. 14198–14199.
        "The constitutional process . . .": Quoted in David E. Rosenbaum, "Senators Unable to Agree on Any Move over Nixon," *NYT,* 8/8/74.
        "that despite our domestic difficulties, . . ." and "expressed their concern": Mansfield and Scott, respectively, Senate speeches, "Bipartisan Foreign Policy," *CR,* 8/7/74, p. 27083.
440   Vote of impeachment by August 22: "Joint Congressional Leadership Meeting in the Speaker's Office," 8/8/74, MMA, Series 22, Box 117, File 7.
        "moving very rapidly": Remarks of Senator Mike Mansfield before the Senate Democratic Conference, 8/8/74, MMA, Series 22, Box 93, File 50.
        "I told them . . .": Nixon, *Memoirs,* p. 1081.
441   "Ford was himself . . .": Mansfield, interview, 10/10/00.
        "a loyal Democrat . . .": Gerald Ford, interview by Missoula Children's Theatre, 9/7/90.
        Ford's son as Senate page: Ludwick, "Mansfield: The Senator from Montana," p. 14.
442   "with the respect . . .": Hildenbrand, Oral History, p. 226.
        "faced up to his responsibility . . .": "Equal Justice under the Law?" *CR,* 9/9/74, pp. 30418–30419.
443   "I had thought that we had left Vietnam . . .": Senate speech, *CR,* 1/21/75, p. 846.
        "At this late date . . .": Senate speech, "The Situation in Southeast Asia," *CR,* 4/15/75, pp. S5931–S5932.
444   "A tragic episode . . .": Senate speech, "When the President and Congress Cooperate," *CR,* 4/30/75, p. 12482.
        "In this he has the concurrence of the premier . . .": Senate speech, "Cambodia," *CR,* 3/10/75, pp. S3532–S3533.
        "10% of Cambodians killed . . .": Mansfield, handwritten notes, undated, MMA, Series 22, Box 115, File 1.
        "Phnom Penh is more anxious . . .": Valeo, "Note for the files," 3/11/75, MMA, Series 22, Box 115, File 1.
445   Preconditions for mission: Valeo to Mansfield, "Suggested Preconditions for an Intercession with Prince Sihanouk in Peking," undated, MMA, Series 22, Box 115, File 1.
        Ford ordered telephone calls: "The War Powers Resolution," undated, Committee Print of House Foreign Affairs Committee, pp. 208–212.
        Ford's briefing of congressional leaders: "Memorandum of Conversation," 5/14/75, National Security Adviser Files, Memcons, Box 11, Gerald R. Ford Library, Ann Arbor, Michigan.
446   Mansfield-Ford telephone call: Mansfield interview, 10/10/00.
        Gallup Poll results: Richard G. Head, Frisco W. Short, and Robert C. McFarlane, *Crisis Resolution: Presidential Decision Making in the* Mayaguez *and Korean*

Confrontations (Boulder, Colo.: Westview Press, 1978), p. 147.

446   "a domestic and foreign triumph": Quoted in Head, Short, and McFarlane, *Crisis Resolution*, p. 141.

Plan to return to China: Telcon (San Clemente) Mansfield/Kissinger, transcript of telephone call, 7/5/72, NSC Files, Box 994, Haig Chron, 7/19–26/72, Nixon Materials.

Kissinger urged Chinese to cooperate: Memoranda of conversation, Kissinger and Ambassador Huang Hua, 7/26/72, 8/26, 9/8, and 10/3/72, RG 59, Records of Policy Planning Staff (Director's Files), 1962–1977, Box 327, China Exchanges, 7/26–10/17/72, NA.

"a most emphatic demonstration . . .": Memorandum, Staff Secretary to Kissinger, 3/2/73, WHCF, Subject Files—FO, EX FO 8, Box 73, 3/2/73, Nixon Materials.

447   Nixon "would do his best": Mansfield memorandum for files, "Meeting at the White House with President Nixon," 4/9/73, MMA, Series 22, Box 103, File 5.

Chinese invitation: Mansfield to Ford, 10/17/74, WHCF, FO 8, Foreign Travel, 10/9/74–10/22/74, Box 35, Ford Library.

President officially approves trip to China: Jerry Jones to William Timmons, 10/18/74, WHCF, FO 8, Foreign Travel, 10/9/74–10/22/74, Box 35, Ford Library.

Chou's health: Dick Wilson, *Zhou Enlai* (New York: Viking, 1984), pp. 286–290.

Chou meeting: Mansfield interviews, 8/28/98 and 3/16/99.

448   "The door between our two countries . . ." and "a buoyant . . .": Quoted in Mansfield's notes, "Chou En lai," 12/12/74, "Hospital," Anne Mansfield Papers.

"a vast nation . . .": Don Oberdorfer, "China: 'Change of Pace,'" *WP,* 12/2/74.

Mansfield-Deng discussion: U.S. Liaison Office Peking to Secstate Washington, "Senator Mansfield's Discussion of World Issues with Vice Premier Teng Hsiao-ping," 12/17/74, Secret (declassified 2001), Presidential Country Files for East Asia and Pacific, Box 15, PRC-State Telegrams, Ford Library.

449   "China's political system . . .": Mike Mansfield, *China: A Quarter Century after the Founding of the People's Republic,* report to the Senate Foreign Relations Committee, 94th Cong., 1st sess., Jan. 1975.

"More confident than ever, . . .": Mansfield, "Chinese Impressions" (handwritten), 1974, no month or day, Salpee Sahagian Papers.

"I got smiles . . .": Salpee Sahagian, interview, 11/4/99.

"the absence of any critical analysis . . .": Michael Lindsay, "Lord Lindsay Answers Senator Mansfield," *Free China Review,* Aug. 1975, MMA, Series 22, Box 112, File 14.

450   "greater degree of knowledge . . .": Mansfield interview, 3/16/99.

Mansfield not inclined to believe Jiang ouster: Donald Anderson, interview, 2/3/99.

451   "it would appear that we remain enmeshed in Taiwan . . .": Mike Mansfield, *China after Mao: Report to the President on a Third Mission to the People's Republic of China,* 10/26/76, Anne Mansfield Papers.

"The national interest is deeply involved, . . .": Mike Mansfield, *China Enters the Post-Mao Era,* report to the Senate Foreign Relations Committee, 11/22/76.

452   "The place . . ." and "There will always be others . . .": Scott and Mansfield, respectively, quoted in "A Time to Go," *Newsweek,* 3/15/76.

"one-sixth of the nation's history . . ." and all other quotations from speeches on 3/4/76: *Tributes to the Honorable Mike Mansfield of Montana in the United States Senate,* 94th Cong., 2d sess., S. Doc. 94-270, 1976.

453   "Other majority leaders, . . .": "Mansfield Steps Down," *Time,* 3/15/76.

"Seldom has a less flamboyant figure . . .": Sam Shaffer, "A Time to Go," *Newsweek,* 3/15/76.

454   "This is not primarily a political loss, . . .": James Reston, "Say It Ain't So, Mike," *NYT,* 3/5/76.

"more effective virtuoso style": "Mike Mansfield's Retirement," *WP,* 3/12/76.

454   "increasingly democratized . . .": Richard E. Cohen, "Marking an End to the Senate's Mansfield Era," *National Journal*, 12/25/76.

     "Much criticism of the modern Senate . . .": Ross K. Baker, "Mike Mansfield and the Birth of the Modern Senate," in Baker and Davidson, *First among Equals*, p. 293.

455   Walked from the chamber: Austin Scott, "Colleagues Hail Mansfield on His Last Day on Hill," *WP,* 9/17/76.

     Sat in rear seat: Martha Angle, "Mansfield Bids Colleagues Simple, Eloquent Goodby," *Washington Star,* 9/17/76; see also, Austin Scott, "Colleagues Hail Mansfield on His Last Day on Hill," *WP,* 9/17/76.

13. AMBASSADOR TO JAPAN

457   "loaf, think and read" and "We will be free . . .": Mike and Maureen Mansfield, respectively, quoted in Katherine Hardin, "For Mike, It's Soon Time to 'Loaf, Think and Read,'" *Helena Independent Record,* 10/30/76.

458   U.S. ambassador to China: "A Post for Mike Mansfield," *Baltimore Sun,* 11/15/76.

     Byrd recommendations: "Byrd Urges President to Appoint Mansfield to Head China Mission," *NYT,* 1/27/77.

     Carter asked Mansfield to serve as ambassador: Jimmy Carter, interview, 4/4/99.

     "As I said to you, . . .": Mansfield to Carter, 3/10/77, *JCL,* WHCF, FO 46. Thanks to Greg Olson for this material.

     Proposal to appoint Mansfield ambassador to Japan: Richard Holbrooke, interview, 4/20/99.

459   Considered senior counselor about Asia: Jimmy Carter, interview, 4/14/99.

     Learned about Japan in 1930s from Kawai: Mansfield interview, 2/28/2000.

     Service on Enemy Alien Hearing Board: Mansfield interview, 10/20/99. See also, "Procedure of Japanese Hearings Being Conducted at Fort Missoula," *Missoulian,* 2/15/42. Prof. Carol VanValkenburg of the University of Montana was particularly helpful in examining this issue and Mansfield's role.

     Supportive of democratization of Japan: Mansfield speech to Foreign Policy Association, New York, 1947, Salpee Sahagian Papers.

     "the key to war . . .": "Senator Urges More Attention to Japan," *Japan News,* Tokyo, 3/30/55.

460   "must literally fish and trade . . .": United Press, "Mansfield Urges Restudy of Program toward Japan," *Mainichi,* 7/13/56.

     Shimoda Conference: Speech, "U.S.-Japanese Relations: Properties, Problems, and Prospects," 9/15/67, Salpee Sahagian Papers.

     Military importance of Bonin Islands: "Talking Points for Senator Mansfield," Department of State, 8/31/67, National Security Archive, Washington, D.C.

     Return of Bonin Islands: "Rusk Throws Cold Water on Mansfield's Suggestion," *Mainichi,* 9/17/67.

     Return of Okinawa to Japan: Yukio Satoh, interview, 1/30/99.

461   "U.S.-Japan relations are good . . .": "The End of the Postwar Era: Time for a New Partnership of Equality with Japan," report to Senate Foreign Relations Committee, 94th Cong., 2d sess., Aug. 1976, p. 13.

     Seven brief notes: Carter notes on meeting with Mansfield, 5/24/77, Office of Staff Secretary, Handwriting File, Box 26, JCL. For details of the positions Carter espoused, see Brzezinski to Carter, "Talking Points for Your Meeting with Mike Mansfield, Tuesday, May 24,1977, at 2:30 p.m." Confidential (declassified 1998), National Security Council file, Name file: "Mansfield, Sen. Mike, 5/77," JCL.

462   Carter and the reprocessing report: William Sherman, interview, 9/16/98.

463   "We are in a genuine bind": Armacost to Brzezinski, "Japan and the Nuclear Reprocessing Issue," 4/18/77, Secret/Sensitive (declassified 1999), Brzezinski Materials.

463   "enormously weaken": Brzezinski to Carter, "Conversations with Fukuda in London,"
       undated [early May 1977], Secret (declassified 1997), Brzezinski Materials.
       Carter had given tentative approval: Brzezinski to Carter, "Japanese Nuclear Talks—
       Negotiating Guidance," 5/31/77, Confidential (declassified 1997), Brzezinski Materials.
       Changes would cost and delay: "Report of the Joint U.S.-Japanese Study Team on
       Scheduled and Alternative Modes for Operating the Tokai Reprocessing Facility," July
       1977, Confidential (declassified 1999), Brzezinski Materials.
       Japanese likely to resist: Brzezinski to Carter, "Japanese Nuclear Talks—Negotiating
       Guidance," 5/31/77, Brzezinski Materials.
464   Signing of cable to Vance: Justin Bloom, interview, 2/4/00.
       "I have been at this post . . .": Cable, Mansfield to Vance, "The Reprocessing Issue
       and Future U.S.-Japan Relations," 7/12/77, Confidential (declassified 1999), Brzezinski
       Materials.
465   "The President feels . . .": Brzezinski to Vance, 7/12/77, Brzezinski Materials.
       "a very critical element": Michael Armacost, interview, 2/7/00.
       "I believe we can find a compromise . . .": Carter to Fukuda, 7/15/77, Confidential
       (declassified 1999), Brzezinski Materials.
       Meeting with Fukuda: Mansfield to Vance, "Effect of Nuclear Reprocessing Issue on
       U.S. Relations with Japan," 7/15/77, Secret (declassified 1999); copy supplied to author
       by Department of State under the Freedom of Information Act (FOIA).
       "very serious blow": Jessica Tuchman Mathews, interview, 1/20/03.
       "turnabout": William Chapman, "U.S.-Japan A-Plant Agreement Seen as Turnabout
       by Carter," WP, 9/2/77.
       "Fukuda and the entire government . . .": Sam Jameson, interview, 1/8/00.
466   "Sometimes I think . . .": Quoted in David S. Broder, "Mike Mansfield's 'New
       Career,' WP, 10/5/77.
       "Big bushes, . . .": Quoted in a pamphlet by Jonathan R. McHale, A History of the
       American Ambassador's Residence in Tokyo, U.S. Embassy Tokyo, 1995.
467   "He was an American . . .": Thomas Foley, interview, 11/18/98.
       "He didn't hesitate . . .": Kimpei Shiba, "Japan: Today and Yesterday," Asahi Evening
       News, 2/29/80.
       "If Lee Iacocca . . .": Quoted in Clyde Haberman, "Mike Mansfield: Mild-mannered
       Diplomat Went Calling on Japan a Decade Ago," Great Falls Tribune, 12/7/86.
       "not quite as difficult . . .": John Needham, UPI Audio, "Interview with Ambassador
       Mansfield," 8/13/80, MMA, Oral History 022-277.
468   "Maureen had no intention . . .": William Sherman, interview, 9/16/98.
       "Maureen spends all her time . . .": Quoted in Keyes Beech, "Mansfield 'Super
       Bigwig' to Japanese," Sunday Oregonian, 10/2/77.
       Limit on invitees: William Sherman, interview, 9/16/98.
       Appeal for more social funds: Memorandum of conversation, Mansfield and Carter,
       10/27/78, Secret (declassified 1999), Subject File (Japan), Box 36-38, Brzezinski Materials.
       "We went through . . ." and other recollections of receptions: Dan Russel, tape-
       recorded recollections, in the possession of the author.
469   Sambo story: See McHale, A History.
       First formal press conference: "Mansfield Mystifies Japanese," NYT, 6/16/77.
470   "100 cents": Sam Jameson, "Mike Mansfield: Head High and Arms Swinging," Asia
       Perspectives, Aug. 2000, p. 6.
       Embassy the largest overseas diplomatic establishment: Andrew H. Malcolm, "Mike
       Mansfield, the Ambassador, Doesn't Miss Senate 'One Bit,'" NYT, 9/15/77.
       "He liked people to speak . . .": Rust Deming, interview, 7/28/98.
       Recounting of incident with Embassy official: Malcolm, "Mike Mansfield, the
       Ambassador," NYT, 9/15/77.

470   Mansfield known to walk: William Clark, interview, 8/29/98.
Visitors to office: Dan Russel, tape-recorded recollections.

471   Story of Japanese academic's wife and "I hoped that by my pouring coffee, . . ." Mansfield interview, 10/29/98.
Visits to prefectures: "Ambassador Mansfield Sees All of Japan 'with His Own Eyes,'" *Sankei Shimbun, Kanagawa* edition (Embassy translation), 9/11/80.
"She enjoyed it . . .": Donald Westmore, interview, 12/30/99.
Sonoda-Mansfield friendship: Yukio Satoh, interview, 1/30/99, and Lewis M. Simons, "Mansfield Holds Respect of Americans, Japanese alike," 4/15/84.

472   "Ambassador Mansfield loved the United States . . .": Sunao Sonoda, *The World, Japan, Love* (Tokyo: Dai-san Seikei Kenkyuukai, 1981).
Relationship with Akihito: Mansfield interview, 1/27/02.
Crown Prince and Princess's trip to United States: Don Oberdorfer and Donnie Radcliffe, "Rallying Round Royalty," *WP,* 10/7/87.
Informal dinner for royal couple: Notations on 9/14/88 dinner in Japan scrapbook, Anne Mansfield Papers.

473   "On reaching 80 years . . .": Quoted in "Happy Birthday, Mike!" *Asahi Evening News,* 3/17/83.
"my personal representative": Carter to Mansfield, 10/25/77, WHCF, Name File: "Mike Mansfield," JCL.

474   Serving "under" a president: Mansfield, interview by Clyde Haberman, *NYT* correspondent, 8/8/86, p. 13, text in the possession of the author.
"My prayers and my hopes . . ." Mansfield to Carter, 12/19/77, WHCF, Subject File: "Public Relations," Box PR 10, JCL. Another example is a handwritten letter from Mansfield to Carter on 6/9/78 after the President's speech at Annapolis on policy toward the Soviet Union, WHCF, Subject File: "Speeches," Box SP 22, JCL.
"It is important . . .": Typewritten note on unmarked stationery, "Pres. and Strauss from Mike Mansfield," 3/7/78, WHCF, Subject File: "Countries," CO 78, Box CO-37, JCL.

475   "increasingly contentious atmosphere": Cable, Mansfield to Holbrooke and Vance, "State of the Relationship," 11/9/77, Confidential (declassified 1999), Brzezinski Materials.
"as usual . . . registers . . .": Memorandum, Armacost to Brzezinski, "Embassy Tokyo's Appraisal of the State of the U.S.-Japan Relationship," 11/9/77, Confidential (declassified 1997), Brzezinski Materials.
"eminently sensible points": Memorandum, Brzezinski to Carter, "The Trade Issue in Our Relations with Japan," undated, Confidential (declassified 1997), Brzezinski Materials.
Toughing of stand made headlines: William Chapman, "U.S., Japan in Trade Row," *WP,* 11/19/77.

476   "It is barely possible . . .": Memorandum, Owen to Carter, "Japan," 12/2/77, Secret (declassified 1999), Brzezinski Materials.
Private appointment with President: Mansfield to Carter 12/19/77, and Carter to Mansfield, 1/11/78, WHCF, Subject File: "Public Relations," Box PR 10, JCL.
"two separate issues . . .": Mansfield interview, 10/8/98.

477   "never seen such a transformation": Brent Scowcroft, interview, 11/14/02.
Forced Carter to drop plans: For an account of the battle over Carter's withdrawal plan, see Don Oberdorfer, *The Two Koreas: A Contemporary History* (New York: Basic Books, 2001), pp. 84–108.
"it would be helpful . . .": Memorandum of conversation, Carter and Mansfield, 2/7/78, Confidential (declassified 2001), National Security Affairs, Subject File: "Far East," Box 6, JCL.
"understand that the attention we paid East Asia . . .": Cable, Mansfield to Carter, 2/16/78, Secret (declassified 1999), Brzezinski Materials.

477   Meeting at White House on 10/27/78: Platt to Brzezinski, "Memorandum of
       Conversation between President Carter and Ambassador Mansfield," 10/31/78, Secret
       (declassified 1999), Brzezinski Materials.
478   Brzezinski and Deng: Patrick Tyler, *A Great Wall* (New York: Public Affairs, 1999), pp.
       253–258.
479   "the first rule . . .": David S. Broder, "Mike Mansfield's New Career," *WP,* 10/5/77.
       "Tell them I am busy, . . .": Quoted by Thomas Foley, interview, 11/18/98.
480   Met governors in Tokyo: Memorandum, Dan Russel to Mansfield, 11/26/86, in the
       possession of the author.
       "I am satisfied . . .": Mansfield to Jones, 8/2/78, MMA, Series 31, Box 1, File 5.
       "it strikes me as a bit out of order . . .": Mansfield to Muskie (in archives as a letter
       even though apparently sent as a cable), 6/8/78, MMA, Series 31, Box 2, File 2.
       Pillsbury fired: Muskie to Mansfield, 7/13/78, MMA, Series 31, Box 2, File 2.
       "a nice enough fellow": Mansfield interview, 10/22/98.
481   "I would like to have . . .": Quoted in William D. James, "Mike Mansfield Is Really
       on the Job for U.S. in Japan," *Great Falls Tribune,* 6/15/80.
       Decision to retire made public: "Mansfield to Retire in Jan.: Spokesman," *Japan
       Times,* 6/17/80.
       Reagan-Mansfield meeting in April 1978: My account of the meeting is taken from
       the reports of two of Reagan's aides who were present, Richard V. Allen (interview,
       10/27/99) and Peter Hannaford (*The Reagans: A Political Portrait* [New York: Coward-
       McCann, 1983]).
483   "Mansfield replied . . .": Howard Simons and William Chapman, "Mansfield Earns
       Respect as Tokyo Envoy," *WP,* 11/28/80.
       Recommendations to Reagan: For Jackson, Mansfield interview, 8/18/99; Glenn, tele-
       phone interview, 3/24/03; Nunn, telephone call from his office, 3/28/03.
       "I did so because he had done a fine job . . .": Gerald Ford to author, 11/24/98.
       "I wanted about six months . . .": Mansfield interview, 8/28/98.
       Motivation was to speed Senate confirmation: Tom Korologos, interview, 3/5/02.
484   "delivered the *coup de maître* . . ." and "It was Haig's idea, . . .": Byrd and Cranston, respec-
       tively, quoted in "Reagan Woos Democrats with a 'Master Stroke,'" *Miami Herald,* 1/8/81.
       Decision to retain Mansfield hailed: Henry Scott Stokes, "Japanese are Pleased to See
       Mansfield Stay as U.S. Ambassador," *NYT,* 1/9/81.
       Plight of auto industry: Stephen D. Cohen, "The Route to Japan's Voluntary Export
       Restraints on Automobiles: An Analysis of the U.S. Government's Decision-Making
       Process in 1981," research paper, in the possession of the author.
       Fraser's boycott threat: Sam Jameson, e-mail to author, 2/20/03.
485   "I hope the big Japanese companies . . .": Mansfield, quoted in Eduardo Lachica,
       "U.S. Is Putting More Pressure on Japan to Locate Car-Making Plants in America,"
       Wall Street Journal, 1/29/80.
       "Japan will play its part . . .": Cable, Mansfield to Reagan and Haig, "U.S. Policy
       toward Japan," 1/26/81, Confidential (declassified 1999), copy obtained by author from
       State Department under FOIA.
       Account of presidential meeting on 3/19/81: Laurence I. Barrett, *Gambling with
       History* (Garden City, N.Y.: Doubleday, 1983), pp. 90–93.
       Japan's "voluntary" limit on imports: Lou Cannon, *Reagan* (New York: Putnam,
       1982), pp. 383–384.
       "Bad policy. . . .": Cable, Haig to Mansfield, "Message to the President," 10/27/81,
       Secret, MMA, Series 24, Scrapbook 235B.
       "if the senator . . .": Quoted by William Clark, interview, 8/29/98.
       Formation of Self-Defense Forces: John K. Emmerson, *Arms, Yen, and Power* (Tokyo:
       Tuttle, 1972), pp. 40–55.

487   "It behooves us to be very cautious . . .": "The End of the Postwar Era: Time for a
New Partnership of Equality with Japan," report to the Senate Foreign Relations
Committee, 94th Cong., 2d Sess., Aug. 1976, pp. 7–8.
        "we do not envision an expanded Japanese military . . .": Memorandum, Brzezinski to
Carter, "Talking Points for Your Meeting with Mike Mansfield, Tuesday, May 24, 1977,
at 2:30 p.m.," Confidential (declassified 1998), NSC File, Name File: "Mansfield, Sen.
Mike," May 1977, JCL.
488   Japan's steady increases in military spending: "Mansfield Satisfied with Japan Defense
Plan," *Daily Yomiuri,* 3/14/80.
        "There was a sense that Mansfield . . .": Nicholas Platt, interview, 10/1/99.
        "We, of course, agree with neither the data . . .": Memorandum, Platt to Komer,
"The New Math on Japanese Defense Spending," 3/24/80, Confidential (declassified
1996), National Security Archive, Washington, D.C.
        "Amb. Mansfield's defensiveness . . .": Memorandum, Komer to Brown, "For
Secdef—Info," 3/28/80, Confidential (declassifield 1996), National Security Archive,
Washington, D.C.
        "Yes, we *are* sending confusing signals, . . .": Memorandum (with attachment),
Komer to Brown. "For Secdef—Info," 8/2/80, Document from National Security
Archive, Washington, D.C.
489   "re-focus our defense discussions . . .": Cable, Mansfield to Reagan and Haig, "U.S.
Policy toward Japan," 1/26/81, Secret (declassified 1999), copy obtained by author from
State Department under FOIA.
        Weinberger had been advocating: Richard Allen, interview, 10/27/99.
        "the approach that I favored . . .": Caspar W. Weinberger, *Fighting for Peace* (New
York: Warner Books, 1990), p. 223.
        Details of the *Nissho Maru* accident and quotations from the investigative report:
Chief of Naval Operations, "Formal Investigation to Inquire into the Circumstances
surrounding the Collision of USS *George* Washington (SSBN-598) and MV *Nissho
Maru* on 9 April 1981," 8/12/81, Secret (declassified 1999), final report of the U.S. Navy's
investigation, copy provided to author in 1999 under FOIA.
490   Wept when informed of accident: Minoru Tamba, interview, 12/7/98.
        "have become a major public issue . . .": William Chapman, "Japanese Official
Skeptical of U.S. Details of Collision," *WP,* 4/14/81.
        "we have to apologize . . .": Quoted by William Clark, interview, 8/29/98.
        "expression of regret": William Chapman, "U.S. Tries to Calm Japan on Sinking of
Freighter," *WP,* 4/19/81.
        Did not know freighter had sunk: Henry Scott Stokes, "U.S. Navy Report on
Collision Denounced in Japan," *NYT,* 5/7/81.
491   Conversation between Mansfield and Clark: William Clark, interview, 8/28/98.
        "The cameras got it. . . .": Mansfield interview, 8/28/98.
        Bowed as deeply as he could: Mansfield interview, 7/31/98.
        "He is a rare diplomat . . .": "An Old Japanese Custom," *Newsweek,* 9/14/81.
        Americans complained he had "kowtowed": Associated Press, "From Montana to
Japan, He's Spanning 80 Years and Still Setting Goals," *Great Falls Tribune,* 3/16/83.
492   "I thought it was the least . . .": Mansfield interview, 4/9/99.
        Nakasone an outstanding leader: Mansfield interview, 7/20/01.
        Informal list of "sexy men": Katharine Graham, *Personal History* (New York: Knopf,
1997), p. 373.
493   "He was the only U.S. ambassador . . .": Kazutoshi Hasegawa, interview, 11/16/98.
        "I found the Prime Minister . . .": Cable, Mansfield to Secstate, "Ambassador
Mansfield's Initial Call on Prime Minister Nakasone," 11/30/82, Confidential (declassified 1999), copy supplied to author by State Department under FOIA.

493   "very straightforward, . . .": Yasuhiro Nakasone, interview, 11/16/98.

494   Defense account increased: Henry Scott Stokes, "U.S. Will Continue to Press Japan on Defense," *NYT,* 1/9/83.

Defense spending 0.98: George P. Shultz, *Turmoil and Triumph* (New York: Scribner's, 1993), p. 180.

495   Exaggerated translation: Don Oberdorfer, "How to Make a Japanese Brouhaha," *WP,* 3/20/83.

"blitzkrieg shock": Yasuhiro Nakasone, interview, 11/16/98.

"There was some enmity . . .": Kazutoshi Hasegawa, interview, 11/16/98.

U.S. deficit in trade with Japanese: Richard Holbrooke, interview, 4/20/99.

Trade imbalance figures: U.S. Census Bureau Web site, ww.census.gov/foreign-trade/balance/c5880.html.

Japan's share of output of goods and services: Jeffrey E. Garten, *A Cold Peace* (New York: Times Books, 1992), p. 9.

"Japan is fast becoming . . .": Soros quoted in pamphlet by Don Oberdorfer, *The Changing Context of U.S.-Japan Relations,* distributed by Japan Society and America-Japan Society, Mar. 1998, pp. 13–14.

496   "At first nobody believed it, . . .": Takakazu Kuriyama, interview, 11/11/98.

"That a greater degree of understanding developed . . .": Mansfield interview, 3/16/99.

"It's easy to blame the Japanese . . .": Quoted in Ronald E. Yates, "The Mansfield Era," *Mainichi Daily News,* 12/28/88.

"Japan must open its markets . . ." Cable, Mansfield to Shultz, "Call on Foreign Minister Abe," 9/21/85, Confidential (declassified 1999), copy supplied to author by Department of State under FOIA.

497   "neither the ambassador . . .": Clyde V. Prestowitz Jr., *Trading Places* (New York: Basic Books, 1988), p. 270.

"For me, the centerpiece . . .": Shultz, *Turmoil and Triumph,* pp. 173–174.

498   "He went to the globe. . . .": George P. Shultz, dedication of George P. Shultz Foreign Service Institute, 5/20/02, DOS Web site: State.Gov.

"I like the old guy": Quoted by Thomas Foley, interview, 11/18/98.

"Mansfield gave one of those amazing, . . .": Lionel Olmer, interview, 2/27/99.

"a virtuoso performance, . . .": Jim Kelly, telephone interview, 8/16/99.

499   Broken record: Shinji Ito, "Mansfield Marks 10 Years as Japan's Link to U.S.," *Japan Times,* 6/11/87.

"Nakasone has issued a number of statements, . . .": Quoted in Margaret Shapiro, "Nakasone Leaves Office with Unusual Legacy," *WP,* 10/31/87.

Tree plantings: Yasuhiro Nakasone, interview, 11/16/98.

500   "There was an awful lot of feeling . . .": Mansfield interview, 11/20/2000.

White House ceremony for service to government: "Mansfield Returns," *NYT,* 3/3/88.

"But the opinions remain clear as glass . . ."Clyde Haberman, "Mansfield, 85, Back in Tokyo for the Finale," *NYT,* 4/5/88.

501   "it is time for us to go": Cable, Mansfield to Shultz, "Message to Secretary from the Ambassador," 11/12/88, Confidential (declassified 1999), copy supplied to author by Department of State under FOIA.

"subject to the will . . .": "Ambassador Michael J. Mansfield's Final Press Conference at the American Embassy," Press Office, U.S. Information Service, U.S. Embassy, Tokyo, 11/14/88.

An extraordinary display: Sam Jameson, interview, 1/8/00, except as noted.

"The Japanese have come upon the world scene . . .": "Ambassador Michael J. Mansfield's Final Press Conference."

502   Presidential Medal of Freedom: "Reagan Awards Medal of Freedom to Shultz, Mansfield," U.S. Information Agency news service, 1/19/89.

502   Japan's highest civilian award: Robert F. Holden, "Mansfield Gets Japan's Highest Civilian Award," U.S. Information Agency news service, 2/2/89.

14. THE FINAL YEARS

503   "I thought he was crazy, . . .": Mansfield interview, 9/9/99.

504   "It was the rough equivalent . . .": Henry James, telephone interview, 10/24/01.

"Are they good people?": Quoted by Stanley Kimmitt, interview, 6/10/02.

"Not too much, . . .": Mansfield, interview by Jim Ludwick, then of the *Missoulian,* 6/213/95, in the possession of the author.

"I've seen too many retired senators . . .": Quoted in Walter R. Mears, "Mansfield Reflects on Career as Senator, Japan Ambassador," *Asahi Evening News,* 4/7/89.

505   "I'm not going to celebrate it. . . .": Quoted in David S. Broder and Don Oberdorfer, "Mike Mansfield, Without Fuss," *WP,* 3/16/93.

"He probably would have opposed it. . .": Tom Kotynski, "'Montana is where my heart is,'" *Great Falls Tribune,* 4/26/92.

"Just as other nations . . .": Quoted in "Senator Mike Mansfield Recipient of the 1990 Sylvanus Thayer Award," *Assembly* (West Point), Jan. 1991.

506   "the feeling of friendliness . . .": Mansfield, interview by Jim Ludwick, then of the *Missoulian,* 6/213/95, in the possession of the author.

Speech on leadership in the Senate: "'The Leaders Lecture Series'—Remarks of Senator Mike Mansfield," *CR,* 3/25/98, pp. S2564-2567.

507   "My darling Mike": Maureen to Mike Mansfield, 3/15/98, Anne Mansfield Papers.

508   "The nicest thing . . .": Quoted in Elaine Woo, "Maureen Mansfield; Wife Inspired Former Senate Majority Leader," *Los Angeles Times,* 9/25/00.

"If me alone, . . .": Mansfield interview, 3/10/99.

"She sat in the shadow": Mansfield, eulogy for Maureen Mansfield, 9/26/00, in the possession of the author.

509   "nobody thought he'd be a candidate . . .": Dr. William Gilliland, telephone interview, 10/25/01.

Did not fear death: Dr. Gilliland, telephone interview, 10/25/01.

INDEX

Newhouse, John, 153

Ne Win, 363–4

New Zealand, 290, 459

Ngo Dinh Diem: assassination of, 117, 139, 151, 196, 200, 201, 215; biography of, 116–7; Buddhist temple attacks, 196, 200; character traits, 120–21, 131–2, 189; military aid, 184–5; overthrow of, 117, 135–9, 141, 151, 200, 215; President, 141; press, 189, 191; Prime Minister, 117, 118; religion, 116–20, 133; support for, 77, 105, 107, 115, 117–21, 128–42, 150, 188–93, 196, 198, 200–1, 295; U.S. visit, 117–8, 141

Ngo Dinh Luyen, 150

Ngo Dinh Nhu, 138, 189–93, 196, 200–1, 215

Nguyen Cao Ky, 277, 295, 304

Nguyen Khanh, 238, 243

Nguyen Van Hinh, 120

Nguyen Van Thieu, 277, 295, 304, 355–6, 413, 429

Nixon, Richard: Acheson, 389; antiballistic missile system, 354, 368; antiwar protests, 313, 370; Asia, leadership, 356–7; breakfast meetings with, 350–51; Bush, 400; Cambodia, 359–60, 366–7, 375–7; China, 3, 127, 350, 360–63, 391–404, 414–24, 446–7; communism stance, 149–50, 349; Congressional activities, 349; domestic policy, 354, 368; Ervin, 433; foreign policy, 142, 352, 371–81, 439–40; Guam Doctrine, 356–7; impeachment of, 432–3, 438–9; Japan, 460–61; Laos, 406–7, 409; on Mansfield, 352–3, 387, 418, 428, 433; NATO, 3, 311, 387–91; pardon of, 442, 455; presidential campaigns, 101, 149–50, 331, 346, 348–50, 389, 429; press, 397–8; resignation of, 3, 352–3, 404–5, 432–3, 438–41; Rockefeller, 401–2; Romania, 394; Scott, 396–7; Taiwan, 451; taping by, 392, 402, 404, 437–9; taxes, 354, 368; on trust, 409; Vice President, 349, 437–8; Vietnam, 3, 313, 350, 352, 354–6, 371–4, 404, 408–13, 424–6; Yom Kippur war, 436–7

Noboru Takeshita, 492, 502

Nolting, Frederick "Fritz," 190, 192, 294

Norodom Sihanouk: China, 360–62, 366, 367–8, 393, 421, 444; envoy request, 358; French rule, 113; Ho Chi Minh, 365; Khmer Rouge, 435, 444–5; leadership, 357–9, 444–5; Mansfield, 358; Nixon, 359; overthrow of, 376; U.S. policy, 214, 358, 365–6; visit to, 293, 358, 364–5

Norstad, Lauris, 389

North Atlantic Treaty Organization (NATO), 3, 311–3, 387–91

Novak, Robert, 206, 257

nuclear power, 92, 461–5

Nuclear Test Ban Treaty, 11, 176, 201–2

Nunn, Sam, 483

O

O'Brien, Larry, 179, 264, 332

O'Connell, Jerry, 45, 46, 48, 49

O'Connor, Stephanie Shea, 10–11

O'Day, Sonny, 17

O'Donnell, Kenneth, 155, 194–6, 250

Ohio National Guard, 379

Olmer, Lionel, 498

Olson, Gregory, 377

Organization of American States, 96, 179

Owen, Henry, 476

P

Pakistan, 392, 399, 400, 401, 403

Pantzer, Robert, 47

Paris Accords, 429

Parsons, J. Graham, 119

Participation Certificates, 323

Pastore, John, 309, 323, 354

Pathet Lao, 113, 162, 165, 169

Pearson, Drew, 64, 81, 109–10

Pell, Claiborne, 190, 290–91, 323

Penn Nouth, 113–4

Pentagon Papers, 184, 187, 267–8, 274, 294–5

Pepper, Claude, 147

Perle, Richard, 483

ABOUT THE AUTHOR

Don Oberdorfer is distinguished journalist in residence and adjunct professor of international relations at the Paul H. Nitze School of Advanced International Studies (SAIS) of Johns Hopkins University. Previously he was a journalist for thirty-eight years, including twenty-five years at the *Washington Post*, the last seventeen of which he served as diplomatic correspondent. He is a graduate of Princeton University, which in 1996 awarded him its annual Woodrow Wilson Award for exemplary service to the nation. He is the author of four previous books: *Tet!* (1971), a political-military history of the turning point of the Vietnam War; *The Turn: From the Cold War to a New Era* (1991), a diplomatic history of the last decade of the Cold War; *Princeton University: The First 250 Years* (1995), an illustrated history of his alma mater; and *The Two Koreas: A Contemporary History* (1997, 2001), a history of the South-North struggle in Korea since 1972. He and his wife, the former Laura Klein, live in Washington, D.C.

This book was published by Smithsonian Books, Washington, D.C. The book printer was The Maple-Vail Book Manufacturing Group in York, Pa. The jacket printer was The Lehigh Press, Inc., in Pennsauken, N.J.

The book was set in Quark 4.04. The body typeface used in this book is set in 11.5 x 15 AGaramons. The display face is set in 18 point AGaramond all caps. The chapter numbers set in 85pt AGaramond Exp.